Criminal Policy Making

The International Library of Criminology, Criminal Justice and Penology
Series Editors: Gerald Mars and David Nelken

Titles in the Series:

Criminal Policy Making

Edited by

Andrew Rutherford

Faculty of Law,
University of Southampton

Dartmouth
Aldershot · Brookfield USA · Singapore · Sydney

Published by
Dartmouth Publishing Company Limited
Gower House
Croft Road
Aldershot
Hants GU11 3HR
England

Dartmouth Publishing Company
Old Post Road
Brookfield
Vermont 05036
USA

British Library Cataloguing in Publication Data
Criminal policy making. – (The international library of
  criminology, criminal justice and penology)
  1. Criminology 2. Crime 3. Crime – Government policy
  I. Rutherford, Andrew, 1940–
  364

Library of Congress Cataloging-in-Publication Data
Criminal policy making / edited by Andrew Rutherford.
        p. cm. — (The international library of criminology, criminal
  justice and penology)
    Includes bibliographical references.
    ISBN 1-85521-782-1 (hardcover)
    1. Criminal justice, Administration of. 2. Criminal law.
  I. Rutherford, Andrew, 1940–   . II. Series: International library
  of criminology, criminal justice & penology.
  HV7405.C76 1997
  364—dc20
                                                                        96-35395
                                                                        CIP

ISBN 1 85521 782 1

Printed in Great Britain by Galliard (Printers) Ltd, Great Yarmouth

Contents

PART IV   CASE STUDIES

PART V   EMERGING ISSUES

Acknowledgements

The editor and publishers wish to thank the following for permission to use copyright material.

Blackwell Publishers for the essay: Willem de Haan (1987), 'Abolitionism and the Politics of "Bad Conscience"', *The Howard Journal*, **26**, pp. 15–32. Copyright © Blackwell Publishers Ltd.

Cambridge Law Journal for the essay: Sir Leon Radzinowicz (1991), 'Penal Regressions', *The Cambridge Law Journal*, **50**, pp. 422–44.

Carfax Publishing Company for the essay: Mary Tuck (1991), 'Community and the Criminal Justice System', *Policy Studies*, **12**, pp. 22–37.

Carnegie-Mellon University Press for the essay: Pieter Spierenburg (1984), 'From Amsterdam to Auburn: An Explanation for the Rise of the Prison in Seventeenth-Century Holland and Nineteenth-Century America', *Journal of Social History*, **4**, pp. 439–61.

Cleveland State University for the essay: Francis A. Allen (1978), 'The Decline of the Rehabilitative Ideal in American Criminal Justice', *Cleveland State Law Review*, **27**, pp. 147–56.

Commentary for the essay: James Q. Wilson (1974), 'Crime and the Criminologists', *Commentary*, pp. 47–53. Reprinted from Commentary, July 1974, by permission; all rights reserved.

Elsevier Science Limited for the essay: Barbara Ann Stolz (1985), 'Congress and Criminal Justice Policy Making: The Impact of Interest Groups and Symbolic Politics', *Journal of Criminal Justice*, **13**, pp. 307–19. Copyright © 1985 Pergamon Press Ltd.

Georgetown University Law Center for the essay: Peter Arenella (1993), 'Rethinking the Functions of Criminal Procedure: The Warren and Burger Courts' Competing Ideologies', *Georgetown Law Journal*, **72**, pp. 185–248. Reprinted with the permission of the publisher, copyright © 1983 and Georgetown University.

Harcourt Brace & Company Limited for the essays: David Garland (1985), 'Politics and Policy in Criminological Discourse: A Study of Tendentious Reasoning and Rhetoric', *International Journal of the Sociology of Law*, **13**, pp. 1–33. Copyright © 1985 Academic Press Inc. (London) Limited; Chrisje Brants and Erna Kok (1986), 'Penal Sanctions as a Feminist Strategy: A Contradiction in Terms? Pornography and Criminal Law in the Netherlands', *International Journal of the Sociology of Law*, **14**, pp. 269–86. Copyright © 1986 Academic Press Inc. (London) Limited; Thomas Mathiesen (1980), 'The Future of Control Systems – the Case of Norway', *International Journal of the Sociology of Law*, **8**, pp. 149–64. Copyright © 1980 Academic Press Inc. (London) Limited; Barry Loveday (1994), 'Government Strategies for Community Crime Prevention Programmes in England and Wales: A Study in Failure?', *International Journal of the Sociology of Law*, **22**, pp. 181–202. Copyright © 1994 Academic Press Limited.

Kluwer Academic Publishers for the essay: Louk H.C. Hulsman (1986), 'Critical Criminology and the Concept of Crime', *Contemporary Crises*, **10**, pp. 63–80. Copyright © Martinus Nijhoff Publishers, Dordrecht. Printed in the Netherlands.

Northern Illinois University Law Review for the essay: James E. Robertson (1984), 'The Role of Ideology in Prisoners' Rights Adjudication: Habilitative Prison Conditions and the Eighth Amendment', *Northern Illinois University Law Review*, **4**, pp. 271–93. Copyright © 1984 Northern Illinois University.

Oxford University Press for the essays: Nils Christie (1977), 'Conflicts as Property', *British Journal of Criminology*, **17**, pp. 1–15. By permission of Oxford University Press; Carol Jones (1993), 'Auditing Criminal Justice', *British Journal of Criminology*, **33**, pp. 187–202. By permission of Oxford University Press; Paul Rock (1995), 'The Opening Stages of Criminal Justice Policy Making', *British Journal of Criminology*, **35**, pp. 1–16. By permission of Oxford University Press.

Sage Publications, Inc. for the essays: Ronald Bayer (1981), 'Crime, Punishment, and the Decline of Liberal Optimism', *Crime and Delinquency*, **27**, pp. 169–90. Copyright © 1981 by Sage Publications, Inc.; Paul J. Brantingham and Frederic L. Faust (1976), 'A Conceptual Model of Crime Prevention', *Crime and Delinquency*, **22**, pp. 284–96. Copyright © 1976 by Sage Publications, Inc.

Sage Publications Ltd for the essays: Jolande uit Beijerse and René van Swaaningen (1993), 'Social Control as a Policy: Pragmatic Moralism with a Structural Deficit', *Social and Legal Studies*, **2**, pp. 281–302. Copyright © 1993 by Sage Ltd. Lucia Zedner (1995), 'In Pursuit of the Vernacular: Comparing Law and Order Discourse in Britain and Germany', *Social and Legal Studies*, **4**, pp. 517–34. Copyright © 1995 by Sage Ltd.

Sweet & Maxwell for the essay: Heike Jung (1993), 'Criminal Justice – A European Perspective', *Criminal Law Review*, April, pp. 237–45.

University of Pennsylvania Law Review and Fred B. Rothman & Company for the essay: Herbert L. Packer (1964), 'Two Models of the Criminal Process', *University of Pennsylvania Law Review*, **113**, pp. 1–68.

Martin J. Wiener (1987), 'The March of Penal Progress?', *Journal of British Studies*, **2**, pp. 83–96. Copyright © 1987 Martin J. Wiener.

Every effort has been made to trace all the copyright holders but if any have been inadvertently overlooked, the publishers will be pleased to make the necessary arrangement at the first opportunity.

Series Preface

The International Library of Criminology, Criminal Justice and Penology, represents an important publishing initiative designed to bring together the most significant journal essays in contemporary criminology, criminal justice and penology. The series makes available to researchers, teachers and students an extensive range of essays which are indispensable for obtaining an overview of the latest theories and findings in this fast changing subject.

This series consists of volumes dealing with criminological schools and theories as well as with approaches to particular areas of crime, criminal justice and penology. Each volume is edited by a recognised authority who has selected twenty or so of the best journal articles in the field of their special competence and provided an informative introduction giving a summary of the field and the relevance of the articles chosen. The original pagination is retained for ease of reference.

The difficulties of keeping on top of the steadily growing literature in criminology are complicated by the many disciplines from which its theories and findings are drawn (sociology, law, sociology of law, psychology, psychiatry, philosophy and economics are the most obvious). The development of new specialisms with their own journals (policing, victimology, mediation) as well as the debates between rival schools of thought (feminist criminology, left realism, critical criminology, abolitionism etc.) make necessary overviews that offer syntheses of the state of the art. These problems are addressed by the INTERNATIONAL LIBRARY in making available for research and teaching the key essays from specialist journals.

GERALD MARS
Professor in Applied Anthropology, University of Bradford
School of Management

DAVID NELKEN
Distinguished Research Professor, Cardiff Law School,
University of Wales, Cardiff

Introduction

Among the core elements of criminal policy is the determination of the boundaries of criminal law, including the defences which are available to suspects and defendants; its reach embraces all stages of the criminal justice process from policing to prison systems with respect to measures taken to combat crime as well as those which share the purpose of protecting individuals from unfair or oppressive treatment. Criminal policy also encompasses the generally neglected issues concerning victims of crime. Finally there is the multi-faceted arena of crime prevention (or, more appropriately, crime reduction) which includes measures to make the commission of crime more difficult and to counter those conditions thought to be conducive to crime. The scope of criminal policy therefore extends far beyond issues of punishment and criminal justice. It covers the 'whole of society's specific response to the problems posed by the phenomenon of crime' (Moriarty, 1977, 144) and also explicitly acknowledges the role played by policy with regards to the problematic concept of crime itself.

The boundaries of criminal policy, therefore, may be regarded in terms of how any state decides who is and who is not a full member (Rock, 1979, 172). Any consideration of the scope of the criminal law serves as a reminder, as Louk Hulsman argues in Chapter 5, that crime should be viewed, not so much as the object, but the product of criminal policy. Indeed, from Hulsman's perspective, the starting point is to avoid presuming an ontological reality to crime. In a rather similar vein, Nils Christie cautions in Chapter 6 that resort to the criminal law often represents a lost opportunity for involving people in matters which are crucially important to them. It is hardly surprising that abolitionists, such as Hulsman and Christie, are to the fore in asserting that it may often be civil procedures such as mediation or, indeed, informal arrangements which offer the most promise.

Borderland issues, ironically always at the heart of criminal policy making, also arise in recognizing that 'non-crime' arenas of policy are crucial to any serious effort to tackle crime (Sampson, 1995). Indeed, the main priorities for the prevention and control of crime are expressed in measures which are not crime-specific, but are aspects of economic and social policy. It is therefore something of a paradox that criminal policy remains at the margins of much of what might be done to reduce crime. Recognition of this basic limitation ensures that priority be given to broader social and economic policies. The essential marginality of criminal policy also provides a safeguard against the intrusive activities inherent to notions such as 'waging war' on crime.

The purpose of this volume is to illuminate those processes which determine the shape and direction of criminal policy within liberal and democratic states.[1] The focus is on the *making* of policy, but it is at once apparent that a distinction cannot easily be drawn and maintained between the formation and implementation phases of the process. Practice, not infrequently, can be seen to be leading and shaping policy. Indeed, as with public policy generally, in searching for origins, there is little which is neat and predictable. Criminal policy is formed as much through an amalgam of pressures as it is by formal plans (Walker, 1977),[2] with chance and happenstance also often playing significant roles.

It is widely agreed that the concept of criminal policy first emerged during the final decade or so of the 19th century. 'The same great spiritual current which has given us social policy has also given us the concept of criminal policy' (Franz von Liszt writing in 1912, quoted by Radzinowicz, 1991, 55). Positivism was at its height, with von Liszt regarding the effective control of the 'irreformable' as the central and most urgent task. Radzinowicz notes that four-fifths of topics taken up by the International Association of Criminal Law during the period 1889–1913 fell within the area of criminal policy. He comments that almost all of these subjects remain topical, although generating much less certainty today that they offer solutions. Within recent historical work, a towering presence is *The Emergence of Penal Policy*, co-authored by Leon Radzinowicz and Roger Hood (1986), volume five of *A History of English Criminal Law*. As Martin Wiener comments in Chapter 1, the scale of the project in terms of original documentation was unprecedented. Covering the 60 years up to the outbreak of the First World War, the authors describe approaches to policy which, while pragmatic and eclectic, were also grounded in classical notions of justice. There was an appreciation too of the limits of criminal policy. 'In the field of criminal justice,' Radzinowicz and Hood concluded, 'the final word belongs, more often than not, in social rather than penal policy' (Radzinowicz and Hood, 1986, 375). An associated and smaller-scale project addressed the formation and development of criminal policy with respect to young people over the period 1914–48, in particular highlighting the role played by 'liberal progressives' whose ideology sprang from 'a similar intellectual heritage with the better known measures which compose the modern welfare state' (Bailey, 1987, 4).

More recently, a study of post-war criminal policy has been undertaken at Cambridge University. Reporting on a preliminary review of the study's major themes, Anthony Bottoms and Simon Stevenson describe their research as being a detailed analysis of policy making in the field of criminal justice in England and Wales between 1945–70 (Bottoms and Stevenson, 1992).[3] Covering a rather wider span of years, 1947–91, is Lord Windlesham's *Responses to Crime: Penal Policy in the Making*, an insider's view which casts fascinating light upon an unusual course of policy developments in England during the 1980s (Windlesham, 1993).[4] Finally, Paul Rock has published an important body of scholarship, starting with his 1979 article, 'Public Opinion and Criminal Legislation'. His main work is to be found in a trilogy, which began with a study of initiatives on crime victims in Canada (Rock, 1986). This was followed by *Helping Victims of Crime* (1990), which must occupy a central place in any bibliography of criminal policy making.[5]

Structural explorations of the origins of criminal policy are exemplified by the pioneering work of Rusche and Kirchheimer (1939), and in more recent years by David Garland (1985, 1990) and Martin Wiener (1990). Commenting upon Radzinowicz and Hood, Wiener argues that these authors 'pass over the wider instrumental and symbolic roles of criminal policy' and thereby avoid 'the deeper waters of politics, social relations, and culture'. David Garland has also insisted that, while values and emotions may be individually experienced, 'they are patterned by cultural frameworks and supported by social structures' (Garland, 1990, 198). As if in response to this structural orientation, Rock has stated that the business of making policy seems to be governed by its own grammar. It is considerably more complicated than the result of intrusive outside forces. Ministries and governments work in an environment of politics, conflicts and crises. But that environment is mediated by a series of lenses, and those lenses are moulded by a busy world manufactured in some small measure by its inhabitants. What is an instance of conflict or crisis, what it signifies and how it is managed must be referred to that inner logic of the policy process, a logic which is more than the simple extension of processes elsewhere (Rock, 1986, 387).

A reasonable conclusion from this divergence of approach is that full recognition be given both to the workings of the 'inner logic' and to the myriad of external structures, processes and pressures.

The formation of criminal policy may also be approached in terms of how it is shaped by a variety of often competing ideologies and beliefs. The core texts on ideology and criminal policy include Radzinowicz (1966) and Packer (1968). Among more recent critical assessments of criminal policy are the work of Stuart Hall and colleagues (Hall et al., 1978) and the creative output of Nils Christie and Thomas Mathiesen, both of Oslo University (see especially, Christie, 1993 and Mathiesen, 1990). In debt to these two Norwegian scholars is an assessment of the impact of influential actors on the criminal policy scene in in three countries during the 1980s (Rutherford, 1996). The human rights dimension to criminal policy has been recently explored by several British academic lawyers (Birks, 1995).

In the United States there have been surprisingly few studies which approach criminal policy in an integrated way. Academic attention has been rather narrowly focused, most often addressing aspects of criminal justice (for significant exceptions see Currie, 1985; Curtis, 1985 and Donziger, 1996). Reflected in this volume (Chapter 8) is the pioneering work of Francis Allen (1964), who argued that the sudden collapse of belief in rehabilitation was one of the most important developments in criminal policy during the 20th century (see also, American Friends Service Committee, 1971). Above all, the demise of the rehabilitative ideal left a values lacunae, prompting Allen, along with others, to worry about future sources of basic decency. In the intervening years conservative and authoritarian ideas have been to the fore, leaving many liberals uncertain as to how humanitarian values might best be protected. Over more recent years there have been collaborative publications by Franklin Zimring and Gordon Hawkins (mostly, but not exclusively, within the realm of penal policy; see Zimring and Hawkins (1991 and 1995)), and the considerable body of work by Michael Tonry (1995 and 1996). The indispensable annual series published by the University of Chicago, *Crime and Justice: A Review of Research*, contains much invaluable source material, as does a collection of essays edited by James Q. Wilson and Joan Petersilia (1995).

No survey of contemporary developments in the shaping of criminal policy making can ignore the work of the conservative commentator and leading American political scientist, James Q. Wilson. In Chapter 10, Wilson suggests that much work in this realm has been distracted by the search for causes, to the detriment of more pragmatic assessments as to what governments might actually do about crime. But many people would regard his distinction between causal analysis and policy analysis as one which carries the probable consequence of encouraging populist and authoritarian solutions. However, criminal policy analysis, when broadly conceived (as opposed to Wilson's restricted definition), remains at a relatively undeveloped stage. One place to begin is with case studies; indeed, the examples presented in Part IV of this volume suggest that this may be promising terrain. A more ambitious approach is to undertake comparative work, although progress in this area – despite the promise of Damaska (1986) – remains tentative (see, e.g., Hood, 1989; Kaiser and Albrecht, 1990, and Graham, 1990a). Writing on the nexus between crime and public policy, Roger Hood has commented that there is '... a vast gulf between studying what goes on in a variety of other countries, and a truly comparative analysis of why those countries may have different legal and social definitions, forms and amounts of crime, different perceptions of and reactions to it, different legal and administrative structures for dealing with it and different avenues and modes for developing, reinforcing and changing policy' (Hood, 1989, 192). A key text is David Downes' comparative study of the Netherlands and England and Wales (Downes, 1988), to which must be added the recent interest by British scholars in developments in Germany (Graham, 1990b; Lacey and Zedner, 1995). The penultimate chapter offers a European perspective. These and other comparative studies are encouraging steps in this direction (see especially Nelken, 1994).

The chapters in this volume are arranged in five sections. Part I, 'Historical and Social Context', opens with an insistence by Martin J. Wiener upon an analysis of discourses that join criminal policy with the wider society. His critique of Radzinowicz and Hood (1986) draws widely on the history of criminal policy, including Bailey (1987), Langbein (1983) and Gatrell (1980).[6] Pieter Spierenburg, author of a classic historical exploration of capital punishment (Spierenburg, 1984), provides the second contribution, in the form of a transatlantic comparison of the origins of the prison. Finally, David Garland argues that several criminological debates of the early years of this century were shaped and determined by the requirements of policy rather than by the results of scientific discourse.

The second section, 'Theoretical Perspectives', opens with a useful model for thinking about criminal policy. Although by no means complete (as the chapter title suggests, it is unduly crime-focused), it remains a useful point of departure. Contributions follow from two of the founding fathers of abolitionism. Louk Hulsman, for many years at Erasmus University (Rotterdam), reminds us of the uncontrollability of criminal justice. For Hulsman, criminal policy means abandoning the notion of crime itself. Nils Christie's concern is that the direct participants should not be deprived of their conflict. In more recent work Christie's mood has darkened as he warns of a burgeoning crime control industry feeding off the unlimited natural resource of 'crime' (Christie, 1993). Some of the difficulties posed by abolitionist perspectives are explored in Chapter 7 by two Dutch criminologists, Chrisje Brants and Erna Kok. The next essays by Francis Allen and Ronald Bayer explore aspects of the collapse of the rehabilitative ideal, with Bayer going on to review the broader decline of liberal perspectives on crime. The section concludes with an early article by James Q. Wilson, prompted by reflections on his experience as an adviser to President Johnson's Crime Commission in the late 1960s, and which reappeared in amended form in his influential book *Thinking About Crime* (1975). Wilson's writings have done more than those of any other scholar to reject the essentially liberal thesis of the Crime Commission (1967) and to encourage hard-nosed approaches to criminal policy.

The ideological cross-currents within which criminal policy is formed are taken a stage further in the essays which make up Part III. The opening chapter by the sociologist, Walter B. Miller, provides a comprehensive framework which, as with Herbert Packer's paper which follows, has to be set against the United States of the late 1960s. Packer's 'two models' of criminal justice has remained a particularly influential scheme for considering issues of both policy and practice. The chapters by Peter Arenella and James E. Robertson explore some of these issues against decisions taken by the US Supreme Court at various stages of the criminal justice process. In Chapter 13, Carol Jones illustrates the increasing impact upon criminal policy of managerialism, including the rapid growth of commercial interests.

The fourth section presents selected policy-making case studies. The first three, by Paul Rock, Mary Tuck (formerly head of the Home Office Research Unit) and Barry Loveday, focus on criminal policy formation in England since the 1980s. Chapters 19 and 20 address policy plans of the late 1970s and mid-1980s in Norway and the Netherlands respectively. Thomas Mathiesen (another founding father of abolitionism) locates the Norwegian white paper of 1978 within its historical and political context. Jolande uit Beijerse and René van Swaaningen provide a critical appraisal of the white paper of 1985 which marked a turning point in Dutch criminal policy. Barbara Ann Stolz's paper examines the variety of interest groups actively engaged at the federal level of policy making in the United States.

'Emerging Issues', the final section, opens with a review of the recent transformation of criminal policy in the Netherlands. Willem de Haan, of Groningen University, traces the decline of liberal and humanitarian values, as exemplified by the group of influential scholars based at Utrecht University a generation or more ago, and the subsequent rise of conservative models of criminal policy. Lucia Zedner's comparative study traces recent ways of thinking about 'law and order' in both Germany and Britain. In the penultimate chapter, a wider European perspective marks Heike Jung's assessment of contemporary criminal policy issues. In conclusion, Sir Leon Radzinowicz succinctly sets forth the key features of authoritarian systems and thereby illuminates the crucial contemporary choices of direction for criminal policy within liberal democratic states.

Clearly much work remains to be done before any definitive study of criminal policy can realistically be expected. The materials assembled for this volume are suggestive as to the scope and depth of the ambitious task ahead.

Notes

1 This volume does not directly address criminal policy making within authoritarian states. For a general discussion see Rock (1979, 171–7); for the extreme case of Germany between 1933–45 see Loewenstein (1936), Wolff (1944) and Muller (1991).
2 In his introduction to this useful collection of papers presented at the 1976 Cropwood Conference, Nigel Walker makes it clear that penal policy was defined sufficiently broadly to mean criminal policy. For a review of penal policy developments in England and Wales, using a narrow definition, see Morgan (1979).
3 This study was funded as part of a major initiative taken in the mid–1980s by the Economic and Social Research Council.
4 The first volume in Lord Windlesham's series was a general overview of issues rather than focusing upon policy. The third volume, addressing policy developments in the early 1990s, was published as this book went to press (Windlesham, 1996).
5 The third volume in the trilogy is Rock (1993); see also Rock (1988, 1994).
6 Further key sources include the work of Douglas Hay and colleagues (Hay et al., 1975), Thompson (1975) and more recently a study of English public executions by Gatrell (1994).

References

Allen, Francis (1964), *The Borderland of Criminal Justice: Essays in Criminology*, Chicago: University of Chicago Press.

American Friends Service Committee (1971), *Struggle For Justice*, New York: Hill and Wang.

Bailey, Victor (1987), *Delinquency and Citizenship: Reclaiming the Young Offender, 1914–1948*, Oxford: Oxford University Press.

Birks, Peter (ed.) (1995), *Pressing Problems of the Law, Volume 1: Criminal Justice and Human Rights*, Oxford: Oxford University Press.

Bottoms, Anthony E. and Simon Stevenson (1992), 'What Went Wrong? Criminal Justice Policy in England and Wales, 1945–70', in David Downes (ed.), *Unravelling Criminal Justice: Eleven British Studies*, London: Macmillan, 1–45.

Christie, Nils (1993), *Crime Control as Industry: Towards Gulags Western Style?*, London: Routledge.

Crime Commission (1967), *The Challenge of Crime in a Free Society*, The President's Commission on Law Enforcement and the Administration of Justice, Washington D.C.: Government Printing Office.

Currie, Elliott (1985), *Confronting Crime*, New York: Pantheon.

Curtis, Lynn A. (1985), *American Violence and Public Policy*, London and New Haven: Yale University Press.

Damaska, M. (1986), *The Faces of Justice and State Authority*, New Haven: Yale University Press.

Donziger, Steven R. (ed.) (1996), *The Real War on Crime*, The Report of the National Criminal Justice Commission, New York: HarperPerennial.

Downes, David (1988), *Contrasts in Tolerance, Post-War Penal Policy in the Netherlands and England and Wales*, Oxford: Oxford University Press.

European Committee on Crime Problems (1975), *Conference on Criminal Policy*, Strasbourg: Council of Europe.

Garland, David (1985), *Punishment and Welfare: A History of Penal Strategies*, Aldershot: Gower.

Garland, David (1990), *Punishment and Modern Society*, Oxford: Oxford University Press.

Gatrell, V.A.G. (1980), 'The Decline of Theft and Violence in Victorian and Edwardian England', in V.A.G. Gatrell et al. (eds), *Crime and the Law: The Social History of Crime in Western Europe since 1500*, London: Europa Publications.

Gatrell, V.A.G. (1994), *The Hanging Tree: Executions and the English People 1770–1868*, Oxford: Oxford University Press.

Graham, John (1990a), *Crime Prevention Strategies in Europe and North America*, Helsinki: Helsinki Institute for Crime Prevention and Control.

Graham, John (1990b), 'Decarceration in the Federal Republic of Germany', *British Journal of Criminology*, **30**, 150–70.

Hall, Stuart et al. (1978), *Policing the Crisis: Mugging, the State, and Law and Order*, London: Macmillan.

Hay, Douglas et al. (eds) (1975), *Albion's Fatal Tree: Crime and Society in Eighteenth Century England*, London: Pantheon.

Hood, Roger (ed.) (1989), *Crime and Criminal Policy in Europe*, Centre for Criminological Research, Oxford: University of Oxford.

Hood, Roger (1990), 'Commentary on International Comparative Research', in Gunther Kaiser and Hans-Jorg Albrecht (eds), *Crime and Criminal Policy in Europe*, Freiburg: Max-Planck Institute, 189–97.

Kaiser, Gunther and Hans-Jorg Albrecht (eds) (1990), *Crime and Criminal Policy in Europe*, Freiburg: Max-Plank Institute.

Lacey, Nicola and Zedner, Lucie (1995), 'Discourses of Community in Criminal Justice', *Journal of Law and Society*, **22** (3), September, 301–25.

Langbein, John H. (1983), 'Albion's Fatal Flaws', *Past and Present*, **98**, 96–120.

Loewenstein, Karl (1936), 'Law in the Third Reich', *Yale Law Journal*, **45**, 719–815.

Mathiesen, Thomas (1990), *Prison on Trial: A Critical Perspective*, London: Sage.

Morgan, Rod (1979), *Formulating Penal Policy: The Future of the Advisory Council on the Penal System*, London: NACRO.

Moriarty, Michael (1977), 'The Policy-Making Process: How It Is Seen from the Home Office' in Nigel Walker (ed.), *Penal Policy-Making in England*, Cambridge: Institute of Criminology, 129–45.

Muller, Ingo (1991), *Hitler's Justice: The Courts in the Third Reich*, London: Tauris.

Nelken, David (1994), 'Who Can You Trust? The Futures of Comparative Criminology' in David Nelken (ed.), *The Futures of Criminology*, London: Sage.

Packer, Herbert L. (1968), *The Limits of the Criminal Sanction*, Stanford: Stanford University Press.

Radzinowicz, Leon (1966), *Ideology and Crime: A Study of Crime and its Social and Historical Context*, London: Heinemann Educational.

Radzinowicz, Leon (1991), *The Roots of the International Association of Criminal Law and their Significance: A Tribute and a Re-assessment on the Centenary of the IKV*, Freiburg: Max-Planck Institute.

Radzinowicz, Leon and Roger Hood (1986), *A History of English Criminal Law and its Administration from 1750, Volume 5: The Emergence of Penal Policy*, London: Stevens.

Rock, Paul (1979), 'Public Opinion and Criminal Legislation' in the European Committee on Crime Policies, *Public Opinion on Crime and Criminal Justice: Collective Studies in Criminological Research*, Vol. XVII, Strasbourg: Council of Europe.

Rock, Paul (1986), *A View from the Shadows*, Oxford: Oxford University Press.

Rock, Paul (1988), 'A Natural History of Research in Policy-Making' in Nigel Fielding (ed.), *Actions and Structures: Research Methods and Social Theory*, London: Sage, 99–116.

Rock, Paul (1990), *Helping Victims of Crime: The Home Office and the Rise of Victim Support in England and Wales*, Oxford: Oxford University Press.

Rock, Paul (1993), *The Social World of an English Crown Court*, Oxford: Oxford University Press.

Rock, Paul (1994), 'The Social Organization of a Home Office Initiative', *European Journal of Criminal Law and Criminal Justice*, **2**, 141–67.

Rock, Paul (1996), *Reconstructing a Women's Prison*, Oxford: Oxford University Press.

Rusche, George and Otto Kirchheimer (1939), *Punishment and Social Structure*, Columbia University Press.

Rutherford, Andrew (1996), *Transforming Criminal Policy*, Winchester: Waterside Press.

Sampson, Robert J. (1995), 'The Community' in James Q. Wilson and Joan Petersilia (eds), *Crime*, San Francisco: Institute for Contemporary Studies, 193–216.

Spierenburg, Pieter (1984), *The Spectacle of Suffering. Executions and the Evolution of Repression: From a Preindustrial Metropolis to the European Experience*, Cambridge: Cambridge University Press.

Thompson, E.P. (1975), *Whigs and Hunters: The Origins of the Black Act*, London: Pantheon.

Tonry, Michael (1995), *Malign Neglect – Race, Crime and Punishment in America*, New York and Oxford: Oxford University Press.

Tonry, Michael (1996), *Sentencing Matters*, New York and Oxford: Oxford University Press.

Walker, Nigel (ed.) (1977), *Penal Policy-Making in England*, Cambridge: Cambridge Institute of Criminology.

Wiener, Martin J. (1990), *Reconstructing the Criminal: Culture, Law, and Policy in England, 1830–1914*, Cambridge: Cambridge University Press.

Wilson, James Q. (1975), *Thinking About Crime*, New York: Basic Books.

Wilson, James Q. and Joan Petersilia (eds) (1995), *Crime*, San Francisco: Institute for Contemporary Studies.

Windlesham, Lord (1993), *Responses to Crime, Volume 2: Penal Policy in the Making*, Oxford: Oxford University Press.

Windlesham, Lord (1996), *Responses to Crime, Volume 3: Legislating with the Tide*, Oxford: Oxford University Press.

Wolff, Hans Julius (1944), 'Criminal Justice in Germany', *Michigan Law Review*, **42**, 1067–88 and **43**, 155–78.

Zimring, Franklin E. and Gordon Hawkins (1991), *The Scale of Imprisonment*, Chicago and London: University of Chicago Press.

Zimring, Franklin E. and Gordon Hawkins (1995), *Incapacitation: Penal Confinement and the Restraint of Crime*, New York and Oxford: Oxford University Press.

Part I
Historical and Social Context

[1]

Reviews

The March of Penal Progress?

History of English Criminal Law and Its Administration from 1750. Vol. 5: The Emergence of Penal Policy. By Sir Leon Radzinowicz and Roger Hood. London: Stevens, 1986. Pp. 1101. £75.

This is the most important work ever written on the history of British penal policy. It is the latest and largest installment of an ambitious project that was begun by Leon Radzinowicz (who was to become the first director of the Institute of Criminology at Cambridge) more than forty years ago. Unlike the first four volumes, which were written solely by Radzinowicz, this volume, the first to appear in eighteen years, is coauthored with Roger Hood, head of the Centre for Criminological Research at Oxford. Although it is the fifth volume in the overall work, it stands complete by itself and is devoted to examining "the endeavours to uncover the roots of crime and to evolve a combination of diverse measures for the control of crime" (p. v) from the 1830s to 1914. It does not simply stand complete; in both bulk and scope it overshadows its predecessors. In nearly 800 pages of heavily annotated text, the two foremost figures of British criminology provide a detailed yet crisp narrative of how a set of central government penal policies evolved. With the aid of half a dozen postgraduate students, several of whom have already made a name for themselves, Radzinowicz and Hood have thoroughly combed the paper mountains of published and unpublished sources, especially the extensive files of the Home Office, many of which have never before been used by historians (their bibliography runs over 250 pages). Before this massive effort even the thoroughness of the previous four volumes pales. The historiography of British criminal justice has never seen such a project.

Radzinowicz and Hood summarize nineteenth-century explanations of crime, assess the character of criminal activity and its measurement, and then turn to focus most of the volume on the development of government policy for dealing with criminals. By taking the story down to 1914, they fill a virtual void in historiography and, for the first time, provide an account of Victorian and Edwardian penal policy as a whole that is firmly grounded in primary sources. In particular, the period after the 1877 nationalization of the prisons has been a virtual terra incognita, which they have now mapped. Their work will be

without question an indispensable reference point for all future historical scholarship as well as a fertile source of reflection on current penal
issues.[1]

However, just because this work is a landmark in scholarship and
is destined to impress its stamp on future conceptions of penal history,
its implicit assumptions and purposes merit careful scrutiny. Running
throughout this work is an underlying framework of "progress," as
defined by modern professional opinion, and a complementary focus
on formal policy formation and application, leaving blurred the social
and psychic fabric within which policy is embedded and from which it
derives its meaning. Presuppositions that encourage development of
certain lines of investigation may foreclose others. Such implicit fore-
closure is evident here. The work seems to be intended to serve not
only as a contribution to modern British history but, even more, as a
reference for present-day policymakers and a guide to how their predecessors handled similar problems. These two aims are not easily
joined.

Through the detailed exposition of volume 5 we can perceive the
lineaments of a tale that might be summarized as follows. Faced with
the newly pressing problem of crime, which appears to be rising at least
until mid-century, "sober" (p. 20) nineteenth-century English policymakers and reformers feel the attraction of, but ultimately refuse to be
"taken in" (p. 287) by, "monolithic" (p. 123) continental criminological philosophies, whether positivist or socialist. They remain, on the
whole, stubbornly empirical and eclectic, keeping their minds on practical questions. For such intellectual restraint they are rewarded by
success, that is, the later nineteenth-century "English miracle" (p.
113) of steadily declining crime rates that culminated, in the last year of
the century, in the lowest levels of indictable crime ever recorded. This
conquest of crime is happily paralleled by a long-term softening of the
severity of punishments, for example, the abolition of transportation,
the gradual disuse of flogging, and fewer executions. Success also is
accompanied by diminishing reliance on a deterrent prison system that

[1] This work supplements, but also greatly extends in period covered and in range,
Sean McConville's thorough but narrow *History of English Prison Administration, 1750–
1877* (Boston, 1981), vol. 1. For the current state of the historiography of penal policy,
see Victor Bailey, ed., *Policing and Punishment in Nineteenth Century Britain* (New
Brunswick, N.J., 1981); Michael Ignatieff, "State, Civil Society, and Total Institutions:
A Critique of Recent Social Histories of Punishment," in *Crime and Justice: An Annual
Review of Research*, vol. 3, ed. Michael Tonry and Norval Morris (Chicago, 1981), pp.
153–92. David Philips, " 'A Just Measure of Crime, Authority, Hunters and Blue Lo-
custs': The 'Revisionist' Social History of Crime and the Law in Britain, 1780–1850," in
Social Control and the State, ed. Stanley Cohen and Andrew Scull (New York, 1983),
pp. 50–73; David Sugarman, J. N. J. Palmer, and G. R. Rubin, "Crime, Law and
Authority in Nineteenth Century Britain," *Middlesex Polytechnic History Journal*
(1983), pp. 28–141; and, most recently, Christopher Harding et al., *Imprisonment in
England and Wales: A Concise History* (London, 1985).

had been established in the climate of fear surrounding the end of transportation. In the last few decades of the century, the length of sentences of imprisonment steadily shorten while even imprisonment itself begins to be resorted to less often. At the same time, this new-found sense of security encourages development of more ambitious policies for the "residuum" of repetitive criminals. "The young potential recidivist, the habitual offender, the confirmed vagrant, the chronic inebriate and the inadequate feeble-minded," they observe, "by their persistency, seemed to invest the problem of crime with a permanence which Victorian society, vigorous and confident as it was, did not wish to accept" (p. 129). The late Victorian years see a hopeful search among reformers and liberal administrators for more transformative alternatives to deterrence for treating members of these categories and for alternatives to incarceration for the general run of offender.

By the Edwardian era these quests begin to bear fruit: older principles of retribution and deterrence, though retaining support among the public and the judiciary, slowly but steadily give way to more flexible and scientific efforts at dealing with criminality. Some of these new efforts fail either when they outrun the nascent supply line of criminological knowledge or when, against their grain, English policy-makers "flirt" (p. 287) with positivist prescriptions for treating deviance as a purely medical problem, neglecting both the rights of the individual and the recalcitrance of human nature. Thus compulsory commitment and treatment of criminal inebriates proves a fiasco, while even more sweeping proposals for "rounding up degenerate stock" are considered but fortunately rejected as un-English. By 1914, however, galvanized by Winston Churchill (a particular hero of this story) and a new generation of reforming officials, penal policy is shaking off these wrong turnings and setting itself firmly on the path toward a system "worthy of a modern, prosperous state and in tune with its developing social conscience" (p. 617).

Good enough, but the trouble is that penal policy is dealt with here as a self-contained and self-explicable sphere whose history can be best understood by working back from later twentieth-century professional perspectives. Policy for Radzinowicz and Hood is practical and responsive: they describe policymakers responding to problems and needs and, in so doing, running into certain "recurring dilemmas" (p. v) from which modern policymakers can learn. These dilemmas include the difficulty of developing methods of dealing with habitual offenders, the question of how to treat political offenders, and the problem of reconciling the claims of predictability and justice with those of equity in sentencing. The agenda for policymakers is largely taken for granted; they do not inquire how these problems came into being and whether criminal policy itself helped to create them. The authors pass over the wider instrumental and symbolic roles of criminal policy to examine which would take them into deeper waters of politics, social relations, and culture. Just as they largely take the problematic concept of crime as a given and note only the "inevitable [quantitative] imperfections of [its] measuring rod" (p. 107), so too they pay only perfunctory attention to the ways in which criminal law and its administration construct the very categories of crime and criminality. Anthropologists in recent years have suggested that we look at law not simply as a description of the rules a society lives by but as "a part of the discourse about good and bad states of society."[2] This insight can be usefully applied not only to law, of course, but to all forms of social rule making, which reveal societies in the ongoing process of constructing themselves. Victorian-Edwardian discourses on crime and its treatment (like the related but better-known discourses on poverty and welfare) are keys to unlocking the political and cultural dynamics of Britain between the Industrial Revolution and the First World War. Yet these are keys that Radzinowicz and Hood show no interest in employing. If the "discourse of crime," in Michelle Perrot's phrase, "reveals the obsessions of a society," we get little sense through these many pages of what such obsessions might be or how they might be interacting or changing.[3] The authors' rationalistic view of policymaking leaves little room for the analysis of discourses that joined penal policy with the wider society.

Certainly, as John Langbein has demonstrated, "legal institutions lead a complex life of their own."[4] Yet, just as in the somewhat analogous case of medical institutions, we have become increasingly aware of how they are nonetheless intricately enmeshed in, and constitutive of, the common life.[5] One indispensable dimension of criminal policy

---

[2] Sally Humphreys, "Law as Discourse," *History and Anthropology* 1, no. 2 (February 1985): 251. See esp. Sally F. Moore, *Law as Process* (London, 1978); and J. L. Comaroff and S. Roberts, *Rules and Processes* (Chicago, 1981).

[3] Michelle Perrot, "Delinquency and the Penitentiary System in Nineteenth Century France," in *Deviants and the Abandoned in French Society,* ed. Robert Forster and Orest Ranum (Baltimore, 1978), p. 219.

[4] John Langbein, "Albion's Fatal Flaws," *Past and Present,* no. 98 (February 1983), pp. 96–120.

[5] If even in a field like medical history—whose subject matter has an undeniable "objective" dimension and whose story is in certain respects at least generally conceded to be progressive—present-minded and internalist forms of explanation have come to be recognized as insufficient, how much more so is this true in the history of criminal policy? This reshaping of medical historiography has gone further in America than in Britain; see, e.g., Charles Rosenberg and Morris Vogel, eds., *The Therapeutic Revolution: Essays in the Social History of American Medicine* (Philadelphia, 1979); Carroll Smith-Rosenberg, "The Hysterical Woman: Sex Roles and Role Conflict in Nineteenth-Century America," in *Visions of Gender in Victorian America,* ed. Carroll Smith-Rosenberg (New York, 1985), pp. 197–216; Martin S. Pernick, *A Calculus of Suffering: Pain, Professionalism, and Anesthesia in Nineteenth-Century America* (New York, 1985); and, from another direction, Paul Starr, *The Social Transformation of American Medicine* (New York, 1982). On one aspect of British medicine, see Roger Cooter, *The Cultural Meaning of Popular Science: Phrenology and the Organization of Consent in Nineteenth-Century Britain* (Cambridge, 1984).

that is given short shrift here is the political—not in the specific sense of political offenders, Chartist, Irish, and suffragette, to which indeed is devoted an illuminating chapter, but rather in the more general sense of its role in articulating state power. For example, the authors stress the later Victorian and Edwardian trend to shorter sentences of imprisonment, a point that valuably corrects careless Foucaultian references to an ever-expanding "carceral archipelago." The marked decline in the average daily population especially of convict prisons indeed demonstrates that to include the later Victorian and Edwardian years in the "era of the prison" without careful qualifications is wrongheaded. Yet Radzinowicz and Hood assume that this fact renders further consideration of "social control" interpretations unnecessary: they caricature these in passing as the exploded "asylum theory" (p. 220) of an inexorable trend toward expanded use of incarceration.[6] However, their argument for liberal progress is left one-sided, for their gaze is solely on the formal penal system, particularly the convict system, and they take little notice of the less obvious but parallel trends to prosecution of nominal offenses that would earlier have been overlooked, to criminalization of a wider range of behavior, and, beyond but not unrelated to the formal system of criminal law, to more extensive supervision of individuals in society at large. Indeed such trends have led V. A. G. Gatrell, who is perhaps the most respected scholar of nineteenth-century criminal statistics, to claim that "as the century wore on, the English judicial system came very near to as total a regulation of even petty—let alone serious—deviance as has ever been achieved."[7]

Radzinowicz and Hood ignore how social regulation was not only extending as imprisonment diminished but how it was in part making it possible for authorities to use the prison less by providing a substitute. Thus in some real sense surveillance and discipline were not necessarily diminishing but were perhaps increasing, though in new forms, and even in the process becoming a cause of the emptying of the jails. To suggest this is not to argue for sinister machinations; these new forms may well have been more popular and less oppressive. Certainly, few prisoners objected to shorter sentences even if they entailed some degree of supervision on release. Indeed there is much evidence of rising popular demand for greater regulation of behavior just as of the economy.[8] However, whether popular or not, such informal regulation

[6] It is significant that Michel Foucault, who for all his irritating imprecision and overreaching raised profound questions, receives in this lengthy work one brief, dismissive mention in a footnote.

[7] V. A. G. Gatrell, "The Decline of Theft and Violence in Victorian and Edwardian England," in *Crime and the Law: The Social History of Crime in Western Europe since 1500*, ed V. Gatrell, B. Lenman, and G. Parker (London, 1980), p. 244.

[8] This is evidenced by the generally successful demands for sanctions against wife beating, child abuse, and deviant sexuality and for raising the age of consent. See George Behlmer, *Child Abuse and Moral Reform in England, 1870–1908* (Stanford, Calif., 1982); and Jeffrey Weeks, *Sex, Politics and Society: The Regulation of Sexuality since 1800* (London, 1981).

calls for the same careful investigation here that is given to formal imprisonment. While it would hardly be reasonable to ask Radzinowicz and Hood to add this assignment to their already full plate, one could ask them to show a sense of this wider context and to remain alert to connections between criminal justice and other facets of social administration such as civil law, welfare policy, and philanthropic activity. In particular, it is highly relevant to their story that the growing supervision of popular behavior by police constables and poor-law guardians—and the later Victorian multiplication of voluntary moral reform activities such as those of the police court "missionaries" of the Church of England Temperance Society, the investigators of the National Society for the Prevention of Cruelty to Children, the Charity Organization Society, the YMCA, the National Vigilance Association, and many others—provided levers of intervention prior to, and often lessening the need for, formal criminal sanctions.

Moreover, they fail to see how the widening application of criminal sanctions that was fostered by broader social changes was itself contributing significantly to the pressure to find ways of dealing with offenders other than uniform and deterrent imprisonment. The later nineteenth-century extension of criminal sanctions to refusal to comply with proliferating public health, welfare, and education regulations and to domestic and sexual behavior (wife beating, child abuse, incest, homosexuality, and certain aspects of prostitution) as well as the stepped-up prosecution of drunkenness and vagrancy were all generating large numbers of offenders who were less suitable for the penalty of imprisonment as it had been shaped in the middle decades of the century. An ever-smaller proportion of prisoners fit the early Victorian stereotypes of Fagins or Sykeses both because of the growing scarcity of such hard-core criminals and because of the growing number of lesser offenders now having run-ins with the expanding law.

In addition, a major procedural change, namely, the vast extension of summary jurisdiction during the Victorian era, which they justly cite as "fostering . . . this retreat from incarceration" (p. 618), nonetheless needs to be considered in wider perspective. The consequences of shifting more and more of the criminal caseload from jury trials to magistrates who act alone have been as yet little explored. One might reasonably suggest that in addition to lowering the scale of punishment, as Radzinowicz and Hood astutely argue, and, more obviously, to preventing a logjam in the courts, it also entailed (even bearing in mind the existing property qualifications for jury service) a significant diminution in popular influence over criminal justice. In fact, this change appears to be a critical link in the long and morally complex shift from dominantly "community" to "state" justice. Like the extension of social regulation, it can be seen as one facet of a movement toward a more bureaucratic, profe sionalized society, one that only the simpleminded would unqualifiedly denounce but, on the other hand, one that cannot be simply labeled as "reform."

Radzinowicz and Hood ignore wider political developments of the Victorian-Edwardian era such as the extension of voting rights, the crystallization of class consciousness, and the emergence of a feminist movement, which were certainly affecting both the definitions of deviance (think of trade union activities or, contrariwise, wife battering) and the regulatory options that were open to the authorities. More generally, such developments were probably encouraging a more "positive" and less "repressive" role for the criminal justice system.[9] These sorts of intersections with criminal policy have only begun to be studied, and there are many other possible interrelations. In any event, an account of the reconstruction of penal policy without any political context can hardly help appearing rather naive.

Not only do the authors miss the subtle network of power relations in which criminal policy was embedded, but they also fail to perceive the cultural character of policy. To place criminal policy within the context of social rule making in the widest sense calls for a second angle of vision in which the articulation of meaning as well as that of power is followed out. Rules about what is illegal and how illegalities are to be dealt with presuppose and, in turn, shape particular definitions of social reality and value. Moreover, such rules serve a variety of purposes, cultural as well as political and administrative. Here the historian of penal policy must try to understand the deeper meanings of principles such as uniformity and deterrence and their abandonment. The transition from nineteenth- to twentieth-century social policy was not simply the replacement of laissez-faire by state intervention but also embodied a movement between one mode of intervention and another, each based on a particular way of conceptualizing human nature, society, and reform. A deterrent criminal law—embodied in an efficient system of police and trial and a feared prison system that stigmatizes inmates while subjecting them to uniform, unvarying, and largely impersonal discipline—can be seen not only as a practical instrument of crime control but also as both expressing and reinforcing a binding system of belief. Deterrence presupposed to some degree the existence of large numbers of responsible individuals who were habituated to calculating the consequences of their actions and regulating their behavior accordingly. As Bentham had declared, "all men calculate, some with less exactness, indeed some with more: but all men calculate."[10] Equally important, deterrent policy also served as a way of fostering such behavior by increasing the incentives to calculate better and to regulate oneself more thoroughly, as Bentham's disciple James Mill had recognized: the principle of utility, he had argued, "marshalls the duties in their proper order, and will not permit mankind to be deluded, as so long they have been, sottishly

---

[9] This is suggested by David Garland, *Punishment and Welfare* (Aldershot, 1985).
[10] Quoted in Ross Harrison, *Bentham* (London, 1983), p. 139.

to prefer the lower to the higher good, and to hug the greater evil, from fear of the less.''[11]

In many ways early and mid-Victorian penal policy, with its intense moralism and its stress on deterrence, fitted within a wider effort at resocialization that Radzinowicz and Hood do not notice. Through civil law, welfare policy, education, and "private" activities such as philanthropy, a population that was undergoing rapid change was enabled (forced?) to adapt to new social conditions while at the same time being provided with a "civil religion" at a time when the effectiveness of traditional religion was receding. The belief in at least the possibility of free will and personal accountability and the concomitant imperative of self-discipline, when embodied in institutions and practices of which criminal justice was one, probably helped many to cope with the impersonal conditions of urban and industrial life. At the same time, such institutionalized beliefs and imperatives constituted an appealing social narrative that reknit the frayed threads of moral community and endowed everyday life with significance.

A penal innovation that Radzinowicz and Hood give much attention to (but in isolation), namely, the special legislation for "habitual criminals" of 1869 and 1871, was paralleled by other measures of deterrent regulation that they fail to mention, including a major effort by the Local Government Board to do away with outdoor relief, legislation to enable boards of guardians to punish parents for neglect of their children, and an education act that granted powers to local authorities against parents for the nonattendance of their children. Behind all these efforts lay the aim of strengthening—creating, if necessary—personal responsibility as the bedrock of social order. The new provisions to encourage cumulative sentencing for habitual criminals were similarly based on "rational voluntarism": they would diminish crime by placing a man's fate clearly in his own hands. As one of their chief proponents, W. Barwick Baker, put it, the offender would "with his eyes open deliberately sentence himself.''[12]

By contrast, interventionist initiatives by the 1890s bear witness to a fading belief in rational voluntarism and to a consequent move away from deterrence as a means of social regulation, which changes the way we interpret the developments that Radzinowicz and Hood list. This shift is best known in regard to the movement of welfare policy toward providing benefits with less or no stigma—the greater availability of poor relief itself but also the expansion of medical services, public employment projects in times of depression, workmen's compensation, and similar initiatives. The same tendency, behind which lay shifts both in the structure of power and in the construction of social values, is evident though less noticed in criminal policy.

[11] Quoted in William Thomas, *The Philosophic Radicals* (Oxford, 1979), pp. 103–4.
[12] W. Barwick Baker, *War with Crime* (London, 1889), p. 31–32.

Radzinowicz and Hood discuss what they take to be three separate developments as isolated phenomena and thus miss the wider implications of a fundamental change of temper that together they reflect. They note that concern was rising about sentencing disparities, and they give a thorough account of efforts to rectify this but provide no evidence to suggest that such disparities were increasing and no explanation of why concern over this perennial situation should have been rising then. Similarly, the 1890s saw a reinvigoration and expansion of efforts to control and treat habitual criminals along with new initiatives to deal with drunkards and the feebleminded. The image of habitual criminals was now coming to merge with that of these other groups, that is, as irresponsible "social wreckage" who required a more direct administration that could address their specific pathologies. Radzinowicz and Hood examine this specialization and redirection of penal policy in great detail but offer little explanation for it beyond noting the general decline of serious crime and the vigor of Victorian optimism. Finally, the prison system that was established by the mid-Victorians was sharply and widely denounced as both a practical failure and a moral stain on society in the 1890s. The entire explanation that the authors offer for this decisive and rather sudden shift in public mood about an institution that had been, in the terms set it a generation before, quite successful (and that was certainly not becoming more harsh) is that "it was a period when all kinds of institutions were being subjected to scrutiny and the prison system too was ripe for reappraisal . . . a new political climate . . . 'the new Liberalism,' gave birth to new approaches to social problems" (p. 575). After this brief gesture toward the misty land of what they call the "more fundamental factors," they return quickly to the more comfortable terrain, clearly landmarked by records of the press and the bureaucracy, of "precipitating circumstances" (p. 575).

Yet each of these three developments can be seen to reflect and encourage a "fundamental factor," namely, the erosion of the image of the responsible individual and the philosophy of deterrence that it underpinned. Underlying a rising dissatisfaction with the disparities between sentences awarded was an increasing intolerance of crimes against the person as compared to crimes against property. Most complaints about sentencing contrasted the severe treatment of thefts with indulgence toward acts of violence. Such complaints suggest several "fundamental" developments at work. From the political perspective there was a shift in social influence away from the almost exclusive preponderance of male property holders who were threatened very little by violence toward those more likely to be victims of it, namely, the poor in general and women in particular, and from the cultural standpoint there was a shift away from a view of deviant behavior as chosen toward seeing it as at least in part beyond individual control. A consistent deterrent philosophy would see no "disparity" in severely punishing a calculated offense like theft with the aim of preventing future occurrences while leniently treating uncalculated crimes that are unlikely to be repeated or imitated, such as men murdering their wives in fits of rage. When the efficacy of deterrence ceases to be accepted automatically, such differences are perceived as unjust disparities. Similarly, the shift in policy in the 1890s away from uniform punishment toward the diagnosis of specialized pathologies and the provision of special treatment for them reflected not only the expanding ambitions of reformers and administrators and the increasing pressures for a more "positive" role for the state noted above but also the diminishing expectations that individuals could and should be held strictly responsible for their behavior or that such deterrent treatment was the surest route to the improvement of that behavior. "Habitual criminals," it was observed in the Home Office in 1900, should "be treated like moral lunatics."[13] More direct methods of dealing with offenders, whether therapeutic or incapacitative, were coming to seem required.

Thus the simultaneous wave of criticism of prison conditions and of the entire existing system of prison discipline, like these other shifts in outlook, need to be understood by more than vague references to humanitarianism or to a "new Liberalism." Dissatisfaction ran across the political spectrum. While Liberals and Radicals provided the sharpest attacks on the prison system, most moderates and even Conservatives agreed that drastic change was needed. As *The Times* noted in 1898, "administrators, no less than irresponsible critics, own that every prison is more or less a failure."[14] This general perception of failure at a time when rates of serious crime and prison populations were reaching new lows is puzzling until it is placed in the context of a rising disillusionment with deterrence joining with a growing inclination to use the state in a more "positive" way, both being shifts in mentality that in turn need to be related to fundamental movements in Victorian politics and culture. "Practical" issues of penal policy remain one-dimensional when separated from seemingly "abstract" processes of defining human nature or the proper role of the state. As these definitions—made daily if implicitly by everyone involved in shaping penal policy—altered, they inevitably changed perceptions of penal institutions and procedures. By the turn of the century, the British penal system had come to seem mindless and pointlessly cruel not because it had altered in such directions but because the political and cultural conditions that had shaped it no longer existed; both the structure of power in society and the implicit descriptions of human nature and social action that were held by those with influence had altered and left the system stranded like a beached whale. All this needs careful investigation and analysis before the detailed history of policymaking that is given by Radzinowicz and Hood can be fully appreciated.

[13] Public Record Office, Home Office 45/10027/A56902C/9.
[14] *The Times* (March 26, 1898).

Without this, their wonderfully thorough account nonetheless lacks depth. They skillfully analyze the views of penal reformers, politicians, and administrators and recount the "precipitating circumstances" that selected certain of these views for implementation. Yet their standard is essentially one of "modernity" and is applied to each on an issue-by-issue basis, obscuring the worldview of the policymaker and the social meanings of his or her discourse by passing over its contemporary functions. It is much as if one were to discuss the literary portrayal of criminals over time without a familiarity with changing genres and changing relations between authors, their writings, and their readers. Or, to adopt the terms of the closer field of the history of medicine, it would be like recounting the evolution of nosologies and therapies for each disease without at the same time excavating the more general conceptions of health and illness from which those nosologies and therapies were derived.

One example will have to suffice here. At several points, Radzinowicz and Hood praise Godfrey Lushington, under secretary at the Home Office during the 1880s and early 1890s, for his libertarian and humane stances in policy debates. They cite his successful opposition to pressures to commit more children to reformatories and "industrial schools" and to extend police supervision from convicts released before their full sentence had been served to first offenders on probation. They also note with great approval his influential criticism to the Gladstone Committee of 1894 of the reformatory ineffectiveness of the existing harsh prison regime. They take these positions as evidence of growing humanitarian and libertarian concern at the highest levels of administration. This there was, and their attention to a figure like Lushington, who was central to the making of criminal policy but virtually unknown to posterity, is welcome and is an example of how the Home Office archives can alter and deepen criminal justice history.

Yet such episodic treatment gives a very misleading picture of Lushington's outlook and concerns. His views, not uncommon in his time, cannot be identified with modern liberalism. His liberalism was of a distinctly Victorian kind, which blended sympathy for the underdog and concern for individual liberty with a strong belief in the necessity and virtue of deterrent social policies. His deepest commitment was to fostering and preserving a society of free and responsible individuals where liability for every action could be clearly located for reward or punishment. Thus he opposed most proposals for increased intervention into personal lives on grounds that from a later twentieth-century perspective seem to mix liberal and conservative values. For example, he resisted the zeal of reformatory activists to incarcerate ever more children not only out of concern for the rights of the children and of their parents but on the grounds of its cost to public funds, fear of the social demoralization and "pauperization" that would result from encouraging parents to shirk their responsibilities, and from a very limited view of the functions of government in general. Radzinowicz and Hood fail to note that among other pressures he resisted were those that called for the first legislation on the prevention of cruelty to children. Issues of child welfare and family rights, which emerged into prominence in the late nineteenth century, provoked more complex responses than is indicated in this work, responses with which humanitarianism and libertarianism were, inconveniently for modern preferences, often at odds.

Similarly, the authors, in highlighting Lushington's criticism of the capacity of the existing prison regime to rehabilitate prisoners, make mention neither of his broader skepticism about the creative possibilities of virtually all institutions nor of his belief in the necessity of a deterrent penal system. He saw little justification for incarcerating anyone except for punishment, but he never doubted the need to punish and, even more, to be seen to punish. Incarceration of child offenders, he felt, might be replaced by whipping and by punishment of their parents. Along these lines he threw his influence against any further disuse of the death penalty and also against suggestions to create less severe forms of penal discipline for "conscience" prisoners or for debt defaulters. Lushington's discourse and actions, whether "liberal" or "conservative," become more coherent and more historically illuminating once placed within the appropriate political and cultural contexts. So too for criminal policy as a whole in this era; as we resist the temptation to see it as either a march in the direction of the present or a casebook of "recurring dilemmas," we gain a window into Victorian and Edwardian life.

Radzinowicz and Hood's impressive work, while an enormous scholarly accomplishment, has major limitations as history. In part these limitations are understandable in light of the historical context of their project itself. The year 1948, when Leon Radzinowicz virtually opened the field of British criminal justice history with the first volume of this project, was a time when pride in British institutions came easily. They had weathered the domestic and international storms of the twentieth century more ably than had any other people. The "British way" of successfully reconciling the rights of the individual and the well-being of the community was the envy of the world and stood in stark contrast to the vicious revolutions and dictatorships of both Right and Left elsewhere. What was true in politics seemed equally clear in everyday life. Britain's pacific and law-abiding nature was remarked on by every foreign visitor and seemed to be embedded in the national character. At such a moment, the outlines of the nation's criminal justice history seemed quite clear: a gradual and more or less continuous advance out of a "medieval" world of disorder and cruelty to the present era, in which serious crime had been largely conquered and criminal justice (barring only a few remnants of that old world under siege, such as hanging) made both humane and efficient. Indeed the year of publication of Radzinowicz's first volume saw the abolition of corporal punishment.

In that volume and in three further volumes that appeared over the following twenty years, Radzinowicz delineated for the first time how the movement for reform of criminal justice arose and advanced in the later eighteenth and early nineteenth centuries. Inhumane corporal and capital punishments were greatly curtailed, and the rights of the accused were extended at the same time that a professional police was created that protected as never before both public security and personal liberty. These developments seemed obviously appropriate and thus required explanation only in a "tactical" sense. There were no uncertainties and no ironies in this sharply drawn account of enlightenment versus prejudice and cruelty and thus no encouragement to see criminal policy as an expression of particular political and cultural structures.

The four decades between Radzinowicz's commencement of the entire undertaking and the completion of the present volume, however, have been eventful and disillusioning. The "British way" of justice has fallen on hard times as crime statistics, prison populations, and public anxiety about "law and order" have all exploded, while criticism of police, judicial, and penal disregard for individual rights has also dramatically mounted. In dramatic contrast to 1948, no consensus and little contentment exists in Britain today about criminal justice policy. These disturbing developments have also contributed to the rapid growth from the 1960s of historical study of crime and criminal justice. Here, as in current policy debates, a rather self-satisfied Whiggish consensus has given way to more critical perspectives and sharper divisions of view. Contemporary failure has opened doors to more questioning and examining of the past.

Yet this drastic change in the context of criminal policy history did not stimulate any corresponding change in the approach taken by this project despite the passage of twenty years and the addition of Roger Hood as coauthor. Certainly, some effect can be seen in their attention to "recurring dilemmas" and in their greater sophistication about the complexities of the process of policy formation. This volume, for instance, shows more sensitivity than does its predecessors to the subjective nature of all sources of information about crime (very much including official statistics) and points out, for example, how aware the Victorians themselves were of the limitations of criminal statistics. Nonetheless, the focus remains on pragmatic grapplings with particular problems that are evaluated by their approach to modern solutions. Radzinowicz's 1948 vision of a gradual advance toward modern enlightenment remains evident. This advance is now seen to be more complicated than it was in the earlier volumes as the line of march at times is pushed back and at times takes false paths that lead to cul-de-sacs. Yet, in the end, it always presses on toward the light.

No doubt the limitations examined here owe much to the nearly overwhelming demands of the task the authors took on. It is certainly enough achievement for any two historians to have examined for the first time the full range of sources for the making of central government penal policy over this long period and to have brought out of this intimidating mass of material the first detailed yet clear, ordered, and discriminating account. Yet, ironically, the very conditions that have admirably fitted the authors for this task may also have worked against a more critical and a more contextual treatment. The very effort to master this vast mass of source material must have discouraged additional efforts of "distancing" and reinterpretation. Even more, their preeminent roles as criminological experts and scientific penal reformers who are consulted by government on current issues may have inclined them to be overly "pragmatic" and teleological in viewing past thinking and action and to prefer to recount the immediate circumstances and explicit arguments involved in the development of policy over entering into the quicksands of "fundamental factors" that are less manageable and less immediately relevant to present policy issues. Although this work is independent in judgment and severely critical of many past policies and policymakers, it nonetheless has something of the quality of an "official" history in its orientation toward the concerns of present policymakers. The civil servants at the Home Office will find this work an invaluable source of perspective; nineteenth-century historians will also find it invaluable, but more as a reference work than as a definitive account of its subject.

The study of British criminal policy as an integral part of social, political, and cultural history for the most part still has to be done. However, thanks to the astute and thorough map of policy debates and their resolutions provided by Radzinowicz and Hood, historians will now be far better equipped for the task.

MARTIN J. WIENER

Rice University

[2]

FROM AMSTERDAM TO AUBURN
AN EXPLANATION FOR THE RISE OF THE PRISON IN SEVENTEENTH-CENTURY HOLLAND AND NINETEENTH-CENTURY AMERICA

The prison and its origins have aroused a good deal of historical interest in recent years.[1] The resultant literature, to which scholars from various disciplines have contributed, is often labelled as 'revisionist'. The label is applied because of a major common characteristic: although these studies diverge on several points, they all react against an older model which presented the rise of the prison simply as the result of the benevolent endeavors of humanitarian reformers. The reaction was of course long overdue. In other fields of historical inquiry serious analysis likewise has been substituted for a naive desire to praise or to blame the actors involved. A disadvantage of the revisionist approach, on the other hand, is its tendency to create a mirror-image of the humanitarian argument. The reformers are now seen as 'bad guys', indifferent to the fate of convicts and bent on creating opportunities for economic gain. The ensuing dichotomy between good and bad should certainly be overcome.[2] Nevertheless, the recent literature represents a very valuable contribution to historical scholarship, because it has placed the rise of imprisonment more firmly in its social context. In America Rothman dealt with the interdependence between various types of institutions and related their emergence to changing attitudes in the Jacksonian era.[3] A different group of scholars, notably Conley and Miller, stressed the role of economic factors in the emergence of prisons.[4] On the other side of the Atlantic authors such as Foucault, Stekl and Ignatieff put forward arguments which were divergent as well but all centered around the social needs for discipline and control.[5] My own work stresses the importance of state formation processes.[6]

The present article attempts to take the discussion further by making a beginning at transatlantic comparison. The comparison will focus on the causes for the establishment of prisons rather than on the details of their functioning once they had been established. My central question is: what was the social context which favored the rise of the prison in Europe and America, respectively? This, it is hoped, may provide a new impetus for historical theorizing about the origins of imprisonment.

The essay deals with Europe first. The earliest phase of Europe's experience with imprisonment will be elucidated, with Amsterdam as the main example. Thereafter the extent to which the European experience sheds light on the problem of the rise of imprisonment in America will be discussed. The first enterprise is a necessary prerequisite for the second. At first sight it may seem only natural to discuss American developments in the early nineteenth centuruy together with simultaneous developments on the other side of the Atlantic. I will demonstrate, however, that the earliest phases of the history of the prison on the two continents are to be situated in the early nineteenth century and in the seventeenth, respectively. In order to discuss causation, therefore, America around 1800 should be compared primarily with seventeenth-century Europe and more specifically with Amsterdam. An older study by Rusche and Kirchheimer acknowledged this difference in timing, but later it tended to be forgotten.[7] In his book on madness, published in 1961, Foucault devoted considerable attention to imprisonment in early modern France, but these data hardly play a role in his 1975 study of French prisons from the Revolution onwards.[8] Therefore it is necessary to pay attention once more to the long-term process in Europe, beginning around 1600. First I will explain, on a general level, how and why the prison emerged in a number of Western-European countries. This is followed by citing an illustrative case, that of Amsterdam. The choice of Amsterdam is not merely one of convenience, since the city was the major model for the rest of the European continent. The Dutch experience is the one that may shed light on developments in North-East America in the late eighteenth and early nineteenth centuries.

Prisons in early modern Europe

A number of German legal historians, writing in the early decades of the twentieth century, dealt with the origins of imprisonment from a European perspective. Several other scholars, inspired by this tradition, devoted articles and a few monographs to individual institutions, notably German and Dutch.[9] All agreed, and for sound reasons, that houses of correction were the first true prisons. The physical restriction of another person's freedom may be a phenomenon as old as mankind itself and confinement in an enclosed space, a more specific act, is probably very ancient too. But the houses of correction, inaugurated from the second half of the sixteenth century onwards, were the first institutions in which the majority of inmates were there to be chastized for a certain time. These houses were different from earlier places of confinement. In the European middle ages people were locked up in dungeons, towers or forts, but imprisonment as a result of a judgment in a trial was very infrequent. The majority of inmates were either kept as a hostage for their creditors or provisionally detained as suspects. These two functions continued to be served in the early modern period but not by the houses of correction. In eighteenth-century London, for example, debtors were locked up in King's bench.[10] Houses of correction, on the other hand, held several categories of deviants such as beggars, prostitutes and thieves.

The historical sequence in Europe justifies a distinction, for analytical purposes, between two Weberian ideal types: jail and prison. A jail mainly holds debtors and persons under provisional detention (in anticipation of or during a trial, and awaiting execution); a few may have been incarcerated for penal purposes. Although some inmates are detained for quite some time, the building is not expressly equipped for long-term stays. There are no arrangements for keeping the inmates busy. A prison primarily keeps delinquents or other deviants who have been sent there to serve a term for purposes of chastisement or correction. The inmates are subjected to a specific regime, which in early modern Europe was usually centered on compulsory labor. The institution is equipped to occupy its inmates, although difficulties may arise in practice. Houses of correction correspond to this ideal type and therefore they can be designated as prisons. In cases where the majority of inmates to be chastised are delinquents sentenced in a criminal trial we may speak of a criminal prison.

The emergence of the house of correction was the culmination of a transformation of attitudes toward the poor in general and beggars and vagrants in particular. In the course of the sixteenth century poverty was increasingly viewed in secular terms as a threat to public order, in Catholic as well as Protestant countries. Although this transformation of attitudes was also influenced by economic developments, it was primarily related to processes of state formation. By the sixteenth century, as a direct concomitant of state formation processes, Western Europe as a whole was a relatively pacified entity for the first time. Pacification served as a major precondition for the rise of confinement. The foundation of houses of correction implied at least two changes of policy. First, the institutions constituted a new and alternative option for dealing with those people who in an earlier period would also have been treated as deviants. In this earlier period they might have been banished, for instance, because the problems of a neighboring town or territory did not bother the judges. In a more pacified society, however, the idea that unwanted atrangers might be kept off the roads is more likely to arise. This idea was realized in the house of correction, being a spatial solution for public order problems. Second, the house of correction was a more visible symbol of repression. It testified to the determination of the authorities to deal with new categories of deviants as well. The latter were the beggars and vagrants, whom the simultaneous change of attitudes toward poverty and idleness had put into such an unfavorable position. In a more pacified society, where private warfare and vendettas have been subdued, it is easier for the authorities to tackle new problems of public order.[11]

Thus the first prisons in Europe were inaugurated because a specific stage in state formation processes, a relative monopolization of violence by monarchs and patriciates, had been reached. England led the way from the middle of the sixteenth century onwards and the Dutch Republic followed around 1600. In the course of the seventeenth century houses of correction were established in many towns in continental Europe. Although most towns did not go so far as to adopt the differentiation that will be shown to have characterized Amsterdam, separate wards were not uncommon. And the three main elements of the Amsterdam prison regime — compulsory labor, physical means of discipline and moderate publicity — were features of houses of correction everywhere.

The emergence of the criminal prison — another development marked in Amsterdam — can also be traced in the Dutch Republic as well as abroad. Most cities in Holland used their houses of correction increasingly as a penal institution from the late seventeenth century onwards, and the institutions severed their ties with poor-relief. The landward provinces, which founded houses of correction in the early eighteenth century, primarily listed delinquents as inmates to be. In seven sample regions from the territory of the Republic between 1700 and 1811 imprisonment in a house of correction accounted for 15.2 pct. of the sentences.[12] In the German countries the criminal prison emerged along other lines, but its rise was equally marked. Originally, houses of correction were not meant for convicts and for a long time the governors conducted a struggle against the judicial bodies who wished them to receive delinquents too. The governors notably opposed the confinement of criminals who had received corporal punishment at the hands of the executioner, which would attach infamy to the institution. By the first half of the eighteenth century, however, the courts had won this struggle and imprisonment in a house of correction had become a common penal option. Houses of correction in the Habsburg Empire likewise evolved into penal institutions.[13] The *hôpitaux généraux* of France remained a sort of asylum, but in the second half of the eighteenth century they were supplemented by new prisons for beggars, which in no way had the character of asylums. In addition, the galleys were put out of service and from 1748 onwards the *bagnes* were in fact workhouses for delinquents.[14] On a European scale, therefore, the rise of the prison should be situated in the seventeenth and that of the criminal prison in the eighteenth century.

This overview may be supplemented by empirical data derived from a case-study. The preceding discussion suggests which features of houses of correction should receive emphasis. The first question is of course: when was the institution established? Further, we have to know whether we may call it a prison: were the inmates really incarcerated or did they enter more or less voluntarily? Was there a labor program or did the institution rather resemble a jail? The next question is 'who were the inmates'? They may be delinquents or other deviants; various categories may be incarcerated together or differentiation may prevail. The length of a prisoner's stay is another crucial variable. Finally, it is important to know whether confinement played a considerable role or only a marginal one in the penal system. For Amsterdam, all these questions can be answered.

The Amsterdam Institutions

As noted above, Amsterdam was exemplary. In fact the city served as a model both within the Republic and abroad, which is attested, among other things, by the large number of foreign visitors to the houses of correction. In the early years of the seventeenth century books and pamphlets about the Amsterdam rasphouse appeared in French and German.[15] Various houses elsewhere in the Republic were consciously modeled on those of Amsterdam. This was the case as early as 1596 in Leiden and as late as 1710 when the Estates of Gelderland founded a prison.[16] Several towns abroad oriented themselves in Amsterdam; directly or indirectly by taking Holland as a whole for a model. The Antwerp magistrates did so in 1613 and the authorities in the German city of Celle did the same in 1732.

The existence of J.N. Jacobsen Jensen's list of foreign visitors[17] enables me to provide a quantitative illustration of the public's interest. It is an inventory of foreigners known to have travelled in the Netherlands prior to 1850. Those coming after 1596, the year in which the rasphouse was opened, number 366, of whom forty-three did not visit Amsterdam. Another forty-five refrained from specifying the places they went to within the city. The remaining 278 are the ones that concern us. They figure in table 1. Over the entire period a third visited one or more of the houses of correction. However, throughout the seventeenth century almost one half did so. This is a relatively high number in view of the many other places of interest. Moreover, these visitors came to Amsterdam for all kinds of different purposes. After 1700 interest in the houses of correction steadily declined. At the end of the eighteenth and in the early nineteenth century the newly built workhouse attracted most visitors.

TABLE 1

Visitors to a house of correction in Amsterdam, 1596-1849

period	visitors to the city	visitors to a house of correction	
	abs.	abs.	pct.
1596-1649	26	12	46
1650-1699	45	21	47
1700-1749	30	11	37
1750-1799	77	24	31
1800-1849	100	23	23
total	278	91	33

(Source: Jensen, 1919)

Amsterdam served as a model not because for some mysterious reason others sought to emulate it, but because the city catered to social needs that were equally felt elsewhere. The house of correction represented one possible solution to problems of control which were common to Western-European countries. Control of the marginal population and discipline of the poor figured prominently among those problems. These were the objectives of Amsterdam's first house of correction, the foundation of which had been decided upon in 1589. Seven years later the first inmates arrived. Although the necessity for an alternative punishment for young thieves had been stressed as the primary motive for establishing a house of correction, beggars and vagrants constituted the principal category of inmates in the early decades of its existence. This emerges from the work of Pontanus, published in 1611.[18] His book is the first in a series of descriptions proclaiming the wonders of the expanding metropolis. According to Pontanus, the problem caused by widespread begging and vagrancy in Holland lay behind the inauguration of the house of correction. He specifically referred to a placard against beggary issued by the provincial Estates in December 1595.[19] That beggars comprised the majority of inmates in the early seventeenth century is confirmed by a booklet, published in 1612, which is devoted entirely to the house of correction. It speaks only of persons asking for alms, being unwilling to work.[20] In 1614 the court ordered the almshouse provosts to pick up everyone illegally asking for alms or wandering about idly and put them in the house of correction without trial. Those rounded up were only taken to court if it was the person in question's fourth arrest.[21]

By this time Amsterdam boasted two houses of correction, since a separate prison for women had been opened in 1597. Thus the city went on a course toward a differentiated system of institutions. The prison for women was called the spinhouse and its male counterpart was soon referred to as the rasphouse. Another major step in the differentiation process was taken in the 1650's, when beggars received their own prison. In 1650 a "workhouse for poor children" was opened and in August 1654 it was officially designated as a prison for beggars and vagabonds.[22] Henceforth the almshouse provosts were ordered to take those arrested by them to the workhouse.[23] Its inmates were beggars of both sexes.

From then on the rasphouse and, to a lesser extent, the spinhouse were truly criminal prisons. The differentiation of institutions was already self-evident to Olfert Dapper, whose description of Amsterdam was published in 1663. Speaking about the rasphouse, he begins by quoting Pontanus. But he immediately adds that he thinks the latter's views on the motives for the house's foundation are incorrect: "It seems rather hard and almost inhuman to put beggars (though some used to steal under that guise) to such heavy labor" [i.e. rasping wood].[24] The real motive, he continues, was "perhaps" that *schepenen* were forced to hang many young thieves, and looked for an alternative. The word "perhaps" betrays the fact that Dapper's conclusions were not based on historical research. For him the connection prison – heavy labor – crime was simply a matter of course. In the less serious case of vagrancy imprisonment took place in the workhouse. At the same time Hans Bontemantel, who was himself *schepen* for several years, testified that the court considered confinement a normal part of the penal system. Imprisonment in a house of correction figures in his rank-order of penalties as a matter of course between whipping indoors and exposure on the pillory.[25] At the end of the century Caspar Commelin sealed the preceding development by inventing a new collective name for the houses of correction. They had always been designated, together with the charitable institutions founded in the middle ages, as *godshuizen*. Commelin separates them from this category and calls them "houses of justice".[26]

One more change was to occur: the detachment of confinement on request from the prison system. From the early years onward those inmates who were not vagrants or delinquents were confined at the instigation of relatives, with the court merely authorizing it. Many of the inmates belonged to the lower classes, but this was not the case with every 'licentious' and 'untractable' person. Even before the opening of the rasphouse there was talk of 'children of good parents' being placed there and in both the rasp and spinhouse a separate ward, called the 'secret place', was soon instituted for this purpose. Its inmates were not obliged to work. It is significant that in these early years respectable families were prepared to have a member confined under the same roof with more marginal persons. But as the houses of correction increasingly evolved into criminal prisons in the course of the seventeenth century, every form of confinement there became associated with the infamous sphere of justice. At the end of the century this led to the emergence of a separate type of institution for confinement on request. Throughout the Republic this institution became known as the *beterhuis*. Although the Amsterdam spin and workhouse continued to accommodate prisoners confined on request, a new institution for the elite founded in 1694. This Amsterdam *beterhuis* was only semi-private; the city leased it to the manager.

At the close of the seventeenth century, therefore, Amsterdam had a

FROM AMSTERDAM TO AUBURN 445

differentiated prison system for male and female criminals (including beggars and vagabonds who were legally delinquents as well) and persons exhibiting undesirable behavior. From the 1650's onwards the rasphouse was unequivocally a criminal prison. The emergence of confinement in private institutions marked the development whereby the older houses became exclusively tools of justice. In the eighteenth century even the rasphouse's secret place served as such a tool. It harbored those among the condemned whom the court wished to bar from public access. These included persons convicted of sodomy, in so far as they were spared the death penalty. The Amsterdam rasphouse may have been the first truly criminal prison in world history.

The differences between the Amsterdam houses of correction and medieval jails can be illuminated further by a look at the former's regime. The programs were fairly uniform. Only the secret places and the *beterhuizen* which succeeded them stand out in this respect, but these are of less concern here. A veritable prison regime was imposed on those confined in the other institutions. They were compelled to work and hence contribute to the cost of their stay. From the early seventeenth century onwards the labor program of the first house of correction consisted solely of rasping wood (hence its name). Blocks of Brazil redwood had to be grated to a pulver, which was used as raw material in the paint industry. The raspers were obliged to produce a minimum amount. This counted as very hard work, as Dapper's remark indicates. The type of work done by the prisoners in the workhouse was lighter. It included hemp-beating, knitting nets and weaving coarse linen and canvas. Sacks were made from the canvas to pack the red powder which the other house of correction produced.[27] The nature of the labor program in the spinhouse is evident from its name. Apart from labor, religious exercises and instruction originally had a prominent place in the projected daily programs. Several historians have stressed this feature, but in fact the original ambitious schemes were soon abandoned of necessity. According to Dapper, in the rasphouse the religious books were simply laid into the cells. One does not expose a preacher or schoolmaster to "a bunch of raging and wild people."[28] The oldest prison was no exception to the rule that practice does not conform to all the rhetoric of the founders.

Visitors were regularly admitted into the houses of correction for a fee. The public could see the condemned in action. It was a reflection of the relatively public character of the entire penal system. Still, the penalty of imprisonment was decidedly less theatrical than punishment on the scaffold. The rise of the prison is a clear expression of the long process which ultimately led to the nineteenth-century privatization of repression. Its twin process was the reduction of the physical element in punishment, and there the houses of correction represented an intermediary stage too. Beatings were a common feature of the maintenance of discipline in the institutions, but still imprisonment was the first form of serious punishment which did not primarily have the infliction of physical suffering as its purpose.

What remains to be demonstrated is the relatively important role of the houses of correction within the penal system in Amsterdam. The available quantitative data make this clear enough. Jean Jüngen studied the court's sentences for the years 1600 and 1614. He found five condemnations to the rasphouse in 1600 out of a total of 130 cases. In 1614 six convicts out of 128 were sent to a house of correction. Three were women condemned to the spinhouse.[29] These are moderate numbers. In those years the majority of inmates were not delinquents serving a court's sentence. My own research covers the years 1650-1750, when all three houses of correction were in operation. It yielded two bodies of data: a complete series of all cases ending in a scaffold punishment and a sample of the remaining cases.[30] The judgment often consisted of several penalties combined. This was notably so in the scaffold series, which would otherwise have counted no confinements at all. The Confinements in the sample include both single cases and those in which it was combined with another penalty (usually banishment).

TABLE 2
Frequency of Confinement in Amsterdam, 1651-1750

A. In the scaffold series

period	number of confinements	percentage from all public sentences
1651-1660	95	37,4
1661-1670	161	53.5
1671-1680	92	48.9
1681-1690	102	49.0
1691-1700	170	47.5
1701-1710	65	34.6
1711-1720	160	34.2
1721-1730	202	43.5
1731-1740	129	46.1
1741-1750	147	52.5

B. In the sample (N = 500 in each period)

period	percentage of confinement
1651-1683	17.4
1684-1716	20.8
1717-1749	20.8

(source: *Sententie-* and *Confessieboeken, Gemeente-archief* Amsterdam.

Table 2 shows that imprisonment followed upon chastisement on the scaffold in a number of cases fluctuating between a third and more than one half. The fluctuations do not betray a specific pattern. It should be noted that the cases without confinement include those where the judgment was capital (13 percent of the entire scaffold series). In the sample the percentage of condemnations to a house of correction stays more or less stable at about one fifth.[31] Since the Amsterdam court judged a declining number of cases in the first half of the eighteenth century, the absolute number of confinements in non-public cases dropped as well. Considering the approximate total of punishments, the annual average of condemnations to a house of correction in non-public cases in the second half of the seventeenth century was about seventy-five. In addition about twelve scaffolded delinquents were imprisoned yearly. After 1700 the total number of confinements declined.

TABLE 3
Long-term confinements in Amsterdam, 1651-1750

A. *Scaffold series* (percentages are from all sentences including confinement)

period	number of terms of five years or longer		number of terms of ten years or longer	
	pct.	abs.	pct.	abs.
1651-1660	41.0	39	14.7	14
1661-1670	28.7	46	4.3	7
1671-1680	21.8	20	6.6	6
1681-1690	58.9	60	29.5	30
1691-1700	59.4	101	25.9	44
1701-1710	56.9	37	26.1	17
1711-1720	81.8	131	51.2	82
1721-1730	75.3	153	44.8	91
1731-1740	78.3	101	53.5	69
1741-1750	68.0	100	52.4	77

B. *Sample* (percentages are from all confinements)

period	percentage of terms of five years or longer	percentage of terms of ten years or longer
1651-1683	0.9	—
1684-1716	6.8	2.3
1717-1749	18.5	4.4

(Source: *Sententie-* and *Confessieboeken,Gemeente-archief* Amsterdam).

Table 3, however, shows that a higher frequency of relatively long terms emerged in the course of the eighteenth century, a development especially marked among the non-public cases. This formed a reaction to the drop in condemnations and it saved the houses of correction from a relative depopulation. The choice of penal options as such was apparently less influenced by capacity-considerations. The combination of the various quantitative trends had its most fateful effect on the rasphouse. The institution's character as a prison for serious delinquents was reinforced in the first half of the eighteenth century. From the 1650's through 1670's an annual average of thirty-eight convicts entered the rasphouse, seven of whom mounted the scaffold. From the 1720's through 1740's the yearly number of scaffolded delinquents confined there was still about seven: this time out of twelve and burdened with longer terms. It should be noted that the real length of a stay in prison was usually shorter than the term set. Most inmates of the houses of correction received reduction for good behavior. This custom had a function similar to the later American 'good time' system.[32] But real length correlated with official term.

It is clear from these figures that the houses of correction played a major role in Amsterdam's penal system. The figures do of course refer to sentenced delinquents only; beggars especially, who were usually confined without a trial, are not included. Further research is needed in order to know to what extent other European cities conformed to the Amsterdam pattern.

Although confinement played a considerable role in the penal system of the Dutch metropolis, it should not be forgotten that public executions and corporal punishment existed alongside it. It was only toward the end of the eighteenth century that a heightened sensitivity with regard to the sight of the scaffold became manifest.[33] This was the case throughout Europe. What happened in Europe after about 1800, therefore, amounted to a new transformation in penal practices and attitudes toward repression, rather than a continuation of the preceding development. Eventually, corporal punishments would be abolished and the death penalty executed indoors. While physical punishment was being debated, experiments were made with new forms of imprisonment which corresponded more closely to the ideal of a privatized repression. The characteristic type of new prison was the penitentiary, a word first used in Britain in the second half of the eighteenth century.[34] The emphasis shifted from compulsory labor and semi-publicity to regimentation, avoidance of contact and, above all, confrontation of the offender with his inner self. Solitary confinement was to promote this confrontation, while the new interest in regimentation and surveillance was reflected most tellingly in the panoptic principle. The experimentation-phase of the first half of the nineteenth century was further characterized by a fresh enthusiasm for the best possible way to set up a prison. This explains the various projects on paper such as Bentham's and the frequent journeys of orientation. Visits to prisons were not only made within Europe but also to America. At this point it may be appropriate to shift the focus to the latter continent.

America before the prison: New Netherland and its neighbors

There is a good reason to consider New Netherland first: the prison system of New Amsterdam's mother-city was already in full operation when the British seized the colony from the Dutch. If there had been houses of correction along the Hudson river by then, we might conclude that imprisonment was easily exportable to distant societies. Compared to the early history of New England, the history of New Netherland has been neglected — certainly as far as criminal justice is concerned. It is worthwhile to dig a little into it. Could Amsterdam's prison system have been exported to the New World in the seventeenth century?

This is not entirely inconceivable, if we realize that the Dutch East India Company opened a spinhouse in Batavia in 1642. But this institution was not a criminal prison and never became one. It was founded because some Christian women led a "scandalous, dirty and licentious life" and its main purpose seems to have been to provide men with the means of ridding themselves of their wives.[35] Its character only faintly resembled that of contemporary houses of correction in Holland.[36] If the founding phrase has any real meaning beyond that of a routine statement, it can be argued why such a spinhouse was not opened in New Amsterdam. The need for protecting the reputation of Christians was less urgent there. The European and Indian communities had little mutual contact save in war. Moreover, the former regarded the latter as savages, to a greater extent than the Asian peoples whom the East India Company dealt with. Consequently, the whites in America were less conscious of having a standard to maintain. The Dutch in New Netherland lacked the Puritans' obsession with morals offenses. Occasionally a prostitute was banished, but on the whole it was not too spectacular.[37]

As New Amsterdam had no spinhouse, it did not establish anything resembling its mother-city's rasphouse either. The New Netherland book of placards, which was begun in 1638 when Willem Kieft became governor, does not refer to such an institution. A few placards threaten with labor in a chain gang along with black slaves, and these laws are significant.[38] Working in a chain gang, or *opus publicum*, was known in Europe too and as a penalty it was older than the house of correction. Where the latter existed, however, *opus publicum* normally fell into disuse. As long as non-capital, serious offenders were occasionally employed to build fortifications and roads, there was even less need for a prison. The absence of a prison from New Amsterdam is attested by a sentence in 1647 when Pieter Stuyvesant condemned one Michiel Piquet to a term of eighteen years in a house of correction. Piquet was sent over to old Amsterdam to be confined in the rasphouse.[39]

This event took place in the first of Stuyvesant's seventeen years of office, when a proper court had not yet come into existence. What about the later years? The city of New Amsterdam got its own court of justice in 1653 and similar courts were subsequently instituted in the settlements on Long Island.[40] New Amsterdam court records are largely unresearched and it would require a large-scale investigation to analyze them thoroughly. Such an investigation would certainly be worthwhile, but for our present purposes it is not necessary to perform it. It is clear enough that these records deal with anything but imprisonment. I examined the year 1663, the last of uninterrupted Dutch rule.[41] Slightly more than half of the cases are civil suits or at least conducted by a private prosecutor. In the others the *schout* is the prosecutor. These are still minor cases and almost always the penalty is a fine. In addition we should consider the activities of the New Netherland Council, which still dealt with judicial matters as well. The contemporary index of the 1663 council minutes contains a page which O'Callaghan lists as 'register of sentences.'[42] The record has twelve entries. Four refer to decisions in conflicts over possession of land or related financial matters. Two men are banished from the province for reasons which remain unclear. One is prosecuted for slander but his begging forgiveness settles the matter. In three cases the extant fragments do not permit a conclusion about their contents. Two men, finally, are condemned for stealing from a ship. They are to be whipped and ordered to return to their service until the money can be restituted.[43]

An exhaustive examination of the records may reveal a few cases of imprisonment, but as a penalty it must have been very rare.[44] Other courts probably followed a similar sentencing policy. Only a tiny fraction of the cases judged by the court of Beverwijk were serious offenses and these were punished corporally.[45] The only location for confinement in New Amsterdam was in the town hall.[46] This was a normal practice adopted from the mother-city: in Amsterdam and other Dutch towns the court convened in the town hall, in the basement of which delinquents in provisional detention were kept together with debtors. These places were jails and so was the place in New Amsterdam's town hall; it was certainly not a prison. There is no trace of a house of correction in New Amsterdam.

Conversely, at least in name, such houses do appear in other colonies at that time. The Massachusetts authorities ordered the building of a house of correction in 1632 and again in 1655, this time for each county. A similar order was given in Pennsylvania in 1683. But the name used should not deceive us. The houses which were constructed or designated were no more than ordinary jails, as was often the case with nominal houses of correction in contemporary England. The one in Philadelphia was actually denoted as a 'cage'. The institution which probably came nearest to a house of correction in seventeenth-century America was the Boston almshouse of 1685, which also served as a place of confinement.[47]

Almshouses were indeed the first 'asylums' in Colonial America, appearing on the scene from the late seventeenth century onwards.[48] The Reformed *diaconie* of New Amsterdam established a refuge for the poor as early as 1653-5, first in a house then in a *bouwerie*.[49] Rothman included almshouses in the network of institutions he studied, but as more or less voluntary places, I would rather consider them separately from prisons, workhouses and madhouses. He further stresses that during the Colonial period most of the poor were assisted at home or in neighboring households.[50] This, however, is a trivial remark, since it has been common practice everywhere in most periods of history. More important are the existence of institutions as such and the mentality which they express. Rothman explains that Colonial attitudes to the poor were not basically repressive, a position also taken by Gary Nash, who argues that in Philadelphia the change toward a new attitude took place on the eve of the Revolution.[51] That is the crucial point. A more benevolent attitude to the poor similarly prevailed in Europe before the sixteenth-century transformation. Still medieval Europe had its voluntary *godshuizen*: almshouses and hospitals. It is clear that charitable institutions do come earlier than prisons. For Europe the actual 'discovery of the asylum' should be situated in the thirteenth century.

As for New York, it does not seem to have played an advanced role among the colonies.[52] In his synthesis of Colonial New York's history, Michael Kammen states that the province remained predominantly Dutch for a generation after 1664.[53] Even so, this means that the reminiscence of Amsterdam had finally faded away by the time of Leisler's rebellion. Only in 1736 did New York City erect its first house of correction.[54] The conclusion must be that there are no grounds for the assumption that the Amsterdam prison system had specific influence upon repression in the New World. How could it have been otherwise? For one thing, Stuyvesant was a Calvinist and a soldier, while the founding fathers of the rasphouse were magistrates and liberals.[55] More important considerations have to do with social structure. The emergence of houses of correction in Europe presupposed a certain stage of state formation and social differentiation, as explained above. This type of social structure did not characterize seventeenth-century America. By 1690 New York City had a few thousand inhabitants and, in many respects, resembled a late medieval town. Like other major Colonial cities it had barely outgrown frontier conditions or differentiated itself from the countryside.[56] The province as a whole was far from pacified or stable, consisting of isolated communities, semi-feudal manors and Indian tribes. No wonder this society only felt a need for quick justice.

The rise of the prison in America

Two conclusions can be drawn from the preceding section. First, for a prison system to be adopted by a society it is not sufficient that its members know about the possibility; the structure of the society must somehow be receptive to it. Second, the discovery of the asylum does not necessarily coincide with the emergence of prisons; in Europe and, to a lesser extent, in America the former antedated the latter. The difference in timing between Europe and America was simply due to the later start of the white societies in the New World. Of course a later start does not necessarily mean late forever. Ideas, technologies and institutions sometimes do migrate from one type of society to another. By the late nineteenth century the North-Eastern part of the USA resembled contemporary Western Europe in many respects. When discussing the rise of imprisonment in America, we have to keep in mind both the late start and the rapid catching up.

As noted above, an embryonic form of imprisonment appeared already in Colonial times. From the second quarter of the eighteenth century onwards institutions resembling European houses of correction were set up in several places. The character of these institutions has not been clearly determined by historical research. Those established in Rhode Island, for example, do not seem to have been penal at all.[57] Connecticut's house of correction in 1727, on the other hand, was meant, among other things, for rogues, vagabonds and beggars.[58] The institution inaugurated in New York in 1736 recalls the Dutch houses of correction in the early years of their existence. Its mixed purpose was threefold: confinement on request of disobedient servants and slaves; poor-relief; imprisonment of beggars, runaway servants and petty offenders condemned at the quarter sessions. In 1775 a new prison was built, which was called the bridewell.[59] It looks as if the coastal towns of New England and the middle colonies made a tentative start with imprisonment in the eighteenth century. Although Rothman's apparent view that these places were all almshouses is hard to accept, he is probably right in stating that we should not overestimate their importance. Penal imprisonment, when it occurred, continued to be executed primarily in jails. Convicts were locked up in the company of debtors and persons under trial in places not very different from an ordinary residence.[60] Between 1691 and 1776 the New York Supreme Court pronounced a prison sentence only nineteen or twenty times. Terms varied from eleven days to a year and a half.[61] Pennsylvania knew life imprisonment for certain felonies but it was hardly ever practiced.[62] Preyer confirms that the prison played but a marginal role in the penal system of all colonies.[63]

The first penal changes after the Revolution which have drawn the attention of historians were those taking place in Philadelphia in the 1790's. Recent studies have dispelled the myths surrounding these events. For one thing, they were not exclusively due to Quaker influence. The society which effectively campaigned for the laws of 1789 and 1790 was dominated by Episcopalians. Second, the experiment with solitary confinement was a rather marginal event. In fact, solitary confinement was only meant for "the more hardened and atrocious offenders".[64] Four out of 117 prisoners condemned in 1795 met this qualification and seven out of 159 in 1796.[65] Imprisonment in the Walnut Street cellhouse thus recalled an earlier Amsterdam practice: in the rasphouse separate confinement had been used from time to time as a disciplinary punishment. The Philadelphia episode was largely over by 1800 when the Walnut Street facility had become overcrowded and in bad state of repair.[66] It was only around 1830, when the penitentiaries in Pittsburgh and Cherry Hill were constructed, that the Pennsylvania system came into existence.[67] Both penitentiaries were designed – rebuilt in the case of Pittsburgh – by the architect John Haviland, who based his designs on a mixture of European models.[68].

By then imprisonment had become a regular practice. Around 1800 prisons were built in several states, but little is known about these early institutions, except in the case of New York.[69] Newgate in Greenwich Village was the first criminal prison in America, receiving felons, of both sexes, only. Just as in Walnut Street, overcrowding soon led it to be considered unsatisfactory.[70] The influx of prisoners reached notorious proportions because of a crime wave in the aftermath of the war with England. As a result, the number of prosecutions increased markedly, for offenses for which imprisonment had become the prescribed penalty in the meantime.[71] This formed the immediate cause for the construction of Auburn, which took place between 1816 and 1823. Two years later its prisoners built Sing Sing.[72]

With Auburn and Sing Sing established, the 'classical' era of American imprisonment had begun. According to Rothman, the 1820's and 1830's constituted the first period that witnessed the building of penal institutions on a large scale.[73] Most other states took New York as their model. The most conspicuous features of Auburn and Sing Sing were congregate labor, coupled with a rule of strict silence and a regime of discipline and humiliation. Their introduction was associated especially with Elam Lynds, who became deputy-keeper of the former institution in 1819. Thus both the Pennsylvania and Auburn systems were in operation by the time when the French inspector-general Charles Lucas published his comparative study of prisons in the USA and Europe and Tocqueville and Beaumont set out on their voyage.[74] Europeans particularly admired the Pennsylvania-style.[75]

The empirical evidence on the beginnings of penal imprisonment in America raises two basic questions. First, why did the prison emerge in the 1820's? Second, why was it that, although Europeans primarily admired the Pennsylvania system, most American prisons were modeled after Auburn? Both questions can be answered by taking the evidence from early modern Europe into account.

The first question has wider implications than an inquiry into concrete, immediate causes such as the crime wave in New York referred to above. We

FROM AMSTERDAM TO AUBURN 453

want to know in which respects the social structure of the early nineteenth century differed from that in the late seventeenth. An explanation in terms of Jacksonian democracy, whatever the merits of that concept, would still remain within the sphere of immediate causes. Moreover, the entirely different political context in which European houses of correction were founded, makes it hard to see this as the cause for the emergence of imprisonment in general. At first sight, economic developments are better suited to serve as an explanatory factor for the rise of prisons. A number of American scholars have argued for that connection. Miller, for example emphasizes that the hard-pressed shoemakers were disproportionately represented among the early prison population: "It hardly seems a coincidence that the shoemakers who were experiencing enormous stress and dislocation in free society were also coming to prison in disproportionate numbers. The prison held a message of deterrence out to the 'undisciplined' workers. The somber penitentiary, the symbol of state coercion at its greatest control and severity, would serve the interests of the emerging capitalist market economy by providing the ultimate 'correction' to the refractory worker."[76]

This type of argument, however, does not lead to a satisfactory explanation. For one thing, it is hardly surprising that repression particularly hit those groups who were in an unfavorable economic position. This also happened at times and places where imprisonment did not figure in the penal system. When houses of correction were established in Amsterdam, it was the marginal population of beggars and vagabonds who were hit hardest. We have to explain why the authorities came to look for a spatial solution to the problems of marginality. This might be because a certain stage of economic growth had been reached, but the comparison between Holland and America renders such a thesis less plausible. In seventeenth-century Europe commercial capitalism prevailed, while the nineteenth-century American North-East witnessed the beginnings of industrialism. If economic processes do not provide the primary explanation, the next step is to inquire whether my argument about state formation processes, developed from the European evidence, can also be valid for America.

Only two authors argue from that point of view. According to Takagi, the essence of the Walnut Street episode was a penal reform designed to give the state more control over repression.[77] The state, of course, is Pennsylvania. Hindus likewise deals with two of the units making up the federation. Massachusetts quickly adopted the new prison system, but antebellum South Carolina had no need for it at all. The two states also differed on other accounts: "Massachusetts consistently sought to bolster the role of formal authority by strengthening its courts, establishing police, and curbing extralegal violence. In South Carolina, however, plantation aristocrats mocked court laws, took their quarrels to the dueling field instead of the courthouse, belatedly established police, supported permanent vigilante organizations, and actually encouraged citizens to find extralegal accommodations rather than increase strife through lawsuits."[78]

Thus both Hindus and Takagi suggest that state formation is an important factor in the rise of imprisonment in America, but they do not provide an analysis of the longer-term process. Takagi refers to a change consisting of judicial centralization, at the expense of the counties, in one of the thirteen ex-colonies. Centralization is an aspect of state formation processes, but not of their earliest phases. In these processes monopolization of violence is the primary element. This aspect has hardly been made an object of systematic study by American historians. Although a literature exists on violence in American history, few studies view the subject from a developmental perspective. Ever since Turner, frontier violence has been considered as a somewhat unfortunate concomitant of the emerging American democracy. It is seldom realized that every region settled successively by whites experienced that development from stateless society to pacified centrally ruled area, which Europe took some seven centuries to complete. At the beginning of this development stood the vigilante movement. The vigilance committee functioned as a private domain of authority and violence in a single community under the leadership of the local elite.[79] The *de facto* fragmentation of authority of which it was an expression, equally prevailed in medieval Europe.

The observations on vigilantism and the differences between regions in America provide a solution to the problem of the emergence of prisons. Late medieval Europe, provincial New York in the middle of the eighteenth century and antebellum South Carolina all witnessed roughly the same degree of (non-) monopolization of violence. The mocking of courts, noted by Hindus, was equally a feature of late medieval Europe.[80] And Douglas Greenberg makes clear that the colony of New York witnessed a high level of private violence and absence of state control up into the 1760's.[81] At the beginning of the nineteenth century a larger area in the North-East had become relatively pacified, but in the South this took a longer time. Thus Holland around 1600 and North-East America in the 1820's, despite many differences, resembled each other in so far as both had recently emerged as relatively pacified entities. The coastal towns of the North had made a tentative start with imprisonment in late Colonial times, because they constituted a more or less settled and pacified fringe. When the North-East as a whole had become pacified the take-off of imprisonment began.

With the problem of the rise of the prison in America solved, it is possible to formulate an answer to the second question. The diverging preferences on either side of the Atlantic can be explained when early modern developments are taken into account. Rusche and Kirchheimer did so almost a half century ago, but they argued from a rather simplistic economic determinism.[82] My own argument stays within the theoretical framework outlined above and, consequently, serves to reinforce it. It is not surprising that Europeans were less excited by the Auburn system, since they had known it for two centuries. It was basically the regime of the house of correction. It is true that the Amsterdam rasphouse neither had a rule of silence nor separated prisoners at night. But its earliest ordinance included such rules as a prohibition of cursing. On the whole, strict regulation characterized the Dutch and German foundations. Just as these earlier institutions, the Auburn-style prisons were in practice workhouses where a severe labor discipline was enforced by the whip.[83] This rather tough repression served the needs of societies which were recently pacified.

The most distinguishing characteristic of the Pennsylvania system was the possibility of solitary confinement twenty-four hours a day. This had not been invented in Philadelphia. English reformers, notably John Howard, had advocated comparable measures and their ideas were echoed by Americans such as Benjamin Rush.[84] In early nineteenth-century Europe the principle of solitary

FROM AMSTERDAM TO AUBURN   455

confinement was discussed extensively, as European policy makers wished to experiment with new forms of imprisonment. Most Americans did not want to experiment; they were just starting with the prison and the Auburn-style suited them well. The Pennsylvania-style remained a minority-system because it served the needs of its society less adequately. In Europe, on the other hand, the rise of the nation-state had brought about a new transformation in repression, as explained at the end of the second section. Mind control became a major objective, and solitary confinement fit into this model. That is why Europeans admired Pennsylvanian practice. Tocqueville explained: "punishment here (. . .) is only directed at a man's mind, but it exerts an incredible influence upon him."[85]

It is easy to be misled by the popularity of American prisons with European visitors. These were not the same kind of people who had flocked to Amsterdam two centuries earlier. The visitors to Holland belonged to the general public; they came for other purposes and saw the houses of correction on their way. Nineteenth-century Europeans visiting American prisons were largely professionals. They were surveying and classifying, in accordance with the emerging 'science' of penology and they were equally interested in new institutions on their own continent. Just as many professionals went to see Geneva's prison, for example.[86] American prisons served as models because Europeans, going through a phase of experimentation, were seeking models. Amsterdam's houses of correction, on the other hand, were exemplary because the city had made what was practiced elsewhere as well into a more elaborate and refined system.

To conclude, it should be noted that in certain respects America did not lag behind Europe. Some penal changes could apparently take effect in spite of a different social context. The humanitarian rhetoric, for example, that became common in Europe from the late eighteenth century onwards, was easily picked up by philanthropists on the other side of the Atlantic. Around 1800 several American states adopted new penal codes which established imprisonment as the penalty for many offenses and reduced the role of corporal punishment. In America legal change preceded the rise of the prison. In Europe, on the other hand, houses of correction had simply been opened without any noteworthy change in formal legislation. For about two centuries the scaffold was used alongside with the prison. North-East America passed over this intermediary phase and, from the beginning, acknowledged imprisonment as the main form of punishment. This did not so much imply a reduction of the physical element in repression, since a stern discipline continued to be enforced within prisons. Consequently, it rather meant a reduction of the public character of repression, substituting physical coercion indoors for the confrontation with the community. The fact that North-East America very rapidly started to execute the death penalty also indoors, is in line with this observation. Massachusetts abolished public executions in 1835, which is earlier than any European country.[87]

The privatization of repression apparently did not necessarily require a preceding evolution of imprisonment. In America it was realized very smoothly during the early years when the prison had appeared on the scene. Consequently, by the latter half of the nineteenth century, there were few outward signs of a difference in modes of repression between the Old World and the New. Both routinely imprisoned delinquents and both witnessed a workers' movement against prison labor.[88] They had arrived at that point, however, by different routes.

Conclusion

The comparison between Western Europe and North-East America has clarified the role of state formation processes in the development of penal systems. Monopolization of violence represents an early phase in these processes and it functioned as a necessary prerequisite for the emergence of the prison, a spatial solution for public order problems. This can be demonstrated for both societies. The take-off of imprisonment occurred just after each society had become a relatively pacified entity. Their early prisons were characterized by compulsory labor enforced through physical discipline.

But from the moment of pacification and the rise of the prison onwards their routes diverged. In Europe violence had been monopolized by monarchs and patriciates. They continued to exercise a relatively personal rule which laid stress on public forms of repression. Consequently the scaffold retained a prominent place alongside the prison for more than two centuries. This slow evolution may have influenced the desire for experimentation and mind control that became so outspoken around 1800. America, on the other hand, hardly experienced this desire. Except in the Old South, monopolization of violence resulted very quickly in relatively impersonal and bureaucratic forms of rule. Consequently, public modes of repression were dispensed with entirely and the prison became the central institution of the penal system.

Erasmus Universiteit Rotterdam   Pieter Spierenburg

FOOTNOTES

An earlier version of this article was presented as a paper at the meeting of the Academy of Criminal Justice Sciences in Louisville, March 1982 and at the symposium "Politics, Economics and the Arts, the Netherlands and the Foundation of the American Republic" at UCLA, April 1982. I am grateful to the participants in both meetings, especially to the discussants, John Conley and Eric Monkkonen, for their comments.

1. Major publications include David J. Rothman, *The Discovery of the Asylum. Social Order and Disorder in the New Republic* (Boston 1971); and see also *Conscience and Convenience. The Asylum and its Alternatives in Progressive America* (Boston, 1980). Michel Foucault, *Surveiller et Punir. Naissance de la Prison* (Paris, 1975). Michael Ignatieff, *A Just Measure of Pain. The Penitentiary in the Industrial Revolution, 1750-1850* (New York, 1978). Hannes Stekl, *Österreichs Zucht- und Arbeitshäuser, 1671-1920. Institutionen zwischen Fürsorge und Strafvollzug* (Vienna, 1978). Michelle Perrot, ed., *L'Impossible Prison. Recherches sur le Système Pénitentiaire au 19e Siècle.Débat avec Michel Foucault* (Paris, 1980). Robert Roth, *Pratiques Pénitentiaires et Théorie Sociale.L'Exemple de la Prison de Genève, 1825-1862* (Geneva, 1981). Jacques G. Petit, ed., *La Prison, le Bagne et l'Histoire.* (Geneva, 1984). Pieter Spierenburg, ed. *The Emergence of Carceral Institutions: Prisons, Galleys and Lunatic Asylums, 1550-1900* (Rotterdam, 1984).

2. Compare Pieter Spierenburg, *The Spectacle of Suffering. Executions and the Evolution of Repression: from a Preindustrial Metropolis to the European Experience* (Cambridge, 1984): 183-5. A good example of a precise analysis in which humanitarian rhetoric is taken seriously is Randall

FROM AMSTERDAM TO AUBURN   457

McGowen, "Humanitarianism and Criminal Law Reform in Early Nineteenth-Century England" (Paper presented at the conference "The History of Law, Labour and Crime," University of Warwick 1983).

3. Rothman, *Discovery of the Asylum*.

4. For example Martin B. Miller, "At Hard Labor: Rediscovering the 19th Century Prison," *Issues in Criminology* 9, 1 (1974): 91-114. John Conley, "Prisons, Production and Profit: Reconsidering the Importance of Prison Industries," *Journal of Social History* 14, 2 (1981): 257-75; see also "Revising Conceptions about the Origin of Prisons: The Importance of Economic Considerations." *Social Science Quarterly* 62, 2 (1981): 247-58: and also "Economics and the Social Reality of Prisons," *Journal of Criminal Justice* 10 (1982): 25-35.

5. Foucault, *Surveiller et Punir*; Stekl, *Österreichs Zucht- und Arbeitshäuser, 1671-1920*; Ignatieff, *A Just Measure of Pain*.

6. Pieter Spierenburg, "Model Prisons, Domesticated Elites and the State: The Dutch Republic and Europe," in Göran Rystad, ed., *Europe and Scandinavia. Aspects of the Process of Integration in the 17th Century* (Lund, 1983), pp. 219-35; see also *The Emergence of Carceral Institutions* and the contribution with Diederiks in Petit, *La Prison, Le Bagne et et l'Histoire*, pp. 43-55.

7. Georg Rusche and Otto Kirchheimer, *Punishment and Social Structure* (New York, 1939).

8. Michel Foucault, *Folie et Déraison, Histoire de la Folie à l'Age classique* (Paris, 1961); see also *Surveiller et Punir*.

9. More detailed information on this subject is to be found in Spierenburg, *The Emergence of Carceral Institutions*; and in the works listed in the bibliography of my own essay in that volume. That essay forms the reference for most of the data discussed in the first section of the present article.

10. Joanna Innes, "The King's Bench Prison in the Later Eighteenth Century: Law, Authority and Order in a London Debtor's Prison." in: John Brewer and John Styles eds., *An Ungovernable People. The English and Their Law in the Seventeenth and Eighteenth Centuries.* (London, 1980) pp. 250-98.

11. Spierenburg, *The Emergence of Carceral Institutions*: pp. 16-24.

12. Herman Diederiks, "Patterns of Criminality and Law Enforcement during the Ancien Regime: The Dutch Case," *Criminal Justice History* I (1980): 281.

13. Stekl, *Österreichs Zucht- und Arbeitshäuser, 1671-1920*.

14. Cf. Zysberg in Spierenburg, *The Emergence of Carceral Institutions*: pp. 78-124.

15. A. Hallema, *In en om de Gevangenis.* (Den Haag, 1936): 32; Amstelodamum, Maandblad, 1939: 181-2 and 1940: 21-2 and 1962: 6-9. In most cases the place of publication is unknown, but at least one pamphlet was printed at Augsburg in 1630.

16. Jan Van Hout, "Rapporten en Adviezen betreffende het Amsterdamse Tuchthuis," ed. A. Hallema, *Bijdragen en Mededelingen van het Historisch Genootschap* 48 (1927): 69-98; A. Hallema, "Het Amsterdamse Tuchthuis in 1710," *Jaarboek Amstelodamum* 45 (1953): 183-92.

17. J.H. Jacobsen Jensen, *Reizigers te Amsterdam. Beschrijvende Lijst van Reizen in Nederland door Vreemdelingen voor 1850.* (Amsterdam, 1919) (Supplement, Amsterdam, 1936).

18. Johannes Isacius Pontanus, *Historische Beschrijvinghe der seer wijt beroemde Coop-Stadt*

Amsterdam (Amsterdam, 1614). I am referring to the Dutch edition. The original Latin one was published in 1611.

19. Pontanus, *Historische Beschrijvinghe*: pp. 132 et seq.

20. *Historie Van de wonderlijcke mirakelen die in menichte ghebeurt zijn ende noch dagelijcx ghebeuren binnen de vermaerde Coop-stad Aemstelredam: In een plaets ghenaempt het Tucht-huys, ghelegen op de Heylighewegh* (Amsterdam 1612).

21. *Handvesten, Ofte Privilegien ende Octroyen mitsgaders Willekeuren, Costumen, Ordonnantien en Handelilngen der Stad Amstelredam*. 3 vols. (Amsterdam, 1748), p. 456. In the same year (1614) the Estates of Holland issued a placard against begging: cf. Groot-Placcaatboek: I 4.

22. J.J.Th. Poederbach, "Het Armenhuis der Stad Amsterdam. Tevens Een en Ander uit den Strijd Tegen de Bedelarij in Vroeger Dagen," *Jaarboek Amstelodamum* 18 (1920): 71-142 (72-83).

23. *Gemeente-Archief* Amsterdam, Keurboek M: fo. 197 vs.

24. Olfert Dapper, *Historische Beschryving der Stadt Amsterdam* (Amsterdam 1663), pp. 425-32.

25. Hans Bontemantel, *De Regeeringe van Amsterdam, soo in' t Civiel als Crimineel en Militaire (1653-1672)*. Ed. G.W. Kernkamp, (2 vols.) ('S Gravenhage, 1897), I, 274-5.

26. Casparus Commelin, Beschrijvinge van Amsterdam. 2 vols. (Amsterdam, 1693): foreword & 507. To be sure, Jan Wagenaar, *Amsterdam in zyne Opkomst, Aanwas, Geschiedenissen, Voorregten, Koophandel, Gebouwen, Kerkenstaat, Schoolen, Schutterye, Gilden en Regeeringe*. 13 vols. (Amsterdam, 1760-1768), writing in the 1760's, again groups them with the *godshuizen* (vol. 8 pp. 233 et seq.) but he was more of an historian.

27. Dapper, *Historische Beschryving der Stadt Amsterdam* (Amsterdam, 1663), pp. 419-20; Bontemantel, *De Regeeringe van Amsterdam*, I, p. 281.

28. Dapper, *Historische Beschryving de Stadt Amsterdam* (Amsterdam, 1663), pp. 425-32.

29. Jean Jüngen, *Een Stad van Justitie?* (MA – thesis, Vrije Universiteit, Amsterdam, 1979) pp. 25 and 63-4.

30. The sources are the *sententie- justitie-* and *confessieboeken* in the *Gemeente-archief* of Amsterdam, from which the tables 2 and 3 were compiled.

31. About five pct. of the cases in all three samples led to a sentence of a short term on bread and water in jail. These sentences are not included in the figures of table 2B.

32. Compare Miller, "At Hard Labor," 91-114.

33. This is discussed in more detail in Spierenburg, *The Spectacle of Suffering*: pp. 183-99.

34. Rod Morgan, "Divine Philanthropy: John Howard Reconsidered," *History* 62 (1977): (401).

35. Quotation from the inaugural statutes: J.A. van der Chijs, *Nederlandsch Indisch Plakaatboek. Eerste Deel, 1602-1642* (Batavia, Den Haag, 1885) p. 576.

36. The inmates were indeed obliged to spin. The status of most Dutch women, however, ensured that they owned slaves, who accompanied them into the spinhouse to do the work.

37. Carl Bridenbaugh, *Cities in the Wilderness. The First Century of Urban Life in America* (New York, 1955), 73.

FROM AMSTERDAM TO AUBURN   459

38. *Plakkaatboek van Nieuw-Nederland* (transcript at the *Gemeentearchief* of Amsterdam, film nr. 3637), 11 July 1642. See also Scott Christianson "Criminal Punishment in New Netherland" (paper prepared for the Rensselaerswyck Seminar III, (Albany 1980): p. 6.

39. A. Hallema, "Nederlandse Invloeden op en Voorbeeld voor het Buitenlands Gevangeniswezen tijdens de Republiek," *Tijdschrift voor Geschiedenis* 69 (1956): 55.

40. Julius N. Goebel Jr., "The Courts and the Law in Colonial New York" in David Flaherty (ed.), *Essays in the History of Early American Law* (Chapel Hill, N.C., 1969) 247.

41. The Amsterdam *gemeente-archief* has copies of all the records.

42. Edmund N. O'Callaghan, *Calendar of Historical Manuscripts in the Office of the Secretary of State* (Albany, 1865) X, 2, p. 466.

43. *Gemeente-Archief* Amsterdam, New Netherland Council Minutes: 1663.

44. Christianson, "Criminal Punishment" p. 7, expresses the same opinion.

45. Lawrence John Decker, *On Pain of Arbitrary Punishment. Court, Crime and Punishment at a Seventeenth Century Frontier Community* (paper) p. 14.

46. Bridenbaugh, *Cities in the Wilderness* p. 75.

47. Ibid: 74-5 and 82. In 1680 the court of New York decided to build a prison for drunken Christians and Indians but nothing much came of it Cf. Julius N. Goebel Jr., and T. Raymond Naughton, *Law Enforcement in Colonial New York* (New York, 1944): p. 690.

48. Albert Deutsch, *The Mentally Ill in America. A History of their Care and Treatment from Colonial Times* (New York, 1937): p. 53.

49. Bridenbaugh, *Cities in the Wilderness*, p. 84.

50. Rothman, *The Discovery of the Asylum*, pp. 30-1.

51. Gary B. Nash, "Poverty and Poor Relief in pre-Revolutionary Philadelphia;" *William and Mary Quarterly* 33 (1976): 3-30 (18-9)

52. Amsterdam's major contribution to the system of repression in New Amsterdam was the latter's adoption of the rattle-watch, which functioned between 1658 and 1682. This watch, however, was on the lookout for Indians rather than for burglars. Bridenbaugh, *Cities in the Wilderness*, pp. 65 and 67; James F. Richardson, *The New York Police. Colonial Times to 1901* (New York, 1970), p. 8.

53. Michael Kammen, *Colonial New York: A History* (New York, 1975): p. 73.

54. Deutsch, *The Mentally Ill in America*: p. 52.

55. To be sure, the West India Company forced a tolerant and liberal policy on Stuyvesant. Cf. George F. Smith, *Religion and Trade in New Netherland, Dutch Origins and American Development* (Ithaca, 1973): p. 23.

56. Kammen, *Colonial New York*: p. 73.

57. Lynne Withey, "Crime, Poverty and Perceptions of Deviance in a Commercial Economy: The Case of Eighteenth-Century Rhode Island" (Paper prepared for the C3-theme of the 7th International Economic History Congress, Edinburgh, 1978), pp. 143-5.

58. Deutsch, *The Mentally Ill in America*, p. 52.

59. Arthur Everett Peterson and George William Edwards, *New York as an Eighteenth Century Municipality* (New York, 1917): pp. 98-9 and 103. A mixture of poor-relief and penal purposes also characterized the Philadelphia bettering house, opened in 1767. Cf. Nash, Poverty and poor-relief, pp. 15-27.

60. Rothman, *The Discovery of the Asylum*, pp. 35-45 and 52-6.

61. Goebel/Naughton, *Law Enforcement in Colonial New York* (New York, 1944): pp. 702-3 (note 139) count 20 cases. Douglas Greenberg, *Crime and Law Enforcement in the Colony of New York 1691-1776* (Ithaca, 1976): p. 125 (note 53) counts 19 cases.

62. Herbert William Keith Fitzroy, "The Punishment of Crime in Provincial Pennsylvania," *Pennsylvania Magazine of History and Biography* 60 (1936): 258.

63. Kathryn Preyer, "Penal Measures in the American Colonies: An Overview," *American Journal of Legal History* 26 (1982).

64. Paul Takagi, "The Walnut Street Jail: A Penal Reform to Centralize the Powers of the State," *Federal Probation* 39, 4 (1975): 18-26.

65. Negley K. Teeters, *The Cradle of the Penitentiary. The Walnut Street Jail of Philadelphia, 1773-1835* (Philadelphia, 1955): p. 39.

66. Martin B. Miller, "Crime, Convicts and Penitentiaries of the North-East 1825-1838" (Paper presented at the meeting of the Academy of Criminal Justice Sciences, Louisville, KY, March 1982): 3.

67. Although even Western penitentiary in Pittsburgh was soon found to be unfit for solitary confinement: Miller, "Crime, Convicts and Penitentiaries:" pp. 1-2.

68. Miller, "At Hard Labor: Rediscovering the 19th Century Prison." *Issues of Criminology* 9, 1 (1974): 95.

69. Blake McKelvey, *American Prisons. A Study in American Social History prior to 1915* (Chicago, 1936): p. 7.

70. Walter David Lewis, *From Newgate to Dannemora. The Rise of the Penitentiary in New York, 1796-1848* (Ithaca, 1965): pp. 29-53.

71. Ibid: 54-5; Miller, "Sinking Gradually into the Proletariat: the Emergence of the Penitentiary in the United States." *Crime and Social Justice* (1980): 38.

72. Lewis, *From Newgate to Dannemora*, pp. 136-7.

73. Rothman, *The Discovery of the Asylum*; see also Michael Stephen Hindus, *Prison and Plantation. Crime, Justice and Authority in Massachusetts and South Carolina, 1767-1878* (Chapel Hill, NC 1980): pp. 162-81 and Paul Boyer, *Urban Masses and Moral Order in America, 1820-1920.* (Cambridge, Mass 1978): pp. 94-6. Rothman's thesis of a relationship with Jacksonian democracy has been contested. See, for example, Martin Miller, "Sinking Gradually into the Proletariat," p. 37.

74. On Lucas: Jacques Petit, "L'Amendement ou l'Entreprise de Réforme Morale des Prisonniers en France au 19e Siècle," *Déviance et Société* 6, 4 (1982): 331-51 (340-6); on Tocqueville/Beaumont: Perrot in Petit, *La Prison le Bagne et l'Histoire.* pp. 103-13.

FROM AMSTERDAM TO AUBURN 461

75. Which has been noted by many authors; see, for example, Kai T. Erikson *Wayward Puritans. A Study in the Sociology of Deviance* (New York, 1966): p. 204; Miller, "At Hard Labor," p. 96; Thomas O. Murton, *The Dilemma of Prison Reform* (New York 1976): pp. 8-9.

76. Miller, "Sinking Gradually into the Proletariat," p. 41. See also Miller, "Crime; Convicts and Penitentiaries," 11-12.

77. Takagi, "The Walnut Street Jail:" p. 24.

78. Hindus, *Prison and Plantation*, p. xxvi. See also the review by Eric Monkkonen (Indiana Law Journal 56,2: 273) who is critical of Hindus' notion of weak and strong states. Just after completing this article I got a copy of Edward L. Ayers, *Vengeance and Justice. Crime and Punishment in the 19th Century American South* (New York, 1984). In chapter 2 Ayers explains that several states in the Old South did in fact establish prisons, so that South Carolina may have been rather exceptional.

79. Richard Maxwell Brown, *Strain of Violence. Historical Studies of American Violence and Vigilantism* (New York, 1975): pp. 95-133. Brown's work comes closest to an analysis of the process of pacification in America, but in the end it appears to have been written from a static perspective. Brown essentially argues for a sort of culture of violence present throughout American history. See, for example, pp. 3-36 and also 56-63 where the association violence-democracy turns up.

80. Spierenburg, *The Spectacle of Suffering*, pp. 6-8.

81. Greenberg, *Crime and Law Enforcement*, pp. 156-87.

82. Rusche/Kirchheimer, *Punishment and Social Structure*, pp. 127-37. This type of economistic argument was recently taken up anew by Dario Melossi and Massimo Pavarini, *The Prison and the Factory. Origins of the Penitentiary System* (London, 1981).

83. Rothman, *The Discovery of the Asylum*, pp. 101-2.

84. Ignatieff, *A Just Measure of Pain*, pp. 93-8; see also Takagi, *The Walnut Street Jail*, p. 21.

85. Quoted by Michelle Perrot in Petit, *La Prison, le Bagne et l'Histoire*, p. 107.

86. Roth, *Pratiques Pénitentiaires et Théorie Sociale*.

87. Hindus, *Prison and Plantation*, p. 201; on the abolition of public punishment in Europe: Spierenburg, *The Spectacle of Suffering*, pp. 196-9.

88. See, for example, Miller, "At Hard Labor:" pp. 103-4; Gordon Wright, *Between the Guillotine and Liberty. Two Centuries of the Crime Problem in France* (New York, 1983): pp. 162-6.

[3]

International Journal of the Sociology of Law 1985, **13**, 1–33

Politics and Policy in Criminological Discourse: A Study of Tendentious Reasoning and Rhetoric

DAVID GARLAND

University of Edinburgh, U.K.

"Perhaps the hardest impression to eradicate is that the criminologist is a penal reformer. ... Strictly speaking, penal reform is a spare-time occupation for criminologists, such as canvassing for votes would be for political scientists. The difference is that the criminologist's spare time occupation is more likely to take this form, and when it does so it is more likely to interfere with what should be purely criminological thoughts" (Walker, 1965, pp. VII–VIII).

Introduction: Criminology and Penal Politics

Throughout the history of their discipline, criminologists have endeavoured to maintain a distinction between what they say as scientists and what they do as political citizens. Indeed this distinction has been so important that a revision of its terms has been seen to lead to a major revision of the discipline itself, as the case of 'radical criminology' makes clear (see Taylor, Walton & Young, 1973, 1975).

The conventional position is that while individual criminologists may well be politically committed — usually to particular penal policies and legal reforms — these concerns and values should be kept quite separate from the "purely logical or purely scientific appreciation of facts" (Walker, 1965; p. vii) which their science demands. In other words, a firm distinction is maintained between criminology as a *scientific discourse* and criminology as a *programme of penal reform*.

Of course no one has ever denied that these two projects have accompanied

0194 – 6595/85/010001 + 33 $03.00/0

2   D. Garland

and complemented one another. Indeed this pairing of 'science' and 'policy-relevance' has been criminology's major asset in the struggle for research funding and institutional recognition (*cf.* Radzinowicz, 1961, p. 179). But nonetheless the convention continues that an interest in matters of policy should not impair one's integrity in matters of science.

That this imperative has been more of an ideal than an actuality does not detract from the point at issue. In fact, those instances where writers have recognisably failed to maintain the separation (and one might include here the case of Cyril Burt) have served only to re-affirm the distinction's importance. On the other hand, this ideal has not been without its detractors. Indeed on occasion the very possibility of distinguishing 'politics' from 'science' has been denied, leaving us with an epistemological nihilism which has no means of knowing the world, only a policy for judging it (for a discussion of this tendency, see Bankowski, Mungham & Young, 1976).

The argument which will be presented here differs from both of these positions. It will proceed not by denying the possibility of such a distinction [1], nor by chastising individual failures to observe it, but by arguing that the concepts and discourse of criminology have been developed in a manner which has silently but steadfastly refused any such distinction, i.e. that criminological discourse has always been 'political'.

Perhaps I can clarify this argument by approaching the issue from a slightly different angle. A related problem is registered in the philosophy of science by the distinction between the 'external' and the 'internal' history of a theory. It is argued by Imre Lakotos (1981), that in order to explain the foundation of a science, its initial orientation and the energy behind its formation, one must make reference to external social, political and cultural conditions. However, once a scientific project is reasonably well-established, these external factors will tend to become marginalised as the internal logics and methods of reasoning of the science itself take over. If this internal scientific take-off occurs, then concepts will be developed, investigation or experiments undertaken, data will be accumulated and analyses refined, in accordance with the increasingly autonomous logic of the discipline. In other words, to the extent that this internal logic asserts itself, the social origins of the science will tend to fade into its pre-history.

This pattern of development has been charted for a number of disciplines, and most notably in regard to the history of statistics in Britain (see McKenzie, 1981) — which in some ways overlaps with the history of criminology. However, if the discipline of statistics has partially succeeded in shrugging off its political parentage, my argument will be that criminology shows no signs of following a similar path of maturation. Indeed it will be argued that this lack of autonomy from politics and 'external' ideologies is an inescapable feature of the discipline of criminology as it has developed in this country over the last 100 years. The aim of this paper will be to move from this initial criticism to a demonstration of precisely *how* such political and ideological elements entered into a discourse which prides itself on its scientificity and value–freedom.

There is no doubt that criminology's initial formation, in the 1870s and 1880s, owes a great deal to external events. I have tried to trace the complex history of these events elsewhere (Garland, 1985), so perhaps I may be forgiven for simply asserting here that criminology is not a product of scientific reasoning and discovery. It is rather a product of the prison, of the institutions and ideologies which individualised and differentiated the criminal, and of the social desire to do so in a thorough and rigorous manner. Criminology, as others have pointed out, is not a science, nor even a knowledge which aspires to scientificity. It is a social–problem–solution which utilises some of the methods and much of the prestige of other scientific disciplines. Its objects of study — and this applies as much to present day criminology as to that of a century ago — are the 'criminal' and the forms of 'criminality'. These objects are neither real entities nor theoretical products but are instead socially-defined problems in need of a scientific solution (see Hirst, 1979). The 'criminal' or his 'criminality' become objects of study precisely because they are chosen targets of particular social policies. Theoretically, the criminal has no more right to a science of his own than do the law-abiding or the 'honest poor' — who in some ways post more difficult questions.

The argument of this essay will be that this ideological foundation — this social problem *raison d'être* — taken together with the reforming concerns of criminologists, crucially affects the subsequent development of the discipline. Instead of settling down to a development which is internally directed in accordance with the patterns of theoretical logic, criminology is continually transformed and directed by external factors — by the demands of penal policy, political viability and ideological conformity.

In other words, criminology's policy programme — its external relations and its external history — continues to assert its ideological effect upon the 'science' of criminology. The two cannot be separated because they are *interdependent* — the science is the programme and the programme is the science. Precisely because criminology's object is a social problem — defined by policies, ideologies and state practices — its 'external' origins will always be internal to it.

Analysing Discourse to Discover Desire

So far it has been suggested that the problem which criminology initially set itself — an investigation of the causes, nature and remedies of criminality — was shaped by 'external' social factors, rather than by scientific reasoning. But this original sin need not have vitiated the discipline's claims thereafter. Is it not possible to study a social problem objectively? Can science not be brought to bear upon society's concerns in an impartial way? Perhaps. But my

4   D. Garland

argument will be that, throughout the development of the criminological discipline, the objectivity of scientific reasoning has continually been displaced by the concern to be practical and 'policy-relevant'. I will argue that several major debates and many of criminology's central concepts owe their elaboration not to the protocols of a scientific discourse but instead to the demands of a penal programme.

The kind of argument I propose to make out faces a problem of evidence. Even if one accepts the initial suggestion as a possible one, what kind of evidence would substantiate it? 'External factors' such as social policy requirements, or even the opinions and political desires of criminologists, do not simply osmose into the conceptual fabric of a discourse. They have to find a discursive place there. That is to say they have to become functioning discursive entities, internal to the structure of the discourse. In other words, to make out such a case, it is necessary to do more than simply point out the desires and politics of criminologists, or the social basis of criminology, and suggest that some influence or orientation was likely. One has to show explicitly and in detail how the concepts, objects and arguments of the discourse reproduced this orientation. We have to show how 'politics' enters into 'discourse' *at the level of discourse*: in the texts and theoretical statements themselves, and not just in their context or deployment.

It is proposed to attempt just this by identifying certain theoretical flaws, evasions and weak arguments in the discourse of criminology and subjecting them to close analysis. Our analysis will scrutinise those points in criminology's conceptual structure where logical argument or empirical data appear to give way to the use of ambiguity and compromise, metaphor and non-sequitor.

It will be argued that in a number of important instances, discursive figures, concepts and devices occur which have no theoretical warrant — either they do not follow from the theory in question, or else they are underdetermined by it — and I will try to show that these are precisely the points at which political desire has interrupted theoretical logic. Criminology's will to truth, such as it is, has been continually compromised by the will to power. Moreover, these unwarranted elements of the discourse are not merely a residue of error which will one day be eliminated. They are functional aspects of criminological discourse which are crucial to criminology's status as a socially authorised knowledge. To eliminate criminology's pragmatic reasoning and tendentious logic — or even to alter their direction — would be to jeopardise its position in the institutions of power. Once again, radical criminology is a case in point, demonstrating that a refusal to adjust theory to the practice of the Establishment can result in practical impotence.

My examples and evidence will be taken, not from contemporary criminology, which has long since won official respect and recognition for its relevance to policy, nor from those earliest texts of a century ago, which took as their task the critique of classical jurisprudence and the construction of a positive criminology. Instead I will be concerned with that period at the turn of the century when the new science of criminology began to settle its internal debates, to organise itself as a professional programme, and to press its claims upon the institutions of law and government.

It was in this period, say from the 1890s to the outbreak of the First World War, that criminology took on the character of an organised professional discipline, with its own infrastructure of associations, journals and conferences, its own conventions of competence and authority. And while these new institutions were dedicated to the furtherance of a theoretical knowledge about crime, they were equally, and explicitly, concerned to press the claims of this new science upon the legislators and the administrators of the institutions of criminal justice.

This practical desire to align penal policy with the principles of positive science set a number of practical problems for the new discipline. First of all, it had to overcome the *resistances* which it faced — from liberal jurists, from conservative penal authorities, and from its own internal debates and divisions. Secondly, it had to make itself *politically relevant* — addressing itself to the problems of the day, aligning itself with social strategies, offering solutions. Finally, it had to make itself *ideologically acceptable* — it had to present itself as compatible with the basic ideological tenets of society's major institutions, and it had to legitimate itself in terms that would prove acceptable. It will be argued that it was these practical–political imperatives as much as any theoretical reasoning which served to direct the development of criminological discourse at the turn of the century, and that this claim can be substantiated by examining a number of specific features of the discipline. The following sections will identify and analyse a number of discursive characteristics and manoeuvres of criminology which seem to me to be following the dictates and vicissitudes of this political programme, rather than the theoretical logic which it claimed for itself.

Discursive Devices in the Quest for 'Policy Relevance'

(a) The pragmatic compromise

The demands of the criminological programme for the individualisation of punishment, and its corollaries of clinical investigations, 'scientific sentencing' and indeterminate treatment terms, faced serious resistance from those forces which supported the tenets of traditional legalism and its procedures. In the face of this opposition, and indeed in regard to the internal divisions which weakened the movement, the most frequent response was a *pragmatic compromise* which effaced theoretical difference in the name of practical unity. The architects of these compromises were sometimes the professional practitioners who stood between the theoretical programme and its practical enactment, but more often the second generation of theorists such

6   *D. Garland*

as Prins, Saleilles and Von Hamel who appear to have been more committed
to political success than theoretical innovation.

In Britain, Sir Evelyn Ruggles-Brise played a key role in this regard, in his
position as Chairman of the Prison Commission between 1895 and 1921.
Moreover, this was a role of which he was fully aware, as his statements
throughout this time make perfectly clear (see Ruggles-Brise, 1901). His
interventions repeatedly sought to reconcile positive criminology with classical
criminal justice by means of various compromise formulations as witness his
changing positions on the crucial question of indeterminate sentencing: at first
asserting weak compromises, e.g. indeterminism only for special cases, never
for ordinary crime (Ruggles-Brise, 1901), then becoming bolder as the
political climate changed [thus by 1914 he was suggesting indeterminate
sentences for everyone below 30 years of age (see Report of the Prison
Commissioners, 1912–1913)].

In much the same vein, Raymond Saleilles (1913; p. 2954) sets out a
convincing theoretical case for individualised treatment, to be decided upon by
an expert sentencing panel of "physicians, directors of reformatory schools,
professional educators, etc.". However, a paragraph later he completely
reverses the logic of his case to maintain that while the 'experts' should decide
upon the *form* of treatment, it should be left to the judge to determine its
duration.

Like Ruggles-Brise, Saleilles is quite explicit about the political destination
of his conceptual manoeuvres. He stresses that the law is by no means
"hospitable to sudden revolution" and insists that "the reconstruction of
penal law requires co-operation" and a united front on "matters of practical
concern" (Saleilles, 1913, preface). (As we shall see, Saleilles himself made an
important contribution to this task of theoretical 'reconciliation' by his efforts
to realign the divergent positions of the 'Italian' and 'neo classical' schools
around a novel conception of 'responsibility'.)

Besides such key individuals, there were a number of organisations
committed to the formation of alliances and the broadening of support for
particular penological reforms. Most prominent amongst these were the
International Union of Criminal Law (founded in 1889 by von Liszt, von Hamel
and Adolphe Prins) and the *American Institute of Criminal Law and Criminology*
(established at the Chicago Conference of 1909). The 'Union' was precisely
that. It was not a school but rather an amalgam or alliance of schools whose
founders "sought to attract the largest number of adherents, even when not
convinced" (Ancel, 1965, p. 48). De Quiros (1911) describes the Union as a
reform movement promoting a kind of "double-entry penology" which, like
Ruggles-Brise, advocated a combination of old and new concepts and
sanctions. And to aid this compromise between legalism and the new
criminology, the schisms, debates and internal divisions of the latter were
glossed over in the Union's texts, or else reduced to the compromise
formations of a pragmatic eclecticism. In much the same way, the American
Institute sought "to co-ordinate the efforts of individuals and organisations",

demonstrating its eclectic approach by translating into English a number of texts representing each of the divergent positions within the new criminology's programme. (See the *Journal of Criminal Law, Criminology and Police Science* 1910–1911, editorial comment.)

It should be understood that the eclecticism of the Union and the other reformers is of a different character from that of Enrico Ferri, Havelock Ellis or the later work of Lombroso. For writers of the latter sort it was the logic of positivist method and the overdetermination of 'criminality' which led to their *theoretical* eclectism or "multi-factorialism". Such a position was quite different from the *pragmatic* electicism of the reformers where theoretical argument was subordinated to political will in the search for alliance and synthesis. Thus Enrico Ferri, himself a theoretical eclectic, violently attacked the 'befogged eclecticism' of the reformers and denounced their "error" of "subjecting science to the state of popular opinion" (Ferri, 1917, pp. 372–3):

> "[Those who] freely invoke a marriage of convenience between the old penal law and the young positive science ... always forget that the new school stands for a complete innovation in scientific method, and that there is no middle term; either one syllogises on crime considered as an abstract juridical being or one studies it as a natural phenomenon' (Ferri, 1917, p. 22).

But if purists like Ferri were unreceptive to this conciliatory approach, there was a much more positive response from the political audience at which this manoeuvre was aimed. Britain in particular was well-known for its resistance to theoretical argument and the pragmatism of its penal establishment. Thomas Hardy may have been exaggerating when he declared that "We Britons hate ideas!", but the need to maintain a 'practical approach' in any new proposals was well known to reformers. As Von Hamel (1911–1921, p. 23) put it:

> "... it has always been one of the most beneficient characteristics of the Anglo-Saxon jurisprudence, that it kept away from purely theoretical reasonings and was influenced mostly by realistic views."

And "beneficient" or not, it was this audience characteristic which motivated many of the pragmatic compromises which feature in the criminological texts and reports of the 1890s and 1900s. For example we find the Gladstone Report endorsing the "learned but conflicting theories" which have subjected "Crime, its causes, and treatment" to "scientific inquiry". However, this endorsement is immediately followed by a reference to "common sense" which counters the implication of these "learned theories" — a "recognition of the plain fact" that most criminals, with important exceptions, are indeed reformable, no matter what these "scientific theories" might imply (Gladstone Report, 1895, p. 8).

The strategic site chosen for these compromise manoeuvres was, of course, the realm of *the practical*. Theoretical difference and conceptual discrepancy

8   *D. Garland*

were made to disappear if divergent positions could be satisfied by a common recommendation or policy objective. The consequence of this was a search for practices which could veil their underlying theoretical disagreements *and* a resulting investment in ambiguity and the kind of 'polysemic' practice which is still the hallmark of British penal policy [2]. William Clarke Hall, grappling with the contending positions of "free-will" and "determinism", attempts just such a resolution:

> "In spite ... of the apparent irreconcilability of these two views in theory, I do not think that they are equally irreconcilable in practice, and it is essential to arrive as far as possible at a common ground of action rather than to investigate and accentuate theoretical and metaphysical differences. If my attempt to do this seems to the scientists crude and superficial it is, I trust, at least practical" (Hall, 1926, p. 15).

In the same mode, Leonard Darwin argues that the preventive detention of habituals, is a point at which 'environmentalists' and 'eugenists' can find "common ground", detention being "the right policy to adopt from whatever direction we approach the subject" (Darwin, 1914–1915, p. 217).

This last example of "reconciliation" is important because it reveals the crucial conceptual point at which disparate theories are linked into a single recommendation. This point of intersection, appearing again and again in these pragmatic formulations, is *the category of the individual*. Moreover the *possibility* of this intersection is precisely related to its political *desirability* which in turn stems from the structured individualism of the law, the courts and political ideology [3].

One would imagine that the position of eugenists and of those criminologists who individualised the sources of crime would be radically incompatible with the theories of environmentalists and social determinists. Yet time and time again a workable compromise was drawn out in which both positions were assimilated behind a single recommendation. Such a paradox was possible because the environmentalists did not take social relations as their object of analysis and transformation, nor even the social phenomenon of crime. Instead, they, like their 'opponents', took as their object *the criminal individual as affected by social factors*. A statement by Boies makes plain this centering of the individual in both kinds of explanation:

> "All the immediate causes of crime are either extraneous or intrinsic *to the individual*. The extraneous causes are the opportunities, incitements, and temptations which his nature is unable to resist. The intrinsic causes are inordinate desires and passions, defective or diseased physical organs or a weakness of moral character which yields to the power of the extraneous influences. The ultimate cause of all crime, therefore, is to be found in the character of the individual" (Boies, 1901, p. 40).

This analytical primacy of the individual stems ultimately from the socially defined nature of criminology's problem — the desire to control individual criminals — and the manoeuvre we are now describing is no more than a return to the individual in the attempt to influence social politics. The focus upon social circumstances which environmentalism suggests is here postponed or marginalised as either a task for the future, or a political impossibility, and what remains is a common concern with the individual, shared by all sides, if for different reasons. Within this logic, environmentalism is transformed from being an argument for social change [as it had been in Ferri (1917)] to being a reason for individual segregation — the removal of the weak individual from a criminogenic environment (see Garafalo, 1914, p. xxxiii).

To summarise then, this focus upon the individual was not just a convenient means of aligning two opposed positions at their point of intersection; it was also, *in itself*, a means of gaining entry into the common sense of British penal policy. For like all 'empiricisms', the anti-theoretical character of the penal authorities rested upon a number of entrenched but unstated theoretical propositions. And the major assumption of that policy was — and *is* — that the individual is always the proper locus of penal intervention and concern [4].

(b) The linking of themes and of categories

Another discursive device at work in these criminological texts involves *the tactical linking of disparate themes and categories*. The linking of *themes* takes place by means of a vertical chain of reference which ties particular penal issues to more general political questions in order to extend popular concern and attract a wider support. The most common linkage of this type draws together questions of the (criminal or deviant) individual, the Nation and the Race in an open appeal to the concerns about "national efficiency" and racial deterioration which were widespread in Edwardian Britain (see Jones, 1971; Searle, 1971). Thus an account of the issues surrounding inebriacy in 1903 is presented as follows:

> "The consequences of alcoholism are well-known and need only to be recapitulated:
> 1. To the individual — degradation of the intellectual faculties and mental degeneration.
> 2. For the descendants — the tendency to drink, epilepsy, insanity, physical sufferings, idiocy, and lastly, extinction of the race.
> 3. From a social point of view, the consequences are increase of mortality, diminution of the number of births, diminution of moral energy and of the rate of intelligence, in a weakening of the life power of the population" (Marr, 1903).

The laconic tone of Dr Marr is no doubt meant to accentuate the devastating consequences of inebriacy for Nation and Race, but it also suggests the ease

10   *D. Garland*

with which these connections could be made by this time. In fact this same
somewhat breathtaking, chain of reference is to be found clearly stated in a
whole series of texts and official statements of this period (see Lydston, 1904;
pp. 37–8; McKenna, 1912; Wilson, 1908, p. vii). Before long, the
associations which were developed at length in these statements had found
expression in a single term. The notion of *"the unfit"* signified all of these
themes and their connections in a condensed form, using an image borrowed
from Social Darwinism. It operated to fix the social significance of the deviant
population in an implicit but incisive manner, automatically raising the focus
from the individual deviant to his or her implications for the Nation and the
Race [5]. It is therefore no surprise to find that when criminals, paupers,
unemployables and the feeble-minded are dealt with by the Cabinet of 1911,
they are presented not as minor and separate issues, but as a common "social
danger" which directly threatens the progress and survival of the nation and
its empire. At the Cabinet meeting of 22 December 1911, Churchill
introduced a paper by Dr. A.F. Tredgold, entitled 'The feeble-minded — a
social danger", which Churchill described as a "concise ... and not
exaggerated statement of the serious problem which we face". Tredgold's
paper states that:

> "... the problem of the feeble-minded is no isolated one, but ... is
> intimately connected with those of insanity, epilepsy, alcholism,
> consumption, and many other conditions of diminished mental and bodily
> vigour. And when we remember that these are the conditions which
> connote social failure and which give rise to such a large proportion of our
> criminals, paupers, and unemployables, we begin to see how far reaching
> the question is."

Having settled the scope of the problem, he then specifies its significance:

> "this brings me to ... the subject of national degeneracy. Now national
> degeneracy is no myth, but a very serious reality. In the past more nations
> have sunk to a position of utter insignificance or have been entirely blotted
> out of existence as a result of the moral, intellectual and physical
> degeneracy of their citizens, than of wars, famines, or any other
> conditions. ... It is impossible for any nation to progress, or even to hold
> its own, which contains a preponderance of individuals who are deficient
> in moral, intellectual and physical vigour. It would be well if we English
> were to ponder these facts. ..." (Tredgold, 1911).

Another linking process, this time of a 'horizontal' kind, operates to bring
together disparate *categories* of the various deviant populations and merge their
characteristics under a single term. This process involves a kind of reasoning
by analogy which argues that several different categories can be commonly
treated in a way that is presently deemed appropriate for only one of them. The
use of the term "moral imbecile" was thus used to link together groups such as
the feeble-minded, the inebriate, the habitual criminal and the vagrant,

extending to the others the *pathological* character of the first. Thus we find Havelock Ellis stressing:

> "... the immense importance of Lombroso's identification of 'moral insanity' with 'instinctive criminality'. Madmen and criminals have been brought into line. They are both recognised as belonging to the same great and terrible family of abnormal, degenerate, anti-social persons. This point will remain unshaken whatever disputes may occur on matters of detail" Ellis (1910; p. 367) [6].

Once again, the success of this manoeuvre is apparent, and its echoes are to be found in official reports, Parliamentary debates, and a multitude texts [7]. As *The Times* declared on 2 October 1911:

> "No study of the problem of crime will, we are convinced, penetrate to all its roots, no measures at once bold and effective are likely to be taken, until the close connection of feeble-mindedness, pauperism and crime is examined and clearly realised."

One very important consequence of these linkages was that they opened up indirect routes of advance for the eugenic programme [8]. As the eugenists themselves realised, their programme was rarely acceptable when presented in explicit terms, and every opportunity was taken to insinuate eugenic demands into other, more respectable projects (see McKenzie, 1981). One such project was criminology and its penological programme, which proved to be a valuable site for a number of displaced eugenic demands.

The infiltration of eugenic terms into penological discourse was encourged by a number of factors. In conceptual terms and orientation the two programmes had much in common, and many criminologists such as Boies, Ellis and Garafalo were committed eugenists. Moreover as Battagliani, Lombroso, and later Goring pointed out, the institutions of penality had a definite eugenic effect of their own, whether it be the 'automatic' effect of the scaffold or long-term imprisonment, or else the more deliberate policies of Broadmoor women's prison [9]. A number of leading eugenists, including Leonard Darwin, Arnold White and Sidney Herbert, argued for penal reforms which would promote eugenic ends, concentrating particularly upon the demand for the preventive detention of habitual petty offenders:

> "... increased periods of detention of habitual criminals would produce both immediate social advantages and ultimate improvements in the racial qualities of future generations, and, if this be the case, the social reformer and the eugenist ought to be able to march together in this path of criminal reform" (Darwin, 1914–1915, p. 212) [10].

The effects of this infiltration can be clearly seen in the terms used by penal reformers when they came to talk of preventive detention. Ruggles-Brise, for example, slips easily into a eugenic terminology, despite the fact that

12   *D. Garland*

"segregation" and "the unfit" are terms which had no previous currency in penological discourse:

> "... the State is justified in segregating, for long periods of time, a dangerous class of offenders, who by their antecedents have proved themselves unfit to be at large" (Ruggles-Brise, 1900, p. 29).

And Sir Robert Anderson and Sir Alfred Wills, while arguing the "humaneness" of preventive detention, explicitly stress the fact that such measures are effective in "preventing [the habitual criminal] propagating and training a new generation of thieves" (Anderson, 1908; Wills, 1907).

Perhaps the greatest eugenic success in infiltrating this field was the famous Goring research on *The English Convict* completed in 1908. This study was the most important official investigation of 'criminality' prior to the First World War, and it is therefore very revealing that the research was conducted under the auspices of Karl Pearson's Biometric laboratory — the scientific nerve centre of the eugenic movement. Nor was the decision to house it there merely a consequence of the laboratory's statistical expertise; the actual terms of the research — ostensibly to 'test' the hypothesis of the Italian School that there is a 'born criminal' — precisely mirror the basic eugenic concerns with heredity, the transmission of 'degenerate' characteristics such as criminality, and the use of anthropometric measurement [11]. It is no surprise then, to find Goring stating the following conclusions:

> "Our figures, showing the comparatively insignificant relation of family and other environmental conditions with crime, and the high and enormously augmented association of feeble-mindedness with conviction for crime, and its well-marked relation with alcoholism, epilepsy, sexual profligacy, ungovernable temper, obstinacy of purpose, and wilful anti-social activity — every one of these being heritable qualities — we think that crime will continue to exist as long as we allow criminals to propagate."

and their eugenic corollaries:

> "Modify opportunity for crime by segregating the unfit ..."

> "Attack the evil at its very root — to regulate the reproduction of those degrees of constitutional qualities — feeble-mindedness, inebriety, epilepsy, deficient social instinct, insanity, which conduce to the committing of crime" (Goring, 1913, quoted in the *Journal of Criminal Law, Criminology and Police Science*, 1914--1915, p. 222).

In the years that followed this publication, more explicit proponents of the eugenic programme refer again and again to Goring's study as solid, official support for their assertions and policies [12]. Moreover a reciprocal reference was also established in the opposite direction, as official statements about habitual crime came to be commonly phrased in a language borrowed from the discourse of eugenics [13].

The Conduct and Resolution of Key Debates

The conceptual manoeuvres which we have described so far took place largely without controversy — or more precisely, in anticipation and evasion of controversy. There were, however, a number of serious and intense theoretical conflicts which did see the light of day, centring upon questions of 'criminal man', 'responsibility' and 'determinism'. Our intention here is to analyse the conduct of these debates and the direction of their paths of resolution in order to identify the ideological and political pressures which helped to shape the eventual theoretical outcomes. It will be argued that these debates had resolutions which were *politically satisfactory* rather than *theoretically adequate*, or at least that their forms of argumentation paid more regard to political tactics than to theoretical logic.

(a) 'The criminal man': differentiation, fatalism and reform

The most renowned and sensational 'discovery' of 19th century criminology was that there existed a distinct and identifiable 'criminal man'. The controversy which followed this contention was world-wide and its echoes resonate to the present day, but it is nonetheless a controversy with very distinct contours and directions. The central points at issue quickly became established as firstly, the implications of this position for penal intervention, and second, the precise way in which the 'criminal type' was to be differentiated from the non-criminal.

The first field of contention is clearly established by Ruggles-Brise when he represented the Italian School's 'criminal type' as:

> "… a race of beings predestined to criminal acts, against whom any
> system of punishment would be futile as by nature such beings would not
> be amenable to the deterrent influences of penal law" (Ruggles-Brise,
> 1921, p. 199).

The fact that this amounts to a gross overstatement of the 'Italian' view (as Ferri and Garafalo never ceased to protest [14]), misrepresenting even the early work of Lombroso, powerfully confirms the importance of this question of "fatalism".

Against this imputed fatalism there was no end of protest [15]. But the attack was launched not so much against the veracity of the proposition, or the evidence for it, but against its *implications* for penal practice:

> "Like all half-truths, it is extremely dangerous…. [It is] what Dr Goring
> calls the great 'superstition' of the day which stands in the way of Prison
> reform, which darkens counsel in dealing with crime, which renders
> rehabilitation difficult, and which stifles and discourages the zeal of the
> philanthropist …" (Ruggles-Brise, 1921, p. 199).

14   *D. Garland*

> "Nothing in the past has so much retarded progress as the conviction ...
> that the criminal is a class by himself, different from all other classes, with
> an innate tendency to crime.... It accounts for the unfavourable and
> sceptical attitude which we still find in many places towards any attempt to
> reclaim the criminal (Ruggles-Brise, 1911, p. 74).

Whatever the theoretical merits or demerits of the proposition, it was too
dangerous to be allowed to circulate. We can see this political closure operate
even more clearly in relation to Dr Goring's study. Here was an official,
British investigation of impeccable scientific credentials (at least in the eyes of
the Prison Commission) which alleged that criminality was indeed an
inherited characteristic. The intervention of Ruggles-Brise to write a preface
to the study, representing it for a popular audience, was therefore crucial.
Here is his rescue manoeuvre in operation:

> "... the criminal diathesis, revealed by the tendency to crime, is affected
> by heredity to much the same extent as other physical and mental
> conditions in man: but this does not mean that a man is predestined to a
> criminal career by a tendency which he is unable to control.... Heritable
> constitutional conditions ... can be regulated, encouraged or stultified by
> training and education ... and it is in the acceptance of this belief that lies
> hope for the race, and encouragement for reformers of all kinds. Its
> acceptance rescues the notion of hereditary criminality from the stigma of
> predestination which necessarily attaches to any idea of a criminal né"
> (Ruggles-Brise, 1913, p. 8).

See how 'science' and statistics quickly give way to their political purposes —
and how in the name of the Race, of hope and of Reform we must *believe* in the
power of intervention. The space for positive intervention — which
criminology constructed and which, ironically, the Italians threatened to
reduce — is thus re-opened by the anxious Chairman of the Prison
Commission. This same 'rescue' operation can be seen in the work of the
reformers of the International Union, their political slogan — "causality and
not fatality of crime" — being designed to ensure that the notion of
determination is retained, but is simultaneously stripped of its self-defeating
possibilities.

The second major line of conflict which followed from Lombroso's notion of
'the criminal man' took up the question of *differentiation*. But it was not so
much concerned with the specific 'anomalies' or 'differences' which
supposedly stigmatised 'the criminal'. Instead it focused upon the *mode of
differentiation* that was implied, attacking the idea of an absolute demarcation
and replacing it with a more sophisticated, more strategic conception. Writers
such as Ruggles-Brise (1911, p. 74), Sante de Sanctis (1914, p. 5) and
Leonard Darwin (1914–1915, p. 207) rejected the notion that criminals were
a "special type" or a "class apart", asserting instead the idea of relative
degrees of criminality, with a *continuum* running between the criminal and
non-criminal, the normal and the pathological:

Politics and policy in criminology   15

> "... criminals are not a class apart, but merely ordinary individuals with
> certain innate qualities exceptionally well marked" (Darwin, 1914–1915,
> p. 207).

> "... defectiveness ... is a relative term only" (Ruggles-Brise, 1913,
> p. vi.).

> "... the anthropological monster' does not exist .... The truth is that these
> [are] deviations from the normal ..." (De Sanctis, 1914–1915).

This rejection of an absolute demarcation, and the substitution of a relative
scale running from the normal to the pathological, carries with it a number of
consequences. Firstly, there is no longer any need to set a fixed, agreed line of
differentiation whereby the criminal can be known absolutely, thereby
relieving criminology of a task which had so far proved impossible. Secondly,
it established a definite place for the expert, for if criminality was a delicate
matter of degree, only the expert could be relied upon to identify its subtle
marks and traces. Ferri recites a tale wherein several uninitiated Conference
members failed to identify any anomalies amongst a group of 'degenerates'
from the Asylum of St Ann in Paris. Cesare Lombroso, "trembling all over
with the tremor of a good bloodhound close to his quarry", confounded them
all by finding in each case numerous serious "stigmata", though "these
anomalies were invisible to the inexpert" (Ferri, 1914–1915, p. 226).
Thirdly, the new continuum establishes a much wider field for intervention —
for two reasons. The declaring of an absolute demarcation which all can agree
(e.g. the insanity rule in McNaughten's case) will necessarily tend to be
restrictive. A continuum, leaving each decision to expert decision in the
individual case, allows a kind of "floating standard", unspecified in advance,
left to experts to define as the occasions arise [16].

The other reason why this marks an extension of intervention is clearly and
simply put by William Clarke Hall when he applies this conception to the
children appearing in his courtroom: "... there can be no such entity as the
completely normal child" (Hall, 1926, p. 31). We can also see from these last
two statements that the rejection of an absolute demarcation of the 'criminal
type' leaves untouched the assumption of *pathology*. The continuum is between
the normal and the *pathological* and it provides the basis and justification for a
potentially infinite field of intervention

The meaning of this debate has become more intelligible in examining its
lines of contest and resolution. But perhaps a deeper significance can also be
suggested. If we were crudely to summarise the conduct of the criminology
programme, we could say that it began by promising to demarcate and
identify the criminal by means of objective, specifiable criteria. Having
convinced its audience of this possibility, it then withdrew the offer of a
publicly specified line of demarcation and instead arrogated to itself *the task of
demarcating*. Moreover, this regrouped strategy has advantages which extend
beyond the promotion of the criminological expert, for in its new form it

16   *D. Garland*

specifies not a norm but an apparatus to enforce norms. It does not so much specify the criminal 'Other' as indicate his existence and set up an apparatus qualified to identify and police 'him'. Thus to extend Foucault's arguments, it justifies an extended form of policing by naming an 'Other' who can never be known in advance of a generalised but closely drawn practice of observation and scrutiny which covers the whole population [17].

(b) Free-will, determinism and the responsible subject

It should be apparent from the above discussion that the new penology was traversed both by theoretical logic and political desire. In consequence it was caught in a contradictory position, *being both for and against determinism*. On the one hand, the notion of determinism supplied criminology's theoretical *raison d'être*, but on the other a total determinism or fatalism would altogether deny its penological intent. On to this contradiction was added a further layer of difficulty by the fact that 'determinism' itself was radically incompatible with the prevailing legal, moral and political conceptions of the free-willed individual. The result was a debate centring upon 'the subject' which was of crucial importance.

As is well-known, the new criminology categorically refused the classical conception of the free-willed criminal actor. This axiomatic difference emerged most forcefully around the practical question of 'responsibility'. In its traditional legal usage, 'responsibility' implied a moral agent, and therefore the denial of free-will entailed a parallel refusal of responsibility and the procedures of social accountability which founded themselves upon the subject's responsibility for his actions (see De Fleury, 1901; Ellis, 1910; Ferri, 1917).

There were some writers such as Ferri and De Fleury who took up this strong position against responsibility, stating it boldly and without compromise [18], but most others were careful to temper their formulations with a degree of caution and respect for tradition. In the face of loud protests that the doctrine of irresponsibility was "demoralising", "subversive" and a "social dissolvent" [19], a more subtle and ambivalent position was elaborated.

Instead of dismissing responsibility as a delusion to be swept away by science, writers such as Saleilles pressed the argument that responsibility was indeed a fiction, but nonetheless a valuable and necessary fiction which should certainly be retained. If 'responsibility' and 'free-will' were subjective illusions, their 'illusory' nature by no means precluded their real-world existence and effects. On the contrary, for "it is as a subjective conception that responsibility is efficient and becomes a conscious motive force". These "fictions" were thus "subjective realities" and, for Saleilles (1913; pp. 158–9), it was "this subjective reality, this mental image and concept that the penal point of view must consider'' [20]. Such fictions may thus be scientifically "false" but nonetheless effective in social terms:

> "It is through the ideal and fictitious that men are governed and societies regulated; and whatever may be said or done, governments and legislation cannot really run counter to factors and phenomena as they exist, for these form the very structure of society.... The way to assure public safety and social protection is not to overthrow the conception of responsibility, but on the contrary to implant it in the conscience of the masses and strengthen it by every remaining vestige of belief.
>
> The conception of responsibility is a principle to be preserved at all costs'' (Saleilles, 1913, p. 154).

We can see the discursive preservation of this concept — and its cost of theoretical incoherence — in the following passages by Ruggles-Brise, where he attempts to accept the propositions of Goring's study without their logically entailed implications of criminal "irresponsibility". He begins by welcoming the "general theory of defectiveness" as laid out by Goring, but warns that: "this theory, however, must not be pressed so far as to affect the liability to punishment of the offender for his act" (Ruggles-Brise, 1913, p. 8). Since no theoretical reason is provided, we can only presume that this "must" is a political imperative and not a conceptual one. He confirms this interpretation later in the same passage when he states:

> "Although ... the fact that on the average, the English prisoner is defective in physique and mental capacity would seem to call in question the whole responsibility of any person guilty of an anti-social act, yet if fully and properly understood, it does not mean more than that in a perfect world where the faculties of each could be fully and highly developed, the problem of punishment would not exist" (Ruggles-Brise, 1913, p. 9).

The Chairman of the Prison Commission is, for once, unable convincingly to rescue political desire from theoretical logic and here retreats into a simple evasion and the nonsense of non-sequitor.

But despite these difficulties of manoeuvre, a compromise position was developed along the following lines. As Saleilles had argued, the fiction of responsibility had to be retained. But if this conception were operationalised in its traditional form, it would leave no place for criminology and its investigation of the causes of the crime [21]. The solution was to retain "responsibility" and "freedom" as general principles — but to put them in question with respect to each individual case. *Responsibility thus became a presumption which was always put in doubt.* The Law would maintain its commitment to responsibility as the normal case, but be willing to accept deviations from this norm, particularly with regard to criminology's special categories — the inebriate, the feeble-minded, the habitual and so on. Consequently, courts would not proceed, as before, by assuming that the

18   *D. Garland*

universal principle of Reason and responsibility would apply in all cases other than those where the accused was palpably insane. Instead, the apparatus of criminology would be called in to investigate the individual in question and establish his relation to the norm. Thus Saleilles' compromise did not demand:

> "the renunciation of the idea of responsibility, but only the renunciation
> of the dangerous and puerile fiction, whereby positive and practical
> *applications* were derived from merely abstract premises" (Saleilles, 1913;
> p. 181, emphasis added).

Criminology thus specifies "a true responsibility in place of an assumed responsibility" substituting "the realities of experience for purely judicial abstractions" (Salailles, 1913, p. 72). It replaces a philosophical principle (all men are free and responsible) with a positive psychology (each man must be investigated, his personality assessed).

Of course this resolution, which finds itself a strategic place between the poles of free-will and determinism, is not without its theoretical plausibility, and the notion of 'soft determinism' has often been developed elsewhere. But here our analysis is concerned less with the 'truth' of the final result than with the *mode of its argumentation*, which is quite evidently directed by practical reasoning and policy requirements.

These arguments of Saleilles which set up this compromise formulation will not be found each time their conclusion is endorsed, although writers such as Havelock Ellis (1910) and Hamblin Smith (1922) did rehearse them explicitly. Instead they came to be expressed in a single term which conveyed the ambivalent combination of freedom and determinism, responsibility and irresponsibility, which Saleilles was at pains to implant into the criminal process. The general term which did duty for this complex range of meanings and significance was the concept of *"character"*. Wherever this compromise position is adopted, its contradictions and ambivalance are covered by this simple term which can convey both the freedom of the normal personality and the irresistable determinants of the pathological. Thus it appears with this function in the work of Ruggles-Brise (1900, p. 57), Goring (1913, p. v), Ellis (1910, pp. ix–x), Garafalo (1914, p. 298), Boies (1901, p. 35) and Darwin (1926, p. 226), as well as in various Official Reports and statutory phrases, most notably the Gladstone Report (1895, p. 30) and the many Acts which followed its recommendations [22].

This compromise between freedom and determinism was based upon a developmental logic. Individuals are somehow "free" to develop their moral character (through the acquisition of habits, discipline, etc.), but a certain stage of maturity, "the fundamental law of physical causality prevails. Freedom prepares the soil, determinism receives the seed and makes it fruitful" (Saleilles 1913, pp. 35). A normal, healthy character, untrammelled by genetic defect or vicious habit, will be able to exercise control and choice. It can therefore be said to be free and responsible. But the crucial point is that this freedom is neither absolute nor essential. It is a contingent and fragile freedom which depends upon the delicate mechanisms of character formation and the vicissitudes of individual and social life. Alongside these responsible individuals are numerous characters which are either unformed or else malformed. The latter category (inebriates, habituals, unemployables, the unfit, etc.) are pathologically determined by their defective character structures. They cannot be deterred or persuaded and so must become the target of a more positive intervention — either a reformative technology or else a preventive segregation. The unformed characters of children and juveniles also present scope for positive transformation, this time the more hopeful forces of training, discipline and education.

By means of this concept of 'character' the classical legal subject is *retained in discourse* (and in ideology) but is at the same time *practically transformed*. Once again, positive psychology is brought into a pragmatic relationship with liberal philosophy. The legal subject is no longer the bearer of an essential Will and Freedom — instead it has become a potentially free character with a psychic structure, a life history and a set of psychological determinants. The practical outcome? Any (ideologically defined) subject who is not careful to obey the law and conventional norms, is at risk of becoming a (criminologically-defined) object to be acted upon.

Given the subjectivity of free-will, the appropriate strategy was one which structured choices — hence the rewards and deterrents of classical criminology. The new subjectivity of character structure, on the other hand, gives rise to a strategy which operates upon that structure and its determinants — to a positive criminology.

It is not difficult to see the deep significance of a debate such as this in the context of British political culture. The 'responsible subject' is an indispensable element of any capitalist society structured around 'free' contract, commodity exchange and representative democracy (Edelman, 1979; Hirst, 1979; Pashukanis, 1978). It allows a morality of individualism which allocates reward and blame 'automatically' to the individual, thereby protecting social relations of wealth and discipline from immediate scrutiny. It is therefore an essential requirement of individualism, competitive enterprise, and the corresponding forms of moral and political rule.

The notion of 'responsibility' must be continually ascribed to individuals (and neither generally denied, nor ascribed elsewhere) if these social requirements are to be met. In denying freedom and responsibility the 'Italian School' allowed itself to be excluded from the terms of serious penal discussion in Britain and elsewhere. But the need to make individuals responsible by forceably ascribing responsibility to them is well met by the Saleilles compromise. Not only did it promise reformative techniques which would construct responsible subjects; its very divisions and distinctions reaffirmed the value of 'responsibility'. Each time a deviant individual was identified as "irresponsible" and in need of treatment, the value of being responsible was

20   *D. Garland*

practically and ideologically reinforced for the rest of the population.

Nor should it surprise us that the term which functioned to promote this outcome was that of 'character'. For 'character' had the crucial advantage of according with both commonsense discourse and the more specialist language of social work and debates about social security [23]. It thus contained within itself a whole array of different connotations, ranging from traditional moral judgments about an individual's worth, through psychological theories of subjectivity and its determinants, to the concern with character formation espoused by both social workers and Imperialist politicians. It thus tied together several distinct chains of reference within a single discursive term while simultaneously containing both poles of the free-will/determinism debate within an ambivalent theory of character formation. As will be clear by now, it was through discursive manoeuvres of precisely this kind that alliances were formed, resistances were overcome, and criminology was elevated to its current social status.

Discursive Tactics and Modes of Representation

At a different discursive level — not of conceptual structure but of the presentational form of argument and justification — we can identify in these criminological texts the operation of certain *discursive tactics* and *modes of representation*. It is not a serious charge against a text or discourse to allege that it utilises the persuasive forms of rhetoric and argument to elaborate its positions: most texts do precisely this. However, these tactics and representational forms can be revealing, particularly when the same few forms appear again and again throughout a multitude of texts and utterances, as they do in the criminological programme. They reveal the political strengths and weaknesses of the programme, the means employed to circumvent resistance, and the chosen forms of legitimation. Consequently, the following discussion of operative metaphors, analogies and imagery is undertaken not to complain that a ''scientific'' discourse employs literary forms to present its arguments (though criminology does so more than most), but to analyse the direction, connotations and representational effects of these discursive forms.

(i) Moving from the 'judicial' to the 'administrative'

Within the texts of criminological writers of this period there is a continual play upon the distinction between 'judicial' and 'administrative'. The judicial sphere is seen to be the proper place for public rules, hearings, the contestation of evidence and the ascription of 'responsibility' and 'guilt', while the sphere of administration is concerned instead with expert knowledge and decision-making, discretionary procedures and the estimation of norms, needs, pathologies and dangers. One finds that the constant tendency of penological texts and reports is to displace argument from the first of these spheres to the second, stressing that any recommendations they make should be understood and evaluated in administrative rather than judicial terms. Thus debates which would formerly have been conducted in terms of justice, desert and retribution are now couched in utilitarian terms, measuring individual welfare against social defence.

Perhaps the clearest example of this manoeuvre is where questions regarding offence-behaviour are displaced by investigations relating to the individual's "mode of life". Numerous texts, and later at least four distinct Reports and several Acts repeat the insistance that the individual "... should be treated not as a criminal, but as a person requiring detention on account of his mode of life" [24]. And of course a major advantage of this concern with character and style of living is that it can demand the incarceration of "persons who have committed no public offence" (Report on Inebriates, 1908) — a situation in which judicial modes would be powerless. Thus a judicially-based authority would have trouble accepting Leonard Darwin's proposal that habitual petty criminals and their descendants should be incarcerated without trial on the grounds of "mental and bodily defects" and "racial danger" (Darwin, 1926, p. 225). But such a procedure could easily be accommodated within an administrative mode.

F.H. Bradley gives perhaps the clearest statement of this reasoning when he insists that dangerous offenders should be regarded as "irresponsible":

> "Justice is the assignment of benefit and injury according to desert.... But if he is not a moral agent I reply, surely what follows is that justice is indifferent to his case. What is just or unjust has nothing to do with our disposal of his destiny. And hence, so long as we do not pretend retributively to punish him, we may cut him off, if that seems best for the general good" (Bradley, 1893–1894, p. 276).

(ii) Appealing to precedent

Another common tactic was the *appeal to precedent* which down-played the novelty of the new programme and represented it as compatible with existing doctrine. Thus the reformatory and industrial schools became the much-quoted precedent for adult reformatories, indeterminate sentences and the "right of the non-responsible offender to special disciplinary and educational treatment" [25]; the practice of supplementing the penal servitude of recidivists with periods of police supervision was used as a justification for the double track system of preventive detention (Ruggles-Brise, 1900, p. 29; 1901, p. 120); and the narrow powers of detention allowed by the Public Health, Lunacy and Poor Law Acts become the legitimatory basis for the very widest kind of restrictions on the liberty of paupers, the feeble-minded and the

22   *D. Garland*

"unemployable" (Report of the Royal Commission on the Feeble-Minded, 1908, p. 325).

There is of course a certain irony involved here, inasmuch as a judicial form of legitimation is being employed to undermine "the Judicial form" itself, and no doubt this says much about the power of both legal and traditional ideologies in this period. But rather more surprising is the speed with which small reforms and tentative innovations, once achieved, themselves came to be cited as important precedents, thereby allowing the programme's success to feed upon itself as further legitimation. Thus we find Ruggles-Brise (1911, p. 3–4) employing the 1908 *Prevention of Crime Act* as a precedent for further use of the indeterminate sentence and the 1908 *Report on Inebriacy* justifying its own proposals by reminding us that:

> "The course of recent legislation shows that the legislature does not now hesitate to enforce restrictions on the liberty of persons whose unchecked vagaries are clearly contrary to the public weal" (Report on Inebriates, 1908).

(iii) Special cases which become the norm

The effect of argument by precedent was frequently to use a special case (e.g. the semi-determinate period of a child's stay at an industrial school) to legitimate a new practice which was significantly different and more general (the indeterminate sentencing of adults to prison custody or labour colonies). In fact as we have seen, criminology operated precisely by producing "special cases" or categories of individual who should not be subject to the normal procedures of legal accountability because of their irresponsible or abnormal characters. However these "special cases", once established, had a tendency to extend their domain — and that of criminology — and we can cite many instances where a special case is established only to have its special features erased in the name of its subsequent extension. Thus we see Ruggles-Brise take pains to argue that the indeterminate sentence is suitable only for the special category of habitual offenders, or else that reformatory treatment can be justified only for juveniles, only to find him in later years arguing that there is no good reason why these practices should not be extended to "ordinary crime" and adult criminals (Report of the Prison Commissioners, 1912–1913, pp. 12–13).

This tactic functions by attacking the points of least resistance in the *status quo*. Categories such as children or the insane, already recognised to be special cases in the eyes of the law and the public, were seized upon and used as *points of entry*, or tactical bridgeheads for the criminological programme [26]. Starting with characters which are obviously *unformed* — namely children — criminology proceeds to add the less obvious cases of firstly the "juvenile adult", then "first offenders" and all offenders under 30 years of age, and finally the full range of "irresponsibles" [27]. In the same way the *malformed* category of the insane undergoes a gradual extension until it includes 'the feeble-minded', 'the inebriate' and 'the habitual' within its terms. What begins as a narrowly-defined special case extends itself indefinitely, and having made its case at either end of the criminal spectrum, criminology turns inwards from the obviously deviant to the apparently normal.

This tactic was important in establishing many of the penal reforms and innovations of the period under study, but it also has a more contemporary relevance. The focus upon exemplary cases to legitimise the non-exemplary by implication is still a major feature of penal discourse, and one which is amplified whenever that discourse enters into the popular idiom. It is therefore no accident that popular discourse about crime and control 'automatically' coheres around images such as "the psychopathic killer", "the asocial youth" or "the ruthless professional" for whom prison is of course "essential — those being the hard cases which settle the direction of uninformed opinion and promote the demand for a general severity. One hardly need add that this works to the detriment of a balanced and fuller view which would give due consideration to the vast majority of offenders who differ radically from the image of these special cases.

(iv) The role of the tactical trade-off

The final notable device which appears in these texts might be termed *the tactical trade-off*. This kind of argument sought to justify severity in one part of the system by reference to other practices where leniency was more apparent:

> "... when we do so much to prevent crime, and to train those youth up, so that they do not pursue criminal avocations, we are bound on the other hand, to be more stringent in the punishment of those who still pursue a course of crime in spite of what we have done for them" (Crofton, 1863, p. xii).

This device was particularly important in the debates surrounding Preventive Detention since on the face of it, an additional sentence of 10 years imprisonment for habitual offenders on top of the proper punishment for their immediate offence was unquestionably severe and difficult to justify. This legitimatory problem was overcome by promising to mitigate the conditions of this detention, 'exchanging' length of detention for leniency of discipline. As a Confidential Memorandum on the Penal Servitude Bill states:

> "It may not be necessary during that period of time, that the punishment should be a severe one. All that is wanted is that they should be under discipline and compulsorily segregated from the outside world. In the case of a conviction for a small offence, e.g. stealing a pair of boots, both judges and public opinion would be averse to the passing of a long sentence.... The new prison rule [states that] ... the ordinary convict discipline will be greatly mitigated ... and thereby seeks to encourage in appropriate cases the passing of long, as opposed to severe, sentences" [28].

24   *D. Garland*

This trade-off tactic is rehearsed on virtually every occasion that Preventive
Detention is officially discussed, as well as being used in a similar fashion to
justify the lengthy detention of inebriates (See Report of the Departmental
Committee on Inebriates, 1908). And perhaps it is not too much to suggest
that the combination of reformatory Borstal provisions for adolescents and
Preventive Detention for adult habituals in the *Prevention of Crime Act 1908*
might be interpreted as a statutory instance of this same tactical device.

(v) Language and metaphor

If one means of justifying severity was to set it off against a purported leniency
elsewhere, another method was to insist upon the severity of the problem
being faced. In this endeavour to characterise the social harm caused by
crime, criminology tended to neglect its concern with scientific measurement
and statistical quantification and to slip into a less rational discursive form.

Thus we find the frequent deployment of a kind of *discursive violence*
whenever harsh measures need to be powerfully justified. And of course these
emotive and alarmist descriptions of criminality go a long way to explaining
the deep sense of social threat and danger evoked by the imaginary figure of
the criminal — both then and now. The following are only the most striking
instances of a violence which is pervasive in this discourse.

Thus W.A. Chapple, the eugenist and M.P. — arguing for a policy of
sterilization:

> "Consider what a burden is the criminal. Every community is more or
> less terrorised by him, our property is liable to be plundered, our houses
> invaded, our women ravished, our children murdered" (Chapple 1904,
> introduction).

And Baron Rafaele Garafalo, invoking a sensationalist statistic to prepare the
reader for his "eliminatory" proposals:

> "... here statistical science steps in. Adding the figures, combining the
> scattered sums of human misery produced by human wickedness, it
> unrolls to us the scenes of a world-appalling tragedy. It shows us a field of
> battle littered with the remains of frightful carnage, it joins in a single
> heartrending cry the groans of the wounded, the lamentations of their
> kindred; it causes to file before us legions of the maimed, of orphans, and
> of paupers; it blinds us with the light of a vast incendiary conflagration
> devouring forests and homes; it deafens us with the yells of an army of
> pirates. And in sinister climax, it reveals to us the author of these scenes of
> desolation — an enemy mysterious, unrecognised by history — we call
> him the CRIMINAL" (Garafalo, 1914, p. xxvii).

In similar terms and for similar purposes, Lydston (1904, p. 569) talks of
"social excreta" which demand "total elimination" and Boies (1893, p. 293)
talks of "the unfit, the abnormals, the sharks, the devil-fish and other

monsters" whom it goes without saying, "ought not to be liberated to destroy and multiply, but must be confined and secluded until they are exterminated". And echoing the more technical but equally violent morphologies of Lombroso and Ferri, Boies describes criminals as:

> "Human deformities and monstrosities, physically illshapen, weak and sickly with irregular features, they bear a sinister ignoble, and furtive expression. They have an inbalanced and distorted cranium, and are of low order of intelligence, and apparently devoid of the nobler sentiments; with a depraved if not utter absence of moral sense or conscience" (Boies, 1893, p. 172).

This tactical symmetry between the form of language and the form of measure being proposed is well brought out in the texts of Thomas Holmes, police court missioner and Secretary of the Howard Association. When he comes to prepare the ground for probation and social work sanctions, his language appropriately moves into a familiar evangelical mode:

> "Even as I sit and write, it is all before me and around. I hear again the horrible speech and diverse tongues. I hear the accents of sorrow and the burst of angry sound. I hear the devil-may-care laugh and the contemptuous expression. I hear the signs and the groans and bitter plaints. I see men shorn of all glory. I see womanhood clothed in shame. I see vice rampant. I see misery crawling ..." (Holmes, 1900, p. 2).

The actual language and modes of representation employed in these discourses are themselves of significance. These terms, styles and literary figures do much more than simply convey propositions or communicate proposals. They simultaneously operate as persuasive devices in the struggle for power *and* help to fix the associations, emotions and responses which these issues popularly evoke. The most obvious illustration of this operation whereby the social meanings and connotations of 'criminality' are discursively constructed, is the use of *metaphor*, and there is a sense in which the chosen metaphors of discourse reveal its social desire — the significance and connotations it would attach to its propositions. Thus for example the scientistic and pathologising tendencies of the criminological programme, as well as its professional ambitions, are well brought out by the medical metaphor which saturates the surface of criminological discourse. And although *The Times* and Ruggles-Brise warn that this metaphor should not be pressed too far (*cf.* the compromises over responsibility, determinism, etc.) we find it appearing in the Parliamentary debates, the Official Reports and even *The Times* itself [29]. It is this metaphor above all else which authorises a language of care and protection to substitute for the more awkward vocabularies of discipline and punishment. Consequently the compulsory detention of paupers becomes "continuous care and treatment", the incarceration of the feeble-minded is rendered as "special protection suited to their needs", which of course must continue as long as is necessary, and

26   D. Garland

Borstal becomes "merely a teaching and training institution" or a "moral hospital" [30].

This medical metaphor also transforms the conception of penal *time* from its negative value as a measure of severity to a more positive statement of the period during which reformative facilities will be offered. It was only through this important inversion that repeated pleas for lengthier sentences could become the mark of the progressive penal reformer [31].

One might also add that it was precisely this metaphor, and its images of treatment, help and care, that necessitated the emphatic and frequently asserted *denial of leniency* which runs through the reformers' texts, striving to restrain the unacceptable connotations which had been set in train [32].

As we have already seen, the images and metaphors of "efficiency", "degeneracy", and "fitness" are also constantly present here, as is the evolutionary analogy from which they derive, linking criminological proposals with the future of the Race and the Empire. In much the same way a recurring description of recidivists as a "blot" or "strain" upon civilisation, operates to link these diverse concerns in a single figure of speech. Finally, there is also a frequent reference to criminals (and sometimes to the whole of the lower classes) as "savages" or "semi-savages" with "a very low order of intellect and a degradation of the natural affections to something little better than animal instincts" (Dendy, 1895, p. 84). The effect of these statements is to do by implication what Garafalo and Ribot do explicitly, viz. to present the deviant population as "beings [who] are completely dehumanised" (Ribot, quoted in Garafalo, 1914, p. 62). Like the violent descriptions noted above, these dehumanising terms allow an escalation to take place in a "war against crime" which is not just metaphorical.

Conclusion: The Political Logic of 'Illogicality'

These detailed discussions of texts and statements should by now have demonstrated that it is not an unwonted cynicism which leads us to talk of 'manoeuvres', 'tactics' and 'political struggles' within criminological and penal discourse. These discursive manoeuvres were clearly motivated rather than accidental. The texts we have examined were not rough-and-ready drafts or careless outbursts — they were rather carefully constructed formulations of a contradictory process wherein theoretical logic is continually interrupted by political desire. The purposes, aspirations and social objectives of organisations and individuals were thus introduced, sometimes crudely, but often very subtly, into these discourses. They can be identified, as we have shown, because they have no theoretical place there — or rather because the theoretical place they carve out for themselves involves arbitrary assumptions, non-sequitors and logical contradictions which become intelligible only through political analysis.

The outcome is an array of texts and supposedly scientific statements which are in fact persuasive documents; they are aimed not at 'truth' but at the political process. Their legacy is a criminology which is eclectic, individualising, pragmatic and often incoherent. Their success is the fact that this same criminology has been adopted, at least in part, into the institutional fabric of our penal institutions and legal process. (For a discussion of the partial institutionalisation of the criminological programme in Britain, see Garland, 1985.)

The main object of this paper has not been to challenge criminology's scientific credentials — which today are widely disputed — or to measure the discipline against some ideal of scientificity which should find even our natural sciences wanting. Rather its point is to show in some detail the discursive processes which constituted this criminology as a silently politicised, pseudo-scientific discourse — to show how its political positions were inscribed, what these positions were, and how they were subsequently denied. The paper thus begins by restating the criticism that criminology is 'ideological', then proceeds to substantiate that claim using textual and circumstantial evidence, while trying more broadly to say a little about the way in which ideology operates through theoretical discourse.

Perhaps the last word should go to Cesare Lombroso, who, after all, must bear much of the credit and much of the blame for the criminology which we inherit today [33]:

> "... nothing is less logical than to try to be too logical: nothing is more imprudent than to try to maintain theories ... if they are going to upset the order of society.... The sociologist must observe still greater circumspection, for if he puts into operation innovations of an upsetting nature he will simply succeed in demonstrating the uselessness and inefficiency of his science" (Lombroso, 1911, p. 209).

Notes

1 Nor would I wish to suggest that socially produced knowledge (scientific or otherwise) can ever be wholly autonomous of social concerns and divisions (i.e. politics). However there are certainly greater and lesser degrees of independence and the argument in this paper is that criminology has less than it claims.

2 The latest penal sanction which means all things to all men (and women) is the community service order. The Report of the Advisory Council on the Penal System (1970, pp. 12–13, para. 33) describes it thus: "to some, it would be a more constructive and cheaper alternative to short sentences of imprisonment; by others it would be seen as introducing into the penal system a new dimension with an emphasis on reparation to the community; others again would regard it as a means of giving effect to the old adage that punishment should fit the crime; while still others would stress the value of bringing offenders into close touch with those members of the community who are most in need of help and support". Baroness Wootton described it as "an undisguised attempt to curry favour with everybody" (Wootton, 1978, p. 178).

28   D. Garland

3 For an extended discussion of this point, see Garland (1983, 1985).
4 This point is not undercut by those policies which have addressed the individual via
   the family unit, for in these cases too *social* relations are ignored in favour of *personal*
   relations.
5 Crackenthorpe (1908, pp. 971–2): "John Bull ... demands that some control
   should be exercised over the unreasonable multiplication of the unfit, whether such
   unfitness be due to drink, feeble-mindedness, insanity, criminality or disease". See
   also Chapple (1904, introduction).
6 See also Lombroso (1911) and Laycock, the alienist, quoted by Ellis (1910, p. 33):
   "... that many or the majority of ... criminals are moral imbeciles is certain".
7 See, for example, the Howard Association (1908, p. 2); Home Secretary Gladstone
   quoted in Hansard, Vol. 190, 1908, Second Reading of the Prevention of Crime
   Bill, at col. 497; the Report of the Departmental Committee on Inebriates (1908,
   p. 26–7) and Boies (1893, 1901).
8 "Eugenics" is the study and deployment of agencies under social control for the
   purpose of improving the 'racial qualities' of future generations, either physically
   or mentally. For a discussion of eugenics in Britain, see McKenzie (1981).
9 cf. Battaglini (1910, p. 15): "Concerning the relationship between eugenics and
   crime, it must be noted that the penal code is *par excellence* a group of eugenic
   measures". Garafalo (1914, p. 252): "... the aim should be only to prevent the
   procreation of individuals who in all likelihood would turn out to be vicious and
   depraved. Not to punish the children of criminals but to prevent their birth....
   Lombroso did not hesitate to ascribe the greater humanity of our times ... to the
   work of capital punishment in improving the human race". See also Goring (1913,
   ch. 5) where he argues that the surprisingly low fertility of convicts is a
   consequence of the frequent desertion of them by their wives. Sir John McDougall
   (1904–1905, p. 24) states that "At Broadmoor, women convicted of infanticide are
   detained until the menopause has occurred".
10 See also Darwin (1926, pp. 219–20): "... it is hoped that in all their decisions in
   regard to setting criminals at liberty [tribunals] would take into consideration
   whether or not consent to be sterilised has been obtained".
11 Goring (1913). An American reviewer of Goring's research noted the heavy bias of
   the work towards questions which would confirm the eugenist views, and away
   from those which might jeopardise them: "We are surprised to note the apparent
   lack of thoroughness Dr. Goring uses in his treatment of environment as a cause of
   criminality. His sub-divisions of the subject are very limited and his data is not of
   large amount: also we consider that some of the most important factors which are
   usually considered prominent as causes, he has passed over entirely" (Newkirk,
   1914–1915, p. 354).
12 cf. Darwin (1914–1915, p. 214) who cites Goring to substantiate the claim that
   "the child of a criminal is at least ten times more likely to enter prison than is the
   child of honest parents". See also Darwin (1926) on "The Juvenile" which is in
   fact a eugenic elaboration of Goring's arguments; and also the significant welcome
   afforded to Goring's book by the *Eugenics Review* of 1914–1915 (Vol. 6).
13 See, for example, the Report of the Prison Commissioners (1913–1914, p. 24):
   "The principal lesson to be learned from this Inquiry is that crime can be
   combatted most effectively by segregation and supervision of the obviously
   unfit ..." Surpisingly, this eugenic influence upon official criminological discourse

has not to my knowledge been noted by the literature, let alone explained or elaborated.

14 See Garafalo (1914, p. xxxi). Lombroso did of course talk of the constitutionally incorrigible offender — the "born criminal" — but this category was not coterminous with the "criminal type".

15 See Ruggles-Brise (1921, p. 199), Hall (1926, p. 18), Saleilles (1913, p. 143), Report of the Departmental Committee on Inebriates (1908, pp. 5–6) and the Report of the Prison Commissioners (1907–1908, p. 13).

16 cf. Donzelot (1979) who uses this metaphor to describe how psycho-analysis can be used to regulate the images of its clients.

17 See Foucault (1980) where he argues that an important effect of criminality is to justify a generalised form of policing which controls and supervises a population much wider than "the criminal class".

18 See Ferri (1917, p. 372) and De Fleury (1901, p. 121): "The criminal is responsible towards society for the dread and antipathy which he inspires only: he is responsible towards himself through a trick of education only, a delusion, which it is no doubt convenient to keep up for the government of children and peoples, but which no jurist or philosopher ought to be able to impose upon himself".

19 See the evidence of the Honorary Secretary of the Personal Rights Association to the Departmental Committee on Inebriates (1908) and De Fleury (1901, p. 121).

20 Essentially the same point has been made more recently in regard to the "subject of ideology", see Hirst (1979) and Althusser (1971).

21 If the offender is deemed to be free and responsible, the cause of his conviction must lie in his freely-willed choice: only when responsibility is questioned do other 'causes' enter into the question.

22 See Garland (1985) for a discussion of how the legislation of the post-Gladstone era embodied these discursive terms and compromise formations.

23 See Garland (1985) for analyses of the social work and social security programmes of this period.

24 See the Report of the Prison Commissioners for 1908–1909; the Majority and Minority Reports on the Poor Law (1909); the Report of the Departmental Committee on Vagrancy (1906); the Report of the Departmental Committee on Inebriates (1908); *The Inebriate Act* of 1908, etc.

25 See, for example, the Report of the Scottish Departmental Committee on Habitual Offenders, etc. (1895, p. xvi); the Report of the Royal Commission on the Feeble-Minded (1908, p. 325); Ruggles-Brise (1901, p. 57).

26 cf. Resolution 5 of the Turin Congress of 1906, quoted in De Quiros (1911, p. 127): "Both in theory and in practice the treatment of young criminals must serve as the prototype for the treatment of adults". L. Hausman, in his preface to Brockway (1928, p. x) makes this tactic explicit: "In this book [the case for scientific penology] is intelligently and moderately stated; and in stressing the overwhelming importance of the treatment of the juvenile offenders, it not only starts its reform proposals at what is obviously the right end, but makes its appeal on ground where public opinion is probably less hardened and less indifferent — and is therefore more readily open to conviction — than in the case of the 'confirmed criminal' ...". The child as a point of entry also had a number of other advantages such as the educational precedent (Hoffding, 1911–1912, p. 696); the attraction of "catching them young" and cutting off the supply of adult criminals

30   *D. Garland*

(the Gladstone Report 1895, p. 11) and the support of a large 'child-saving' lobby.
27 For evidence of this use of analogy to extend the category of the 'responsible', see
    the Mental Deficiency Bill 1913, Second Reading Debate, Hansard, Vol. 53,
    especially the contribution of L. Scott, M.P.; the Second Reading Debate on the
    Inebriates Bill 1912, Hansard, Vol 37, especially C. Bathurst, M.P. The term
    "juvenile–adult" was developed for this purpose by Ruggles-Brise (1901, p. 92)
    "... a person cannot be regarded as fully responsible before the age of 21 ... and it
    has been observed by scientific authority that the citizens of the poorer classes
    develop physically [and hence mentally and morally] much later than those of the
    more favoured classes, even as late as 25 or 26".
28 The Memorandum is contained in the file on "Habitual Criminals" in Public
    Records Office category P. Com. 7. 286.
29 For examples of this, see Barman (1934, p. 43); Ritchie (1894–1895, p. 422);
    Baker (1898, introduction); Boies (1901, p. 435); *The Times*, 30 October 1900;
    Ruggles-Brise (1901, p. 106); the Gladstone Report (1895,, p. 9); the Majority
    Report of the Royal Commission on the Poor Law (1909, R. 212); McLean, M.P.
    quoted in Hansard, Vol. 190 (1908) in the Second Reading Debate on the
    Prevention of Crime Bill, at col. 485. See also *The Times*, 21 April 1911 where it is
    suggested that the U.S. penal authorities have taken the medical metaphor *too*
    seriously, and have jeopardised the valuable sentiment of social revulsion against
    crime and criminals.
30 See the Majority Report of the Royal Commission on the Poor Law (1909);
    Chapple, M.P. quoted in Hansard, Vol. 65 (20 July 1914) at col. 125.
31 See Ruggles-Brise (1921, p. 93); the Report of the Prison Commissioners
    (1900–1901, p. 13); Report of the Prison Commissioners (1901–1902, p. 14);
    Ruggles-Brise (1899, p. 19–20; 1901, p. 57).
32 See Garafalo (1914, p. 136); Ruggles-Brise (1925, p. 12); Tallack (1895, p. 103);
    Morrison (1904, p. 105); Report of the Prison Commissioners (1912–1913,
    pp. 22–3).
33 Without wishing to suggest that nothing has happened in the discipline of
    criminology over the last 100 years, it is nonetheless true that the criminological
    problematic described in this essay remains firmly in place. (See, for example, any
    recent volume of the *British Journal of Criminology*.) Arguments and techniques have
    become more refined, studies and data have accumulated, but the discipline still
    revolves around the concept of criminality, its causes and its remedies. It is a
    discourse fixed in a socio-political space, a technical auxilliary of the welfare state,
    which endlessly reproduces itself and the policies it supports. Of course this
    problematic and its favoured policies have been subjected to challenge, especially
    since the 1960s, but the most successful challenges have been those which have
    entirely revised the terms of analysis. Thus when writers like Stuart Hall and his
    co-authors (1978) produce *Policing the Crisis* — a study of crime which displaces the
    criminal, correctionalism and individualism — they are manifestly not doing
    criminology in any conventional sense of that term.

References

Althusser, L. (1971) *Lenin and Philosophy and Other Essays*. New Left Books: London.
Ancel, M. (1965) *Social Defence*. Routledge & Kegan Paul: London.

Politics and policy in criminology   31

Anderson, R. (1908) Criminals and crime: a rejoinder. *The Nineteenth Century* **LXIII**.
Baker, T.B. (1898) *War With Crime*. Longmans: London.
Bankowski, Z., Mungham, G. & Young, P. (1976) Radical criminology or radical criminologist? In *Contemporary Crises*.
Barman, S. (1934) *The English Borstal System*. P.S. King & Son: London.
Battaglini, G.Q. (1910) Eugenics and the criminal law. *The American Journal of Criminal Law, Criminology and Police Science* **5**.
Boies, H.M. (1893) *Prisoners and Paupers*. Putnams: New York.
Boies, H.M. (1901) *The Science of Penology*. Putnams: London.
Bradley, F.H. (1893–1894) Some remarks on punishment. *The International Journal of Ethics* **IV**.
Brockway, A.F. (1928) *A New Way with Crime*. Williams & Norgate: London.
Chapple, W.A. (1904) *The Fertility of the Unfit*. Whitcombe & Tombs: Melbourne.
Crackenthorpe, M. (1908) Eugenics as a social force. *The Nineteenth Century* **LXIII**.
Crofton, W. (1863) Evidence to the Carnarvon Commission, quoted in *The Carnarvon Report, 1863*, at p. xii.
Darwin, L. (1914–1915) The habitual criminal. *The Eugenics Review* **6**.
Darwin, L. (1926) *The Need for Eugenic Reform*. John Murray: London.
De Fleury, M. (1901) *The Criminal Mind*. Downey & Co: London.
Dendy, H. (1895) The industrial residuum. In *Aspects of the Social Problem*, (Bosanquet, B., Ed.). Macmillan: London.
De Quiros, B. (1911) *Modern Theories of Criminality*. Heinemann: London.
De Sanctis, S. (1914–1915) Review of Goring. *The Journal of Criminal Law, Criminology and Police Science* **5**.
Donzelot, J. (1979) *The Policing of Families*. Hutchinson: London.
Edelman, B. (1979) *Ownership of the Image: Elements for a Marxist Theory of Law*. Routledge & Kegan Paul: London.
Ellis, H.H. (1910) *The Criminal* (1st edit. 1889). Contemporary Science Series: London.
Eugenics Review, The. (1914–1915) Eugenic Education Society: London.
Ferri, E. (1914–1915) Review of Goring's 'The English Convict'. *The Journal of Criminal Law, Criminology and Police Science* **5**.
Ferri, E. (1917) *Criminal Sociology*. Heinemann: London.
Foucault, M. (1980) Prison talk. In *Michel Foucault: Power/Knowledge*, (Gordon, C., Ed.). Harvester: Brighton.
Garafalo, R. (1914) *Criminology*. Heinemann: London.
Garland, D. (1983) Durkheim's theory of punishment: a critique. In *The Power to Punish*, (Garland, D. & Young, P., Eds). Heinemann: London.
Garland, D. (1985) *Punishment and Welfare*. Heinemann: London.
Gladstone Report, The (1895) Report of the Departmental Committee on Prisons P.P. 1895, LVI.
Goring, C. (1913). *The English Convict*. Prison Commission.
Hall, S. *et al.*, (1978) *Policing the Crisis*. London: Macmillan.
Hall, W. C. (1926) *Children's Courts*. G. Allen & Unwin: London.
Hirst, P. (1979) *On Law and Ideology*. Macmillan: London.
Hoffding, H. (1911–1912) The state's authority to punish crime. *The Journal of the American Institute of Criminal Law and Criminology* **2**.
Holmes, T. (1900) *Pictures and Problems from London Police Courts*. Edward Arnold:

32   *D. Garland*

London.
Howard Association (1907–1910) *Crime of the Empire and Its Treatment*. Annual Reports of the Howard Association for promoting the most efficient means of penal treatment and crime prevention (1907), (1908), (1909), (1910), London.
Jones, G. S. (1971) *Outcast London: A Study in the Relationships between Classes in Victorian Society*. Clarendon Press: Oxford.
Journal of Criminal Law, Criminology and Police Science, The. (1910–1911) 1, "Editorial Comment".
Lakatos, I. (1981) History of science and its rational reconstruction. In *Scientific Revolutions*. (Hacking, E., Ed.). Oxford University Press: Oxford.
Lombroso, C. (1911) *Crime, Its Causes and Its Remedies*. Heinemann: London.
Lydston, G.F. (1904) *The Diseases of Society (The Vice and Crime Problem)*. Publisher?: London.
Marr, Dr (1903) Quoted in the Scottish Department file on "Lunacy and alcoholic excess", Scottish Public Records Office, HH 59/13.
McDougall, Sir J. (1904–1905) Quoted in *The Transactions of the Medico-Legal Society* 2.
McKenna (1912) Home Secretary McKenna, quoted in *Hansard* 1912, Vol. 39. Second Reading Debate on the Mental Deficiency Bill, at col. 641.
McKenzie, D. (1981) *Statistics in Britain, 1835–1930*. Edinburgh University Press: Edinburgh.
Morrison, W.D. (1904) *The Treatment of Prisoners*. Humanitarian League: London.
Newkirk, H.D. (1914–1915) Review of Goring's 'The English Convict'. *The Journal of Criminal Law, Criminology and Police Science* 5.
Pashukanis, E.B. (1978) *Law and Marxism: A General Theory*, (Arthur, C., Ed.). Ink Links: London.
Radzinowicz, L. (1961) *In Search of Criminology*. Heinemann: London.
Report of the Select Committee of the House of Lords on the Present State of Discipline in Gaols and Houses of Correction (1863) (The Carnarvon Report) P.P. 1863, IX.
Report of the Prison Commissioners (1900–1901) P.P. 1902, XLV.
Report of the Prison Commissioners (1901–1902) P.P. 1902, XLVI.
Report of the Departmental Committee on Vagrancy (1906) P.P. 1906, CIII.
Report of the Prison Commissioners (1907–1908) P.P. 1908, LII.
Report of the Royal Commission on the Care and Control of the Feeble-Minded (1908) P.P. 1908, XXXIX.
Report of the Departmental Committee on the Operation of the Law Relating to Inebriates and to their Detention in Reformatories and Retreats (1908) P.P. 1908, XII.
Report of the Royal Commission on the Poor Law and Relief of Distress (1909) (The Majority Report) P.P. 1909, XXXVII.
Report of the Royal Commission on the Poor Law and Relief of Distress (1909) (The Minority Report) P.P. 1909, XXXVII.
Report of the Prison Commissioners (1912–1913) P.P. 1914, XLV.
Report of the Prison Commissioners (1913–1914) P.P. 1914, XLV
Report of the Advisory Council on the Penal System (1970) (The Wootton Report) H.M.S.O.: London.
Ritchie, D.G. (1894–1895) Free-will and responsibility. *The International Journal of Ethics* 5.
Ruggles-Brise, E. (1899) Some Observations on the Treatment of Crime in America.

P.P. 1899, XLIII.

Ruggles-Brise, E. (1900) The indeterminate sentence. Paper given to the 6th International Penitentiary Congress, 1900. Contained in P.R.O. P. Com. 7 286.

Ruggles-Brise, E. (1901) Report on the Proceedings of the Fifth and Sixth International Penitentiary Congresses. P.P. 1901, XXXIII.

Ruggles-Brise, E. (1911) Report on the Proceedings of the Eighth International Penitentiary Congress. P.P. 1911, XXXIX.

Ruggles-Brise, E. (1913) Preface to C. Goring, *The English Convict*. Prison Commission.

Ruggles-Brise, E. (1921) *The English Prison System*. Macmillan: London.

Ruggles-Brise, E. (1925) *Prison Reform at Home and Abroad*. Macmillan: London.

Saleilles, R. (1913) *The Individualisation of Punishment*. Heinemann: London.

Scottish Departmental Committee on Habitual Offenders, Vagrants, Beggars, Inebriates and Juvenile Delinquents (1895) P.P. 1895, XXXVII.

Searle, G.R. (1971) *The Quest for National Efficiency*. Blackwell: Oxford.

Smith, M. (1922) *The Psychology of the Criminal*. Methuen: London.

Tallack, W. (1895) *Penological and Preventive Principles*. Wertheimer, Lea & Co.: London.

Taylor, I., Walton, P. & Young, J. (1973) *The New Criminology*. Routledge & Kegan Paul: London.

Taylor, I., Walton, P. & Young, J. (1975) *Critical Criminology*. Routledge & Kegan Paul: London.

Tredgold, A.F. (1911) The feeble-minded — a social danger. Paper circulated to the Cabinet by W. Churchill on 22 December 1911; see P.R.O. Cab. 37/108.

Von Hamel, J.A. (1911–1912) The indeterminate sentence. *The Journal of the American Institute of Criminal Law and Criminology* 2.

Walker, N. (1965) *Crime and Punishment in Britain*. Edinburgh University Press: Edinburgh.

Wills, A. (1907) Criminals and crime. *The Nineteenth Century* LXII.

Wilson, A. (1908) *Education, Personality and Crime*. Greening & Co.: London.

Wootton, B. (1978) *Crime and Penal Policy: Reflections on Fifty Years Experience*. George Allen & Unwin: Hemel Hempstead.

Date received: May 1984

Part II
Theoretical Perspectives

[4]

A Conceptual Model of Crime Prevention

PAUL J. BRANTINGHAM
Associate Professor, School of Criminology, Florida State University

FREDERIC L. FAUST
Associate Professor, School of Criminology, Florida State University

Crime prevention is the professed mission of every agency found within the American criminal justice system. In practice, the term "prevention" seems to be applied confusingly to a wide array of contradictory activities. This confusion can be avoided through the use of a conceptual model that defines three levels of prevention: (1) primary prevention, *directed at modification of criminogenic conditions in the physical and social environment at large;* (2) secondary prevention, *directed at early identification and intervention in the lives of individuals or, groups in criminogenic circumstances; and* (3) tertiary prevention, *directed at prevention of recidivism. The use of such a conceptual model helps to clarify current crime prevention efforts, suggests fruitful directions for future research by identifying current lacunae in practice and in the research literature, and may ultimately prove helpful in addressing the seemingly endless debate between advocates of "punishment" and advocates of "treatment."*

PREVENTION, probably the most overworked and least understood concept in contemporary criminology, might be defined simply as any activity, by an individual or a group, public or private, that precludes the incidence of one or more criminal acts. But caution is warranted here, for the simplicity is deceptive. Can crime prevention be logically conceived to encompass such divergent actions as long-term incarceration and pretrial diversion from the justice system? Solitary confinement and remedial reading instruction? The improvement of automotive antitheft devices and the development of neighborhood recreation centers? Or psychosurgery and the levying of fines? Considering the goal definition of crime prevention, the answer might well be "yes." But where means are concerned, the matter is heavily clouded by definitional ambiguity and theoretical contradiction.

The purpose of the following discussion, then, is threefold: (1) to examine briefly the philosophical roots and related definitional issues of crime prevention; (2) to outline a conceptual framework that will provide a more useful understanding of crime prevention; and (3) to specify the most fruitful direction for the development of theory, research, and programing in crime prevention. Considering the present state of competing and contradictory views on the prevention of

284

criminal behavior, we judge this to be a timely endeavor.

Punishment, Treatment, and Crime Prevention

Punishment is a persistent problem for social theorists: its definition is elusive and its justification is debatable.[1] Nevertheless, a definition of the standard case of punishment, roughly acceptable to utilitarians, seems to have evolved from the work of Antony Flew.[2] Under this definition, punishment is (1) a painful or unpleasant consequence (2) intentionally imposed by other persons (3) upon an offender (4) for his offense against legal rules (5) under authority of the legal system against which the offense was committed.[3] The paramount utilitarian justification for the imposition of punishment has been that it will prevent crime.[4]

Recent scholarship has shown, however, that the ethical issues involved in the application of painful or unpleasant consequences to individual men by agents of legal systems cannot properly be circumscribed by the concept of punishment. Troublesome children, retarded people, madmen, and drug abusers are all currently subject to treatment through legal process at the hands of what Kittrie has called the "therapeutic state."[5] The actual consequences accruing to people being treated differ very little from the consequences accruing to people being punished.

Herbert Packer has observed that punishment and treatment can be distinguished primarily by the *purpose* for which the consequence is imposed: crime prevention or retribution, or both, in the case of punishment; social protection or individual betterment, or both, in the case of treatment.[6] But that distinction blurs when social protection is equated with prevention of social harms (including crimes) in the more aggressive literature of deterministic criminology.[7] This blurring of a weak distinction increases in many legislative formulations. "Prevention of harm to self or others," for instance, is the seventh most frequently mandated ground for exercise of juvenile court jurisdiction

---

1. Recent collections which probe the debate between utilitarians and retributionists include Jeffrie G. Murphy, *Punishment and Responsibility* (Belmont, Calif.: Wadsworth, 1973); Rudolph J. Gerber and Patrick D. McAnany, *Contemporary Punishment* (South Bend, Ind.: University of Notre Dame Press, 1972); Stanley E. Grupp, *Theories of Punishment* (Bloomington, Ind.: Indiana University Press, 1971).

2. Antony Flew, "The Justification of Punishment," *Philosophy*, October 1954, pp. 291 *et seq.* Those who have adopted Flew's position include H. L. A. Hart, *Punishment and Responsibility* (New York: Oxford University Press, 1968), and Herbert L. Packer, *The Limits of the Criminal Sanction* (Stanford, Calif.: Stanford University Press, 1968).

3. Packer attempted to make the definition workable for both utilitarians and retributionists by adding a sixth condition to the standard case adduced by Flew: "That it be imposed for the dominant purpose of preventing offenses against legal rules or of exacting retribution from offenders, or both." Packer, *op. cit. supra* note 2, p. 31.

4. Cesare Beccaria, *On Crimes and Punishments*, Henry Paolucci, trans. (Indianapolis: Bobbs-Merrill, 1963), pp. 42, 93-94; Jeremy

Bentham, *An Introduction to the Principles of Morals and Legislation* (New York: Haffner, 1948); Packer, *op. cit. supra* note 2, p. 31.

5. Nicholas N. Kittrie, *The Right to Be Different: Deviance and Enforced Therapy* (Baltimore, Md.: Johns Hopkins University Press, 1971).

6. Packer, *op. cit. supra* note 2, pp. 25-30.

7. Barbara A. Wootton, *Crime and the Criminal Law* (London: Stevens, 1963); Marc Ancel, *Social Defence* (New York: Schocken, 1966); Karl Menninger, *The Crime of Punishment* (New York: Viking 1968).

P. J. BRANTINGHAM, F. L. FAUST

in American juvenile court legislation.[8] The British Mental Health
Act of 1959 provides for compulsory hospital commitment of the
retarded, psychopathic, or mentally
ill person in the interest of his
health or safety, or for the protection of others.[9]

Though punishment and treatment are generally regarded as
closely related concepts, one common conceptual tie has not been
developed. Both the general justification of punishment and treatment
and the specific justification of
particular forms of punishment and
treatment, as well as hybrid peno-
therapeutic practices such as probation and halfway house confinement, are considered to be crime
prevention. We suggest that analysis
of this common conceptual goal—
crime prevention—may be the key
to a better understanding of the
definitional and ethical distinctions
between punishment and treatment.

One of the more striking features
of the Anglo-American system of
criminal justice is a divergence between systemic activity and systemic
ideology. The system[10] in action
deals in *post hoc* assessment, of
culpability and assignment of punishment. Police arrest offenders
after the offense occurs; courts
adjudicate offenders after the offense occurs; prisons punish offend-

ers after the offense occurs.[11] Yet
each major element of the criminal
justice system professes a special
calling to prevent crime. Thus, says
the American Bar Association,
"Police administrators. . .character-
ize prevention as their primary
goal."[12] The President's Crime
Commission pointed out that "It is
generally assumed that police have
a preventive. . .role as well."[13] And
the recent report by the National
Advisory Commission on Criminal
Justice Standards and Goals defined
the primary goal of police as crime
prevention.[14]

According to the American Law
Institute, the prime purpose of a
penal code is "to forbid and prevent" crimes, and the principal
purpose of sentencing and treatment of offenders is "to prevent
the commission of offenses."[15]

---

11. The juvenile justice system, compulsory
narcotics addict commitment schemes, eugenic
sterilization laws, and sexual psychopath laws
have all tried to deal with potential offenders
before any offense has been committed. All
have been under serious attack of late as distri-
butively unjust.

12. American Bar Association Project on
Standards for Criminal Justice, *Standards Relating to the Urban Police Function*, approved
draft (Chicago: American Bar Association,
1973), p. 56. The standards also point out that
the first commissioner of the London Metropolitan Police set crime prevention as the *first*
priority for the new police—ahead of apprehension and prosecution of offenders. *Id.*, pp. 55-
56. The standards themselves, however, reverse
that order, giving apprehension first priority
and prevention second priority out of a ranked
list of eleven priorities. *Id.*, § 2.2.

13. President's Commission on Law Enforce-
ment and Administration of Justice, *Task Force
Report: The Police* (Washington, D. C.: U. S.
Govt. Printing Office, 1967), p. 13.

14. National Advisory Commission on Crim-
inal Justice Standards and Goals, *A National
Strategy to Reduce Crime* (Washington, D. C.:
U. S. Govt. Printing Office, 1973), pp. 103-05.

15. American Law Institute, *Model Penal
Code*, Proposed Official Draft (Philadelphia:
American Law Intitute), § § 1.02, pp. 2-3.

---

8. From a list of thirty-four such grounds
compiled in Frederick B. Sussman and Frederic
S. Baum,. *Law of Juvenile Delinquency*, 3rd.
ed. (Dobbs Ferry, N.Y.: Oceana, 1968), p. 12.

9. Mental Health Act 1959 § 26; cf. § § 60,
61, permitting commitment of retarded, psychopathic, or mentally ill convicts to the same mental hospitals in lieu of sentence.

10. It is a "system" in the formal sense—a set
of elements which interact in some significant
way. We do not imply that the interaction is
necessarily smooth or efficient.. The criminal
justice system is amazingly inefficient.

Since courts necessarily make contact with suspected actual offenders and convicted offenders rather than potential offenders, prevention takes two forms: general deterrence through exemplary sentencing and special deterrence through selective sentencing involving combinations of punishment and treatment. The goal of sentencing courts is crime prevention.[16]

The preventive purpose of correctional agencies is less directly expressed than that of police or courts but appears strongly in the American Correctional Association's equation of modern penology with "rehabilitation"—the reform or control of offenders so that they will not commit new crimes when released from custody or supervision.[17] Of course, the historical penitentiary was designed to serve general and special deterrence purposes. The goal of the correctional subsystem, then, is to prevent recidivism.

Outside of the criminal justice system, many community organizations and agencies engage in activities of which crime prevention is at least one of the major purposes. These include such diverse programs as parent education, mental health services, recreational activities, vocational education and employment counseling, drug abuse treatment services, remedial academic classes, public information programs on

protection of self and property, crisis intervention telephone services, school programs on youth and the law, and so forth. Every public reference to crime prevention is coupled with a proposal for some form of further community involvement in reducing the opportunity for, deterring, or treating criminality.

Clearly, with each of the major criminal justice subsystems as well as several noncriminal justice systems being committed to crime prevention, the concept must have wide temporal and behavioral scope —so wide, in fact, that it is of dubious value without definitional refinement.

A Paradigm for Analysis of Crime Prevention

A legitimate argument may be made that each of the subsystems referred to above poaches on the crime prevention functions of the others—business organizations engage in security and law enforcement activities, community agencies provide services to probationers and parolees, police engage in adjudication and correctional activities through informal probation and cautioning schemes, prosecutors and probation officers become involved in detective work, and correctional officers investigate and adjudicate rule violations by in-custody offenders. Most of the time, however, the preventive activities of noncriminal justice programs, police, courts, and correction are substantially different. The points of distinction may be identified most clearly by the level or stage in the development of criminal behavior at which intervening activity is implemented. Since it is similarly conceived as intervention at dif-

---

16. R. M. Jackson, *Enforcing the Law*, rev. ed. (Harmondsworth, England: Penguin, 1971), pp. 311-30.

17. American Correctional Association, *Manual of Correctional Standards*, 3rd ed. (College Park, Md.: American Correctional Association, 1966), pp. 6-12. *See* also the ACA's statement on objectives of the correctional system: "Simply stated, the basic goal of a correctional system is to provide public protection by aiding in the prevention of crime." *Id.*, p. 1.

ferent developmental levels, the public health model of disease prevention is analogous and useful.[18]

The public health model posits three levels of activity.[19] *Primary* prevention identifies disease-creating general conditions of the environment and seeks to abate those conditions (e.g., sewage treatment, mosquito extermination, small-pox vaccination, job-safety engineering, personal hygiene education). *Secondary* prevention identifies groups or individuals who have a high risk of developing disease or who have incipient cases of disease and intervenes in their lives with special treatments designed to prevent the risk from materializing or the incipient case from growing worse (e.g., chest x-rays in poor neighborhoods, special diets for overweight executives, rubella vaccinations for prospective but not-yet-expectant mothers, dental examinations). *Tertiary* prevention identifies individuals with advanced cases of disease and intervenes with treatment to prevent death or permanent disability (e.g., stomach pumping for poisoning, open-heart surgery for defective heart valves, radiation therapy for some forms of cancer), provides rehabilitation services for

those persons who must live under the constraints of permanent disability (e.g., Braille training for the blind, prosthetic limbs for amputees), and provides a measure of relief from pain and suffering for individuals with incurable diseases (e.g., opiate therapy for terminal cancer patients, leper colonies).[20] Tertiary prevention, then, aims at three forms of prevention: (1) prevention of death or disability; (2) prevention of a decline to a less adequate level of social, economic, and physical activity; (3) prevention of more physical and social pain than necessary in an inevitable demise.

Crime prevention can be conceptualized as operating at these same three levels.[21] (See Figure 1).

---

18. We recognize the risk inherent in borrowing a conceptual model from medicine. Criminology is only just beginning to recover from the damage done by the Positivist School's use of the medical analogy of crime as disease. In borrowing from public health concepts here, we have modified the public health model to fit the criminological situation rather than vice versa.

19. Hugh R. Leavell and E. Gurney Clark, *Preventive Medicine for the Doctor in His Community: An Epidemiological Approach*, 3rd ed. (New York: McGraw-Hill, 1965), pp. 19-28. We are indebted to Jack Wright, of the Florida Department of Health and Rehabilitative Services, for bringing the public health paradigm to our attention.

20. We have modified the groups of activity within the primary, secondary, and tertiary classifications described above to facilitate their use for criminological purposes. *See* Leavell and Clark, *op. cit. supra* note 19, pp. 20-21. For an argument that an unmodified public health model is not useful to criminological thinking, even in the drug abuse area, see Richard Brotman and Frederic Suffet, "The Concept of Prevention and Its Limitations," *Annals of the American Academy of Political and Social Science,* January 1975, pp. 55-56.

21. Lejins has developed a tripartite classification of crime prevention which cuts orthogonally across our model. Thus, he describes (1) punitive prevention (a primary and tertiary form), (2) corrective prevention (a primary and secondary form), and (3) mechanical prevention (a primary and tertiary form). Peter Lejins, "The Field of Prevention," *Delinquency Prevention: Theory and Practice*, William Amos and Charles Wellford, eds. (Englewood Cliffs, N. J.: Prentice-Hall, 1967), pp. 1-21. Wolfgang's tripartite categorization of prevention appears to be a breakdown of secondary and tertiary forms of prevention. Marvin E. Wolfgang, "Urban Crime," *The Metropolitan Enigma*, James Q. Wilson, ed. (New York: Anchor Books, 1970), p. 299. The Florida State Bureau of Criminal Justice Planning has developed a typology of crime prevention programs which also cuts across our model. It defines programs of prevention aimed at (1) the initiating conditions of

FIGURE 1

MODELS OF PREVENTION

PUBLIC HEALTH PARADIGM

PRIMARY

Health Promotion
- health education
- general social & physical well-being programs
- nutrition
- genetics
- periodic examinations

Specific Protection
- personal hygiene
- specific immunizations
- job safety engineering
- environmental sanitation

SECONDARY

Early Diagnosis
- case finding
- screening
- selective examinations

Disability Limitation
- treatment for advanced disease

TERTIARY

Rehabilitation
- retraining
- community placement and support

CRIMINOLOGICAL PARADIGM

PRIMARY
- environmental design
- general social and physical well-being programs
- crime prevention education

SECONDARY
- early identification
- pre-delinquent screening
- individual intervention
- neighborhood programs

TERTIARY

Reform
- community treatment
- institutional treatment
- punishment

Rehabilitation
- training
- support
- surveillance

Incapacitation
- institutional custody

P. J. BRANTINGHAM, F. L. FAUST

Primary crime prevention identifies conditions of the physical and social environment that provide opportunities for or precipitate criminal acts. Here the objective of intervention is to alter those conditions so that crimes cannot occur. *Secondary* crime prevention engages in early identification of potential offenders and seeks to intervene in their lives in such a way that they never commit criminal violation. *Tertiary* crime prevention deals with actual offenders and involves intervention in their lives in such a fashion that they will not commit further offenses. With this classification in view, let us examine the relationship of these levels of crime prevention to contemporary issues in criminal justice. For the purpose of analysis, we will consider the three levels of crime prevention in reverse order.

Application of the Model

The correctional subsystem within the criminal justice system is charged with tertiary prevention. The optimistic—perhaps heroic—assumption is made that, through effective intervention, the offender will be fully restored to a permanent, functional level of socially acceptable behavior. For those offenders whose behavior is not amenable to modification through known forms of punishment or treatment, tertiary prevention aims to provide such control of the offender's behavior as is necessary to protect society and elicit the highest and most sustained level of con-

forming behavior possible.[22] The preventive aspect of intervention at this level may be found in the notion that such intervention keeps society from being placed at increased risk, keeps the offender from being placed at greater risk for his own harmful behavior and from the excessive retaliation of others,[23] and keeps conditions from occurring which offer no opportunity and encouragement for whatever higher level of conforming behavior the offender might be capable of achieving at some future time.

For offenders whose criminal behavior is not amenable to correction through known forms of punishment and treatment and who are seen as potentially dangerous to society, the traditional societal reaction has been incapacitation—the imposition of lifetime or long-term confinement in a secure setting. This confinement has been justified as societal protection.[24] Theoretically, it is assumed that the behavior of offenders in this category might improve to some degree but not

---

22. Capital punishment does not fall within this conceptual model without straining the analogy considerably since the legal and ethical tenets of public health medicine do not include the intentional infliction of death, regardless of the patient's medical threat to the health of others. If we do strain the analogy, however, the death penalty might be viewed as the most extreme form of tertiary prevention, with general deterrence feedback to the primary prevention level.

23. Canadian Committee on Correction, *The Basic Principles and Purposes of Criminal Justice* (Ottawa: Queen's Printer, 1969).

24. Capital punishment is excluded from consideration here and is not treated seriously within the general model of crime prevention, since the principal justification for imposition of the death penalty is retribution rather than any utilitarian judgment that the offender is not amenable to reform or rehabilitation and is too dangerous for less final methods of incapacitation.

---

crime (primary prevention) and (2) the sustaining conditions of crime (secondary prevention). Florida Bureau of Criminal Justice Planning and Assistance, *The Florida Annual Action Plan for 1974* (Tallahassee, Fla., 1974), pp. 1-21.

sufficiently to warrant their release from custody in the near future. But still, any behavioral improvement is desirable. Toward this end, the President's Crime Commission recommended that offenders of this type be transferred to special institutions that would "encourage the development of more imaginative programs for long-term prisoners—special industries, perhaps greater independence and self-sufficiency within the confines of a secure institution."[25] For those offenders who are not seen as potentially serious threats to society, the correctional system combines rehabilitation and reform to elicit more conforming behavior. The hope is that the behavioral improvements for these prisoners will be sufficient to inhibit further illegal activities.

Effective tertiary prevention is the primary goal of the correctional subsystem. It is also one of the goals of the courts and the probation and parole service as these subsystems interact and interlink with correction. Effective tertiary prevention is, and always has been, more ideal than actual. But the justification of particular forms of both punishment and treatment is grounded on their efficacy in achieving this level of prevention. As a result, corporal punishment has been generally abolished because it fails to prevent recidivism rather than because it is inhumane, even though a case can be made for it on retributive grounds. Other forms of punishment such as imprisonment and other forms of

treatment such as castration of sexual offenders are currently under attack because they fail to reduce recidivism below the levels attained by cheaper and less drastic methods. On the other hand, forms of punishment such as fines and forms of treatment such as psychosurgery, which promise improved tertiary prevention, are currently fashionable even though retributive and humanitarian problems are raised.[26]

Secondary prevention is the level at which crime prevention is most fervently pursued in research and program funding. Courts, probation and parole services, general social services, educational institutions, planners, private citizens, and police all engage in secondary prevention. It is argued that poverty, low educational level, lack of vocational skills, minority status, and poor physical and mental health are all associated with criminal activity. The assumption is that these social and physical problems are causally related to crime, although most current research rejects the causal link.

Without question, the great bulk of intervention activities labeled "crime prevention" must be categorized as secondary prevention—i.e., early identification of potential offenders, followed by action designed to reduce the risk of future involvement in more serious forms of antisocial behavior, particularly

---

25. President's Commission on Law Enforcement and Administration of Justice, *Task Force Report: Corrections* (Washington, D. C.: U. S. Govt. Printing Office, 1967), p. 58. (Our italics.)

26. See generally, Alan R. Mabe, ed., *New Techniques and Strategies for Social Control: Ethical and Practical Limits*, a special issue of *American Behavioral Scientist*, May-June 1975, for a group of articles probing state-of-the-art issues in behavioral control. Note that the ethical and legal issues surrounding such modes of behavioral control make them politically vulnerable as secondary and tertiary prevention techniques. See, e. g., "Clockwork Orange Projects Banned," *Crime & Delinquency*, July 1974, pp. 314-15.

criminal behavior. For example, during the 1960's, massive federal, state, and local programs were mounted to identify and deal with problems of school drop-outs, vocationally untrained and economically disadvantaged youth, physically and mentally handicapped individuals, minority group members, etc., with the assumption that such intervention would curb and reverse the increasing crime rates.[27] While these endeavors have been launched toward laudable objectives, they have frequently rested on the false assumption that they were striking at the root "cause" of crime and delinquency when, instead, they were dealing only with observable symptoms.[28]

Primary prevention—identification of those conditions of the physical and social environment that provide opportunities for or precipitate criminal behavior and the alteration of those conditions so that no crimes occur—is clearly the ideal objective. In fact this is the objective that is posited as the justification for most secondary prevention activities, but obviously the identification of incipient cases implies that the opportunity for primary prevention (in those instances at least) has already passed. With a few notable exceptions, there has been little systematic study of primary prevention of criminal behavior.[29] The work ac-

complished at this level has been largely pursued along one of three lines: (1) psychological immunization from certain types of behavioral tendencies, (2) preclusion of criminal activity by redesign of the physical environment, and (3) general "deterrence" of criminal activity by exemplary sentences and the presence of correctional facilities. The first two directions of inquiry have raised serious ethical and legal questions, to say nothing of the problem of resource allocation for implementation on a scale large enough to affect crime rates significantly.

Directions for Crime Prevention

Using the three-part model we can classify criminal justice system activities and noncriminal justice system activities designed to prevent crime. As can be seen by examining Figures 2 and 3, most crime prevention activity has occurred in secondary and tertiary prevention. Less effort has been spent on primary prevention.

Tertiary prevention, currently, consists mostly of efforts to "treat" offenders, but this "treatment" is given in the absence of knowledge and competence to permanently "reform" tendencies toward illegal behavior. Most of what is done in the name of "treatment" is, in reality, little more than an effort to help offenders cope and to control them through externally imposed pressures. If this fact were more widely recognized in contemporary correction and the widespread myth of available effective treatment were dispelled until human behavior is more fully understood, then resources could be more appropriately allocated between

27. Peter Marris and Martin Rein, *Dilemmas of Social Reform*, 2nd ed. (Chicago: Aldine, 1973); Daniel P. Moynihan, *Maximum Feasible Misunderstanding* (New York: Free Press, 1968).

28. C. Ray Jeffery, *Crime Prevention through Environmental Design* (Beverly Hills, Calif.: Sage, 1971).

29. *Ibid.*; Oscar Newman, *Defensible Space* (New York: Macmillan, 1972).

control activities and much needed behavioral research. For example, probation and parole officers recognize that their job has dimensions of both control and treatment—i.e., on the one hand, surveillance and serving as a source of information and, on the other, some type of therapeutic counseling. The type of training that probation and parole personnel generally receive, however, places great emphasis on the treatment function and virtually ignores control technology. As a result, these persons frequently spend the largest share of their time and effort attempting to accomplish an unrealistic therapeutic task and resist the performance of less interesting and often routine control activities which could produce more effective results. Further, the control relationship between correctional personnel generally and offenders and their families might be considerably strengthened if the delusion of effective treatment, and the subsequent disillusionment of failure, were removed.

This leads to the conclusion, then, that the rhetoric of effective treatment should be dropped, except for those few activities where the consequences of therapeutic intervention have been rigorously tested and the outcome can be predicted with confidence (e.g., the controlled use of chemotherapy in certain cases of aggressive behavior, or brain surgery where tumors are determined to be the cause of acts of violence). Such a narrowing of the operational definition of treatment is quite consistent with legal arguments and recent court decisions relating to the "right to treatment" and would help to put the justification for coerced loss of liberty into proper perspective.[30]

Clearly differentiating between rehabilitative control and treatment in tertiary prevention may spare many offenders imprisonment for nonexistent therapy, in favor of more humane and economical rehabilitative programing. Research is also needed in the other forms of tertiary prevention; e.g., special deterrence, postadjudicative diversion, and the deterrent effect of arrest and prosecution.

At the level of secondary prevention, there is certainly a need for continued research that will lead to the development of more accurate diagnostic instruments for the early identification of potential offenders and more effective intervention approaches. At present, however, the inadequate state of knowledge precludes such diagnosis and intervention, except in rather rare instances, and suggests that premature and inappropriate assignment of the "potential offender" label contributes to the crime problem.[31] Thus, as with tertiary prevention, effective intervention at the secondary level will have to await the scientific achievement of a more complete understanding of human behavior in general and criminal behavior in particular and careful evaluation of existing secondary prevention schemes.

On the basis of the foregoing discussion, it should come as no surprise that primary prevention is viewed as the most fruitful direction for the future development of

30. Kittrie, *op. cit. supra* note 5; Beverly G. Toomey, Clifford E. Simonsen, and Harry E. Allen, "Right to Treatment: Issues and Prospects," *Proceedings of the 20th Annual Southern Conference on Corrections* (Tallahassee, Fla.: Florida State University, 1975).

31. Frederic L. Faust, "Delinquency Labeling—Its Consequences and Implications," *Crime & Delinquency,* January 1973, pp. 41-48.

P. J. BRANTINGHAM, F. L. FAUST

FIGURE 2

PREVENTION ACTIVITIES OF THE CRIMINAL JUSTICE SYSTEM

	PRIMARY	SECONDARY	TERTIARY
POLICE	GENERAL DETERRENCE (through "presence") CITIZEN EDUCATION PROGRAMS	INTELLIGENCE OPERATIONS SOCIAL SERVICE OPERATIONS (athletic programs, family crisis units, sensitivity training) PATROL PEACE-KEEPING ACTIONS ("move-along" orders, stop-and-frisk contacts) INTERVENTION AND DIVERSION (drunk detoxification, juvenile supervision)	ARREST AND PROSECUTION MISDEMEANOR CORRECTIONAL INSTITUTIONS
COURTS	GENERAL DETERRENCE (through "exemplary" sentences)	PRE-ADJUDICATION DIVERSION	POST-ADJUDICATION DIVERSION, REFORM, REHABILITATION, AND INCAPACITATION (through sentence)
CORRECTION	GENERAL DETERRENCE (through existence)	OPERATION OF DIVERSION PROGRAMS	REFORM (through punishment, community treatment, institutional treatment) REHABILITATION (through aftercare support, training, and surveillance) INCAPACITATION (through custody)

FIGURE 3

PREVENTION ACTIVITIES OUTSIDE THE CRIMINAL JUSTICE SYSTEM

	PRIMARY	SECONDARY	TERTIARY
PRIVATE CITIZENS	HOUSEHOLD AND BUSINESS SECURITY PRECAUTIONS; GENERAL CHARITY	BIG BROTHER PROGRAMS; DELINQUENCY SPECIFIC SOCIAL ACTIVITIES	CORRECTIONAL VOLUNTEERS
SCHOOLS	GENERAL EDUCATION	PRE-DELINQUENT SCREENING; EDUCATIONAL INTERVENTION PROGRAMS	PROSECUTION OF TRUANTS AND DELINQUENTS; INSTITUTIONAL EDUCATION PROGRAMS
BUSINESS	SECURITY PROVISIONS	EMPLOYEE SCREENING	PROSECUTION OF OFFENDERS; HIRING OF EX-OFFENDERS
PLANNERS	MODIFICATION OF PHYSICAL ENVIRONMENT TO REDUCE CRIMINAL OPPORTUNITY; MODIFICATION OF SOCIAL ENVIRONMENT TO REDUCE IMPULSIONS TOWARDS CRIMINAL BEHAVIOR	CRIME LOCATION ANALYSIS FOR NEIGHBORHOOD EDUCATION AND MODIFICATION PROGRAMS; CRIMINAL RESIDENCE STUDY FOR NEIGHBORHOOD SOCIAL WORK	INSTITUTIONAL DESIGN
RELIGIOUS AND SOCIAL AGENCIES	MORAL TRAINING; FAMILY EDUCATION; GENERAL SOCIAL WORK	WELFARE SERVICES: Child Protection, Programs for Disadvantaged & Pre-Delinquent Youth, Crisis Intervention	AFTERCARE SERVICES

theory, research, and programing insofar as preventing criminal behavior is concerned. Perhaps the most cogent argument in support of this position is that presented by C. Ray Jeffery in his *Crime Prevention through Environmental Design.*[32] The logic that crime can most effectively be curbed by altering conditions that precipitate or provide opportunities for criminal behavior can hardly be challenged. The problems of implementation, however, are staggering—not just problems of required resources and legal and ethical considerations (these have always been major challenges to the advancement of science), but more significantly the necessary shift in public policy from almost total commitment to crisis intervention to an equally strong commitment to long-range behavioral research.

Such a shift is by no means impossible, but under the most ad-

vantageous conditions it would be ponderously slow in taking place and the question of how to deal with the crime problem in the interim is legitimately raised.

The answer, of course, is that we cannot turn our backs on the problem while we work to influence public policy toward basic behavioral research and wait for the products of that research. Rather, we can place greater emphasis on more effective rehabilitative control, on the one hand, and basic research in primary prevention (involving limited pilot and demonstration projects), on the other, using a significant share of the resources currently being expended on ineffective secondary and tertiary prevention programs. We entertain no illusions about the problems to be confronted in this endeavor. It is certainly an ambitious goal, but it holds promise for ultimately preventing much, if not most, criminal behavior before rather than after it has occurred.

---

32. Jeffery, *op. cit. supra* note 28.

[5]

Contemporary Crises 10: 63–80 (1986)

Critical criminology and the concept of crime

LOUK H.C. HULSMAN
Erasmus University, Rotterdam, The Netherlands

1. Are criminal events exceptional?: Problematizing the normal outlook on crime

Traditionally we are accustomed to regard criminal law and criminal justice systems, as systems which have been devised by man (society) and are under his (its) control. We are inclined to consider 'criminal events' as exceptional, events which differ to an important extent from other events which are not defined as criminal. In the conventional image, criminal conduct is considered as the most important cause of these events. Criminals are – in this view – a special category of people, and the exceptional nature of criminal conduct, and/or of the criminal, justify the special nature of the reaction against it. The public debate about the criminal justice system (c.j.s.) and its possible reform, almost always takes place in our (Western) type of society, within this limited framework. Proposals for reform take for granted that the c.j.s. must become better equipped to 'deal with social problems which are defined as offences'. Furthermore, one should minimize as much as possible the social costs of this method and distribute them as justly as possible. In addition, the impression exists among many people that the development of the criminal law is one of slowly progressing humanisation.

The scope of the debate is further restricted by the view that reform has to remain within the limits of what is acceptable to 'public opinion'. Public opinion is understood in this view not so much as construct – largely reflecting the visible part of the c.j.s. practice – but as a representation of attitudes existing independently of this practice.

This picture of the reality of criminal justice appears untenable, on the basis of the direct experiences of those participating in face-to-face relationships with and within the system, as well as on the basis of scientific research.

The special form of cooperation between the police, the courts, the prison system, the ministry of justice, other departments and Parliament which we describe as the criminal justice system, is extremely difficult to control. Attempts at reform, as even the most recent history shows, often have completely different results from those intended.[1]

In one of the preparatory papers of the United Nations Secretariat (1975) for the 5th United Nations Congress on Crime Prevention and the Treatment of Offenders in Geneva, the following statement was made:

64

One of the problems is that it is taken for granted that such a complex
structure (the criminal justice system) indeed works as a system, that the
several sub-systems share a set of common goals, that they relate to each
other in a consistent manner and that the interrelationship constitute the
particular structure of the system enabling it to function as a whole with a
certain degree of continuity and within certain limitations. However, in
countries where researchers and policy makers have undertaken a critical
examination of the structure of their criminal justice systems, they have
found that there are few common aims, that there is considerable diffusion
of duties and responsibilities and little or no co-ordination between the subsystems and that there are often differing views regarding the role of each
part of the system. In short, they have found a serious lack of cohesion
within the system. Yet, when people talk about the criminal justice system
as a whole they implicitly and explicitly assume that the system functions
well and is effectively controlled. They also assume that it is a system
oriented toward goals that are designed to meet the needs of the community. (p. 16)

The uncontrollability of the c.j.s. is of course not an exclusive property of that
system. It is one of the big problems of our type of society that through the
increase in the size of organisations, division of labour, professionalisation,
and the interdependence of larger units, man is losing his grip on, and contact
with, the environment and is alienated from it. It is however certainly a fact
that this process manifests itself most clearly in the present day c.j.s. This is
particularly alarming, since the typical products of the system are the infliction
of suffering and stigmatisation.

One of the most important causes of the difficulty in controlling the c.j.s. is
that there is hardly any feedback of information which is relevant to the way
that those directly involved have experienced the event. This is inherent in the
structure of the system. Conflicts which occur in society between persons or
groups are defined in the penal system not in terms of the parties involved, but
rather in terms of the regulations (criminal legislation) and the organisational
requirements of the system itself. The parties directly involved in a conflict can
exert little influence on the further course of events once a matter has been
defined as criminal and as such has been taken up by the system. We shall
return to this aspect of the c.j.s. later.

The idea that the development of the criminal laws is one of slowly progressing humanisation deserves also a critical note. Quantitatively the impression is
certainly not accurate. The number of convicted people per 100,000 population shows a strong cyclic movement. This cycle of the number of convictions
has in many countries in the industrialised world for some times been moving
upwards.

To assess the qualitative aspect of the development is more difficult. It is true that the application of the death penalty has been greatly reduced in recent centuries, and in normal times has even vanished in many countries. The same can be said of many forms of corporal punishment. Progress has also been made in improving the regime in the prison system. We must however be careful about simply concluding from this that there has been a qualitative humanisation. The 'degree of suffering' in the penal measures is not an absolute. To a large extent it consists of the difference between the normal living situation of people, and that which is created by the intervention of the c.j.s. The latter has always drawn its clientele mainly from the most disadvantaged sections of the population and still does so. The living standards of those same sections have in Europe improved considerably in recent years. The improvements inside prisons during the last 30 years, however, do not appear to have kept pace. If this supposition is correct, then the degree of suffering from the penal sanction has in a sense increased.

People who are involved in 'criminal' events do not appear in themselves to form a special category of people. Those who are officially recorded as 'criminal' constitute only a small part of those involved in events that legally are considered to require criminalisation. Among them young men from the most disadvantaged sections of the population are heavily over-represented.

Within the concept of criminality a broad range of situations are linked together. Most of these, however, have separate properties and no common denominator: violence within the family, violence in an anonymous context in the streets, breaking into private dwellings, completely divergent ways of illegal receiving of goods, different types of conduct in traffic, pollution of the environment, some forms of political activities. Neither in the motivation of those who are involved in such events, nor in the nature of the consequences or in the possibilities of dealing with them (be it in a preventive sense, or in the sense of the control of the conflict) is there any common structure to be discovered. All these events have in common, is that the c.j.s. is authorised to take action against them. Some of these events cause considerable suffering to those involved, quite often affecting both perpetrator and victim. Consider for example traffic accidents, and violence within the family. The vast majority of the events which are dealt with within the c.j.s. in the sphere of crime, however, would not score particularly high on an imaginary scale of personal hardship. Matrimonial difficulties, difficulties between parents and children, serious difficulties at work and housing problems will, as a rule, be experienced as more serious both as to degree and duration. If we compare 'criminal events' with other events, there is – on the level of those directly involved – nothing which distinguishes those 'criminal' events intrinsically from other difficult or unpleasant situations. Nor are they singled out as a rule by those directly involved themselves to be dealt with in a way differing radically from

66

the way other events are dealt with. Last, not least, some of these events are
considered by those directly involved (and sometimes also by 'observers') as
positive and harmless.

It is therefore not surprising that a considerable proportion of the events
which would be defined as serious crime within the context of the c.j.s., remain
completely outside that system. They are settled within the social context in
which they take place (the family, the trade union, the professional association, the circle of friends, the workplace, the neighbourhood) in a similar way
as other non-criminal trouble.[2]

All this means that there is no 'ontological reality' of crime.

**2. Critical criminology and the concept of crime: what has been problematised
and what not?**

Critical criminology has naturally problematised and criticised many of the
'normal' notions about crime which I have just described. The contribution to
this form of 'debunking' varies according to the different perspectives of the
stream of critical criminology involved. In a certain period, marxist criminology predominantly took the stand that 'crime' was a product of the capitalistic
system, and that crime would disappear if a new society took birth. In this
perspective the disappearance of 'crime' was seen as a disappearance of the
'problematic situations' which are supposed to trigger the criminalisation
processes. Disappearance of crime was not seen as: 'the disappearance of
criminalisation processes *as an answer* to problematic situations'. In a later
stage, critical criminology problematised the class-biased and 'irrational' aspects of the processes of primary and secondary criminalisation. In those
endeavours the 'functionality' as well as the 'legal equality principle', which
are so often invoked as legitimation of processes of primary criminalisation,
were de-mystified. On the basis of such a de-mystification, critical criminology
has argued for partial decriminalisation, a more restrictive policy with respect
to recourse to criminal law, radical non-intervention with respect to certain
crimes and certain criminals. It has pointed to the far more weighty crimes of
the powerful and asked for a change in criminal justice activities from the weak
and the working class towards 'white collar crime'. It has pictured the war
against crime as a sidetrack from the class struggle, at best an illusion invented
to sell news, at worst an attempt to make the poor scape goats. With very few
exceptions however, the concept of crime as such, the ontological reality of
crime, has not been challenged.

Two recent books by critical criminologists (D.F. Greenberg 1981; J. Lea
and J. Young 1984) show clearly the lack of interest of critical criminology in
criticising the 'concept of crime' as such. Greenberg dedicates in his – in other

respects most interesting – book, less than one page to the question 'what is crime'. He mentions in this page only examples of critical criminologists who point out that other behaviours should be criminalised (violations of fundamental human rights and white collar crime). The examples he gives show that the critical criminologists he is referring to, do not challenge the ideas that: (1) it makes sense to construct a uniform scale of degree of harm; (2) harm should be attributed in the context of a criminal justice system to individuals; (3) malice is an element of crime; (4) malice can be determined in a criminal justice procedure; (5) crime is (or should be) the top of 'evil harm' as it is attributed to individuals.

The non-problematized character of crime as a concept is still clearer in the last book of Lea and Young. Their book belongs to the stream of the 'new realists' in critical criminology. Not only that they do not problematise the five points I mentioned above. On the contrary, they positively subscribe to many of those conventional wisdoms on crime. I cite some examples: 'crime is the end-point of a continuum of disorder' (p. 55), 'crime is the tip of the iceberg, it is a real problem in itself, but it is also a symbol for a far greater problem;' (p. 55), 'we argued that what is necessary, is a double thrust against both types of crime' (p. 73; the both types of crime which are referred to are street crime and corporate crime), 'street crime is the most transparent of all injustices. It is a starting point for all double thrust against crime on all levels. If we concentrate on it alone, as the political right would wish, we are actively engaged in a process of diversion from the crimes of the powerful. If we concentrate solely on the latter, as many on the left would have us to do, we omit what are real and pressing problems for working class people and loose the ability to move from the immediate to encompass the more hidden and thus demonstrate *the intrinsic similarity of crime at all levels of our society.*' (p. 75; italics by me).

There is also another rather recent trend which starts to problematise the concept of crime as such (Baratta 1983; Hulsman and Bernard-de Célis 1982; Landreville 1978; A. Normandeau 1984). This approach focusses on the fact that there is no 'ontological reality' of crime. It tries to reorganise the debate within criminology and criminal policy with this fact as a starting point. This leads to the *abolition* of criminal justice as we know it. Because 'crime as an ontological reality' is the corner stone of such a type of criminal justice. The '*why*' and '*how*' of this approach will be dealt with in the following sections.

3. What does it mean when we do not problematise (and reject) the concept of crime?

When we do not problematise (and reject) the concept of crime it means that we are stuck in a catascopic view on society in which our informational base (as

68

well the 'facts' as their 'interpretational frame') depends mainly on the institutional framework of criminal justice. It means therefore that we do not take effectively into account the critical analyses of this institutional framework by 'critical criminology'. I will not try to give an exhaustive list of all those findings of critical criminology which we leave then out of consideration. It suffices here to give some important examples. These examples will touch upon the questions of primary criminalisation, the *false consciousness* created by unequal secondary criminalisation linked with a certain type of mass media coverage, the dark figure and the contribution of interactionism to the understanding of social processes.

Primary criminalisation

(1). The ideological foundation for centralised law as a basis for criminalisation
The ideological foundation for written centralised law as a basis for criminalisation lies in a legal view on the world. In this legal view the concept of 'society' has a key role. Let us take a critical look at this concept.

In the legal view, 'society' consists of the formal institutions of the state on one hand and of individuals on the other. When we look at the historical development of this idea we see that it has two different sources. A religious one: God's chosen people which were ruled by the ten commandments. A secular one: People binding themselves together 'freely' by a social contract.

It is this legal view on 'society' which pervades the political discourse and also the discourse as it is often pursued in a sociological and criminological context. In such a view society is seen as an aggregation of people over which a state claims jurisdiction. This aggregation of people is then presented as having the properties of a *group*: people who share values and meanings in common, who engage in continued social interaction and who belong together by a ritualistic bounding. It is however clear that most aggregations of people, called in this way 'society', do *not* possess the properties of a group. In a group, people arrive at a similarly structured sense of what life is about. Shared direct experience is a necessary condition to arrive at such a state. This shared direct experience is lacking in the state society. The common experiences in the state society are to a high degree limited to mass media and formal institution-based *indirect* experience. Even this common indirect experience is often grossly exaggerated by the people producing the political and scientific discourses; they generalise unreflectedly their own experience to other 'members' of the 'society'. The members of e.g. the 'society of criminology' in all their national differentiation posess probably much more the character of a group – not because of that membership, but because of their shared experiences in life – then members of a state society. An important part of the function of social regulation can only be fulfilled in a satisfactory way in a group context, because it has to be based on cognitive consensus.

The disarray caused by the unreflected attribution of group properties to the 'members' of the state society is clearly shown in the historical comparisons between state societies and tribal and acephalous societies. In such comparisons the social function of the tribe is often attributed to the state society. This reinforces naturally the idea that the state has the properties of a group. In such a comparative context, it is in my opinion more fruitful to compare (some) neighbourhoods, professional groups, circles of friends, social movements, recreational clubs, work settings, (private and public) as tribes. In such a view the state-society would be seen as a context in which a high degree of tribal interaction (co-operation and conflict) is going on and in which many data about those intertribal contacts are being gathered. Such a view on the state-society in comparison to tribal social organisation would be naturally incomplete and would have to take into account, that 'present day 'industrial' social formations' differ from their traditional counterparts in the sense that the traditional tribes knew less overlapping memberships than the modern tribes and that the mobility between tribes (the *change* of tribe) is much easier in modern social formations than in traditional ones.

The *anascopic* view on social life, implied in the image of a society as a conglomerate of tribes, has in comparison to the *catascopic* prevailing view, the advantage of making it easier to understand many of the findings of traditional and critical criminology (as the very high figures of unrecorded 'crime') and to promote an emancipatory and libertarian stand to issues of social regulation and social control.

In such a perspective not the individual but the 'intermediate institutions' – the modern tribes – would be seen as the buildingstones of the state-society. Many functions of social regulation can only be fulfilled in a 'tribe', because – to be realistic – they have to be founded on a cognitive consensus between those who interact. This cognitive consensus cannot be supposed to exist outside the context of those intermediate institutions.

(2). The unequal powerrelations, the peculiarity of political processes and the legal technicalities involved in legislative processes
There is a large body of research which shows how the processes of primary criminalisation are influenced by factors which have nothing to do with the negativity of the situations they are supposed to create a remedy for, nor with the existence of (other) resources which in fact could provide under certain circumstances a remedy for problematic situations (Report on Decriminalisation, Council of Europe 1980). This whole body of knowledge is neglected when we take the image of negativity (and of remedies against it) as it results from taking uncritically those primary criminalisation processes as a starting point for our views on social life and its problems.

70

Unequal secondary criminalisation and its link with the mass media

Urban areas in the industrialised world are characterised by the extreme social segregation that occurs within them. To a large degree, class is segregated from class, young from old, rich from poor. This creates a situation of mass ignorance; direct information about many aspects of life about what is going on in such a 'society' is not any more available. In such a state of affairs everybody is to a large degree dependent on the mass media for his opinions on the 'society' he lives in. This is true for the life worlds in so far as other life worlds are concerned, and it is equally true for that part of the system world which is involved in scientific research (criminology) and crime policy. This dependence on mass media information is particularly strong in cases in which certain activities are criminalised. The risk of criminalisation forces people to hide those activities. Direct information about what is going on in the life world in which those illegal activities take place is therefore more difficult to get. Victims of criminalised activities, in so far as they seek contact with the police and the judiciary, are obliged to speak the language of the system. They have to submit themselves to the interpretational frame which their stronger counterparts offer. Also from victims of criminalised activities reliable informations is difficult to get.

The type of information however which the mass media portray, is what is 'newsworthy'. In brief, it selects events which are a-typical, present them in a stereotypical fashion, contrast them against a backcloth of normality which is over-typical. This brings about a mystification about the world which is in contact with criminal justice. It is to this mystification that criminologists submit when they continue to use the concept of crime.

Dark figure

The studies which criminology has done in the field of the 'dark figure' and more specifically in the field of 'unrecorded crime' are of great importance. The findings of those studies have nevertheless not yet been integrated in criminological theory and in criminal policy practice. It is also striking that many conclusions on the basis of dark figure studies show, that many criminologists have been insufficiently aware of the limited way in which victim surveys can give insight in unrecorded crime. In my opinion the amount of unrecorded crime is systematically *under*estimated. Anyway, there is no doubt that *actual criminalisation* of criminalisable events – even in the field of traditional crime – is a very rare event indeed. In a country like Holland, far less than one percent of those criminalisable events is actually criminalised in the courts. Non-criminalisation is the rule, criminalisation a rare exception.

71

This fact is not taken into account if one looks at social reality taking as a starting point criminal justice.

Interactionism

The contribution of interactionism to sociology has made us aware of the importance of defining processes for the construction and the understanding of social reality. This showed also how differences in power relations influenced the social reality in the first place by the intermediary of those defining processes. The impact of criminal justice on social life is not in the first place exercised by direct intervention by its agents and not by the threat of repression. It orients the view and practices of policy makers and policy implementators of various disciplines from the concrete realities of the different life worlds towards the legal part of the system world (Hulsman 1984). *A criminology which continues to incorporate in its own 'language' the concepts which play a key role in this process, can never take an external view on this reality and is therefore unable to demystify it.*

My conclusion is that critical criminology has to abandon a catascopic view on social reality, based on the definitional activities of the system which is the subject of its study, and has instead to take an anascopic stance towards social reality. This makes it necessary to abandon as a tool in the conceptual frame of criminology the notion of 'crime'. Crime has no ontological reality. Crime is not the *object* but the *product* of criminal policy. Criminalisation is one of the many ways to construct social reality. In other words, when someone (person or organisation) wants to criminalise, this implies that he:

a. deems a certain 'occurence' or 'situation' as undesirable;
b. attributes that undesirable occurence to an individual;
c. approaches this particular kind of individual behaviour with a specific style of social control: the style of punishment;
d. applies a very particular style of punishment which is developed in a particular (legal) professional context and which is based on a 'scholastic' (last-judgement) perspective on the world. In this sense the style of punishment used in criminal justice differs profoundly from the styles of punishment in other social contexts;
e. wants to work in a special organizational setting: criminal justice. This organizational setting is characterized by a very developed division of labour, a lack of accountability for the process as a whole and a lack of influence of those directly involved in the 'criminalised' event on the outcome of the process.

72

Two remarks have to be added to this rather 'streamlined' description of the specificity of the 'criminal way' to construct reality.

When we look at criminal justice processes in a more detailed way we see that within the timespan criminal justice deals with an individual, other styles of social control like the therapeutical and the compensatory ones can also play a role. Generally this 'blurring' of different styles of social control within a criminal justice process does not impair the predominance of the punishment style of social control.

In many instances the way in which cases are dealt with in criminal justice is influenced by 'negotiation'. This negotiation is however not a negotiation, between the parties implied in the 'original event', but between professionals, whose main interest is not related to the original event, but to their daily work in criminal justice.

How should we now proceed to liberate criminology from criminal justice and to develop within criminology an anascopic view? In the next section I will try to develop the outlines for such an approach.

3. Developing an anascopic view

Defining and dealing with trouble outside a formal context

When does trouble occur? Pfohl (1981) defines it as follows:

> Trouble can be defined as that situation which occurs when (1) people are not ritualisticly linked to a relatively similar sense of how life is and should be structured and (2) the lack of such links results in conflict over ways of thinking, feeling and acting.

Pfohl restricts himself in this definition to trouble which finds his source in a social conflict. We can extend his approach however to the way we are relating our lives to 'nature'. Trouble occurs also when 'nature' interferes differently from the way we expect it to 'behave'.

Pfohl distinguishes two types of rituals, which are essential to minimize trouble. The first when succesfully enacted prevent trouble. These are *rituals or primary ordering*. The second attend to the presence of trouble. They are *rituals of reordering*. When succesful they curtail or contain trouble.

Trouble (or *problematic situations*) are thus defined as events which are in a negative way deviating from the order in which we see and feel our lives rooted.

When we discuss problematic situations we should keep one thing in mind. It is wrong to think about problematic situations as situations which could be eradicated in social life. They are part of life. People need problematic situations in the same way as food and air. More important then to prevent problematic situations is to try to influence societal structures in such a way that people can cope and deal with problems in a way which permits growth and learning and avoids alienation.

To avoid 'reifying' problematic situations it seems useful to make a distinction between:

1. situations which are considered problematic, by all those directly concerned with that situation;
2. situations which are considered problematic by some of those directly involved and not by others;
3. situations which are not considered problematic by those directly involved but only by persons or organisations not directly involved.

One of the consequences of the prevailing catascopic view on questions of trouble and order is that contrary to the abundance of concepts which can be brought to bear when we try to explain and understand *formal* processes of societal regulation, there is a scarcity of concepts when we use an anascopic perspective in a scientific context.

To understand the varieties in the way different participants construct meanings on the basis of 'what occurs', it could be helpful to use as analytical tool two concepts: (1) frame of interpretation, and (2) focus.

Within the *frame of interpretation* we can make a distinction between *natural* and *social* frames of interpretation. In a natural frame of interpretation a negative occurence is an 'accident'. What happens is attributed to 'nature'.

Within the *social* frame of interpretation we can distinguish between more *person oriented* and more *structure oriented* varieties. The more person oriented varieties can be subdivided according to different 'styles' of social control: *penal, compensatory, therapeutic, conciliatory, and educational* (Black 1976; Meclintock 1980).

When people give meaning to life they do not necessarily use the same 'material'. When people are at a given moment involved in an interaction which started for two of them already the day before and for the third one on this given moment, there is a good chance that the two first ones will take in the construction of reality the interaction of the earlier day into account. Their focus for the definition of the situation will be wider than for the third one who got only on this given moment involved. The 'raw material' on which the social reality is constructed is different.

Let us 'play' a moment with this concepts on the basis of some examples of social life.

A road accident occurs. Two cars hit eachother. One of the drivers is seriously injured. The other – uninjured driver – had had during the day serious trouble in his job and after his work had drunk whisky to get rid of his tension.

74

We can easily imagine different people involved in such an accident define it in very different ways. One person could apply a *natural frame of interpretation*. He attributes this injury to the clash of two vehicles. This you can expect to happen when you drive a certain number of miles, like you catch from time to time a cold. For him the trouble will lie in the process of healing. Perhaps he will in the future not want to expose himself to the risk of driving and use public transport instead. Another person could apply a *social* frame of interpretation in a *structure oriented* variety. He could attribute his injury to the societal organization of traffic. He could get interested in a political activity to make road traffic more safe. A third person could apply a *person oriented* variety of the social frame. He could make either himself or the other driver responsible for the accident and depending on the 'style' involved in this person oriented variety he would ask for *punishment, compensation,* etc.. It is likely that the focus used in defining the event would differ between the two drivers. The injured driver would start from the accident. The other driver would see the accident perhaps in relation with the trouble he had in his job and his drinking.

The initial definition of an event is likely to change over time. If the injured driver initially defined the event in the punishment variety of the person oriented frame of interpretation and he became confronted with the other driver – showing concern over his injury – his definition of the event would perhaps change.

The television set. Five students live together in a house. At a certain evening one of them gets angry and throws the television set from the staircase. The roommates could easily take very different views on this event. One could construct the event in the *penal* frame. He would 'blame' the perpetrator and ask for his eviction from the house. Another could take a more liberal view and apply the *compensatory* frame of interpretation. 'Everybody has a right to his anger – he says – but one is responsible for his actions. He has to buy a new television set and everything is OK'. A third student, not used to such expressions of anger could get very upset and ask for medical help to control such outbursts. He would apply the *therapeutical* frame of interpretation. The fourth student may apply the *conciliatory* frame of interpretation. He could interpret the event as a sign of tension in the group and ask for a collective self-examination with respect to the mutual relations.

The different frames of interpretation applied by the participants could be related to a different focus on what was going on in their common life. Those who applied the penal and the conciliatory frame of interpretation linked the shattered television set probably with other experiences in their mutual interactions.

The defaulter. We have a family. The family expects everyone to be in time for the meal. One of the family members breaks this rule. He comes regularly too late for dinner. It is easy to imagine that the family members define this event by applying the person oriented drame of interpretation in its *penal* variation. Reproof is administered; perhaps reinforced after recidivism by 'fine' (a cut in pocketmoney). This reproof may lead to a change in the situation in the sense that the family member involved conforms more to the rule. It may also lead to an escalation of the situation. Imagine that the involved family member stops altogether to appear at the meals. Perhaps he even leaves the house.

In many families in such a case one would change of frame of interpretation and also change with respect to the 'focus' applied to the situation. In the beginning a narrow focus was applied. One looked only at the moment of appearance at the table. Now a broader focus of interpretation in the family is brought into bearing. Instead of penal frame of interpretation, a *therapeutic* or a *conciliatory* frame of interpretation is applied. Because things are considered now to be more 'serious' one leaves the penal frame of interpretation – which is in many families reserved only for minor events – and turns to a therapeutical or conciliatory frame of interpretation. There follows a collective inquiry in what is wrong with the family (in which also the rules within the family may be a topic of discussion) – the conciliatory model – or the family asks for the aid of an outsider expert to advise about the way to act with the defaulter – the therapeutic model.

We see also in this example how the concept of 'frame' and 'focus' can help us to describe and understand differences in the 'construction' of situations and in reactions to – for an outsider – comparable occurences. The *additional* information contained in this last example is the flexibility which may exist in a social context to switch from one frame of interpretation and one focus to another and more particularly that a penal frame of interpretation in 'normal' life may very often be applied for *minor* events and other frames of interpretation for events which are considered important.

I choose my examples in such a way that they could easily relate to the direct experience of my readers. This implies naturally the risk that a reader will say: Yes I see that such an approach makes sense in the sphere of life you are talking about, but does it apply also in those spheres of life to which a definition of serious crime relates? I am convinced that the variety in frames of interpretation, in focus and in dynamics of the process of definition exist in those areas not less than in the areas I took my examples from. Here are two examples:

Some years ago Molukkans captured a Dutch train. One of the hostages was killed. Several of the hostages became friends with those Molukkans and visit them now still in prison. Perhaps you will answer me: 'Clear, Stockholm syndrome'. (That is, the psychiatric explanation for those hostages who do not conform to the c.j.s. stereotypes of victims' hate; and vengeance but who develop an understanding of and bond with their aggressors. According to this

76

explanation, such hostages are 'pathological'). So here is another example. In Holland, policemen on duty who kill another person are practically never declared guilty of a homicide. But burglars and other 'troublesome rascals' (Spector, 1981) who kill are condemned under this incrimination.

The meanings which those directly involved (and observers) bestow upon situations influence how they will deal with them. Laura Nader (1981) distinguishes the following procedures people use in dealing with trouble:

– *lumping it*. The issue or problem that gave rise to a disagreement is simply ignored and the relationship with the person who is part of the disagreement is continued.

– *avoidance or exit*. This option entails withdrawing from a situation or curtailing or terminating a relationship by leaving.

– *coercion*. This involves unilateral action.

– *negotiation*. The two principle parties are the decision makers, and the settlement of the matter is one to which both parties agree, without the aid of a third party. They do not seek a solution in terms of rules, but try to create the rules by which they can organize their relationship with one another.

– *mediation*. Mediation, in contrast, involves a third party who intervenes in a dispute to aid the principals in reaching an agreement.

– other procedural modes that are used in attempts to handle trouble are *arbitration* and *adjudication*. In *arbitration* both principals consent to the intervention of a third party whose judgement they must agree to accept beforehand. When we speak about *adjudication* we refer to the presence of a third party who has the authority to intervene in a dispute whether or not the principals wish it.

The list of ways of dealing with trouble which Nader gives is by no means exhaustive. People can address themselves for help to different professional or non-professional settings. They may engage in a 'ritual of reordering' which does not involve the other person earlier implied in the problematic situation (Pfohl 1981).

People may also engage in collective action to bring about a structural change in the situations which cause them trouble (Abel 1982).

Which of these many courses of action will an involved person choose?

The meaning which a directly involved person bestows upon a situation will influence, as we saw, his course of action. That course of action will also be influenced by the degree to which different strategies to deal with trouble are available and accessible for him. In other words the degree to which he has a real possibility of choice. This degree of choice is largely influenced by his place in the network of power which shapes his environment and by his practical possibilities to change the 'tribes' of which he is a part for other ones.

Formal and informal ways of defining trouble and dealing with it compared

The process of bestowing, meaning of what is going on in life is flexible in face to face relations in sofar as those involved in this process feel relatively 'free' to each other as equal human beings. In other words: if they feel not constrained by the requirements of organizational or professional roles and they are not caught in a power relation which prevents some of the parties to take fully part in this process. This flexibility has many advantages. It increases the possibilities to reach by negotiation a common meaning of problematic situations. It provides also possibilities for learning. Experience can teach people that the application of a certain frame of interpretation and a certain focus does not lead very far in certain sectors of life.

This flexibility is often lacking when situations are defined and dealt with in a highly formalized context. The more such a context is specialized, the more the freedom of definition – and thus of reaction – is limited by a high degree of division of labour or by a high degree of professionalization. In such a case it depends on the type of institution which has – fortuitously – taken the case up which definition and which answer will be given. It is improbable that a definition and a reaction provided for in such a context corresponds with the definition and reactions of the direct involved.

There are however important differences in the degree of flexibility which formal institutions involved in a problematic situation show. In many countries we find a high degree of flexibility in parts of the police organization e.g. the neighbourhood police. The same may be true, of the first echelons of the health and social work system. Of all formalized control systems the criminal justice system seems the most inflexible. The organizational context (high division of labour) and the internal logic of its specific frame of interpretation (peculiar style of punishment in which a gravity scale modeled according to the 'last judgement' plays an overriding role) contribute both to this inflexibility. Another factor in the particularly alienating effect of criminal justice involvement in problematic situations is its extreme narrow focus: only very specific events modeled in accordance with a legal incrimination may be taken into account and these may only be considered as they were supposed to be on a certain moment in time. The dynamic side of constructing reality, lacks completely in this particular system. Thus the construction of reality as it is pursued in criminal justice will practically never coincide with the dynamics of the construction of reality of the direct involved. In criminal justice one is generally deciding on a reality which exists only within the system and finds seldom a counterpart in the outside world.

It may illuminate the questions we are dealing with to compare in a very global way the processes of constructing the reality in a criminal justice system with those in a civil justice system. In a criminal justice system it is a formal

78

organization separated from the direct involved people which decides about the preliminary definition of the case (police or public prosecutor). In civil justice it is one of the direct involved parties who decides about the preliminary definition and the other party has an opportunity to contribute to the definition on the same level as the plaintiff. It is true that they may be – even in civil justice – considerably limited in their freedom of definition by the constraints which a formal legal system puts on the (legal) relevance of certain definitions. The constraints in civil justice – although also alienating for the directly involved parties – are however considerably less severe than in criminal justice. A third important difference is that the directly involved parties have no influence in the consequenses of a judgement in criminal justice. The execution of a sentence takes place on the initiative of a formal organization.

In civil justice the consequences of a judgement are in the hands of one of the parties and very often the existence of such a judgement has not bereft the loosing party of all bargaining power. A civil judgement changes the power relation between involved parties but leaves them room for further negotiation. After the judgement they can interact on the basis of their own dynamic definition of the situation.

5. Conclusion

What would be the task of a critical criminology which has abandoned according to the view developed above, 'crime' as a conceptual tool? The main tasks of such a critical criminology can be summarized as follows:

a. continue to describe, explain and demystify the activities of criminal justice and its adverse social effects. This activity should however be more directed than up till now to the definitory activities of this system. To do that, it would be necessary to compare in concrete fields of human life the activities of criminal justice (and their social effects) with those of other formal control systems (legal ones, like the civil justice systems, and non-legal ones, like the medical and social work system). The activities of those formal control systems with respect to a certain area of life should be at the same time compared with informal ways of dealing with such an area of life. In such a task, critical criminology can be stimulated by the developments in (legal) anthropology and in a more general way by sociology in an interpretative paradigm. This implies abandoning 'behavior' and deviance as a starting point for analysis and adopting instead a situation-oriented approach, micro and macro.

b. Illustrate – but only as a way of example without pretending to be a 'science of problematic situations' – how in a specific field problematic situations could be addressed at different levels of the societal organisation without having recourse to criminal justice.

c. Study strategies how to abolish criminal justice; in other words, how to liberate organisations like the police and the courts of a system of reference which turns them away of the variety of life and the needs of those directly involved.

d. One of these strategies ought to be to contribute to the development of another overall language in which questions related to criminal justice and to public problems which generate claims to criminalisation, can be discussed without the bias (Cohen, 1985) of the present 'control babble'.

Notes

1. During the period of the seventies there was in Holland general governmental agreement on the desirability of reducing custodial sentences considerably, a goal endorsed by a large majority in Parliament. And yet the number of custodial sentences imposed during that period, and their average duration, continued to increase.

2. The International Society of Penal Law adopted at the world congress in Cairo in 1984 a resolution on mediation which supports this view. The preamble reads: 'This phenomenon of informal diversion of these occurances which would be crimes if they were evaluated by criminal law, but which are either not preceived as such by those directly involved or are simply not reported to criminal justice agencies, plays an important role in the prevention and control of crime . . . This is true whether an offence is serious or minor. Attempts at formal diversion should not interfere with such informal controls . . . *Revue internationale de droitpenal* 3/4, 1985, Editions Eres, Toulouse, p. 21.

References

Abel, R. (ed.) (1982), *The Politics of Informal Justice*. New York: Academic Press.

Baratta, A. (1983), 'Sur la criminologie critique et sa function dans la politique criminelle,' Vienna: World Society of Criminology.

Black, D. (1976), *The Behavior of Law*. New York: Academic Press.

Cohen, S. (1985), *Visions of Social Control*. Cambridge: Polity Press.

Council of Europe (1980), 'Report on Decriminalisation,' Strasbourg.

Greenberg, D.F. (ed.) (1981), *Crime and Capitalism*, Palo Alto: Mayfield.

Hulsman, L. and Bernat de Célis, J. (1982), *Peines Perdues*, Paris. See also: Sistema penal y seguridad ciudadena: heia una alternativa (1984) Barcelona: Ariel.

Hulsman, L. (1985), 'Drug Policy as a Source of Drug Problems and a Vehicle of Colonisation and Repression,' Herman Rosera Cueva (ed.), Instituto de criminologia, Universidad Central, Quito. *Trigesimo quinto course international de criminologia*.

Landreville (1978), 'Reform et abolition de la prison: illusion ou réalité?' *8me Congres Internationale de Criminologie*, Lison.

Lea, J. and Young, J. (1986), *What is to Be Done About Law and Order?* Harmondsworth: Penguin.

Meclintock, F. (1980), 'The Future of Imprisonment in Britain.' In: A. Bottoms and R. Preston (eds.), *The Coming Penal Crisis*, Edinburgh.

80

Normandeau, A. and Bernat de Célis, J. (1984), 'Alternatives to the Criminal Justice System. An Abolitionist Perspective.' International Centre for Comparative Criminology, Université de Montréal.

Pfohl, S.J. (1981), 'Labelling Criminals.' In: H.L. Ross (ed.), *Law and Deviance*, Beverly Hills: Sage.

Spector, M. (1981), 'Beyond Crime: Seven Methods to Control Troublesome Rascals.' In: H.L. Ross (ed.), *Law and Deviance*, Beverly Hills: Sage.

[6]

THE BRITISH JOURNAL
OF
CRIMINOLOGY

| Vol. 17 | January 1977 | No. 1 |

CONFLICTS AS PROPERTY*

NILS CHRISTIE (*Oslo*) †

Abstract

CONFLICTS are seen as important elements in society. Highly industrialised societies do not have too much internal conflict, they have too little. We have to organise social systems so that conflicts are both nurtured and made visible and also see to it that professionals do not monopolise the handling of them. Victims of crime have in particular lost their rights to participate. A court procedure that restores the participants' rights to their own conflicts is outlined.

Introduction

Maybe we should not have any criminology. Maybe we should rather abolish institutes, not open them. Maybe the social consequences of criminology are more dubious than we like to think.

I think they are. And I think this relates to my topic—conflicts as property. My suspicion is that criminology to some extent has amplified a process where conflicts have been taken away from the parties directly involved and thereby have either disappeared or become other people's property. In both cases a deplorable outcome. Conflicts ought to be used, not only left in erosion. And they ought to be used, and become useful, for those originally involved in the conflict. Conflicts *might* hurt individuals as well as social systems. That is what we learn in school. That is why we have officials. Without them, private vengeance and vendettas will blossom. We have learned this so solidly that we have lost track of the other side of the coin: our industrialised large-scale society is not one with too many internal conflicts. It is one with too little. Conflicts might kill, but too little of them might paralyse. I will

* Foundation Lecture of the Centre for Criminological Studies, University of Sheffield, delivered March 31, 1976. Valuable comments on preliminary drafts of the manuscript were received from Vigdis Christie, Tove Stang Dahl and Annika Snare.
† Professor of Criminology, University of Oslo.

I

NILS CHRISTIE

use this occasion to give a sketch of this situation. It cannot be more than a sketch. This paper represents the beginning of the development of some ideas, not the polished end-product.

On Happenings and Non-Happenings

Let us take our point of departure far away. Let us move to Tanzania. Let us approach our problem from the sunny hillside of the Arusha province. Here, inside a relatively large house in a very small village, a sort of happening took place. The house was overcrowded. Most grown-ups from the village and several from adjoining ones were there. It was a happy happening, fast talking, jokes, smiles, eager attention, not a sentence was to be lost. It was circus, it was drama. It was a court case.

The conflict this time was between a man and a woman. They had been engaged. He had invested a lot in the relationship through a long period, until she broke it off. Now he wanted it back. Gold and silver and money were easily decided on, but what about utilities already worn, and what about general expenses?

The outcome is of no interest in our context. But the framework for conflict solution is. Five elements ought to be particularly mentioned:

1. The parties, the former lovers, were in *the centre* of the room and in the centre of everyone's attention. They talked often and were eagerly listened to.

2. Close to them were relatives and friends who also took part. But they did not *take over*.

3. There was also participation from the general audience with short questions, information, or jokes.

4. The judges, three local party secretaries, were extremely inactive. They were obviously ignorant with regard to village matters. All the other people in the room were experts. They were experts on norms as well as actions. And they crystallised norms and clarified what had happened through participation in the procedure.

5. No reporters attended. They were all there.

My personal knowledge when it comes to British courts is limited indeed. I have some vague memories of juvenile courts where I counted some 15 or 20 persons present, mostly social workers using the room for preparatory work or small conferences A child or a young person must have attended, but except for the judge, or maybe it was the clerk, nobody seemed to pay any particular attention. The child or young person was most probably utterly confused as to who was who and for what, a fact confirmed in a small study by Peter Scott (1959). In the United States of America, Martha Baum (1968) has made similar observations. Recently, Bottoms and McClean (1976) have added another important observation: "There is one truth which is seldom revealed in the literature of the law or in studies of the administration of criminal justice. It is a truth which was made evident to all those involved in this research project as they sat through the cases which made up our sample. The truth is that, for the most part, the business of the criminal courts is dull, commonplace, ordinary and after a while downright tedious ".

But let me keep quiet about your system, and instead concentrate on my

CONFLICTS AS PROPERTY

own. And let me assure you: what goes on is no happening. It is all a negation of the Tanzanian case. What is striking in nearly all the Scandinavian
cases is the greyness, the dullness, and the lack of any important audience.
Courts are not central elements in the daily life of our citizens, but peripheral
in four major ways:—

1. They are situated in the administrative centres of the towns, outside the
territories of ordinary people.

2. Within these centres they are often centralised within one or two large
buildings of considerable complexity. Lawyers often complain that they need
months to find their way within these buildings It does not demand much
fantasy to imagine the situation of parties or public when they are trapped
within these structures. A comparative study of court architecture might
become equally relevant for the sociology of law as Oscar Newman's (1972)
study of defensible space is for criminology. But even without any study, I
feel it safe to say that both physical situation and architectural design are
strong indicators that courts in Scandinavia belong to the administrators of
law.

3. This impression is strengthened when you enter the courtroom itself—
if you are lucky enough to find your way to it. Here again, the periphery of
the parties is the striking observation. The parties are represented, and it is
these representatives and the judge or judges who express the little activity
that is activated within these rooms. Honoré Daumier's famous drawings
from the courts are as representative for Scandinavia as they are for France.

There are variations. In the small cities, or in the countryside, the courts
are more easily reached than in the larger towns. And at the very lowest end
of the court system—the so-called arbitration boards—the parties are sometimes less heavily represented through experts in law. But the symbol of the
whole system is the Supreme Court where the directly involved parties do not
even attend their own court cases.

4. I have not yet made any distinction between civil and criminal conflicts. But it was not by chance that the Tanzania case was a civil one. Full
participation in your own conflict presupposes elements of civil law. The key
element in a criminal proceeding is that the proceeding is converted from
something between the concrete parties into a conflict between one of the
parties and the state. So, in a modern criminal trial, two important things
have happened. First, the parties are being *represented*. Secondly, the one
party that is represented by the state, namely the victim, is so thoroughly
represented that she or he for most of the proceedings is pushed completely
out of the arena, reduced to the triggerer-off of the whole thing. She or he is
a sort of double loser; first, *vis-à-vis* the offender, but secondly and often in a
more crippling manner by being denied rights to full participation in what
might have been one of the more important ritual encounters in life. The
victim has lost the case to the state.

Professional Thieves

As we all know, there are many honourable as well as dishonourable reasons
behind this development. The honourable ones have to do with the state's

3

NILS CHRISTIE

need for conflict reduction and certainly also its wishes for the protection of
the victim. It is rather obvious. So is also the less honourable temptation for
the state, or Emperor, or whoever is in power, to use the criminal case for
personal gain. Offenders might pay for their sins. Authorities have in time
past shown considerable willingness, in representing the victim, to act as
receivers of the money or other property from the offender. Those days are
gone; the crime control system is not run for profit. And yet they are not
gone. There are, in all banality, many interests at stake here, most of them
related to professionalisation.

Lawyers are particularly good at stealing conflicts. They are trained for
it. They are trained to prevent and solve conflicts. They are socialised into a
sub-culture with a surprisingly high agreement concerning interpretation of
norms, and regarding what sort of information can be accepted as relevant
in each case. Many among us have, as laymen, experienced the sad moments
of truth when our lawyers tell us that our best arguments in our fight against
our neighbour are without any legal relevance whatsoever and that we for
God's sake ought to keep quiet about them in court. Instead they pick out
arguments we might find irrelevant or even wrong to use. My favourite
example took place just after the war. One of my country's absolutely top
defenders told with pride how he had just rescued a poor client. The client had
collaborated with the Germans. The prosecutor claimed that the client
had been one of the key people in the organisation of the Nazi movement. He
had been one of the master-minds behind it all. The defender, however, saved
his client. He saved him by pointing out to the jury how weak, how lacking
in ability, how obviously deficient his client was, socially as well as organisa-
tionally. His client could simply not have been one of the organisers among
the collaborators; he was without talents. And he won his case. His client
got a very minor sentence as a very minor figure. The defender ended his
story by telling me—with some indignation—that neither the accused, nor
his wife, had ever thanked him, they had not even talked to him afterwards.

Conflicts become the property of lawyers. But lawyers don't hide that it is
conflicts they handle. And the organisational framework of the courts underlines this point. The opposing parties, the judge, the ban against privileged
communication within the court system, the lack of encouragement for
specialisation—specialists cannot be internally controlled—it all underlines
that this is an organisation for the handling of conflicts. *Treatment personnel*
are in another position. They are more interested in *converting the image of the
case from one of conflict into one of non-conflict.* The basic model of healers is not
one of opposing parties, but one where one party has to be helped in the
direction of one generally accepted goal—the preservation or restoration of
health. They are not trained into a system where it is important that parties
can control each other. There is, in the ideal case, nothing to control, because
there is only one goal. Specialisation is encouraged. It increases the amount
of available knowledge, and the loss of internal control is of no relevance. A
conflict perspective creates unpleasant doubts with regard to the healer's
suitability for the job. A non-conflict perspective is a precondition for defining crime as a legitimate target for treatment.

4

CONFLICTS AS PROPERTY

One way of reducing attention to the conflict is reduced attention given to the victim. Another is concentrated attention given to those attributes in the criminal's background which the healer is particularly trained to handle. Biological defects are perfect. So also are personality defects when they are established far back in time—far away from the recent conflict. And so are also the whole row of explanatory variables that criminology might offer. We have, in criminology, to a large extent functioned as an auxiliary science for the professionals within the crime control system.We have focused on the offender, made her or him into an object for study, manipulation and control. We have added to all those forces that have reduced the victim to a nonentity and the offender to a thing. And this critique is perhaps not only relevant for the old criminology, but also for the new criminology. While the old one explained crime from personal defects or social handicaps, the new criminology explains crime as the result of broad economic conflicts. The old criminology loses the conflicts, the new one converts them from inter-personal conflicts to class conflicts. And they are. They are class conflicts—also. But, by stressing this, the conflicts are again taken away from the directly involved parties. So, as a preliminary statement: Criminal conflicts have either become *other people's property*—primarily the property of lawyers—or it has been in other people's interests to *define conflicts away*.

Structural Thieves

But there is more to it than professional manipulation of conflicts. Changes in the basic social structure have worked in the same way.

What I particularly have in mind are *two types of segmentation* easily observed in highly industrialised societies. First, there is the question of segmentation *in space*. We function each day, as migrants moving between sets of people which do not need to have any link—except through the mover. Often, therefore, we know our work-mates only as work-mates, neighbours only as neighbours, fellow cross-country skiers only as fellow cross-country skiers. We get to know them as *roles*, not as total persons. This situation is accentuated by the extreme degree of division of labour we accept to live with. Only experts can evaluate each other according to individual—personal—competence. Outside the speciality we have to fall back on a general evaluation of the supposed importance of the work. Except between specialists, we cannot evaluate how good anybody is in his work, only how good, in the sense of important, the role is. Through all this, we get limited possibilities for understanding other people's behaviour. Their behaviour will also get limited relevance for us. Role-players are more easily exchanged than persons.

The second type of segmentation has to do with what I would like to call our re-establishment of caste-society. I am not saying class-society, even though there are obvious tendencies also in that direction. In my framework, however, I find the elements of caste even more important. What I have in mind is the segregation based on biological attributes such as sex, colour, physical handicaps or the number of winters that have passed since birth. Age is particularly important. It is an attribute nearly perfectly synchronised to a modern complex industrialised society. It is a continuous variable where

5

NILS CHRISTIE

we can introduce as many intervals as we might need. We can split the population in two: children and adults. But we also can split it in ten: babies, pre-school children, school-children, teenagers, older youth, adults, pre-pensioned, pensioned, old people, the senile. And most important: the cutting points can be moved up and down according to social needs. The concept " teenager " was particularly suitable 10 years ago. It would not have caught on if social realities had not been in accordance with the word. Today the concept is not often used in my country. The condition of youth is not over at 19. Young people have to wait even longer before they are allowed to enter the work force. The caste of those outside the work force has been extended far into the twenties. At the same time departure from the work force—if you ever were admitted, if you were not kept completely out because of race or sex-attributes—is brought forward into the early sixties in a person's life. In my tiny country of four million inhabitants, we have 800,000 persons segregated within the educational system. Increased scarcity of work has immediately led authorities to increase the capacity of educational incarceration. Another 600,000 are pensioners.

Segmentation according to space and according to caste attributes has several consequences. First and foremost it leads into a *depersonalisation* of social life. Individuals are to a smaller extent linked to each other in close social networks where they are confronted with *all* the significant roles of the significant others. This creates a situation with limited amounts of information with regard to each other. We do know less about other people, and get limited possibilities both for understanding and for prediction of their behaviour. If a conflict is created, we are less able to cope with this situation. Not only are professionals there, able and willing to take the conflict away, but we are also more willing to give it away.

Secondly, segmentation leads to destruction of certain conflicts even before they get going. The depersonalisation and mobility within industrial society melt away some essential conditions for living conflicts; those between parties that mean a lot to each other. What I have particularly in mind is crime against other people's honour, libel or defamation of character. All the Scandinavian countries have had a dramatic decrease in this form of crime. In my interpretation, this is not because honour has become more respected, but because there is less honour to respect. The various forms of segmentation mean that human beings are inter-related in ways where they simply mean less to each other. When they are hurt, they are only hurt partially. And if they are troubled, they can easily move away. And after all, who cares? Nobody knows me. In my evaluation, the decrease in the crimes of infamy and libel is one of the most interesting and sad symptoms of dangerous developments within modern industrialised societies. The decrease here is clearly related to social conditions that lead to increase in other forms of crime brought to the attention of the authorities. It is an important goal for crime prevention to re-create social conditions which lead to an increase in the number of crimes against other people's honour.

A third consequence of segmentation according to space and age is that certain conflicts are made completely invisible, and thereby don't get any

6

CONFLICTS AS PROPERTY

decent solution whatsoever. I have here in mind conflicts at the two extremes of a continuum. On the one extreme we have the over-privatised ones, those taking place against individuals captured within one of the segments. Wife beating or child battering represent examples. The more isolated a segment is, the more the weakest among parties is alone, open for abuse. Inghe and Riemer (1943) made the classical study many years ago of a related phenomenon in their book on incest. Their major point was that the social isolation of certain categories of proletarised Swedish farm-workers was the necessary condition for this type of crime. Poverty meant that the parties within the nuclear family became completely dependent on each other. Isolation meant that the weakest parties within the family had no external network where they could appeal for help. The physical strength of the husband got an undue importance. At the other extreme we have crimes done by large economic organisations against individuals too weak and ignorant to be able even to realise they have been victimised. In both cases the goal for crime prevention might be to re-create social conditions which make the conflicts visible and thereafter manageable.

Conflicts as Property

Conflicts are taken away, given away, melt away, or are made invisible. Does it matter, does it really matter?

Most of us would probably agree that we ought to protect the invisible victims just mentioned. Many would also nod approvingly to ideas saying that states, or Governments, or other authorities ought to stop stealing fines, and instead let the poor victim receive this money. I at least would approve such an arragement. But I will not go into that problem area here and now. Material compensation is not what I have in mind with the formulation " conflicts as property ". It is the *conflict itself* that represents the most interesting property taken away, not the goods originally taken away from the victim, or given back to him. In our types of society, conflicts are more scarce than property. And they are immensely more valuable.

They are valuable in several ways. Let me start at the societal level, since here I have already presented the necessary fragments of analysis that might allow us to see what the problem is. Highly industrialised societies face major problems in organising their members in ways such that a decent quota take part in any activity at all. Segmentation according to age and sex can be seen as shrewd methods for segregation. Participation is such a scarcity that insiders create monopolies against outsiders, particularly with regard to work. In this perspective, it will easily be seen that conflicts represent a *potential for activity, for participation.* Modern criminal control systems represent one of the many cases of lost opportunities for involving citizens in tasks that are of immediate importance to them. Ours is a society of task-monopolists.

The victim is a particularly heavy loser in this situation. Not only has he suffered, lost materially or become hurt, physically or otherwise. And not only does the state take the compensation. But above all he has lost participation in his own case. It is the Crown that comes into the spotlight, not the victim. It is the Crown that describes the losses, not the victim. It is the Crown

7

NILS CHRISTIE

that appears in the newspaper, very seldom the victim. It is the Crown that gets a chance to talk to the offender, and neither the Crown nor the offender are particularly interested in carrying on that conversation. The prosecutor is fed-up long since. The victim would not have been. He might have been scared to death, panic-stricken, or furious. But he would not have been un-involved. It would have been one of the important days in his life. Something that belonged to him has been taken away from that victim.[1]

But the big loser is us—to the extent that society is us. This loss is first and foremost a loss in *opportunities for norm-clarification*. It is a loss of pedagogical possibilities. It is a loss of opportunities for a continuous discussion of what represents the law of the land. How wrong was the thief, how right was the victim? Lawyers are, as we saw, trained into agreement on what is relevant in a case. But that means a trained incapacity in letting the parties decide what *they* think is relevant. It means that it is difficult to stage what we might call a political debate in the court. When the victim is small and the offender big—in size or power—how blameworthy then is the crime? And what about the opposite case, the small thief and the big house-owner? If the offender is well educated, ought he then to suffer more. or maybe less, for his sins? Or if he is black, or if he is young, or if the other party is an insurance company, or if his wife has just left him, or if his factory will break down if he has to go to jail, or if his daughter will lose her fiancé, or if he was drunk, or if he was sad, or if he was mad? There is no end to it. And maybe there ought to be none. Maybe Barotse law as described by Max Gluckman (1967) is a better instrument for norm-clarification, allowing the conflicting parties to bring in the whole chain of old complaints and arguments each time. Maybe decisions on relevance and on the weight of what is found relevant ought to be taken away from legal scholars, the chief ideologists of crime control systems, and brought back for free decisions in the court-rooms.

A further general loss—both for the victim and for society in general—has to do with anxiety-level and misconceptions. It is again the possibilities for personalised encounters I have in mind. The victim is so totally out of the case that he has no chance, ever, to come to know the offender. We leave him outside, angry, maybe humiliated through a cross-examination in court, without any human contact with the offender. He has no alternative. He will need all the classical stereotypes around " the criminal " to get a grasp on the whole thing. He has a need for understanding, but is instead a non-person in a Kafka play. Of course, he will go away more frightened than ever, more in need than ever of an explanation of criminals as non-human.

The offender represents a more complicated case. Not much introspection is needed to see that direct victim-participation might be experienced as painful indeed. Most of us would shy away from a confrontation of this character. That is the first reaction. But the second one is slightly more posi-tive. Human beings have reasons for their actions. If the situation is staged so that reasons can be given (reasons as the parties see them, not only the selection lawyers have decided to classify as relevant), in such a case maybe the situation would not be all that humiliating. And, particularly, if the situa-

---

[1] For a preliminary report on victim dissatisfaction, see Vennard (1976).

8

CONFLICTS AS PROPERTY

tion was staged in such a manner that the central question was not meting out guilt, but a thorough discussion of what could be done to undo the deed, then the situation might change. And this is exactly what ought to happen when the victim is re-introduced in the case. Serious attention will centre on the victim's losses. That leads to a natural attention as to how they can be softened. It leads into a discussion of restitution. The offender gets a possibility to change his position from being a listener to a discussion—often a highly unintelligible one—of how much pain he ought to receive, into a participant in a discussion of how he could make it good again. The offender has lost the opportunity to explain himself to a person whose evaluation of him might have mattered. He has thereby also lost one of the most important possibilities for being forgiven. Compared to the humiliations in an ordinary court—vividly described by Pat Carlen (1976) in a recent issue of the *British Journal of Criminology*—this is not obviously any bad deal for the criminal.

But let me add that I think we should do it quite independently of his wishes. It is not health-control we are discussing. It is crime control. If criminals are shocked by the initial thought of close confrontation with the victim, preferably a confrontation in the very local neighbourhood of one of the parties, what then? I know from recent conversations on these matters that most people sentenced are shocked. After all, they prefer distance from the victim, from neighbours, from listeners and maybe also from their own court case through the vocabulary and the behavioural science experts who might happen to be present. They are perfectly willing to give away their property right to the conflict. So the question is more: are *we* willing to let them give it away? Are we willing to give them this easy way out? [2]

Let me be quite explicit on one point: I am not suggesting these ideas out of any particular interest in the treatment or improvement of criminals. I am not basing my reasoning on a belief that a more personalised meeting between offender and victim would lead to reduced recidivism. Maybe it would. I think it would. As it is now, the offender has lost the opportunity for participation in a personal confrontation of a very serious nature. He has lost the opportunity to receive a type of blame that it would be very difficult to neutralise. However, I would have suggested these arrangements even if it was absolutely certain they had no effects on recidivism, maybe even if they had a negative effect. I would have done that because of the other, more general gains. And let me also add—it is not much to lose. As we all know today, at least nearly all, we have not been able to invent any cure for crime. Except for execution, castration or incarceration for life, no measure has a proven minimum of efficiency compared to any other measure. We might as well react to crime according to what closely involved parties find is just and in accordance with general values in society.

With this last statement, as with most of the others I have made, I raise many more problems than I answer. Statements on criminal politics, particularly from those with the burden of responsibility, are usually filled with

---

[2] I tend to take the same position with regard to a criminal's property right to his own conflict as John Locke on property rights to one's own life—one has no right to give it away (*cf*. C. B. MacPherson (1962)).

NILS CHRISTIE

answers. It is questions we need. The gravity of our topic makes us much too pedantic and thereby useless as paradigm-changers.

A Victim-Oriented Court

There is clearly a model of neighbourhood courts behind my reasoning. But it is one with some peculiar features, and it is only these I will discuss in what follows.

First and foremost; it is a *victim-oriented* organisation. Not in its initial stage, though. The first stage will be a traditional one where it is established whether it is true that the law has been broken, and whether it was this particular person who broke it.

Then comes the second stage, which in these courts would be of the utmost importance. That would be the stage where the victim's situation was considered, where every detail regarding what had happened—legally relevant or not—was brought to the court's attention. Particularly important here would be detailed consideration regarding what could be done for him, first and foremost by the offender, secondly by the local neighbourhood, thirdly by the state. Could the harm be compensated, the window repaired, the lock replaced, the wall painted, the loss of time because the car was stolen given back through garden work or washing of the car ten Sundays in a row? Or maybe, when this discussion started, the damage was not so important as it looked in documents written to impress insurance companies? Could physical suffering become slightly less painful by any action from the offender, during days, months or years? But, in addition, had the community exhausted all resources that might have offered help? Was it absolutely certain that the local hospital could not do anything? What about a helping hand from the janitor twice a day if the offender took over the cleaning of the basement every Saturday? None of these ideas is unknown or untried, particularly not in England. But we need an organisation for the systematic application of them.

Only after this stage was passed, and it ought to take hours, maybe days, to pass it, only then would come the time for an eventual decision on punishment. Punishment, then, becomes that suffering which the judge found necessary to apply *in addition to* those unintended constructive sufferings the offender would go through in his restitutive actions *vis-à-vis* the victim. Maybe nothing could be done or nothing would be done. But neighbourhoods might find it intolerable that nothing happened. Local courts out of tune with local values are not local courts. That is just the trouble with them, seen from the liberal reformer's point of view.

A fourth stage has to be added. That is the stage for service to the offender. His general social and personal situation is by now well-known to the court. The discussion of his possibilities for restoring the victim's situation cannot be carried out without at the same time giving information about the offender's situation. This might have exposed needs for social, educational, medical or religious action—not to prevent further crime, but because needs ought to be met. Courts are public arenas, needs are made visible. But it is important that this stage comes *after* sentencing. Otherwise we get a re-emergence of

CONFLICTS AS PROPERTY

the whole array of so-called "special measures"—compulsory treatments—
very often only euphemisms for indeterminate imprisonment.

Through these four stages, these courts would represent a blend of elements
from civil and criminal courts, but with a strong emphasis on the civil side.

A Lay-Oriented Court

The second major peculiarity with the court model I have in mind is that it
will be one with an extreme degree of lay-orientation. This is essential when
conflicts are seen as property that ought to be shared. It is with conflicts as with
so many good things: they are in no unlimited supply. Conflicts can be cared
for, protected, nurtured. But there are limits. If some are given more access
in the disposal of conflicts, others are getting less. It is as simple as that.

Specialisation in conflict solution is the major enemy; specialisation that in
due—or undue—time leads to professionalisation. That is when the specialists
get sufficient power to claim that they have acquired special gifts, mostly
through education, gifts so powerful that it is obvious that they can only be
handled by the certified craftsman.

With a clarification of the enemy, we are also able to specify the goal; let
us reduce specialisation and particularly our dependence on the professionals within the crime control system to the utmost.

The ideal is clear; it ought to be a court of equals representing themselves.
When they are able to find a solution between themselves, no judges are
needed. When they are not, the judges ought also to be their equals.

Maybe the judge would be the easiest to replace, if we made a serious
attempt to bring our present courts nearer to this model of lay orientation.
We have lay judges already, in principle. But that is a far cry from realities.
What we have, both in England and in my own country, is a sort of specialised
non-specialist. First, they are used *again and again*. Secondly, some are even
trained, given special courses or sent on excursions to foreign countries to
learn about how to behave as a lay judge. Thirdly, most of them do also
represent an extremely *biased sample* of the population with regard to sex,
age, education, income, class [3] and personal experience as criminals. With
real lay judges, I conceive of a system where nobody was given the right to
take part in conflict solution more than a few times, and then had to wait
until all other community members had had the same experience.

Should lawyers be admitted to court? We had an old law in Norway that
forbids them to enter the rural districts. Maybe they should be admitted in
stage one where it is decided if the man is guilty. I am not sure. Experts are
as cancer to any lay body. It is exactly as Ivan Illich describes for the educational system in general. Each time you increase the length of compulsory
education in a society, each time you also decrease the same population's
trust in what they have learned and understood quite by themselves.

Behaviour experts represent the same dilemma. Is there a place for them in
this model? Ought there to be any place? In stage 1, decisions on facts,
certainly not. In stage 3, decisions on eventual punishment, certainly not.
It is too obvious to waste words on. We have the painful row of mistakes from

[3] For the most recent documentation, see Baldwin (1976).

NILS CHRISTIE

Lombroso, through the movement for social defence and up to recent attempts to dispose of supposedly dangerous people through predictions of who they are and when they are not dangerous any more. Let these ideas die, without further comments.

The real problem has to do with the service function of behaviour experts. Social scientists can be perceived as functional answers to a segmented society. Most of us have lost the physical possibility to experience the totality, both on the social system level and on the personality level. Psychologists can be seen as historians for the individual; sociologists have much of the same function for the social system. Social workers are oil in the machinery, a sort of security counsel. Can we function without them, would the victim and the offender be worse off?

Maybe. But it would be immensely difficult to get such a court to function if they were all there. Our theme is social conflict. Who is not at least made slightly uneasy in the handling of her or his own social conflicts if we get to know that there is an expert on this very matter at the same table? I have no clear answer, only strong feelings behind a vague conclusion: let us have as few behaviour experts as we dare to. And if we have any, let us for God's sake not have any that specialise in crime and conflict resolution. Let us have generalised experts with a solid base outside the crime control system. And a last point with relevance for both behaviour experts and lawyers: if we find them unavoidable in certain cases or at certain stages, let us try to get across to them the problems they create for broad social participation. Let us try to get them to perceive themselves as resource-persons, answering when asked, but not domineering, not in the centre. They might help to stage conflicts, not take them over.

Rolling Stones

There are hundreds of blocks against getting such a system to operate within our western culture. Let me only mention three major ones. They are:
1. There is a lack of neighbourhoods.
2. There are too few victims.
3. There are too many professionals around.

With lack of neighbourhoods I have in mind the very same phenomenon I described as a consequence of industrialised living; segmentation according to space and age. Much of our trouble stems from killed neighbourhoods or killed local communities. How can we then thrust towards neighbourhoods a task that presupposes they are highly alive? I have no really good arguments, only two weak ones. First, it is not quite that bad. The death is not complete. Secondly, one of the major ideas behind the formulation ' Conflicts as Property ' is that it is neighbourhood-property. It is not private. It belongs to the system. It is intended as a vitaliser for neighbourhoods. The more fainting the neighbourhood is, the more we need neighbourhood courts as one of the many functions any social system needs for not dying through lack of challenge.

Equally bad is the lack of victims. Here I have particularly in mind the lack of personal victims. The problem behind this is again the large units in

CONFLICTS AS PROPERTY

industrialised society. Woolworth or British Rail are not good victims. But again I will say: there is not a complete lack of personal victims, and their needs ought to get priority. But we should not forget the large organisations. They, or their boards, would certainly prefer not to have to appear as victims in 5000 neighbourhood courts all over the country. But maybe they ought to be compelled to appear. If the complaint is serious enough to bring the offender into the ranks of the criminal, then the victim ought to appear. A related problem has to do with insurance companies—the industrialised alternative to friendship or kinship. Again we have a case where the crutches deteriorate the condition. Insurance takes the consequences of crime away. We will therefore have to take insurance away. Or rather: we will have to keep the possibilities for compensation through the insurance companies back until in the procedure I have described it has been proved behond all possible doubt that there are no other alternatives left—particularly that the offender has no possibilities whatsoever. Such a solution will create more paper-work, less predictability, more aggression from customers. And the solution will not necessarily be seen as good from the perspective of the policy-holder. But it will help to protect conflicts as social fuel.

None of these troubles can, however, compete with the third and last I will comment on: the abundance of professionals. We know it all from our own personal biographies or personal observations. And in addition we get it confirmed from all sorts of social science research: the educational system of any society is not necessarily synchronised with any needs for the product of this system. Once upon a time we thought there was a direct causal relation from the number of highly educated persons in a country to the Gross National Product. Today we suspect the relationship to go the other way, if we are at all willing to use GNP as a meaningful indicator. We also know that most educational systems are extremely class-biased. We know that most academic people have had profitable investments in our education, that we fight for the same for our children, and that we also often have vested interests in making our part of the educational system even bigger. More schools for more lawyers, social workers, sociologists, criminologists. While I am *talking* deprofessionalisation, we are increasing the capacity to be able to fill up the whole world with them.

There is no solid base for optimism. On the other hand insights about the situation, and goal formulation, is a pre-condition for action. Of course, the crime control system is not the domineering one in our type of society. But it has some importance. And occurrences here are unusually well suited as pedagogical illustrations of general trends in society. There is also some room for manoeuvre. And when we hit the limits, or are hit by them, this collision represents in itself a renewed argument for more broadly conceived changes.

Another source for hope: ideas formulated here are not quite so isolated or in dissonance with the mainstream of thinking when we leave our crime control area and enter other institutions. I have already mentioned Ivan Illich with his attempts to get learning away from the teachers and back to active human beings. Compulsory learning, compulsory medication and compulsory consummation of conflict solutions have interesting similarities.

NILS CHRISTIE

When Ivan Illich and Paulo Freire are listened to, and my impression is that they increasingly are, the crime control system will also become more easily influenced.

Another, but related, major shift in paradigm is about to happen within the whole field of technology. Partly, it is the lessons from the third world that now are more easily seen, partly it is the experience from the ecology debate. The globe is obviously suffering from what we, through our technique, are doing to her. Social systems in the third world are equally obviously suffering. So the suspicion starts. Maybe the first world can't take all this technology either. Maybe some of the old social thinkers were not so dumb after all. Maybe social systems can be perceived as biological ones. And maybe there are certain types of large-scale technology that kill social systems, as they kill globes. Schumacher (1973) with his book *Small is Beautiful* and the related Institute for Intermediate Technology come in here. So do also the numerous attempts, particularly by several outstanding Institutes for Peace Research, to show the dangers in the concept of Gross National Product, and replace it with indicators that take care of dignity, equity and justice. The perspective developed in Johan Galtung's research group on World Indicators might prove extremely useful also within our own field of crime control.

There is also a political phenomenon opening vistas. At least in Scandinavia social democrats and related groupings have considerable power, but are without an explicated ideology regarding the goals for a reconstructed society. This vacuum is being felt by many, and creates a willingness to accept and even expect considerable institutional experimentation.

Then to my very last point: what about the universities in this picture? What about the new Centre in Sheffield? The answer has probably to be the old one: universities have to re-emphasise the old tasks of understanding and of criticising. But the task of training professionals ought to be looked into with renewed scepticism. Let us re-establish the credibility of encounters between critical human beings: low-paid, highly regarded, but with no extra power—outside the weight of their good ideas. That is as it ought to be.

REFERENCES

BALDWIN, J (1976) "The Social Composition of the Magistracy" *Brit. J Criminol.*, **16,** 171–174.

BAUM, M. AND WHEELER, S. (1968). "Becoming an inmate," Ch. 7, pp. 153–187, in Wheeler, S. (ed.), *Controlling Delinquents*. New York: Wiley.

BOTTOMS, A. E. AND McCLEAN, J. D. (1976). *Defendants in the Criminal Process.* London: Routledge and Kegan Paul.

CARLEN, P. (1976). "The Staging of Magistrates' Justice." *Brit. J. Criminol.*, **16,** 48–55.

GLUCKMAN, M. (1967). *The Judicial Process among the Barotse of Northern Rhodesia* Manchester University Press.

KINBERG, O., INGHE, G., AND RIEMER, S. (1943). *Incest-Problemet i Sverige.* Sth.

14

CONFLICTS AS PROPERTY

MacPHERSON, C. B. (1962). *The Political Theory of Possessive Individualism: Hobbes to Locke.* London: Oxford University Press.

NEWMAN, O. (1972). *Defensible Space: People and Design in the Violent City.* London: Architectural Press.

SCHUMACHER, E. F. (1973). *Small is Beautiful: A Study of Economics as if People Mattered.* London: Blond and Briggs.

SCOTT, P. D. (1959). "Juvenile Courts: the Juvenile's Point of View." *Brit. J. Delinq.,* **9,** 200–210.

VENNARD, J. (1976). "Justice and Recompense for Victims of Crime." *New Society,* **36,** 378–380.

[7]

International Journal of the Sociology of Law 1986, **14**, 269–286

Penal Sanctions as a Feminist Strategy: a Contradiction in Terms? Pornography and Criminal Law in the Netherlands

CHRISJE BRANTS AND ERNA KOK

Willem Pompe Instituut, University of Utrecht, Janskerkhof 16, 3512 BM Utrecht, The Netherlands

Introduction

One of the first things that the student of law in the Netherlands learns, is that penal law must always be *ultimum remedium:* a last resort, but a resort nevertheless. If all else fails, penal law, with its drastic and far-reaching sanctions, is expected to prevent, avenge and in the long run perhaps even eradicate social evils.

The criminal justice climate in the Netherlands has always been mild in comparison with that of its immediate neighbours. During the 1970s, the influence of critical criminology and abolitionism made itself felt and it became milder still. Decriminalisation and depenalisation became official policies in a number of fields and, while not everyone agreed that the criminal justice system, and prison sentences in particular, are ineffective and unjust and their social cost too high, there was to some extent consensus on the necessity of exploring other means of social control.

During the 1980s, Holland, like so many other European countries, has moved politically to the right. This shift has brought not only Thatcherism as an answer to the Dutch disease in the economic field, but also an ideological change in criminal justice policy. The latest government report on crime and crime control (Samenleving en Criminaliteit, 1985) paints a sombre picture of Dutch society: crime is rampant, soft-soaping has made it worse, what is needed now is an unequivocal answer by the criminal justice system. There are to

270   *C. Brants and E. Kok*

be less suspended sentences, more prisons, less rights for suspects, etc., etc.,
The social cost might be high, but society, apparently, is willing to pay.

Reliance on criminal law as an answer to otherwise seemingly unsolvable
social problems, however, is not the prerogative of law and order adepts. Faith
in the *ultimum remedium,* with the emphasis on *remedium,* is so deeply entrenched
that many, in themselves progressive, groups and movements who see
criminal justice *in theory* as conservative and conducive to the status quo, advocate its practical application to behaviour which they see as intrinsically des-
erving of punishment. They claim an ulterior motive for this apparent paradox, for the use of penal law is seen as a means of promoting more fundamental social change.

The environmental movement is a good example, but the women's movement too, both in the Netherlands and abroad, has repeatedly intervened in
the criminal justice debate with an eye to contributing, in the long run, to a
solution of the structural problems of inequality between men and women.
More especially, the women's movement has advocated the use of penal sanctions in order to oppose (sexual) violence against women. These are not merely
pleas for bloody vengeance against the male aggressor. A great deal of emphasis is also laid on better help and facilities for the victim, on solutions in civil
law suits (such as a court injunction not to visit the area where the victim lives)
and on legislative measures which will go to the very heart of fundamental
inequality and economic dependence, e.g. in social security and divorce law
(see also: Marsh, Geist & Caplan, 1982). Yet, while the women's movement
has not pinned its faith exclusively to penal law, the use of criminal prosecution and penal sanctions as a short-term strategy often seems to be a matter of
course.

Matters of course, however, entail some risk, for the need to examine critically the premises upon which they are based no longer exist. Moreover, the less
pleasant or even contradictory effects are inclined to be seen as inevitably,
something which — unfortunately or not — just can't be helped. Such in-
evitabilities and matters of course, but postulated by men about women, are
precisely what the women's movement has been seeking to undermine, also in
the field of criminal justice ('If a girl says no she means yes'; 'battered wives
ask for it'; 'if you must wear mini-skirts . . .').

The result of feminist 'subversion' has been, in many cases, to increase the
rate of prosecutions for rape, to stimulate the extension of its legal definition, to
re-open the debate on pornography and the criminal code. Unintentionally, it
has brought the women's movement closer to conservative and punitive forces
in the no-nonsense society of the 1980s.

Dilemmas

In a polemical discussion with one of the public prosecutors in the Netherlands, who had publicly reproached the women's movement for advocating an
undifferentiated and unmercifully hard policy with regard to the criminalisa-

tion and prosecution of rape, Jeanne Doomen wrote that the onus of proof should not lie with the women's movement, and that "women have the right to remain vague" as far as the problems of penal sanctions are concerned (Doomen 1979, pp.134–135). This is all very well as a polemical argument, although it avoids a number of fundamental questions and moreover allows 'the other side' to propose the solutions and therefore set the limits of the debate. We are now seven years further on. Perhaps the time has come to take a critical look at the use of penal sanctions as a feminist strategy.

In this paper we propose to examine a number of dilemmas which, in our view, are inherent in a strategy which seeks to employ the ideological weapon of criminal law as a means of promoting a better and more just social order.

Indeed, at a theoretical level, the use of penal sanctions as a feminist strategy might even be said to be a contradiction in terms. For if penal law itself is an expression of male ideology, as has been repeatedly contended by feminist writers, how can it ever serve to undermine the masculinist bias and resulting inequalities in society? A more practical problem arises when we consider the result of criminological reasearch into the actual effect of punishment in the sense of both general and individual deterrence. At the very best, it is highly debateable whether prison sentences achieve much more than a temporary removal from society, much vicarious suffering on the part of innocent wives and children and re-affirmation in prison of the values which put the offender there in the first place. Also an all-male prison must surely be one of the strongest masculinist fortresses imaginable. What then is to be expected of (new) penal sanctions and their enforcement against the perpetrators of violence against women? And finally, there is a dilemma of conscience. Progressive jurists and criminologists have repeatedly advocated the reduction rather than the extension of the scope of penal law. Sympathy towards critical criminology and legal theory or practice and sympathy towards the feminist struggle could become an awkward combination. Does the end ever justify the means, and shall we not find ourselves involved in some dubious coalitions and our strategy put to purposes for which it was never intended?[1].

Although these dilemmas are inherent in the use of criminal law in general and apply whatever the seriousness of the offence, it will be clear that seriousness could be a criterion for determining whether the means may, after all, be justified. We have chosen to illustrate the dilemmas above by tracing the debate on pornography and criminal law in the Netherlands. Unlike, for example rape, the seriousness and social injuriousness of which is undisputed, there is no such consensus on the harmful effect of pornography. Indeed, the harm it does is most likely to be on an ideological and immaterial level. The criminalisation of pornography is therefore highly arbitrary. Why should a photograph of two adults copulating, be it in a somewhat unusual position, be more harmful and offensive than the (German) advertising slogan: "What is the difference between a woman and a carpet?" (See Spaink, 1982, illustration opp. p.129). Pornography also poses a number of problems where funda-

272	*C. Brants and E. Kok*

mental rights and freedoms are concerned (notably the freedom of expression). And while the prosecution and punishment of rapists might be said to realise at least some of the traditional goals of penal law (retribution and the protection of society — at least temporarily and from one offender), the aim of effective criminalisation of pornography is by no means clear.

Finally, during the past few years, a public debate on pornography and criminal law in the Netherlands has been the result of feminist intervention in the legislative process, culminating in new criminal legislation. Advocates and adversaries of the Pornography Bill opposed each other not only in their views on the phenomenon of pornography but also in their appreciation of the use of criminal law to contain it. Before we take a closer look at this debate, let us first briefly outline the legal history of pornography in the Netherlands.

Pornography and Criminal Law in the Netherlands

Criminal legislation with regard to pornography in the Netherlands has never been particularly intensive. "The first codified penal provision on pornography was to be found in section 287 of the French Code Pénal which came into force in 1811 during the Napoleonic occupation of the Netherlands and was not replaced until the introduction of the present Dutch Penal Code in 1886. Section 287 prohibited the distribution of images and "pamphlets" in contravention of proper morals. The prohibition was purely a matter of public order.

Section 240 of the Penal Code of 1886 prohibited the showing and distribution of "indecent pamphlets". As the section appears in a sequence of sexual crimes, it is evident that sexual decency was at stake, although the legislator evidently considered his duties to be limited and the concern was for the protection of decency against public and involuntary violation only. As a result only those pornographic manifestations with which one could be confronted "unexpectedly" — songs, pictures, pamphlets etc. were punishable by law. The authorities took no steps against books of "indecent" content, for one is rarely caught unawares by the content of a book. And there was no remedy for voluntary corruption of morals (de Hullu, 1984, p.16). The increasing influence of the social-democratic, but more especially religious, parties on the political scene, meant a good deal of pressure on the authorities — and an increasing willingness on their part — to intervene actively in social life, even if this would mean intervention in the private lives of individuals.

In 1911, a whole package of legislation was passed aimed at bringing the corruption of morals to a halt. It is known as the morality laws of Regout, after the minister who was the driving force behind it. As well as provisions against abortion, neo-Malthusianism and homosexuality, there were also new provisions on pornography. Writings and objects could now also be classed as indecent under section 240 of the Penal Code. Moreover, the "production, for distribution" of pornography and its import and export were also made punishable, the latter for reasons of "international pressure" (Schalken, 1972, p.23). Finally, the maximum punishment was increased, while new sections (240 bis and 451 bis) were added, aimed explicitly at protecting young people under 16 from corruption.

The morality laws of 1911 have been portrayed as the triumph of religious *petit bourgeois* politics at the expense of reigning liberalism. Regout as the embodiment of "generations long yearning for revenge" (Kempe, 1976, p.62). In reality, however, anxiety about "the decline of public morals" was widespread, in both religious and non-religious circles, especially with regard to the increasing numbers of illegal abortions after 1900. Some liberals and feminists were also unhappy about neo-Malthusianist practices and propaganda (de Bruyn, 1979, pp. 40 and 90). And prostitution was everybody's worry. The prohibition of brothels (section 250 PC) received hearty support from the women's organisation which concerned itself extensively with matters of morality (Posthumus & Waal, 1977, p.86), while the socialists' emancipatory aspirations went hand in hand with an ethical revival that led to an almost religious moral attitude in matters of sex (de Bruyn, 1979, p.93).

In this climate, the almost universal condemnation of pornography as a possible source of corruption is hardly surprising and Regout was able to simply ignore the arguments of principle against criminalisation put forward during the parlimentary debate. That '1911' was no political accident is demonstrated by the fact that later (in 1927 and 1934) the penal provisions on pornography were extended and tightened up until they eventually took on the form they were to keep until 1985[2].

The debate on pornography was not re-opened until the 1960s; years in which liberation was the key-word, the old order rocked on its foundations and the sexual revolution — subsequently to be recognised as not as revolutionary as it might have been — demanded freedom of experience and expression for all the infinite variations of human sexuality. Pornography was no longer a source of corruption worthy of public attention, but of, be it dubious, pleasure and in any event the adult citizen's private business to which he (and perhaps even she) was free to turn without interference by the state. All of this made the enforcement of section 240 of the Penal Code extremely problematic.

It is, therefore, hardly surprising that the burgeoning notion of decriminalisation brought great relief in matters of morality at the end of the 1960s. The provisions on homosexuality, contraceptives and abortion disappeared from the Penal Code one after another.

In 1970 the Advisory Committee on Morality Laws (the Committee-Melai) was installed. Its task was to advise on the possibilities of bringing the laws of morality into harmony with changing social attitudes. In doing so, the committee was to achieve a balance between the individual's freedom to determine his or her own behaviour on the one hand, and, on the other, the duty to respect the feelings and personal integrity of others (Schalken, 1974, pp.214–215). The committee's second interim report (1973) dealt with porno-

274   *C. Brants and E. Kok*

graphy. With a view to performing its balancing act, it proposed, as far as adults were concerned, to limit the criminalisation of pornography to unexpected confrontation.

The same tendency towards liberalisation is also apparent in the jurisprudence of those years. In the Chick decision[3], the High Court's ruling amounted to a limited definition of the concept of decency: the meaning of the term was not to be derived from the feelings of an elite of high moral standing, but from the "reigning morals in this country, which are determined by the views of an important majority of the Dutch people" (HR, 17 November 1970, NJ, 1971, 374).

A similar limited definition was later to be applied to the term 'shocking". One can only be shocked by involuntary and unexpected confrontation, not by voluntarily reading or looking at pornography. In the Deep Throat decision[4], the High Court ruled that the legal concept "shocking . . . is not applicable in cases in which admission to the showing (of the film) is limited to persons of 18 years and older who, before they entered the cinema, were unequivocally warned of the special and immodest nature of the film they were about to see, for of such persons it can be said that it was their intention to watch that film, in spite of said nature, and they they would, therefore, not be shocked by it" (HR, 28 November 1978, NJ, 1979,93).

The 'Bill on the Amendment of section 240 Penal Code and other provisions' which was presented in Parliament at the end of 1979 (HeK 1978/79, 15836 no. 2) took the same line as the Advisory Committee and the High Court: adults were to be protected against unexpected confrontation only (so that once again books no longer come under the provision), while young persons under 16 were to enjoy an extra measure of protection. During the parliamentary debate another provision was added aimed explicitly at combatting child pornography. It was the result of the work of a small number of American 'moral crusaders' who depicted the Netherlands as one of the largest producers of child pornography, thanks to the liberal criminal justice climate. At the end of 1984, the matter made the headlines for weeks in the national and international press.

In the beginning, not many reactions to the Bill were forthcoming. A number of minor legal flaws were discovered, but there was nothing resembling a public debate and nothing to indicate that, politically, there were still some hard nuts to crack. The situation changed, however, from 1980 and especially 1981 onwards. The women's movement raised a vehement protest against what they considered to be the liberalisation of pornography. One of the most powerful arguments was the alleged relationship between freely obtainable pornography and an increase in sexual violence against women. "Pornography is the theory, rape the practice" became the slogan around which the anti-porn lobby organised and its aim was to "Keep porn in penal law" (Quispel, 1981).

The ensuing debate was conducted on the basis of a number of misunderstandings and often at cross-purposes. To start with, there was — and is — no question of pornography's disappearing from criminal law; the Bill merely proposed to adapt the legal text to the jurisprudence of the High Court. It would be wrong to conclude that the criminal justice authorities were or are contemplating any drastic change in policy. Then there was the theory that a direct relationship exists between consuming pornography and actually committing violent sexual offences. No one was able to come up with unequivocal scientific proof that this is the case — or, for that matter, that it is not. A great deal of time was spent in proving and disproving the social injuriousness of adult pornography, but the definitions of injuriousness were not always the same. While the women's movement was often referring to the ideological reinforcement of prevailing male values (power, aggression, possession, sexual prowess, etc.) which also underlie attitudes towards rape, its, predominantly male, opponents were thinking along much more one-dimensional lines and demanding proof that the consumer of pornography was likely to go out and rape someone afterwards (see e.g. de Hullu, 1984.).

And finally, there was the question of criminal law. The women's movement repeatedly expressed the belief that pornography belonged in the Penal Code and demanded consistent enforcement of its provisions. Right- and left-wing liberals remarked that women's liberation had apparently brought forth a new generation of morality freaks bent on destroying the sexual revolution and once again limiting the personal freedom of the individual. It was unfortunate, but only to be expected, that the women's movement found itself hand-in-hand with the Christian Democrats and other religious parties and involved in a crusade against sex and other immoralities in general. Moreover, women were accused by the left of pursuing "law and order" — tactics which would eventually erode fundamental rights and freedoms, notably the freedom of expression.

And yet, there is no real evidence in the feminist literature produced during the pornography debate that women object to sex, or to pictures of it, nor that they are prepared to walk blindly on with Dame Justice (see, e.g. Spaink, 1982.). What they seek to achieve through the criminal justice system is certainly not a merciless campaign of revenge against men in general, whom they see by definition as dirty, immoral and lusting after power. But what is their aim? Can it be achieved with the help of criminal justice and, if so, how? Although the Pornography Bill has now been passed[5] it still makes sense to examine the motives and expectations which led the women's movement to advocate penal law as a means of helping to solve what it sees as part of a much greater social problem.

For while the Bill which eventually became law is the embodiment of jurisprudence very much in tune with the ideas of the sexual revolution and in no way the ideological instrument which women had hoped it would be, it could be said (with the benefit of hindsight) that the outcome of the pornography debate — defined as "a slap in the face for the women's movement" by feminists and their opponents alike — was no more than could be expected.

276   C. Brants and E. Kok

Pornography and Penal Law, a Problematic Issue

While, as we have said, six years ago it might have been legitimate to demand the effective criminalisation and penalisation of offences against women, including pornography, and then leave it at that, in our view the time is ripe, not only for an evaluation of what we have accomplished — which is not the aim of this paper — but also for a critical examination of the use of penal sanctions as a feminist strategy. What do we hope to accomplish, what can we hope to accomplish by intervention in the criminal justice debate? The debate on pornography in the Netherlands ended in the formal legalisation of the existing situation, and apart from the provisions on child pornography, in all likelihood the result of American intervention — the Dutch government is extremely susceptible to suggestions that the penal climate in the Netherlands promotes crime — little has been achieved by way of innovation and there is even less guarantee that the laws on pornography will actually have any effect in reducing the amount produced and distributed. Not only did the women's movement in Holland fail to convince its opponents that the end justified the means, the question was never asked explicitly. Neither was there any debate on what that end is, or whether the proposed means would, indeed could, bring it any closer.

The objections to pornography which have been formulated by the women's movement are not directed against portraying or describing people engaged in sexual activities. Rather, they concern the way in which such activities are described or portrayed, and the way in which a substantial amount of pornography is produced: snuff movies, using children and the exploitation of (illegal) immigrant women. More fundamentally, they concern the implicit ideological message contained in pornography and its possible effect in reinforcing male notions on sexual domination and therefore lowering the threshold of actual sexual violence.

Susan Griffin (1982) has argued that pornography is essentially the ritual exorcism of the fear of the female and all it stands for in our culture. Its definition is therefore a great deal broader than the legal concept of indecent: any objectivation of woman, any portrayal of woman as a thing, as something to be consumed — a common trick in advertising — is an expression of the pornographic mind which dominates our culture and influences the daily thoughts and lives of men *and* women. Not only are the latter the victims of the pornographic mind in the most usual sense of the word, it also influences their most fundamental notions of the way society and social relations work and should work. The argument — often heard during the pornography debate in Holland — that porn is not a man's thing, as many women buy and consume it and derive pleasure from it, may be unsympathetic, but it is not entirely without truth. And in this sense, but in this sense only, there is also some truth in the notion of victim-precipitation. This makes the question of what we can expect from criminal law all the more pertinent.

It would go beyond the scope of this paper to delve into explanations of the hegemony of sexism as a dominant ideology (see on this matter Groenendijk, 1983 and Vintgens, 1983). If we take as our starting point pornography as a more or less excessive expression of a sexist culture, in which the ideological message is not so much concerned with the sexual as with the confirmation and perpetuation of social power relations, then it will be clear that the ultimate goal of criminalisation has a much wider scope than the mere prohibition of production and distribution. Ultimately, criminal law must help serve to eradicate sexism by stamping out the excesses, so that a more just society will guarantee the equality, safety and physical and mental integrity of all individuals. That is no small matter. If criminal law can help perform this gargantuan task, then perhaps the end does justify the means, despite the social cost of its enforcement. But can it?

Criminal legislation and the enforcement of criminal law are social processes, which cannot be separated from existing economic and other social networks and relations of power. The patriarchal — and sometimes downright sexist — nature of society, as expressed in pornography, is reflected in (criminal) law and in the way in which it is enforced. A much-debated example of this is to be found in the law on rape. It would be impossible to discuss all the literature on this subject here. In short we may say that, during the 1970s, women all over the world expressed their concern and indignation about the enforcement of the penal provisions on rape. Convincingly they argued that rape is an offence which reflects the dominant masculinist and sexist ideology; that this not only applies to the actual offence, but also to its legal definition and the criminal justice authorities' policing and prosecution policy; that the result is a stereotype of the rapist (pathological, immigrant, lower-class) which draws attention away from the large majority of rapists who do not fit this pattern; that *their* victims are greeted with cynical unbelief by the police and the courts: did they, by any chance 'ask' for it, did they perhaps even enjoy it? The true nature of rape — the violation of physical integrity and the right of sexual self-determination disappears behind an effective and closed ideological network of criminal law which is self-perpetuating, for the ideology and its consequences are contained in the legal definition and further expressed in its enforcement (see Weis & Weis, 1975, Leuw, 1982, Vorrink, 1982).

There is no earthly reason to suppose that the law on pornography will be any different. Just as it once reflected the result of a clash of interests between liberal and religious parties, in which the latter came out on top (not only because they were politically stronger, but more especially because they were able to appeal to prevailing attitudes in society), so it now reflects the liberal and libertarian attitudes of the sexual revolution, including the sexist ideology which underlies the prevailing interpretation of sexual "freedom". As it now stands, criminal law cannot protect against the dissemination of that ideology; in a sense it even protects the dissemination itself. Since the Deep Throat ruling, adults may watch and read whatever they want, as long as they are

278   *C. Brants and E. Kok*

informed beforehand what to expect. It is not the underlying ideas that are reprehensible, but the fact that some people might be shocked and must therefore be forewarned. Let us compare the situation with racism and the dissemination of racist ideas which is, at least in theory, considered reprehensible enough to warrant criminalisation in the Netherlands. In the privacy of one's home, one can, of course, tell offensive racist jokes without risking prosecution. But to hang a notice on the door: "Nigger jokes told here" would practically guarantee a visit by the criminal justice authorities. In other words, a public exhibition of racist ideas, however forewarned the public might be, is a crime. Since the Deep Throat case, upon which the penal provisions on pornography are based, forewarned is not only forearmed, but also exonerated.

However, before the above leads us to conclude that the use of penal sanctions is, and always will be, a contradiction in terms and, by definition, a hopeless prospect as far as pornography is concerned, let us examine more closely how criminal legislation on pornography functions. This could provide some insight into the likely effect of penal provisions with regard to our second dilemma: can we expect them actually to prevent the most offensive and excessive expressions of sexism? We shall return to the first — as yet unsolvable — dilemma later.

Functions of Criminal Legislation and the Law on Pornography

Theoretically, one of the distinctions most commonly drawn is that between the instrumental and symbolic functions of criminal law.

Criminal legislation can be called instrumental if it represents an attempt by the state to influence directly and immediately the behaviour of individuals with a view to regulating specific social relations — e.g. economic relations (Bunt and de Roos, 1983). Instrumental is not the same as effective: it is an 'attempt' at regulation by means of legislation and its goal is not retribution but rather deterrence. As we are dealing here with criminal legislation, the power actually to act is not given until after the event.

The deterrent effect of such legislation is seen as doubly inherent in the provisions themselves. On the one hand, they express the prohibited nature of the behaviour concerned. On the other, the penalty they contain is expected to act as sufficient deterrent to most people. The former aspect is, of course, highly problematic if the prohibition concerns behaviour that, in itself, reflects generally accepted norms and values, so that the borderline between what is allowed and what is not is not only very finely drawn, but also the result of the policy of the day and open to debate. The latter is mainly a matter of weighing the risk and cost of incurring a penalty against the gains of infringing the law. The larger the 'profit', the less the deterrent effect, especially if the penalty is mild and the risk of prosecution unlikely.

The criminal justice authorities in the Netherlands have had plenty of time to judge both aspects of deterrence in the field of economic crime. There too, prohibited behaviour is deeply rooted in generally accepted economic practices. The perpetrators's goal in itself is legitimate, his means of attaining it, however, prohibited by the state as non-constructive. Such prohibitions are unlikely to be deterrent in the first sense. At the same time, discovery is unlikely, owing to the fact that the behaviour is so widespread, and the penalties mild in comparison with the potential profit, so that the risk is well worth taking.

Pornography, too, is big business, with a gigantic turnover and a well-nigh insatiable market. The police are overworked and understaffed, as are the courts, and priorities lie elsewhere. Drugs and organised crime are Public Enemy Number One at present in Holland, and while there is some indication that money from organised crime goes into the pornography business, the only people likely to be caught are those who sell forbidden pornography under the counter. The penalties, a maximum of three-months imprisonment or a fine of 10,000 guilders, are merely a drop in the ocean when the profit runs into millions and, anyway, the maximum penalty is rarely imposed and fines, not prison sentences, are the rule in such cases. Moreover, penal provisions are unlikely to make much impression on behaviour so well entrenched in the prevailing ideology (see, for a similar argument with regard to rape and white-collar crime, Walsh & Schram, 1980).

The women's movement is not concerned with regulating sexism by attempts to remove its excesses, nor with short-term effects on behaviour, although both would be welcome. Rather, women are concerned with undermining a socially harmful ideology. What they expect from criminal legislation is not to be found at the instrumental level, for they are at pains to point out that their concern is with the symbolic function of penal law (Spaink, 1982; Acker & Rawie, 1982, pp. 134–154).

What is meant by the symbolic function of penal law? Criminal legislation can be symbolic in that it serves to satisfy different — conflicting — interests. This is the sense in which the Norwegian sociologist of law, Aubert (1966), uses the term. The penal provision is not meant to work: it reflects a compromise, with one party satisfied by the symbolic repudiation of certain behaviour and the other by the fact that symbolic is exactly what it is likely to remain. There is rarely any question of effective enforcement for matters of enforcement were never at stake. The penal provision is not so much a symbol as a paper tiger. Now, it may be to the advantage of some (political) interests to work for the symbolic criminalisation of pornography. The Dutch coalition parties, Christian Democrats and right-wing liberals, have been at loggerheads before now on morality issues (abortion, for example). Penal provisions on pornography which will be difficult — perhaps impossible — to enforce effectively are likely to satisfy both and provide a means of saving the coalition an awkward choice: the moral point has been made, but people remain "free to do as they choose" (the liberal election slogan).

Symbolic, however, as used by the women's movement in the pornography debate, has a much more far-reaching meaning: it refers to criminal legislation as a reflection of the norms and values to which great, if not supreme, importance is attached. In principle, murder is a criminal offence, for in our culture the intrinsic value of human life renders it, without exception, worthy of protection by the state; the criminalisation of theft reflects basic notions on property as an unassailable right. Criminalisation is one of the means of stressing the interests which can count on state protection and its moral connotations serve to help establish basic ideas on right and wrong, good and bad. In this sense, it is not so much symbolic, as ideological.

In criminal legislation which is instrumental only, or which is purely symbolic, this ideological function is lacking to a great extent. On the other hand, if criminal law is to have any ideological impact, it must also be instrumental, but credibly so, for the public prosecution of infringement must be accepted as just retribution and effective deterrence: justice done and seen to be done. As it now stands, Dutch criminal law on pornography does not express a social desire to protect the intrinsic dignity and integrity of women. At most, it is a symbolic gesture, morally satisfying to Christian Democratic politics, which makes some pretence at protecting youth and the public order from the destructive influence of sex. And for that reason — and for the reasons set out above — its instrumental effect is likely to be negligible. It is a far cry from an ideological instrument of social change.

Again we are faced with the contradiction in terms. To write off the strategy of criminalisation, however, would be to define social processes, norms and values as static and unchangeable, while we see criminal law as part of a process of social control which is dynamic and by no means dependent on norms and values which are fixed for eternity. But if we are to use criminal law and its enforcement as a means of promoting ideological change, we must exploit its ideological potential. In Holland, this means forgetting about specific provisions on pornography, for their connotation is sexual, their effect mostly party political and their usefulness as a means of combatting either the ideology underlying pornography or its excesses practically nil.

A Possible Way Out

How does one go about exploiting the ideological potential of criminal law? Not by becoming involved in party-political debates in which the issue at stake is the symbolic criminalisation of behaviour, nor by advocating penal provisions intended to function at a purely instrumental level. While it was, of course, never the intention of the women's movement in Holland that this should be the case, as it turned out it was precisely what happened in the pornography debate. To put it plainly, women backed the wrong horse.

It could be said that the very fact of intervention in a criminal legislation debate has some ideological effect, for it puts the issues at stake on the public agenda. In the case of pornography in Holland, however, the women's movement was drawn into an argument concerning fundamental rights and freedoms in which the opponent was allowed to determine the limits and definitions of such rights. The freedom of expression is never an absolute freedom, but liberals and socialists alike were given ample opportunity to argue that the right to read and look at pornography is one of (sexual) self-determination. There were several reasons why women in Holland were unable to produce a compelling counter-argument and themselves set the pace. One was that they answered the sociological and psychological 'proof' of the harmless nature of pornography put forward by their opponents with 'proof' of their own drawn from other research and the debate dwindled into "yes it is", "no it isn't". Secondly, by latching onto the existing laws on pornography, they were unable to widen its definition and lose the sexual connotation. Thirdly, this put them, politically on the wrong side of the fence and unwittingly and unwillingly in the company of right-wing (religious) groups. Fourthly, they failed to see the true nature of the pornography provisions as they stood, and still stand, be it amended.

Section 240 of the Dutch Penal Code is not, and never has been, a means of opposing the violent, dehumanising elements of pornography. Neither is it suited to repressing the excesses which occur during the production stage. Indeed, there is no need for a separate provision in this case, for the Penal Code is amply provided with provisions of a less symbolic and instrumental nature (manslaughter, assault, slave-traffic, kidnapping, forcing a person to endure or participate in immoral acts, blackmail, threatening with violence, etc.). The Dutch Penal Code also contains a number of provisions which are primarily intended to function ideologically (the provisions on discrimination)[6]. At present, they have nothing whatever to do with pornography, they concern insult to groups of people for reasons of race, religion or other fundamental convictions, inciting to hatred, discrimination or violent action against such groups, publishing insulting or discriminatory statements, supporting or participating in discriminatory activities. By extending the scope of these provisions with the words "for reasons of sex", they would also cover pornography in a much wider sense than its current meaning.

There are, of course, a number of pitfalls involved here too. To start with, these provisions were introduced in the Netherlands in order to fulfil international obligations stemming from the Treaty of New York (1966). They are intended to eventually help exterminate racism. Holland is a country where racism is not rife, but it certainly does exist and it is a matter of debate whether criminal law will indeed have the effect intended. However, when this legislation was passed, the public debate at least centred around the real issue. Here too, the matter of the freedom of expression came up. Parliament and press were unanimous in maintaining that the freedom of expression must yield to the right of all people to be protected against discrimination.

In order to actually bring pornography under the anti-discrimination provisions, the Penal Code must be amended yet again. This will involve a great deal of political work on the part of the women's movement. We are still, of

282   *C. Brants and E. Kok*

course, faced with the contradiction-in-terms dilemma, but at least we will
have put the debate on the plane where it belongs and this alone will be a
contribution to any eventual ideological change.

If, and it is a big if, pornography can be brought under the anti-
discrimination legislation, it will again be up to women themselves to ensure
its enforcement. One of the problems will be the definition of discrimination
and insult in connection with pornography. In the Netherlands, only the
Public Prosecutor has the power to instigate prosecution and he therefore determines the limits of criminal jurisprudence. It would be a great improvement
if more women were to fulfil the office of Prosecutor (and judge). The number
of women studying law in the Netherlands is growing and we may be optimistic as to the chances of greater female participation in influential positions
within the criminal justice in the future.

There is also an exception to the rule that the enforcement of criminal justice
depends on the Prosecutor. Section 12 of the Code on Criminal Procedure
allows the victims to request prosecution if the Prosecutor fails to do so. Not
only could this give women the opportunity of provoking trial cases, it could
also be a powerful means of publicity for initiatives on the part of the women's
movement. For, since 1985, not only individual victims but also organisations
promoting interests directly harmed by the decision not to prosecute, come
under section 12[7].

While the anti-discrimination provisions could, perhaps, serve the ideological function to which feminists have pinned their hopes when advocating the
use of penal sanctions, and while their implementation could be a means of
reinforcing their ideological scope, we still have not dealt with the third
dilemma: does the end justify the means?

It is a difficult question. The answer is 'yes', if the end is indeed the eventual
eradication of sexism and the means really are a means of attaining it. But let
us have no illusions about criminal law. At best, it is the lesser of a number of
evils, justifiable only if the basic conditions in society allow for insufficient
informal non-legal remedies. Our concern must be with developing such basic
conditions and with keeping criminal law where it belongs, in the margin,
ultimum remedium with the emphasis on *ultimum*. We must also not allow ourselves to forget that, by invoking the criminal justice system, we are appealing
to forces which are beyond our control and which, given the present political
situation with its increasing reliance on law and order methods, may very well
get out of hand. There remains, therefore, the danger of rubbing the lamp once
too often and letting the genie escape.

Notes

1 A recent incident in the Netherlands is illustrative for the pitfalls which may lie
   ahead. Owing to the shortage of cells created by the intensified 'war against crime',
   the public prosecutor's office is regularly obliged to release suspects from preventive

detention because there is simply no room for them. At the height of the debate on the necessity for five new prisons, the public prosecutor in Amsterdam released the suspect in a particularly offensive and frightening case of sexual assault. Although one of the victims managed to obtain a civil court injunction against the offender during the ensuing public hue and cry, the lasting result was that the shortage of cells in general was taken up by the media as the overriding issue. A new prison will open shortly in Amsterdam. (See Hes, 1985 *Offenders and victims in cases of sexual violence feel used by the Public Prosecutor*).

2 Until 1985,the criminal provisions on pornography read:

"*Section 240 Penal Code.* 1. The person who exhibits, distributes or shows writings, pictures or objects which he knows to be indecent, or who produces, imports, transports, exports or stocks such pictures, writings or objects, or who offers the same, or makes their obtainability known, either publicly or by means of written information, will be subject to a penalty of at most one year imprisonment or a fine of six thousand guilders. The same penalty will apply to the person who knowingly and publicly repeats the content of such writings.

2. The person who exhibits, distributes or shows indecent writings, pictures or subjects of which he has serious reason to believe that they are indecent, or who produces, imports, tranports, exports or stocks such writings, pictures or objects, or who offers the same, or makes their obtainability known, either publicly or by means of written information, will be subject to a penalty of at most six months imprisonment or detention or a fine of six thousand guilders. The same penalty will apply to the person who publicly repeats the content of such writings of which he has serious reason to believe that they are indecent.

3. A person guilty of the offences sub 1, who has made of such offences a profession or custom, will be subject to a penalty of at most two years imprisonment or a fine of ten thousand guilders.

Section 240 bis. 1. The person who offers, gives, temporarily or otherwise, or shows a minor, or whom he has reason to expect that he has not yet reached the age of eighteen years, any indecent writings, picture or object, or by means of terminating a pregnancy will, if the content of those writings or if the picture, object or means are known to him, be subject to a penalty of at most six months imprisonment or a fine of the third category.

2. The same penalty will apply to the person who, in the presence of a minor as above, publicly repeats the content of indecent writings, if that content is known to him.

3. The person who offers, gives, temporarily or otherwise, or shows to a minor as above, any indecent writings, picture or object or any means of terminating a pregnancy, or who publicly repeats in the presence of the same the content of indecent writings, will if he has serious reason to believe that those writings, picture or object are indecent, or that those means are the means of terminating of a pregnancy, be subject to a penalty of at most three months imprisonment or detention or a fine of the second category.

Section 451 bis. 1. A penalty of at most two months detention or a fine of the second category, will apply to:

1: the person who openly exhibits, offers or shows, in places open to public traffic, any writings, of which the readable title, cover or content is likely to stimulate the lust of young persons.

284   *C. Brants and E. Kok*

2: the person who, in places open to public traffic, publicly repeats the content of any writings likely to stimulate the lust of young persons.
2. The same penalty will apply to:
1: The person who offers, gives, temporarily or otherwise, or shows to a minor any writings, picture or object likely to stimulate the lust of young persons.
2: The person who publicly repeats in the presence of a minor the content of such writings".

3 *Chick* is a pornographic magazine, known especially for its personal column, usually accompanied by photgraphs of men and women seeking contact with others of like disposition.

4 Deep Throat is the film in which Linda Lovelace starred. It was shown openly in spite of a ban in order to provoke the trial-case which led to such important jurisprudence.

5 The Bill on pornography was finally passed in Parliament on February 7 1985. In future, the sections of the Penal Code will read:
"*Section 240:* The person who knows or has serious reason to believe that a picture or object is indecent, and nevertheless
1. shows or offers that picture or object in a place open to public traffic, or
2. sends that picture or object to another, but not on request, will be subject to a penalty of at most two months imprisonment or a fine of the third category.
Section 240a: The person who gives, offers or shows to a minor whom he knows or should suspect to be under 16 years of age, any picture or object which can be considered harmful to persons under sixteen years of age, will be subject to a penalty of at most two months imprisonment or a fine of the second category.
Section 240b: The person who distributes or exhibits, or produces for distribution or exhibition, or imports, exports, transports or stocks any image — or information containing the same — of sexual behaviour in which a a person apparently not yet sixteen years of age is involved, will be subject to a penalty of at most three months imprisonment or a fine of the third category".

6 *Section 137d:* The person who publicly, by word of mouth or by means of writings or pictures, incites to hate against or discrimination of others, or to violent action against others or their property, for reasons of race, religion or other fundamental convictions, will be subject to a penalty of, at most, one year imprisonment or a fine of the third category.
Section 137c: The person who publicly, by word of mouth or by means of writings or pictures, wilfully insults a group of persons for reasons of race, religion or other fundamental convictions, will be subject to a penalty of at most one year imprisonment or a fine of the third category.
Section 137e: The person who, other than for reasons of business,
1: publishes an utterance which he knows or has reason to believe to be insulting to a group of persons for reasons of race, religion or other fundamental convictions, or which incites to hate or discrimination of a group of persons for said reasons, or who
2: distributes or stocks with a view to publication, an object which he knows or has reason to believe to contain such an utterance, will be subject to a penalty of at most six months imprisonment or a fine of the third category.
2. If the person guilty of the offences above, has committed them in the course of his occupation, while less than 5 years have passed since a conviction for a similar

offence, he may be banned from holding that occupation.

Section 429 ter: The person who participates in, or provides financial or other support for activities aimed at discrimination of persons for reasons of race, will be subject to a penalty of at most two months detention or a fine of the third category."

7 *Section 12 Code of Criminal Procedure:* 1. If a criminal offence is not prosecuted, or the prosecution therefore dropped, parties with a direct interest may appeal in writing against that decision to the Court of Appeal in the district in which the decision was taken.

2. Parties with a direct interest include legal persons who, considering their aims and actual activities, are given to the promotion of interests such as have been harmed by the decision not to prosecute (further).

References

Acker, H. & Rawie, M. (1982) *Sexueel geweld tegen vrouwen en meisjes*. Ministry for Social Affairs and Employment: The Hague.

Aubert, V. (1966) Some social functions of legislation. *Acta Sociologica* **10**, 99–110.

de Bruyn, J. (1979) *Geschiedenis van de abortus in Nederland*. van Gennep: Amsterdam.

van de Bunt, H. G. & de Roos, Th. (1983) Zwarte toga's contra witte boorden. *Recht en Kritiek* **9**, 6–50.

Doomen, J. (1979) Justitie en het overmannen van vrouwen. *Ars Aequi* **28**, 134–135.

Griffin, S. (1982) *Pornography and Silence, Culture's Revenge against Nature*. Women's Press: London.

Groenendijk, H. (1983) Vrouwelijke sexualiteit uit het kader van pornografie. *Tijdschrift voor Vrouwenstudies* **4**, 352–372.

Hes, J. (1985) Het Openbaar Ministerie als aangeklaagde partij en het straatverbod in kort geding. *Nemesis* **1**, 315–320.

de Hullu, J. (1984) *Strafrechtelijke en sociaal-wetenschappelijke gronden voor de strafbaarstelling van pornografie*. Gouda Quint: Arnhem.

Leuw, E. (1982) De traditionele en feministische visie op (fysieke) sexuele victimisering. *Tijdschrift voor Criminologie* **24**, 257–278.

Marsh, J. C., Geist, A. & Caplan, N. (1982) *Rape and the Limits of Law Reform*. Aubern House: Boston, Massachusetts.

Pitch, T. (1985) Critical Criminology, the Construction of Social Problems and the Question of Rape. *International Journal of the Sociology of Law* **13**, 35–47.

Posthumus, W. H. van de Groot & de Waal, A., Eds (1979) *Van moeder op dochter: de maatschappelijke positie van de vrouw*. Sun: Bijmegen.

Quispel, Y. (1981) Porno nu niet de strafwet halen. *KRI*, Sept./, 9–12.

Samenleving en Criminaliteit, IIeK, 1984/1985, nos 1 and 2.

Schalken, T.M. (1972) *Pornografie en Strafrecht, beschouwingern over het pornografiebegrip eun zijn juridische hanteerbaarheid*. Gouda Quint: Arnhem.

Schalken, T. M. (1974) Tweede interimrapport van de adviescommissie zedelijkheidswetgeving (pornografir en schennis van de eerbaarheid). *Delikt en Delinkwent*, 214–225.

Spaink, K., Ed. (1982) *Pornografie: bekijk 't maar*. van Gennep: Amsterdam.

Vintgens, K. (1983) Porno in tekst en contekst. *Tijdschrift voor Vrouwenstudies* **4**, 406–417.

286   *C. Brants and E. Kok*

Vorrink, L. (1982) De beeldvorming ten aanzien van sexueel geweld. *Tijdschrift voor Criminoligie* **24,** 294–309.

Walsh, M. E. & Schram, D. D. (1980) The victim of white-collar-crime: accuser or accused?. In *White Collar Crime, Theory and Research* (Geis, G. and Stotland, E., Eds). Sage: London, pp. 32–51.

Weis, K. & Weis S. (1975) Victimology and the justification of rape. In *Victimology, a New Focus*, vol. V (Drapkin, S. I. and Viano, E., Eds). Heath: Lexington, Massachusetts, pp. 3–28.

[8]

ADDRESS

THE DECLINE OF THE REHABILITATIVE IDEAL IN AMERICAN CRIMINAL JUSTICE*

FRANCIS A. ALLEN**

THESE COMMENTS DO NOT CONSTITUTE A SET OF PERFECTED CONCLUSIONS; rather, what is being presented is in the nature of an interim report. Because this is true, I do not have a printed text. I shall be speaking very informally, and on the basis of notes.

If there is any one characteristic of modern legal thought more important than any other it is the modern concern with issues of public policy. This has not always been true; at other times other interests appeared to dominate, such as the construction of elegant structures of precedents or questions of the historical validity of legal doctrine. Yet the modern fixation on public policy has not resulted, by and large, in highly sophisticated techniques of policy analysis. There has been much talk about policy science. We have borrowed from other disciplines, such as economics, and have enriched our vocabularies with talk about "cost-benefit ratios." I have no doubt that these accretions to our language have at times added significantly to our thought; although there are times when one almost concludes that the new phrases are chiefly useful to young faculty members demonstrating their command of fashionable language in their tenure articles. We do not do very much by way of auditing the performance of regulatory schemes initiated by the law, with the result that often we literally do not know what we are doing. Nor are we doing much to find out.

One of the areas of policy analysis insufficiently explored involves the impact of new knowledge on the law. The questions have not been ignored, as is demonstrated by the interests of a group of American legal historians in the impact of new technology on the law in nineteenth-century America. Yet I think most would agree that we are far from being able to state useful generalizations about the distribution of knowledge in this society, and about the tortuous course taken by knowledge as it moves out of the laboratory and the library and eventually to the court house or legislative hall.

What may be even more surprising is that in a democratic society we have not really been much concerned about the impact of changes in public attitudes and opinion on the law. One of the most forthright discussions of these matters is still Dicey's LAW AND PUBLIC OPINION IN ENGLAND,[1] but that book was originally published in 1905. Among other things, Dicey argues that in many areas the law tends to lead a life of its own, that new law is to some

---

* This Address was delivered as the Twelfth Cleveland-Marshall Fund Lecture, by Professor Allen on April 13, 1978, at the Cleveland-Marshall College of Law of the Cleveland State University.
** A.B., Cornell College; L.L.B., Northwestern University; Edson R. Sunderland Professor of Law, University of Michigan Law School.
[1] A. DICEY, LAW AND PUBLIC OPINION IN ENGLAND (1905).

extent generated by old law, and that in many instances there is no such thing as *a* public opinion, but rather many public opinions involving different segments of the community, only some of which are influential on legal development.

The decline of what I have called the rehabilitative ideal seems to me to offer a prime opportunity to consider the effect of changes in public attitudes on the policy of the law. I say a prime opportunity because we are talking about a series of ideas that has dominated thought about criminal justice in this country throughout most of the 20th century. Indeed, the origins of these ideas lie in the previous century and in even earlier history. Within the space of a single decade, perhaps less, there has been a precipitous falling off of support for the rehabilitative ideal in almost all segments of public opinion. This, of course, raises the question of why this has occurred and what its significance may be.

Consideration of these events may contribute to modern thought about public policy in the criminal law. If one, for example, is interested in maintaining or expanding a rehabilitative approach to penal treatment, it may be important to understand what limitations on such efforts are imposed by the present temper of public opinion. But there is another justification, and I confess that this has become increasingly interesting to me. The decline of the rehabilitative ideal may be of importance not only to those professionally interested in problems of crime and punishment, but also to those who may find in it insights about the society of which the criminal law is a part. More and more scholars in the universities are discovering that a useful approach to the understanding of contemporary society is to see it through the eyes of the legal system. Holmes, as usual, has the exact phrase. "The law is a small subject," he wrote, "though . . . it leads to all things. . . ."[2]

I now come to the unhappy point in the lecture in which it is necessary to define terms. Nothing is better calculated to produce glazed looks on the face of an audience. It reminds me of an incident when I was a young, and, of course, a brash, law teacher. I was sitting at lunch at the Northwestern University Law School with some of my elderly colleagues, that is to say, persons in their late thirties and forties. The conversation was going full tilt when, very rudely, I interrupted one of my venerable colleagues to say: "But you certainly can't talk about that without defining your terms." My wonderful friend, Professor Nat Nathanson, whom I had confronted, smiled his lovely smile and said: "Define the terms and kill the conversation." He then proceeded without taking further notice of my presence. I hope that the modest effort I shall make in defining my terms will not kill the communication between us; for I believe that a word needs to be said about the meaning of the phrase "the rehabilitative ideal." My efforts at definition will be brief and not very elaborate.

When I speak of the rehabilitative ideal I refer to the notion that the sanctions of the criminal law should or must be employed to achieve fundamental changes in the characters, personalities, and attitudes of convicted offenders, not only in the interest of the social defense, but also in the interests of the well-being of the offender himself. This appears to be a

---

[2] THE HOLMES-EINSTEIN LETTERS 37 (J. Bishop ed. 1964).

simple idea, and it may be difficult to understand how it has come to be the source of such vigorous public controversies.

Actually the formula, as stated, doesn't tell one much. Obviously, it makes a great deal of difference how important one regards the rehabilitative object in comparison to other purposes of criminal punishment. Is rehabilitation to be regarded as the predominant purpose of criminal treatment or even the exclusive justification for criminal sanctions, as has, in fact, been asserted by some enthusiasts during the twentieth century; or is rehabilitation to be taken as only one of the goals of criminal punishment, other goals including things like the deterrence of crime, incapacitation of dangerous people, or even the expression of our feelings of moral indignation produced by the crime that was committed? The difference is great, for the latter view may result in our giving up rehabilitative aspirations in cases in which other objectives are thought to be of vital importance.

It also makes a great deal of difference about how one views the techniques of rehabilitation. Those techniques have in the past included the use of the whip and the club. On the other hand, the techniques espoused have included depth psychology, or drastic therapies like psycho-surgery, behavior modification, and the like. On still other occasions the rehabilitative techniques have included efforts to overcome illiteracy and training in job skills. It follows that although the general formula may be stated with some ease, there are many varieties of the rehabilitative ideal.

As was said earlier, there have been major defections from the rehabilitative ideal in very recent years. Until the mid-sixties or even the early seventies, the rehabilitative ideal was, by all odds, the dominant American theory of penal treatment. The support in the public and on the bench was perhaps not as enthusiastic as in the academic halls, but there was a wide consensus that the objective of criminal justice, however infrequently attained, ought to be rehabilitation. There are various ways the dominance of the idea can be illustrated. Almost all of the characteristic innovations in criminal justice in the 20th century are related to the rehabilitative ideal: the juvenile court, systems of probation and parole, the indeterminate sentence, the promise (if not the reality) of therapeutic programs in the prisons. Moreover, the rehabilitative ideal dominated the research interests of scientific criminology in this country. Typically, criminology was not much interested in such issues as the definition of criminal behavior, or the procedures by which criminality is determined. The criminologist took the convicted offender as a given, and proceeded to think about how a different and better person could be made out of him. This is one of the interesting instances of how an over-arching ideology determines what kinds of questions will be researched. One of the consequences of this was that until the last decade there has been no comprehensive effort to research the question of the deterrent efficacy of legal sanctions. A good deal of work in this area is now being done, but most of it has its origins in the last decade.

We, today, suddenly find ourselves in a situation in which there has been a massive desertion from the rehabilitative ideal and its assumptions. The significant thing is not so much that the general public has abandoned the rehabilitative ideal, or that the media have, or that the politicians have. In this country about once every seven years, since the American Revolution, we

150   *CLEVELAND STATE LAW REVIEW*   [Vol. 27: 147

suddenly discover that we have a crime problem. And each time we discover it we forget that it ever happened before. But the significance of this occasion is not simply that we are agitated about high crime rates, but that there has been a desertion of the rehabilitative ideal by the academic community; and that has not happened before.

This certainly is not to say that the rehabilitative ideal is dead. Some years ago it was fashionable to say that God is dead — a casualty of the modern world. The Association of the Bar of the City of New York published a book in the early 1970s with a question for its title, Is LAW DEAD?.[3] I do not assert that the rehabilitative ideal is dead; but I do assert that it is languishing. There are many groups in the community that support it with about the same undiluted enthusiasm as in the past; the Quakers, for example, have long identified with the rehabilitative ideal and with reservations continue to do so. There is substantial support for the continuation of the old ideology from the "helping professions," many members of which may be said to have a kind of vested interest in its maintenance. The fact is that hundreds of millions of dollars are being appropriated by Congress for rehabilitative objectives. It may be that there is something fundamental in American character that embraces the notion of rehabilitation.

Yet however casual one's interest in the system of criminal justice may be, I think that one can hardly miss the massive desertions from the standard of the rehabilitative ideal. It shows up in all sorts of ways. There are sentencing statutes now being passed expressly stating that rehabilitative considerations shall not be taken into account with reference to certain kinds of sentencing. It is really inconceivable that such provisions could have been enacted as recently as ten years ago. There is a great impatience with discretion in sentencing; a great desire for something called certainty in sentencing; a great impatience with high levels of criminality; strong support for vigorous measures of law enforcement; strong support for the notion of mandatory minimum sentences; and strong support for the elimination of the parole function altogether. All these things are grist for the mill in the new age that has followed the dominance of the rehabilitative ideal.

So there has been a precipitous and remarkable shift of opinion, more thorough-going than anything I can recall over a comparable period involving significant issues of legal policy. It will be useful if we can gain some notions about the "why" of these occurences.

There is a book written by a lawyer-sociologist, Anthony Platt and entitled THE CHILD SAVERS[4] that may be helpful in getting into the question. Some of you may know the book. The title is sardonic. The book consists of Professor Platt's version of the history of the juvenile court movement; it is angry and tendentious and fun because it is so angry. Platt's theory is that, in its origins, the juvenile court is a product of the milk-and-water values of the wives of the prosperous Chicago bourgeoisie in the last quarter of the 19th century, which women insisted on imposing those values on the children of the immigrant population. What was true of the origins is true of the subsequent history of

---

[3] Is LAW DEAD? (E. Rostow ed. 1971).
[4] A. PLATT, THE CHILD SAVERS (1977).

the juvenile court: a continuing effort to impose middle-class standards on the poor and oppressed groups within society.

It is no part of my purpose to analyze or quarrel with this thesis. But in thinking about the Platt book this interesting question arises: Can you ever have a viable, flourishing rehabilitative ideal in a society unless the dominant segments of the society are confident of their values, so confident that they are willing to use the public force to impose them on society as a whole? And I wonder if that is not likely to be true also, of any society that would satisfy the requirements of Professor Platt.

At this point I am going to advance a proposition. It is an analytic proposition, not an empirical statement, and relates to what characteristics a society must possess in order to maintain a flourishing rehabilitative ideal. Then I shall try to test that proposition by looking at two very different societies in which the rehabilitative ideal flourished. Finally, I shall ask whether those conditions are satisfied in modern America. My proposition is in two parts. First, you cannot have a flourishing rehabilitative ideal unless the society as a whole has a strong faith in the malleability of human behavior and human character. It ought not to be supposed that no society could exist without that faith. The Calvinist society of Geneva with beliefs in predestination and the fixity of behavior types might constitute one example. A society founded on the assumptions of the Italian School of criminology may provide a more modern possibility. Lombroso, the leader of that School, talked about "born criminals" and viewed crime as the product of basic biological constitutional factors. If one accepts those assumptions, then penal policy is likely to be largely incapacitative, not rehabilitative in character; and in fact members of the Italian School espoused extensive use of capital punishment. There is something inherently anti-rehabilitationist about capital punishment. It is more likely, however, that this lack of faith will be expressed in somewhat different ways in the present age: that is, a society which at least in theory retains its belief that people can be made better, but which also reveals a fundamental skepticism about the capacity of its institutions to produce desirable changes in human character and behavior. This is more likely the realistic situation we shall have to survey.

Thus, one of the analytic conditions for the rehabilitative ideal is a faith in the malleability of human beings. The second proposition is that there must be a sufficient consensus of values to permit practical agreement on what it means to be rehabilitated. An example is in order. The well-known psychiatrist, Eric Fromm puts this case in one of his books. A patient comes to a psychiatrist complaining of neurotic symptoms, and the therapist discovers a deep conflict in him. The patient has been educated as an architect and his dearest wish is to practice that profession. His father, however, insists that the young man enter the family business which is facing economic difficulties. And the son sacrifices his own inclinations and aspirations and gives up his profession. The question is, of what does the cure consist in this case? What does it mean to be rehabilitated? How do you distinguish the cure from the disease? Should the objective of therapy be to cause the young man to adapt to the decision he has made in order that he can function effectively in the family business; or should the objective be to strengthen the resolve of the young man to break away from his family ties and proceed with the realization of his own ambitions?

There is a value choice to be made. Determining the ends of rehabilitation is surrounded by value choices. And the second condition for a flourishing rehabilitative ideal is, not unanimity of values in society, but a workable consensus on what it means to be rehabilitated.

As I indicated, I shall look at twó societies in which the rehabilitative ideal strongly established itself. The first is 19th century America, particularly pre-Civil War America. This was the great age of reform in America, reform associated not only with penal matters but with almost all aspects of life. This is not to say that the rehabilitative ideal was invented in the United States, it most clearly was not. One finds expressions of the rehabilitative ideal in the Old Testament, particularly the assertion that the purpose of chastisement is to make the victim a better person. The idea is repeated in the Greek plays, in Plato, and in the writings of medieval churchmen. Versions of the idea are repeated again and again in the reformist writings in the 18th century both in France and England.

Nevertheless, there is real basis for saying that the first practical institutional expressions occurred in the United States. The notion of the malleability of institutions was widely discussed in the Jacksonian period. Illustrative is a famous lecture by Ralph Waldo Emerson, entitled, interestingly enough, "Man the Reformer".[5] Emerson says that "[i]n the history of the world the doctrine of Reform had never such scope as at the present hour [present being 1841]. . . . [There is] not a kingdom, town, statute, rite, calling, man, or woman, but is threatened by the new spirit."[6] The spirit he refers to is, of course, the spirit of reform.

Looking specifically at the area of the criminal law, one will discover that the modern penitentiary system was founded in the states of Pennsylvania and New York. The central concept of the penitentiary system was, however bizarre the methods employed to achieve it, that criminal penalties should be imposed for the purposes of improving the character, the attitudes, the behavior of persons subjected to penal treatment. Of course, the closer you get to a society the more complicated it appears. This applies to generalizations about the reformist character of ante-bellum America. The fact is, for example, that a good many people associated with the penitentiary movement, and particularly those who really knew something about it, were skeptical about the reform capacities of the penitentiary system. And if one looks at the works of novelists like Hawthorne and Melville, he finds a spirit being expressed quite different from a vibrant enthusiasm about the possibilities of malleability of human beings, for changes for the better. This is true, and yet it seems quite accurate to say that one of the dominant strands of the 19th century America was faith in the malleability of human beings for the better, not only in the criminal law, but generally.

Did early 19th century America have a consensus of values that made rehabilitation feasible? It was a pluralistic society; there were conflicts in values then as now, and in some areas the conflicts were as intense as those

---

[5] R. EMERSON, NATURE ADDRESSES AND LECTURES (1886).
[6] *Id.* at 228.

today. But there were certain kinds of accord that can be safely identified; and one of the most interesting of these is the high regard expressed for the family. The 19th century, some historians have said, was a period in which there was a great surge of domesticity; that is, a rising evaluation of the importance of the nuclear family. The family remained largely immune from the attacks of the times on almost all other institutions. Some attacks on the family came from the extreme fringes of the feminist movement, but even that movement was, by and large, predicated on the assumption of the essential importance of the family and its sanctity. This is important, for if you look at the juvenile court statute in your state today, very likely you will find that the sanctions imposed by the court are directed to be as near as may be to those imposed by wise parents in a family setting. The notion of the family as a model of rehabilitation has been very important. So in summary it can be said that early 19th century America was a society in which the rehabilitative ideal found strong expression. It was a society that revealed faith in the malleability of human nature, and one in which there was a workable consensus about what rehabilitation means.

The second example of a society in which the rehabilitative ideal has flourished is one of a very different kind. I refer to modern China. That country may be said to be the clearest and most enthusiastic adherent to its own version of the rehabilitative ideal in the world today. Modern China is a society that probably believes more strongly in the malleability of human nature than any other. The official line is "Every peasant a sage." One of the manifestations of this is the remarkable faith that that society has in education — the belief that the way to solve social problems is through the devices of education. I shall not pause because of passing time to go into the details, but my assertion is that modern China, like early 19th century America, is a society that reveals those characteristics specified for a thriving rehabilitative ideal: faith in malleability of human nature and accord on the values relating to what it means to be rehabilitated.

The interesting question, of course, is whether those conditions are now satisfied in this society. If they are missing, this may give some clues about why the rehabilitative ideal has declined in these times. What are the institutions that we have traditionally relied on to change human nature for the better? The answer would certainly include the family, the schools, religion, and what might broadly be called therapy. This is not meant to be an exhaustive list. My gloomy conclusion is that in each of these areas there has been a precipitous loss of confidence in the capacity of the institution to make desirable changes in human character.

First, the family. We talk about family dissolution, violence within the family, child abuse, spousal violence. We note the fact, for it is a fact, that the family has suffered in importance because many of its functions have been taken over by other agencies, and quite deliberately so. The family has lost significance as an economic unit. There are not very many of us engaged in family farming these days, in an undertaking in which every member of the family has an economic role to play. We have delegated to public schools, to government, important aspects of the family — to adolescent peer groups, to self-styled experts on child-rearing and marital counseling. The paternalism of government is so pervasive that we almost forget that it occurs. One of the best illustrations of this can be found in the current discussions of the proposal of the Federal Trade Commission to regulate advertising directed to children. I certainly do not want to devalue the merits of that proposal, for there may be a very good case to be made for it. I am inclined to think that there is. But in the Task Force Report of the Commission, there is a passage which, when thought about, boggles the mind. The statement is by a psychiatrist. The reason for government regulation, he says, is that if the parent tries to control what his children see on television, there will be an unhappy confrontation between parent and child. The notion that it is the function of government, and the federal government at that, to introduce itself between parent and child in the interests of family harmony, is a concept a little hard to accomodate.

One can also say that there has been a very significant change in the definition of what the family is. It makes a great deal of difference whether you regard the family as a kind of hierarchy in which there are mandated mutual obligations or whether you look on the family as a kind of arrangement of convenience to advance the personal self-satisfactions of each member of the family group. The modern literature on the family indicates that the second definition is becoming the dominant mode. With that being the dominant mode, one is not likely to put many chips on the family as a dynamic force for creating desirable traits of character and attitudes. The family is a tough institution, and it is not ready to be buried; but if we compare the role of the family as an instrumentality for producing desirable character today with that in earlier periods, we shall certainly find significant changes since the high point in domesticity reached in the 19th century.

What about the public school? It is the American tradition that public schools are a marvelous instrumentality for producing the kind of character that makes a democratic society possible. That faith begins at least with Thomas Jefferson and includes many 19th century reformers like Horace Mann. Is that the aspiration we hold for the public school today? One of the things most distressing today is not so much that citizens will not vote for schools levies, but the decline in our aspirations for the schools, the decline in our confidence in what the schools can accomplish. Instead of looking at the public schools as that great instrumentality for making the democratic way possible, the most we now demand, and that very tentatively, is that high school students shall have acquired basic literacy before graduating. And there are a great many public school people who say that that demand is too severe, and that all kinds of evil things can occur if you try to enforce it. This is in sharp contrast to the Chinese view of education as a solution to all problems. Time does not permit me to discuss religion. I am interested in the implications of the "born again" movement, but I shall not pause to talk about them.

What about therapy? This is a hard and complicated issue. It is certainly true that the kinds of therapy directed to making people adjust to their circumstances is not in great repute among young people in these times. On the other hand, we are afflicted by a kind of pervasive psychologism in this country which oozes out of television talk shows and situation comedies and in a whole literature of self-improvement, written, however, by persons other than the self to be improved. This psychologism performs the alchemy of transforming what are basically fundamental moral and ethical issues or basic issues of public policy into occasions for therapeutic manipulation. Despite the decline in the rehabilitative ideal, I see no corresponding decline in this pervasive psychologism. On the other hand, this kind of psychologism is directed to providing ease, comfort and excuse. It is not directed to bringing people together for the purpose of achieving major social objectives.

This does not present an inspiring view of the modern world. I am saying that there has, in fact, developed in this country a serious loss in the vibrancy of expectations about the capacity of our institutions to affect human character and behavior for the better. I also conclude that there has been a decline in the consensus of values relevant to the ends of rehabilitation, even though I shall not be able to develop that point in detail. Whatever the intellectual case against the rehabilitative ideal may be (and there is a case to be made) the decline in the rehabilitative ideal is not primarily the product of the case made. The decline is much more closely related to various cultural phenomena, most of which are not directly associated with criminal justice at all.

And so we enter a new era. It is an era in which we are very much concerned about granting discretion to public officials. This is one of the legacies of Viet Nam and Watergate. It is an era in which we are very much concerned in seeing that criminal sentences are certain, that criminal penalties are vigorously imposed. No doubt many of these tendencies are well justified by the circumstances of the times. But we need to understand that every stance that one takes toward a complex social issue has its own distinctive and peculiar pathologies. We ought not to think that in choosing a stance one can avoid fundamental difficulties. And the new stance in criminal justice today produces such difficulties. For example, if you say that it is a bad thing (and it is) to impose widely different penalties on two people who have done the same thing, one is recognizing a genuine problem of injustice that has caused deep concern, and properly so. But the other side of the coin is that there is another kind of injustice that results from providing the same penalty to persons who have done different things. It brings to mind the statement of Justice Frankfurter in a different context: "[T]here is no greater inequality than the enforced equality of unequals."[7] And one of the problems of present sentencing schemes is that in the effort to avoid disparities resulting from punishing people differently who have done the same thing, we may now tend to punish people the same way who have committed crimes in very different circumstances. The possibilities of legal definitions being made sufficiently precise to avoid that problem are very remote.

Maybe we don't know very much about how to make prisoners better — I think we don't. But the whole history of the prison indicates that we know a great deal about how to make them worse; so that even if the rehabilitative ideal is rejected, no sane society can avoid the problem of how to mitigate the harms created by its own penal efforts. We are going to have to worry about this unless we are simply blind. That means that some of the same concerns

---

[7] FRANKFURTER, *The Zeitgeist and the Judiciary*, in LAW AND POLITICS 6 (A. MacLeish & E. Prichard, Jr. eds. 1971).

that were rampant during the dominance of the rehabilitative ideal will have to be considered again.

There is another thing, and with this I shall conclude. I was one of those who vigorously criticized the rehabilitative ideal, and I remain a critic of many of its modern manifestations. But one of the things the rehabilitative ideal did was to focus attention on the individual human being caught up in the system of criminal justice. The question is, if you forswear the rehabilitative ideal, where will the impetus come from to advance the essential decency of the system? Many of the present tendencies tend toward a kind of war theory of criminal justice. We are really not dealing with individuals, according to this view, but with the "criminal classes". Mr. Nixon talked about a war between the "peace forces" and the "criminal forces" — there is a great deal of this ideology at work in the modern period. One of the consequences of the rehabilitative ideal was that there were compassionate people in institutions concerned about individual people. And even if they didn't succeed in affecting the recidivism rate, every so often they did useful things for individuals. Where is this impulse to come from in the future? I believe no matter how heinous the crime committed by the offender, we as a society cannot afford to deny him opportunities for self-improvement. I say those opportunities must be provided, that compassion and decency require that we do, and that this is true whether we embrace the rehabilitative ideal or not. I have a feeling too, that it would probably be a good thing if, now that we have become innoculated against the extravagant claims made on behalf of rehabilitation, we went back to the drawing board again and looked at some sorts of peripheral things like employment training to see if, just possibly, we might be able to accomplish something a little like rehabilitation in some cases. It may be possible in this way to succeed very modestly in rehabilitating the rehabilitative ideal.

[9]

Crime, Punishment, and the Decline of Liberal Optimism

Ronald Bayer

Postwar American liberalism was an optimistic ideology assuming the possibility of resolving the problems of the social order within the context of capitalism. That optimism has now been shattered, with liberals exhibiting great pessimism about the possibility of fashioning policy that can meet the challenge of the times. In this essay, this transformation is traced through an analysis of the shifting perspective of liberalism on crime and punishment. A review of the journals of liberal opinion between 1945 and 1975 reveals a growing recognition of the seriousness of urban crime and a profound shift from the rehabilitative ideology to a more punitive response to criminals. The distinction between conservative social thought and the liberal critique of that outlook has thus begun to vanish.

American liberal thought has held out the possibility of resolving the problems of the social order within the context of advanced capitalism. It has brought to these problems the Enlightenment faith in the perfectability of man, the American dream of a "new Adam," and a belief in the utility of applying scientific rationality to policy making. In short, as a system of belief American liberalism has been optimistic, asserting not only the necessity of social reform and melioration but their possibility as well.

At its height, liberalism presented itself vigorously and self-confidently. Nothing reflected this mood so clearly as the dismissal of conservative and pessimistic formulations as merely backward, irrational, and selfish. Lionel Trilling captured this spirit in his introductory remarks to *The Liberal Imagination*:

> In the United States at this time liberalism is not only the dominant but even the sole intellectual tradition. For it is the plain fact that nowadays there are no conservative or reactionary ideas in general circulation. . . . This does not mean, of course, that there is no impulse to conservatism or to reaction. . . . But the conservative impulse and the reactionary impulse do not, with some ecclesiastical exceptions, express themselves in ideas but only in action or in irritable mental gestures which seek to resemble ideas.[1]

RONALD BAYER: Associate in Policy Studies, Institute of Society, Ethics and the Life Sciences, Hastings Center, Hastings-on-Hudson, New York.

1. Lionel Trilling, *The Liberal Imagination* (Garden City, N.Y.: Doubleday Anchor, 1950), p. vii.

Having shed the limitations of nineteenth century individualism and joined Keynesian economic theory with a nonideological, pragmatic commitment to social welfare programs, liberalism proclaimed its capacity to mobilize the political and intellectual resources necessary for social and economic reconstruction in the period immediately following World War II. Not only could liberalism generate a critical analysis of American social life and institutions, but it could also fashion policies designed to achieve changes consonant with that analysis.

The mood of self-confidence has been shattered. More than three decades after the end of World War II, liberalism appears to have lost its sense of vision, of mission. It is not simply that liberals seem incapable of formulating policy directed at resolving problems that their analysis of society has highlighted; more important, they lack a sense of confidence regarding the efficacy of their proposed interventions. As caution and pessimism have replaced optimism, liberalism has lost not only its vigor, but its luster as well.

In this essay I will examine this transformation as it has affected liberal social thought about crime and punishment. Because the problem of crime has come increasingly to haunt urban life, it presents a significant example of the difficulty liberals have faced in their efforts to respond to grave social problems. Because the question of the appropriate social response to the criminal has always been of deep concern to liberals, the changing attitude toward punishment provides a clear example of the collapse of the liberal faith in its capacity to fashion effective social policies and institutions. It is the exhaustion of the rehabilitative ideology, which was associated for so long with the liberal posture on crime and punishment, that marks this change.

As a way of tracing the course of liberal social thought, I have chosen to examine the writings on crime and punishment in six journals of opinion that have been identified with the various currents of postwar liberalism: *Commentary, Commonweal, The Nation, The New Republic, The Progressive,* and *The Reporter.* Editorials, articles, and book reviews published between 1945 and 1975 were read to determine not only what was said, but also how statements were presented. It was the language, the diction, and the tone of this material that most engaged my attention.[2]

OF CRIMES

The desire to probe both the social structure and the personality of the individual law breaker to gain a greater understanding of the causes of crime is explicable primarily in terms of the liberal belief that only such understanding can make possible the suppression of crime and restoration of social peace.

2. All citations in the *Reader's Guide to Periodical Literature* related to crime and punishment that were indexed between 1945 and 1975 were read for this study. *The Progressive,* which has something of a regional flavor, was included even though it was not indexed in the *Reader's Guide* until after 1973.

Crime, Punishment, and the Decline of Liberal Optimism 171

The possibility of such understanding seemed plausible as sociologists, criminologists, and psychologists entered the twentieth century confident about the prospect of applying the canons of science to human affairs. In the belief that a scientific understanding of crime was both necessary and, in principle, attainable, and in the belief in the desirability and possibility of formulating rational policies derived from such knowledge, liberalism exhibited its faith in the promise of the social sciences. It is this that explains the characteristic concern of liberals with the "root causes" of crime. As Sybelle Bedford wrote, in *The Nation*, "To punish criminals without attempting to understand them or to change the soil which continues to produce them is as dangerous as it is shortsighted."[3]

In this perspective, the personal guilt of the criminal was of relatively little interest. Indeed, it was precisely in the extent to which liberals were to de-emphasize the moral categories traditionally associated with the discussion of crime that they were to distinguish themselves from conservative authors.

> It is vain to try to write about the particular motivation of an individual who succumbs and commits a crime. The general public maladies that lead or tempt to crime are everybody's fault to the degree that each could, with justly demanded effort, work against the general demoralizing conditions.[4]

Thus, if there was blame to be attributed, it was shifted from the criminal—the target of traditional moral discourse—to the society as a whole. "It is virtually impossible to think of anyone or any agency that must not take a share of the blame."[5] The concept of blame was transformed from a claim against the criminal into a demand that the community itself change.

At times, the attempt to unravel the dilemma of criminality led to suggestions that the criminal is merely a distorted reflection of American society "whose culture is frankly materialistic, predatory and acquisitive, . . . frequently draw[ing] an extremely tenuous line between the legitimate and the illegitimate."[6] More typically, however, liberal authors focused on the conditions of lower-class life, especially conditions in the urban ghettos.[7] Economic deprivation—specifically, chronic unemployment—was causally linked with crime against property.[8] Such crime was perceived as an instrument for acquiring goods that could not be obtained legally, and, furthermore, as an expression of rebellion against the order of things.

During the early 1970s, for example, when American social life and institutions had been subjected to protests and to demonstrations against the war in

3. Sybelle Bedford, "Generations on the Gallows," *Nation*, Dec. 2, 1973, p. 395.
4. "Crime Waves and Scapegoats," *Commonweal*, Aug. 9, 1946, p. 396.
5. "More Crime," *Commonweal*, May 9, 1952, p. 109.
6. Alfred Hassler, "The Best Is Still a Prison," *Nation*, Dec. 11, 1954, p. 515.
7. See, for example, Robert Sherill, "A Talk with Ramsey Clark: Justice in a Torn Nation," *Nation*, Dec. 7, 1970, p. 588.
8. See, for example, Frank Remington, "The Challenge of Crime," *New Republic*, May 20, 1967, p. 40; TRB, "Crime Fighting," *New Republic*, Nov. 11, 1974, p. 4.

Vietnam, with the memory of ghetto rebellions still fresh, editors of *The Nation* responded to the statement that lower-class crime was merely a form of primitive social protest by describing it as "a primitive form, but nevertheless protest."[9] Not only property crime but also assault and murder could be seen from this perspective. Commenting on the attack by two young black men on Senator Stennis in Washington, D.C., the editor of *The Nation* argued, "In a predominantly racist acquisitive society like ours the lunatic fringe of the underdog population will not only rob but kill to satisfy the hatreds that society has bred in them."[10]

The main current of liberal thought tended to stress the social roots of crime, but there was considerable interest, especially in the decade between the mid-1950s and the mid-1960s, in the psychological bases of crime. This was in part the result of efforts to explain the persistence of crime in societies where, it was assumed, the socioeconomic conditions associated with criminality in the United States no longer prevailed. Terence Morris wrote, in *The Nation*, "The problem of crime is scarcely new; what is new is the realization that in a society such as modern Britain, with its 'welfare state,' the simple theory that crime stems from poverty, economic inequity and their associated evils is no longer tenable."[11]

Another important factor in the interest in the psychodynamic dimensions of crime was the ascendant status of American psychiatry in the postwar period. Psychological variables were especially valuable in explaining the seemingly senseless violence associated with murder[12] and sexual offenses.[13] In their capacity to demystify the horrendous, psychiatric explanations provided the kind of knowledge that could permit the reassertion of reason in the face of the disturbingly unreasonable. Yet although there was considerable support in the liberal journals for extending the influence of psychiatric explanations of crime, never, even in the period of psychiatry's greatest popularity, did psychiatric explanations rival socioeconomic interpretations.

The tendencies noted above took on sharper definition in the discussion of juvenile crime. Not only because of the danger such crime seemed to pose, but also because it seemed to clash with conventional expectations of how the young should behave, the search for explanations of juvenile delinquency often took on anguished tones. If the criminality of the adult represented

9. "The Price of Repression," *Nation*, Aug. 31, 1970, p. 131.

10. "The Logic of Inversion," *Nation*, Feb. 19, 1973, p. 229.

11. Terence Morris, "Social Values and the Criminal Act," *Nation*, July 4, 1959, p.6. See also Laurence Malkin, "Britain's Aristocrats of Crime," Sept. 22, 1966, pp. 46–48; Michael Fooner, "Crime and Affluence: The Case of the Culpable Victim," *Nation*, Mar. 6, 1967, pp. 307–08.

12. Hale Champion, "The Nice Murder: Search for a Motive," *Nation*, Mar. 22, 1958, pp. 255–57.

13. Ralph Branacle and F. Lovell Bixby, "How to Treat Sex Offenders," *Nation*, Apr. 6, 1957, p. 295. See also "Sex-Killer at 18," *Nation*, June 8, 1957, p. 49; Robert Coles, "Anatomy of Perversion," *New Republic*, Oct. 16, 1965, pp. 25–27.

Crime, Punishment, and the Decline of Liberal Optimism   173

social failure, how much more so was this case with the person who had
barely entered puberty. In an otherwise unsympathetic report on four boys
who had engaged in acts of brutality and violence, Marya Mannes wrote, in
The Reporter, "We must find the causes of this susceptibility in the young,
this vacuum that can be filled with violence, this boredom that can be relieved
by the suffering of others. What is it that they miss and do not have."[14]

As was the case with criminality more generally, many efforts to explain
juvenile delinquency merely entailed an undifferentiated listing of the full
range of social problems. From war and militarism on an international scale[15]
to the threatened and precarious structure of the family on the most intimate
level, it was an "interaction of staggeringly complex and multiform social
factors"[16] that was perceived as producing the young criminal. So closely was
the delinquent linked with social malaise that one writer in *The Nation* entitled his article "The Delinquent Society or Juvenile?"[17] "The forces impel-
ling delinquency pervade our whole social structure. . . . A theory that could
be used most profitably by investigators is that juveniles in America are growing up in a delinquent society."[18] Like the argument that adult criminality was
but a reflection of societal norms, juvenile delinquency was depicted as mirroring American life: "For the heart of this problem does not lie in defects
which are alien to the mainstream of an otherwise wholesome society. On the
contrary, juvenile delinquency in America is largely a reflection of institutions, values and ideals which typify our way of life."[19]

As in efforts to discover specific factors contributing to the prevalence of
criminality among adults, great emphasis was placed on the role of poverty
and racism in the "creation" of juvenile delinquency. But when one aspect of
the socioeconomic situation was stressed, it was unemployment. Like a *leitmotif*, the effect of joblessness ran through discussions attempting to make
sense of both long-term trends in crime among juveniles and the apparent
periodic surges in such activity. A comparison of two editorials in *The Nation*
written some twenty-five years apart reveals the persistence of both this
theme and the language used to present it. Writing about juvenile delinquency
among Mexican-American youths in Los Angeles in 1950, Carrey
McWilliams noted,

14. Marya Mannes, "The Night of Horror in Brooklyn," *Reporter*, Jan. 27, 1955, p. 26.
15. See Charles J. Dutton, "Young Destroyers," *Commonweal*, Sept. 14, 1945, pp. 524–26;
"Youth in a Violent Age," *Commonweal*, Sept. 10, 1954, p. 550.
16. "Juvenile Delinquency," *Commonweal*, Sept. 6, 1957, p. 555.
17. Milton L. Barron, "The Delinquent Society or Juvenile?" *Nation*, June 5, 1954, p. 483.
18. Ibid.
19. Irving Sarnoff, "Bad Boys, Bad Times," *New Republic*, Jan. 8, 1960, p. 12. This type of
document was, however, subject to attack. Albert K. Cohen was extremely critical of "the tempting and widespread tendency to explain delinquency as a natural and obvious consequence of
whatever other features of our society we happen to find objectionable." But even Cohen refers
to delinquency as the product of society. Albert K. Cohen, "The Fortress of Delinquency," *Nation*, Jan. 10, 1959, p. 37.

> The cause of the current acts of juvenile delinquency is not mysterious. The youngsters of many underprivileged groups first to bear hard times are beginning to feel the economic squeeze with their parents unemployed. They are painfully poor and since they in turn find it increasingly difficult to get part time jobs they swarm about the city streets with nothing to do, frustrated in all their desires.[20]

A 1975 article on California once again discussed the effects of the post–Vietnam War economic slump: "As the depression continues juvenile crime may well increase, exacerbating what was a major social problem even before recent hard times began to be felt."[21]

Usually, those emphasizing conditions of economic deprivation did not exhibit antagonism toward explanations stressing familial or psychodynamic orientations. But there were exceptions. Some felt that a stress on more personal characteristics shifted attention from the issue of class, thus obscuring the extent to which juvenile delinquency was an outgrowth of the American social structure. The role of Richard Cloward and Lloyd Ohlin's *Delinquency and Opportunity* in buttressing this antipsychological position is worth noting.[22] Kenneth Keniston was especially critical, in a *Commentary* article, of research inspired by the proposition that "bad families make bad boys":

> The roots of delinquency go beyond the boys and their families to our society, which permits the preconditions of delinquency—social disintegration, deterioration, and marginality—which offers working class children few prospects as dignified, exciting and challenging as truancy, gang warfare, vandalism and theft.[23]

Those who minimized the role of socioeconomic factors tended to suggest that the undeniable overrepresentation of the poor and especially of the black and Hispanic underclass in the official statistics on delinquency was an artifact of police practices. That is, while the juvenile "crimes" of the middle class were processed through unofficial channels and were resolved informally, those of the poor became the target of law enforcement.[24] Reference to delinquency in Scandinavia served to highlight the persistence of juvenile delinquency, even in societies characterized by relative social equality. Even *The Nation*, which normally stressed the relationship between juvenile crime and poverty, published analyses making use of a transnational, transclass approach to delinquency. In "Fagin's Children," the writer contended that ef-

20. Carrey McWilliams, "Nervous Los Angeles," *Nation*, June 10, 1950, p. 570.
21. "Bad Is No Good," *Nation*, June 14, 1975, p. 710.
22. Richard Cloward and Lloyd Ohlin, *Delinquency and Opportunity* (Glencoe, Ill.: Free Press, 1960). See Donald Cook, "Delinquency and the Goods of the World," *New Republic*, Apr. 24, 1961, pp. 21–24.
23. Kenneth Keniston, "Entangling Juvenile Delinquency," *Commentary*, June 1960, p. 491.
24. Milton L. Barron, "Class and Delinquency," *Nation*, Aug. 18, 1956, pp. 143–45; Joseph Margolis, "Rebellion or Delinquency," *Nation*, July 15, 1961, p. 31; Joseph P. Fitzpatrick, "They're Sending Delinquents Back Home," *Commonweal*, Feb. 2, 1973, pp. 395–98.

Crime, Punishment, and the Decline of Liberal Optimism   **175**

forts to see delinquency in terms of economic status created "stereotypes." Such class perspectives tended to inhibit the capacity to see "a *person* with real problems that are both his and ours."[25]

Despite the conflicts between those who stressed sociocultural conditions and those presenting psychodynamic explanations of delinquency, it is clear that virtually all writers in the liberal journals were uncomfortable with the prospect of holding juveniles fully accountable for their crimes. Whether they were seen as the distorted products of deprivation, bad families, or injured psyches, young criminals were "products." The deterministic view of behavior in analyses of the roots of delinquency, while not leading to recommendations for automatic and complete exculpation of delinquents, provided a powerful source of mitigation. Blameworthiness remained, but in attenuated form. There was, however, no room for the harsher notions of personal evil and wickedness.

The focus on root causes had yet another significant consequence. To the extent that crime was perceived as a product of the social order or psychiatric disturbance, the possibility of eliminating such behavior was made contingent on efforts directed beyond the criminal's instant offense. Indeed, characteristic of virtually all liberal writing in the 1950s and 1960s was the view that "law and order" are only attainable as a result of profound social changes.[26] Even suggestions that specific reforms to upgrade the efficiency of the criminal justice system might have a salutary effect on the crime problem were always presented within the context of an argument for more far-reaching changes. Thus, Alexander Bickel wrote in *The New Republic*, "Until we successfully attack the underlying conditions, the crime problem calls for . . . more professional police work. . . . That would be the beginning of a fight if not against the causes of crime at least against its high incidence."[27]

It was the liberal assertion of the primacy of "root causes" that inspired James Q. Wilson's attack in a 1971 issue of *Commentary* magazine. Arguing that such a focus had had disastrous consequences for the capacity to formulate social policies to reduce the level of criminal activity, he noted, "It almost literally became a mark of one's acceptability as a liberal that one would have nothing to do with any of these issues [such as] crime, except to say that the 'only' cure of crime was to 'solve the underlying problems of poverty and racism.' "[28] Declaring such a perspective profoundly mistaken, Wilson went on to say, "Here as with many social problems it is necessary to deal with symptoms *before* one can deal with causes."[29] Three years later, the

25. "Fagin's Children," *Nation*, Oct. 29, 1973, p. 422.

26. For an assessment of this position, see Herbert L. Packer, "Revolving Door Millenium," *New Republic*, Nov. 15, 1969, pp. 24–26.

27. Alexander M. Bickel, "How to Beat a Crime," *New Republic*, Aug. 23, 1969, p. 12. See also Frank Serri, "Conviction Hoax," *Nation*, Nov. 4, 1968, pp. 464–65.

28. James Q. Wilson, "Crime and the Liberal Audience," *Commentary*, January 1971, p. 77.

29. Ibid. Emphasis supplied.

implications of Wilson's argument were made more explicit in his "Crime and the Criminologists," also published in *Commentary*. Distinguishing between "causal" and "policy" analysis, he stated, "Ultimate causes cannot be the object of policy efforts precisely because being ultimate they cannot be changed."[30] Among those unchangeable features associated with crime were the values of the lower class.

That this argument against the primacy of root causes appeared in *Commentary* is not surprising. Of the six journals discussed in this paper, it made the most marked break in the mid-1960s with the traditional liberal posture on a range of sociopolitical issues, including crime and punishment. For some this suggested that *Commentary* was "no longer liberal"—had, in fact, become a major forum for neoconservative thought. For others it reflected a major transformation within liberalism itself.

Given the extent to which the liberal journals exhibited a strong commitment to viewing crime as a reflection of psychological, socioeconomic, and cultural dysfunction in postwar American society, it is significant that crime as a political issue was first pressed by conservative political figures and commentators. The reluctance to confront crime as a discrete problem, the efforts at evasion and denial, as well as the profound discomfort that marked the first attempts by liberals to respond to the conservative challenge reflected liberal uncertainty regarding both the motivations of those who raised the issue and the course public policy would take in dealing with the crimes of the ghettos' poor.

For the most part,[31] direct discussion of the extent of crime before the mid-1960s was restricted to juvenile delinquency[32] and property crime stemming from America's narcotics policies.[33] It was the effort of Barry Goldwater to use the problems of crime and civil disorder in his 1964 presidential campaign that forced liberals to respond. Characteristic of the first commentaries in the liberal journals were efforts to dismiss the statistical indications of a crime wave as an artifact of the police reporting system. Writing in *Commonweal*, Will Sparks[34] acknowledged the emergence of an ill-defined anxiety regarding crime and expressed concern about conservative exploitation of that fear. The fear was not, he claimed, founded upon social reality: "There is no rational reason to believe that city streets have become spectacularly more dangerous in the last three years, or the last thirty."[35] Similarly, George Sha-

30. James Q. Wilson, "Crime and the Criminologists," *Commentary*, July 1974, p. 49.
31. An exception is "Just the Facts," *Commonweal*, Aug. 13, 1954, p. 454.
32. For example, McWilliams, "Nervous Los Angeles"; "Teenage Violence," *Commonweal*, Aug. 31, 1956, pp. 528–29; Virginia P. Held, "What Can We Do about 'JD'?" *Reporter*, Aug. 20. 1959, pp. 12–18.
33. Ronald Bayer, "Liberal Opinion and the Problem of Heroin Addiction," *Contemporary Drug Problems*, Spring 1975, pp. 93–118.
34. Will Sparks, "Terror in the Streets?" *Commonweal*, June 4, 1965, p. 346.
35. Ibid.

Crime, Punishment, and the Decline of Liberal Optimism   177

doan, in *The Nation,* wrote, "The facts do not accord with this outcry."[36] The refusal to acknowledge a rational basis for the fear of crime led liberal writers to suggest that those who raised the issue did so in order to draw upon racist fears and anger provoked by the civil rights movement and to galvanize political pressures against the procedural advances in criminal law being instituted under the guidance of the activist Warren Court. Justice J. Skelly Wright of the United States Court of Appeals thus warned in *The New Republic* of a "new McCarthyism, with crime in the streets replacing communism as the danger to be eradicated."[37]

It was not until 1966 that a serious liberal effort to confront directly the growing popular concern about crime emerged. Acknowledging that conservatives had successfully used the issue, the editors of *Commonweal* wrote,

> Crime is properly a liberal concern because it hurts most severely precisely those groups in society about which liberals have been most concerned. Poor people have always been the most frequent victims of criminality and the situation has not changed despite middle class worries to the contrary.[38]

Here, then, was a device for recognizing the crime problem without yielding a concern for the dispossessed. Without having to deny that those who committed street crimes were victims of social injustice, liberals could select an even more disadvantaged group for special consideration—the victims of the victims. The liberal journals continued to publish articles critical of the statistical reliability[39] of data used to suggest a crime wave, analyses suggesting that any increases in crime were the result of demographic changes in the population, and attacks on the motivations of those who raised crime as a political issue[40]; but the conservative monopoly with regard to concern for safe streets had been broken. In 1967, *The Reporter* echoed *Commonweal* in its position that "crime in the streets is a far more serious and terrifying problem for Negroes than it is for other Americans."[41] *The New Republic,* despite a lingering suspicion about official crime statistics, admitted that "there is widespread concern about crime in this country and it is justified."[42]

As the fear of crime continued to intensify, and as crime was linked, by conservatives, not only with the patterns of civil disobedience that characterized the early civil rights struggle but also with ghetto rebellions and campus unrest, the journals began to express grave concern regarding the capacity of

36. George Shadoan, "Behind the Crime Scare," *Nation,* May 10, 1965, p. 495.

37. J. Skelly Wright, "Crime in the Streets and the New McCarthyism," *New Republic,* Oct. 9, 1965, pp. 10–11.

38. "Crime in the Streets," *Commonweal,* Dec. 9, 1966, p. 281.

39. John Leo, "Crime Statistics: The Great Juggling Act," *Commonweal,* Oct. 6, 1967, pp. 9–10; Gilbert Geis, "Crime and Politics," *Nation,* Aug. 14, 1967, pp. 115–16.

40. TRB, "Stamping Out Crime," *New Republic,* Dec. 10, 1966, p. 4.

41. "The President on Crime," *Reporter,* Feb. 23, 1967, p. 16.

42. "Armed and Dangerous," *New Republic,* Nov. 25, 1967, pp. 8–10.

liberal institutions to survive under conditions of disruption. Thomas R.
Brooks thus wrote in *Commonweal*, "There will be no end to police vigilantism until we do something about crimes, riots and violence. People want
an end to such social disturbances, or at least want them reduced to manageable proportions."[43] And Alexander Bickel asserted in *The New Republic*,
"No society will long remain open and attached to peaceable politics and the
decent and controlled use of public force if fear for personal safety is the
ordinary experience of large numbers."[44] Of special concern during this period were the efforts of Lyndon Johnson and Richard Nixon to press federal
crime control legislation, aspects of which involved threats to the constitutional guarantees liberals considered vital to the judicial process.[45]

The shift in the stance of liberals in this period with regard to crime is
highlighted by the way "TRB" in *The New Republic* adjusted the quality and
tone of his remarks on this issue between 1968 and 1971. In 1968, rejecting
the assertion that crime was a fabrication of conservative political forces, he
wrote, "Crime is not a nightmare of the rightwing. It is real and menacing."[46]
In the summer of the next year, decrying the rise in rapes, robberies, and
murders, he focused his attention on the impact of crime on blacks. Portraying the virtual imprisonment of a poor black Baltimore woman who was too
fearful to step out of her home on a hot August night, he lashed out against
the "terror" induced by crime in the streets.[47] By 1971, his language had become more strident. Referring to crime as a "cancerous evil," he went on to
say, "Americans are afraid to walk the streets at night. It is one of the most
shocking changes of a lifetime."[48] "Menace," "terror," "cancerous evil"; with
each account the concern mounted.

Even *The Nation*, which had appeared reluctant to take on the problem of
street crime, did so beginning in 1970,[49] as its editorials and articles began to
reflect the sense of urgency that since the 1960s had become more common in
the other journals of liberal opinion.[50]

It is, therefore, surprising that Michael Novak could write as late as 1974
about the "liberal neglect" of the crime problem. His analysis is significant,
however, in that it captures the extent to which this issue had begun to assume
a preeminent status among liberals and the extent to which earlier reluctance
to face the problem had become a source of acute embarrassment:

43. Thomas R. Brooks, "Law and Order," *Commonweal*, Sept. 27, 1968, p. 653.
44. Alexander M. Bickel, "Crime, the Courts and the Old Nixon," *New Republic*, June 15,
1968, p. 8.
45. TRB, "From Washington," *New Republic*, May 18, 1968, p. 4; Bickel, "How to Beat a
Crime"; "Full of Flees," *New Republic*, June 27, 1970, pp. 7–8.
46. TRB, "Law and Order," *New Republic*, June 29, 1968, p. 5.
47. TRB, "Poultice on Crime," *New Republic*, Aug. 9, 1969, p. 6.
48. TRB, "Crime Fighting," p. 6.
49. "Lawlessness and Crime," *Nation*, June 29, 1970, p. 770–71.
50. See also "What the Muggings Mean," *Nation*, Oct. 9, 1972, pp. 292–93; and "Logic of
Inversion."

> Before there is a civil right to vote, there needs to be a civil right not to be lynched—and not to be mugged, robbed or physically harassed. Many of the poor and a good portion of the middle class have lost this civil right during the last ten years. . . . The left stands for civil rights, but it has not, alas, been a champion of this civil right. A person who is concerned about crime . . . is considered to be turning "conservative." Blindness![51]

Crime had thus become an issue about whose importance liberals and conservatives could increasingly agree. Writing in *Commentary*, Wilson applauded this new consensus: "Crime and disorder have perhaps ceased to be ideological issues and have become practical issues—which is what they should have been all along."[52]

But crime was not merely a "practical" issue. For most liberal authors it stood as a symptom of the wide range of socioeconomic problems that lay at the root of dangerous, disruptive, and fear-inspiring behavior. The recognition that there was a real problem of urban crime was especially distressing because it suggested the need, at least in the short run, to develop policies directed at reestablishing civil order and safe streets, policies that would necessitate use of the apparatus of social control against the urban poor. That this recognition occurred just as liberals had begun to lose confidence in the capacity of the criminal justice system to correct, cure, and rehabilitate, when punishment as a justification for the criminal sanction was assuming a surprising vitality in the liberal journals, made this juncture of considerable importance.

. . . AND THEIR PUNISHMENT

No aspect of public policy with regard to criminal behavior has evoked more wrathful condemnation on the part of liberals than capital punishment. Although it has assumed a relatively marginal status among the range of available penalties, it has stood symbolically for all that liberals have held anathema in the criminal justice system. As an unwelcome inheritance from the era preceding the rise of the penitentiary and the emergence of rehabilitative thought, it has seemed an atrocious reminder of the practices that predated modern penology. Although it was *The Nation* that made this issue a cause of preeminent concern, for none of the journals was it a matter of minor interest. It is because there was such an outpouring of opinion on capital punishment, and because of its symbolic status, that it is possible to use capital punishment as a prism through which to refract the liberal perspective on social policy toward criminals.

The liberal opposition to capital punishment has been founded in part upon a utilitarian conception of law, retribution being rejected as an inappropriate

51. Michael Novak, "Liberal Neglect," *Commonweal*, Feb. 8, 1974, p. 456.
52. Wilson, "Crime and the Liberal Audience," p. 71.

justification for public policy. Capital punishment is seen as nothing more than an act of societal vengeance, satisfying "primitive" needs for retaliation, a penalty fueled by anger and passion.

If capital punishment is the inheritance of the premodern past against which liberals have directed their implacable opposition, abolition being the only acceptable goal, the penitentiary has held a very different position in liberal thought. A child of modern penology, it has served as a target for an endless series of denunciations because of its failure to fulfill its multiple purposes. The commitment to rehabilitation has provided the basis for criticism of penal practices as tending to create an institution serving retributive rather than rehabilitative ends. Long before Attica emerged as a symbol of the crisis in American penology, the liberal journals were a forum for scathing condemnation of prison conditions and practices. Whether directed at Ohio,[53] Georgia,[54] Missouri,[55] or Arkansas,[56] the muckraking tales were the same. Throughout the 1950s and 1960s a succession of horrors was presented to the readers of these journals: deplorable overcrowding, working conditions (for those who were not forcibly kept idle) resembling servitude, brutality and corporal punishment by guards, unbridled discretionary authority exercised by those who capriciously administered the details of the day-to-day lives of inmates, and violence directed by strong prisoners against the weaker.

As prisoners began to organize themselves,[57] to present their demands formally through official channels and less formally through violent outbursts,[58] the journals responded with great sympathy. To those who felt that conditions behind prison walls might become too comfortable, the editors of *The Nation* responded, "And the bloody minded need not worry that conditions will become too good for the scoundrels. The essence of jail is that the gate is locked; no amount of justice and common decency on the inside will make that fact more than endurable."[59]

This concern about the quality of life in prison derived its force in part from a diffuse humanitarian impulse which has characterized liberal social thought. The language most often used in the denunciations conveys a sense of outrage which cannot be reduced to mere instrumental concerns regarding the capacity of the prison to rehabilitate the criminal.

While acknowledging the need to protect the community from those who were dangerous, liberals in the postwar period pressed to make the prison perform its rehabilitative function. In so doing, they carried forward the tradi-

53. "The Ohio Criminals," *Commonweal*, Apr. 6, 1948, p. 393.
54. Dora Byron, "Georgia Rockpile," *Nation*, June 29, 1957, pp. 568–69.
55. Patrick J. Buchanan, "The Pen That Just Grew," *Nation*, Nov. 16, 1964, pp. 355–57.
56. "Prison Politics," *New Republic*, Apr. 6, 1968, p. 7.
57. Ronald Goldfarb, "Rapping with Convicts," *New Republic*, July 19, 1969, pp. 21–23.
58. "Life in Prison," *Commonweal*, Mar. 6, 1953, pp. 543–44.
59. "Union Stripes," *Nation*, Oct. 31, 1966, p. 436.

tion of penal reform that had emerged at the very moment of the prison's birth. "A good correctional institution is more than a gleaming edifice. . . . It is a workshop of a team of skilled people concerned to turn social failures into useful citizens."[60] The imagery in this passage is striking. There are no criminals described here but "social failures" who, like the raw material processed in any workshop, must be transformed—not in this case by mere laborers, but instead by "skilled people."

Reliance upon experts in the process of rehabilitation suggested the necessity of altering the staffing patterns of courts and prisons. Needed were not just lawyers but also persons skilled in diagnosis and classification; not just guards, but also counselors, therapists, and teachers.[61] Resistance to such change was attributed to official reluctance to make the necessary investment in new resources and an irrational attachment to the efficacy of the punitive model.[62] Writing of a failed effort to transform the particularly backward penal system of Arkansas, Robert Pearman commented,

> Rockefeller promised to hire a professional penologist to run the state prison system. But that implies a tremendous outlay of funds. None of that is possible as long as counting house standards are applied to the penal system. The Arkansas prison would have to stop making money and start remaking men.[63]

Stinginess was juxtaposed with humanitarian considerations with respect to reformation, and the production of profits was pitted against the reproduction of men.

With the failure of punitive penal policies to meet the demands of social defense, prevailing practice was denounced as shameful and criticized as ineffective. Strong doubts about the deterrent effects of the criminal law and a belief that the prison was itself a criminogenic force in society merged to make the rehabilitative model the choice dictated by reason. Punishment, as Gresham Sykes wrote in *The Nation*, is a luxury:

> Even if the necessary conditions for punishment's effectiveness could prevail it is still doubtful if punishment is the best way to reduce crime and delinquency. Punishment under ideal conditions may deter some potential offenders. But we have come to realize that a society in which men conform to the law through fear is hardly preferable to a society in which the only answer to the deviant is vengeance. The objective—for practical reasons if for no other—is rehabilitation, the transformation of the offender to a point where he willingly follows the dictates of the law. Punishment in short may be a luxury that we can ill afford.[64]

60. Morris, "Social Values and the Criminal Act," p. 8.
61. Graham Hughes, "The Futility of Punishment," *Nation*, Nov. 30, 1957, p. 414.
62. Gresham Sykes, "The Luxury of Punishment," *Nation*, July 18, 1959, p. 33.
63. Robert Pearman, "Arkansas Prison Farm: The Whip Pays Off," *Nation*, Dec. 26, 1966, p. 704.
64. Sykes, "Luxury of Punishment," p. 33. See also Maxwell King, "Four Inmates Speak," *New Republic*, July 4, 1970, p. 23.

The tenacious hold of the ideal of rehabilitation upon liberals during the postwar period is suggested by the extent to which it seemed capable of surviving what might have been mortal blows to a less resilient position. The indeterminate sentence was an integral part of the rehabilitative orientation toward criminals, with the duration of the offender's sentence to be determined not by past deeds but rather by progress made toward "socially useful" roles.[65] The discretion allowed both judges and parole boards under this system was extraordinary. Yet when concern first began to mount regarding the evident disparity of sentences among persons who had committed similar crimes, there was no suggestion that the judge's capacity to tailor sentences for purposes of rehabilitation be abandoned.[66] As the harmful effects of imprisonment, under the best of circumstances, became a focus of discussion in the mid-1960s it was the ideology of rehabilitation that both suggested the necessity of limiting the time criminals were incarcerated and recommended alternative forms of social control that might be brought to bear on the criminal offender.[67]

While the ideology of rehabilitation served primarily as a critical force in the discussion of the adult prison, the situation was more complex with regard to the juvenile justice system. There the ideology had attained a hegemonic status, serving as the official justification for a nonadversarial legal procedure through which juveniles who engaged in criminal activities and those whose noncriminal behavior suggested the need for preventive state intervention were committed to institutions for "care," "treatment," and rehabilitation. It was obvious, however, to careful observers writing in the liberal journals that cant was more in evidence than was the practice of rehabilitation. George Edwards, a former juvenile court judge, expressed distress with the obvious shortcomings of the system while holding out the prospect for improvement: "We cannot say the juvenile court theory has failed for we have not armed our courts with the tools, we have not brought together our government and our people to grapple with the problem of juvenile delinquency by applying fully the available knowledge."[68] More resources, greater effort, more serious commitment—these were the ingredients necessary to realize the promise of rehabilitation.

With the growing preoccupation during the 1960s with procedural protection of offenders and increasing suspicion of the benevolent justifications for incarceration of mental patients, the juvenile justice system was subjected to

65. "James V. Bennett's Prisons," *New Republic*, Sept. 12, 1964, p. 5.

66. William H. Dempsey, Jr., "Justice by Geography," *Commonweal*, Nov. 21, 1958, p. 203; "Unjust and Unequal," *Nation*, Dec. 30, 1967, p. 708.

67. "The High Cost of Imprisonment," *Nation*, Dec. 26, 1966, p. 693; Ronald Goldfarb, "The Conspiracy for Correctional Reform," *New Republic*, Dec. 13, 1969, p. 15.

68. George Edwards, "Judge, I Told That Boy . . . ," *New Republic*, Mar. 28, 1960, p. 15; see also "The School Crime Wave," *Nation*, Mar. 30, 1964, pp. 310–11; "Challenges of Delinquency," *Commonweal*, June 9, 1967, pp. 331–32.

Crime, Punishment, and the Decline of Liberal Optimism   183

ever greater scrutiny.[69] Justice David Bazelon, who had been among the most articulate judicial proponents of the rehabilitative ideal, clearly expressed the dilemma in a *New Republic* article:

> I do not find it objectionable to deprive the child of procedural safeguards if the individualized treatment he is supposed to get requires the sacrifice and if the new procedures are reasonably fair. We should not blind ourselves though to what individualized treatment in our juvenile courts really is.[70]

Thus, while demanding unembellished frankness regarding practices carried out in rehabilitative settings, Bazelon sustained a commitment to rehabilitation as an ideal, and to its capacity to provide a critical perspective.

The commitment to a nonpunitive criminal justice system, to a system that conceived its primary function as rehabilitation and was therefore forward looking in orientation, provided liberals with a set of critical standards with which to judge prevailing penal practices. Yet the content of this stance was surprisingly ambiguous. Outrage against overcrowding, against poor classificatory systems for prisoners, and against inadequate "services"—it was as if "the rehabilitative" could be best defined in terms of what it was not.

Beyond the symbolic attachment to rehabilitation, the apparent coherence of the liberal perspective seemed to vanish. Specificity regarding particular techniques of rehabilitative intervention engendered considerable conflict and disagreement. At times, there was an outright rejection of the practices that were the very expression of a corrective-reformative orientation. As mentioned above, since it was psychiatry that had assumed professional responsibility in the postwar era for the transformation of discordant behavior, the problematic nature of the liberal commitment to rehabilitation is most evident in the liberal journals' treatment of psychiatric practice in the criminal justice system.

There was little disagreement among liberals about the desirability of replacing the M'Naghten rule, which had, since the nineteenth century, governed the definition of criminal insanity and set the terms for the role of psychiatric evidence in that determination. Authors writing in the six journals typically supported the broadest possible role for the expert witness in determining the extent to which mental disorder affected the defendant's capacity to act in a "responsible" manner. While aware that the insanity defense created many problems, liberal writers rejected suggestions that it be abandoned. Thus, in a critical review of Thomas Szasz's *Law, Liberty and Psychiatry*, Justice Wright argued,

> It would of course be less troublesome if we handled the mentally ill as Dr. Szasz suggests. But inconvenient as it may be, our mores require a humanitarian ap-

69. James Symington, "Youth, Crime, and the Great Society," *Reporter*, Feb. 24, 1966, pp. 41–43.
70. David Bazelon, "Justice for Juveniles," *New Republic*, Apr. 22, 1967, p. 15.

proach—an approach which not only protects society but preserves the dignity
of human beings who "know not what they do."[71]

It was during the mid-1950s that the most optimistic expressions about the
potential contribution of psychiatry to the rehabilitative process were to be
found. That optimism was a reflection of psychiatry's own sense of self-confidence. Writing in *The Nation*, Derrick Sington stated,

> The truth is that the constructive civilized alternative to execution or veritable
> life imprisonment for the "dangerous" and "twisted" criminal has not yet been
> fully accepted in any country. . . . That alternative is the cure and rehabilitation
> of people who are offenders because they have become deformed in mind and
> spirit. . . . The modern weapon of psychotherapy and psychoanalysis offers the
> brightest hope. . . . The world is only on the threshold of the curative approach
> to crime.[72]

In contrast to prevailing practices in the United States, Sington portrayed a
model prison in Utrecht, Holland, where each prisoner, committed for an indeterminate period, faced a psychoanalyst four or five times a week.

Yet at the very time such enthusiasm was in evidence, both caution and
alarm also found expression in the liberal journals. Thus, in a three-part series
published in *The New Republic*[73] Walter Goodman presented with obvious
discomfort the vision of Benjamin Karpman, who would replace the jailer
with a nurse and the judge by a psychiatrist "whose sole attempt will be to
treat and cure the individual."[74] For Goodman as well as other authors,[75] a
profound threat was perceived in the possible abrogation of the rule of law by
psychiatric experts. Warning of a "brave new world" which would seek to
remake the criminal, Charles Curran wrote, "The rule of law deprives the
criminal of his liberty but it leaves him his personality. Those who support a
psychiatric perspective would deprive him of both."[76] By the end of the next
decade this same suspicion would begin to assume a dominant status in the
liberal journals. In the reviews that greeted Karl Menninger's *The Crime of
Punishment*, this is unmistakably clear.[77]

71. J. Skelly Wright, "The Mentally Ill: Stepchildren of the Law," *New Republic*, May 9,
1964, pp. 24–27. For a contrary view of Szasz, see George P. Elliot, "The Free Criminal," *Commentary*, March 1964, pp. 78–80.

72. Derrick Sington, "Redeeming the Murderer," *Nation*, Feb. 9, 1957, p. 117.

73. Walter Goodman, "Lawyers, Psychiatrists and Crime," *Nation*, Aug. 1, 1955, pp. 13–16;
Aug. 8, 1955, pp. 14–17; Aug. 15, 1955, pp. 12–15.

74. Ibid., Aug. 8, 1955, p. 17.

75. For example, Victor Ferkiss, "A Life for a Life?" *Commonweal*, Oct. 7, 1955, p. 12. In
Michael Maccoby, "Violence and the Mass Media," *New Republic*, Jan. 14, 1957, pp. 19–20,
there is a strong attack on the implications of Dr. Frederic Werthan's "expert" opinion regarding
the relationship between violence in the media and actual violent behavior.

76. Charles Curran, "The Law of the Gallows," *New Republic*, Nov. 18, 1957, p. 20.

77. William Ryan, "The Crime of Punishment," *Commonweal*, Jan. 24, 1969, p. 533; Christopher D. Stone, "Crises and Criminality," *Nation*, Apr. 21, 1969, pp. 510–13.

Crime, Punishment, and the Decline of Liberal Optimism   185

If ambivalence characterized the discussion of the role of psychiatry in its most general form, no such uncertainty is to be found in material on the techniques of behavior modification. Unlike the more traditional forms of therapy, the newer approaches were perceived as short-circuiting the autonomy of the prisoner. They appeared to be a threat to the very dignity that rehabilitation, in contrast to punishment, was supposed to enhance. This view is clear in the reaction provoked by psychiatrists' rather primitive effort to change prisoners' behavior by playing tape-recorded messages during sleeping hours. Worried about mental and moral "forced feeding," *Commonweal's* editors went on to raise important questions about the meaning of "voluntary" participation in experimental treatment by those incarcerated in penal institutions.[78] Echoing these concerns, the editors of *The Nation*, which tended to be the journal most receptive to expanding the role of psychiatry in prisons, wrote, "Clearly the future with which Aldous Huxley dealt in *Brave New World* is overtaking us with awesome rapidity."[79]

If Huxley and Orwell provided the images that haunted liberals during the 1950s and 1960s, by the 1970s, with an increasingly sophisticated psychiatric technology at hand, it was Stanley Kubrick who served this function. Whether referring to the attempt to establish a special institution at Butner, North Carolina,[80] the START program in the federal prisons,[81] or the Medical-Psychiatric Diagnostic Unit at California's Vacaville prison,[82] it was *A Clockwork Orange* that provided the backdrop. The difference between Huxley and Orwell, on the one hand, and Kubrick, on the other, is instructive. In the writings of the former, malcontents are "adjusted" to an evil society. In Kubrick's work, sympathy is evoked on behalf of a clearly vicious man who has been subjected to behavioral engineering.

> What is happening at Vacaville is only a sample of what's happening all over the world, as technological tools come into the hands of psychiatrists and bureaucrats. . . . More and more political considerations become paramount in psychiatry—openly within the Soviet Union, more subtly in the United States.[83]

And so psychiatry, which was to make possible the cure of the "crippled" criminal, was transformed instead into a "weapon" to be used against prisoners in revolt against the very institutional settings that liberals had so forcefully criticized from the perspective of the ideology of rehabilitation. In its

78. "Talking Pillows," *Commonweal*, Dec. 27, 1957, p. 327.

79. "Hypnopaedia," *Nation*, Jan. 25, 1958, p. 62.

80. Mark Pinsky, "Who Is Dr. Groder: Alarms in the Prison Grapevine," *Nation*, Oct. 5, 1975, pp. 294–97.

81. Clay Steinman, "Behavior Modification: The Case of the Frightened Convict," *Nation*, Dec. 3, 1973, pp. 590–93.

82. Bernard Weiner, "Prison Psychiatry: The Clockwork Cure," *Nation*, Apr. 3, 1972, pp. 433–36.

83. Ibid.

preoccupation with the maintenance of prison discipline, institutional psychiatry was seen as a threat to the dignity of those whom it attempted to control, and as particularly insidious because it masked its role through the appropriation of the symbols of rehabilitation.

It is clear that by the end of the 1960s there was a growing uneasiness with the implications of the forward-looking, nonpunitive penal philosophy. But none of the criticisms yet had the quality of a fundamental judgment on both liberal correctional ideology and the practices reflecting, even if imperfectly, that perspective. The rebellion at Attica and its bloody suppression accelerated the growth of discontent. While the liberal journals were fiercely critical of Governor Nelson Rockefeller's response to the crisis,[84] more important, they did not publish the kinds of demands one would have expected to issue from those committed to humane rehabilitative institutions. In the post-Attica period, many began to assert that it was the ideology of rehabilitation itself that lay at the root of the most undesirable features of prevailing penal practice.[85]

Although brief, the first major statement in the liberal journals reflecting this mood appeared in a *Commonweal* article by Donald G. Shockley. Attacking the indeterminate sentence, the most obvious manifestation of the rehabilitative posture, he went on to argue against earlier liberal assumptions, claiming that the correctional system had failed "not because it lacked modern buildings, adequate budgets and trained professionals, but because its basic assumptions are false."[86] Previously, the rehabilitative ideology had served as the reference point for criticisms of the prison system; now the ideology itself was the subject of criticism. "The point at which radical change must occur is in the basic concept of rehabilitation and not at the level of mere tinkering with program structures and personnel."[87]

The arguments which had received only skeletal expression in Shockley's essay were given extended discussion in Robert Martinson's "Paradox of Prison Reform,"[88] a four-part series published by *The New Republic*. After a historical review of the rise of the "age of treatment" in correction, Martinson presented a detailed summary of the available evidence regarding the efficacy

84. See, for example, John Leo, "Vietnam at Home," *Commonweal*, Oct. 1, 1971, pp. 6–7; Peter Steinfels, "How We Perceive the Enemy," *Commonweal*, Oct. 1, 1971, pp. 7–8; "Dead End at Attica," *New Republic*, Sept. 25, 1971, pp. 9–10; "Slaughter at Attica," *Nation*, Sept. 27, 1971, pp. 258–59.

85. See, for example, the Report of the Twentieth Century Fund Task Force on Criminal Sentencing, *Fair and Certain Punishment* (New York: McGraw-Hill, 1976); and the Report of the Committee for the Study of Incarceration, issued under the authorship of Andrew von Hirsch, *Doing Justice: The Choice of Punishments* (New York: Hill & Wang, 1976).

86. Donald G. Shockley, "Reforming Prison Reform," *Commonweal*, Sept. 24, 1971, p. 498.

87. Ibid.

88. Robert Martinson, "The Paradox of Prison Reform," *New Republic*, Apr. 1, 1972, pp. 23–25; Apr. 8, 1972, pp. 13–15; Apr. 15, 1972, pp. 17–19; Apr. 29, 1972, pp. 21–23.

Crime, Punishment, and the Decline of Liberal Optimism   187

of correctional therapy. No mode of treatment was shown to have a predictably positive effect on the recidivism of former prisoners. He attacked the practice of rehabilitation as resting upon a "dangerous myth," one that permitted experts to impose "unasked-for help" and to exercise disturbingly broad discretionary authority.

With rehabilitation characterized as a myth, a justification for conditions prevailing in America's prisons, Martinson was able to argue that the ideology which had at one time been a critical force had been pressed into the service of the status quo: "The myth of correctional treatment is now the main obstacle to progress; it has become the last line of defense of the prison system."[89] Martinson argued that the prison should be used only for that "small number" of criminals who could not be handled in less restrictive ways. But for these persons the prison would be seen as a secure facility designed to protect the public, not as a setting for rehabilitation. Prisons, he concluded, "cannot be reformed and must be gradually torn down. But let us give up the comforting myth that the remaining facilities (they will be prisons) can be changed into hospitals."[90]

These pessimistic conclusions, at such a distance from the hopes of the liberal reformers of earlier years, were most forcefully presented by David J. Rothman. Writing in *The Nation*, he said,

> Given the tradition of reform without change and the broad consensus that we do not know how to rehabilitate offenders, we now find ourselves in a unique position. We should therefore take advantage of this special moment to impose a different model on the incarceration system. Heretofore, at the heart of the penal system or of parole and probation was a "success" model: we could reform the deviant. As an alternative, I believe we may accomplish more by frankly adopting a "failure" model by recognizing our inability to achieve such heady and grandiose goals as eliminating crime and remaking offenders. Let us accept failure and pursue its implications.[91]

In recognizing the failure, not only of incarceration but also of less restrictive and less costly modes of social defense against crime, those who urged a rethinking of the function of the criminal law pressed reformers to set more limited tasks while acknowledging the relative intractability of criminality under prevailing socioeconomic circumstances.

With the acknowledged failure of rehabilitation, punishment began to resurface as an appropriate justification for the criminal justice system. Retribution was no longer anathema. Deterrence, so long considered a quaint inheritance from an earlier era, became respectable once more. The efficient functioning of the repressive apparatus of the state became a legitimate object

89. Martinson, "Planning for Public Safety," *New Republic*, Apr. 29, 1972, p. 23.
90. Ibid.
91. David Rothman, "Prisons: The Failure Model," *Nation*, Dec. 21, 1974, p. 657.

of concern.[92] Discretionary authority, exercised by judges and parole boards and defended in an earlier period, was increasingly perceived as inimical to the ends of justice.[93] That in almost every instance it was argued that prison sentences be dramatically reduced and that the exercise of punitive authority be measured, restrained, and "economical" does not alter the fact that the justification being put forward for the exercise of such authority was starkly at variance with previous liberal positions.

Actually, it is remarkable that the ideology of rehabilitation had held so central a position for so long. Had the liberal understanding of the roots of crime stressed the psychological characteristics of the individual offender, such a perspective would have been fully understandable. Yet, as I have shown, this was not the case. Far more important to the liberal outlook was an emphasis on the role of socioeconomic factors. Thus, the "fit" between the liberal explanation of crime and liberal recommendations regarding policy toward criminals was always rather poor.[94] What the ideology of rehabilitation had permitted was the formulation of short-term options that suggested the possibility of controlling the criminal without harming him. With the abandonment of rehabilitation as a legitimate ideology for the practice of crime control, it was necessary for liberals to confront the distasteful fact that social defense against criminals entails punishment.

It would be a serious mistake to conclude that as a consequence of this shift the liberal concern with prison conditions and prison reform has diminished. The journals continue to publish muckraking exposés and to present programs for reform. What has changed, however, is the perspective from which this material is written. There are still appeals to the rehabilitative ideal,[95] but they have taken an increasingly marginal role. More central is a general humanitarian outrage against deplorable living conditions and brutality,[96] as well as an insistence that due process safeguards be extended to those behind prison walls.[97] Animating these criticisms is a liberalism of procedural rights and limited state authority rather than a liberalism of social reform.[98]

92. David J. Rothman, "You Can't Reform the Bastile," *Nation*, Mar. 19, 1973, p. 366; and Novak, "Liberal Neglect," p. 456.

93. See, for example, Donald Barlett, "Justice in Philadelphia," *New Republic*, May 20, 1973, pp. 19–21; "Criminal Sentences: Law without Order," *New Republic*, May 5, 1973, p. 31; Larry Schultz, "Waifs of the Courts: The Problem of Problem Children," *Nation*, Oct. 29, 1973, pp. 426–29; "Sense in Sentencing," *Nation*, May 4, 1974, p. 549.

94. This was acknowledged with candor by *The Nation*, in "Crime Cures," Feb. 23, 1974, p. 230.

95. For example, Alain Woodrow, "France's Atticas," *Commonweal*, Apr. 28, 1972, pp. 187–89; and James Higgins, "Buckley: Sheriff of Middlesex," *Nation*, Jan. 24, 1972, pp. 101–03.

96. For example, see Michael Meltsner, "Brave Journalism," *New Republic*, Apr. 6, 1974, pp. 31–32; Richard L. Fricker, "Oklahoma's 'Hard Line' Prison," *Progressive*, March 1975, pp. 31–32; David Underhill, "Prison Justice in Alabama: The Shadow of Southern History," *Nation*, June 21, 1975, pp. 749–54.

97. For example, "The Hole," *Nation*, Dec. 7, 1974, p. 582; Henry A. Giroux, "A Blow for Prison Justice," *Progressive*, March 1975, pp. 10–11.

98. von Hirsch, *Doing Justice*.

Crime, Punishment, and the Decline of Liberal Optimism   189

With these changes the gulf with respect to the issue of crime separating liberal and more conservative writers has all but vanished.[99]

CONCLUSIONS

When liberals have attempted to explain the transformation of their perspective on crime and its punishment, they have most often suggested that the weight of "scientific evidence" in recent years has made it impossible to sustain a faith in the ideal of rehabilitation. Furthermore, they have argued that it has become increasingly obvious that the institutional reflections of that ideal have revealed themselves to be profoundly flawed when judged from the standpoint of other liberal values, the most important being those governing limitations on state authority. Although the importance to liberal perceptions of recent studies cannot be denied, explanations of the transformation that are based on such "facts" are ultimately unsatisfactory. That prisons fail to affect recidivism rates[100] and that those who are incarcerated under indeterminate sentencing procedures spend longer periods in prison than do those sentenced under less discretionary schemes have long been known.[101]

Wilson has underscored the element of "rediscovery" in an essay on the renewal of interest in punishment among liberals and others committed to rehabilitation. He has stated,

> The renewed respectability . . . of the concept of punishment derives . . . from the various empirical inquiries the results of which have been so consistent and the implications of which so clear that they could no longer be neglected (though they were neglected for the better of half a century).[102]

Thus, although Wilson cites the importance of the "empirical inquiries," he too acknowledges that findings critical of rehabilitative prison practice have been available—although "neglected"—for 50 years. Indeed as Michel Foucault has so masterfully shown, the criticisms made of the prison today are virtually the same as those made 150 years ago, at the very moment of the prison's "birth."[103]

---

99. See, for example, J. Anthony Luckas, "Muckraking à la Mode," *New Republic*, Oct. 20, 1973, pp. 29–30; Wilson, "Crime and the Criminologists"; Marc F. Plattner, "Neo-Abolitionism," *Commentary*, January 1974, pp. 80–82. Differences in emphasis and tone are, however, still quite obvious. The topics marked by the sharpest disagreement pertained to the rights of persons accused of crime and those sentenced to prison.

100. Blake McKelvey, *American Prisons: A History of Good Intentions* (1936; reprint ed., Montclair, N.J.: Patterson Smith, 1977), p. 299.

101. Edward Lindsey, "Historical Sketch of the Indeterminate Sentence and Parole," *Journal of the American Institute of Criminal Law and Criminology*, 1925, pp. 9–126; and Alan Dershowitz, "Indeterminate Confinement: Letting the Therapy Fit the Crime," *University of Pennsylvania Law Review*, vol. 123 (1974), pp. 297–339.

102. James Q. Wilson, "The Political Feasibility of Punishment," in *Justice and Punishment*, J. Cederblom and William Blizek, eds. (Cambridge, Mass.: Ballinger, 1977), p. 111.

103. Michel Foucault, *Discipline and Punish: The Birth of the Prison* (New York: Pantheon Books, 1977), pp. 269–70.

What, then, accounts for these "rediscoveries," for the end of "neglect"? Wilson argues that this is the cumulative effect of repeated discoveries that many of the social programs associated with liberalism simply do not work:

> The changes in elite views on criminal justice, particularly among liberals, were contemporaneous with and no doubt linked to a generalized liberal disenchantment with the efficacy of planned social change. The recognition that we were not "curing" criminals was part and parcel of the awareness that we were not "curing" alcoholism, drug addiction, broken homes or low school achievement scores either.[104]

I would argue that although Wilson is certainly correct, his analysis provides only a partial answer. Failures have not always resulted in "disenchantment." Indeed, the history of penal reform shows that during the period of rehabilitation's popularity, each failure prompted a demand for more experimentation, more expertise, more resources. The disenchantment about which Wilson writes is related to a much more profound and far-reaching phenomenon: the collapse of the liberal faith in the capacity of man to compel the world, both natural and social, to provide an endless series of benefits. Although each failure adds to the pessimistic conclusion, it only derives its meaning from that conclusion.

In writing about the emergence of psychiatry in the United States, Norman Dain notes that "the optimistic approach to man's nature"[105] had as much to do with the belief in the curability of insanity as did medical discoveries. It is the collapse of that optimism rather than any series of failures that accounts for the very bleak view of the possibility of solving the problems of crime.

With the emergence of pessimism—characterized by the open recognition of both the seriousness of crime and the failure of rehabilitation—the liberal outlook has increasingly begun to resemble the conservative perspective against which it had set itself in opposition during much of the postwar period. With the end of optimism, the quality that most distinguished American liberal social thought from conservatism's "irritable mental gestures," in the words of Trilling, has been lost. That is a loss of incalculable significance, one that is bound to affect every aspect of American social life and thought.

104. Wilson, "Political Feasibility of Punishment," p. 112.
105. Norman Dain, *Concepts of Insanity in the United States 1789–1865* (New Brunswick, N.J.: Rutgers University Press, 1964), p. xiv.

[10]

Crime and the Criminologists

James Q. Wilson

THE "social-science view" of crime is thought by many, especially its critics, to assert that crime is the result of poverty, racial discrimination, and other privations, and that the only morally defensible and substantively efficacious strategy for reducing crime is to attack its "root causes" with programs that end poverty, reduce discrimination, and meliorate privation. In fact, however, at the time when their views on crime were first sought by policymakers (roughly, the mid-1960's), social scientists had not set forth in writing a systematic theory of this sort. I recently asked three distinguished criminologists to nominate the two or three scholarly books on crime which were in print by mid-1960 and which were then regarded as the most significant works on the subject. There was remarkable agreement as to the titles: *Principles of Criminology*, by Edwin H. Sutherland and Donald R. Cressey, and *Delinquency and Opportunity*, by Richard A. Cloward and Lloyd E. Ohlin. Agreement was not complete on the validity of the views expressed in these books. Quite the contrary; criminologists then and now debate hotly and at length over such issues as the cause of crime. But these two books, and others like them, are alike in the way questions are posed, answers are sought, and policies are derived—alike, in short, not in their specific theories of delinquency, but in the general perspective from which those theories flow. And this perspective, contrary to popular impression, has rather little to do with poverty, race, education, housing, or the other objective conditions that supposedly cause crime. If anything, it directs attention away from factors that government can control, even if only marginally, to move beyond the reach of social policy altogether. Thus when social scientists were asked for advice by national policymaking bodies on how to reduce crime, they could not respond with suggestions derived from and supported by their

JAMES Q. WILSON is Henry Lee Shattuck Professor of Government at Harvard and has often written on issues of crime in this and other periodicals. His books include *Varieties of Police Behavior* and, most recently, *Political Organizations*. Another version of the present essay was presented as a paper at a conference on "Intellectuals, Knowledge, and the Public Arena" at the University of Massachusetts in Amherst this past May.

scholarly work. In consequence, such advice as they did supply tended to derive from their general political views rather than from the expert knowledge they were presumed to have.

I

IN the 1960's the prevalent social-science perspective on crime found its most authoritative development in the treatise by Sutherland and Cressey whose seventh edition appeared in 1966, just after President Johnson appointed his crime commission. In this work Sutherland and Cressey reviewed various "schools of criminology" and faulted all but the "sociological" approach, according to which criminal behavior is learned by a person in intimate interaction with others whose good opinion he values and who define crime as desirable. The "classical" theories of Bentham and Beccaria were rejected because their underlying psychological assumptions—that individuals calculate the pains and pleasures of crime and pursue it if the latter outweigh the former—"assume freedom of the will in a manner which gives little or no possibility of further investigation of the causes of crime or of efforts to prevent crime." The hedonistic psychology of Bentham, in short, suffered from being "individualistic, intellectualistic, and voluntaristic." Theories based on body type, mental abnormality, or mental illness were also rejected because the available data were inconsistent with them. Criminals were no more likely than law-abiding persons to have a certain stature, to be feeble-minded, or to suffer from a psychosis.

As for poverty—defined as having little money—Sutherland and Cressey's references to its impact were few and skeptical. Sutherland was quoted from his earlier writings as observing that while crime was strongly correlated with geographic concentrations of poor persons, it was weakly correlated (if at all) with the economic cycle. That is, crime might be observed to increase as one entered a poor neighborhood, but it was not observed to decrease as neighborhoods generally experienced prosperity. Furthermore, Albert K. Cohen (to whom Sutherland and Cressey refer approvingly) had shown that much of the delinquency found among working-class boys was

47

48/COMMENTARY JULY 1974

"non-utilitarian"—that is, consisted of expressive but financially unrewarding acts of vandalism and hell-raising—and that these acts were more common among this group than among middle-class boys. If economic want were the cause of crime, one would predict that delinquency for gain would be more common among those less well-off and delinquency for "fun" more common among the better-off. Yet the opposite seemed to be the case. "Poverty as such," Sutherland concluded, "is not an important cause of crime."

Nor could being a member of a minority group and experiencing the frustrations produced by discrimination explain crime for Sutherland and Cressey: while the experience of Negroes, whose crime rate was high, might support a theory, that of the American Japanese, whose crime rate was low, refuted it. Poverty and racial segregation might serve to perpetuate crime, however, to the extent that these factors prevented persons from leaving areas where crime was already high and thus from escaping those personal contacts and peer groups from which criminal habits were learned.

THERE were in 1966 other theories of crime in addition to Sutherland and Cressey's. Most of these were reviewed in their treatise and though criticisms were sometimes made, the governing assumptions of each were quite compatible with what the authors described as the sociological approach. Sheldon and Eleanor Glueck, for example, produced in the 1950's a major effort to predict delinquency, and while the idea of predicting delinquency became controversial on grounds of both fairness and feasibility, their empirical data on factors that helped cause delinquency were not seriously challenged. They argued and supplied data to show that among the key variables distinguishing delinquents from non-delinquents were those related to family conditions—chiefly stability, parental affection, and the discipline of children. Walter B. Miller also argued that delinquency was in large part an expression of the focal concerns of lower-class youth. Toughness, masculinity, "smartness," the love of excitement, and a desire for personal autonomy were valued by lower-class persons to a greater degree than by middle-class ones, and acting on the basis of these values, which were maintained by street-corner gangs, inevitably placed many lower-class boys (and some girls) in conflict with the laws of the middle class. Albert K. Cohen further suggested that delinquency was in part the result of lower-class youth striving, not simply to assert their focal values, but to repudiate those middle-class values which they secretly prized.

These and other sociological theories of crime, widely known and intensely discussed in the 1960's, had certain features in common. All sought to explain the causes of delinquency, or

at least its persistence. All made attitude formation a key variable. All stressed that these attitudes were shaped and supported by intimate groups—the family and close friends. All were serious, intelligent efforts at constructing social theories, and while no theory was proved empirically, all were consistent with at least some important observations about crime. *But none could supply a plausible basis for the advocacy of public policy.*

This was true for several reasons. By directing attention toward the subjective states that preceded or accompanied criminal behavior, the sociological (or more accurately, social-psychological) theories directed attention toward conditions that cannot be easily and deliberately altered. Society, of course, shapes attitudes and values by its examples, its institutions, and its practices, but only with great difficulty, slowly and imprecisely. If families inculcate habits of virtue, law-abidingness, and decorum, it is rarely because the family is acting as the agent of society or its government, but rather because it is a good family. If schools teach children to value learning and to study well, it is not simply because the schools are well-designed or generously supplied but because attitudes consistent with learning and study already exist in the pupils. One can imagine what government might do if it wished to make good families even better or successful pupils even more successful: more resources might be offered to reduce burdens imposed by want, but the gains, if any, would likely be at the margin.

If it is difficult by plan to make the good better, it may be impossible to make the bad tolerable so long as one seeks to influence attitudes and values directly. If a child is delinquent because his family made him so or his friends encourage him to be so, it is hard to conceive what society might do about this. No one knows how a government might restore affection, stability, and fair discipline to a family that rejects these characteristics; still less can one imagine how even a family once restored could affect a child who by now has left the formative years and in any event has developed an aversion to one or both of his parents. Government could supply the lower class with more money, of course, but if a class exists because of its values rather than its income, it is hard to see how, in terms of the prevailing theory, increasing the latter would improve the former.

If, similarly, the lower class has focal concerns that make crime attractive or even inevitable, it is not clear how government could supply it with a new set of values consistent with law-abidingness. Indeed, the very effort to inculcate new values would, if the sociological theory is true, lead the members of that class to resist such alien intrusions all the more vigorously and to cling to their own world-view all the more strongly. Peer groups exist, especially for young people, as a way of defending their members from an alien, hostile, or indifferent larger society and for supplying them with a mutually satisfactory basis for self-respect. A deviant peer group—one that encourages crime or hell-raising—would regard any effort by society to "reform" it as confirmation of the hostile intent of society and of the importance of the group.

II

THE problem lies in confusing causal analysis with policy analysis. Causal analysis attempts to find the source of human activity in those factors which themselves are not caused—which are, in the language of sociologists, "independent variables." Obviously nothing can be a cause if it is in turn caused by something else; it would then only be an "intervening variable." But ultimate causes cannot be the object of policy efforts precisely because, being ultimate, they cannot be changed. For example, criminologists have shown beyond doubt that men commit more crimes than women and younger men more (of certain kinds) than older ones. It is a theoretically important and scientifically correct observation. Yet it means little for policymakers concerned with crime prevention since men cannot be changed into women nor made to skip over the adolescent years. Not every primary cause is itself unchangeable: the cause of air pollution is (in part) certain gases in automobile exhausts, and thus reducing those gases by redesigning the engine will reduce pollution. But social problems—that is to say, problems occasioned by human behavior rather than mechanical processes—are almost invariably caused by factors that cannot be changed easily or at all, because human behavior ultimately derives from human volition—tastes, attitudes, values, or whatever—and these aspects of volition are in turn formed either entirely by choice or are the product of biological or social processes that we cannot or will not change.

It is the failure to understand this point that leads statesman and citizen alike to commit the causal fallacy—to assume that no problem is adequately addressed unless its causes are eliminated. The preamble to the UNESCO charter illustrates the causal fallacy: "Since wars begin in the minds of men it is in the minds of men that the defenses of peace must be constructed." Yet the one thing we cannot easily do, if at all, is change, by plan and systematically, the minds of men. If peace can only be assured by doing what we cannot do, then we can never have peace. If we regard any crime-prevention or crime-reduction program as defective because it does not address the "root causes" of crime, then we shall commit ourselves to futile acts that frustrate the citizen while they ignore the criminal.

Sutherland and Cressey commit the fallacy; yet, being honest scholars, they provide evidence in their own book that it *is* a fallacy. "At present," they write, "the greatest need in crime prevention is irrefutable facts about crime causation and sound means for transforming that knowledge into a program of action." Suppose it could be shown that their own theory of crime causation is irrefutably correct (it may well be). That theory is that individuals commit crime when they are members of groups—families, peers, neighborhoods—which define criminal behavior as desirable. The policy implication of this, which the authors draw explicitly, is that the local community must use the school, the church, the police, and other agencies to "modify" the personal groups in which crime is made to appear desirable. No indication is given as to how these agencies might do this and, considering what the authors and other sociologists have said about the strength and persistence of family and friendship ties, it is hard to see what plan might be developed.

But we need not merely raise the theoretical difficulties. A series of delinquency-prevention programs have been mounted over the decades, many if not most of which were explicitly formed on the strategy of altering primary-group influences on delinquents. Almost none can be said on the basis of careful, external evaluation to have succeeded in reducing delinquency. Sutherland and Cressey describe one of the most ambitious of these, the Cambridge-Somerville Youth Study in the late 1930's. The differences in crime between those youths who were given special services (counseling, special educational programs, guidance, health assistance, camping trips) and a matched control group were insignificant: " 'the treatment' had little effect." Perhaps a better program would have had better results, though it is striking that for some a "better" youth project is one that moves beyond merely providing concentrated social-welfare services to deliquents because these services do not address the "real" cause of crime. William and Joan McCord, in *Origins of Crime*, for example, draw the lesson from the Cambridge-Somerville study that the true causes of delinquency are found in the "absence of parental affection" coupled with family conflict, inconsistent discipline, and rebellious parents. They are quite possibly correct; indeed, if I may speak on the basis of my own wholly unscientific observation, I am quite confident they are correct. But what of it? What agency do we create, what budget do we allocate, that will supply the missing "parental affection" and will restore to the child consistent discipline supported by a stable and loving family? When it comes to the details of their own proposals, they speak of "milieu therapy" in which the child is removed from his family and placed in a secure and permissive therapeutic environment of the sort developed by Dr. Bruno Bettleheim for autistic

50/COMMENTARY JULY 1974

children. Conceding that such a program is frightfully expensive, they urge that we attempt to reach fewer children than under conventional programs, and presumably keep each child for a relatively long period. That parents, children, taxpayers, or courts might object to all this is not considered.

Attempts to explain the causes of crime not only lead inevitably into the realm of the subjective and the familial, where both the efficacy and propriety of policy are most in doubt; they also lead one to a preference for the rehabilitative (or reformation) theory of corrections over the deterrence or incapacitation theories. Sutherland and Cressey recognize this: "On a formal level it may be observed that attempts to explain criminal behavior have greatly abetted at least the official use of the treatment reaction." One may deter a criminal by increasing the costs or reducing the benefits of crime, but that strategy does not deal with the "causes" of criminality, and hence does not go to the "root" of the problem. Stated another way, if causal theories explain why a criminal acts as he does, they also explain why he *must* act as he does and therefore they make any reliance on deterrence seem futile or irrelevant. Yet when Sutherland and Cressey come to consider the consequences of treating criminals in order to reform them, as opposed to punishing in order to deter them, they forthrightly admit that "there is no available proof" that treatment increased or decreased crime, and that "the methods of reformation . . . have not been notably successfuly in reducing crime rates." Careful reviews of the major efforts to rehabilitate criminals amply support this judgment.*

Policy analysis, as opposed to causal analysis, begins with a very different perspective. It asks, not what is the cause of a problem, but what is the condition one wants to bring into being, what measure do we have that will tell us when that condition exists, and finally what policy tools does a government (in our case, a democratic and libertarian government) possess that might, when applied, produce at reasonable cost a desired alteration in the present condition or progress toward the desired condition? In this instance, the desired condition is a reduction in specified forms of crime. The government has at its disposal certain policy instruments—rather few, in fact—that it can use: it can redistribute money, create (or stimulate the creation of) jobs, hire persons who offer advice, hire persons who practice surveillance and detection, build detention facilities, illuminate public streets, alter (within a range) the price of drugs

and alcohol, require citizens to install alarm systems, and so forth. It can, in short, manage to a degree money, prices, and technology, and it can hire people who can provide within limits either simple (e.g., custodial) or complex (e.g., counseling) services. These tools, if employed, can affect the risks of crime, the benefits of non-criminal occupations, the accessibility of things worth stealing, and the mental state of criminals or would-be criminals. A policy analyst would ask what feasible changes in which of these areas would, at what cost (monetary and non-monetary), produce how much of a change in the rate of a given crime. He would suspect, from his experience in education and social services, that changing the mental state of citizens is very difficult, quite costly, hard to manage organizationally, and may produce many unanticipated side-effects. He would then entertain as a working hypothesis that, given what he has to work with, he may gain more by altering risks, benefits, alternatives, and accessibility. He would not be sure of this, however, and would want to analyze carefully how these factors are related to existing differences in crime by state or city, and then would want to try some experimental alterations in these factors before committing himself to them wholesale.

In sum, the criminologist, concerned with causal explanations and part of a discipline—sociology—which assumes that social processes determine behavior, has operated by and large within an intellectual framework that makes it difficult or impossible to develop reasonable policy alternatives and has cast doubt, by assumption more than by argument or evidence, on the efficacy of those policy tools, necessarily dealing with objective rather than subjective conditions, which society might use to alter crime rates. A serious policy-oriented analysis of crime, by contrast, would place heavy emphasis on the manipulation of objective conditions, not necessarily because of a belief that the causes of crime are thereby being eradicated, but because behavior is easier to change than attitudes, and because the only instruments society has for altering behavior in the short run require it to assume that people act in response to the costs and benefits of alternative courses of action. The criminologist assumes, probably rightly, that the causes of crime are determined by attitudes which in turn are socially derived, if not determined; the policy analyst is led to assume that the criminal acts *as if* crime were the product of a free choice among competing opportunities and constraints. The radical individualism of Bentham and Beccaria may be scientifically questionable, but it *is* prudentially necessary.

The other most important work of the 1960's in the field of criminology, *Delinquency and Opportunity* by Richard A. Cloward and Lloyd E.

---

* See, for example, Leslie T. Wilkins, *Evaluations of Penal Measures* (Random House, 1969), and Robert Martinson, "What Works? Questions and Answers About the Rehabilitation of Prisoners" (*Public Interest*, Spring 1974).

Ohlin, would appear to be an exception to the general criminological perspective of the day. Writing in 1960, Cloward and Ohlin developed an influential theory of delinquency in big cities. A delinquent gang (or "subculture"—the terms are used, for reasons not made clear, interchangeably) arises in response to the conflict that exists between socially-approved goals (primarily monetary success) and socially-approved means to realize those goals. Certain youths, notably of the lower class, desire conventional ends but discover that there are no legitimate means to attain them; being unable (unwilling?) to revise these expectations downward, they experience frustration and this may lead them to explore illegitimate ("nonconforming") alternatives. Some lower-class youth may aspire to middle-class values ("money and morality," as the authors put it) while others may aspire only to success in lower-class terms (money alone). The barriers to realizing those aspirations are found in part in cultural constraints derived from the immigrant experience (Southern Italians and Sicilians, for example, allegedly do not value schooling highly), but in larger part in structural difficulties, chiefly the fact that education is costly in money outlays and foregone earnings.

In its brief form, the theory of Cloward and Ohlin would seem to be in sharp contrast to the general sociological perspective. Delinquency may in their view be learned from peers, but it is learned because of the gap between aspirations and opportunities, and opportunities in turn are objective conditions determined by government and the social system. Education, they claim, is the chief source of opportunity. One therefore expects them to end their book with a call for cheaper, more readily available educational programs. But they do not. Indeed, less than one page is devoted to policy proposals, amounting essentially to one suggestion: "The major effort of those who wish to eliminate delinquency should be directed to the reorganization of slum communities." No explanation is offered of what "slum reorganization" might be, except for several pages that decry "slum disorganization." Their analysis leads the reader toward the material desires of life as the key factor (indeed, that is all the lower classes are supposed to value), but stops short of telling us how those material desires are to be realized. Their theory states that "each individual occupies a position in both legitimate and illegitimate opportunity structures" (they rightly note that this is a "new way" of viewing the problem), but they do not speak of the costs and benefits of illegitimate as opposed to legitimate opportunities. Instead, the individual who is confronted with a choice among kinds of opportunities does not *choose*, he "learns deviant values" from the "social structure of the slum."

Thus, when the authors come to speak of policy, they have little to say about what determines the choice of illegitimate opportunities (nobody has chosen anything, he has only "learned" or "assimilated"), and thus they have no theoretical grounds for suggesting that the value of legitimate "opportunities" should be increased (e.g., better-paying jobs for slum youth), or that the benefits of illegitimate ones should be decreased (e.g., more certain penalties for crime), or that "opportunities" for goal gratification be replaced by direct goal gratification (e.g., redistributing income).

III

Explaining human behavior is a worthwhile endeavor; indeed, for intellectuals it is among the most worthwhile. Those who search for such explanations need not justify their activity by its social utility or its policy implications. Unfortunately, neither intellectuals nor policymakers always understand this. If the government becomes alarmed about crime, it assumes that those who have studied crime most deeply can contribute most fully to its solution. Criminologists have rarely sought to show statesmen the error of this assumption. Much of their writing is "practical," much of their time is "applied." To a degree, of course, criminological knowledge may assist criminologists' actions: careful study and conscientious learning can help one avoid obvious errors, attack popular myths, and devise inventive proposals. But it is also likely that the most profound understanding may impede or even distort, rather than facilitate, choice, because much of this knowledge is of what is immutable and necessary, not of what is variable or contingent.

In the mid-1960's, when the federal government turned toward social scientists for help in understanding and dealing with crime, there was not then in being a body of tested or even well-accepted theories as to how crime might be prevented or criminals reformed, nor was there much agreement on the causes of crime except that they were *social*, not psychological, biological, or individualistic. In fact, there was not even much agreement that crime was a major and growing problem—scholars noted the apparent increase in crime rates, but (properly) criticized the statistical and empirical weaknesses in these published rates. While these weaknesses did not always lead the critics to conclude that crime was in fact not increasing, some scholars did draw that conclusion tentatively and their criticisms encouraged others to draw it conclusively.

Nor were scholars very farsighted. Having established beyond doubt that crime rates were strongly related to age differences, few scholars (*none* that I can recall) noted the ominous consequences for crime of the coming-of-age in the 1960's of the products of the postwar "baby boom." Similarly, while some scholars had shown

52/COMMENTARY JULY 1974

by cross-sectional studies that the proportion of a city's population that was nonwhite was powerfully correlated with assaultive crimes, few to my knowledge drew the obvious implication that, unless this correlation was spurious, the continued in-migration of blacks to large cities would inflate crime rates. Once the various national commissions were underway, however, scholars associated with them (notably the group associated with the Task Force on the Assessment of Crime, under the direction of Lloyd Ohlin) began to work vigorously on these issues and produced a number of reports that showed vividly the impact of demographic changes on crime rates.

The major intellectual difficulty governing the relationship of social scientists to policymakers with respect to crime was not the presence or absence of foresight, however, but rather the problem of how to arrive at policy proposals in the absence of scientific knowledge that would support them. The crime commission did not develop new knowledge as to crime prevention or control; as Professor Ohlin later described it, existing "social-science concepts, theories, and general perspectives were probably of greater utility to the staff and the commission in forming the final recommendations than the inputs from new knowledge development efforts." What were these "concepts, theories, and general perspectives"? One, cited by Ohlin, consisted of "grave doubts" about the effectiveness of the criminal-justice system and of rehabilitation and treatment programs. From this, Ohlin and his colleagues drew the conclusion that "the criminal-justice system should be used only as a last resort in the control of undesirable conduct." From that inference, in turn, the commission adopted the view that offenders should be "diverted" from the system and recommended a broad policy of "deprisonization."

There are no doubt ample grounds in humane sentiment for finding fault with prisons, but at the time of the commission's work there were scarcely any well-established *scientific* grounds. That "treatment" had failed seemed clear, but "non-treatment" had failed just as clearly: persons on probation might be no more likely to "recidivate" than those in prison, but neither were they much less likely. As for deterrence, there was, when the commission deliberated and Professor Ohlin advised, virtually *no* scientific material on whether prison did or did not deter. It was not until 1966, fifty years after criminology began as a discipline in this country and after seven editions of the leading text on crime had appeared, that there began to be a serious and sustained inquiry into the consequences for crime rates of differences in the certainty and severity of penalties. In any case, the commission scarcely dealt with the deterrence or incapacitation functions of prison.

In short, criminology could not form the basis for much policy advice to the commission. Yet that did not prevent criminologists from advising. Professor Ohlin is entirely honest about this: "The relevant social-science literature was descriptive and analytical. There were relatively few experimental or controlled studies of the effectiveness of particular programs or policies. ... Sociologists serving as consultants to the commission proved reluctant to draw out ... action recommendations. ... When they did try to do this, the recommendations were often *more influenced by personal ideological convictions than by appropriately organized facts and theories ...*" [emphasis added].

Social scientists did not carry the day on the commission (they could not, for example, get their view on marijuana accepted), but the effect of their advice, based on personal belief rather than scholarly knowledge, was clear. Working with sympathetic commission members in small task forces, the advisers stimulated and participated in a process that—as Professor Ohlin later put it—"led to far more liberal recommendations by the commission than one would have thought possible at the outset given the conservative cast of its membership."

There is nothing whatsoever wrong with social scientists trying to persuade others of their policy beliefs, just as there is nothing wrong with lay commission members trying to persuade sociologists of their beliefs. There *is* something wrong with a process of persuasion colored by the mistaken notion that one party is an "expert" whose views are entitled to special consideration because of their evidentiary quality. There is no way of knowing to what extent commission members believed what the sociologists were saying was true, as opposed to merely plausible or interesting. But based on my own experience in advising national commissions, including the crime commission, I am confident that few social scientists made careful distinctions, when the chips were down, between what they knew as scholars and what they believed as citizens, or even spent much time discussing the complex relationships between knowledge and belief. I certainly did not, and I do not recall others doing so.

IV

H AVING alluded to my own role as a policy adviser, let me amplify on that experience to reinforce, by self-criticism, the point I am making. I was not in 1966 a criminologist, nor am I now. I came to crime, if I may put it that way, as a consequence of my study of police administration and its political context, and found myself labeled an "expert" on crime because of that interest and perhaps also because of the desire of governmental consumers of "expertise" to inflate, by wishful thinking, the supply of such persons to equal the demand for their services.

Once I found myself, willy-nilly, in the crime business, I found that my ideas on the subject—apart from those formed by my own empirical research on policing—were inevitably influenced by the currents of academic opinion about me. The effect of these currents is not to persuade one of what is true, but to persuade one of what is important. In my case, I did not absorb from criminological writings a set of policy conclusions about whether criminals can be deterred or rehabilitated, but I did absorb a set of interesting facts about crime: for example, that crimes are age-specific, that victims contribute to their victimization in most assaultive crimes, and that published crime rates are unreliable. All of these things were (and are) true, but of course they are not directly related to the policy question of what is to be done about crime.

In short, I did not, any more than Professor Ohlin, have in 1966-68 empirically supported policy advice to offer statesmen dealing with crime. What I then realized, as did Professor Ohlin, was that many of those seated about me, urging in the strongest tones various "solutions" to crime, were speaking out of ideology, not scholarship. Nor was this only true of my colleagues on the crime commission. Walter Reckless, for example, in the 1967 edition of his text, *The Crime Problem*, states flatly that punishment "does not . . . prevent crime," though he adduces no systematic

evidence to warrant such a conclusion. Charles R. Tittle and Charles H. Logan provide other examples of this unsupported assertion in their review of the more recent literature on deterrence, a review that nevertheless concludes by observing that "almost all research since 1960 supports the view that negative sanctions are significant variables in the explanation of conformity and deviance. . . . Sanctions apparently have some deterrent effect under some circumstances."

What I only later realized was that criminologists, and perhaps sociologists in general, are part of an intellectual tradition whose focal concerns are with those aspects of society that are, to a great extent, beyond the reach of policy and even beyond the reach of science. Those matters that are within the reach of policy have been, at least for many criminologists, defined away as uninteresting because they were superficial, "symptomatic," or not of "causal" significance. Sociology, for all its claims to understand structure, is at heart a profoundly subjectivist discipline. When those who practice it are brought forward and asked for advice, they will say either (if conservative) that nothing is possible, or (if liberal) that everything is possible. That most sociologists are liberals explains why the latter reaction is more common even though the presuppositions of their own discipline would more naturally lead to the former.

Part III
Ideological Framework

[11]

THE JOURNAL OF CRIMINAL LAW AND CRIMINOLOGY
Copyright © 1973 by Northwestern University School of Law

Vol. 64, No. 2
Printed in U.S.A.

IDEOLOGY AND CRIMINAL JUSTICE POLICY: SOME CURRENT ISSUES

WALTER B. MILLER*

There is currently in the United States a wide-spread impression that our country is experiencing a major transitional phase—a period in which long-established social arrangements and the moral and conceptual notions that undergird them are undergoing substantial change. Optimists see this process as a transition from one relatively effective social order to another; pessimists see it as a one-way passage to catastrophe.

It is hard to judge the validity of these conceptions. Few generations have been free from the conviction that the nation was in the throes of "the crisis of our times," and such perceptions have not always corresponded with judgments of later historians.[1]

Since criminal behavior, ways of thinking about crime, and methods of dealing with crime make up an intrinsic component of any social order, the notion of a transitional phase also affects the perceptions and actions of both criminals and criminal justice system personnel. As soon as one considers crime as one facet of a larger set of social and historical shifts, however, a paradox emerges. One gets an impression both of striking and substantial change, and striking and substantial stability.

This paradox seems to apply equally to crime and to societal response to crime. On the one hand, patterns of contemporary criminal behavior reflect substantial shifts—e.g., a massive increase in drug use and drug-related crimes, a new dimension of political motivation affecting many adult prisoners. On the other hand, an impression of changelessness and stability is evident in the relatively unchanging nature of youth crime and periodic attention to youth gang violence.[2]

A similar paradox affects those responsible for making and implementing criminal justice policy. On the one hand, we seem to be in the midst of a radical shift in conceptualizing and coping with crime, indicated by a host of current slogans such as decentralization, decriminalization, deinstitutionalization, victimology and others. On the other hand, there is a surprising sameness in the basic issues which these slogans reflect—issues such as free will versus determinism, individual rights versus state's rights, concentration versus

* Visiting Research Fellow, Center for Criminal Justice, Law School of Harvard University. Ph.D., 1954, Harvard University.

This paper is an expanded and modified version of an address presented in April 1972 as the first annual Pinkerton lecture of the School of Criminal Justice of the State University of New York at Albany. The author is much indebted for critical reactions to earlier versions of the paper to Richard Myren, Vincent O'Leary, Abraham Blumberg, Lloyd Macdonald, Gary Marx, and the staff members and fellows of the Center for Criminal Justice at Harvard Law School, James Vorenberg, Director. A shortened version of the original presentation has been published by Pinkerton's Incorporated, New York City.

[1] A few examples of perceptions that "our times" are witnessing radical or unprecedented changes are found in selected excerpts from statements published in 1874, 1930, and 1939, respectively.

Society has grave charges to answer in regard to its influence on the present and rising generation.... The social conditions of the present age are such as to favor the development of insanity. The habits inculcated by ... growing wealth ... among individuals of one class and the stinging poverty ... of another ... nurture dispositions which might ... under more equitable distributions ... have died out. Have we not seen [youth] emerging from the restraints of school, scoffing at the opinions of the world, flouting everything but their own conceit...?

Dickson, *The Science and Practice of Medicine in Relation to Mind, and the Jurisprudence of Insanity* (1874), quoted in M. ALTSCHULE, ROOTS OF MODERN PSYCHIATRY 122, 133 (1957).

In our nineteenth century polity, the home was a chief reliance ... discipline was recognized as a reality ... the pressure of the neighborhood ... was strong ... in the urban industrial society of today there is a radical change.... This complete change in the background of social control involves much that may be easily attributed to the ineffectiveness of criminal justice....

Pound, *Criminal Justice in America* (1930), quoted in F. TANNENBAUM, CRIME AND THE COMMUNITY 29 (1938).

Men's ways of ordering their common lives have broken down so disastrously as to make hope precarious. So headlong and pervasive is change today that ... historical parallels are decreasingly relevant ... because so many of the variables in the situation have altered radically ....Professor James T. Shotwell recently characterized "the anarchy we are living in today" as "the most dangerous since the fall of Rome."

R. LYND, KNOWLEDGE FOR WHAT 2, 11 (1939).

[2] An analysis involving long-term trends in youth gang violence and periodically recurrent representations of such violence as a new phenomenon engendered by contemporary conditions is included in Miller, *American Youth Gangs: Past and Present*, in A. BLUMBERG, ISSUES IN CRIMINOLOGY (in preparation).

diffusion of power. Do these concerns represent progressive movement or merely contemporary replays of ancient dramas?

Intriguing as it might be to explore these issues with respect to the behavior of both those who engage in crime and those who attempt to deal with it, I shall treat only the latter. The terms "criminologist" or "criminal justice personnel" will be used here to refer to those persons who maintain some consistent responsibility for dealing with criminals and their behavior.

One may seek to escape this paradox by employing the concept of "ideology." Ideology is also a central element in the complex patterns of change and stability, and a key to their understanding. A useful point of departure may be found in a quotation from Myrdal's *An American Dilemma*:

The place of the individual scientist along the scale of radicalism-conservatism has always had strong influences on both the selection of research problems and the conclusions drawn from research. In a sense, it is the master scale of biases in social science.[3]

It is this master scale, and its influence on the field of criminal justice, which will be my major concern here.

The term "ideology" may be used in many ways.[4] It will be used here only to refer to a set of general and abstract beliefs or assumptions about the correct or proper state of things, particularly with

[3] G. MYRDAL, AN AMERICAN DILEMMA: THE NEGRO PROBLEM AND MODERN DEMOCRACY, 1038 (1944). Myrdal's citation of the "radicalism-conservatism" scale is part of an extended discussion of sources of bias in works on race-relations, appearing as Appendix 2, "A Methodological Note on Facts and Valuations in Social Science," at 1035-64. His entire discussion is germane to issues treated in this article.
[4] A classic treatment of ideology is K. MANNHEIM, IDEOLOGY AND UTOPIA (1936). *See* ch. II.1 "Definition of Concepts." *See also* G. MYRDAL, *supra* note 3, at 1035-64. There is an extensive literature, much of it sociological, dealing with ideology as it relates to a wide range of political and social phenomena, but the specific relation between ideology and criminal justice has received relatively little direct attention. Among more recent general discussions are E. SHILS, THE INTELLECTUALS AND THE POWERS (1972); Orlans, *The Political Uses of Social Research*, 393 ANNALS AM. ACAD. POLIT. & SOC. SCI. 28 (1971); Kelman, *I.Q., Race, and Public Debate*, 2 HASTINGS CENTER REP. 8 (1972). Treatments more specific to crime and criminal justice appear in L. RADZINOWICZ, IDEOLOGY AND CRIME (1966); Andanaes, *Punishment and the Problem of General Prevention*, 8 INT'L ANNALS CRIMINOLOGY 285 (1969); Blumberg, *The Adversary System*, in C. BERSANI, CRIME & DELINQ. 435 (1970); Glaser, *Criminology and Public Policy*, 6 AM. SOCIOLOGIST 30 (1971).

respect to the moral order and political arrangements, which serve to shape one's positions on specific issues. Several aspects of ideology as used in this sense should be noted. First, ideological assumptions are generally pre-conscious rather than explicit, and serve, under most circumstances, as unexamined presumptions underlying positions taken openly. Second, ideological assumptions bear a strong emotional charge. This charge is not always evident, but it can readily be activated by appropriate stimuli, in particular by direct challenge. During the process of formation, ideological premises for particular individuals are influenced by a variety of informational inputs, but once established they become relatively impervious to change, since they serve to receive or reject new evidence in terms of a self-contained and self-reinforcing system.

The major contention of this presentation is that ideology and its consequences exert a powerful influence on the policies and procedures of those who conduct the enterprise of criminal justice, and that the degree and kinds of influence go largely unrecognized. Ideology is the permanent hidden agenda of criminal justice.

The discussion has two major aims. First, assuming that the generally implicit ideological basis of criminal justice commands strong, emotional, partisan allegiance, I shall attempt to state explicitly the major assumptions of relevant divergent ideological positions in as neutral or as nonpartisan a fashion as possible. Second, some of the consequences of such ideologies for the processes of planning, program, and policy in criminal justice will be examined.

I shall use a simple conceptual device for indicating ideological positions—a one-dimensional scale that runs from five on the right to zero in the middle to five on the left. Various ideological positions under consideration will be referred to this scale, using the terms "left" and "right" in an attempt to achieve neutrality. Although not all eleven possible distinctions will be made in every analysis, five scale distinctions on each side seem to be the minimum needed for present purposes. Later discussions will in some instances attribute considerable importance to differences as small as one scale degree.

The substance of ideologically divergent positions with respect to selected issues of current concern will be presented in three ways. Positions will be formulated first as "crusading issues"—

shorthand catchwords or rallying cries that furnish the basic impetus for action or change in the criminal justice field. Such catch phrases are derived from a deeper and more abstract set of propositions as to desired states or outcomes. These will be designated "general assumptions." Third, differentiated positions will be delineated for all points along the full range of the scale—extreme right to extreme left—for three major policy issues.[5]

[5] The substance of ideologically-relevant statements formulated here as crusading issues, general assumptions, or differentiated positions was derived from examination and analysis of a wide range of materials appearing in diverse forms in diverse sources. Materials were selected primarily on the basis of two criteria: that they bear on issues of current relevance to criminal justice policy, and that they represent one possible stance with respect to issues characterized by markedly divergent stances. With few exceptions, the statements as formulated here do not represent direct quotes, but have been generalized, abstracted or paraphrased from one or more sets of statements by one or more representatives of positions along the ideological scale. A substantial portion of the statements thus derived were taken from books, articles, speeches, and media reporting of statements by the following: Robert Welch, writer; John Schmitz, legislator; Gerald L. K. Smith, writer; Meyer Kahane, clergyman; Edward Banfield, political scientist; William Loeb, publisher; George Wallace, government; Julius Hoffman, jurist; L. Patrick Gray III, lawyer; William Rehnquist, jurist; William Buckley, writer; Spiro Agnew, government; Robert M. McKiernan, police; Howard J. Phillips, government; Lewis F. Powell Jr., jurist; Andrew Hacker, political scientist; Kevin Phillips, writer; Victor Reisel, labor; Albert Shanker, educator; Fred P. Graham, lawyer/writer; Warren Burger, jurist; James Q. Wilson, political scientist; Hubert H. Humphrey, legislator; James Reston, writer; Jacob Javits, legislator; Ramsey Clark, lawyer; Tom Wicker, writer; Earl Warren, jurist; James F. Ahearn, police; Henry Steele Commager, historian; Alan Dershowitz, lawyer; Julian Bond, legislator; Herbert J. Gans, sociologist; Ross K. Baker, political scientist; Russell Baker, writer; William Kunstler, lawyer; Benjamin Spock, physician; Noam Chomsky, anthropologist; Richard Cloward, sociologist; Herman Schwartz, lawyer; Richard Korn, sociologist; Michael Harrington, writer; Richard Quinney, sociologist; Frank Reissman, sociologist; Tom Hayden, writer; Eldridge Cleaver, writer; H. Bruce Franklin, professor; Abbie Hoffman, writer; Phillip Berrigan, clergyman; Jerry Rubin, writer. Among a range of non-academic reports, pamphlets, and periodicals which served as sources for statements by these and other persons were: JOHN BIRCH SOCIETY REPRINT SERIES; ERGO: THE RATIONAL VOICE OF LIBERTARIANISM; NEW SOLIDARITY: NATIONAL CAUCUS OF LABOR COMMITTEES; THE HASTINGS CENTER REPORT; S.D.S. NEW LEFT NOTES; Guardian; Ramparts; National Review; The Nation; The New Republic; The New York Review; Commentary; Fortune; Time; Life; Newsweek; New York Times; New York Times Magazine; The Washington Post; The Manchester Union Leader. It should be noted that the substance of materials appearing in published sources represents the publicly-taken positions of the individuals involved. The relation between public positions and

IDEOLOGICAL POSITIONS

Right: Crusading Issues

Crusading issues of the right differ somewhat from those of the left; they generally do not carry as explicit a message of movement toward new forms, but imply instead that things should be reconstituted or restored. However, the component of the message that says, "Things should be different from the way they are now," comes through just as clearly as in the crusading issues of the left. Current crusading issues of the right with respect to crime and how to deal with it include the following:

1. *Excessive leniency toward lawbreakers.* This is a traditional complaint of the right, accentuated at present by the publicity given to reform programs in corrections and policing, as well as to judicial activity at various levels.

2. *Favoring the welfare and rights of lawbreakers over the welfare and rights of their victims, of law enforcement officials, and the law abiding citizen.* This persisting concern is currently activated by attention to prisoners' rights, rehabilitation programs, attacks on police officers by militants, and in particular by a series of well-publicized Supreme Court decisions aimed to enhance the application of due process.

3. *Erosion of discipline and of respect for constituted authority.* This ancient concern is currently manifested in connection with the general behavior of youth, educational policies, treatment of student dissidents by college officials, attitudes and behavior toward law-enforcement, particularly the police.

4. *The cost of crime.* Less likely to arouse the degree of passion evoked by other crusading issues, resentment over what is seen as the enormous and increasing cost of crime and dealing with criminals—a cost borne directly by the hard working and law abiding citizen—nevertheless remains active and persistent.

5. *Excessive permissiveness.* Related to excessive leniency, erosion of discipline, and the abdication of responsibility by authorities, this

"actual" or private positions can be very complex, ranging from "close" to "distant" along a "degree of correspondence" axis, and with variation involving changes over time, differences according to the sub-issue involved, nature of audience addressed, and other factors.

trend is seen as a fundamental defect in the contemporary social order, affecting many diverse areas such as sexual morality, discipline in the schools, educational philosophies, child-rearing, judicial handling of offenders, and media presentation of sexual materials.

Right: General Assumptions

These crusading issues, along with others of similar import, are not merely ritualized slogans, but reflect instead a more abstract set of assumptions about the nature of criminal behavior, the causes of criminality, responsibility for crime, appropriate ameliorative measures, and, on a broader level, the nature of man and of a proper kind of society. These general assumptions provide the basic charter for the ideological stance of the right as a whole, and a basis for distinguishing among the several subtypes along the points of the ideological scale. Major general assumptions of the right might be phrased as follows:

1. The individual is directly responsible for his own behavior. He is not a passive pawn of external forces, but possesses the capacity to make choices between right and wrong—choices which he makes with an awareness of their consequences.

2. A central requirement of a healthy and well functioning society is a strong moral order which is explicit, well-defined, and widely adhered to. Preferably the tenets of this system of morality should be derived from and grounded in the basic precepts of a major religious tradition. Threats to this moral order are threats to the very existence of the society. Within the moral order, two clusters are of particular importance:

   a. Tenets which sustain the family unit involve morally-derived restrictions on sexual behavior, and obligations of parents to maintain consistent responsibility to their children and to one another.

   b. Tenets which pertain to valued personal qualities include: taking personal responsibility for one's behavior and its consequences; conducting one's affairs with the maximum degree of self-reliance and independence, and the minimum of dependency and reliance on others, particularly public agencies; loyalty, particularly to one's country; achieving one's ends

through hard work, responsibility to others, and self-discipline.

3. Of paramount importance is the security of the major arenas of one's customary activity—particularly those locations where the conduct of family life occurs. A fundamental personal and family right is safety from crime, violence, and attack, including the right of citizens to take necessary measures to secure their own safety, and the right to bear arms, particularly in cases where official agencies may appear ineffective in doing so.

4. Adherence to the legitimate directives of constituted authority is a primary means for achieving the goals of morality, correct individual behavior, security, and other valued life conditions. Authority in the service of social and institutional rules should be exercised fairly but firmly, and failure or refusal to accept or respect legitimate authority should be dealt with decisively and unequivocally.

5. A major device for ordering human relations in a large and heterogeneous society is that of maintaining distinctions among major categories of persons on the basis of differences in age, sex, and so on, with differences in religion, national background, race, and social position of particular importance. While individuals in each of the general categories should be granted the rights and privileges appropriate thereto, social order in many circumstances is greatly facilitated by maintaining both conceptual and spatial separation among the categories.

Left: Crusading Issues

Crusading issues of the left generally reflect marked dissatisfaction with characteristics of the current social order, and carry an insistent message about the desired nature and direction of social reform. Current issues of relevance to criminal justice include:

1. *Overcriminalization.* This reflects a conviction that a substantial number of offenses delineated under current law are wrongly or inappropriately included, and applies particularly to offenses such as gambling, prostitution, drug use, abortion, pornography, and homosexuality.

2. *Labelling and Stigmatization.* This issue is

based on a conception that problems of crime are aggravated or even created by the ways in which actual or potential offenders are regarded and treated by persons in authority. To the degree a person is labelled as "criminal," "delinquent," or "deviant," will he be likely to so act.

3. *Overinstitutionalization.* This reflects a dissatisfaction over prevalent methods of dealing with suspected or convicted offenders whereby they are physically confined in large institutional facilities. Castigated as "warehousing," this practice is seen as having a wide range of detrimental consequences, many of which are implied by the ancient phrase "schools for crime." Signalled by a renewed interest in "incarceration," prison reform has become a major social cause of the left.

4. *Overcentralization.* This issue reflects disatisfaction with the degree of centralized authority existing in organizations which deal with crime—including police departments, correctional systems, and crime-related services at all government levels. Terms which carry the thrust of the proposed remedy are local control, decentralization, community control, a new populism, and citizen power.

5. *Discriminatory Bias.* A particularly blameworthy feature of the present system lies in the widespread practice of conceiving and reacting to large categories of persons under class labels based on characteristics such as racial background, age, sex, income level, sexual practices, and involvement in criminality. Key terms here are racism, sexism, minority oppression and brutality.

Left: General Assumptions

As in the case of the rightist positions, these crusading issues are surface manifestations of a set of more basic and general assumptions, which might be stated as follows:

1. Primary responsibility for criminal behavior lies in conditions of the social order rather than in the character of the individual. Crime is to a greater extent a product of external social pressures than of internally generated individual motives, and is more appropriately regarded as a symptom of social dysfunction than as a phenomenon in its own right. The correct objective of ameliorative

efforts, therefore, lies in the attempt to alter the social conditions that engender crime rather than to rehabilitate the individual.

2. The system of behavioral regulation maintained in America is based on a type of social and political order that is deficient in meeting the fundamental needs of the majority of its citizens. This social order, and the official system of behavioral regulation that it includes, incorporates an obsolete morality not applicable to the conditions of a rapidly changing technological society, and disproportionately geared to sustain the special interests of restricted groups, but which still commands strong support among working class and lower middle class sectors of the population.

3. A fundamental defect in the political and social organization of the United States and in those components of the criminal justice enterprise that are part of this system is an inequitable and unjust distribution of power, privilege, and resources—particularly of power. This inequity pervades the entire system, but appears in its more pronounced forms in the excessive centralization of governmental functions and consequent powerlessness of the governed, the military-like, hierarchical authority systems found in police and correctional organization, and policies of systematic exclusion from positions of power and privilege for those who lack certain preferred social characteristics. The prime objective of reform must be to redistribute the decision-making power of the criminal justice enterprise rather than to alter the behavior of actual or potential offenders.

4. A further defect of the official system is its propensity to make distinctions among individuals based on major categories or classes within society such as age, sex, race, social class, criminal or non-criminal. Healthy societal adaptation for both the offender and the ordinary citizen depends on maintaining the minimum separation—conceptually and physically—between the community at large and those designated as "different" or "deviant." Reform efforts must be directed to bring this about.

5. Consistent with the capacity of external societal forces to engender crime, personnel of

official agencies play a predominantly active role, and offenders a predominantly reactive role, in situations where the two come in contact. Official agents of behavioral regulation possess the capacity to induce or enhance criminal behavior by the manner in which they deal with those who have or may have engaged in crime. These agents may define offenders as basically criminal, expose them to stigmatization, degrade them on the basis of social characteristics, and subject them to rigid and arbitrary control.

6. The sector of the total range of human behavior currently included under the system of criminal sanctions is excessively broad, including many forms of behavior (for example, marijuana use, gambling, homosexuality) which do not violate the new morality and forms which would be more effectively and humanely dealt with outside the official system of criminal processing. Legal codes should be redrafted to remove many of the behavioral forms now proscribed, and to limit the discretionary prerogatives of local authorities over apprehension and disposition of violators.

An Ideological Spectrum: Differentiated Positions of Left and Right

The foregoing ideologically-relevant propositions are formulated as general assumptions common to all those designated as "left" or "right." The present section will expand and differentiate these generalized propositions by distributing them along the ideological scale proposed earlier. Charts I, II, and III (See Appendix) present thirty differentiated positions with respect to three major issues of relevance to criminal justice policy. Statements concerning each issue are assigned ten positions along scales running from right five through left five. The three issues are: conceptions as to the causes of crime and the locus of responsibility for criminality; conceptions of proper methods of dealing with offenders; conceptions of proper operating policies of criminal justice agencies. Not included in these tables is a theoretically possible "centrist" position.

Several features of the charts in the appendix should be noted. Statements representing ideologically-influenced positions on the scale are formulated in a highly condensed and simplified manner, lacking the subtleties, qualifications, and supporting arguments which characterize the actual stances of most people. The basic model is that of an "ideal type" analysis which presents a series of simplified propositions formulated to bear a logical relationship to one another and to underlying abstract principles, rather than to reflect accurately the actual positions of real people.[6] Few readers will feel entirely comfortable with any of the statements exactly as phrased here; most will feel instead that given statements might reflect the general gist of their position, but with important qualifications, or that one can subscribe to selected parts of statements at several different points along the scale. On the other hand, few readers will fail to find some statements with which they disagree completely; it is most unlikely, for example, that one could support with equal enthusiasm the major tenets attributed here to positions at left four and right four.

In "placing" oneself with respect to the scaled positions outlined here, one should look for those statements with which one feels least uncomfortable rather than expecting to find formulations which correspond in all respects to his viewpoint. The process of ascertaining discrepancies between actual positions and those represented here as "pure" examples of rightist or leftist ideology serves one of the purposes of ideal-typical analysis; few are ideological purists, but this type of analysis makes it possible to identify positions which correspond more or less closely to ideological orthodoxy. Those whose positions are closer to the extremes will feel least comfortable with statements attributed to the opposing side of the spectrum; those closer to "centrist" positions will tend to find orientations congenial to their own at a larger number of scale positions, possibly including positions on both sides of the spectrum.

To say that the statements show some logical relationship to one another and to underlying principles is not to say that they are logically consistent; in fact, several obvious inconsistences appear in the charts. For example, right five maintains that criminals are unwitting puppets of a radical

---

[6] The classic application of ideal-type method is that of Max Weber. *See, e.g.*, the discussion of Weber's method and typology of authority and coordination in A. Henderson & T. Parsons, Max Weber: The Theory of Social and Economic Organization 98, 329 (1947). In the field of criminology, MacIver applies ideal-type analysis to discussions of social causality in general and crime causality in particular. R. MacIver, Social Causation, 174 *passim* (1942). Neither of these applications directly parallels present usage, but underlying principles are similar.

conspiracy and, at the same time, holds that they are responsible for their own behavior. Left four calls for maximum access to information concerning the inner workings of criminal justice agencies and, at the same time, advocates minimum access by employers, personnel departments and others to criminal records of individuals. If one fails to find in internal consistency the "logical" basis for these propositions, where do the logical relationships lie?

Although some degree of logical inconsistency is likely in almost any developed set of propositions about human behavior, the consistency in the above propositions lies largely in the degree to which the interests of particular classes of persons are supported, defended, and justified. The inconsistencies often lie either in the means advocated to achieve such ends or in the rationales used to defend or exculpate favored interests and condemn opposing ones. In the above examples, if one assumes that a basic interest of left four is maximum protection of and support for actual or putative offenders, then these ends are served in the one instance by maximum access to information which might reveal errors, inequities or violations in their treatment by criminal justice officials, and in the other by denying to potential employers and others access to information that might jeopardize their welfare. Similarly, in attempting to reconcile the apparent contradiction in assertions that offenders are pawns of a radical conspiracy and also that they are directly responsible for their behavior, a rightist could argue that offenders are indeed responsible for their behavior, and that they make a deliberate personal choice to follow the crime-engendering appeals of the radicals.

While statements at different scale positions frequently present differing orientations to the same sub-issue (*e.g.*, scope of criminal law, appropriate degree of restraint of offenders, extent to which "rehabilitation" should be an objective), not all of the statements on each major issue treat all of the included sub-issues. The positioned statements are defective with respect to "dimensionality," the possibility of full scalability across all issues. Each of the included sub-issues represents an independently scalable dimension. The "cause" issue incorporates approximately 14 distinguishable dimensions or sub-issues, the "offender" issue 15, and the "agencies" issue 18. To include a separate statement for each dimension at each scale position for all three issues would require a minimum of 470 statements—an impractical

number for a presentation at this level. Selection of sub-issues and their assignment to given positions was guided by an attempt both to produce internally-coherent statements and to cover a fairly broad range of sub-issues.

One often finds convergences at the extremes of a distribution of ideological positions. Several instances can be found in the charts; for example, both right five and left five attribute criminality to deliberate or systematic efforts or policies of highly-organized interest groups, although of differing identities (radicals, the ruling class). If quantifiable weights can be assigned to the scalable dimensions of the chart, two major types of distribution are included—"opposition" and "convergence" distributions. "Opposition" distributions occur where the maximum weight or magnitude is found at one extreme of the scale and the minimum at the other, with intermediate positions showing intermediate values. Examples may be found in the sub-issues "degree of coercive power to be exercised by official agencies"; (left five espouses the minimum degree, right five the maximum, with others occupying intermediate positions), and "degree of personal culpability of offenders" (right five maximum, left five minimum, others in between). Policy disputes involving this type of distribution tend to be most difficult to resolve.

In "convergence" distributions similarities or partial similarities are found in the positions of those at opposing ends of the spectrum. One instance is found in attitudes toward rehabilitation of offenders—an objective strongly opposed by partisans at both left four and right four, although for different reasons. A rather complex but crucial instance is found in the statements concerning "localized" versus "centralized" authority. Both left four and right four call for increased local autonomy, whereas the more "moderate" of both left and right favor continued or increased federal authority and support for criminal justice programs and operations. The apparent convergence of the extremes is, however, complicated by a number of factors. One relates to which branch of government exercises authority; another relates to the particular policy area at issue. Those at left four are not adverse to strong federal initiatives to improve social-service delivery capacity of local welfare agencies. Those at right four, while decrying the iron grip of federal bureaucrats over local affairs, are not adverse to strong federal initiatives to improve technological capacity of local police forces.

The more extreme leftists seek greatly increased local autonomy for citizen control over police and correctional operations, but welcome strong federal power in formulating and enforcing uniform civil rights measures. The more extreme rightists adamantly oppose the use of centralized power to enforce "mixing" of racial and other social categories or to compel uniform operations of local police, courts and corrections, but welcome strong federal power in the development and maintenance of military forces, or a strong federal investigatory branch with the power to probe corruption and collusion in local programs, particularly those of left-oriented agencies.

The unifying principle behind these apparent contradictions is the same as that noted for intra-position inconsistencies; ideologically-derived objectives are supported despite possible discrepancies involving the means to achieve them or the identity of sources of support. An additional dimension of considerable importance is also involved—that of time. Ideological positions of left and right are delineated on the basis of a given point in time earlier designated as "current." But specific stances of the left and right can change rapidly in response to changing circumstances, or they can even reverse themselves. Moreover, some of the "crusading issues" currently fashionable will become passé in the near future.

The "decentralization" issue again provides a good example. Whether one favors more or less power for "centralized" or federal agencies depends on the current ideological complexion of the several federal departments or branches. Viewed very broadly, in the early 1930's the left looked to the executive branch as a prime source of support for policies they favored, and the right to the judicial and legislative; in the 1960's the left viewed both the executive and judicial as allies, the legislature as a potential source of opposition, and sought more power for the High Court and the Presidency. At present the right views the executive as supportive, and the left looks to the legislature as an ally in an attempt to curb the power of the presidency. Reflecting these shifts have been changes in attitudes of the left and right toward "local control." While traditionally a crusading issue of the right (state's rights), the banner for community control was taken up in the 1960's by the left as an effective method of bypassing entrenched political power at the local level—primarily with respect to civil rights. Recently the

trend has begun to reverse because of a resurgence of the right's traditional "anti-big-government" stance and an increasing resort to local control by community groups pursuing rightist causes (*e.g.*, exclusion of blacks from white schools).

Further detailed analyses of convergences and divergences, consistencies and contradictions, past, present and future fashions of both these issues and others could be developed. It might be useful at this point, however, to briefly consider a more fundamental level—the basic philosophical underpinnings of the two sides—and to compress the variety and complexity of their varied positions into a single and simple governing principle.

For the right, the paramount value is order—an ordered society based on a pervasive and binding morality—and the paramount danger is disorder—social, moral and political. For the left, the paramount value is justice—a just society based on a fair and equitable distribution of power, wealth, prestige, and privilege—and the paramount evil is injustice—the concentration of valued social resources in the hands of a privileged minority.

Few Americans would quarrel with either of these values since both are intrinsic aspects of our national ideals. Stripped of the passion of ideological conflict, the issue between the two sides could be viewed as a disagreement over the relative priority of two valuable conditions: whether *order with justice*, or *justice with order* should be the guiding principle of the criminal justice enterprise.

These are ancient philosophical issues, and their many aspects have been argued in detail for centuries. Can both order and justice be maximized in a large, heterogeneous, pluralistic society? Can either objective be granted priority under all circumstances? If not, under what circumstances should which objective be seen as paramount? It might appear that these issues are today just as susceptible to rational discussion as they have been in the past; but this is not so, because the climate militates against such discussion. Why this is so will be considered shortly—after a brief discussion of the ideologies of the formal agencies of criminal justice.

IDEOLOGICAL COMPLEXION OF CRIMINAL JUSTICE
AGENCIES

The ideological positions of four major professional fields will be discussed—academic criminology, the police, the judiciary, and corrections. Rather than complex analysis or careful delineation, tentative impressions will be offered. Each system will be characterized on a very gross level, but it is important to bear in mind the possibility that there is as much ideological variability within each of the several systems as there is among them. Of particular importance within these systems are differences in age level, social class and educational level, and rank.

Academic Criminologists: This group is included not out of any presumption about the importance of the role they play, but rather because academic criminology provides the platform from which the present analysis is presented. Probably the most important point to make here is that the day-to-day ideological environment of the average academic criminologist, viewed within the context of the total society, is highly artificial; it reflects the perspectives of a deviant and unrepresentative minority. Academic criminology, reflecting academic social science in general, is substantially oriented toward the left, while the bulk of American people are oriented toward the right.[7] Further-

[7] Several recent studies provide indirect evidence of differences between academics and the general public in the likelihood that one will characterize his ideological position as "right" or "left." Of 60,000 professors surveyed by the Carnegie Commission, approximately 70% characterized themselves as "left" or "liberal," and fewer than 25% as "conservative" or "middle-of-the-road." A survey of social science professors by Everett Ladd and Seymour Lipset showed that approximately 70% voted against the "conservative" presidential candidate in 1972, compared with approximately 75% against four years before. These studies were reported in Hacker, *On Original Sin and Conservatives*, N.Y. Times, Feb. 25, 1973, § 6 (Magazine) at 13. Henry Turner and Carl Hetrick's survey of a systematic sample of members of the American Political Science Association showed that approximately 75% characterized themselves as Democrats (among academics "Democratic" almost invariably means "liberal", whereas it generally means "conservative" in blue collar populations), a percentage which had remained stable for ten years. Those designating themselves as "Republicans" had declined to about 10% at the time of the survey. Turner and Hetrick's survey also showed that the Democratic majority was significantly more active in publication and political activity than the non-Democratic minority. H. Turner & C. Hetrick, Political Activities and Party Affiliations of American Political Scientists, (paper delivered at the 1971 Meetings of the American Political Science Association).

By comparison, a Gallup survey conducted in 1972 found that 71% of a systematically-selected sample of voters designated themselves as "conservative" (41%) or "Middle-of-the-road" (30%), with 24% characterizing themselves as "liberal." A survey by Daniel Yankelovich during the same period found that 75% of the voters surveyed viewed themselves as "conservative" (37%) or "moderate" (38%), and 17% as "liberal" (15%) or "radical" (2%). *See* Rosenthal, *McGovern is Radical or Liberal to Many in Polls*, N.Y.

more, the members of the large liberal academic majority do proportionately more writing and speechmaking than those of the small conservative minority, so that their impact on the ideological climate exceeds even their large numbers. If the proportion of right-oriented persons in academic criminology comes close to being just the reverse of that in the general population, then this marked ideological divergence certainly has implications for those situations in which academicians come in contact with the public, particularly where they interact with representatives of other criminal justice branches. It also has an important impact on their own perceptions of the ideological positions of the public and other criminal justice professionals.

Police: The bulk of police officers have working-class backgrounds, and the contemporary working class is substantially rightist. Archie Bunker is a caricature, but the reality he exaggerates is a significant one. Rightist ideology in one of its purest versions may be found in the solemn speeches of Officer Joe Friday to temporarily discouraged young police officers or disgruntled citizens. Among police departments, differences in ideological complexion are found in different regions (for example, West Coast departments generally have higher proportions of college-trained personnel), different sized communities, and departments with different personnel policies. Within departments, age differences may be important (some younger officers are less rightist), as well as differences in rank and function (some departments have more liberally-oriented chiefs or research and planning personnel). The majority of working police professionals, however, subscribe to the ideological premises here designated as "rightist."

Judiciary: The legal and judicial field is probably characterized by greater ideological diversity than either the police or corrections. One reason is that leftist positions are more common among those with college degrees than among those with less education. Since college education is a prerequisite to formal legal training, lawyers are more likely to

Times, Aug. 27, 1972, at 34, col. 3. An earlier poll by Yankelovich of American college students, seen by many as among the most liberal of large population categories, showed that approximately 70% reported themselves as holding "mainstream" positions, and that among the remainder, conservatives outnumbered left-wing radicals by two-to-one. D. YANKELOVICH, THE CHANGING VALUES ON CAMPUS: POLITICAL AND PERSONAL ATTITUDES OF TODAY'S COLLEGE STUDENTS (1972).

have been exposed to the leftward orientation characteristic of most academic faculties, particularly those of the larger and more prestigious universities.[8] Judges show enormous variation in ideological predilections, probably covering the full range from right five to left four. Variation is related to factors such as the law school attended, size of jurisdiction, social status of jurists and their clientele, region, level of the court. While public attention is often directed to the actions of highly moralistic, hard line judges at right four and five positions, such jurists are probably becoming less common.

Ideological orientations of the legal profession have recently been subject to public attention, particularly in connection with two developments. First, the Supreme Court has in the recent past been associated with a series of decisions that reflect basic tenets of the left. Included have been such issues as increased protection for the rights of suspected and accused persons, inadmissibility of illegally-obtained evidence, minimization of distinctions based on race, reduction of discretionary powers of law-enforcement personnel, and reduction of judicial discretion in juvenile proceedings.[9]

These decisions and others were perceived by the right as posing a critical threat to an established balance of power and prerogatives between law-enforcement personnel and offenders, seriously endangering the law-enforcement process and the security of the public.

The second development is the emergence during the past ten years of a group of young left-oriented lawyers whose influence is probably disproportionate to their small numbers. Able, dedicated, active on a variety of fronts, many representing low-income or black clients, their activities became best known in connection with Federal Anti-Poverty programs. Many of these lawyers have assumed positions along the ideological scale as far left as the left three and left four positions.

Despite these well-publicized manifestations of leftward orientations in some sectors of the legal profession, it is unlikely that a substantial proportion of the profession consistently espouses the tenets of the left, particularly those of left three and beyond. The more liberal judges are generally found in federal and higher-level state courts, but conservative views are still common among jurists of the lower level courts, where the great bulk of day-to-day legal business is transacted. Moreover, as part of the ideological shifts noted earlier, the Burger court is regarded by the right with considerably less antipathy than the Warren court.[10]

---

[8] Hacker states that "... the higher one climbs on the prestige ladder [of American colleges and universities] the less likely are conservatives to be found on the faculty." Hacker, *supra* note 7, at 71.

[9] Issues involved here fall into two general clusters: those affecting the rights and resources available to law-enforcement officials relative to those available to persons suspected, accused, or convicted of crimes; those relating to the conceptual or physical separation or combining of major population categories. Stands of the right and left with respect to the first cluster have been delineated in several places (right crusading issue 2; left general assumptions 3, 5; right policies respecting offenders 3, 4, respecting agencies 3, 4; left policies respecting offenders 3, 4, respecting agencies 3, 4). Major decisions of the United States Supreme Court during the 1960's which appear to accord with ideological stances of the left and to run counter to those of the right include: Mapp v. Ohio, 367 U.S. 643 (1961), which reduced resources available to law-enforcement officials and increased resources available to the accused by extending limitations on the admissibility of illegally-obtained evidence; Escobedo v. Illinois, 378 U.S. 478 (1964), and Miranda v. Arizona, 384 U.S. 436 (1966), which reduced the power of law-enforcement officials to proceed with criminal processing without providing suspects with knowledge of and recourse to legal rights and resources; *In re* Gault, 387 U.S. 1 (1967), which reduced the power of judges to make dispositions in juvenile proceedings and increased the legal rights and resources of defendants; Katz v. United States, 389 U.S. 347 (1967), which reduced prerogatives of law-enforcement officials with respect to the gathering of evidence by increasing protection of suspects against intrusions of privacy; Gilbert v. California, 388 U.S. 263 (1967), and United States v. Wade, 388

U.S. 218 (1967), which decreased the freedom of law enforcement officials to seek identification of suspects, and increased the legal rights and resources available to suspects.

With respect to the second cluster, separation of population categories, stands of the right are delineated under general assumption 5, sources of crime 4, policies respecting criminal justice agencies 4, and of the left under crusading issue 5 and general assumption 4. The landmark decision here was Brown v. Board of Education, 347 U.S. 483 (1954), which held that racially segregated public education was *per se* discriminatory. While preceding the above-cited decisions by about a decade, *Brown* set a precedent for later court actions which provided support for the diminution of categorical segregation, as favored by the left, and reduced support for the maintenance of such separation, as espoused by the right.

[10] It has been widely held that the Burger Court, reflecting the influence of right-oriented Nixon appointees such as Justices Rehnquist and Powell, would evince marked support for rightist ideological premises, stopping or reversing many of the initiatives of the Warren Court in areas such as equal protection and due process. This viewpoint is articulated by Fred P. Graham, who writes, "Mr. Nixon's two new justices are strikingly like his first two appointments in conservative judicial outlook, and ... this cohesion is likely to produce a marked swing to the right—par-

Corrections: Corrections, the current hot spot of the criminal justice field, probably contains a mixture of ideological positions, with the bulk of correctional personnel ranged along the right. The average lower-echelon corrections employee has a working-class background similar to that of the average patrolman, and thus manifests the rightist orientation characteristic of that class. As in the case of police, age may be an important basis for differentiation, with older officials more likely to assume right-oriented positions. Among other bases are size of the institution and age level of the bulk of inmates. Juvenile corrections tends to have a higher likelihood of left-oriented staff, both at administrative and lower-echelon levels.

Prison reform is currently one of the most intense crusading issues of the left. While most reform efforts are exerted by persons not officially part of the correctional system, there has been some influx of left three and four persons into the official system itself, particularly among younger staff in juvenile correction facilities.

CONSEQUENCES OF IDEOLOGY

If, as is here contended, many of those involved in the tasks of planning and executing the major policies and procedures of our criminal justice system are subject to the influence of pervasive ideological assumptions about the nature of crime

---

ticularly on criminal law issues . . . ." Graham, *Profile of the "Nixon Court" Now Discernible*, N.Y. Times, May 24, 1972, at 28, col. 3. *See also* Graham, *Supreme Court, in Recent Term, Began Swing to Right That Was Sought by Nixon*, N.Y. Times, July 2, 1972, at 18, col. 1; *Nixon Appointees May Shift Court on Obscenity and Business*, N.Y. Times, October 2, 1972, at 16, col. 4. However, Gerald Gunther, in a careful review of the 1971 term of the Burger court, characterizes the court essentially as holding the line rather than moving to reverse the directions of the Warren Court or moving in new directions of its own. Gunther writes "There was no drastic rush to the right. The changes were marginal . . . . The new Court . . . has shown no inclination to overturn clear, carefully explained precedent." Gunther, *The Supreme Court 1971 Term, Foreword: In Search of Evolving Doctrine on a Changing Court: A Model for Newer Equal Protection*, 86 HARV. L. REV., 1, 2–3 (1972). *Cf.* Goldberg, *Supreme Court Review 1972, Foreword—The Burger Court 1971 Term: One Step Forward, Two Steps Backward?*, 63 J. CRIM. L.C. & P.S. 463 (1972). Although the court has shown an inclination to limit and specify some of the broader decisions of the Warren Court (*e.g.*, limiting rights to counsel at line-ups as dealt with in *Gilbert* and *Wade*, *see* Graham, July 2, 1972, *supra*), there does not appear at the time of writing any pronounced tendency to reverse major thrusts of Warren Court decisions relevant to presently-considered ideological issues, but rather to curb or limit momentum in these directions.

and methods of dealing with it—assumptions which are largely implicit and unexamined—the question then arises: what are the consequences of this phenomenon?

While both the crusading issues and graded ideological positions presented earlier were phrased to convey the tone of urgent imperatives, the assumptions from which they arise were phrased in relatively neutral terms as a set of general propositions about the nature, causes, and processes of coping with crime. So phrased and so regarded, these assumptions are susceptible to rational consideration. Their strengths and weakness can be debated, evidence can be employed to test the degree of validity each may possess, contradictions among them can be considered, and attempts made to explain or reconcile differences among them. Formulated and used in this manner, the question arises: why are they characterized here as "ideological?"

The scale of ideology presented comprises a single major parameter—substantive variation along a left-right scale with respect to a set of issues germane to crime and the criminal justice process. But there is an additional important parameter which must also be considered: that of intensity—the degree of emotional charge which attaches to the assumptions. It is the capacity of these positions to evoke the most passionate kinds of reactions and to become infused with deeply felt, quasi-religious significance that constitutes the crucial element in the difference between testable assumptions and ideological tenets. This dimension has the power to transform plausibility into ironclad certainty, conditional belief into ardent conviction, the reasoned advocate into the implacable zealot. Rather than being looked upon as useful and conditional hypotheses, these assumptions, for many, take the form of the sacred and inviolable dogma of the one true faith, the questioning of which is heresy, and the opposing of which is profoundly evil.

This phenomenon—ideological intensification—appears increasingly to exert a powerful impact on the entire field. Leslie Wilkins has recorded his opinion that the criminal justice enterprise is becoming progressively more scientific and secularized;[11] an opposite, or at least concurrent, trend is here suggested—that it is becoming progressively more ideologized. The consequences are many.

[11] Wilkins, *Crime in the World of 1990*, 4 FUTURES 203 (1970).

Seven will be discussed briefly: Polarization, Reverse Projection, Ideologized Selectivity, Informational Constriction, Catastrophism, and Distortion of Opposing Positions.

Polarization. Polarization is perhaps the most obvious consequence of ideological intensification. The more heavily a belief takes on the character of sacred dogma, the more necessary it becomes to view the proponents of opposing positions as devils and scoundrels, and their views as dangerous and immoral. Cast in this framework of the sacred and the profane, of virtuous heroes and despicable villains, the degree of accommodation and compromise that seems essential to the complex enterprise of criminal justice planning becomes, at best, enormously complicated, and at worst, quite impossible.

Reverse Projection. This is a process whereby a person who occupies a position at a given point along the ideological scale perceives those who occupy any point closer to the center than his own as being on the opposite side of the scale. Three aspects of this phenomenon, which appears in its most pronounced form at the extremes of the scale, should be noted. First, if one grants the logical possibility that there can exist a "centrist" position—not a position which maintains no assumptions, but one whose assumptions are "mixed," "balanced," or not readily characterizable—then this position is perceived as "rightist" by those on the left, and "leftist" by those on the right.

A second aspect concerns the intensity of antagonism often shown by those occupying immediately adjacent positions along the ideological scale. Perhaps the most familiar current manifestation of this is found in the bitter mutual denunciations of those classified here as occupying the positions of left four and left five. Those at left four are often taken by those at left five as far more dangerous and evil than those seen as patent facists at right four and five. Left fours stand accused as dupes of the right, selling out to or being coopted by the establishment, and blunting the thrust of social activism by cowardly vaccilation and compromise.

A third aspect of reverse projection is that one tends to make the most sensitive intrascale distinctions closest to the point that one occupies. Thus, someone at right four might be extremely sensitive to differences between his position and that of an absolute dictatorship advocate at right five, and at

the same time cast left four and five into an undifferentiated class of commies, communist dupes and radicals, quite oblivious to the distinctions that loom so large to those who occupy these positions.

Ideologized Selectivity. The range of issues, problems, areas of endeavor, and arenas of activity relevant to the criminal justice enterprise is enormous. Given the vastness of the field relative to the availability of resources, decisions must be made as to task priorities and resource allocation. Ideology plays a paramount but largely unrecognized role in this process, to the detriment of other ways of determining priorities. Ideologized selectivity exerts a constant influence in determining which problem areas are granted greatest significance, which projects are supported, what kinds of information are gathered and how research results are analyzed and interpreted. Divergent resource allocation policies of major federal agencies can be viewed as directly related to the dominant ideological orientation of the agency.

Only one example of ideologized selectivity will be cited here. The increasing use of drugs, soft and hard, and an attendant range of drug-related crime problems is certainly a major contemporary development. The importance of this problem is reflected in the attention devoted to it by academic criminologists. One major reason for this intensive attention is that explanations for the spread of drug use fit the ideological assumptions shared by most academicians (drug use is an understandable product of alienation resulting from the failure of the system to provide adequate meaning and quality to life). Also one major ameliorative proposal, the liberalization of drug laws, accords directly with a crusading issue of the left—decriminalization.

Another contemporary phenomenon, quite possibly of similar magnitude, centers on the apparent disproportionate numbers of low-status urban blacks arrested for violent and predatory crimes, brought to court and sent to prison. While not entirely ignored by academic criminologists, the relatively low amount of attention devoted to this phenomenon stands in sharp contrast to the intensive efforts evident in the field of drugs. Important aspects of the problem of black crime do not fit the ideological assumptions of the majority of academic criminologists. Insofar as the issue is studied, the problem is generally stated in terms of oppressive, unjust and discriminatory behavior by society and its law-enforcement agents—a formulation that accords with that tenet of the left which assumes the capacity of officials to engender crime by their actions, and the parallel assumption that major responsibility for crime lies in conditions of the social order. Approaches to the problem that involve the careful collection of information relative to such characteristics of the population itself as racial and social status run counter to ideological tenets that call for the minimization of such distinctions both conceptually and in practice, and thus are left largely unattended.

Informational Constriction. An attitude which is quite prevalent in many quarters of the criminal justice enterprise today involves a depreciation of the value of research in general, and research on causes of crime in particular. Several reasons are commonly given, including the notion that money spent on research has a low payoff relative to that spent for action, that past research has yielded little of real value for present problems, and that research on causes of crime in particular is of little value since the low degree of consensus among various competing schools and theorists provides little in the way of unified conclusions or concrete guidance. Quite independent of the validity of such reasons, the anti-research stance can be seen as a logical consequence of ideological intensification.

For the ideologically committed at both ends of the scale, new information appears both useless and dangerous. It is useless because the basic answers, particularly with respect to causes, are already given, in their true and final form, by the ideology; it is dangerous because evidence provided by new research has the potential of calling into question ideologically established truths.

In line with this orientation, the present enterprise, that of examining the influence of ideology on criminal justice policy and programs, must be regarded with distaste by the ideologically intense—not only because it represents information of relevance to ideological doctrine, but also because the very nature of the analysis implies that ideological truth is relative.

Catastrophism. Ideological partisans at both extremes of the scale are intensely committed to particular programs or policies they wish to see effected, and recurrently issue dire warnings of terrible castastrophes that will certainly ensue unless their proposals are adopted (Right: Unless the police are promptly given full power to curb criminality and unless rampant permissiveness toward criminals is halted, the country will surely be faced with an unprecedented wave of crime and violence; Left: Unless society promptly decides to provide the resources necessary to eliminate poverty, discrimination, injustice and exploitation, the country will surely be faced with a holocaust of violence worse than ever before). Such predictions are used as tactics in a general strategy for enlisting support for partisan causes: "Unless you turn to us and our program . . . ." That the great bulk of catastrophes so ominously predicted do not materialize does not deter catastrophism, since partisans can generally claim that it was the response to their warnings that forestalled the catastrophe. Catastrophism can thus serve to inhibit adaptation to real crises by casting into question the credibility of accurate prophets along with the inaccurate.

Magnification of Prevalence. Ideological intensification produces a characteristic effect on perceptions of the empirical prevalence of phenomena related to areas of ideological concern. In general, targets of ideological condemnation are represented as far more prevalent than carefully collected evidence would indicate. Examples are estimates by rightists of the numbers of black militants, radical conspirators, and welfare cheaters, and by leftists of the numbers of brutal policemen, sadistic prison personnel, and totally legitimate welfare recipients.

Distortion of the Opposition. To facilitate a demonstration of the invalidity of tenets on the opposite side of the ideological scale it is necessary for partisans to formulate the actual positions of the opposition in such a way as to make them most susceptible to refutation. Opposition positions are phrased to appear maximally illogical, irrational, unsupportable, simplistic, internally contradictory, and, if possible, contemptible or ludicrous. Such distortion impedes the capacity to adequately comprehend and represent positions or points of view which may be complex and extensively developed—a capacity that can be of great value when confronting policy differences based on ideological divergencies.

IMPLICATIONS

What are the implications of this analysis for those who face the demanding tasks of criminal justice action and planning? It might first appear that the prescription would follow simply and directly from the diagnosis. If the processes of formulating and implementing policy with respect to crime problems are heavily infused with ideological doctrine, and if this produces a variety of disadvantageous consequences, the moral would appear to be clear: work to reverse the trend of increased ideological intensification, bring out into the open the hidden ideological agenda of the criminal justice enterprise, and make it possible to release the energy now consumed in partisan conflict for a more direct and effective engagement with the problem field itself.

But such a prescription is both overly optimistic and overly simple. It cannot be doubted that the United States in the latter 20th century is faced with the necessity of confronting and adapting to a set of substantially modified circumstances, rooted primarily in technological developments with complex and ramified sociological consequences. It does not appear too far-fetched to propose that major kinds of necessary social adaptation in the United States can occur only through the medium of ardently ideological social movements—and that the costs of such a process must be borne in order to achieve the benefits it ultimately will confer. If this conception is correct, then ideological intensification, with all its dangers and drawbacks, must be seen as a necessary component of effective social adaptation, and the ideologists must be seen as playing a necessary role in the process of social change.

Even if one grants, however, that ideology will remain an inherent element of the policy-making process, and that while enhancing drive, dedication and commitment it also engenders rigidity, intolerance and distortion—one might still ask whether it is possible to limit the detrimental consequences of ideology without impairing its strengths. Such an objective is not easy, but steps can be taken in this direction. One such step entails an effort to increase ones' capacity to discriminate between those types of information which are more heavily invested with ideological content and those which are less so. This involves the traditional distinction between "fact" and "value" statements.[12] The present delineation of selected

[12] The classic formulations of the distinction between "factual" and "evaluative" content of statements about human behavior are those of Max Weber.

ideological stances of the left and right provides one basis for estimating the degree to which statements forwarded as established conclusions are based on ideological doctrine rather than empirically supportable evidence. When assertions are made about what measures best serve the purposes of securing order, justice, and the public welfare, one should ask "How do we know this?" If statements appear to reflect in greater or lesser degree the interrelated patterns of premises, assumptions and prescriptions here characterized as "ideological," one should accomodate one's reactions accordingly.

Another step is to attempt to grant the appropriate degree of validity to positions on the other side of the scale from one's own. If ideological commitment plays an important part in the process of developing effective policy, one must bear in mind that both left and right have important parts to play. The left provides the cutting edge of innovation, the capacity to isolate and identify those aspects of existing systems which are least adaptive, and the imagination and vision to devise new modes and new instrumentalities for accomodating emergent conditions. The right has the capacity to sense those elements of the established order that have strength, value, or continuing usefulness, to serve as a brake on over-rapid alteration of existing modes of adaptation, and to use what is valid in the past as a guide to the future. Through the dynamic clash between the two forces, new and valid adaptations may emerge.

None of us can free himself from the influence of ideological predilections, nor are we certain that it would be desirable to do so. But the purposes of effective policy and practice are not served when we are unable to recognize in opposing positions the degree of legitimacy, validity, and humane intent they may possess. It does not seem unreasonable to ask of those engaged in the demanding task of formulating and implementing criminal justice policy that they accord to differing positions that measure of respect and consideration that the true idealogue can never grant.

See, e.g., A. HENDERSON & T. PARSONS, *supra* note 6, at 8 *passim*. See also G. MYRDAL, *supra* note 3.

APPENDIX

CHART I

SOURCES OF CRIME: LOCUS OF RESPONSIBILITY

Left	*Right*
5. Behavior designated as "crime" by the ruling classes is an inevitable product of a fundamentally corrupt and unjust society. True crime is the behavior of those who perpetuate, control, and profit from an exploitative and brutalizing system. The behavior of those commonly regarded as "criminals" by establishment circles in fact represents heroic defiance and rebellion against the arbitrary and self-serving rules of an immoral social order. These persons thus bear no responsibility for what the state defines as crime; they are forced into such actions as justifiable responses to deliberate policies of oppression, discrimination, and exploitation.	5. Crime and violence are a direct product of a massive conspiracy by highly-organized and well-financed radical forces seeking deliberately to overthrow the society. Their basic method is an intensive and unrelenting attack on the fundamental moral values of the society, and their vehicle is that sector of the populace sufficiently low in intelligence, moral virtue, self-control, and judgment as to serve readily as their puppets by constantly engaging in those violent and predatory crimes best calculated to destroy the social order. Instigators of the conspiracy are most often members of racial or ethnic groups that owe allegiance to and are supported by hostile foreign powers.
4. Those who engage in the more common forms of theft and other forms of "street crime" are essentially forced into such behavior by a destructive set of social conditions caused by a grossly inequitable distribution of wealth, power, and privilege. These people are actually victims, rather than perpetrators of criminality; they are victimized by discrimination, segregation, denial of opportunity, denial of justice and equal rights. Their behavior is thus a perfectly understandable and justified reaction to the malign social forces that bring it about. Forms of crime perpetrated by the wealthy and powerful—extensive corruption, taking of massive profits through illicit collusion, outright fraud and embezzlement—along with a pervasive pattern of marginally legal exploitative practices—have far graver social consequences than the relatively minor offenses of the so-called "common" criminal. Yet these forms of crime are virtually ignored and their perpetrators excused or assigned mild penalties, while the great bulk of law-enforcement effort and attention is directed to the hapless victims of the system.	4. The bulk of serious crime is committed by members of certain ethnic and social class categories characterized by defective self-control, self-indulgence, limited time-horizons, and undeveloped moral conscience. The criminal propensities of these classes, which appear repeatedly in successive generations, are nurtured and encouraged by the enormous reluctance of authorities to apply the degree of firm, swift, and decisive punishment which could serve effectively to curb crime. Since criminality is so basic to such persons, social service programs can scarcely hope to affect their behavior, but their low capacity for discrimination makes them unusually susceptible to the appeals of leftists who goad them to commit crimes in order to undermine the society.
3. Public officials and agencies with responsibility for crime and criminals must share with damaging social conditions major blame for criminality. By allocating pitifully inadequate resources to criminal justice agencies the government virtually assures that they will be manned by poorly qualified, punitive, moralistic personnel who are granted vast amounts of arbitrary coercive power. These persons use this power to stigmatize, degrade and brutalize those who come under their jurisdiction, thus permitting them few options other than continued criminality. Society also manifests enormous reluctance to allocate the resources necessary to ameliorate	3. The root cause of crime is a massive erosion of the fundamental moral values which traditionally have served to deter criminality, and a concomitant flouting of the established authority which has traditionally served to constrain it. The most extreme manifestations of this phenomenon are found among the most crime-prone sectors of the society—the young, minorities, and the poor. Among these groups and elsewhere there have arisen special sets of alternative values or "countercultures" which actually provide direct support for the violation of the legal and moral norms of law-abiding society. A major role in the alarming increase in crime and vio-

CHART I—*Continued*

the root social causes of crime—poverty, urban deterioration, blocked educational and job opportunities—and further enhances crime by maintaining widespread systems of segregation— separating race from race, the poor from the affluent, the deviant from the conventional and the criminal from the law-abiding.

lence is played by certain elitist groups of left-oriented media writers, educators, jurists, lawyers, and others who contribute directly to ciminality by publicizing, disseminating, and supporting these crime-engendering values.

2. Although the root causes of crime lie in the disabling consequences of social, economic, and educational deprivation concentrated primarily among the disadvantaged in low-income communities, criminal behavior is in fact widely prevalent among all sectors of the society, with many affluent people committing crimes such as shoplifting, drunkenness, forgery, embezzlement, and the like. The fact that most of those subject to arrest and imprisonment have low-income or minority backgrounds is a direct consequence of an inequitable and discriminatory application of the criminal justice process—whereby the offenses of the more affluent are ignored, suppressed, or treated outside of a criminal framework, while those of the poor are actively prosecuted. A very substantial portion of the crime dealt with by officials must in fact be attributed to the nature of the criminal statutes themselves. A wide range of commonly pursued forms of behavior such as use of drugs, gambling, sexual deviance—are defined and handled as "crime", when in fact they should be seen as "victimless" and subject to private discretion. Further, a substantial portion of these and other forms of illegal behavior actually reflect illness—physical or emotional disturbance rather than criminality.

2. A climate of growing permissiveness and stress on immediate personal gratification are progressively undermining the basic deterrents to criminal behavior—self-discipline, responsibility, and a well-developed moral conscience. The prevalent tendency by liberals to attribute blame for criminality to "the system" and its inequities serves directly to aggravate criminality by providing the criminal with a fallacious rationalization which enables him to excuse his criminal behavior, further eroding self-discipline and moral conscience.

1. Crime is largely a product of social ills such as poverty, unemployment, poor quality education, and unequal opportunities. While those who commit crimes out of financial need or frustration with their life conditions deserve understanding and compassion, those who continue to commit crimes in the absence of adequate justification should in some degree be held accountable for their behavior; very often they are sick or disturbed persons who need help rather than punishment. Officials dealing with crime are often well-meaning, but they sometimes act unjustly or repressively out of an excessively narrow focus on specific objectives of law-enforcement. Such behavior in turn reflects frustration with the failure of society to provide them adequate resources to perform their tasks for which they are responsible, as it also fails to provide the resources needed to ameliorate the community conditions which breed crime.

1. The behavior of persons who habitually violate the law is caused by defective upbringing in the home, parental neglect, inadequate religious and moral training, poor neighborhood environment, and lack of adequate role-models. These conditions result in a lack of proper respect for the law and insufficient attention to the basic moral principles which deter criminality. The federal government also contributes by failing to provide local agencies of prevention and law-enforcement with sufficient resources to perform adequately the many tasks required to reduce or control crime.

CHART II

MODES OF DEALING WITH CRIME: POLICIES WITH RESPECT TO OFFENDERS

Left	*Right*
5. Since the bulk of acts defined as "crime" by the ruling classes simply represent behavior which threatens an invalid and immoral social system, those who engage in such acts can in no sense be regarded as culpable, or "criminal". There is thus no legitimate basis for any claim of official jurisdiction over, let alone any right to restrain, so-called offenders. Persons engaging in acts which help to hasten the inevitable collapse of a decadent system should have full and unrestrained freedom to continue such acts, and to be provided the maximum support and backing of all progressive elements. The vast bulk of those now incarcerated must be considered as political prisoners, unjustly deprived of freedom by a corrupt regime, and freed at once.	5. Habitual criminals, criminal types, and those who incite them should bear the full brunt of social retribution, and be prevented by the most forceful means possible from further endangering society. Murderers, rapists, arsonists, armed robbers, subversives and the like should be promptly and expeditiously put to death. The more vicious and unregenerate of these criminals should be publicly executed as an example to others. To prevent future crimes, those classes of persons who persistently manifest a high propensity for criminality should be prevented from reproducing, through sterilization or other means. Those who persist in crimes calculated to undermine the social order should be completely and permanently removed from the society, preferably by deportation.
4. All but a very small proportion of those who come under the jurisdiction of criminal justice agencies pose no real danger to society, and are entitled to full and unconditional freedom in the community at all stages of the criminal justice process. The state must insure that those accused of crimes, incarcerated, or in any way under legal jurisdiction be granted their full civil rights as citizens, and should make available to them at little or no cost the full range of legal and other resources necessary to protect them against the arbitrary exercise of coercive power. Criminal justice processing as currently conducted is essentially brutalizing—particularly institutional incarceration, which seriously aggravates criminality, and which should be entirely abolished. "Rehabilitation" under institutional auspices is a complete illusion; it has not worked, never will work, and must be abandoned as a policy objective. Accused persons, prisoners, and members of the general public subject to the arbitrary and punitive policies of police and other officials must be provided full rights and resources to protect their interests—including citizen control of police operations, full access to legal resources, fully developed grievance mechanisms, and the like.	4. Dangerous or habitual criminals should be subject to genuine punishment of maximum severity, including capital punishment where called for, and extended prison terms (including life imprisonment) with airtight guarantees that these be fully served. Probation and parole defeat the purposes of public protection and should be eliminated. Potential and less-habituated criminals might well be deterred from future crime by highly visible public punishment such as flogging, the stocks, and possibly physical marking or mutilation. To speak of "rights" of persons who have chosen deliberately to forfeit them by engaging in crime is a travesty, and malefactors should receive the punishment they deserve without interference by leftists working to obstruct the processes of justice. "Rehabilitation" as a policy objective is simply a weakly disguised method of pampering criminals, and has no place whatever in a proper system of criminal justice. Fully adequate facilities for detection, apprehension, and effective restraint of criminals should be granted those police and other criminal justice personnel who realize that their principal mission is swift and unequivocal retribution against wrongdoers and their permanent removal from society to secure the full protection of the law-abiding.
3. Since contacts with criminal justice officials—particularly police and corrections personnel—increase the likelihood that persons will engage in crime, a major objective must be to divert the maximum number of persons away from criminal justice agencies and into service programs in the community—the proper arena for helping offenders. There should be maximum use of probation as an alternative to incarceration, and parole as an	3. Rampant permissiveness and widespread coddling of criminals defeat the purposes of crime control and must be stopped. Those who persist in the commission of serious crime and whose behavior endangers the public safety should be dealt with firmly, decisively and forcefully. A policy of strict punishment is necessary not only because it is deserved by offenders but also because it serves effectively to deter potential criminals among the general public.

CHART II—*Continued*

alternative to extended incarceration. However, both services must be drastically overhauled, and transformed from ineffective watchdog operations manned by low-quality personnel to genuine and effective human services. Institutionalization should be the alternative of last resort, and used only for those proven to be highly dangerous, or for whom services cannot be provided outside of an institutional context. Those confined must be afforded the same civil rights as all citizens, including full access to legal resources and to officially-compiled information, fully-operational grievance mechanisms, right of petition and appeal from official decisions. Every attempt must be made to minimize the separation between institution and community by providing frequent leaves, work-release furloughs, full visitation rights, full access to citizen's groups. Full rights and the guarantee of due process must be provided for all those accused of crimes—particularly juveniles, minorities, and the underprivileged.

A major effort must be directed toward increasing the rights and resources of officials who cope with crime, and decreasing the rights and resources—legal, statutory, and financial—of those who use them to evade or avoid deserved punishment. Predetention measures such as bail, suspended sentences and probation should be used only when it is certain that giving freedom to actual or putative criminals will not jeopardize public safety, and parole should be employed sparingly and with great caution only in those cases where true rehabilitation seems assured. The major objective both of incarceration and rehabilitation efforts must be the protection of law-abiding society, not the welfare of the offender.

2. Since the behavior of most of those who commit crimes is symptomatic of social or psychological forces over which they have little control, ameliorative efforts must be conducted within the framework of a comprehensive strategy of services which combines individually-oriented clinical services and beneficial social programs. Such services should be offered in whatever context they can most effectively be rendered, although the community is generally preferable to the institution. However, institutional programs organized around the concept of the therapeutic community can be most effective in helping certain kinds of persons, such as drug users, for whom external constraints can be a useful part of the rehabilitative process. Rehabilitation rather than punishment must be the major objective in dealing with offenders. Treatment in the community—in group homes, halfway houses, court clinics, on probation or parole—must incorporate the maximum range of services, including vocational training and placement, psychological testing and counselling, and other services which presently are either unavailable or woefully inadequate in most communities. Where imprisonment is indicated, sentences should be as short as possible, and inmates should be accorded the rights and respect due all human beings.

2. Lawbreakers should be subject to fair but firm penalties based primarily on the protection of society, but taking into account as well the future of the offender. Successful rehabilitation is an important objective since a reformed criminal no longer presents a threat to society. Rehabilitation should center on the moral re-education of the offender, and instill in him the respect for authority and basic moral values which are the best safeguards against continued crime. These aims can be furthered by prison programs which demand hard work and strict discipline, for these serve to promote good work habits and strengthen moral fiber. Sentences should be sufficiently long as to both adequately penalize the offender and insure sufficient time for effective rehabilitation. Probation and parole should not be granted indiscriminately, but reserved for carefully selected offenders, both to protect society and because it is difficult to achieve the degree of close and careful supervision necessary to successful rehabilitation outside the confines of the institution.

1. Effective methods for dealing with actual or putative offenders require well-developed and sophisticated methods for discriminating among varying categories of persons, and gearing treatment to the differential needs of the several types thus discriminated. A major goal is to insure that those most likely to benefit from psychological counseling and

1. An essential component of any effective method for dealing with violators is a capability for making careful and sensitive discriminations among various categories of offenders, and tailoring appropriate dispositional measures to different types of offenders. In particular, the capacity to differentiate between those with a good potential for reform and those with

CHART II—*Continued*

other therapeutic methods will receive the kinds of treatment they need, rather than wasting therapeutic resources on that relatively small group of offenders whose behavior is essentially beyond reform, and are poor candidates for rehabilitation. All those under the jurisdiction of criminal justice agencies should be treated equitably and humanely. Police in particular should treat their clients with fairness and respect—especially members of minority groups and the disadvantaged. Careful consideration should be given before sentencing offenders to extended prison terms to make sure that other alternatives are not possible. Similarly, probation and parole should be used in those cases where these statutes appear likely to facilitate rehabilitation without endangering public safety. Prisoners should not be denied contact with the outside world, but should have rights to correspondence, visiting privileges, and access to printed and electronic media. They should also be provided with facilities for constructive use of leisure time, and program activities aimed to enhance the likelihood of rehabilitation.

a poor potential will ensure that the more dangerous kinds of criminals are effectively restrained. Probationers and parolees should be subject to close and careful supervision both to make sure that their activities contribute to their rehabilitation and that the community is protected from repeat violations by those under official jurisdiction. Time spent in prison should be used to teach inmates useful skills so that they may re-enter society as well-trained and productive individuals.

CHART III

MODES OF DEALING WITH CRIME: POLICIES WITH RESPECT TO CRIMINAL JUSTICE AGENCIES

Left	*Right*
5. The whole apparatus of so-called "law-enforcement" is in fact simply the domestic military apparatus used by the ruling classes to maintain themselves in power, and to inflict harassment, confinement, injury or death on those who protest injustice by challenging the arbitrary regulations devised by the militarists and monopolists to protect their interests. To talk of "reforming" such a system is farcical; the only conceivable method of eliminating the intolerable injustices inherent in this kind of society is the total and forceful overthrow of the entire system, including its so-called "law-enforcement" arm. All acts which serve this end, including elimination of members of the oppressor police force, serve to hasten the inevitable collapse of the system and the victory of progressive forces.	5. Maximum possible resources must be provided those law-enforcement officials who realize that their basic mission is the protection of society and maintenance of security for the law-abiding citizen. In addition to substantial increases in manpower, law-enforcement personnel must be provided with the most modern, efficient and lethal weaponry available, and the technological capacity (communications, computerization, electronic surveillance, aerial pursuit capability) to deliver maximum force and facilities possible to points of need—the detection, pursuit, and arrest of criminals, and in particular the control of terrorism and violence conducted or incited by radical forces.
4. The entire American system of criminal justice must be radically reformed. Unless there is a drastic reduction in the amount of power now at the disposal of official agencies—particularly the police and corrections, a police state is inevitable. In particular, unchecked power currently possessed by poorly qualified, politically reactionary officials to deal with accused and suspected persons as they see fit must be curtailed; their behavior brutalizes and radicalizes the clients of the system. To these officials, "dangerous"	4. The critical crime situation requires massive increases in the size of police forces and their technological capacity to curb crime—particularly in the use of force against criminals and radical elements. It is imperative that police command full freedom to use all available resources, legal and technical, without interference from leftist elements seeking to tie their hands and render them impotent. The power of the courts to undermine the basis of police operations by denying them fundamental legal

CHART III—*Continued*

usually means "politically unacceptable". Increasing concentration of power in entrenched bureaucracies must be checked, and the people given maximum rights to local control of their own lives, including the right to self protection through associations such as citizens councils and security patrols to counter police harassment and brutality and to monitor the operations of local prisons. Means must be found to eliminate the extensive corruption which pervades the system—exemplified by venal criminality within police departments and the unholy alliance between organized crime, corrupt politicians, and those who are supposedly enforcing the laws. Most of the criminal offenses now on the books should be eliminated, retaining only a few truly dangerous crimes such as forceful rape, since most of the offenses which consume law-enforcement energies have no real victims, and should be left to private conscience. However, statutes related to illegality by business interests, bureaucrats, corporations and the like should be expanded, and enforcement efforts greatly increased. Virtually all prisons should be closed at once, and the few persons requiring institutional restraint should be accommodated in small facilities in local communities.

powers must be curbed. The nation's capacity for incarcerating criminals—particularly through maximum security facilities—must be greatly expanded, and prison security strengthened. The "prison reform" movement rests on a mindless focus on the welfare of convicted felons and a blind disregard for the welfare of law-abiding citizens. Particularly pernicious is the movement now underway to unload thousands of dangerous criminals directly into our communities under the guise of "community corrections" (halfway houses, group homes, etc.). The local citizenry must unite and forcefully block this effort to flood our homes and playgrounds with criminals, dope addicts, and subversives. Increasing concentration of power in the hands of centralized government must be stopped, and basic rights returned to the local community—including the right to exclude dangerous and undesirable elements, and the right to bear arms freely in defense of home and family. Strict curbs must be imposed on the freedom of the media to disseminate materials aimed to undermine morality and encourage crime.

3. The more efficiency gained by law enforcement agencies through improvements in technology, communications, management, and so on, the greater the likelihood of harrassment, intimidation, and discrimination directed against the poor and minorities. Improvements in police services can be achieved only through fundamental and extensive changes in the character of personnel, not through more hardware and technology. This should be achieved by abandoning antiquated selection and recruitment policies which are designed to obtain secure employment for low-quality personnel and which systematically discriminate against the minorities and culturally disadvantaged. Lateral entry, culture-free qualification tests, and other means must be used to loosen the iron grip of civil-service selection and tenure systems. The outmoded military model with its rigid hierarchical distinctions found among the police and other agencies should be eliminated, and a democratic organizational model put in its place. The police must see their proper function as service to the community rather than in narrow terms of law-enforcement. As part of their community responsibility, law enforcement agencies should stringently limit access to information concerning offenders, especially younger ones, and much of such information should be destroyed. There must be maximum public access to the inner operations of police, courts and prisons by insuring full flow of

3. Law enforcement agencies must be provided all the resources necessary to deal promptly and decisively with crime and violence. Failure to so act encourages further law breaking both by those who are subject to permissive and inefficient handling and by those who become aware thereby how little risk they run of being caught and penalized for serious crimes. The rights of the police to stringently and effectively enforce the law must be protected from misguided legalistic interference—particularly the constant practice of many judges of granting freedom to genuine criminals laboriously apprehended by the police, often on the basis of picayune procedural details related to "due process" or other legalistic devices for impeding justice. The scope of the criminal law must be expanded rather than reduced; there is no such thing as "victimless" crime; the welfare of all law-abiding people and the moral basis of society itself are victimized by crimes such as pornography, prostitution, homosexuality and drug use, and offenders must be vigorously pursued, prosecuted, and penalized. Attempts to prevent crime by pouring massive amounts of tax dollars into slum communities are worse than useless, since such people can absorb limitless welfare "benefits" with no appreciable effect on their criminal propensities. Communities must resist attempts to open up their streets and homes to hardened criminals through halfway houses and other forms of "community corrections".

CHART III—*Continued*

information to the media, full accountability to and visitation rights by citizens and citizen groups, and full public disclosure of operational policies and operations. The major burden of corrections should be removed from the institutions, which are crime-breeding and dehumanizing, and placed directly in the communities, to which all offenders must at some point return.

2. A basic need of the criminal justice system is an extensive upgrading of the quality of personnel. This must be done by recruiting better qualified people—preferably with college training, in all branches and at all levels, and by mounting effective in-service training programs. Higher quality and better trained personnel are of particular importance in the case of the police, and training must place more stress on human relations studies such as psychology and sociology, and relatively less stress on purely technical aspects of police work. Quality must be maintained by the development and application of performance standards against which all personnel must be periodically measured, and which should provide the basis for promotion. Sentencing procedures must be standardized, rationalized, and geared to specific and explicit rehabilitative objectives rather than being left to the often arbitrary and capricious whims of particular judges. Corrections as well as other criminal justice agencies must be made more humane and equitable, and the rights of prisoners as individuals should be respected. Attempts should be made to reduce the degree of separation of prison inmates from the outside world. Changes in both legislation and law enforcement policies must be directed to reducing the disparities in arrest rates between richer and poorer offenders, so that commensurately fewer of the poor and underprivileged and more of the better off, are sought out, convicted, and imprisoned. Promising programs of humane reform must not be abandoned simply because they fail to show immediate measurable results, but should receive continued or increased federal support.

1. There must be better coordination of existing criminal justice facilities and functions so as to better focus available services on the whole individual, rather than treating him through disparate and compartmentalized efforts. This must entail better liaison between police, courts and corrections and greatly improved lines of communication, to the end of enabling each to attain better appreciation, understanding and knowledge of the operational problems of the others. Coordination and liaison must also increase between the criminal justice agencies and the general welfare services of the community,

2. There should be substantial increases in the numbers and visibility of police, particularly in and around schools, places of business, and areas of family activity. Although a few bad apples may appear from time to time, the bulk of our police are conscientious and upstanding men who deserve the continued respect and support of the community, and who should be granted ample resources to do the job to which they are assigned. Some of the proposed prison reforms may be commendable, but the burden to the taxpayer must never be lost sight of: most of the reforms suggested or already in practice are of dubious benefit or yield benefits clearly not commensurate with their costs. More effort should be directed to prevention of crime; in particular, programs of moral re-education in the schools and communities, and the institution of safeguards against the influence of those in the schools, media and elsewhere who promote criminality by challenging and rejecting the established moral values which serve to forestall illegal and immoral conduct.

1. The operations of the police should be made more efficient, in part through increased use of modern managerial principles and information processing techniques. Police protection should focus more directly on the local community, and efforts should be made to restore the degree of personal moral integrity and intimate knowledge of the local community which many older policemen had but many younger ones lack. Prison reform is important, but innovations should be instituted gradually and with great caution, and the old should not be discarded until the new is fully proven to be adequate. There

162   *WALTER B. MILLER*   [Vol. 64

CHART III—*Continued*

which have much to contribute both in the way of prevention of crime and rehabilitation of criminals. Local politicians often frustrate the purposes of reform by consuming resources in patronage, graft, and the financial support of entrenched local interests, so the federal government must take the lead in financing and overseeing criminal justice reform efforts. Federal resources and standards should be utilized to substantially increase the level and quality of social service resources available to criminal justice enterprises, promulgate standardized and rationalized modes of operation in local communities, and bring administrative coherence to the host of uncoordinated efforts now in progress.

should be much better coordination among law enforcement agencies, to reduce inefficiency, wasteful overlap, and duplication of services. The federal government must assume a major role in providing the leadership and financial resources necessary to effective law-enforcement and crime control.

ERRATA

In the March, 1973 issue:

At p. 111: footnote *, first sentence, should read: "Assistant Professor of Sociology, Associate of the Center for Russian and East European Studies, University of Michigan."

At p. 114, Table 4: footnote 3, first sentence, should read: "Totals greater than 1005 are too large to be attributable to rounding errors."

At p. 114, Table 4: insert figure "3" in columns headed "Moscow" and "Briansk."

[12]

University of Pennsylvania Law Review

FOUNDED 1852

Formerly
American Law Register

| Vol. 113 | November 1964 | No. 1 |

TWO MODELS OF THE CRIMINAL PROCESS *

Herbert L. Packer †

There are two more or less separable complexes of issues which need to be investigated as one approaches the central question of the limits of criminal law. One complex of issues concerns what may be called the ideology of the criminal law, such as questions about the nature and purposes of criminal punishment. This is generally recognized as relevant to what I have termed the central question.[1] There does not seem to be an equivalent recognition of the relevance of the other complex of issues, which concerns what may be called the processes of the criminal law.[2] The major premise of this Article is that the shape of the criminal process has an important bearing on

---

* This Article is a sketch for a portion of a work in progress concerning the criteria that a rational lawmaker should consider in determining what kinds of conduct to treat as criminal. Legal thought has not had much to say on this question: little enough if by "legal thought" we mean thought about law; less still if by it we mean thought by lawyers.

The present Article is intended as a prolegomenon directing attention to a group of problems necessarily affecting the behavior content of the criminal law. Its appearance in this forum, given its nontechnical nature, can be explained only by giving a broad construction to the "we" in Holmes's aphorism that "what we need at this time is education in the obvious more than investigation of the obscure."

It would be both premature and presumptuous to identify all those who have aided in the enterprise whose first fruits are presented here. The burden of my gratitude cannot, however, be evaded by the Dean and Faculty of the University of Pennsylvania Law School, whose generous hospitality during a sabbatical year provided the ideal environment for pursuing the subject of these reflections.

† Professor of Law, Stanford University. B.A. 1944,.LL.B. 1949, Yale University. Member, New York Bar.

[1] See, e.g., Devlin, The Enforcement of Morals (1959) ; Hart, Law, Liberty, and Morality (1963).

[2] There has been a tendency among students of the criminal process to treat procedural issues as if their resolution had nothing to do with judgments about the substantive uses of the criminal law, which apparently are thought to be immutable. See, e.g., Barrett, *Police Practices and the Law—From Arrest to Release or Charge*, 50 Calif. L. Rev. 11, 20 (1960).

questions about the wise substantive use of the criminal sanction. Its minor premise is that important trends in the development of the criminal process that are now underway make the task of appraising the uses of the criminal sanction an especially timely one.

We will start by considering the spectrum of choices that is at least in theory open in fixing the shape of the criminal process and by proposing a device for identifying and appraising the poles and the distance between them. The device, a pair of models, will then serve as a framework for considering the dynamism that appears to characterize present-day trends in the evolution of the criminal process. Finally, after a summation of the trends and an attempt to evaluate their continued potency, some tentative suggestions will be advanced about the relevance of the criminal process to the elaboration of criteria for the substantive invocation of the criminal sanction.

I. VALUES AND THE CRIMINAL PROCESS

A. Why Build Models?

People who commit crimes appear to share the prevalent impression that punishment is an unpleasantness that is best avoided. They ordinarily take care to avoid being caught. If arrested, they ordinarily deny their guilt and otherwise try not to cooperate with the police. If brought to trial, they do whatever their resources permit to resist being convicted. And, even after they have been convicted and sent to prison, their efforts to secure their freedom do not cease. It is a struggle from start to finish. This struggle is often referred to as the criminal process, a compendious term that stands for all the complexes of activity that operate to bring the substantive law of crime to bear (or to avoid bringing it to bear) on persons who are suspected of having committed crimes. It can be described, but only partially and inadequately, by referring to the rules of law that govern the apprehension, screening, and trial of persons suspected of crime. It consists at least as importantly of patterns of official activity that correspond only in the roughest kind of way to the prescriptions of procedural rules. As a result of recent emphasis on empirical research into the administration of criminal justice, we are just beginning to be aware how very rough the correspondence is.[3]

---

[3] See, *e.g.*, Goldstein, *Police Discretion Not To Invoke the Criminal Process: Low-Visibility Decisions in the Administration of Criminal Justice*, 69 YALE L.J. 543 (1960); LaFave, *Detention for Investigation by the Police: An Analysis of Current Practices*, 1962 WASH. U.L.Q. 331. Both articles are based to some extent on material gathered in the American Bar Foundation Survey of the Administration of Criminal Justice in the United States.

At the same time, and perhaps in part as a result of this new accretion of knowledge, some of our lawmaking institutions—and particularly the Supreme Court of the United States—have begun to add measurably to the prescriptions of law that are meant to govern the operation of the criminal process. This accretion has become, in the last few years, exponential in extent and velocity. We are faced with an interesting paradox: the more we learn about the Is of the criminal process, the more we are instructed about its Ought and the greater the gulf between Is and Ought appears to become. We learn that very few people get adequate legal representation in the criminal process; we are simultaneously told that the Constitution requires people to be afforded adequate legal representation in the criminal process.[4] We learn that coercion is often used to extract confessions from suspected criminals; we are then told that convictions based on coerced confessions may not be permitted to stand.[5] We discover that the police in gathering evidence often use methods that violate the norms of privacy protected by the fourth amendment; we are told that evidence so obtained must be excluded from the criminal trial.[6] But these prescriptions about how the process ought to operate do not automatically become part of the patterns of official behavior in the criminal process. Is and Ought share an increasingly uneasy co-existence. Doubts are stirred about the kind of criminal process we want to have.

The kind of criminal process we have is an important determinant of the kind of behavior content that the criminal law ought rationally to comprise. Logically, the substantive question may appear to be anterior: decide what kinds of conduct one wants to reach through the criminal process, and then decide what kind of process is best calculated to deal with those kinds of conduct. It has not worked that way. On the whole, the process has been at least as much a Given as the content of the criminal law. But it is far from being a Given in any rigid sense.

The shape of the criminal process affects the substance of the criminal law in two general ways. First, one would want to know, before adding a new category of behavior to the list of crimes and therefore placing an additional burden on the process, whether it is easy or hard to employ the criminal process. The more expeditious the process, the greater the number of people with whom it can deal and, therefore, the greater the variety and, hence, the amount of anti-

---

4 Gideon v. Wainwright, 372 U.S. 335 (1963).

5 *E.g.*, Haynes v. Washington, 373 U.S. 503 (1963); Escobedo v. Illinois, 378 U.S. 478 (1964).

6 Mapp v. Ohio, 367 U.S. 643 (1961).

social conduct that can be confided in whole or in part to the criminal law for inhibition. On the other hand, the harder the process is to use, the smaller the number of people who can be handled by it at any given level of resources devoted to staffing and operating it. The harder it is to put a suspected criminal in jail, the fewer the number of cases that can be handled in a year by a given number of policemen, prosecutors, defense lawyers, judges and jurymen, probation officers, etc. A second and subtler relationship exists between the characteristic functioning of the process and the kinds of conduct with which it can efficiently deal. Perhaps the clearest example, but by no means the only one, is in the area of what have been referred to as victimless crimes, *i.e.*, offenses that do not result in anyone's feeling that he has been injured so as to impel him to bring the offense to the attention of the authorities. The offense of fornication is an example. In a jurisdiction where it is illegal for two persons not married to each other to have sexual intercourse, there is a substantial enforcement problem (or would be, if the law were taken seriously) because people who voluntarily have sexual intercourse do not often feel that they have been victimized and therefore do not often complain to the police. Consensual transactions in gambling and narcotics present the same problem, somewhat exacerbated by the fact that we take these forms of conduct rather more seriously than fornication from the standpoint of the criminal law. To the difficulties of apprehending a criminal when it is known that he has committed a crime are added the difficulties of knowing that a crime has been committed. In this sense the victimless crime always presents a greater problem to the criminal process than does the crime with an ascertainable victim. But this problem may be minimized if the criminal process has at its disposal measures that are designed to enhance the probability that the commission of such offenses will become known. If suspects may be entrapped into committing offenses, if the police may arrest and search a suspect without evidence that he has committed an offense, if wiretaps and other forms of electronic surveillance are permitted, it becomes easier to detect the commission of offenses of this sort. But if these measures are prohibited and if the prohibitions are observed in practice, it becomes more difficult, and eventually there may come a point at which the capacity of the criminal process to deal with victimless offenses becomes so attentuated that a failure of enforcement occurs.

In both of these ways, the characteristics of the criminal process bear a relationship to the central question of what the criminal law is good for. Both a general assessment of whether that process is a high-speed or a low-speed instrument of social control and a series of specific assessments of its fitness for the handling of particular kinds of antisocial behavior are called for if we are to have a basis for elaborating the criteria that ought to affect the invocation of the criminal sanction. How can we provide ourselves with an estimate of the criminal process that pays due regard to its static and dynamic elements? There are, to be sure, aspects of the criminal process that vary only inconsequentially from place to place and from time to time. But its dynamism is clear—clearer today, perhaps, than ever before. We need to have an idea of the potentialities for change in the system and the probable direction that change is taking and may be expected to take in the future. We need to detach ourselves from the welter of more or less connected details that make up an accurate description of the myriad ways in which the criminal process does operate or may be likely to operate in midtwentieth-century America so that we can begin to appraise the system as a whole in terms of its capacity to deal with the variety of substantive missions we confide to it.

One way to do this kind of job is to abstract from reality, to build a model. In a sense that is what an examination of the constitutional and statutory provisions that govern the operation of the criminal process would produce. This, in effect, is the way analysis of the legal system has traditionally proceeded. The method has considerable utility as an index of current value choices; but it produces a model that will not tell us very much about some important problems that the system encounters and that will only fortuitously tell us anything useful about how the system actually operates. On the other hand, the kind of model that might emerge from an attempt to cut loose from the law on the books and to describe, as accurately as possible, what actually goes on in the real-life world of the criminal process would so subordinate the inquiry to the tyranny of the actual that the existence of competing value choices would be obscured. The kind of criminal process we have depends importantly on certain value choices that are reflected, explicitly or implicitly, in its habitual functioning. The kind of model we need is one that permits us to recognize explicitly the value choices that underlie the details of the criminal process. In a word, what we need is a *normative* model, or rather two models, to let us perceive the normative antinomy that runs deep in the life of the criminal law. These models may not be labelled Good and Bad, and I hope they will not be taken in that sense. Rather, they represent an attempt to abstract two separate value systems that compete for attention in the operation of the criminal process. Neither is presented as either corresponding to reality or as representing what the criminal process ought to be. The two models merely afford a convenient way to talk about the operation of a process whose day-to-day functioning involves a constant series of minute adjustments between the competing demands of two value systems and whose normative future likewise involves a series of resolutions, of greater or lesser magnitude, of the tensions between mutually exclusive claims.

I call these two models the Due Process Model and the Crime Control Model. In the next section I shall sketch their animating presuppositions, and in succeeding sections I shall present the two models as they apply to a selection of representative problems that arise at successive stages of the criminal process. As we examine in succession this sampling of stage and substage of the criminal process on which the models operate, we will move from the description of the model stages to two further inquiries: first, where on a spectrum between the extremes represented by the two models do our present practices seem approximately to fall; second, what appears to be the direction and thrust of current and foreseeable trends along each such spectrum?

There is a risk in an enterprise of this sort that is latent in any attempt to polarize. It is, simply, that values are too various to be pinned down to yes or no answers. When we polarize, we distort. The models are, in a sense, distortions. The attempt here is only to clarify the terms of discussion by isolating the assumptions that underlie competing policy claims and examining the conclusions to which those claims, if fully accepted, would lead. This Article does not make value choices, but only describes what are thought to be their consequences.

B. *Values Underlying the Models*

In this section we shall develop two competing systems of values, the tension between which accounts for the intense activity now observable in the development of the criminal process. The models we are about to examine attempt to give operational content to these conflicting schemes of values. Like the values underlying them, the models are polarities. Just as the models are not to be taken as describing real-world situations, so the values that underlie them are not to be regarded as expressing the values held by any one person. The values are presented here as an aid to analysis, not as a program for action.

1. Some Common Ground

One qualification needs to be made to the assertion of polarity in the two models. While it would be possible to construct models that exist in an institutional vacuum, it would not serve our purposes to do so. We are not postulating a criminal process that operates in any kind of society at all, but rather one that operates within the framework of contemporary American society. This leaves plenty of room for polarization, but it does require the observance of some limits. A model of the criminal process that left out of account relatively stable and enduring features of the American legal system would not have much relevance to our central task. For convenience, these elements of stability and continuity can be roughly equated with minimal agreed limits expressed in the Constitution of the United States and, more importantly, with unarticulated assumptions that can be perceived to underlie those limits. Of course, it is true that the Constitution is constantly appealed to by proponents and opponents of many measures that affect the criminal process. And only the naive would deny that there are few conclusive positions that can be reached by appeal to the Constitution. Yet assumptions do exist about the criminal process that are widely shared and that may be viewed as common ground for the operation of any model of the criminal process. Our first task is to clarify these assumptions.

First, there is the assumption implicit in the ex post facto clause of the Constitution [7] that the function of defining conduct that may be treated as criminal is separate from and anterior to the process of identifying and dealing with persons as criminals. How wide or narrow the definition of criminal conduct must be is an important question of policy that yields highly variant results depending on the values held by those making the relevant decisions.[8] But that there must be a means of definition that is in some sense separate from and anterior to the operation of the process is clear. If that were not so, our efforts to deal with the phenomenon of organized crime would appear ludicrous indeed (which is not to say that we have by any means exhausted the potentialities for dealing with that problem within the limits of this basic assumption).

A related assumption that limits the area of controversy is that the criminal process ordinarily ought to be invoked by those charged with the responsibility for doing so when it appears that a crime has been committed and that there is a reasonable prospect of apprehending and convicting its perpetrator. Although the area of police and prosecutorial discretion not to invoke the criminal process is demonstrably broad, it is common ground that these officials have no general dispensing power. If the legislature has decided that certain conduct is to be treated as criminal, the decision-makers at every level of the

---

[7] U.S. CONST. art. 1, § 9.
[8] See Note, *The Void-for-Vagueness Doctrine in the Supreme Court*, 109 U. PA. L. REV. 67 (1960).

8   *UNIVERSITY OF PENNSYLVANIA LAW REVIEW*   [Vol.113:1

criminal process are expected to accept that basic decision as a premise for action. The controversial nature of the occasional case in which that is not the role played by the relevant decision-makers only serves to highlight the strength with which the premise holds.[9] This assumption may be viewed as the other side of the ex post facto coin. Just as conduct that is not proscribed as criminal may not be dealt with in the criminal process, so must conduct that has been denominated as criminal be so treated by the participants in the process.[10]

Next, there is the assumption that there are limits to the powers of government to investigate and apprehend persons suspected of committing crimes. I do not refer to the controversy (settled recently, at least in broad outline) as to whether the fourth amendment's prohibitions against unreasonable searches and seizures applies to the states with equal force as to the federal government.[11] Rather, I refer to the general assumption that there is a degree of scrutiny and a degree of control that have to be exercised with respect to the activities of law enforcement officers, that the security and privacy of the individual may not be invaded at will. It is possible to imagine a society in which not even lip service is paid to this assumption. Nazi Germany approached but never quite reached this position. But no one in our society would maintain that every individual may be taken into custody at any time and held without any limitation of time during the process of investigating his possible commission of crimes, or that there should be no form of redress for violation of at least some standards for official investigative conduct. Although this assumption may not appear to have much in the way of positive content, its absence would render moot some of our most hotly controverted problems. If there were not general agreement that there must be some limits on police power to detain and investigate, the very controversial provisions of the Uniform Arrest Act,[12] permitting the police to detain for questioning for a short period even though they do not have grounds for making an arrest, would be a magnanimous concession by the all-powerful state rather than, as it is now perceived, a substantial expansion of police power.

Finally, there is a complex of assumptions embraced within terms like "the adversary system," "procedural due process," "notice and an opportunity to be heard," "day in court," and the like. Common to them all is the notion that the alleged criminal is not merely an object to be acted upon, but an independent entity in the process who may,

---

[9] *E.g.*, Poe v. Ullman, 367 U.S. 497 (1961).
[10] HALL, GENERAL PRINCIPLES OF CRIMINAL LAW 382-87 (2d ed. 1960).
[11] Mapp v. Ohio, 367 U.S. 643 (1961); Ker v. California, 374 U.S. 23 (1963).
[12] See pp. 28-29 *infra*.

if he so desires, force the operators of the process to demonstrate to an independent authority (judge and jury) that he is guilty of the charges against him. It is a minimal asumption. It speaks in terms of "may," not "must." It permits but does not require the accused, acting by himself or through his own agent, to play an active role in the process; by virtue of that fact, the process becomes or has the capacity to become a contest between, if not equals, at least independent actors. Now, as we shall see, much of the space between the two models is occupied by stronger or weaker notions of how this contest is to be arranged, how often it is to be played, and by what rules. The Crime Control Model tends to deemphasize this adversary aspect of the process; the Due Process Model tends to make it central. The common ground, and it is an important one, is that the process has, for everyone subjected to it, at least the potentiality of becoming to some extent an adversary struggle.

So much for common ground. There is a good deal of it, even on the narrowest view. Its existence should not be overlooked because it is, by definition, what permits partial resolutions of the tension between the two models to take place. The rhetoric of the criminal process consists largely of claims that disputed territory is "really" common ground; that, for example, the premise of an adversary system "necessarily" embraces the appointment of counsel for everyone accused of crime, or conversely, that the obligation to pursue persons suspected of committing crimes "necessarily" embraces interrogation of suspects without the intervention of counsel. We may smile indulgently at such claims; they are rhetoric and no more. But the form in which they are made suggests an important truth: that there *is* a common ground of value assumption about the criminal process that makes continued discourse about its problems possible.

2. Crime Control Values

The value system that underlies the Crime Control Model is based on the proposition that the repression of criminal conduct is by far the most important function to be performed by the criminal process. The failure of law enforcement to bring criminal conduct under tight control is viewed as leading to the breakdown of public order and thence to the disappearance of an important condition of human freedom. If the laws go unenforced, which is to say, if it is perceived that there is a high percentage of failure to apprehend and convict in the criminal process, a general disregard for legal controls tends to develop. The law-abiding citizen then becomes the victim of all sorts of unjustifiable invasions of his interests. His security of person and property is sharply diminished and, therefore, so is his liberty to function as a member of society. The claim ultimately is that the criminal process is a positive guarantor of social freedom.[13] In order to achieve this high purpose, the Crime Control Model requires that primary attention be paid to the efficiency with which the criminal process operates to screen suspects, determine guilt, and secure appropriate dispositions of persons convicted of crime.

Efficiency of operation is not, of course, a criterion that can be applied in a vacuum. By "efficiency" we mean the system's capacity to apprehend, try, convict, and dispose of a high proportion of criminal offenders whose offenses become known. In a society in which only the grossest forms of antisocial behavior were made criminal and in which the crime rate was exceedingly low, the criminal process might require many more man-hours of police, prosecutorial, and judicial time per case than ours does, and still operate with tolerable efficiency. On the other hand, a society that was prepared to increase substantially the resources devoted to the suppression of crime might cope with a rising crime rate without sacrifice of efficiency while continuing to maintain an elaborate and time-consuming set of criminal processes. However, neither of these hypotheses corresponds with social reality in this country. We use the criminal sanction to cover an increasingly wide spectrum of behavior thought to be antisocial, and the amount of crime is very large indeed. At the same time, while precise measures are not available, it does not appear that we are disposed in the public sector of the economy to increase very drastically the quantity, much less the quality, of the resources devoted to the suppression of criminal activity through the operation of the criminal process. These factors have an important bearing on the criteria of efficiency and, therefore, on the nature of the Crime Control Model.

The model, in order to operate successfully, must produce a high rate of apprehension and conviction and must do so in a context where the magnitudes being dealt with are very large, and the resources for dealing with them are very limited. There must then be a premium on speed and finality. Speed, in turn, depends on informality and on uniformity; finality depends on minimizing the occasions for challenge. The process must not be cluttered with ceremonious rituals that do not advance the progress of a case. Facts can be established more quickly through interrogation in a police station than through the formal process of examination and cross-examination in a court; it follows that extrajudicial processes should be preferred to judicial processes, informal to formal operations. Informality is not enough; there must

---

13 For a representative statement see Barrett, *supra* note 2, at 11-16.

also be uniformity. Routine stereotyped procedures are essential if large numbers are being handled. The model that will operate successfully on these presuppositions must be an administrative, almost a managerial, model. The image that comes to mind is an assembly line or a conveyor belt down which moves an endless stream of cases, never stopping, carrying the cases to workers who stand at fixed stations and who perform on each case as it comes by the same small but essential operation that brings it one step closer to being a finished product, or, to exchange the metaphor for the reality, a closed file.

The criminal process, on this model, is seen as a screening process in which each successive stage—prearrest investigation, arrest, post-arrest investigation, preparation for trial, trial or entry of plea, conviction, and disposition—involves a series of routinized operations whose success is gauged primarily by their tendency to pass the case along to a successful conclusion.

What is a successful conclusion? One that throws off at an early stage those cases in which it appears unlikely that the person apprehended is an offender and then secures, as expeditiously as possible, the conviction of the rest with a minimum of occasions for challenge, let alone postaudit. By the application of administrative expertness, primarily that of the police and prosecutors, an early determination of probable innocence or guilt emerges. The probably innocent are screened out. The probably guilty are passed quickly through the remaining stages of the process. The key to the operation of the model as to those who are not screened out is what I shall call a presumption of guilt. The concept requires some explanation, since it may appear startling to assert that what appears to be the precise converse of our generally accepted ideology of a presumption of innocence can be an essential element of a model that does correspond in some regards to the real-life operation of the criminal process.

The presumption of guilt allows the Crime Control Model to deal efficiently with large numbers. The supposition is that the screening processes operated by police and prosecutors are reliable indicators of probable guilt. Once a man has been investigated without being found to be probably innocent, or, to put it differently, once a determination has been made that there is enough evidence of guilt so that he should be held for further action rather than released from the process, then all subsequent activity directed toward him is based on the view that he is probably guilty. The precise point at which this occurs will vary from case to case; in many cases it will occur as soon as the suspect is arrested or even before, if the evidence of probable guilt that has come to the attention of the authorities is

sufficiently strong. But in any case, the presumption of guilt will begin
to operate well before the "suspect" becomes a "defendant."

The presumption of guilt is not, of course, a thing. Nor is it
even a rule of law in the usual sense. It simply exemplifies a complex
of attitudes, a mood. If there is confidence in the reliability of informal administrative factfinding activities that take place in the
early stages of the criminal process, the remaining stages of the
process can be relatively perfunctory without any loss in operating
efficiency. The presumption of guilt, as it operates in the Crime
Control Model, is the expression of that confidence.

It would be a mistake to think of the presumption of guilt as the
opposite of the presumption of innocence that we are so used to
thinking of as the polestar of the criminal process and which, as we
shall see, occupies an important position in the Due Process Model.
The presumption of innocence is not its opposite; it is irrelevant to
the presumption of guilt; the two concepts embody different rather
than opposite ideas. The difference can perhaps be epitomized by an
example. A murderer, for reasons best known to himself, chooses to
shoot his victim in plain view of a large number of people. When the
police arrive, he hands them his gun and says: "I did it, and I'm
glad." His account of what happened is corroborated by several eye-
witnesses. He is placed under arrest and led off to jail. Under these
circumstances, which may seem extreme but which in fact characterize with rough accuracy the factfinding situation in a large
proportion of criminal cases, it would be plainly absurd to maintain
that more probably than not the suspect did not commit the killing.
But that is not what the presumption of innocence means. It means
that until there has been an adjudication of guilt by an authority
legally competent to make such an adjudication, the suspect is to be
treated, for reasons that have nothing whatever to do with the probable
outcome of the case, as if his guilt is an open question.

The presumption of innocence is a direction to officials how they
are to proceed, not a prediction of outcome. The presumption of
guilt, however, is basically a prediction of outcome. The presumption
of innocence is really a direction to the authorities to ignore the presumption of guilt in their treatment of the suspect. It tells them, in
effect, to close their eyes to what will frequently seem to be factual
probabilities. The reasons why it tells them that are among the
animating presuppositions of the Due Process Model, and we will
come to them shortly. It is enough to note at this point that the
presumption of guilt is descriptive and factual; the presumption of
innocence is normative and legal. The pure Crime Control Model finds

unacceptable the presumption of innocence although, as we shall see, its real-life emanations are brought into uneasy compromise with the dictates of this dominant ideological position. For this model the presumption of guilt assures the dominant goal of repressing crime through highly summary processes without any great loss of efficiency (as previously defined), for in the run of cases, the preliminary screening processes operated by the police and the prosecuting officials contain adequate guarantees of reliable factfinding. Indeed, the position is a stronger one. It is that subsequent processes, particularly of a formal adjudicatory nature, are unlikely to produce as reliable factfinding as the expert administrative process that precedes them. The criminal process thus must put special weight on the quality of administrative factfinding. It becomes important, then, to place as few restrictions as possible on the character of the administrative factfinding processes and to limit restrictions to those that enhance reliability, excluding those designed for other purposes. As we shall see, the desire to avoid restrictions on administrative factfinding is a consistent theme in the development of the Crime Control Model.

For this model the early administrative factfinding stages are centrally vital. The complementary proposition is that the subsequent stages are relatively unimportant and should be truncated as much as possible. This, too, produces tensions with presently dominant ideology. The pure Crime Control Model has very little use for many conspicuous features of the adjudicative process and in real life works a number of ingenious compromises with it. Even in the pure model, however, there have to be devices for dealing with the suspect after the preliminary screening process has resulted in a determination of probable guilt. The focal device, as we shall see, is the plea of guilty; through its use adjudicative factfinding is reduced to a minimum. It might be said of the Crime Control Model that, reduced to its barest essentials and when operating at its most successful pitch, it consists of two elements: (a) an administrative factfinding process leading to exoneration of the suspect, or to (b) the entry of a plea of guilty.

3. Due Process Values

If the Crime Control Model resembles an assembly line, the Due Process Model looks very much like an obstacle course. Each of its successive stages is designed to present formidable impediments to carrying the accused any further along in the process. Its ideology is not the converse of that underlying the Crime Control Model. It does not deny the social desirability of repressing crime, although its critics have been known to claim so. Its ideology is composed of a

complex of ideas, some of them based on judgments about the efficacy
of crime control devices.   The ideology of due process is far more
deeply impressed on the formal structure of the law than is the ideology
of crime control; yet, an accurate tracing of the strands of which it is
made is strangely difficult.[14]   What follows is only an attempt at an
approximation.

The Due Process Model encounters its rival on the Crime Control Model's own ground in respect to the reliability of factfinding
processes.   The Crime Control Model, as we have suggested in a
preliminary way, places heavy reliance on the ability of investigative
and prosecutorial officers, acting in an informal setting in which their
distinctive skills are given full sway, to elicit and reconstruct a tolerably
accurate account of what actually took place in an alleged criminal
event.   The Due Process Model rejects this premise and substitutes
for it a view of informal, nonadjudicative factfinding that stresses
the possibility of error: people are notoriously poor observers of disturbing events—the more emotion-arousing the context, the greater the
possibility that recollection will be incorrect; confessions and admissions by persons in police custody may be induced by physical or
psychological coercion, so that the police end up hearing what the
suspect thinks they want to hear rather than the truth; witnesses may
be animated by a bias or interest that no one would trouble to discover
except one specially charged with protecting the interests of the
accused—which the police are not.   Considerations of this kind all
lead to the rejection of informal factfinding processes as definitive of
factual guilt and to the insistence on formal, adjudicative, adversary
factfinding processes in which the factual case against the accused is
publicly heard by an impartial tribunal and is evaluated only after the
accused has had a full opportunity to discredit the case against him.
Even then the distrust of factfinding processes that animates the Due
Process Model is not dissipated.   The possibilities of human error
being what they are, further scrutiny is necessary, or at least must be
available, lest in the heat of battle facts have been overlooked or
suppressed.   How far this subsequent scrutiny must be available is
hotly controverted today; in the pure Due Process Model the answer
would be: at least as long as there is an allegation of factual error that
has not received an adjudicative hearing in a factfinding context.   The
demand for finality is thus very low in the Due Process Model.

This strand of due process ideology is not enough to sustain the
model.   If all that were at issue between the two models was a series of

---

14 For a perceptive account dealing with a wider spectrum of problems than those
posed by the criminal process, see Kadish, *Methodology and Criteria in Due Process
Adjudication—A Survey and Criticism*, 66 YALE L.J. 319 (1957).

questions about the reliability of factfinding processes, we would have but one model of the criminal process, the nature of whose constituent elements would pose questions of fact, not of value. Even if the discussion is confined for the moment to the question of reliability, it is apparent that more is at stake than simply an evaluation of what kinds of factfinding processes, alone or in combination, are likely to produce the most nearly reliable results. The stumbling-block is this: how much reliability is compatible with efficiency? Granted that informal factfinding will make some mistakes that will be remedied if backed up by adjudicative factfinding, the desirability of providing this backup is not affirmed or negated by factual demonstrations or predictions that the increase in reliability will be x percent or x plus n percent. It still remains to ask how much weight is to be given to the competing demands of reliability (a high degree of probability in each case that factual guilt has been accurately determined) and efficiency (a process that deals expeditiously with the large numbers of cases that it ingests). Just as the Crime Control Model is more optimistic about the unlikelihood of error in a significant number of cases, it is also more lenient in establishing a tolerable level of error. The Due Process Model insists on the prevention and elimination of mistakes to the extent possible; the Crime Control Model accepts the probability of mistakes up to the level at which they interfere with the goal of repressing crime, either because too many guilty people are escaping or, more subtly, because general awareness of the unreliability of the process leads to a decrease in the deterrent efficacy of the criminal law. On this view reliability and efficiency are not polar opposites but rather complementary characteristics. The system is reliable *because* efficient; reliability becomes a matter of independent concern only when it becomes so attenuated as to impair efficiency. All of this the Due Process Model rejects. If efficiency suggests shortcuts around reliability, those demands must be rejected. The aim of the process is at least as much to protect the factually innocent as it is to convict the factually guilty. It somewhat resembles quality control in industrial technology: tolerable deviation from standard varies with the importance of conformity to standard in the destined use of the product. The Due Process Model resembles a factory that has to devote a substantial part of its input to quality control. This necessarily reduces quantitative output.

    This is only the beginning of the ideological difference between the two models. The Due Process Model could disclaim any attempt to provide enhanced reliability for the factfinding process and still produce a set of institutions and processes that would differ sharply from those posited by the demands of the Crime Control Model. Indeed, it may not be too great an oversimplification to assert that in point of historical development the doctrinal pressures that have emanated from the demands of the Due Process Model have tended to evolve from an original matrix of concern with the maximization of reliability into something quite different and more far-reaching.[15] This complex of values can be symbolized although not adequately described by the concept of the primacy of the individual and the complementary concept of limitation on official power.

The combination of stigma and loss of liberty that is embodied in the end result of the criminal process is viewed as being the heaviest deprivation that government can inflict on the individual. Furthermore, the processes that culminate in these highly afflictive sanctions are in themselves coercive, restricting, and demeaning. Power is always subject to abuse, sometimes subtle, other times, as in the criminal process, open and ugly. Precisely because of its potency in subjecting the individual to the coercive power of the state, the criminal process must, on this model, be subjected to controls and safeguards that prevent it from operating with maximal efficiency. According to this ideology, maximal efficiency means maximal tyranny. And, while no one would assert that minimal efficiency means minimal tyranny, the proponents of the Due Process Model would accept with considerable equanimity a substantial diminution in the efficiency with which the criminal process operates in the interest of preventing official oppression of the individual.

The most modest-seeming but potentially far-reaching mechanism by which the Due Process Model implements these antiauthoritarian values is the doctrine of legal guilt. According to this doctrine, an individual is not to be held guilty of crime merely on a showing that in all probability, based upon reliable evidence, he did factually what he is said to have done. Instead, he is to be held guilty if and only if these factual determinations are made in procedurally regular fashion and by authorities acting within competences duly allocated to them. Furthermore, he is not to be held guilty, even though the factual determination is or might be adverse to him, if various rules designed to safeguard the integrity of the process are not given effect: the tribunal that convicts him must have the power to deal with his kind of case ("jurisdiction") and must be geographically ap-

---

15 It is instructive to compare, for example, the emphasis on diminished reliability in early coerced confession cases like Brown v. Mississippi, 297 U.S. 278 (1936), with the subsequent development of a rationale that stresses the assertedly limited roles assigned to the state and the accused in an adversary system, *e.g.*, Rogers v. Richmond, 365 U.S. 534 (1961).

propriate ("venue"); too long a time must not have elapsed since the offense was committed ("statute of limitations"); he must not have been previously convicted or acquitted of the same or a substantially similar offense ("double jeopardy"); he must not fall within a category of persons, such as children or the insane, who are legally immune to conviction ("criminal responsibility"); and so on.   None of these requirements has anything to do with the factual question of whether he did or did not engage in the conduct that is charged as the offense against him; yet favorable answers to any of them will mean that he is legally innocent.   Wherever the competence to make adequate factual determinations lies, it is apparent that only a tribunal that is aware of these guilt-defeating doctrines and is willing to apply them can be viewed as competent to make determinations of legal guilt. The police and the prosecutors are ruled out by lack of capacity in the first instance and by lack of assurance of willingness in the second. Only an impartial tribunal can be trusted to make determinations of legal as opposed to factual guilt.

In this concept of legal guilt lies part of the explanation for the apparently quixotic presumption of innocence of which we spoke earlier. A man who after police investigation is charged with having committed a crime can hardly be said to be presumptively innocent, if what we mean is factual innocence.   But if any of a myriad of legal doctrines may be appropriately invoked to exculpate this particular accused, it is apparent that as a matter of prediction it cannot be said with any confidence that more probably than not he will be found guilty.

Beyond the question of predictability this model posits a functional reason for observing the presumption of innocence: by forcing the state to prove its case against the accused in an adjudicative context, the presumption of innocence serves to force into play all the qualifying and disabling doctrines that limit the use of the criminal sanction against the individual, thereby enhancing his opportunity to secure a favorable outcome.   In this sense the presumption of innocence may be seen to operate as a kind of self-fulfilling prophecy.   By opening up a procedural situation that permits the successful assertion of defenses that have nothing to do with factual guilt, it vindicates the proposition that the factually guilty may nonetheless be legally innocent and should therefore be given a chance to qualify for that kind of treatment.

The possibility of legal innocence is expanded enormously when the criminal process is viewed as the appropriate forum for correcting its own abuses.   This notion may well account for a greater amount of the distance between the two models than any other.   In theory the

Crime Control Model can tolerate rules that forbid illegal arrests, unreasonable searches, coercive interrogations, and the like if their enforcement is left primarily to managerial sanctions internally imposed. What it cannot tolerate is the vindication of those rules in the criminal process itself through the exclusion of evidence illegally obtained or through the reversal of convictions in cases where the criminal process has breached the rules laid down for its observance. The availability of these corrective devices fatally impairs the efficiency of the process. The Due Process Model, while it may in the first instance be addressed to the maintenance of reliable factfinding techniques, comes eventually to incorporate prophylactic and deterrent rules that result in the release of the factually guilty even in cases in which blotting out the illegality would still leave an adjudicative factfinder convinced of the accused's guilt.[16]

Another strand in the complex of attitudes that underlies the Due Process Model is the idea—itself a shorthand statement for a complex of attitudes—of equality. This notion has only recently emerged as an explicit basis for pressing the demands of the Due Process Model, but it appears to represent, at least in its potential, a most powerful norm for influencing official conduct. Stated most starkly, the ideal of equality holds that "there can be no equal justice where the kind of trial a man gets depends on the amount of money he has." [17]

The factual predicate underlying this assertion is that there are gross inequalities in the financial means of criminal defendants as a class, that in an adversary system of criminal justice, an effective defense is largely a function of the resources that can be mustered on behalf of the accused, and that a very large proportion of criminal defendants are, operationally speaking, "indigent" [18] in terms of their ability to finance an effective defense. This factual premise has been strongly reinforced by recent studies that in turn have been both a cause and an effect of an increasing emphasis upon norms for the criminal process based on the premise.

The norms derived from the premise do not take the form of an insistence upon governmental responsibility to provide literally equal

---

[16] This tendency, seen most starkly in the exclusionary rule for illegally seized evidence, Mapp v. Ohio, 367 U.S. 643 (1961), is also involved in the rejection of the "special circumstances" approach to testing the deprivation of counsel, Gideon v. Wainwright, 372 U.S. 335 (1963), and in the apparently similar trend in confession cases, Mallory v. United States, 354 U.S. 449 (1957); Escobedo v. Illinois, 378 U.S. 478 (1964).

[17] Griffin v. Illinois, 351 U.S. 12, 19 (1956).

[18] The vacuity of the concept of indigence is exposed in ATT'Y GEN. COMM. ON POVERTY AND THE ADMINISTRATION OF FEDERAL CRIMINAL JUSTICE, REPORT 7-8, 40-41 (1963) [hereinafter cited as ATT'Y GEN. REP.].

opportunities for all criminal defendants to challenge the process. Rather, they take as their point of departure the notion that the criminal process, initiated as it is by government and containing as it does the likelihood of severe deprivations at the hands of government, imposes some kind of public obligation to ensure that financial inability does not destroy the capacity of an accused to assert what may be meritorious challenges to the processes being invoked against him.[19]

The demands made by a norm of this kind are likely by its very nature to be quite sweeping. Although its imperatives may be initially limited to determining whether in a particular case the accused was injured or prejudiced by his relative inability to make an appropriate challenge, the norm of equality very quickly moves to another level on which the demand is that the process in general be adapted to minimize discriminations rather than that a mere series of *post hoc* determinations of discrimination be made or makeable.

It should be observed that the impact of the equality norm will vary greatly depending upon the point in time at which it is introduced into a model of the criminal process. If one were starting from scratch to decide how the process ought to work, the norm of equality would have nothing very important to say on such questions as, for example, whether an accused should have the effective assistance of counsel in deciding whether to enter a plea of guilty. One could decide, on quite independent considerations, that it is or is not a good thing to afford that facility to the generality of persons accused of crime. But the impact of the equality norm becomes far greater when it is brought to bear on a process whose contours have already been shaped. If our model of the criminal process affords defendants who are in a financial position to consult a lawyer before entering a plea the right to do so, then the equality norm exerts powerful pressure to provide such an opportunity to all defendants and to regard the failure to do so as a malfunctioning of the process from whose consequences the accused is entitled to be relieved. In a sense that has been the role of the equality norm in affecting the real-world criminal process. It has made its appearance on the scene comparatively late [20] and has therefore encountered a situation in which, in terms of the system as it operates, the relative financial inability of most persons accused of crime sharply distinguishes their treatment from the small minority of the financially capable. For that reason its impact has already been substantial and may be expected to be even more so in the future.

---

[19] *E.g., id.* at 8-11.
[20] Griffin v. Illinois, 351 U.S. 12 (1956), is generally regarded as being the first decision of the Supreme Court explicitly and exclusively grounded on the equality norm.

20 *UNIVERSITY OF PENNSYLVANIA LAW REVIEW* [Vol.113:1

There is a final strand of thought in the Due Process Model whose presence is often ignored but which needs to be candidly faced if thought on the subject is not to be obscured. That is a mood of skepticism about the morality and the utility of the criminal sanction, taken either as a whole or in some of its applications. The subject is a large and complicated one, comprehending as it does much of the intellectual history of our times.[21] To put the matter *in parvo*, one cannot improve upon the statement by Professor Paul Bator:

> [I]n summary we are told that the criminal law's notion of just condemnation and punishment is a cruel hypocrisy visited by a smug society on the psychologically and economically crippled; that its premise of a morally autonomous will with at least some measure of choice whether to comply with the values expressed in a penal code is unscientfic and outmoded; that its reliance on punishment as an educational and deterrent agent is misplaced, particularly in the case of the very members of society most likely to engage in criminal conduct; and that its failure to provide for individualized and humane rehabiliation of offenders is inhuman and wasteful.[22]

This skepticism, which may be fairly said to be widespread among the most influential and articulate of contemporary leaders of informed opinion, leads to an attitude toward the processes of the criminal law which, to quote Mr. Bator again, engenders

> a peculiar receptivity toward claims of injustice which arise within the traditional structure of the system itself; fundamental disagreement and unease about the very bases of the criminal law has, inevitably, created acute pressure at least to expand and liberalize those of its processes and doctrines which serve to make more tentative its judgments or limit its power.[23]

In short, doubts about the ends for which power is being exercised create pressure to limit the discretion with which that power is exercised.

The point need not be pressed to the extreme of doubts about or rejection of the premises upon which the criminal sanction in general rests. Unease may be stirred simply by reflection on the variety of uses to which the criminal sanction is put and by judgment that an increasingly large proportion of those uses may represent an unwise

---

21 A portion of the work in progress of which this paper is a part is concerned with the impact of modern skeptical doubts on the ideology of the criminal law.

22 Bator, *Finality in Criminal Law and Federal Habeas Corpus for State Prisoners*, 76 HARV. L. REV. 441, 442 (1963).

23 *Id.* at 442-43.

invocation of so extreme a sanction.[24] It would be an interesting irony if doubts about the utility of certain uses of the criminal sanction prove to contribute to a restrictive trend in the criminal process that in the end requires a choice among uses and finally an abandonment of some of the very uses that stirred the original doubts.

There are two kinds of problems that need to be dealt with in any model of the criminal process. One is what the rules shall be. The other is how the rules shall be implemented. The second is at least as important as the first. As we shall see time and again in our detailed development of the models, the distinctive difference between the two models is not only in the rules of conduct that they lay down, but also in the sanctions that are to be invoked when a claim is presented that the rules have been breached and, no less importantly, in the timing that is permitted or required for the invocation of those sanctions.

As I have already suggested, the Due Process Model locates at least some of the sanctions for breach of the operative rules in the criminal process itself. The relation between these two aspects of the process—the rules and the sanctions for their breach—is a purely formal one unless there is some mechanism for bringing them into play with each other. The hinge between them in the Due Process Model is the availability of legal counsel. This has a double aspect: many of the rules that the model requires are couched in terms of the availability of counsel to do various things at various stages of the process—this is the conventionally recognized aspect; beyond it, there is a pervasive assumption as to the necessity for counsel in order to invoke sanctions for breach of any of the rules. The more freely available these sanctions are, the more important is the role of counsel in seeing to it that the sanctions are appropriately invoked. If the process is seen as a series of occasions for checking its own operation, the role of counsel is a much more nearly central one than is the case in a process that is seen as primarily concerned with expeditious determination of factual guilt. And if equality of operation is a governing norm, the availability of counsel to some is seen as requiring it for all. Of all the controverted aspects of the criminal process, the right to counsel, including the role of government in its provision, is the most dependent on what one's model of the process looks like, and the least susceptible of resolution unless one has confronted the antinomies of the two models.

I do not mean to suggest that questions about the right to counsel disappear if one adopts a model of the process that conforms more or

---

[24] See pp. 66-68 *infra.*

less closely to the Crime Control Model, but only that such questions become absolutely central if one's model moves very far down the spectrum of possibilities toward the pure Due Process Model. The reason for this centrality is to be found in the shared assumption underlying both models that the process is an adversary one in which the initiative in invoking relevant rules rests primarily on the parties concerned, the state and the accused. One could construct models that placed central responsibility on adjudicative agents such as committing magistrates and trial judges. And there are, as we shall see, marginal but nonetheless important adjustments in the role of the adjudicative agents that enter into the models with which we are concerned.[25] For present purposes it is enough to say that these adjustments *are* marginal, that the animating presuppositions that underlie both models in the context of the American criminal system relegate the adjudicative agents to a relatively passive role and therefore place central importance on the role of counsel.

One last introductory note. What assumptions do we make about the sources of authority to shape the real-world operations of the criminal process? What agencies of government have the power to pick and choose between their competing demands? Once again, the limiting features of the American context come into play. Ours is not a system of legislative supremacy. The distinctively American institution of judicial review exercises a limiting and, ultimately, a shaping influence on the criminal process. Because the Crime Control Model is basically an affirmative model, emphasizing at every turn the existence and exercise of official power, its validating authority is ultimately legislative (although proximately administrative). Because the Due Process Model is basically a negative model, asserting limits on the nature of official power and on the modes of its exercise, its validating authority is judicial and requires an appeal to supra-legislative law, to the law of the Constitution. To the extent that tensions between the two models are resolved by deference to the Due Process Model, the authoritative force at work is the judicial power, working in the distinctively judicial mode of invoking the sanction of nullity. That is at once the strength and the weakness of the Due Process Model: its strength because in our system the appeal to the Constitution provides the last and the overriding word; its weakness because saying no in specific cases is an exercise in futility unless there is a general willingness on the part of the officials who operate the process to apply negative prescriptions across the board. It is no accident that statements reinforcing the Due Process Model come from

---

[25] As, for example, in the role of judge in the plea of guilty. See pp. 46-51 *infra*.

the courts while at the same time facts denying it are established by the police and prosecutors.

II. THE MODELS IN OPERATION

We turn now to some details of the Crime Control and Due Process Models. This is an effort, first, to convey a sense of the extraordinary complexity of the criminal process, no matter which model one visualizes as corresponding more closely to reality; even the Crime Control Model is a formidable consumer of human resources. Again, we shall try to document the existence throughout the process of recurrent themes that divide the two models, posing an essentially limited number of basic choices for shaping its real-life structure. Finally, this assortment of instances will serve to document the minor premise of the Article: that the present real-world criminal process tends by and large to resemble the Crime Control Model but that the current trend is pushing it a significant distance down the spectrum toward the Due Process Model.

There are various ways of dividing the criminal process for purposes of description and analysis. We shall view it as consisting of three major stages or periods: the period from arrest through the decision to charge the suspect with a crime; the period from the decision to charge through the determination of guilt; and the stage of review and correction of errors that have occurred during the earlier periods. From the first period I have chosen two problems to illustrate the contrasting requirements of the two models: arrests for investigation, and detention and interrogation after a "lawful" arrest. From the second period I have again selected two problems: pretrial detention and the plea of guilty. From the third stage I have selected problems of direct appeal and collateral attack that raise issues of equality of access to the courts, of the special problems of criminal justice in a federal system, and of retroactivity in the application of changed norms in the criminal process. Finally, there is a postscript on the pervasive and strategically crucial problem of access to counsel.

The themes here dealt with could be developed through application of the model technique to many other problems of the criminal process, including electronic surveillance, discovery in criminal cases, the presentation of the insanity defense, and the institution of the jury trial. As to each of these, and others as well, it can be asserted with some confidence that the antinomies of the two models show up in the same or similar form as those chosen for discussion, and also that an examination of the situation and the trend would produce

24   *UNIVERSITY OF PENNSYLVANIA LAW REVIEW*   [Vol.113:1

conclusions in line with those reached on the basis of the examples presented here.

A. From Arrest to Charge

1. Arrests for Investigation

The act of taking a person into physical custody is ordinarily spoken of as an arrest. The term "arrest" carries with it important legal consequences, so that great controversy attends the question whether certain forms of physical restraint, such as stopping a person on the street for questioning, or taking him to the station house for a brief period of questioning without then and there intending to prefer any particular charge against him, is "really" an arrest. Since our discussion of the competing norms will refer to a number of different kinds of restraining conduct that may or may not be thought of as desirable depending on the dictates of the particular model, there is no reason not to refer indifferently to all of them as arrests, with the understanding that the term is used in the sense of physical description, not of operational legal norm.

Two crucial issues arise at this stage of the process: (1) on what basis are the police entitled to make an arrest, and (2) what consequences, if any, will flow from their making an "illegal" arrest? These are the issues that divide our two polar models, and that may in addition be thought of as representing a paradigm of the kind of division that will occur over numerous other issues that arise in the process of investigation and apprehension.

The Crime Control Model. Of course the police should be entitled to arrest a person when they have probable cause to think that he has committed a particular criminal offense, but it would be absurd to suggest that an arrest is permissible *only* in that situation. The slight invasion of personal freedom and privacy involved in stopping a person on the street to ask him questions, or even taking him to the station house for a period of questioning and other investigation, is justified in a wide variety of situations that only by the exercise of hypocrisy could be described as involving "probable cause." To give only a few examples: (1) people who are known to the police as previous offenders should be subject to arrest at any time for the limited purpose of determining whether they have been engaging in antisocial activities, especially when a crime has taken place of the sort they have committed in the past and it is known that it was physically possible for them to have committed it; (2) anyone who behaves in a way that arouses suspicion that he may be up to no good should be subject to arrest for investigation; it may turn out that he has committed an offense, but more importantly, the very fact of stopping him for questioning, either on the street or at the station house, may prevent the commission of a crime; (3) those who make a living out of criminal activity should be made to realize that their presence in the community is unwanted if they persist in their criminal occupations; periodic checks of their activity, whether or not they involve an arrest, will help to bring that attitude home to them.

In short, the power of the police to arrest people for the purpose of investigation and prevention is one that must exist if the police are to do their job properly; the only question is whether arrests for investigation and prevention should be made hypocritically and deviously, or openly and avowedly. It causes disrespect for law when there are great deviations between what the law on the books authorizes the police to do and what everyone knows they actually do.

The police have no reason to abuse this power by arresting and holding law-abiding people. The innocent have nothing to fear. It is enough of a check on police discretion to let the dictates of police efficiency determine under what circumstances and for how long a person may be stopped and held for investigation. But if laws are thought to be required limiting police discretion to make an arrest, they should either provide very liberal outer limits so as to accommodate all possible cases or, preferably, should require nothing more explicit than behavior that is reasonable under all the circumstances.

The question of appropriate sanctions for breach of whatever rules are devised to limit police arrest powers is, as a practical matter, at least as important to the ends of crime control as is the nature of the substantive rules themselves. The most appropriate sanction is discipline of the offending policemen by those best qualified to judge whether his conduct has lived up to professional police standards—his superiors in the police department. Discipline by his superiors may make him a better policeman; in cases where that seems improbable, he should be dismissed from the force. Civil remedies for the arrested person, administered in the ordinary courts, are also a possibility, although they are less likely to serve the end of educating the erring police officer. The one kind of sanction that should be completely inadmissible is the kind that takes place in the criminal process itself: dismissal of prosecution, suppression of evidence, etc. That kind of sanction for police misconduct simply gives the criminal a windfall without affecting the conduct of the erring police. This is particularly true in the light of the fact that any set of rules for the governance of police conduct is apt to be quite technical, leading to a certain

number of good faith mistakes.[26] The policeman who made the
mistake may never know or be only dimly aware that his conduct resulted in a criminal's going free. His own conduct is much more
likely to be changed by measures that affect him personally and that
do not have the fortuitous effect of conferring benefit on the criminal
and thus reducing the effectiveness of law enforcement.

There are, generally speaking, two kinds of devices for giving
the police adequate scope in making arrests for investigation. The
first is what might be called the direct method: explicitly providing
broad powers to stop and question persons, irrespective of whether they
are reasonably suspected of having committed a particular crime. The
second is the indirect method: framing broad enough definitions of
criminal conduct to give the police the power to arrest on the orthodox
"probable cause" basis a wide variety of people who are engaged in
suspicious conduct. Vagrancy laws, disorderly conduct laws, and
laws making it a crime not to give an account of oneself in response
to police interrogation are all examples. It is not too important which
of these methods is used; often a combination of the two will produce
the desired result.

The Due Process Model. It is a basic right of free men—basic
in the sense that his other rights depend upon it—not to be subject to
physical restraint except for good cause. The only measurable standard of cause is the time-honored prescription that no one may be
arrested except upon a determination—preferably made independently
by a magistrate in deciding whether to issue a warrant, but in situations
of necessity by a police officer acting upon probative data subject to
subsequent judicial scrutiny—that a crime has probably been committed, and that he is the person who probably committed it. Any
less stringent standard opens the door to the probability of grave
abuse, as repeated investigations of police practices have shown. A
society that covertly tolerates indiscriminate arrest is hypocritical; but
one that approves its legality is well on the way to becoming totalitarian in nature.

It is far from demonstrable that broad powers of arrest for
investigation are necessary to the efficient operation of the police.
The argument that they are necessary is open to a serious charge of
inconsistency since it is also argued that changes in the law are
necessary to bring it into conformity with prevalent though unacknowledged practices. If arrests for investigation are actually now

---

[26] See the famous *mot* of Mr. Justice Cardozo in People v. Defore, 242 N.Y. 13,
21, 150 N.E. 585, 587 (1926): "the criminal is to go free because the constable has
blundered."

tolerated on a wide scale, it makes no sense to assert that legalizing them is necessary to protect efficiency from being impaired. In the end, however, arguments about what is required by efficiency are wide of the mark. A totally efficient system of crime control would be a totally repressive one since it would require a total suspension of rights of privacy. We have to be prepared to pay a price for a regime that fosters personal privacy and champions the dignity and inviolability of the individual. That price inevitably involves some sacrifice in efficiency; consequently, an appeal to efficiency alone is never sufficient to justify any encroachment on the area of human freedom. It must be shown that efficient law enforcement will be so heavily impaired by failure to adopt the proposed measure that the minimal conditions of public order necessary to provide the environment in which individuals can be allowed to enjoy the fruits of personal freedom will in themselves cease to exist or be gravely impaired. No one has seriously suggested that we are at or near that point.

The practical consequence of enlarging police authority to detain individuals for questioning is not likely to be that all classes of the population will thereupon be subjected to interference. If that were the consequence, the practice would carry its own limiting features because the popular outcry would be so great that these measures could not long be resorted to. The danger, rather, is that they will be applied in a discriminatory fashion to precisely those elements in the population—the poor, the ignorant, the illiterate, the unpopular—who are least able to draw attention to their plight and to whose sufferings the vast majority of the population are the least responsive. Respect for law, never high among minority groups, would plunge to a new low if what the police are now thought to do sub rosa became an officially sanctioned practice.

The need, then, is not to legalize practices that are presently illegal but widespread. Rather, it is to reaffirm their illegality and at the same time to take steps to reduce their incidence. This brings us to the question of sanctions for illegal arrests. To the extent possible, these sanctions should be located within the criminal process itself; since it is the efficiency of that process that they seek so mistakenly to promote, the process should penalize, and thus label as inefficient, arrests that are based on any standard less rigorous than probable cause. Of course and as a minimal requirement, any evidence that is obtained directly or indirectly on the basis of an illegal arrest should be suppressed. Beyond that, any criminal prosecution commenced on the basis of an illegal arrest should be dismissed, preferably with prejudice, but at the least with the consequence that the entire process, if it is to be re-invoked, must be started over again from scratch, and all records, working papers, and the like prepared in the course of the first illegal proceeding impounded and destroyed.

Many illegal arrests do not result in criminal prosecution (one of their undoubted vices) and are therefore not amenable to sanctions imposed in the criminal process itself. A variety of devices should be marshalled to provide effective sanctions against arrests for investigation. The ordinary tort action against the policeman has been demonstrated to be of very limited utility. It should be supplemented by provision for a statutory action against the governmental unit employing the offending policeman, with a high enough minimum recovery to make suit worthwhile. Since an important public service is performed by attorneys who bring suits against errant police officers, there should also be provision for allowing adequate attorney's fees in cases where the action is successful. Measures of this kind will give governmental units a stake in proper police activity and an incentive to discourage illegal activity that they do not now have. Direct disciplinary measures against the offending police officer are also desirable, but it is unrealistic to expect these to be initiated by a departmental authority. Outside scrutiny is needed, both to insure that the law is being impartially enforced and, perhaps even more importantly, to reassure the general public that the police are not a law unto themselves. To this end there is need to set up civilian (i.e., nonpolice) boards to which complaints about illegal police activity may be directed and which can at least initiate, if not conduct, disciplinary proceedings in cases where preliminary investigation shows that the complaint may be meritorious.

The Situation and the Trend. The legal power of the police to stop persons on the street, search them for weapons, and require them to answer questions about their identity and business is ambiguous.[27] There is no doubt that the police, like any other person, may approach others and ask them questions. The question is what the police may do if the person refuses to stop or to answer questions. Strangely enough, there is no authoritative holding on whether the police may constitutionally be authorized to restrain a person who refuses to stop and answer questions when there is no probable cause to arrest him. The proposed Uniform Arrest Act would give the police the power to "stop any person abroad who he has reasonable ground to suspect is committing, has committed or is about to commit a crime,

---

[27] The confused state of the law has been demonstrated by many commentators. *E.g.*, Remington, *The Law Relating to "On the Street" Detention, Questioning and Frisking of Suspected Persons and Police Arrest Privileges in General*, 51 J. CRIM. L., C. & P.S. 386 (1960).

and may demand of him his name, address, business abroad and whither he is going." [28]   It goes on to provide that any person so questioned who fails to give a satisfactory account of himself may be "detained" for further questioning and investigation, the period of such "detention" not to exceed two hours.   The Act has been adopted by only three states and has apparently been construed out of existence in one of them.[29]   It is silent on the question of remedies available to a person wrongfully detained under its provisions.

"There is no doubt that it is common police practice to stop and question suspects as to whom there are no sufficient grounds for arrest." [30]   The knowledgeable commentator who expressed that opinion goes on to say that its truth is not easy to document.   It is also clear that many persons so stopped who do not give a satisfactory account of themselves are taken to the station house for further investigation.   In the District of Columbia,[31] where the police had an explicit category of arrest denominated as a "taking into custody without probable cause," a recent study showed that in a one-year period there were 3,743 such arrests.   This represented less than one percent of the total arrests in the District—415,925—during the period.   But since such arrests are apparently made only for investigation of felonies, the more relevant figure is the percentage of arrests for felonies that fall into the category of arrests for investigation.   Here the percentage is twenty-eight, or about one in every four felony arrests. Most such arrests were made on the street, but a substantial proportion were made in the suspects' homes.

The present sanctions for illegal arrest are essentially as follows: exclusion in a criminal prosecution of evidence obtained by a search conducted incident to an illegal arrest; [32] tort action against the offending police officer; [33] complaint to the police department which, with rare exceptions, disposes of the complaint through departmental channels and without "civilian" scrutiny.[34]

Recent Supreme Court decisions make it quite clear that if the detention of suspects in the absence of probable cause must be justified by the constitutional standards that prevail for a technical "arrest,"

---

[28] The text of the act is set forth in Warner, *The Uniform Arrest Act*, 28 Va. L. Rev. 315, 320-21 (1942).

[29] De Salvatore v. State, 52 Del. 550, 163 A.2d 244 (1960).

[30] Remington, *supra* note 27, at 389.

[31] Wash., D.C., Commissioners' Comm. on Police Arrests for Investigation, Report and Recommendations 9 (1962).

[32] Mapp v. Ohio, 367 U.S. 643 (1961).

[33] See Foote, *Tort Remedies for Police Violations of Individual Rights*, 39 Minn. L. Rev. 493 (1955).

[34] See Note, *The Administration of Complaints by Civilians Against the Police*, 77 Harv. L. Rev. 499 (1964).

such detention would be held to be a violation of the fourth amendment.[35] And it seems quite likely that detention, whether on the
street or at the station house, would be considered an arrest (or to
use the language of the fourth amendment, a "seizure") in the constitutional sense.[36] If this judgment is right, it would follow that the
provisions of the Uniform Arrest Act, referred to earlier, would now
be held unconstitutional by the Supreme Court, even though there
might have been substantial doubt about that proposition as recently
as 1941, when the act was first proposed.

It is one thing for a court to declare a procedure unconstitutional.
It is quite another to translate that declaration into operative fact. By
and large, all that courts have available is the sanction of nullity. They
can reverse criminal convictions based on evidence obtained through
an unlawful arrest. They can (and perhaps will) go farther and
reverse such convictions or nullify at an earlier stage of the process
whenever it is shown that an illegal arrest has taken place. But that
is still only a retail operation, and the problem is a wholesale one.

One indication of further trend may be that the Commissioners of
the District of Columbia, acting in response to the study already described, have directed the police department to discontinue the practice
of making arrests for investigation.[37] That action, not in itself perhaps
of major significance, may provide a microcosmic example of a process
that appears to be underway on many fronts in the administration
of criminal justice in this country. The legal norm ostensibly says one
thing. There is some suspicion that actual practice is quite different.
However, it is only when investigation of the actual practice, spurred
by developing legal norms, shows the magnitude of the discrepancy
that the tension between norm and practice is partially resolved by
reform. The increase in visibility itself contributes to the evolution
and refinement of the norm, which in turn stimulates and keeps alive an
interest in the development of actual practice. How long such a cycle
of reform may sustain itself is not clear. It does seem, however, that
such a cycle is now underway in the area of arrests for investigation
and that it is slowly but perceptibly pushing practice in the direction
of the Due Process Model.

---

[35] See, *e.g.*, Henry v. United States, 361 U.S. 98 (1959); Johnson v. United
States, 333 U.S. 10, 15-16 (1948).

[36] The question of when a technical "arrest" takes place was left open in Henry
v. United States, 361 U.S. 98 (1959), and Rios v. United States, 364 U.S. 253 (1960).
Cf. United States v. Bonnano, 180 F. Supp. 71 (S.D.N.Y. 1960). *But see* United
States v. Bufalino, 285 F.2d 408, 420 n.3 (2d Cir. 1960).

[37] But not without some backing and filling. See Kamisar, *On the Tactics of
Police—Prosecution Oriented Critics of the Courts*, 49 CORNELL L.Q. 436, 444-45
(1964).

2. Detention and Interrogation After a "Lawful" Arrest

Once a person suspected of crime has been taken into custody, someone has to decide whether a prosecution should be formally initiated and, if so, what specific offense or offenses should be charged. Typically, this is a job for the prosecutor; yet, at this point he will ordinarily not even know that the suspect is in custody. Furthermore, there is a question whether the charge against the suspect ought not to be evaluated by some impartial authority in order to determine whether he should be held for judicial action. Since there is also a question whether the suspect should be held in custody until his guilt is adjudicated or released pending that determination, an occasion needs to be afforded for making that decision. Both of these decisions— whether or not to hold for the institution of charges and, if so, whether or not to release pending further steps in the process—are, in theory at least, made at a preliminary hearing before a judicial officer who, when he sits in this capacity, is known as a magistrate. This occasion provides typically a terminus ad quem for the initial investigatory and apprehending phase of the criminal process, a mechanism for turning the criminal investigation into a criminal prosecution.

However, prior to the independent magisterial hearing, it must be determined to what extent the accused may be required to cooperate in the postarrest investigation: (1) May the police hold the accused indefinitely or must they bring him before a magistrate at some particular time? (2) If the latter, what sanctions, if any, should be imposed for failure to comply with the requisite time limits? (3) May the suspect be interrogated by the police during this time and, if so, under what limitations? (4) If the accused admits his guilt during this period, what restrictions, if any, are there on the use that may be made of this evidence at his trial? (5) Should the accused be entitled to the assistance of counsel during the time between his arrest and the preliminary hearing and, if so, under what conditions and with what consequences for failure by the police to adhere to those conditions?

The Crime Control Model. The police cannot be expected to solve crimes by independent investigation alone. The best source of information is usually the suspect himself. Without his cooperation many crimes could not be solved at all. The police must have a reasonable opportunity to interrogate the suspect in private before he has a chance to fabricate a story or to decide that he will not cooperate. The psychologically optimal time for getting this kind of cooperation from the suspect is immediately after his arrest, before he has had a chance to rally his forces. Any kind of outside interference is likely to

32   *UNIVERSITY OF PENNSYLVANIA LAW REVIEW*   [Vol.113:1

diminish the prospect that the suspect will cooperate in the interrogation; therefore, he should not be entitled to summon his family or friends, and most importantly, he should not be entitled to consult a lawyer. The first thing that a lawyer will tell him is to say nothing to the police. Once he obtains that kind of reinforcement, the chances of getting any useful information from him sink to zero.

Of course, the police should not be entitled to hold the suspect indefinitely for interrogation nor would they want to do so. The point of diminishing return in interrogation is reached fairly soon, and, anyhow, the police do not have extensive enough resources to be able to go on interrogating indefinitely. But no hard and fast rule can be laid down about how long the police should be permitted to interrogate the suspect before bringing him before a magistrate. The gravity of the crime, its complexity, the amount of criminal sophistication that the suspect appears to have, all of these are relevant factors in determining how long he should be held. The standard ought to be the length of time under all the circumstances during which it is reasonable to suppose that legitimate techniques of interrogation may be expected to produce useful information, or that extrinsic investigation may be expected to produce convincing proof either of the suspect's innocence or of his guilt.

The suspect should not be held incommunicado under normal circumstances. His family is entitled to know where he is; but they should not be entitled to talk with him, since that may impair the effectiveness of the interrogation. Occasionally, it may be justifiable not to notify them at all, as where a confederate is still at large and does not know that his partner in crime has been apprehended.

The point of all these illustrations, however, is that hard and fast rules cannot be laid down if police efficiency is not to be impaired. It follows that good faith mistakes in applying these rules in any given case should not be penalized. If the police err by holding a suspect too long, he has no complaint, because by hypothesis they have some basis for belief that he has committed a crime. The public has a complaint to the extent that police resources are thereby demonstrated to be used inefficiently; but the redress for that is intradepartmental discipline in flagrant cases and a general program of internal administrative management that minimizes such occasions.

Any trustworthy statement obtained from a suspect during a period of police interrogation should of course be admissible into evidence against him. Criminal investigation is a search for truth, and anything that aids the search should be encouraged. There is, to be sure, a danger that occasionally police will not live up to professional standards and will use coercive measures to elicit a confession from a suspect. That is not to be condoned, but at the same time we should keep in mind that the evil of a coerced confession is that it may result in the conviction of an innocent man. There is no way of laying down hard and fast rules about what kinds of police conduct are coercive. It is a factual question in each case whether the accused's confession is unreliable. A defendant against whom a confession is introduced into evidence should have to convince the jury that the circumstances under which it was elicited were so coercive that more probably than not the confession was untrue. In reaching a determination on that issue, the trier of fact should of course be entitled to consider the other evidence in the case and, if it points toward guilt and tends to corroborate the confession, should be entitled to take that into account in determining whether, more likely than not, the confession was untrue.

To say this is not to say that the unlawful use of force by the police on an accused is ever to be condoned. It is simply to say that its use is not in itself determinative of the reliability of a confession and should therefore not in itself be conclusive against the admissibility of a confession. The sanctions available for mistreating a person in custody are ample, if vigorously pursued, to ensure that this kind of conduct will be found only in rare instances. It is through the raising of professional standards by internal administrative methods, rather than through the happenstance outcome of a criminal prosecution, that improper police conduct is being eliminated.

It follows a fortiori from what has been said that factors less probably coercive than the use of force, like an overly long period of detention unaccompanied by physical abuse, should not count conclusively against the admissibility of a confession.

The Due Process Model. A valid decision to arrest must be based on probable cause to believe that the suspect has committed a crime. To put it another way, the police should not arrest unless on the basis of the information at that time in their hands a case exists that, subject to the vicissitudes of the litigation process, seems likely to result in a conviction. It follows that if proper arrest standards have been employed, there is no necessity to obtain additional evidence from the mouth of the defendant. He is to be arrested so that he may be held to answer the case against him, not so that a case against him that does not exist at the time of his arrest can be developed.

Once a suspect has been arrested, he should be brought before a magistrate without unnecessary delay, which is to say, as soon as it is physically possible to do so, once the preliminary formalities of recording his arrest have been completed. Anyone who is held in arrest has the right to test the legality of his arrest, *i.e.*, whether there is probable cause to hold him, in a judicial proceeding. As a practical matter that right is diluted through delay unless the accused is promptly brought before a magistrate. Since a suspect is entitled to be at liberty pending the judicial determination of his guilt or innocence, there must be as promptly as possible after arrest a proceeding in which the conditions of his release, as for example on bail, are determined. This right, too, is diluted by delay unless the suspect is promptly brought before a magistrate. And the suspect is entitled to the assistance of counsel, a right that he most acutely needs to enjoy as soon as he is arrested. As a practical matter he is unlikely to receive that right unless he is promptly advised of it. Once again, his prompt production before an impartial judicial officer is necessary if his right is not to be diluted by delay.

It is never proper for the police to hold a suspect for the purpose of interrogation or investigation. Of course, some interval of time must always elapse between his arrest and his production before a magistrate, and it would be unrealistic to expect the police to maintain complete silence toward him during that period. However, there is a decisive difference between an interrogation conducted during the relatively brief span of time necessary to get the suspect before a magistrate and an interrogation whose length is measured by the time necessary to get him to confess. Any such interrogation should by that fact alone be held illegal.

As soon as a suspect is arrested, he should be told by the police that he is under no obligation to answer questions, that he will suffer no detriment by refusing to answer questions, that he may answer questions in his own interest to clear himself of suspicion, but that anything he says may be used in evidence, and, above all, that he is entitled to see a lawyer if he wants to do so.

If the suspect does make self-incriminatory statements while under arrest and before he is brought before a magistrate, their admissibility in evidence against him should be barred under any of the following conditions: (1) the failure of the police to apprise him of his rights, including his right to the assistance of a lawyer; (2) the fact that the confession was made during a period of detention that exceeded what was necessary to get him promptly before a magistrate; or (3) that the confession was made under other coercive circumstances, such as the use of force against him. Any confession made under these circumstances should be regarded as "involuntary" and should be excluded at the trial. Any further evidence secured on the basis of an involuntary confession should likewise be excluded at the trial to deprive the police of any incentive to obtain such a confession.

The rationale of exclusion is not that the confession is untrustworthy, but that it is at odds with the postulates of an accusatory system of criminal justice in which it is up to the state to make its case against a defendant without forcing him to cooperate in the process. It follows, then, that the existence of other evidence of guilt has no bearing on the admissibility of the confession or on the necessity for reversing a conviction based in part on such a confession. It also follows that the procedure for determining the admissibility of a confession must be such as to avoid any possibility of prejudice to the defendant through the process of determining admissibility. Specifically, in a jury trial the issue of the admissibility of a confession should be litigated on a record made before the judge and out of the hearing of the jury so that the trial judge has the clear and undivided responsibility for deciding whether the jury should hear the confession, and so that a reviewing court can have an unambiguous basis for deciding whether the trial judge reached the proper conclusion.

The Situation and the Trend. The power of the police to interrogate a suspect between his arrest and his production before a magistrate is generally recognized; but there is a strong and apparently accelerating judicial trend toward limiting the duration and the circumstances of such interrogation. The Supreme Court has laid down increasingly strict standards for determining when a confession is "involuntary" and therefore inadmissible in evidence against the accused.[38] It has become clear that the criterion of voluntariness is not the trustworthiness of the confession, but rather its compatibility with the asserted postulates of an accusatorial system in which the case against the accused must be established "by evidence independently and freely secured" and which precludes the state "by coercion [to] prove its charge against an accused out of his own mouth." [39] Although the criterion has ostensibly been applied on a case-by-case basis, there appears to be a trend toward general and automatic standards for determining whether the circumstances of the interrogation were such as to be "inherently coercive." This trend has been most dramatically manifested in federal criminal prosecutions where the Supreme Court, in an exercise of its supervisory power over the administration of federal criminal justice, has laid down a rule rejecting confessions that are secured during a period of detention that exceeds what is required

---

[38] See, *e.g.*, Haynes v. Washington, 373 U.S. 503 (1963), and Gallegos v. Colorado, 370 U.S. 49 (1963), neither of which involved particularly gross forms of "coercion."

[39] Rogers v. Richmond, 365 U.S. 534, 541 (1961).

to bring the accused before a magistrate "without unnecessary delay." [40]
The states have so far been left free of this requirement and have, in
general, not applied it to their criminal prosecutions.   However, the
length of detention has been a factor conspicuously stressed by the
Supreme Court in reversing state criminal convictions based in part
on a confession, and there have been intimations that the federal rule
or something like it may eventually be applied to the states.[41]   Apart
from specific intimations in confession cases, there has been a general
tendency to extend restrictions originally applied to federal prosecutions to state prosecutions as well.[42]   There has been a concomitant
tendency to move from rules that require case-by-case determination
of prejudice to the accused to rules setting forth general standards
of police and prosecutorial conduct.[43]   These developments may well
presage the ultimate extension to state criminal prosecutions of a rule
outlawing the admissibility of confessions secured during a period of
detention whose length and purpose is determined by the dictates of
efficiency in securing confessions rather than by the unavoidable lapse
of time between arrest and production before a magistrate.

It has become a firmly established principle that convictions based
in part on involuntary confessions (so deemed by increasingly rigorous
standards) must be reversed regardless of the strength of other evidence of guilt in the case.   And, in a most recent development, the
states have been told that they must establish procedures for litigating
the admissibility of confessions that do not give juries a clandestine
opportunity to hold either the substance of a confession or the fact
that one was made against the defendant.[44]

Running through most of the problems that arise during this
preliminary phase of the criminal process is the pervasive theme of
access to counsel.   It has a twofold relationship with the other problems posed for resolution by our competing models of the process,
acting as both their cause and effect.   The importance of counsel is
either enhanced or diminished depending on the view one takes of
the rules that ought to govern arrest, search, and interrogation.   On
the other hand, if one starts with a position on the utility or disutility

---

[40] McNabb v. United States, 318 U.S. 332 (1943) ; Mallory v. United States,
354 U.S. 449 (1957).

[41] Perhaps directly, by giving that rule constitutional status, *cf.* Wong Sun v.
United States, 371 U.S. 471 (1963), or indirectly, through a requirement of access
to counsel immediately after arrest, *cf.* Escobedo v. Illinois, 378 U.S. 478 (1964).

[42] *Compare* Mapp v. Ohio, 367 U.S. 343 (1961), *with* Wolf v. Colorado, 338 U.S.
25 (1949). *Compare* Gideon v. Wainwright, 372 U.S. 335 (1963), *with* Betts v. Brady,
316 U.S. 455 (1942). *Compare* Malloy v. Hogan, 378 U.S. 1 (1964), *with* Adamson
v. California, 332 U.S. 46 (1947).

[43] *Compare* Rochin v. California, 342 U.S. 165 (1952), *and* Irvine v. California,
347 U.S. 128 (1954), *with* Mapp v. Ohio, 367 U.S. 643 (1961).

[44] Jackson v. Denno, 378 U.S. 368 (1964).

of counsel at this stage of the process, that view is itself likely to be determinative of many of the other rules. And, as a practical matter, the availability of counsel is bound to have important consequences for the effectiveness with which the applicability of the governing rules, whatever they may be, is challenged.

A concrete instance of this ubiquitous problem is the question whether the admissibility of a confession should be conditioned on access to counsel during the period between arrest and production before a magistrate. So far, the Supreme Court has not placed this general limitation on the admissibility of confessions. The point at which access to counsel becomes an absolute limitation on interrogation has been somewhat later—roughly the point at which the suspect, upon being formally charged with a crime by indictment or information, becomes "the accused." However, there are signs that this point may be pushed back to an earlier stage in the criminal process. In a number of cases in which confessions have been held involuntary, some stress has been laid upon the "special circumstance"—among others—that the suspect was denied an opportunity to consult a lawyer or was not informed of his right to remain silent. More significantly, the Court has just held, by a bare majority, that a "principal suspect" who is induced to confess by an interrogation conducted despite his express requests to see his lawyer and despite his lawyer's attempts to see him is entitled to have his confession excluded from evidence.[45] While the court spoke of the "particular circumstances" of the case, this decision casts considerable doubt on the continued vitality of cases decided only a few years ago in which confessions secured under similar conditions were upheld.[46] It seems very unlikely that this view, if it continues to be adhered to by a majority of the Court, can be confined to explicit requests for legal assistance. The ignorant, inexperienced defendant, for whom the Court has shown special solicitude in the past, no less than the sophisticate who knows his rights and tries to insist upon them, will presumably be afforded equivalent protection, which may ultimately mean that no confession will stand unless given by a defendant who, having been fully advised by the police of his right to remain silent and to consult a lawyer, nonetheless "freely" chooses to speak. Needless to say, any such rule as that would be only inches away from one that ruled out of evidence any statement made by an accused to the police before his production before a magistrate.

---

[45] Escobedo v. Illinois, 378 U.S. 478 (1964).
[46] See Crooker v. California, 357 U.S. 433 (1958); Cicenia v. Lagay, 357 U.S. 504 (1958).

It may be worthwhile calling attention to features of this development that are typical of what seems to be a general tendency in the evolution of the criminal process: (1) a tendency to apply to the states the somewhat more rigorous rules first laid down for federal prosecutions; (2) a tendency to move from case-by-case adjudication to the laying down of broad rules of administration; (3) a tendency to narrow the area of police discretion. What all of this seems to portend is a criminal process that is being forced increasingly to take on the contours of the Due Process Model, at least in terms of the norms that ostensibly govern it.

B. From Charge to Guilt Determination

1. Pretrial Detention

Some interval of time must always elapse between the decision to hold a person for trial adjudication and the adjudication itself. What is to be done with the person who is charged with a crime but not yet convicted of it? The answer has important consequences for the shape of the subsequent proceedings; indeed, it may determine whether there will be any subsequent proceedings, since a decision that the defendant will remain in custody once he has been charged may itself induce him to plead guilty, thereby short-circuiting the part of the process concerned with guilt determination and moving directly to the question of ultimate disposition.

In our system the question, baldly put, is bail or jail: will the defendant be able to provide the required financial assurance that he will appear for trial or will he, for lack of such provision, be kept in custody until the case against him has been prepared for trial and he is brought before the court either to stand trial or to plead guilty? The issues that divide the two models run much deeper, posing as they do questions that are begged by existing institutional arrangements. What reasons justify keeping a defendant in custody before his guilt has been formally adjudicated? Is the only relevant consideration the likelihood that he will not appear for trial? If so, are financial deterrents the only, or the most appropriate, means of assuring presence at trial? If not, what other considerations are relevant? The possibility that the defendant may tamper with the evidence, as by intimidating prospective witnesses? The possibility that he may commit other offenses while he is at large? The degree of probability that he is guilty of the offense charged against him? Questions of this order, which are blurred in the day-to-day administration of the criminal law, may be clarified by examining them in the context of our polarized models.

The Crime Control Model. The vast majority of persons charged with crime are factually guilty. An arrest that results in a charge being placed has behind it a double assurance of reliability: the judgment of the police officer who made the arrest is supported by that of the prosecutor who has decided that there is enough evidence to hold the defendant for trial. For all practical purposes, the defendant is a criminal. Just because the assembly line cannot move fast enough for him to be immediately disposed of is no reason for him to go free. If he does go free, he may not appear for trial, a risk that is heightened when he has a strong consciousness of guilt and a lively expectation of probable punishment. If he does not appear voluntarily, we will have to devote some of our limited resources to tracking him down and bringing him in. That may be tolerable when it occurs sporadically and on a small scale; but if large numbers of people are turned loose before trial, the chances are that the problem will get out of hand, and we will be faced with a vicious circle; the more people fail to appear, the more people will be encouraged not to appear, and the whole system will collapse.

Failure to appear is not the only risk involved in pretrial liberty. The prospect that known criminals will commit further crimes while at large awaiting trial is in itself an adequate reason for not fostering pretrial liberty as the norm. The resulting danger to property and to human life is inexcusable because it is so easily avoidable.

Even for first offenders and others who do not present any obvious danger of repetition while awaiting trial, there are good reasons why pretrial liberty should not be available as a matter of right. Courts are inclined to be lenient with first and other minor offenders. Their prosecutions are apt to be dismissed in a large proportion of cases because it is not worthwhile to use the limited resources available to law enforcement agencies to prosecute them. If they are not dismissed, they may nonetheless be put on probation or fined or given suspended sentences, all dispositions which fall short of exercising any significant effect on their future conduct. For many such persons, a short period spent in jail awaiting trial is not only a useful reminder that crime does not pay, but also the only such reminder they are likely to receive.

Other considerations apart, it is likely that a significantly higher percentage of defendants who now plead guilty would elect to stand trial if they could be at liberty pending trial. People who know that they are guilty tend to accept their punishment if, in order to gamble on the off-chance of an acquittal, they have to spend weeks or months in jail awaiting trial. But if they are released pending trial, the in-

40   *UNIVERSITY OF PENNSYLVANIA LAW REVIEW*   [Vol.113:1

centive to plead guilty is greatly reduced.   The inevitable delays of the process, as well as those that are not so inevitable but can be induced by carelessness or bad faith, would then work in favor of the defendant rather than, as is the situation when he is in custody, against him.   It is unlikely that there would be a significant rise in the percentage of defendants eventually found not guilty because these people are, by hypothesis, probably guilty.   There would be some rise, partly attributable to the disappearance of witnesses through delays in bringing the case to trial, partly attributable to the fact that some defendants whom we know are guilty will be exculpated through human error—by judges, jurors, or prosecutors.   But the danger is only secondarily that some few defendants will be exculpated who otherwise would not.   The main risk is that the increased consumption of time required to litigate cases that do not really need to be litigated would put an intolerable strain on what is already an overburdened process.   That consideration alone argues against a policy that makes pretrial liberty the norm.

These arguments against automatic pretrial liberty are not necessarily arguments in favor of the present bail system, under which there is a nominal right to pretrial liberty, which is in practice not a right at all because of the power of the committing magistrate to set bail in an amount which the defendant is unlikely to be able to afford.   However, that system works well enough in practice, even if its supposed premise is at odds with the postulates underlying this model.   Preferably the courts, with the expert help of the police and the prosecutors, should select those people who, for whatever reason, ought not to be at liberty pending formal adjudication of guilt, and see to it that they are not.

There are, it is true, injustices in the bail system that are not required by the demands of the Crime Control Model.   There is no reason, for example, why defendants who are ultimately convicted and sentenced to prison terms should not have time spent in pretrial custody credited against their postconviction prison terms.   And there may be many instances in which police efficiency would be promoted by not cluttering station houses and detention centers with minor offenders.   For these, the use of summons instead of arrest or release after arrest without the posting of bail may be desirable in the interest of cutting down the use of police for convoy duty through the pretrial pipeline.   However, if pretrial detention is to be mitigated or avoided for some people, it ought to be done explicitly for the purpose of promoting the efficiency of the crime control process rather than because of any abstract "right" to pretrial liberty.   In cases of serious crime, at the least, the confinement of the defendant before adjudication of guilt serves the ends of the process and should be regarded as the norm. If the present system of requiring bail for some reason or other stopped producing a high rate of pretrial confinement, it would have to be replaced by one that did.

The Due Process Model. A person accused of crime is not a criminal. The sharpest distinction must be observed between the status of the defendant and of the person who has been duly convicted of committing a crime. Perhaps the most important and certainly the most obvious operational distinction between the two lies in the issue of physical restraint. Pending the formal adjudication of guilt by the only authority with the institutional competence to decree it— a court—the status of the accused cannot be assimilated to that of the convicted in this most important respect. There are practical as well as ideological reasons why this should be so. An accused who is confined pending trial is greatly impeded in the preparation of his defense. He needs to be able to confer on a free and unrestricted basis with his attorney, something notoriously hard to do in custody. He may be in the best position to interview and track down witnesses in his own behalf, which he cannot do if in jail. His earning capacity is cut off; he may lose his job; his family may suffer extreme economic hardship—all in advance of any determination of guilt. Furthermore, the economic and other deprivations sustained as a result of pretrial confinement all act as coercive measures that inhibit the accused's will to resist. He is rendered more likely to waive the various safeguards to unjust conviction which the system provides by agreeing to plead guilty. When this happens on a large scale, the adversary system as a whole suffers because its vitality depends on effective challenge.

A person accused of crime is entitled to freedom except to the extent necessary to serve the legitimate ends of a legal system. The only legitimate end that is threatened by an absolute right to be free pending trial is the assurance that a defendant will not subvert the orderly processes of criminal justice by deliberately absenting himself at the time and place appointed for trial. If persons accused of crime could with impunity fail to appear, the premise of cooperation on which a system of pretrial liberty depends could not in practice be realized. Hence, it is important that the right to pretrial liberty be exercised in a way that does not jeopardize the process as a whole.

The historic way in which the right to pretrial liberty has been vindicated is through the institution of bail. It has been thought that the requirement of a financial deterrent to flight would adequately protect the viability of the system while ensuring that the defendant could in fact enjoy liberty before trial. This has been manifested through a constitutional guarantee of an absolute right to bail in noncapital cases, expressed in the form that "excessive bail shall not be required." [47] But the constitutional guarantee should properly be understood not merely as a guarantee that "reasonable" bail will be set, but rather as a guarantee that the defendant will be released pending trial on the basis of bail or whatever other device or combination of devices will insure his presence at trial without defeating his right to be free on grounds that have nothing to do with the assurance of his presence. Bail is simply an instance, not the exclusive means, of assuring presence at trial. If the institution of bail does not adequately promote the desired combination of goals, then the spirit of the constitutional guarantee requires that alternative means be developed. Such alternatives include nonfinancial deterrents to flight, such as criminal penalties for nonappearance, the use of summons rather than arrest (with its attendant physical custody) as an initial process in criminal cases, release of arrested defendants on their own recognizance or in the custody of some responsible person, use of cash bail rather than bail bonds, and the like.

Where bail is used, it must be set with regard to the circumstances of the individual case rather than on a mechanical basis. Thus, the nature of the offense charged is only one of several elements to be taken into account in making the bail decision, and if bail is set mechanically on the basis of a schedule for certain offenses, that may in itself be an effective denial of the defendant's right. Essentially, bail-setting must be a factfinding process in which the financial resources of the defendant, his roots in the community, the nature and circumstances of the offense charged, and other relevant factors are all taken into account in arriving at an individualized decision as to the minimum level of bail required to assure a reasonable probability of his appearance for trial. It is, of course, completely inadmissible to set bail at a figure that the defendant is thought to be unable to meet. Speedy appellate review must be available to correct errors of that sort, which is yet another reason why the bail decision must initially be made on the basis of a record that others can subsequently appraise. To the extent that adequate investigative and other factfinding resources are not brought to bear, the defendant should be entitled to go free on nominal bail or no bail. The period of custody should in no event exceed the minimum required after arrest to ascertain the relevant facts about the suspect's situation. Normally,

---

[47] U.S. CONST. amend. VIII.

that should be done by the time the committing magistrate has made the decision to hold the arrested person for subsequent proceedings.

There remains, however, a large class of persons for whom any bail at all is "excessive bail." They are the people loosely referred to as "indigents." Studies of the operation of the bail system have demonstrated that even at the very lowest levels of bail—say five hundred dollars—where the bail bond premium may be only twenty-five or fifty dollars, there is a very substantial percentage of persons who do not succeed in making bail and are therefore held in custody pending trial.[48] It may be that the decision not to seek bail in many of these cases is a voluntary one: a man who knows that he is factually guilty may simply decide that it isn't worth his while to spend money on a bail bond premium. However, many people who are eventually adjudged guilty do post bond and are released pending trial. Their consciousness of guilt may be just as great as the poor man's, but they avail themselves of their right to be free pending a formal adjudication of guilt. It discriminates unfairly against the poor to deny them the same right simply because for them the marginal utility of the bail money is higher than it is for the rich. At any rate, it is clear that if all persons in custody were informed of their right to be free on the basis of nonfinancial conditions if they so elect, many of those who presently spend days, weeks, or months in custody awaiting trial would avail themselves of these devices. It seems to follow that a system that conditions pretrial freedom on financial ability is discriminatory. Indeed, given the malfunctioning of the present system, viewed from the standpoint of the financially disadvantaged, it may well be that the bail system should be ruled out for rich and poor alike. One need not pursue the argument to that extreme, however, to recognize that a system that conditions pretrial release exclusively or even predominantly on the provision of financial assurances of presence at trial is a seriously defective one.

Other asserted bases for pretrial detention are either entirely without merit or present special problems that need to be handled on a more discriminating basis than a general rule permitting detention before guilt-determination. It is antithetical to our conceptions of justice to permit pretrial detention to be used as a kind of informal punishment in advance of (or instead of) a formal determination of guilt and sentence. To speak of the possibility that the accused may commit *further* crimes if left at large begs the question, since it has not yet been determined that he has committed any crime at all. Many of the limitations on substantive criminal enactments safeguard us

[48] *E.g.*, ATT'Y GEN. REP. 67, 135 Table IV. See generally FREED & WALD, BAIL IN THE UNITED STATES: 1964, at 9-21 (1964).

44   *UNIVERSITY OF PENNSYLVANIA LAW REVIEW*   [Vol.113:1

against being punished for a mere propensity to commit crime. The logic of preventive detention would extend to persons newly released from prison; why not re-arrest them and lock them up because they may commit another crime?

The problem of what to do with "dangerous" people who have not been convicted of committing crimes is a troublesome one. It far transcends the preventive detention of persons accused of crime. The solution, if there is one, must include setting standards for determining who is "dangerous" and providing the minimal procedural due process safeguards of notice and a hearing for persons sought to be confined on this ground. Whatever the solution, it cannot bypass these basic due process requirements by permitting the indiscriminate preventive detention of people who are accused of crime. The problem can, in any event, be minimized by shortening the interval between charge and trial.

In some cases there may be a possibility that the defendant if left at large will threaten witnesses, destroy evidence, or otherwise impede the preparation of the case against him. This is said to be particularly likely in the case of organized criminals. The argument is a little difficult to understand. The higher the degree of organization involved, the less likely it would seem to be that the personal attention of the defendant would be required to promote obstructive tactics. To the extent that there is a threat of this kind, it can be dealt with in other ways: by giving witnesses police protection, by placing the accused under injunction backed by the contempt power, by providing criminal penalties for tampering with witnesses, and the like. The vice of detaining a defendant before he actually does anything bad is obvious: it penalizes him for a mere disposition, something totally unprovable, thus opening the way for the most widespread abuses. At the first concrete sign that the accused has engaged in obstructive activities, it is altogether proper to seek to confine him on the basis of proof that obstructive activities have taken place. But there is all the difference between so doing on the basis of proof after the fact and on the basis of suspicion before the fact.

In summary, then, pretrial liberty should be the norm; the only exception that the criminal process as such should recognize ought to be the assurance of the accused's presence at trial; assuring his presence ought to be accomplished by measures other than detention; and detention should never be resorted to merely because the accused is unable to provide financial deterrents to nonappearance.

The Situation and the Trend. The legal norm embraced in the eighth amendment which forbids the requirement of excessive bail is construed to confer an absolute right to pretrial release on reasonable bail in noncapital cases.[49]   Bail in turn is required to be set solely with respect to assuring defendant's presence at trial; other considerations are inadmissible.   The federal standards are echoed by those prevailing in the states.   While it has not been authoritatively so held, it appears that the federal constitutional provision on bail would be held applicable to the states.[50]   There is at the present time very little appellate control over bail-setting.   The court of first instance has wide discretion: bail is ordinarily set pretty much on the basis of the offense charged; bail reductions are usually ordered only when the bail set in a particular case is thought to be out of line for the particular offense charged.   There is no general right to be free if one is unable to provide bail; the accused's remedy is said to be to move for prompt trial.[51]

In practice there is very little judicial control over bail practices. Bail is set mechanically.[52]   There is almost never any investigation of the circumstances of a particular accused or the likelihood that he will appear for trial.   Bail or jail therefore becomes a question answered solely on the basis of a defendant's financial resources and his ability to obtain a professional bondsman to post bail for him.   On the whole it is the alleged gangster or hardened criminal who is freed on bail and the first or sporadic offender who stays in jail.   Furthermore, the system in practice permits and fosters the setting of bail in amounts that ensure that defendants will remain in jail; there is no question but that bail is widely used for purposes that are supposedly denied it by the legal norm, because of the unavailability of prompt remedial measures, the discretionary nature of the bail decision, and the lack of assistance of counsel in calling attention to infractions of the legal norms.   It is a notable fact that the unbailed defendant is also to a large extent the unrepresented defendant.[53]   The combination of factors alluded to makes the constitutional guarantee to a large extent nugatory in practice.   If the legal norm is thought of as conforming in most respects to the Due Process Model, it is evident that the practical reality indicates a situation much closer to the Crime Control Model.

There exists today a widespread, vocal, and increasingly influential dissatisfaction with the operation of a system that places prime reliance on the use of financial devices for assuring presence

---

49 See Stack v. Boyle, 342 U.S. 1 (1951).

50 See *In re* Shuttlesworth, 369 U.S. 35 (1962).

51 See United States v. Rumrich, 180 F.2d 575 (2d Cir. 1950).

52 FREED & WALD, *op. cit. supra* note 48, at 18-21.

53 ATT'Y GEN. REP. 70-72.

at trial.[54] Unlike most of the other model trends we are considering, this one is not primarily judicial in character. There have been no path-setting decisions creating new norms, as in the areas of investigatory practices or right to counsel. Rather, the trend has been so far manifested by the work of governmental and extragovernmental groups, who have revealed in detail the present state of affairs and framed new norms responsive to the needs believed to emerge from factual revelations. Experiments are now underway designed to demonstrate the efficacy of other means of assuring presence at trial: improved factfinding mechanisms to determine whether an individual accused is a good risk for release without financial conditions; the use of cash deposits in an amount equal to what would otherwise be the bail bond premium, in order to reduce reliance on the professional bondsman; initiating criminal prosecutions by summons rather than arrest in minor cases, among others. A bill has been introduced in the Senate, supported by all members of the Subcommittee on Constitutional Rights of the Committee on the Judiciary, that would preclude the pretrial detention of an accused solely on the ground that he is financially unable to make bail.[55] The special problem of bail in civil rights cases is receiving considerable attention and may provoke judicial trends that will promote greater conformity with the Due Process Model generally.

Where all this ferment will lead is difficult to say, but undeniably the ferment is there. It seems safe to predict that in the foreseeable future legislation and court rulings will advance rather than retard the trend toward conformity with the Due Process Model. There will be an indeterminate but significant increase in the percentage of criminal defendants who are at liberty pending trial, accompanied by an indeterminate but significant increase in the number of criminal defendants who do not plead guilty to the initial charge against them, but who either succeed in obtaining a more advantageous outcome through plea bargaining or who elect to put the prosecution to its proof in a trial.

2. The Plea of Guilty

The vast majority of criminal prosecutions terminate with the entry of a plea of guilty. The plea rather than the trial is the dominant

---

[54] This dissatisfaction was epitomized and brought to a focus in the National Conference on Bail and Criminal Justice held in Washington, D.C., on May 27-29, 1964, under the cosponsorship of the United States Department of Justice and the Vera Foundation, a private organization concerned with remedying deficiencies in the present bail system. FREED & WALD, BAIL IN THE UNITED STATES: 1964 (1964), was prepared as a working paper for this conference and contains extensive documentation of the present situation and current trends, as well as a valuable bibliography on the bail problem.

[55] S. 2838, 88th Cong., 2d Sess. (1964).

mode of guilt-determination. It is widely asserted that any significant increase in the number of criminal prosecutions going to trial would result in a breakdown of the criminal justice system. The institution of the guilty plea is itself affected by factors operating at earlier levels of the criminal process, notably by the availability vel non of pretrial liberty and of the assistance of counsel. It seems clear both as a matter of logical inference and of demonstrable fact that a defendant who is out on bail and who enjoys the services of a lawyer is less likely to plead guilty than is one who lacks one or both of these advantages. It is of course possible that in many cases the advantages referred to are banked in the form of an advantageous plea-bargain rather than of insistence on a trial on the merits. Nonetheless, it appears likely that there would be a substantial shift in the proportion of cases going to trial if factors at earlier stages of the process operated with uniform frequency in favor of the defendant. Thus, if there were a reduction of twenty-five percent in the number of cases in federal courts disposed of on guilty pleas, there would be roughly twice the number of trials that are now held.[56]

What do our two models tell us about the guilty plea? From the host of relevant aspects of this institution we will briefly examine these: Under what circumstances, if any, should a plea of guilty be set aside as "involuntary"? To what extent should a defendant who pleads guilty have the assistance of counsel? What obligation, if any, does the judge who receives the plea have to satisfy himself as to the factual and legal guilt of the accused?

The Crime Control Model. The purpose of the arraignment, at which the defendant is required to plead to the charge against him, is to dispose of as large a proportion of cases as possible without trial. It is in the interest of all—the prosecutor, the judge, and the defendant—to terminate without trial every case in which there is no genuine doubt as to the guilt of the defendant. If the earlier stages of the process have functioned as they should, only a very small proportion of cases should at this point remain in that category. There is also an irreducible minimum of cases where so much is at stake—either because of the gravity of the offense or the position of the defendant—that there is no reasonable possibility of compromise. The murderer and the bank president charged with income tax evasion have

---

[56] Approximately 80% of criminal defendants disposed of in the federal courts from 1956 through 1962 entered pleas of guilty or *nolo contendere*. See Note, *Guilty Plea Bargaining: Compromises by Prosecutors To Secure Guilty Pleas*, 112 U. PA. L. REV. 865 & n.4 (1964). Assuming that the rest stood trial and that all those included in the hypothesized 25% reduction also were to stand trial, the present 20% who stand trial would grow to 40%.

this in common: they have little to lose by going down fighting. Aside from these two categories of case where the will to litigate is strong, all criminal cases ought normally to be terminated by plea. If this general criterion is accepted, the details follow without much trouble.

There is a distinct social advantage to terminating criminal proceedings without trial whenever the defendant is willing to do so. Any number of subtle interacting factors may make a defendant willing; it would be an endless operation and essentially a self-defeating one, in terms of the objectives of the process, to inquire into the precise nature of these factors in any large number of cases. For example, the judge in accepting a plea of guilty may of course inquire whether any promises have been made to the defendant, since a promise of leniency by the police or the prosecutor is one which cannot be delivered and is evidence of poor prosecutorial performance. But if the judge does discover that an improper promise has been made, the proper course is not to reject the plea but rather to set the defendant right about the legal situation and then permit him to enter the plea if he so wants. In the overwhelming majority of cases, then, the function of an inquiry by the judge is to provide an assurance of regularity on the record, not to protect any special right of the defendant. It is also perfectly proper for the judge to make it clear that a defendant who pleads guilty can expect greater leniency in sentencing than one who insists on putting the state to the time and expense of a trial.

The general run of criminal defendants are capable of making up their own minds as to whether they want to plead guilty. If a defendant has a lawyer and wants to consult him about the guilty plea, that is proper. But the state should be under no obligation to provide counsel for a defendant at arraignment. All that is required for a plea of guilty is that the defendant understand its nature and consequences in a general kind of way, and that he enter it of his own free will. The judge's duty is to ensure that these conditions are met. It would involve a needless duplication of resources to insist that a defense lawyer as well as a judge must participate in the entry of a guilty plea.

The judge need not inquire into the factual circumstances underlying the commission of the offense except to the extent that he deems it desirable in helping him to perform his sentencing function. Cases do not reach this stage of the criminal process unless there is substantial evidence of guilt. Any requirement that the judge inquire into the issue of guilt before accepting a plea would impair the efficiency of the process and undermine the purpose of the plea of guilty by converting the arraignment into an abbreviated trial on the merits.

A fortiori, there should be no inquiry into the availability of defenses that do not go to the issue of factual guilt. It is cause for congratulation, not alarm, when a defendant who is factually guilty is convicted and sentenced despite the existence of possible defenses that have nothing to do with the merits of the case. One of the great strengths of the guilty plea is that it serves to bypass issues that can only result in a weakening of effective criminal justice. If a defendant is conscious of his own guilt and willing to accept his punishment, it does neither him nor the community any service to inquire into possible errors made at earlier stages of the process that might serve to enable him to escape his just deserts.

The Due Process Model. The arraignment is the fulcrum of the entire criminal process. It is at this point that one of two things happens: either the possible errors and abuses at the earlier, largely unscrutinized stages of the process are exposed to judicial scrutiny, or they are forever submerged in a plea of guilty. The guilty plea is not only a device for expediting the handling of criminal cases; it is a kind of Iron Curtain that cuts off, almost always irrevocably, any disinterested scrutiny of the earlier stages of the process. Guilty pleas should therefore be disfavored. There may indeed be a serious question whether they should ever be permitted at all; but it is clear that they should be hedged about with safeguards designed both to cut down their incidence and to prevent them from being used in cases where possibly meritorious challenges to the process exist.

No kinds of pressure, either by the prosecutor or the judge, should be brought to bear on a defendant to induce him to plead guilty. Plea-bargaining by a defendant who is adequately advised by counsel may, under careful supervision by the judge, be an acceptable way of terminating a criminal case. But the prosecutor, in order to avoid any possibility of coercive pressure, should never take the lead in proposing or suggesting a compromise plea. It is manifestly improper for a judge to use his sentencing discretion to coerce a guilty plea, either by threatening severe punishment in a particular case or by reserving lenient treatment, as for example probation, for defendants who plead guilty. A criminal defendant is entitled to have the charges against him tried in the manner prescribed by law, no matter how overwhelming the evidence of guilt may be thought to be. A criminal trial is not to be viewed as an undesirable burden, but rather as the logical and proper culmination of the process. It follows that it defeats the ends of the system to penalize a defendant for insisting on a trial or to intimidate him by threatening him with unpleasant consequences if he does insist.

No one should be permitted to plead guilty without the assistance of counsel. If a criminal defendant cannot receive a fair trial without counsel, how much less likely is he to have enjoyed fair process if he has to resolve the highly technical and complex strategic problems involved in a guilty plea without expert assistance? It is doubtful whether waiver of counsel should ever be allowed at this stage. As a practical matter, there is unlikely to be such a waiver if the judge, on hearing that a defendant wishes to plead guilty, informs him that he is reluctant to accept a plea at this time, explains the advantages of consultation with counsel, and offers to appoint a lawyer immediately.

Even if these restrictions are faithfully observed, it is probable that a high proportion of criminal defendants will choose to plead guilty. The question then arises what guarantees of procedural regularity the judge should endeavor to provide before, in effect, closing the door to further scrutiny by accepting the plea. He ought, in the first place, to require the prosecutor to summarize the evidence against the defendant, indicating what the testimony will be and by whom it will be provided. He should satisfy himself that there is probably sufficient evidence to sustain a conviction on the charge or charges against the defendant. He should also satisfy himself as to the admissibility under applicable rules of evidence of the testimony proposed to be elicited. Beyond satisfying himself about the evidence, the judge should also take this occasion to probe, with the assistance of the prosecutor and the defense counsel, the possible existence of abuses at earlier stages of the process, such as illegally obtained evidence, improper confessions, failure to provide counsel at an appropriate stage, length of pretrial detention, and the like, in order to determine their possible bearing on the adverse termination of the proceeding by acceptance of a plea of guilty. Only after he is satisfied that the record is clear in these two general respects—the establishment of guilt and the absence of abusive practices at earlier stages of the process—should the judge accept a plea of guilty. To the extent that these protective measures are not employed, the defendant should be entitled at a later time to move to set aside the plea of guilty and to stand trial.

The Situation and the Trend.[57] Although reliable data are hard to come by, it is highly probable that any general view of the guilty plea in this country at the present time would disclose practices that conform far more closely to the Crime Control than to the Due Process Model. Pressures from earlier phases of the process particularly on

---

[57] There is an excellent exposition of the present situation as well as a detailed examination of judicial decisions contributing to the trend herein described in Note, 112 U. Pa. L. Rev. 865 (1964).

those defendants who are not at liberty after arrest and who do not have the assistance of counsel, plus pressures exerted at or about the time of arraignment, tend strongly to militate toward the entry of pleas of guilty. The assistance of counsel, to the extent that it is available at arraignment, is perfunctory in the majority of cases. Waiver is easily accomplished and widespread. And the role of the judge is a relatively passive one, with no generally effective pattern of inquiry into factual guilt or into the possibility of abuses at earlier stages of the process.

There are some signs, however, that the plea of guilty may be receiving increasingly close scrutiny. If the prosecutor enters into a plea arrangement that depends on promises he is unable to fulfill, some courts have taken the view that the resulting plea should be set aside as "involuntary." [58] There also seems to be a trend developing toward stricter standards for appraising the defendant's understanding of the nature and consequences of the plea. The full impact of *Gideon v. Wainwright* is yet to be determined, but it would appear that pleas of guilty entered without the assistance of counsel may prove vulnerable, quite apart from the probability that implementation of *Gideon* will insure the participation of counsel in a higher proportion of guilty pleas than has hitherto been the case.

It seems unlikely that the practice of guilty plea bargaining will itself come under attack. Rather, the trend seems to be toward regulating and equalizing the conditions under which the bargaining takes place. Greater insistence upon the participation of defense counsel and a more active role for the trial judge will probably characterize the development of plea bargaining. To the extent that this turns out to be an accurate forecast, the institution of the guilty plea will hold its place as the fulcrum of the criminal process only at the cost of a greater input of resources and, therefore, a diminution in "efficiency" as measured by the dictates of the Crime Control Model.

C. *Review of Errors in the Guilt-Determination Process*

Although it is probably common ground today that any criminal process ought to provide some opportunity for correcting some errors that have occurred at earlier stages in the process, it need be kept in mind that the institution of appellate review in criminal cases is less than one hundred years old. If it would indeed "go against the grain, today, to make a matter as sensitive as a criminal conviction subject to unchecked determination by a single institution," [59] that fact is a

---

[58] See Machibroda v. United States, 368 U.S. 487 (1962) ; Dillon v. United States, 307 F.2d 445, 449-50 (9th Cir. 1962) (dictum).
[59] Bator, *supra* note 22, at 453.

52   *UNIVERSITY OF PENNSYLVANIA LAW REVIEW*   [Vol.113:1

striking testimonial to the dynamic character of the criminal process and to the consequent fluidity of what may usefully be regarded as the range of practicable alternatives. Even if there is general agreement that in some sense appellate review is a necessary feature of the process, the terms on which review should be available divide the two models: What kinds of issues should be reviewable, "legal" issues only or "factual" determinations as well? What financial barriers to review, if any, should be allowed? Should review be automatically available, or should some screening devices be used to prevent frivolous appeals from being taken? If errors are found, what standards should determine the outcome of review—must the defendant show that the outcome would probably have been different but for the error, or should some errors count as conclusive, and if so, which ones? What is the permissible timing of review, *i.e.*, to what extent is review to be limited to a continuation of the original process—"appeal"—or permitted also to take place in a fresh proceeding—"collateral attack"?

It will be convenient to divide the subject of review in accordance with the distinction just made between appeal and collateral attack, since the distinction has become thoroughly ingrained in our thinking about the criminal process. There is another reason for observing it: the opportunity that it affords to depart from the assumption that we are dealing with a wholly unitary system of criminal justice and to examine in one hotly contested instance the impact of federalism on the shape of the criminal process. For this purpose we will make the artificial and somewhat misleading assumption that review by appeal concerns review within a unitary system while review by collateral attack concerns federal review of state criminal processes, for the limiting purpose of selecting a few representative problems whose solutions divide our two models.

1. Appeal

The general role of an appeal system is, of course, strongly conditioned by assumptions about what has occurred in previous stages of the process. The Crime Control Model, as we have seen, places very heavy emphasis upon the plea of guilty as the central guilt-determining device. The comparatively few cases that it confides to a more formal adjudicative process are those in which there is thought to be some doubt about the factual guilt of the accused. Those doubts are supposed to be resolved by the trier of fact. Accordingly, the role of an appellate review system is highly marginal: it is available to correct those occasional slips in which the trier of fact either makes a plain error about factual guilt or makes some kind of procedural mistake so gross as to cause with some high degree of probability a substantial diminution in the reliability of the guilt-determining process.

In contrast the appellate stage in the Due Process Model is seen as having a much broader function. It operates, true, to correct errors in the assessment of factual guilt (at least when they have redounded to the detriment of the accused), but that is only the beginning of its function. It serves, more importantly, as the forum in which infringements on the rights of the accused, as laid down in the model, that have accumulated at earlier stages of the process, are to be redressed and their repetition in later cases deterred. The appellate forum, seen as having distance from and independence of the police-prosecutor nexus into which the trial court is so often drawn, is both guardian and vindicator of the Due Process Model. While the appellate stage is seen in the Crime Control Model as being a remote and marginal appendage of the process as a whole, it is perceived in the Due Process Model as being qualitatively crucial and quantitatively significant. Important differential consequences follow for the resolution in the two models of problems of access and scope.

The Crime Control Model. Once a determination of guilt has been made, either by entry of a plea or by adjudication, the paramount objective of the criminal process should be to carry out the sentence of the court as speedily as possible. We must be able to say that people who violate the law will be swiftly and certainly subjected to punishment. This end will be undermined if the process permits, and hence invites, delays in the execution of sentences. Finality of guilt determination is therefore the most important point of departure for evaluating any system of review. To put the matter bluntly, appeals should be so effectively discouraged that the mere taking of an appeal should be in itself a fairly reliable indicator that the case contains substantial possibility of error going to the issue of factual guilt.

If appeal in criminal cases is available as a matter of right, restrictions must be imposed to ensure that the right is exercised responsibly. Specifically, the costs of an appeal, filing fees, printing costs for the record and briefs, and most importantly, counsel fees, should not be waived or publicly defrayed unless the appeal is screened and determined to be probably meritorious. This screening power should be lodged in the court that has made the determination of guilt, since it is the tribunal most likely to be familiar with the case and therefore most likely to be able to make an expeditious determination of probable merit. A decision not to permit an appeal by a person unable to finance his own appeal should be conclusive, subject only to review for gross abuse of discretion. While in theory the same procedure should probably apply to all appeals, such a limitation may be sufficient, since in practice the financial burden of an appeal not defrayed by the state may adequately impede frivolity. Bail pending an appeal should be allowable only as a matter of grace and should be withheld where the issues raised on appeal do not appear to be substantial.

No issue should be raisable on appeal that was not raised at an earlier stage of the process. No conviction should be reversed for the insufficiency of evidence unless the appellate tribunal finds that no reasonable trier of fact could have convicted on the evidence presented. Appeals against a verdict of acquittal should be available to the prosecution to the same extent as appeals against a conviction are available to the defense. Errors not going to the sufficiency of the evidence to establish factual guilt—errors in the admission or exclusion of evidence, in the trial court's instructions, or in the conduct of the prosecutor or the trial judge—should not provide a basis for reversal of a conviction on appeal unless it is found that in the absence of the error or errors the result would probably have been different. Further, no errors should suffice for reversal if the appellate court concludes on a review of all the evidence that the factual guilt of the accused was adequately established.

The Due Process Model. The initial forum in which abuses of official power should be corrected in the criminal process is the trial. However, they are not always corrected there, and, indeed, the trial process may itself be a fertile source of additional abuses. If they are not corrected, they do not come to public attention since the trial process is in the great run of cases only slightly more visible than the police and prosecutorial processes that precede it. The right of appeal is an important safeguard for the rights of the individual accused. Beyond that, it plays an essential role in the lawmaking process; it is only the existence of a steady flow of criminal cases on the appellate level that provides the raw material for the elaboration of those very rights. If the Due Process Model is to retain its dynamic character, there must be full and unrestricted access to the appellate phase of the process.

There should be no limitations on the convicted defendant's right to appeal. Financial restrictions are as much out of place here as they are at other levels of the process. If the appellant cannot afford to pay a filing fee, it must be waived; if he cannot afford to buy a transcript, it must be given to him; if he cannot afford to hire a lawyer, he must be assigned one. This last point is especially important; whether reversible errors justifying an appeal have occurred is uniquely a matter on which the convicted defendant needs the help of a lawyer; there is no more technical aspect to the criminal process. No lawyer will advise an appeal where grounds for appeal are lacking, but only a lawyer can tell whether the grounds exist or not; for at this stage of the process, it is legal errors rather than factual guilt that are primarily at issue. And, while bail pending appeal raises different and more restrictive issues than does the question of liberty pending trial, it is important that the discretion to allow bail pending appeal not be manipulated coercively to discourage the pursuit of any appeal that has a semblance of merit. Where discretionary judgments of this kind are inevitable, they ought to be lodged with the appellate court rather than with the trial court.

While it should not be possible to sit by silently and allow errors to go unchallenged at the trial level, appellants should not be held rigidly to a requirement that the errors of which they complain must have been challenged below. The appellate court should be entitled to notice any plain error prejudicial to the rights of an accused. No unitary standard for determining reversible error can be advanced; even cumulative and repetitive errors of an insubstantial kind should suffice for reversal. Of course, any error abridging basic rights of the defendant —rights to be free of illegal searches and seizures, not to be coerced into confessing, and not to be forced to incriminate himself—should be ground for reversal irrespective of the strength of the rest of the case. To say that is simply to repeat that the process itself must afford remedies for its abuse and deterrents against the misuse of official power. The appellate process should afford similar sanctions against abuses that occur for the first time at the trial level, such as prosecutorial misconduct, prejudicial publicity, and ineffective counsel. The reversal of a criminal conviction is a small price to pay for an affirmation of proper values and a deterrent example of what happens when those values are slighted. When an appellate court finds it necessary to castigate the conduct of the police, the prosecutor, or the trial court, but fails to reverse a conviction, it simply breeds disrespect for the very standards it is trying to affirm.

The Situation and the Trend. Appeals are taken in only a small proportion of criminal cases. The appeal is the apex of the pyramid and represents a final screening from a group of cases whose number has been sharply reduced through previous screenings. Nonetheless, the appeal is important out of all proportion to numbers because it is the level of the criminal process at which the governing legal norms are made explicit. There appears to be a fairly constant relationship between the number of appeals taken in criminal cases and the proportion of convictions that are reversed. Unsuccessful appeals are by and

56   *UNIVERSITY OF PENNSYLVANIA LAW REVIEW*   [Vol.113 :1

large not very significant legally; it is the successful appeal, in which
reasons of more or less general applicability are given for reversing a
conviction, that is significant for the laying down of operative norms.
Consequently, the larger the absolute number of appeals taken, the
greater the number of reversals there probably tends to be, and the
more complex, precise, and thickly textured are the inhibitory norms
that tend to be established.   In a very real sense, therefore, the question of access to the appellate process is strategically crucial to the
struggle between the two models.   The fewer appeals there are, the
likelier it is that Crime Control norms will prevail; the more appeals
there are, the likelier it is that Due Process norms will prevail.

There is no level of the criminal process at which the triumph
of the Due Process Model, at least in terms of asserted norms, has
been more speedily and more completely established than on the question of access to the appellate process.   Only a decade ago there were
significant differences in legal norm between the treatment of appeals
by those who could afford to finance them and those who could not.
The factual disparities doubtless remain; but the legal norms have
been drastically pushed toward the Due Process end of the spectrum.
In a series of pathbreaking decisions, the Supreme Court has established, on the state and federal levels alike, that the situation of financially incapable persons must be substantially improved.   If a transcript
of the trial proceedings is necessary for appellate purposes, the state
must supply one to persons who cannot buy their own.[60]   The screening
of appeals as a prerequisite to relief from financial barriers has been
sharply eased, perhaps virtually eliminated.[61]   And the right to counsel
on appeal has been assured.[62]   Here as elsewhere, of course, the development of Due Process norms has preceded their translation into operative fact, and the process of providing the resources necessary to make
the developing norms generally operative has barely begun.[63]

On issues of scope and standards of review, the trend seems un-
mistakeably to be toward the norms posited in the Due Process Model.
Errors that are denominated "constitutional" are more and more being
viewed as grounds for automatic reversal without regard to the sufficiency of evidence of factual guilt.   And even nonconstitutional errors
are being treated as calling for reversal in the teeth of what have previously been regarded as well-established rules requiring an assessment

---

[60] Griffin v. Illinois, 351 U.S. 12 (1956).

[61] See Draper v. Washington, 372 U.S. 487 (1963) ; Coppedge v. United States,
369 U.S. 438 (1962).

[62] See Douglas v. California, 372 U.S. 353 (1963).

[63] See ATT'Y GEN. REP. 90-115.

of the record as a whole.[64] It is not surprising that this should be so. The appellate process is the forum par excellence for assertion of the norms that make up the Due Process Model. What can be observed on the appellate level today is merely an affirmation of the increased emphasis on Due Process norms in the criminal process as a whole.

2. Collateral Attack

Should the criminal process end with a determination of guilt that is subject to review on direct appeal? The question may arise whether or not an appeal is actually taken. It becomes particularly acute when the determination of guilt is made by a plea of guilty, since in that situation an appeal is as a practical matter highly unlikely. The issue is complicated by the coexistence of state and federal law and of state and federal forums for deciding questions that arise in criminal cases.

Assume that a state's criminal process has resulted in a determination of guilt, and the accused, now a state prisoner, asserts in a federal habeas corpus proceeding that he is being held in custody in violation of the Constitution and laws of the United States, alleging that rights established under the fourteenth amendment have been abridged at some stage of the state criminal process.

It is obvious that one important dimension of the problem involves the delineation of what those fourteenth amendment rights are thought to be. We can say with rough accuracy that such tenets of the Due Process Model as have been translated into legally binding imperatives, insofar as they apply to state criminal prosecutions, have been grounded in the commands of the fourteenth amendment. The substantive questions, then, on collateral attack, raise the whole range of dynamically evolving dictates of the Due Process Model that we have been examining. The procedural issues to which we now turn are all aspects of a single basic problem: to what extent should federal collateral attack on state criminal convictions be permitted to invoke the expanding tenets of the Due Process Model to nullify state criminal convictions? Three representative issues will serve to illustrate the distance between the two models with respect to this crucial procedural problem: (1) If a federal fourteenth amendment claim has been asserted by the habeas corpus petitioner at any point in the state criminal process and has been considered and rejected on the merits by a state court, may the petitioner relitigate the issue in a federal habeas corpus proceeding? (2) If the federal habeas petitioner has failed to avail himself of an oppor-

---

[64] See, *e.g.*, People v. Modesto, 59 Cal. 2d 722, 382 P.2d 33, 31 Cal. Rptr. 225 (1963). See generally WITKIN, CALIFORNIA CRIMINAL PROCEDURE 733-43 (1963), for a documentation of the trend in one jurisdiction by a commentator generally unsympathetic to it.

58   *UNIVERSITY OF PENNSYLVANIA LAW REVIEW*   [Vol.113:1

tunity to raise a fourteenth amendment issue in the state criminal process and is therefore barred by state procedural rules from now raising the issue, may he nonetheless secure a federal determination? (3) If the governing legal norms have been changed since a state prisoner was convicted so that contentions formerly rejected are now viewed as established rights, may he secure relief, *i.e.*, are changes in the law "retroactive"? Affirmative answers to each of these questions tend to provide a broad scope for judicial vindication of the Due Process Model; negative answers tend to perpetuate the prevalence of the Crime Control Model, notwithstanding the fact that the norms now on the books tend toward the tenets of the Due Process Model.

We need not spell out in detail the positions that the two models reach on these representative issues; they are implicit in what has been said earlier about the operations of the model at the appellate level.

The Situation and the Trend. Until 1953 it was "at most doubt-ful" [65] whether federal constitutional claims raised and decided on the merits in state criminal cases could be re-examined by a federal court in a habeas corpus proceeding. The landmark decision in *Brown v. Allen* [66] held that they could. Since that time there has been an increasing number of petitions for habeas corpus filed by state prisoners. The Supreme Court has recently reaffirmed the doctrine of *Brown v. Allen*, and has laid down rules considerably more favorable to habeas petitioners than contemporary practice in the lower federal courts has provided for determining the circumstances under which habeas petitioners are entitled to have an evidentiary hearing on the under-lying merits of their fourteenth amendment claims.[67]

At the same time that the Court opened the door to determination of federal claims already heard in a state court, it appeared to close the door to a first determination in a federal court of a fourteenth amendment claim that state courts had refused to hear because of some state procedural default by the petitioner.[68] In subsequent years there was lively controversy over the circumstances in which a procedural default by a state prisoner should not be counted against him for habeas purposes.[69] The controversy has been at least temporarily resolved by a Supreme Court decision setting forth in the most sweep-

---

[65] The phrase is Professor Bator's. Bator, *supra* note 22, at 463.

[66] 344 U.S. 443 (1953).

[67] Townsend v. Sain, 372 U.S. 293 (1963).

[68] See Brown v. Allen, 344 U.S. 443, 482 (1953).

[69] *Compare* Hart, *Foreword: The Time Chart of the Justices, the Supreme Court, 1958 Term*, 73 Harv. L. Rev. 84, 101-22 (1959), *with* Reitz, *Federal Habeas Corpus: Impact of an Abortive State Proceeding*, 74 Harv. L. Rev. 1315 (1961).

ing terms that a federal habeas court may, and in the ordinary case should, determine federal claims even though the petitioner has failed to avail himself of state remedies once, but no longer, open to him.[70] So, for example, a state prisoner who contends that his conviction was based on a coerced confession but who failed to appeal from that conviction and was therefore barred from receiving a state determination is no longer barred from seeking release on federal habeas.

The combined effect of the doctrines of *Brown v. Allen* and *Fay v. Noia* gives the federal courts a broad supervisory power over the administration of state criminal justice. The amplitude of this spatial reach is matched in the temporal dimension by a doctrine, yet to be made explicit by the Supreme Court but apparently emerging from a number of its summary dispositions, that changes in fourteenth amendment doctrine are to be deemed retroactive. Thus, a state prisoner convicted on the basis of illegally obtained evidence before *Mapp v. Ohio*,[71] or without the provisions of counsel before *Gideon v. Wainwright*,[72] or, presumably, on the basis of a confession secured during a period of interrogation without the aid of counsel before *Escobedo v. Illinois*,[73] or of comment on his failure to testify in his own behalf before *Malloy v. Hogan*[74] may now be entitled to release on habeas corpus.

Of course, formidable obstacles stand in the way of any individual prisoner's success in pressing an application for habeas corpus. Working in most cases without the aid of counsel, he must convince a federal district judge, one of a notably unsentimental group of men, that there is arguable merit to his cause before he will even be given a hearing on his allegations. But with all the difficulties that collateral attack presents for the prisoner seeking to invoke it, it is undeniable that the remarkable broadening of its theoretical availability that has been taking place in recent years constitutes a powerful weapon for maintaining, capitalizing upon, and expanding the influence of the Due Process Model on the criminal processes of the state and the nation.

D. Access to Counsel: A Postscript

At every stage in the criminal process, as we have seen, our two models divide on the role to be played by counsel for the accused. In

---

[70] Fay v. Noia, 372 U.S. 391 (1963).

[71] 367 U.S. 643 (1961).

[72] 372 U.S. 335 (1963).

[73] 378 U.S. 478 (1964).

[74] 378 U.S. 1 (1964) (the fourteenth amendment makes the privilege against self-incrimination as embodied in the fifth amendment binding on the states).

the Crime Control Model, with its administrative and managerial bias, he is a mere luxury; at no stage is he indispensable, and only in the very small proportion of cases that go to trial and the even smaller proportion that are reviewed on appeal is he to be regarded as more than merely tolerable. The Due Process Model, with its adversary and judicial bias, makes counsel for the accused a crucial figure throughout the process; on his presence depends the viability of this Model's prescriptions. The decision in *Gideon v. Wainwright*, that the states must provide counsel for criminal defendants who are financially unable to provide their own, is therefore the longest single step so far taken by any institution of government in moving the norms of the criminal process toward the Due Process Model. Many issues posed by this development remain to be clarified. In what kinds of criminal prosecutions does the right to assigned counsel apply? In "serious" offenses only? If so, what are the criteria of "seriousness"? When does the right to counsel "begin" and "end"? Are the limits the same for assigned counsel as for privately retained counsel? Does the guarantee require the reversal of convictions obtained before the decision in *Gideon*? Looming behind these questions are even more portentous ones: Does the effective assistance of counsel require that the state provide financial compensation for the lawyers who serve? Must provision be made for other expenses of an effective defense? The emerging shape of the criminal process will be substantially affected by the answers given to questions such as these.

It can be asserted, without depreciating the importance of questions of this order, that *Gideon* will remain for a long time the watershed decision in the evolution of the criminal process. It may also be the most durable.[75] Even if the cycle of change turns out to be near its end, the norms of the process have been ineradicably changed, and in far more than the mere insistence that counsel must be provided. *Gideon* makes no sense except on the acceptance of premises, all the stronger for being unarticulated, about the adversary and judicial quality of the criminal process. As long as *Gideon* remains in the law, there is in the normative content of state criminal processes a core of meaning that rests on the Due Process Model and provides a base for expansion of Due Process norms to other aspects of the process.

Yet *Gideon* and decisions like it do not alone determine the shape of the criminal process. The response of other institutions of

---

[75] *Gideon* was decided by a unanimous Court, although there were four opinions and although two members, Justices Clark and Harlan, did not join in the opinion of the Court.

government is equally important in determining whether the necessary resources will be provided to make the norm something more than a ground for reversing a few convictions. The implementation of *Gideon* may provide a paradigm of the tension between forces of change and of inertia. No one can doubt that the norms of the criminal process have been moved rapidly and spectacularly down the spectrum toward the Due Process Model. But a parallel development in the real-world operation of the process remains for the future. No estimate of direction and velocity for the criminal process can be realistic that fails to appraise not only the normative revolution that has occurred, but the forces of change and inertia that will govern the extent to which that revolution becomes a reality.

III. The Trend and Its Impact: A Tentative Appraisal

The criminal process as it actually operates in the large majority of cases probably approximates fairly closely the dictates of the Crime Control Model. Such systematically-gathered evidence as we have, reinforced by the impressionistic "feel" for the situation that is widely current in our culture, suggests that the real-world criminal process tends to be far more administrative and managerial than it does adversary and judicial. Yet, as we have seen, the officially determined norms of the process are rapidly providing a view that looks more and more like what has been described in these pages as the Due Process Model.

It would be unnecessarily repetitive at this point to recapitulate this development in detail. Its principal thrusts have been to "judicialize" each stage of the criminal process, to enhance the capacity of the accused to challenge the operation of the process (both at the time adverse action is taken or threatened and subsequently), and to equalize the capacity of all persons accused of crime to take advantage of the opportunities thus created. In theory at least, to revert to a figure suggested at an earlier point in this Article, the process is being turned from an assembly line into an obstacle course. That is by far the dominant normative trend. We must now try to appraise its durability.

There are some fairly obvious negative factors. First, the trend as it has so far developed is based almost exclusively on judicial decisions. Indeed, it has been derived from the lead taken by one judicial institution, the Supreme Court of the United States. Changes in attitude toward the criminal process or changes in personnel on the Court (which may come to the same thing) can slow or reverse the trend in two ways. First and more obviously, decisions can be overruled.

Much of the development of the last decade has been accomplished by overruling earlier precedents; decisional instability has been a feature of its evolution, and there is no reason to suppose that it can work in only one direction. Some of the most crucial decisions have been the result of closely divided judgments. Minorities within the Court have made powerful appeals to the reason of another day. A second, subtler, and probably more serious threat to the continued strengthening of the Due Process trend is that the Court, out of a diminished enthusiasm either for the principles involved or for the continued combat their vindication entails, might cease or slacken its scrutiny of the criminal process as it operates in both state and federal criminal courts. It is well to remember that the Court's jurisdiction in these matters is almost entirely discretionary and exemplary. Any perceptible slackening in the pace or the tone of its oversight will quickly convey a message to the lower courts who are necessarily the first-line custodians of the process' norms. That is not to say that the process of change can only be maintained if the Court continues to set new norms. We may well be coming to the point at which tightening the very open-textured pronouncements of the past decade will be the main task of a Court that continues to be committed to promoting the goals of the Due Process Model. But that sort of consolidating effort, no less than the innovating effort that has been going on, requires constant attention. Whether the Court will be willing or able to supply this steady and unspectacular kind of leadership remains to be seen.

Instability of decision and slowing of pace aside, there is another major reason why the predominantly judicial character of the trend we have been examining is a potential source of weakness. With insignificant exceptions, the courts can intervene in the criminal process only to impose the sanction of nullity. That is powerful enough, especially when applied conscientiously by courts of first instance, but the sanction of nullity has its limitations. A court cannot ordain, administer, and finance an adequate system for providing the assistance of counsel to persons unable to finance their own. It can only refuse to validate criminal proceedings that are the product of inadequate systems or of no system at all. And, by and large, it can only invalidate such proceedings as happen to be brought before it for scrutiny, typically requiring at some point the initiative of counsel whose very absence gave rise to the original objection. If it is the strength of courts that they can only deal, as Professor Freund has said, at retail, it is their weakness too. The sanction of nullity applied on a retail basis may provide the goad for change; but it is not a sufficient instrument of change.

That brings us to a second and related cautionary note about the durability of the trend toward the Due Process Model. However diffused among governmental and extragovernmental agencies the capacity for promoting change in the criminal process may be, few would be disposed to deny the centrality of legislative assistance. Yet the legislative response has been slow and grudging. A single instance will suffice. It has been over twenty-five years since the decision in *Johnson v. Zerbst*[76] that persons accused of crime in federal courts are entitled to have counsel appointed for them if they are unable to hire their own. Repeated attempts have been made to get the Congress to set up a system for appointing and compensating defense counsel in the various federal districts. Finally, after a President explicitly made this an aspect of his program and an Attorney General put the force of his office behind a specific set of plans, both for the first time, bills to this end were this year passed in both houses of Congress and have finally been enacted into law.[77]

The lesson of this experience seems clear. The legislative process is not, at best, a fast one. Powerful interests must normally be mobilized in order to get legislation approved. Reform in the criminal process has very little political appeal. There is no constituency of any consequence behind it, aside from a few professional organizations whose concern tends to exist in inverse ratio to their power. If it has taken twenty-five years to bring *Johnson v. Zerbst* to the brink of puberty, how long will the childhood of *Gideon v. Wainwright* have to last?

Inertia is not the only force to be contended with. Hostility to the Due Process Model and its works is widely shared and is effectively mobilized by police and prosecutorial organizations. Every significant move in the Due Process direction has been greeted with predictions of an imminent breakdown in the criminal process. Because judicial activity has been based on the high ground of the Constitution, there have been not many instances of legislative riposte, although examples do exist. But those who unhesitatingly give an affirmative answer to the rhetorical question, "Are the courts handcuffing the police?" need not get their prescriptions enacted into law; theirs is the status quo, and they can maintain it well enough by resisting legislative efforts to provide the resources required to translate Due Process prescriptions into operative fact.

Behind all this stands that enigmatic force, public opinion. Just where it stands we cannot know. Television and the other mass media

---

[76] 304 U.S. 458 (1938).
[77] Criminal Justice Act, Pub. L. No. 455, 88th Cong., 2d Sess. (Aug. 20, 1964) (33 U.S.L. WEEK 19 (Stat. Aug. 25, 1964)).

seem to be making the defender of the accused into a folk hero. Yet one suspects that a substantial if not a preponderant segment of the public has little sympathy with the tenets of the Due Process Model. It is hard to think that the balance of advantage in the criminal process, if that is a reckonable entity, now lies with the accused.[78] Yet there is some evidence that at least a segment of the public believes that it does, and that the pendulum has swung dangerously away from order. When speculations of this sort become the stuff of political campaigns, it is evident that there are powerful currents running against the trend. Who can say what will happen to the Due Process Model?

These doubts may conduce to a picture too one-sided for accuracy. One of the most powerful features of the Due Process Model is that it thrives on visibility. People are willing to be complacent about what goes on in the criminal process as long as they are not too often or too explicitly reminded of the gory details. The more often specific cases are brought to light of invasions of privacy, of coerced confessions, of excessive bail, of lengthy periods of pretrial detention, and of deprivations of the assistance of counsel, the harder it becomes to maintain that the process should go on being primarily administrative and managerial. At root, the Due Process Model depends on the functioning of what has been called the sense of injustice. No one, Supreme Court Justices included, is immune to the force of the horrible example. And therein lies the Due Process Model's peculiar strength. It is self-sustaining because its own operations uncover the raw material that fuels its continued growth. It would take a conspiracy of silence to check the mobilization of energies that perpetuates the Due Process revolution.

That is a conspiracy we are not likely to get. To start at the small end, the renaissance of criminal studies that has taken place in this country in the last fifteen or twenty years has produced a generation of scholars uniquely knowledgeable about and alert to the problems of the criminal process. They, in turn, are having an impact on students of the law that may well reverse the historic tendency of the American bar to ignore the problems of the criminal law and give us, if not a corps of professionals, at least a generation of dedicated amateurs. These tendencies are also producing a new journalism about the criminal process whose publicists will help to ensure that the subject does not drop out of sight. The Due Process Model is to a significant extent the model of the schools. The next generation of lawyers and judges will have cut their teeth on its tenets. Cultural lag, then, is on the side of the Due Process Model.

---

[78] See Goldstein, *The State and the Accused: Balance of Advantage in Criminal Procedure*, 69 YALE L.J. 1149 (1960).

Beyond the immediate arena of the criminal law, there are growing interests in national life that may be expected as a kind of by-
product to foster the development of the Due Process Model. Two in
particular may be mentioned—civil rights and poverty. The criminal
process has been and will probably continue to be an important forum
in the struggle over civil rights. The coercive use of the criminal
process—police brutality, arrests on inadequate grounds, denial of bail
or excessively high bail, denial of access to counsel, prejudiced tri-
bunals—has focused and will continue to focus attention on the problem of adequate challenge in the process, that mainspring of the Due
Process Model. Just as the Jehovah's Witnesses made much of our
law on free speech, so may the Negro demonstrators be expected to
make much of our law on the criminal process. Beyond that, the
plight of the Negro as criminal defendant out of all proportion to his
numbers in the population may be expected to produce legislative and
extragovernmental interest in the workings of the criminal process.
The problem of poverty is not far removed. As we have seen, an important dimension of the Due Process ideology is in its insistence upon
equality in the operation of the criminal process. The problem of
crime is to an important extent a problem of poverty. The current
national interest in poverty cannot fail, first indirectly and then directly,
to confront the manifold relationships between poverty and the criminal process. We have it on high authority that poverty and the administration of criminal justice must be dealt with together in the formulation of national policies.[79] Unless the current that now appears to be
running so strongly toward governmental concern in the problem of
poverty is abruptly reversed, the exponents of the Due Process Model
may expect to find powerful official support that has not hitherto
been available in their cause.

One can do no more than venture a guess about the continuation
of present trends in the criminal process. In the short run, at least,
it seems probable that the development and consolidation of norms
drawn from the Due Process Model will not slacken. In particular
norms that require the equalization of opportunity to challenge the
process are likely to become firmly established. This trend, as symbolized by the decisions on the right to assigned counsel, may in the
end be a far more momentous one than trends expanding particular
substantive rights of the accused. If those rights are not further
extended, or even if they are curtailed, there will remain a list of opportunities to challenge the operation of the process that far exceeds the

---

[79] See Address by Attorney General Robert F. Kennedy, University of Chicago
Law School, May 1, 1964.

66   *UNIVERSITY OF PENNSYLVANIA LAW REVIEW*   [Vol.113:1

present capacity of criminal defendants to use it. If the recent trends toward the prescriptions of the Due Process Model in such matters as powers of arrest, use of illegally obtained evidence, confessions during police interrogation, pretrial liberty, and early access to counsel were now to come to an abrupt halt—an unlikely eventuality—the theoretical operation of the process would still look very much like the Due Process Model. The burning question will be whether the great mass of criminal defendants, who are financially unable to invoke the challenges now available to them, will find their capacity to do so materially improved by measures designed more closely to assimilate their opportunities to those presently enjoyed by the small minority of the fully able. The interest now being displayed by governmental and extra-governmental organizations in devising ways to implement this norm of the Due Process Model suggests that this trend is both durable and influential.

What are the implications for the criminal sanction of the trend toward the Due Process Model? If it tends to become not merely a legal norm but an operational fact that the accused will have a much better opportunity to challenge the operation of the process than he presently enjoys, what, if anything, should that fact have to say to our hypothetical rational legislator [80] as he ponders the uses and limits of the criminal sanction? The problems are, of course, somewhat interdependent, in that official decision-makers will have a great deal to say about the extent to which the developing Due Process Model is allowed to become operational fact. Let us, nonetheless, make the simplifying assumption that to a degree the trend in the process is irreversible and that, for whatever complex of reasons and however reluctantly, the rational legislator finds himself confronted by a Given so far as the changed mechanics of the criminal process are concerned.

The criminal process now looks to him as if it is becoming a somewhat unwieldy instrument of public policy, especially for dealing with large numbers of defendants. It is not to the same extent the low-cost, high-speed process envisioned in the Crime Control Model and reflected in the present real-world situation. At the level of resources presently devoted to its operation, the capacity of the criminal process for dealing with its rapidly increasing annual intake must be seriously impaired.

One line of solution is to throw more resources into the operation of the process—more policemen, more prosecutors, more judges, and more supporting services of all kinds. While there has undoubtedly been an expansion in the public resources devoted to the criminal

---

[80] See note accompanying title *supra.*

process, perhaps even greater than would have been called for by increases in population or the so-called crime rate, we have not so far been noted for the steadiness of our attention to the resource needs of the process. Indeed, no systematic work has been done on the extent of those needs. Beyond that, even if conscious choice were to lead in that direction, there may come a point at which the quality of life in a free society is adversely affected by increases in the proportion of public resources employed to detect, prosecute, and punish activity that has been defined as criminal. Some increase in the resources available for operation of the process is undoubtedly warranted, even apart from the demands of the shift toward the Due Process Model that we have been exploring; but a conscious choice to meet the problems created by that shift entirely or even predominantly through increasing the resources of crime control seems unwise, if there is an alternative.

The alternative that I would commend to the rational legislator is to reexamine the uses now being made of the criminal sanction with a view toward deciding which uses are relatively indispensable and which might with safety (and perhaps even with some net gain to the public welfare) be restricted or relinquished. There is nothing inherent in the nature of things about the penal code of any time and place. The behavior content of the criminal law has expanded enormously over the past century, mainly because declaring undesirable conduct to be criminal is the legislative line of least resistance for coping with the vexing problems of an increasingly complex and interdependent society. As a result we have inherited a strange mélange of criminal proscriptions, ranging from conduct that offers the grossest kind of threat to important social interests to conduct whose potentiality for harm is trivial or nonexistent.

It is always in order to question the uses made of this most awesome and coercive of sanctions. It is especially appropriate to do so at a time when the processes that are invoked to apply the criminal sanction are undergoing a profound change that renders them unsuitable for being lightly employed. What we require is a set of criteria for distinguishing the "mandatory" uses of the criminal sanction from the "optional" ones. Particular attention need be paid to that large group of consensual offenses in which it is not always easy to say who is being injured and by whom. Offenses of that kind—narcotics, gambling, and alcoholism are three statistically conspicuous examples—afford a special opportunity to canvass the important question of alternatives to the criminal sanction. And through that kind of examination, the foundation that we do not now have for a jurisprudence of sanctions may eventually be laid. It may be predicted that the change in our model of the criminal process will provide not merely a reason for pressing an inquiry into the appropriate criteria for legislative invocation of the criminal sanction, as has been argued in this Article, but also the source of some valuable clues to what some of those criteria ought to be.

[13]

BRIT. J. CRIMINOL. VOL. 33 NO. 2 SPRING 1993

AUDITING CRIMINAL JUSTICE

CAROL JONES*

This paper addresses the impact of economy, efficiency, and effectiveness — the 'three Es' upon agencies of the criminal justice system (police and prosecution, forensic investigation, courts, probation services, and prisons) in the 1980s in Britain. It also asks whether what is happening to criminal justice signifies a shift from 'rule of law' towards 'managerial justice'. It argues that the emphasis upon 'consumer control' has led not to more public accountability but to increased central control of criminal justice practice. Finally, it raises the issue of whether these trends form part of a wider political strategy to 'manage' social tensions within British society wrought by the return to notions of 'free market' capitalism, enterprise culture, and the 'strong state'.

The Promise of Auditing

Efficient, effective, and economic management formed part of the political agenda of the 'Thatcher revolution' which promised consumers greater control over their own lives. Time-wasting and unresponsive institutions were to be made more accountable to 'customer needs'. To this end, there were to be changes in the way services were paid for and delivered, e.g. by charging and contracting out (Gamble 1989). By the end of the 1980s, the provision of education, health, and housing, as well as criminal justice, had begun to be restructured on these principles.

The application of auditing methods to public administration stems partly from a modernist faith in 'administration by experts', and partly from the need for economic stringency. The remit of the Rayner Efficiency Unit, set up in 1979, was to generate improved efficiency within Whitehall. Civil servants needed to adopt a more 'business-like approach'; the existing administration of government was deemed too costly and too inefficient, lacking any evidence to suggest that existing policies were being effective. The guiding principles of managerialism were:

the pursuit of efficiency, effectiveness and value for money; responsibility is to be decentralised, lower level operatives made aware of and accountable for the costs of their operations, targets are to be established . . . In brief, we are offered a world where bureaucrats (and ministers) are redefined as *accountable managers*, public sector operations sub-divided into *businesses*, and the public seen as the *customer*. (Gray and Jenkins 1986: 171)

Within the first six years of the Rayner initiative a total of 266 efficiency scrutinies were conducted (Public Accounts Committee 1985), and by 1986 an estimated £950 million had been saved. The economic impact of Rayner was thus substantial. Crucially, Rayner also concluded that lasting reform in public sector administration required two sorts of changes: changes in culture, and changes in institutions. This meant a longer-term shift in the way the British public sector was managed. In effect, Rayner set in train a shift

* Dr Carol Jones is in the Department of Sociology, University of Hong Kong.
The original version of this paper was presented at the British Criminology Conference in York, 1991.

187

CAROL JONES

away from the hierarchical decision-making of bureaucrats and professionals towards 'consumer power'. This displacement of professional hegemony formed part of Thatcherism's wider political agenda. The professionals, in their turn, argued that certain cherished beliefs about the aims of public sector services were being irrevocably displaced; the ethos of public sector provision would never be the same again.

Social auditing promised to end this 'producers' cartel'. It offered policy-makers a kit of tools whereby they could better evaluate whether the money being put into curing social problems was being used to best effect. It also promised to open up to scrutiny the previously closed world of professional and bureaucratic decision-making. It would tell us whether those charged with the 'good stewardship' of service provision were acting in the public interest. Auditors would become society's 'watchdogs of the night'.

The Construction of The Consumer

As McSweeney has pointed out, this faith in 'the reforming and revelatory power' of auditing arose 'in a period of economic constraint [and] pressure on public expenditure' (McSweeney 1988: 29–43). There was a need to cut inflation and stabilize the economy. Public discontent with an inefficient public sector provided the New Right with a justification for making radical changes in the character—and not simply the form—of public sector services. State intervention in public service provision was to be minimized, creating opportunities for free market competition in the provision of public services and increasing the power of 'consumer control' over the service providers. This active reduction of the role of the state was eased by a powerful rhetoric of consumer sovereignty. Individuals were to be given back that control over their own lives which the state had taken away. Recipients of services were reconstituted as 'consumers' whose level of service provision would depend upon their ability to pay. The police _force_ became the police _service_, 'clients' became 'customers', and 'contract' became the favourite metaphor for this new relationship between the citizen and the state. Accountability was defined 'more in terms of meeting market demands than of upholding cultural values': 'The change in management style then became a metaphor for more significant changes ... from liberal to utilitarian, from ... critical to conformist values, from humanity to technocracy' (Scott 1989: 13, 16). The new focus was on 'good management rather than good policy' (Greenwood and Wilson 1989).

Effects on the Criminal Justice System

How did these changes affect criminal justice? Have they resulted in the filching away of rights or do citizens now have more control over the criminal justice system? I have chosen to examine these issues by scrutinizing changes in the police, the forensic science service, the courts, the probation service, and the prison service. I aim to show that, despite a powerful rhetoric of community participation and 'consumer responsiveness', the old hierarchy still operates within the same power structure 'behind a false front' (Pascal 1989: 84; see also Newton 1970). Central government has devolved some powers in order to maintain its dominance—democratizing institutions is one means whereby the elite can incorporate potential challengers to its authority into the system. Auditing has contributed to this process in four ways: by (1) elevating the achievement of economy, efficiency, and effectiveness over principled criminal justice policy;

(2) dismantling central structures of accountability in favour of localized discretionary powers; (3) emphasizing consumer satisfaction as the goal of criminal justice policy; and (4) encouraging the breakdown of formal constitutional boundaries between the agencies of social control.

The police

The Financial Management Initiative (FMI) launched in 1982 required the police to state clear policy objectives and to measure performance. The Home Office found it highly problematic to arrive at a clear statement of its policy objectives. How did one measure the effectiveness of the police? What counted as an effective performance? What was the relationship between the resources put into police investigation and its output? What, indeed, *was* its output? The Home Office did not know the answers. Nor was there much enthusiasm for asking the 'right' questions. For decades, it had proceeded on the basis of public acquiescence in its decisions. It had 'always' been assumed that policies such as an increase in police establishment automatically had some beneficial effect on law and order. But it was now required to specify exactly what that effect was. Both increases *and* decreases in the crime rate might mean that the police were being more effective; equally, they might indicate the influence of outside factors beyond police control (Audit Commission 1990c). Even where changes in policing practice *are* associated with a downturn in crime, there is no guarantee that the relationship is causal. Using crime rates and clear-up rates as indicators of police performance was also profoundly problematic, though they are often favoured by the police force itself, which puts forward 'little other quantified evidence of its success' (Audit Commission 1990).

The Audit Commission took its base-line from a statement by the first Commissioner of the Metropolitan Police in 1829: "The protection of life and property, the preservation of public tranquillity, and the absence of crime, will alone prove whether [the efforts of the police] have been successful, and whether the objects for which the police have been appointed have been attained.' On the basis of these criteria, after 160 years the police were clearly failing in their role: 'Crime levels are higher than most citizens would wish to see, and are currently rising' (Audit Commission 1990c: 3). Clearly, the police force was felt not to be providing 'value for money'.

A major obstacle to improvement was the 'culture' of policing and the hierarchical nature of police decision-making: 'Perhaps the single greatest handicap to securing improved value for money . . . is what might be termed management style or the prevailing culture of the organisation. Time and again possibilities are blocked—or slowed down—by cultural constraints.' Any successful organization, 'especially one involving political choice and action affecting the general public', required some guiding concept—'a set of values and aspirations', clarity of purpose and an 'explicit vision of the future' (Audit Commission 1984: 6). FMI's push to improve police efficiency thus entailed changes in the 'culture of policing'. Delegated responsibility and individual initiative were to take the place of hierarchical decision-making. Junior officers were to be involved in the formuation of higher-level aims and 'every officer needs to know how he or she can contribute to the overall aims and objectives of the force' (Audit Commission 1990c: 14). This would increase the 'sense of ownership' of the organization's objectives throughout the workforce 'securing participation in decision-making and planning and sharing information'. This, in turn, would

CAROL JONES

'reinforce throughout the organisation a commitment to serving the public, so that responsiveness is built into the way individuals view their personal responsibilities' (Audit Commission 1984: 12).

The effect of this devolved financial and management structure was to shift police policy-making towards local initiatives and community responsiveness. Moreover, the evaluation of policing was also to change towards 'customer satisfaction'. Structured local research would enable the police and public to decide what priorities should be set and what their order should be, which offences the police ought to devote most time to combating, and so forth. Public opinion 'quality inspection' reports were to be published in the local media, generating local debate about the general aims of policing.

The police response to FMI and 'Policing by Objectives' was to engage in large-scale number-crunching for no particular purpose (National Audit Office 1991). 'Policing by Objectives' was criticized for leading to 'management by numbers'. However, neither the Audit Commission nor the Audit Office arrived at a definition of 'Policing by Objectives' which went beyond that of meeting customer requirements. The Audit Commission also suggested that the police generate income by charging a realistic rate for services provided to sports venues, escorting abnormal loads, executing magistrates' courts' warrants, etc. One issue which arises from all this is who exactly are the consumers of police services, and 'What should a police force be expected to provide free of charge as part of its normal public service, and what should it provide only if a charge for that service is paid?' (Audit Commission 1990*b*: 4). The Commission's tentative answer to this question is that it must be right to provide basic emergency services free. Clearly there is potential here for the development of two-tier policing: those who can pay receive private policing tailored to their needs; those who cannot pay receive a lesser service. The danger is that those who do not pay become those who are at best irrelevant to policing policy, and at worst its target.

How far, than, has the power to make policing policy really been relocated among 'managers' and 'consumers' at the local level? On the one hand, some writers argue that FMI has led to a transformation in police authority deliberations:

Councillors are now better informed about the realities of day to day policing and are generally less likely to strike irresponsible postures about it. At one extreme there are now fewer councillors who judge it to be impertinent to ask the police penetrating questions about policy. At the other extreme, there are also fewer councillors who never fail to take an opportunity to embarrass the police or publicly attack them. (Morgan 1990: 18, 19)

Arguably, all consultative committees do is provide a gloss of community homogeneity over the ethnic, social, and economic differences within 'communities'. Typically, such 'community' bodies completely omit those who have, in Scraton's terminology, been pushed to the edge of mainstream class locations, such as the poor, the young, the unemployed, the old, women, and black people (Scraton *et al.* 1987: ix). But the apparent consensus about policing achieved by this consultative process legitimizes the disciplining of those at the periphery. Moreover, it has also been argued that local consultative committees have provided a means whereby local political elites can be co-opted by police professionals to support their claim for more resources.

Such local accountability structures may help explain why the development of an authoritarian state in Britain has been accompanied not by conflict but by consensus (Norrie and Adelman 1989: 117). The Police and Criminal Evidence Act 1984 not only

AUDITING CRIMINAL JUSTICE

increased police powers but also placed a duty on the police authorities to 'make arrangements for obtaining the views of people ... about matters concerning the policing of the area and for obtaining their co-operation in preventing crime' (Gordon 1987: 136). These consultative committees were *only* consultative; they were not a step towards greater accountability of the police to the public:

Rather they have been set up precisely at a time when demands for accountability reached a new height ... consultation will divert attention from accountability and will help co-opt some of those, particularly those in the middle ground of politics, who are genuinely concerned by police malpractices and might otherwise move in the direction of demanding accountability ... The creation of consultative committees, however, is not just a government and police smokescreen or public relations exercise. It is not just *against* accountability—it is *for* the co-optation of the community into policing. (Gordon 1987: 136)

Community participation is thus a double-edged sword: it improves the image of the police but it also improves their intelligence-gathering capacity. Community policing and consumer consultation may, then, represent forms of surveillance and control of communities:

Community policing offers no prospect of greater democratic control of the police and policing. Indeed, community policing has come to the fore precisely at the same time as there has been widespread demand for greater public accountability and control of the police. Control of community policing remains firmly in the hands of the police ... Instead we must locate community policing in the context of the increasing disciplining of society by the state. (Gordon 1987: 141)

Norrie and Adelman (1989: 117) cite police attempts to establish 'policing by consent' as co-extensive with increases in police powers. They argue that 'important sections of the working class in addition to the middle class have been drawn into supporting police actions'. In the property-owning, share-holding democracy of the 1980s, the affluent working class came to have a real stake in the successful maintenance of law and order—measures to reduce the high crime levels of inner-city working-class areas hold a real populist appeal. Managerialist policies on policing have consolidated this appeal by emphasizing the 'service nature' of policing and the enfranchisement of local communities in policing policy. These processes of co-optation and consultation assist in the separation of what Gilroy and Sim (1987: 99) term the 'reputable from the slag citenzry'. Community consultation is thus an effective means of 'soft cop' policing designed to contain passive social unrest (Sim *et al.* 1987: 4). However radical 'consumer responsive policing' may seem, it thus operates within a very particular and restrained political agenda: 'It is a fundamental misunderstanding of what the police do to evaluate them as just another municipal agency delivering services ... The important question is whom the police serve and how they serve them' (Brown 1981: 283–4).

While the debate about whether policing has become more 'consumer responsive' is important, it misses the fact that, despite all the talk of devolved decision-making, there has actually been a real shift towards a more centralized control of policing. About 70 per cent of the cost of running provincial police forces is met by central government. The Home Office reimburses police authorities with 51 per cent of their net expenditure. Other support comes from the Department of the Environment and the revenue support grant. While each police authority is charged with determining the number of

CAROL JONES

officers in its force, its decision is subject to Home Office approval. Moreover, 'the Home Office is able to pick and choose which bids to accept and, in effect, to determine the establishment of each force. This does not sit happily with the police authority's responsibility under the tripartite structure' (Audit Commission 1990*a*: 2). The controls placed by the Home Office on police capital expenditure are also more detailed than those of almost any other local authority service. This makes it difficult for local police authorities to plan: 'All these problems reduce local accountability and work against value for money' (Audit Commission 1991*a*). These restrictions mean that local police forces cannot be 'consumer responsive'. As the Audit Commission itself points out: 'A balance has always been struck between the interests of central government, local government and the police service itself. But the balance has now tilted so far towards the centre that the role of local police authorities is significantly diminished' (Audit Commission 1991*a*: 6).

What becomes clear is that despite a rhetoric of consumer enfranchisement, the power to order criminal justice is increasingly shifting towards the centre. Whoever controls finance ultimately controls the agenda. At the same time, the power of local 'decision-makers' to oppose central government policies has been rendered less effective—the dismantling of centralism has led to the relative absence of national structures of accountability. Power has become diffused: 'A limited amount of devolution at local level can therefore be seen as a method of bolstering up an overall movement towards greater centralization in the system' (Pascal 1989: 87). The attraction of managerialism as a political strategy is that it keeps the rhetoric of criminal justice intact while demolishing the structures which, however imperfectly, previously enabled their realization.

The Forensic Science Service

If there has been a greater centralization of control over police practice, the opposite would seem to be true of the Forensic Science Service (FSS). If the key role played by forensic expertise in securing convictions is to be retained against a barrage of criticism, forensic science must be seen to be independent of the police and prosecution. Thus in 1991, after a series of damaging revelations concerning the accuracy and impartiality of Home Office scientists, the FSS became an 'Executive Agency', open to all 'customers' of forensic service, including the defence.

At first sight, this appears to be a move towards a fairer system of justice. In the past, the state has been criticized for having a monopoly of forensic science services, to the disadvantage of defendants. However, the change in FSS operation was stimulated not by a desire for equal access to justice but by a search for a more economic, efficient, and effective service.

What exactly has this pursuit of effectiveness meant for forensic science? Initial changes led the FSS away from policing priorities towards its own administrative goal of high casework throughput within laboratories. Conscious of its need to become more efficient, economic, and effective, as well as to improve its public image as an independent service, the FSS sought to establish a greater distance from the police. Some laboratories began to turn away cases on the grounds that they were not cost-effective. A large-scale murder case, for example, could tie up laboratory staff, time, and equipment for a substantial period, thereby reducing the throughput of other

AUDITING CRIMINAL JUSTICE

casework, and contributing to a lower overall 'efficiency rate' for the laboratory. Laboratories thus grew more selective about the types of cases they were prepared to investigate. This policy of selectivity led to strained relations with the police, who quickly learnt what kinds of cases it was 'pointless' to submit for forensic analysis.

In time, the FSS was criticized for no longer meeting police demands and being less responsive to the government's strong 'law and order' policy. In the light of the growing rate of crime (particularly serious crime involving complex forensic investigation of a large number of exhibits), FMI looked at ways of pricing forensic science and ways of saving police time and money by using forensic science to identify 'blind alleys' as well as to obtain convictions. This led to a debate about the proper goals of the FSS and the appropriate funding basis for its work. The outcome was a new definition of FSS effectiveness which stressed the service's ability to deliver policing needs. What was wanted was an FSS which had a clear view of its role as an arm of police investigation but nevertheless managed to preserve its public image of impartiality. Thus the First Report of the Home Affairs Committee on The Forensic Science Service took the view that the main functions of the service were to provide scientific resources to assist the police in the investigation and detection of crime and to assist the courts in the administration of justice (Ramsay 1986). FSS scientists argued that closer links with the police would compromise their independence. This claim was met by the argument that greater co-operation with the police would ensure higher efficiency, more effectiveness, and greater economy. In 1987 Touche Ross recommended a number of changes in the FSS, most significant of which was the recommendation that the police should pay for forensic support according to the use they make of it. Police forces should play a greater role in determining how much was spent on forensic science, and what kinds of equipment FSS laboratories should stock. The financial and managerial restructuring of the FSS thus had significant implications for the embedded nature of its material and cognitive commitments.

A more efficient, effective, and economic FSS would thus become a sharper tool of crime control. It was also, incidentally, to become a more dedicated tool of conviction. At first sight, however, this is not at all clear. The new FSS 'executive agency' was to be open to both the police and other users, such as the defence and civil clients. This seemed to promise a more even-handed approach. However, the Touche Ross report included one crucial proviso. It argued that the market for income generation from other sources (defence, commerce, industry, etc.) should be explored *only* once the needs of the police had been met. This effectively stymied the promise of independence. The police are the largest user of forensic science and there is always a list of cases pending analysis, frequently requiring results for presentation in court by fixed deadlines. In effect, therefore, changing the funding base of the FSS made it highly dependent upon one single customer. Rather than gaining greater independence, FSS facilities became a more dedicated arm of prosecution, with deeper—but less visible— ties with the police.

The Prosecution and the Courts

Thus far I have argued that there has been a consolidation of state control in the investigative branches of criminal justice. I now turn to examine the impact of managerialism upon the agencies of prosecution and trial.

CAROL JONES

In its report on the Procurator Fiscal Service in Scotland, the National Audit Office pointed out that the aims and objectives of the Procurator Fiscal Service were nowhere defined in statute nor formally set out elsewhere. This absence of clear aims and consistent objectives hardly sat well with the notion of a service described by the National Audit Office as 'a cornerstone of the Scottish criminal justice system'. Moreover, even where limited performance measures were available—such as time limits—these were generally not being met. There were also substantial variations between jurisdictions in the time taken for cases to come to trial, with one court taking forty-five weeks to process cases. There had been substantial increases in resources in recent years, and whereas in private industry this would have been expected to lead to an improvement in the output of the service, no improvement in prosecution practice had been forthcoming; indeed, things seemed to have become worse. The service was thus inefficient.

Criticisms of the Crown Prosecution Service (CPS) proceeded along similar lines. The National Audit Office specifically noted that since the introduction of the CPS in 1986, the quality of case preparation had deteriorated—there was limited evidence to suggest that the dismissal of some cases was attributable to poor work by CPS lawyers themselves (National Audit Office 1989*a*: 13). Costs had also increased since, in the absence of CPS lawyers, the service had employed local lawyers as its agents. The introduction of the CPS had not reduced court delays—in fact, Home Office statistics suggested that there had been a significant increase in the time taken to process cases through the magistrates' courts (National Audit Office 1989*b*: 13). Finally, the introduction of the CPS had produced no significant improvement in the conviction rate.

Seeking ways of evaluating the efficiency and effectiveness of these two prosecution services, the National Audit Office looked to key performance indicators such as case discontinuance, conviction and acquittal rates, processing delays, and costs as indicators of 'value for money' (National Audit Office 1989*b*: 2). It found that 7.5 per cent of cases brought before the magistrates' courts were dropped. In Scotland, the 'equivalent' discontinuance rate was 17 per cent. In England, two-thirds of these discontinued cases were not being dropped by the CPS until the day of trial, thus taking up scarce court time. Variations in conviction rates between regions were also noted, as were differences in the rate of dismissals (the proportion of cases in which the accused was found not guilty) and judgment quality (the proportion of trials where the case was dismissed by the magistrates before the defence was presented).

In defence of the rate of discontinuance, the DPP suggested that it might be a positive indication that the CPS was acting independently of the police that 'we are not rubber stamping every decision that a police officer has made and letting it go through on the nod' (Public Accounts Committee 1990*a*: 8). Despite the rationale of the CPS as an independent agency, the National Audit Office found that efficient jurisdictions (i.e. those with a low discontinuance rate) achieved their success by *greater* alignment between the police and prosecution. *Closer* police/prosecution liaison thus equals more 'efficient' prosecution.

In Scotland, a major finding of the National Audit Office was that procurators fiscal were dropping cases for a variety of reasons, only some of which were good legal reasons (e.g. insufficiency of evidence). Some cases were marked 'no pro' due to staff shortages and caseload backlogs. In Glasgow and Edinburgh 25 per cent of cases were being

AUDITING CRIMINAL JUSTICE

marked 'no pro', while in Hamilton—another very busy court—the 'no pro' rate was only 9 per cent. The 'no pro' rate did not, therefore, depend on the size of workload. Despite these 'anomalies' the National Audit Office regarded the fact that 90 per cent of cases prosecuted ended in a plea of guilty as a confirmation that the fiscal service *was* doing a good job, i.e. selecting cases correctly. Efficiency thus came to be equated with convictions.

Delay in case processing was identified by the National Audit Office as the single most important obstacle to achieving economy, efficiency, and effectiveness in the criminal justice system. Ways of securing more and earlier pleas of guilty were examined, but the principle of pursuing more and earlier guilty pleas itself was never questioned—an efficient policy clearly being one which produced convictions at the lowest administrative and financial cost. Though this push for reduced court delay is supported by the view that 'justice delayed is justice denied', it must be recognized that this search for efficiency may itself undercut substantive justice ends. In some UK courts, for example, cases 'turn around' in three to four weeks. Moreover, research suggests that busy courts with high caseloads can also be fast courts, and that such courts also experience low rates of adjournment and high rates of contested trial (see e.g. Church *et al.* 1978). The downside to this rosy picture is that courts can become 'too efficient'. Case turn-round times can become *too short*—lawyers go to trial inadequately prepared, there is no time to prepare a proper defence, review the evidence, or interview witnesses. Justice speeded up may also, therefore, be justice denied.

In 1991 a steering group was set up to develop an 'action plan' for remedying court delay. The group recommended a national guideline of eight weeks between entry of a not guilty plea and summary trial (Law Society 1991). For accused held in custody, a national guideline of fourteen days should apply between entry of the plea and summary trial. It also recommended that defendants should be able at committal proceedings to indicate whether they intended to plead guilty to any of the charges 'And, to discourage those committed for trial from entering "tactical not guilty pleas", attention should be drawn to the likelihood that an early plea of guilty might attract a discount on sentence.' Another recommendation was that defendants be required to state the nature of their defences at direction hearings: 'substantial savings in court time could accrue from this procedure' (p. 3). Further recommendations included refusing adjournments to accused who delay seeking legal advice.

Similar remedies were discussed by the 8th World Conference on Procedural Law, which looked at the question of efficiency in the appellate courts. Solutions included reducing the size of the appeal court, restrictions on the right to appeal, restrictions on the content of the appeal so that certain types of issues may not be re-opened on appeal nor new matters introduced, restricting appeal only to those cases where the decision of the court of first instance is 'clearly wrong', and introducing penalties for parties to discourage 'inefficient' handling of appeals (Jolowicz 1989: 86 ff.).

Expansion (more judges, more courts), restriction (fewer judges, fewer courts, fewer cases), and efficiency (better management) were all devices aimed at making appeal courts more efficient by controlling the number of appeals actually launched and/or heard (Public Accounts Committee 1990*b*: ix). Other popular 'efficiency devices' include the introduction of pre-trial review, use of skeleton arguments, paper procedures, advanced disclosure, greater use of para-legals and para-judicials, diversion of

CAROL JONES

cases out of the criminal justice system, the introduction of alternatives to the criminal justice system, and refusal of legal aid for 'frivolous' cases. Legal aid was originally introduced 'so that no-one will be financially unable to prosecute a just and reasonable claim or defend a legal right' (Law Society 1991: 18). In the mid-1980s limits were set on such welfarism. The cost of criminal legal aid was said to be 'spiralling out of control', the 'lax' administration of legal aid was identified as a 'cause' of court delay— 'too many' frivolous cases were going to trial because they were legally aided. A report by the National Audit Office in 1991 spoke of the widespread failure of justices' clerks, magistrates, and officials to scrutinize legal aid applications. Similar accusations were repeated in 1992. Local administration of legal aid has all but disappeared, making it easier to institute central government policy of 'rolling back' legal aid expenditure.

Underlying these proposals to restrict access to justice (and/or penalize parties who insist upon their due process rights) is the notion that some kinds of litigation amount not to a *use* of process but to an *abuse* of process. The managerial dream is that the 'problem' of court delay will go away if only such cases can be weeded out of the system. Contested cases are slow and costly, and half the time the accused is found not guilty; late pleas of guilty are also administratively inconvenient. The ideal-type efficient criminal justice system would thus appear to be a 'trial-free' system, in which fewer people would use the formal processes of law, while those who do would plead guilty and the few who go to trial would never be allowed to appeal. As far as the managers of the system are concerned, the exercise of due process rights thwarts the efficiency and effectiveness of the system. Improvement involves curtailing due process 'trappings', providing structural opportunities for 'opting out' of trial and applying penalties to those who 'opt in'.

Clearly, there are several issues of substantive justice involved here. The most striking is not that the criminal justice system depends for its survival upon citizens' abdication of their due process rights; this is nothing new. What is new is that there is now in the ascendant an ideology which wholly legitimates the pursuit of administratively rational ends over substantive justice goals. Managerial changes designed to improve the efficiency of the courts and prosecution thus clearly entail substantive justice implications. The 'problem' of court overload may not be resolved without compromising and sacrificing some of the traditional values of the legal system (Jolowicz 1989: 93). The more general dilemma is the question of 'how much of the "trappings" of formal due process' can be exchanged in the name of the efficient processing of caseloads:

The danger is that the value of efficiency, which too often is translated simply into the variable of state costs, is taken for granted as equal to or greater in importance than the need to preserve longstanding and valuable safeguards in procedure. We might call this the simple meaning of a trade-off between efficiency and justice. (Garth 1989: 278)

But the symbolic value of due process means that it is sometimes prudent to meet expensive procedural demands where this secures other social goals such as political legitimacy. This is what Mashaw would count as necessary 'given the contingencies of modern government, to effect the liberal State's promise to construct a legal order that supports privacy, equality and comprehensibility in public decisional processes' (Mashaw 1985: 201). In the 1980s, however, these goals—and the philosophy of the

AUDITING CRIMINAL JUSTICE

'liberal State' which provided their political underpinning — receded as the principal ends of the criminal justice system.

The Probation Service

I have suggested that changes in the agencies of investigation, prosecution, and trial have led to greater central control over criminal justice policy and a 'rolling back' of welfarism and due process rights. This movement has been accompanied by a rhetoric of greater consumer choice and state disengagement. What I have tried to delineate are the financial and organizational mechanisms by which this change has been instituted and justified. In particular, it becomes clear that where local criminal justice agencies depend for their finance upon central government funds, central government is able to set their agendas. Nowhere is this more apparent than in the probation service. The Home Office supplies 80 per cent of funding for local authority probation services in England and Wales; it can and does determine the agenda for probation. How it chooses to exercise this power has been influenced by audits which suggest that the service is inefficient and ineffective — probation has little impact on re-offending rates, or on the number of people sent to prison (National Audit Office 1989*c*: 4).

On the issue of who determines the deployment of probation resources—the professional probation workers or central government—the National Audit Office left no doubt: it was the clear duty of the Home Office to make sure that the money was spent economically and efficiently. The Home Office has thus retained overall control of probation strategy. It was criticized for failing to investigate the causes of wide differences in resource consumption between probation services and responded by producing national standards for community service in April 1989. These were 'designed to improve the profile of community service, in the eyes of sentencers particularly, as an alternative to custody by demonstrating that it is uniformly tough and demanding on offenders'. This call for national standards and uniformity conflicted with the notion of professional autonomy in judging local 'consumer' needs—local autonomy providing a flexibility more suited to grass-roots probation work (National Audit Office 1989*c*). In the auditors' view, however, finite resources gave rise to the need to 'harness probation work more closely to central policy objectives'. Probation officers should concentrate on diversion of offenders to non-custodial disposals. By 1989 the Audit Commission was clearly spelling out the options for the probation service: 'The Probation Service is therefore at a critical point. It can either move to the forefront of the Government's penal policy; or it could find that another agency is given responsibility for new community options and, perhaps, part of its existing workload' (Audit Commission 1989: 6; Fowles 1990: 82–100).

Despite a more generalized rhetoric of devolved management and local responsiveness, the guiding principles of probation were not, then, to be decided locally on the basis of consumer need. Central government goals of relieving pressure on overcrowded prisons and reducing the rates of re-offending took priority. Probation did not appear to be contributing to these aims. To do so, it had to concentrate upon the supervision of offenders subject to non-custodial orders. This met all three of its goals of reintegrating offenders into the community, prevention or reduction of re-offending, and diversion from custody. Since through-care only met two of these goals, it had lower priority (Public Accounts Committee 1990*b*).

CAROL JONES

What at first sight appeared to be simply a management reorganization of probation thus became a critical re-evaluation of its substantive goals. A new definition of what counted as effective probation was produced. Auditing gave central government a crucial additional tool with which to enforce its 'law and order' agenda.

The Prison Service

The conflict between the 'three Es' and substantive penal policy objectives was also apparent in the 'Fresh Start' Initiative introduced into the prison service in 1987. A 1985 study concluded that the prison service could be maintained at the existing regime level with an immediate reduction of 15–20 per cent in total officers' hours worked (Woolf 1991: 340). 'Fresh Start' involved 'the complete phasing out of overtime' (p. 340). Where officers worked additional hours, they would receive time off in lieu. This would amount to savings equivalent to 4.5 working hours for each officer. The Prison Officers Association challenged the claim that there was a 15 per cent inefficiency in the use of staff hours. It held that 'techniques which measure, for example, the flow of a car assembly line, cannot be related to the running of a prison . . . time taken in dealing with any particular inmate depends on the type of inmate and the nature of his problems' (p. 342).

One aim of 'Fresh Start' was to enhance job satisfaction and increase tranquillity within the prison system. However, instead of improving the quality of prison life for prisoners and staff, the result was low morale, a sharp reduction in staffing levels, and a deleterious effect on the quality of regimes. Staff felt disappointed, 'devalued and unfairly treated' (p. 347). In their view, the pursuit of efficiency and economy directly impoverished the substantive formal goals of the system.

The Woolf Report continued the 'managerialist' approach by recommending a more visible leadership at the top of the Prison Service accompanied by greater delegation of power at local level. On this view, management should be an 'enabling process' (p. 295). Higher-level management should *enable* governors to govern; governors should *enable* their staff to look after prisoners. Woolf also recommended the use of 'contracts' throughout all levels of the Prison Service. At the highest level, the contract would be between the Director General of the Prison Service and the Secretary of State, and would take the form of a 'corporate plan' detailing the tasks and objectives of the service. At the lower levels, area managers were to 'contract' with the governors of establishments in their area, setting out the level of service to be provided, 'how this is to be met within the resources available and objectives for change in respect of local or national (i.e. strategic) priorities in the year ahead' (p. 297). Prisoners were also to be afforded the chance of making a 'contract', in return for what the prison would provide for the prisoner:

The prisoner would agree to comply with the responsibilities which the 'contract' placed upon him . . . The prisoner would also receive progressively more under his 'contract' as he progressed through his sentence. On the other hand, he could lose for a period of time some of the features of his 'contract' in consequence of any finding of ill discipline. The 'contract' would therefore be a way of introducing greater incentives into the system . . . A prisoner could not be obliged to enter into a 'contract' but it would be very much in his interests to do so. If he did not do so, he would still receive the ordinary regime in the prison, but he might not receive opportunities that

AUDITING CRIMINAL JUSTICE

were extended to those who were prepared to take on the responsibilities laid down by the 'contract'. The 'contract' could be developed, as in the Netherlands, by offering the prisoner more if he were prepared to submit voluntarily to obligations which he would not otherwise have, urine tests for drugs, for example, on returning from home leave. (p. 302)

This generates an image of the individual prisoner controlling his or her own destiny, while in practice the true balance of power within prisons has not shifted at all. One aspect of the classical idea of the law of contract is that it 'facilitates a subtle form of domination, no less effective for being the product of an agreement than if it were imposed directly by the state' (Collins 1986: 13). This arises because 'some bargaining partners enjoy such strong advantages that they may routinely dominate others through contractual arrangements' (Collins 1986: 12). This is clearly the case with prison–prisoner 'contracts'. Moreover, it is not clear what remedy the prisoner has if the prison authorities fail to deliver their side of the bargain. Woolf's 'contract' is not the same as a legally enforceable contract. This being so, the prisoner cannot sue the authorities for their failure to deliver the promised 'goods' and 'services'. The positions of the two parties to the contract are therefore patently unequal with regard to setting the terms of the contract and enforcing these terms. Not only does the contract metaphor mask the locus of power within the prison, it also disables protest by recourse to a rhetoric of voluntariness and consent.

Conclusions

I have argued that the auditing process has had a profound impact upon the practice of criminal justice in Britain. Clearly, the process has a good side in so far as it has made more explicit the value preferences underlying the criminal justice system. It has also subjected criminal justice agencies to an unprecedented degree of scrutiny—the hearings of the Public Accounts Committee, which summons top civil servants and officials to answer criticisms made by the National Audit Office, have provided parliamentary accountability of a particularly robust kind. Officials are frequently placed in 'the hot seat'. Senior law officers have been brought for the first time before a Committee of Parliament to answer criticisms, and their evidence has been published. Arguably, the National Audit Office, the Audit Commission, and the Public Accounts Committee are fulfilling the promise of 'social accounting' to render key organizations more open to public scrutiny.

At first sight, therefore, the traditional structures of accountability appear to be reinforced by the new system. The contrary view argues that auditing undermines these traditional structures. Instead of officials being responsible to ministers for their decisions, ministers are forced to rely upon the professional values of accountants and auditors (Clark 1975: 30). Accountants are no longer simply providers of financial information; they are in the forefront of decision-making. Policy-making thus moves outside recognized political channels.

The National Audit Office recommendation of greater liaison between all agencies of the criminal justice system (courts, police, prosecution) also weakens traditional constitutional boundaries. The pursuit of economy and effectiveness thus encourages a more intricate meshing of criminal justice agencies, whose efficiency and effectiveness are increasingly defined in terms of their 'success rate': i.e. convictions. The auditing

CAROL JONES

process itself also enables central government to penetrate criminal justice agencies more effectively and less obtrusively. Standardization creeps through the system via a new route. National application of the 'three Es' undercuts local distinctiveness and professional autonomy. It may also cut across national boundaries. For example, procurators fiscal in Scotland were literally 'called to account' because their practices did not accord with a set of criteria formulated in another legal system. What is marketed as a 'hands off' policy may thus actually result in a 'receding locus of power' (Noble and Pym 1989: 28) which masks a more intricate realignment of the forces of law and order and removes existing—if imperfect—channels of accountability.

   Cumulatively, there has also been a shift away from a formal commitment to rational justice and 'rule of law' to 'managerial justice'. While managerialism may pay lip-service to all the 'three Es', the 1980s saw the 'ascendancy of economy' over efficiency and effectiveness (Gray 1986), resulting in a 'managerial myopia' and 'a concern with short-term managerial innovation at the expense of a long term focus' (Gray and Jenkins 1984: 425). 'Value for money' translated not only into a greater emphasis upon crime control but also into 'more crime control with fewer resources'. This produced a new definition of what the criminal justice system was for: the rights of accused persons were inefficient and uneconomic 'trappings'; due process of law was too expensive, too inefficient, and too ineffective—it 'let too many guilty persons go free'. Thus the tenets of auditing, allied to those of managerialism and devolved control, came to underpin an increasingly 'crime control'-oriented legal system.

   I have argued that the construction of the consumer as a participant in the management of his or her own life served as a useful ideological strategy for stabilizing this increasing focus on 'law and order' in society. This was particularly crucial at a time when the 'postwar consensus' appeared to be breaking down, where the policy was 'not to integrate the poor and underprivileged but to manage their protest' (Norrie and Adelman 1989: 123). I have also argued that despite the rhetoric of consumer power there has in fact been a greater centralization of control over criminal justice practices. This undercuts the notion of consumers being able to make strategic choices among competitors in a free market.

   The increase in managerial discretion is also quite at odds with the tenets of 'rule of law' ideology, though the rhetoric of freely contracting consumers is the epitome of that bourgeois individualism found in rule of law ideology. It provides a gloss of equality where none exists. It legitimizes a system of settled—or emerging—inequalities. Managerialism undercuts the distinction between formal legal rationality and techno-cratic rationality. It also undercuts the 'traditional apparatuses of justice' (Damaska, cited in Heydebrand 1991) and increasingly legitimizes a 'relatively naked emphasis within the criminal justice system upon criminalisation and the suppression of resistance, and a relative de-emphasising of the formal norms and values of individual justice' (Norrie and Adelman 1989: 15). Typically, sociologists have predicted that a move away from formal legal rationality will result in a move towards technocratic justice. Managerialism is a hybrid form which intercepts these boundaries. It is pragmatic and instrumentalist but it is also flexible and informal, substituting discretion and 'the right of management to manage' for explicit legal rules, formal procedural norms, the principle of precedent, and due process of law (Heydebrand 1991). In this respect, managerialism shares what Heydebrand has termed the 'tendencies of de-juridification and de-stratification' which characterize technocratic

AUDITING CRIMINAL JUSTICE

decision-making (Heydebrand 1991: 8). The 'virtue' of managerialism is that it is divorced from any substantive normative or political values. Indeed, it transforms the absence of principled policy (for example, along lines of justice and fairness) from a vice into a virtue.

REFERENCES

AUDIT COMMISSION (1984), *Economy, Efficiency and Effectiveness: The Audit Commission Handbook on Improving Economy, Efficiency and Effectiveness in Local Government*. London: HMSO.

—— (1989), *The Probation Service: Promoting Value for Money*. London: HMSO.

—— (1990a), Police Papers, no. 6, *Footing the Bill: Financing Provincial Police Forces*. London: HMSO.

—— (1990b), Police Papers, no. 7, *Taking Care of the Coppers: Income Generation by Provincial Police Forces*. London: HMSO.

—— (1990c), Police Papers, no. 8, *Effective Policing: Performance Review in Police Forces*. London: HMSO.

—— (1991a), Police Papers, no. 9, *Reviewing the Organisation of Provincial Police Forces*. London: HMSO.

—— (1991b), Police Papers, no. 10, *Pounds and Coppers: Financial Delegation in Provincial Police Forces*.

BROWN, M. (1981), *Working the Street: Police Discretion and the Dilemmas of Reform*. London: Russell Sage Foundation.

CHURCH, T., CARLSON, A., LEE, J., and TAN, T. (1978), *Justice Delayed*. Virginia: National Center for State Courts.

CLARK, J. M. (1975), 'Towards a Concept of Social Value', in L. J. Siedler and L. Siedler, eds., *Social Accounting: Theory, Issues, Cases*. Los Angeles: Melville Publishing.

COLLINS, H. (1986), *The Law of Contract*. London: Weidenfeld & Nicolson.

FOWLES, A. J. (1990), 'Monitoring Expenditure on the Criminal Justice System', *Howard Journal*, 29/2: 82–100.

GAMBLE, A. (1989), 'Privatisation, Thatcherism and the British State', *Journal of Law and Society*, 16/1.

GARTH, B. G. (1989), 'Improvement of Civil Litigation by Lessons Derived from Administrative Procedures', in Wedekind, ed.

GLATTER, R., ed. (1989), *Educational Institutions and their Environments: Managing the Boundaries*. Milton Keynes: Open University Press.

GORDON, P. (1987), 'Community Policing: Towards the Local Police State?', in Scraton, ed.

GRAY, A. (1986), *The Background in Policy Management and Policy Assessment*. London: Royal Institute of Public Administration.

GRAY, A., and JENKINS, W. T. (1984), 'Lasting Reforms in Civil Service Management', *Political Quarterly*, 55/4: 425.

—— (1985), *Administrative Politics in British Government*. Brighton: Harvester.

—— (1986), 'Accountable Management in British Government: Some Reflections on the Financial Management Initiative, *Financial Accountability and Management*, 2/3: 171–87.

GREENWOOD, J., and WILSON, D. (1989), *Public Administration in Britain Today*. London: Unwin Hyman.

HEYDEBRAND, W. (1991), 'Technocratic Justice and the Rule of Law: The Transformation of the Disputing Process and Law Enforcement in the United States and Germany', paper

CAROL JONES

presented to the joint conference of the Law and Society Association and the Research Committee on the Sociology of Law of the International Sociological Association, Amsterdam, 28 June.

JOLOWICZ, J. A. (1989), 'Managing Overload in Appellate Courts: "Western Countries"', in Wedek ', ed.

LAW SOCIETY (1991), *Law Society Gazette*, no. 8, Wed. 27 Feb.

MASHAW, J. L. (1985), *Due Process in the Administrative State*. New Haven: Yale University Press.

MORGAN, R. (1990), *Policing by Consent: Current Thinking in Police Accountability in Great Britain*, Social Science Research Centre and Department of Sociology Occasional Paper. Hong Kong: University of Hong Kong.

McSWEENEY, B. (1988), 'Accounting for the Audit Commission', *Political Quarterly*, 59: 28–43.

NATIONAL AUDIT OFFICE (1989a), *Review of the Crown Prosecution Service*. London: HMSO.

—— (1989b), *The Prosecution of Crime in Scotland: Review of the Procurator Fiscal Service*. London: HMSO.

—— (1989c), *Home Office: Control and Management of Probation Services in England and Wales*. London: HMSO.

—— (1991), *Promoting Value for Money in Provincial Police Forces*. London: HMSO.

NEWTON, K. (1970), *The Theory of Pluralistic Democracy*. Oxford: Oxford University Press.

NOBLE, T., and PYM, B. (1989), 'Collegial Authority and the Receding Locus of Power', in T. Bush, ed., *Managing Education: Theory and Practice*. Milton Keynes: Open University Press.

NORRIE, A., and ADELMAN, S. (1989), 'Consensual Authoritarianism and Criminal Justice in Thatcher's Britain', *Journal of Law and Society* 16/1: 112–29.

PASCAL, C. (1989), 'Democratized Primary School Government', in R. Glatter, ed., *Educational Institutions and their Environments: Managing the Boundaries*. Milton Keynes: Open University Press.

PUBLIC ACCOUNTS COMMITTEE (1985), *39th Report: The Rayner Scrutiny Programme 1979–1983*. London: HMSO.

—— (1990a), *2nd Report: Review of the Crown Prosecution Service*. London: HMSO.

—— (1990b), *7th Report: Home Office: Control and Management of Probation Services in England and Wales*. London: HMSO.

RAMSAY, M. (1986), *The Effectiveness of the Forensic Science Service*, Home Office Research and Planning Unit. London: HMSO.

SCOTT, P. (1989), 'Accountability, Responsiveness and Responsibility', in Glatter, ed.

SCRATON, P., ed. (1987), *Law, Order and the Authoritarian State*. Milton Keynes: Open University Press.

SCRATON, P., SIM, J., and GORDON, P. (1987), 'Crime, the State and Critical Analysis', introduction to Scraton, ed.: 1–71.

STEWART, A., and BURRIDGE, R. (1989), 'Housing Tales of Law and Space', *Journal of Law and Society*, 16/1: 65–83.

WEDEKIND, W., ed. (1989), *Proceedings of the 8th World Conference on Procedural Law: Justice and Efficiency*. The Hague: Kluwer.

WOOLF, LORD (1991), *Prison Disturbances April 1990* (The Woolf Report), Cmnd. 1456. London: HMSO.

[14]

Rethinking the Functions of Criminal Procedure: The Warren and Burger Courts' Competing Ideologies*

PETER ARENELLA**

Did the Burger Court bring the so-called criminal procedure revolution of the 1960s to an abrupt halt? Did it launch a counter-revolution? Has it promoted "law and order" without regard to the procedural rights of the accused or the suspected? Or has the Burger Court, no less than its predecessor, been the victim of grossly exaggerated criticism? . . . It may well be that the intensity of the civil libertarian criticisms of the Burger Court in the police practices area relates less to what the Court has done . . . than to what the critics fear[ed] it [would] do.[1]

Yale Kamisar—1983

The Warren Court's criminal procedure decisions that regulated the investigative aspects of law enforcement are neither very radical nor very great departures from traditional fourth and fifth amendment values. These decisions have been reaffirmed by the Burger Court's decisions of the last decade. Some of the Warren Court's holdings have been limited, but others are more firmly entrenched now than ever before and perhaps have been extended by recent decisions. Thus, the Burger Court hardly can be characterized as a tribunal set upon the task of dismantling piece by piece the work of its predecessor.

In his successful 1968 campaign, President Nixon won much popular support for his stated goal of changing the Court to redress the imbalance he perceived in decisions favoring criminal defendants. He appointed four justices in as many years and, as a consequence, dramatically changed the face of the Court. Nonetheless, while the personnel changed, the Court adhered to its basic regard for constitutional values.[2]

Stephen Saltzburg—1980

What functions are served by criminal procedure? For the most part, American criminal justice scholarship has assumed that the answers to this question

* © 1983 by Peter Arenella.
** Professor of Law, Boston University School of Law. B.A. 1969, Wesleyan University; J.D. 1972, Harvard University. I would like to thank Ken Simons, Larry Sager, Steve Shiffrin, Yale Kamisar, Colin Diver, John Leubsdorf, Ron Allen, Steve Schulhofer, and Peter Westen for their invaluable critiques of earlier drafts of this article.

1. Kamisar, *The Warren Court (Was It Really So Defense-Minded?), The Burger Court (Was It Really So Prosecution-Oriented?) and Police Investigatory Practices*, in THE BURGER COURT: THE COUNTER-REVOLUTION THAT WASN'T 62, 62-63, 90 (V. Blasi ed. 1983) (footnote omitted).

2. Saltzburg, *Foreword: The Flow and Ebb of Constitutional Criminal Procedure in the Warren and Burger Courts*, 69 GEO. L.J. 151, 208-09 (1980).

are obvious and noncontroversial.[3] Consequently, many American scholars have skirted this fundamental issue by trotting out tired cliches like truth-discovery, crime control, and the protection of individual rights.

The shallowness of such answers is highlighted by the recent debate about whether the Burger Court has significantly departed from the Warren Court's approach to criminal procedure. The debate has been couched in terms that prevent meaningful comparison of the two Courts' decisions. Commentators ask whether the Burger Court has engaged in a "counter-revolution." Many criminal defense specialists think that it has. The criminal defense bar no longer believes that the United States Supreme Court is the most appropriate forum in which to seek vindication for the rights of the accused.[4] On the other hand, recent academic commentary has suggested that there is less here than meets the eye. Indeed, there is a growing academic consensus, espoused by such notable figures as Yale Kamisar,[5] Jerold Israel,[6] Stephen Saltzburg,[7] and Louis Michael Seidman,[8] that the popular perception of a Burger Court counter-revolution greatly exaggerates the differences between the two Courts.[9]

These scholars insist that the Burger Court has reaffirmed the basic structural elements of the Warren Court's due process revolution. Kamisar, Saltzburg, and Israel focus on doctrinal developments. They argue that the Warren Court was not as "liberal" as its conservative critics portrayed it and that the Burger Court is not as "conservative" as its civil libertarian critics claim.[10] Seidman focuses on the discrepancy between the Burger Court's rhetoric about "factual guilt," speed, efficiency, and finality and what the Court has actually done. Seidman points out that the Burger Court has not embraced a pure "guilt or innocence" model of criminal procedure that would force our system to focus primarily on accurate determinations of guilt in individual cases. Like its predecessor, the Burger Court has been quite willing to use the criminal process "for social engineering, even when this pursuit of

---

3. Notable exceptions include: Alschuler, *The Changing Plea Bargaining Debate*, 69 CAL. L. REV. 652 (1981); Damaska, *Evidentiary Barriers to Conviction and Two Models of Criminal Procedure: A Comparative Study*, 121 U. PA. L. REV. 506 (1973); Griffiths, *Ideology in Criminal Procedure or a Third "Model" of the Criminal Process*, 79 YALE L.J. 359 (1970).

4. This popular perception among the practicing bar helps to explain the revitalized interest in state constitutional law as an independent source of norms regulating state criminal justice officials. *See* Brennan, *State Constitutions and the Protection of Individual Rights*, 90 HARV. L. REV. 489, 502 (1977). Heeding Justice Brennan's advice, many criminal defense specialists have begun to rely more heavily on state constitutional provisions to support their requests for further judicial support of individual rights.

5. *See* Kamisar, *supra* note 1.

6. *See* Israel, *Criminal Procedure, The Burger Court and the Legacy of the Warren Court*, 75 MICH. L. REV. 1319 (1977).

7. *See* Saltzburg, *supra* note 2.

8. *See* Seidman, *Factual Guilt and the Burger Court: An Examination of Continuity and Change in Criminal Procedure*, 80 COLUM. L. REV. 436 (1980).

9. For a notable exception to this view, see Chase, *The Burger Court, the Individual, and the Criminal Process: Directions and Misdirections*, 52 N.Y.U. L. REV. 518 (1977). Professor Chase's excellent article focuses on significant substantive and methodological differences between the Warren and Burger Courts' articulation of criminal procedure doctrine. For further discussion of these doctrinal differences, see *infra* notes 236-323 and accompanying text.

10. *See* Kamisar, *supra* note 1, at 67-68; Saltzburg, *supra* note 2, at 152-54; Israel, *supra* note 6, at 1321-24.

broad social goals conflicts with the need to reach factually reliable judgments in individual cases."[11] While Seidman readily concedes that the Burger Court has been more sympathetic to "crime control" concerns than the Warren Court, he concludes that "the extent of even this change is easy to overstate."[12] In essence, all of these scholars agree that the Burger Court's greater emphasis on crime control values is merely a little fine tuning.

My contention is that much of this debate is shallow,[13] that it avoids basic questions about the specific functions of American criminal procedure, and that it accordingly fails to illuminate fundamentally different approaches to the criminal process. Of course, both Courts have attempted to accommodate the tensions between the protection of individual rights and the state's need to detect and punish criminal activity quickly and efficiently. This "similarity" between the two Courts' approaches to criminal procedure is trivial; any Supreme Court would make such accommodations. The Warren and Burger Courts' attempts to do so simply reflect the fact that criminal procedure serves functions apart from promoting reliable guilt determinations. No Supreme Court would risk undermining its own legitimacy, or that of the criminal justice system, by promoting order without law. Couching the debate in these terms leads one to an obvious and thoroughly uninteresting conclusion.

The questions that must be addressed to compare the two Courts' approaches are actually more important than the initial inquiry about whether a "counter-revolution" has occurred: What are the purposes served by American criminal procedure? How have the two Courts attempted to implement them? This inquiry must consider, for example, whether the Burger Court's concept of individual rights and fair process norms differs in content and justification from the Warren Court's view of these norms. How different are the two Courts' views about the appropriate allocation of power in our criminal justice system? Does the Burger Court's image of the functions served by American criminal procedure differ significantly from that of the Warren Court? If it does, can we use this image to describe some of the continuities and discontinuities between the two Courts' legal rules?[14]

This article attempts to answer these questions. Its conclusion is simple: The academic consensus about the Burger Court ignores or minimizes the degree to which the Court's rhetoric and doctrine reflect a vision of criminal law's goals and procedural functions that differs significantly from that espoused by the Warren Court. Viewed from this perspective, there is more here than meets the eye.[15]

---

11. Seidman, *supra* note 8, at 437.

12. *Id.*

13. I do not mean to disparage the value of the doctrinal analysis that Kamisar, Israel, Saltzburg, and Seidman have presented in their writings. Many of the footnotes to this article reflect their insights about specific doctrinal developments.

14. I am not suggesting that a particular vision of criminal procedure's functions can, by itself, *explain* why the Court decided a case in a particular manner. I am suggesting that many of the Warren and Burger Courts' decisions *reflect* a different approach to criminal procedure's functions. I believe that these differences would have been even greater if the Burger Court had the freedom to ignore Warren Court precedents.

15. Whether the two Courts' competing visions of criminal procedure's functions have dramatically altered existing legal practices is a separate question that merits an independent essay. *See infra* notes 230 & 252 (discussing impact of Warren Court's decisions).

Part I examines the major arguments supporting the academic consensus. It suggests that Kamisar, Israel, Saltzburg, and Seidman have effectively repudiated some exaggerated descriptions of the differences between the two Courts while unduly minimizing the significance of their conflicting visions of criminal procedure's functions.

To demonstrate the importance of these differences, one must start with a clear conception of the functions served by our procedural system. Unfortunately, American scholarship has identified these functions too abstractly. Scholarly references to reliable and efficient truth-discovery, deterrence of future criminality, and protection of individual rights provide an inadequate and misleading list of these functions. Part II breaks down these hoary generalizations into more concrete statements of the purposes served by American criminal procedure. First, criminal procedure must provide a process that vindicates substantive criminal law goals.[16] This procedural mechanism must determine substantive guilt reliably, authoritatively, and in a manner that promotes the criminal law's sentencing objectives. Second, criminal procedure must provide a dispute resolution mechanism that allocates scarce resources efficiently and that distributes power among state officials.[17] Finally, criminal procedure can perform a legitimation function[18] by resolving state-citizen disputes in a manner that commands the community's respect for the fairness of its processes as well as the reliability of its outcomes. Criminal procedure can serve this function by articulating fair process norms that attempt to validate the state's exercise of coercive power over its citizens.

Part III uses this analysis to reconstruct two "models"—the "due process" and "crime control" perspectives[19]—that some commentators have used to describe competing themes in our criminal justice system. It suggests that these reconstructed models actually describe competing ideological visions of how our system serves criminal procedure's functions. Both models describe a set of values, beliefs, attitudes, and ideas about our criminal justice system that are held by many legal actors within the system and that are reflected in some

---

16. *See infra* notes 82-88 and accompanying text.

17. *See infra* note 89 and accompanying text.

18. *See infra* notes 90-137 and accompanying text. One can define "legitimation" in several different ways. When a Court articulates a positive legal doctrine that legalizes a specific practice, the Court has "legitimated" that practice. This narrow use of "legitimate," however, does not imply that the Court's legalization of the act conveys any message about the act's moral desirability. One can also use the concept to refer to an evaluative statement by the Court that attempts to justify a specific practice as morally desirable. This evaluative use of the term "legitimate" does not imply that the Court's justification or approval necessarily causes people to believe in the act's ethical validity. Finally, one can use the concept to refer to official communications that not only approve a practice or institution but have the *effect* of actually inducing public acceptance and obedience to the legal order because of the public's belief in its "legitimacy." I am using the term "legitimation" in these last two senses. At the very least, American criminal procedure attempts to justify the state's use of coercion by articulating fair process norms that place some substantive and procedural limits on the state's exercise of power. Whether this attempt to ethically validate the state's use of coercion actually provides people with an independent reason to believe in the criminal justice system's "legitimacy" apart from their own self-interest or normative values is subject to serious question. See generally Hyde, *The Concept of Legitimation in the Sociology of Law*, 1983 WIS. L. REV. 379, for an excellent critique of this "Weberian" use of the term "legitimacy." See also *infra* note 231 for a critique of the assumption made by some critical legal theorists that our system's due process ideology induces community acceptance of an unjust criminal justice system.

19. *See* H. PACKER, THE LIMITS OF THE CRIMINAL SANCTION 153 (1968).

of its institutions and practices. Both models are prescriptive as well as descriptive. They make competing normative claims about the validity of procedural functions and the relative weight that should be attached to valid procedural objectives when they conflict with each other. Finally, both ideologies have programmatic content because they suggest doctrinal courses of action that would implement their vision of how the process should function. Consequently, both ideological models provide a source for legitimate arguments that courts may use to shape legal doctrine in criminal procedure.[20]

Part IV uses the two models' distinctive programmatic and doctrinal themes to describe some of the major doctrinal differences between the Warren and Burger Courts. It suggests that the Burger Court's treatment of *Fay*, *Miranda*, and *Mapp* reflects some of the basic themes of crime control ideology.

I. REEVALUATING THE WARREN COURT'S "REVOLUTION" AND THE BURGER COURT'S "COUNTER-REVOLUTION"

To speak of a judicial "revolution" or "counter-revolution" in criminal procedure is to suggest that the Supreme Court has done something that radically changes our criminal justice system. Most commentators agree that the Warren Court's "revolution" in criminal procedure consisted of a dramatic change in the system's normative aspirations.[21] The Warren Court acted as the system's moral conscience by articulating the ideals that should regulate the conduct of criminal justice officials in investigating criminal activity and adjudicating guilt. These commentators suggest that the norms espoused by the Court were not novel.[22] What was new was the Court's willingness to apply these federal constitutional norms to state criminal justice systems by selec-

---

20. Of course, a constitutional interpretivist would argue that the Supreme Court should not interpret the Bill of Rights to promote any particular ideological vision of criminal procedure's functions unless compelling evidence indicates that the Framers themselves had adopted that vision. Absent evidence of such an intent, interpretivists would insist that the Court has no business imposing its own ideological preconceptions about criminal procedure's goals.

Even defenders of constitutional interpretivism, however, concede the inevitability of courts interpreting the Bill of Rights from a functional rather than a historical perspective. According to Henry Monaghan,

> Candor requires that one recognize that the common law approach, and not the statutory approach, best describes the development of constitutional law under the bill of rights. Substantive elaboration of the bill of rights has increasingly followed the incremental, case-by-case method employed by common law judges. Viewed retrospectively, this was perhaps inevitable. Courts have had to cope with the relative paucity and indeterminacy of the underlying historical materials, as well as the difficulty of relating ancient norms to a world radically different from that of the Framers. Not surprisingly, as the text got older and interpretative materials accumulated, "the focus of professional and judicial attention . . . [shifted] from the . . . text and history to the . . . norm[s] to be derived by analysis and synthesis of the judicial precedents."

Monaghan, *Our Perfect Constitution*, 56 N.Y.U. L. REV. 353, 393 (1981) (footnotes omitted).

21. *See, e.g.*, Allen, *The Judicial Quest for Penal Justice: The Warren Court and the Criminal Cases*, 1975 U. ILL. L.F. 518, 525.

22. *See id.* at 521; Seidman, *supra* note 8, at 440 & n.17. This consensus view unduly minimizes the extent to which the Warren Court offered an expansive interpretation of the privilege against self-incrimination. The Court's generous interpretation of what constitutes fifth amendment compulsion in *Miranda* indicated that much less pressure to confess rendered a statement "compelled" under the privilege than what would have been necessary to establish its involuntariness under the due process clause.

tively incorporating them through the due process clause of the fourteenth amendment.[23] The Warren Court's "revolution" lay in its attempt to secure state conformity with these due process ideals.

The Court attempted to implement these norms by granting criminal defendants procedural safeguards at the police station,[24] at line-ups,[25] at trial,[26] and on appeal.[27] Some of these safeguards promoted the system's capacity to adjudicate guilt more reliably.[28] Many of them, however, impaired the state's capacity to detect and punish guilty offenders in order to ensure that the criminal process treated all criminal suspects with dignity and respect.[29]

The Warren Court relied on the educational and deterrent effect of reversed convictions to enforce these fair process norms. Since the Court could review only a few criminal procedure decisions each term, it also expanded the federal courts' habeas corpus power to consider federal constitutional claims denied by state courts.[30] This expansive view of habeas corpus provided a federal forum for the protection of fair process norms that state courts might have been reluctant to enforce because of the norms' tendency to frustrate the state's capacity to determine guilt reliably. Although such review impaired the system's speed, efficiency, and finality, as well as raising comity concerns, the Warren Court's "dialectical federalism"[31] ensured that some meaningful federal-state dialogue concerning the elaboration of these norms would occur.

How much this normative revolution transformed the day-to-day functioning of state criminal justice systems is a subject of considerable controversy.[32] Many scholars have described the institutional factors that limited the Warren Court's ability to implement its ideals.[33] A review of these institutional constraints demonstrates the wisdom of Professor Allen's observation that "[o]ne devising institutions for Utopia would not likely delegate so large a responsi-

---

23. Allen, *supra* note 21, at 527.

24. *See* Miranda v. Arizona, 384 U.S. 436, 479 (1966).

25. *See* United States v. Wade, 388 U.S. 218, 227 (1967) (defendant has right to counsel at post-indictment line-up).

26. *See* Griffin v. California, 380 U.S. 609, 615 (1965) (fifth amendment forbids both comment by prosecution on defendant's refusal to testify and instructions to jury that defendant's trial silence is evidence of guilt).

27. *See* Douglas v. California, 372 U.S. 353, 357-58 (1963) (indigent entitled to appointed counsel at state mandatory appeal stage); Griffin v. Illinois, 351 U.S. 12, 18-19 (1956) (indigent defendant has right to obtain free trial transcripts in order to ensure adequate appellate review).

28. *See, e.g.,* Stovall v. Denno, 388 U.S. 293, 302 (1967) (due process mandates exclusion of out-of-court identification based on unnecessarily suggestive identification procedure); Pointer v. Texas, 380 U.S. 400, 407-08 (1965) (defendant has constitutional right to confront and cross-examine witnesses at trial); Brady v. Maryland, 373 U.S. 83, 87, 90-91 (1963) (prosecutor has duty to disclose exculpatory evidence to defendant at trial).

29. *See, e.g.,* Miranda v. Arizona, 384 U.S. 436, 460 (1966) ("the constitutional foundation underlying the privilege [against self-incrimination] is the respect a government—state or federal—must accord to the dignity and integrity of its citizens").

30. *See* Fay v. Noia, 372 U.S. 391, 398-99, 435 (1963) (federal courts retain power to decide merits of federal constitutional claim despite state procedural forfeiture of claim unless defendant deliberately bypassed state opportunity to raise claim).

31. *See* Cover & Aleinikoff, *Dialectical Federalism: Habeas Corpus and the Court*, 86 YALE L.J. 1035 (1977).

32. *See, e.g.,* Alschuler, *Plea Bargaining and Its History*, 79 COLUM. L. REV. 1, 37-38 & n.209 (1979). For further analysis of this question, *see infra* notes 230 & 252.

33. *See, e.g.,* Allen, *supra* note 21, at 526-29; Amsterdam, *The Supreme Court and the Rights of Suspects in Criminal Cases*, 45 N.Y.U. L. REV. 785, 786-93 (1970).

bility for maintaining the integrity of the criminal justice process to the courts."[34]

First, the Court can neither allocate the resources nor make all of the structural changes needed to provide for adversarial guilt adjudication in most cases. While the Warren Court reduced some of the systemic pressures that discouraged defendants from exercising their right to trial,[35] it was ultimately dependent on the states' willingness to fashion and pay for significant structural reform of the trial system.

Second, serious institutional constraints limited the Court's capacity to regulate the conduct of state criminal justice officials. In many cases, legislative inertia left the Court as the sole regulator of law enforcement conduct. The absence of any supporting legislative or administrative rulemaking in these cases impaired the Court's capacity to supervise police behavior effectively.[36] Regulating by default, the Court was forced to rely solely on the parties and the lower courts to articulate the competing policies raised by a constitutional challenge to a particular law enforcement practice. Such adversarial presentations of competing policy considerations often made it difficult for the Court to evaluate either the need for or significance of the challenged police practice or the availability and cost of less intrusive alternatives.[37]

Moreover, the impact of the Warren Court's decisions on the day-to-day functioning of the system depended heavily on the lower courts' interpretation and application of the Court's doctrine. As the primary judicial regulators of police conduct, the lower courts could either dilute or expand the Warren Court's procedural safeguards. To a considerable extent, judicial implementation of the Warren Court's due process norms rested on the lower courts' sympathy or hostility to the values served by the Court's doctrine.[38]

Finally, the Court's primary regulatory sanctions, exclusionary rules and reversals of convictions, have their own transaction costs. First, these sanctions impair the system's capacity to promote substantive criminal law goals. Second, they may undermine public confidence in the judicial system when guilty defendants are released in order to vindicate fair process norms that the public often views as mere technicalities.[39]

Acting as the system's moral conscience is never an easy task, especially when a Court articulates aspirations that the public does not understand or share.[40] Doing so during a time of escalating crime rates and growing public anxiety about the system's capacity to protect its citizens from street violence almost proved fatal. The Warren Court was an easy scapegoat because the Justices could not enter the public forum to answer their critics. Political scientists did point out that the judiciary was not responsible for the socioeconomic and demographic forces generating increases in criminal activity.

---

34. Allen, *supra* note 21, at 523.
35. *See infra* text accompanying notes 236-40.
36. *See* Allen, *supra* note 21, at 541-42; Amsterdam, *supra* note 33, at 810-15.
37. *See* Amsterdam, *supra* note 33, at 787-90.
38. *Id.* at 791-92.
39. *See* Illinois v. Gates, 103 S. Ct. 2317, 2342 (1983) (White, J., concurring) (excluding reliable evidence of guilt in cases when police acted in "good faith" may weaken community confidence in integrity of criminal justice system).
40. *See generally* F. GRAHAM, THE SELF-INFLICTED WOUND (1970).

Criminal Policy Making

Several commentators demonstrated that the conservative critique of decisions like *Miranda* exaggerated their impact on effective law enforcement.[41] But few members of the public actually read the Court's opinions or the work of its academic defenders. Richard Nixon's charge that the Warren Court was soft on crime contributed to his election in 1968 because it reflected the public's belief that procedural technicalities were preventing the police from stopping crime.[42]

Liberal defenders of the Warren Court's legacy feared that President Nixon would fulfill his campaign pledge to appoint "law and order" Justices who would narrow the scope and practical effect of landmark decisions like *Mapp*,[43] *Miranda*,[44] and *Fay*.[45] Nixon fueled these fears of a conservative "counter-revolution" when he appointed Warren Burger as the new Chief Justice. Indeed, Nixon made it clear to the public that Burger's conservative views about law and order were the prime reason for his appointment to the Court.[46] By 1972, Nixon had appointed four Justices (Burger, Blackmun, Powell and Rehnquist) and commentators were referring to the "Nixon" Court.[47] By 1976, the Burger Court's "counter-revolution" appeared to be in place.

At a rhetorical level, the Burger Court consistently criticized procedural safeguards erected by the Warren Court that frustrated the system's capacity to determine factual guilt efficiently, quickly, and conclusively.[48] At a doctrinal level, the Burger Court undermined the constitutional rationales of both *Miranda* and *Mapp*. Finding that a police violation of *Miranda* did not constitute a "core" violation of the privilege against self-incrimination,[49] the Court permitted statements taken in violation of *Miranda* to be used as impeachment evidence.[50] Having concluded that *Mapp*'s exclusionary rule was not a personal constitutional right of the defendant,[51] the Burger Court only applied the rule to those procedural contexts in which the rule's speculative deterrent benefit outweighed its tangible cost of excluding reliable evidence. The Court used this balancing analysis to justify its restriction of the exclusionary rule to

---

41. *See, e.g.*, Burger & Wettick, Miranda *in Pittsburgh—A Statistical Study*, 29 U. PITT. L. REV. 1 (1967) (*Miranda* has not significantly impaired ability of law enforcement agencies to apprehend and convict criminals); Note, *Interrogations in New Haven: The Impact of* Miranda, 76 YALE L.J. 1519 (1967) (immediate impact of *Miranda* on police capacity to elicit incriminating admissions not significant).

42. *See 63% in Gallup Poll Think Courts Are Too Lenient on Criminals*, N.Y. Times, Mar. 3, 1968, at 40, col. 3 (66% in poll disagreed with Warren Court decision restricting police tactics in obtaining confessions); *cf. 81% in a Poll See Law Breakdown*, N.Y. Times, Sept. 10, 1968, at 31, col. 1 (81% in Harris Poll felt there was breakdown of "law and order").

43. Mapp v. Ohio, 367 U.S. 643 (1961).

44. Miranda v. Arizona, 384 U.S. 436 (1966).

45. Fay v. Noia, 372 U.S. 391 (1963).

46. *See* L. LEVY, AGAINST THE LAW 14 (1974).

47. *See, e.g., id.* at 48.

48. *See, e.g.*, Schneckloth v. Bustamonte, 412 U.S. 218, 245, 249 (1973).

49. Michigan v. Tucker, 417 U.S. 433, 450-52 (1974).

50. Oregon v. Hass, 420 U.S. 714, 722 (1975) (voluntary statements obtained in violation of *Miranda* inadmissible in prosecutor's case-in-chief but admissible for impeachment purposes if statements' trustworthiness satisfies legal standards); Harris v. New York, 401 U.S. 222, 224-25 (1971) (same).

51. *See* United States v. Janis, 428 U.S. 433, 446 (1976) (exclusionary rule judicially created remedy and not personal constitutional right of defendant); United States v. Calandra, 414 U.S. 338, 348 (1974) (same).

the trial itself.[52]

In other decisions, the Burger Court refused to apply the fourth amendment's warrant requirement to a broad range of police investigatory practices,[53] weakened the strength of the warrant's particularity requirement,[54] enhanced the power of the police to stop and frisk,[55] diluted the prosecutor's duty to disclose exculpatory evidence,[56] discouraged the use of civil suits to remedy alleged police and prosecutorial misconduct,[57] and curtailed the privilege against self-incrimination.[58]

All of these decisions appeared to validate the worst fears of those civil libertarians who wished to preserve the Warren Court's legacy. It seemed only a matter of time before the Burger Court completely destroyed the doctrinal pillars of the Warren Court revolution—*Miranda*, *Mapp*, *Wade*, and *Fay*. The Burger Court, however, did not totally follow this scenario. Instead of overruling *Miranda*, the Burger Court applied it to police custodial interrogations occurring outside the police station[59] and offered a "fairly generous reading"[60] of what constituted interrogation. Despite rhetoric about narrowing the scope of habeas corpus to guilt-related claims,[61] the Burger Court reaffirmed the use of habeas corpus to relitigate constitutional claims that protect societal values having little to do with the system's function of reliably determining guilt.[62]

By 1982, several prominent criminal procedure scholars had written articles

---

52. *Janis*, 428 U.S. at 458; *Calandra*, 414 U.S. at 350-51.

53. *See* United States v. Martinez-Fuerte, 428 U.S. 543, 566 (1976) (no warrant required to authorize vehicle stops at fixed immigration checkpoints); South Dakota v. Opperman, 428 U.S. 364, 375-76 (1976) (no warrant required to authorize routine police inventory search of lawfully impounded vehicles); United States v. Watson, 423 U.S. 411, 423-24 (1976) (no arrest warrant required when police make felony arrest in public).

54. *See* Andresen v. Maryland, 427 U.S. 463, 481-82 (1976) (warrant specifying items to be seized, along with "other fruits, instrumentalities and evidence of crime at this [time] uncertain," satisfies particularity requirement of fourth amendment).

55. *See* Adams v. Williams, 407 U.S. 143, 146-48 (1972) (police may rely on informant's tip that defendant possessed narcotics and gun to make forcible stop and conduct limited weapons search to protect officer's safety during stop).

56. *See* United States v. Agurs, 427 U.S. 97, 108, 112 (1976) (where defendant fails to make "specific" request for exculpatory evidence, prosecutor's failure to disclose exculpatory evidence only violates due process if omitted evidence, evaluated in context of entire record, creates reasonable doubt of guilt).

57. *See* Imbler v. Pachtman, 424 U.S. 409, 427 (1976) (state prosecutor immune from civil suits under 42 U.S.C. § 1983 for alleged constitutional violations of defendants' rights when prosecutor acting within scope of his duties in initiating and pursuing criminal investigation); Rizzo v. Goode, 423 U.S. 362, 379-80 (1976) (principles of comity and federalism bar federal court's prophylactic injunctive remedy against local police misconduct). For a remarkable illustration of the Burger Court's unwillingness to have courts supervise police conduct, see Los Angeles v. Lyons, 103 S. Ct. 1660, 1670 (1983).

58. *See* Fisher v. United States, 425 U.S. 391, 409-10 (1976). For a discussion of *Fisher*, see Arenella, Schmerber *and the Privilege Against Self-Incrimination: A Reappraisal*, 20 AM. CRIM. L. REV. 31 (1982) [hereinafter cited as Arenella, *Reappraisal*], and *infra* note 260.

59. *See* Rhode Island v. Innis, 446 U.S. 291, 301 (1980) (*Miranda* safeguards apply whenever person in custody is subject to either express questioning or to any words or actions that police should know are reasonably likely to elicit incriminating response from suspect).

60. Kamisar, *supra* note 1, at 68.

61. *See, e.g.*, Schneckloth v. Bustamonte, 412 U.S. 218, 266 (1973) (Powell, J., with Burger, C.J., & Rehnquist, J., concurring) (when constitutional claim does not bear on guilt or innocence, federal habeas review should be limited to whether petitioner received fair opportunity to adjudicate that claim in state courts).

62. *See* Rose v. Mitchell, 443 U.S. 545, 559 (1979) (racial discrimination claims in selection of state grand jury support issuance of federal habeas corpus writ even though guilt established beyond reasonable doubt at trial free of constitutional error).

suggesting that reports of a Burger Court counter-revolution were greatly exaggerated. To support their thesis, Kamisar, Israel, and Saltzburg focused primarily on doctrinal developments. While conceding that the Burger Court's rhetoric is very different, they insisted that it was more important to compare what the two Courts actually did rather than what they said. Their examination of the two Courts' decisions led them to conclude that the Warren Court was not as "pro-defendant" as its conservative critics portrayed it and that the Burger Court was not as "pro-government" as its civil libertarian critics claimed.

For example, they pointed out that the Warren Court consistently considered and protected law enforcement interests. Indeed, Kamisar suggested there were really two Warren Courts. The "first" Warren Court constitutionalized state criminal procedure by applying traditional fourth, fifth, and sixth amendment values to the states through the due process clause of the fourteenth amendment. The "second" Warren Court reacted to the considerable public hostility aroused by "liberal" decisions like *Miranda* by beginning "a process many associate only with its successor—a process of reexamination, correction, consolidation, erosion, or retreat, depending upon your viewpoint."[63] In several landmark decisions, this "second" Warren Court enhanced police investigatory powers. It was the Warren Court that abolished the mere evidence rule,[64] upheld the informer's privilege,[65] and constitutionalized electronic surveillance.[66] It was the Warren Court that validated the power of police to stop and frisk without probable cause[67] and to conduct undercover operations free of fourth amendment constraints.[68]

Turning to the Burger Court, Kamisar, Israel, and Saltzburg noted that the Court reaffirmed the basic structural element of the Warren Court's due process revolution by its begrudging acceptance of the selective incorporation doctrine. Although conceding that the Burger Court has limited the scope and effect of some of the Warren Court's procedural safeguards, they insisted that doctrinal pillars like *Miranda* and *Mapp* remain standing, if somewhat battered. Once again, Kamisar suggested there were two Burger Courts. Admittedly, the "first" Burger Court showed considerable hostility to the basic pillars of the Warren Court "revolution." But,

> [i]n the past few years, . . . a significantly less police-oriented "sec-

---

63. Kamisar, *supra* note 1, at 67.

64. *See* Warden v. Hayden, 387 U.S. 294, 310 (1967) (no viable reason to distinguish intrusions to secure "mere evidence" from intrusions to secure fruits, instrumentalities, or contraband of crime). It should be noted that the mere evidence rule had been diluted beyond recognition long before the Warren Court formally buried it.

65. *See* McCray v. Illinois, 386 U.S. 300, 305 (1967) (no constitutional duty to disclose informant's identity when issue is whether probable cause existed for arrest or search and not whether defendant guilty or innocent); *cf.* Roviaro v. United States, 353 U.S. 53, 64-65 (1957) (duty to disclose informer's identity at trial if informer's testimony critical to guilt determination).

66. *See* Katz v. United States, 389 U.S. 347, 359 (1967); Berger v. New York, 388 U.S. 41, 63 (1967).

67. *See* Terry v. Ohio, 392 U.S. 1, 30 (1968) (when unusual or suspicious activity leads police to conclude criminal activity afoot, police may stop suspect without probable cause and, if officer also has reasonable suspicion that individual armed and dangerous may conduct limited protective search of suspect's outer clothing). For a discussion contrasting the Warren and Burger Courts' treatment of *Terry*, see *infra* notes 259 & 311.

68. *See* Hoffa v. United States, 385 U.S. 293, 302-03 (1966) (no fourth amendment violation when defendant consents to informer's presence and voluntarily confides wrongdoings to informer).

ond" Burger Court seems to have emerged, one that has given interrogation within the meaning of *Miranda* a fairly generous reading, reinvigorated *Miranda* safeguards when a suspect has invoked his right to counsel, revivified and even expanded the *Massiah* doctrine . . . [and] underscored the centrality of the search warrant requirement in all investigations with the exception of automobile searches.[69]

While I agree with many of these commentators' specific observations, I fail to see how any of them address, much less answer, the question of whether the Burger Court's approach to criminal procedure differs substantially from that of the Warren Court. That both Courts have attempted to accommodate the tension between efficient crime control and protection of individual rights is not only unsurprising, it is inevitable.[70] Nor is it remarkable that the Burger Court has accepted the Warren Court's selective incorporation of most of the Bill of Rights as a *fait accompli* and has failed to overrule Warren Court landmarks like *Miranda* and *Mapp*. To wage such a frontal assault on Warren Court precedents and the principle of stare decisis would weaken the distinction between law and politics that any Court must maintain to sustain its own legitimacy.

What Kamisar, Israel, and Saltzburg have done is to knock down some exaggerated descriptions of the differences between the two Courts. I do not mean to belittle the significance of their work or the potency of the stereotypes they have attacked. One need only look at the impact that the shrill critique of the Warren Court had in the late sixties to appreciate both the power of exaggerated stereotypes and the value served by repudiating them. Nevertheless, vital questions about the Warren and Burger Courts' approaches to criminal procedure remain unanswered because, for the most part, they have not been asked. The issue is not simply which side wins more frequently but whether any distinctive pattern emerges as to how the two Courts view the functions served by American criminal procedure.

To his credit, Louis Michael Seidman addressed this question in his fascinating article, *Factual Guilt and the Burger Court: An Examination of Continuity and Change in Criminal Procedure*.[71] Seidman criticized the Warren Court for

---

69. Kamisar, *supra* note 1, at 68. Yale Kamisar wrote these words in 1981. Decisions like Oregon v. Bradshaw, 103 S. Ct. 2830, 2835 (1983) (police may renew interrogation of suspect who has asserted his right to counsel when suspect "initiates" conversation by asking where police are taking him), United States v. Place, 103 S. Ct. 2637, 2645 (1983) ("canine sniff" of luggage by well-trained narcotics detection dog not a fourth amendment "search"), Illinois v. Gates, 103 S. Ct. 2317, 2332 (1983) (overruling *Aguilar-Spinelli* rule for evaluating probable cause determination based partially on hearsay information), and United States v. Knotts, 103 S. Ct. 1081, 1086-87 (1983) (tracking movement of chemical drum in car by monitoring beeper attached to drum not fourth amendment search because defendant had no expectation of privacy in car's movement on public streets), have prompted Kamisar to reassess his view of this "second" Burger Court. *See* 5 J. CHOPER, Y. KAMISAR & L. TRIBE, THE SUPREME COURT: TRENDS AND DEVELOPMENTS 1982-1983, at — (1984) (forthcoming) ("Although I stand by what I said about the Burger Court as of 1981, I would not write that essay the same way today. For now I fear that a 'third' Burger Court is emerging, one much more like the 'first' Burger Court than the 'second.'").

70. *See infra* notes 82-137 and accompanying text.

71. Seidman, *supra* note 8.

its naive ambition of "trying to do too much with too little."[72] His critique of the Warren Court, however, was not simply that it lacked the institutional resources and capability to implement its norms effectively. Seidman argued that the Warren Court used criminal procedure to serve "unrealistically broad social ends"—racial justice, economic equality, and limited government—that had little to do with criminal procedure's "central mission" of reliably determining guilt and innocence:[73]

> The conflicts between these competing demands which the Court placed on an already overburdened system are plain enough. For example, there is an obvious tension between the trial as a method of making individualized factual judgments concerning guilt and innocence and the trial as a method of fighting proxy battles over issues of social policy. Individualized truth is often the first casualty in large-scale struggles over the meaning of social justice.[74]

Seidman's critique of the Warren Court rests on two critical assumptions. First, Seidman assumed that there is a pure "guilt or innocence" model of criminal procedure that the Warren Court rejected so that it could use criminal procedure to promote other social values. Adoption of this pure guilt or innocence model

> would require forsaking goals outside the immediate, guilt-determining function of the system and concentrating our focus so as to assure that, at a minimum, we are in fact punishing the guilty while vindicating the innocent. It would require abolition of "technical" rules that obstruct discovering and acting upon the truth in criminal cases. *It would mean emphasizing result instead of process.*[75]

Second, Seidman argued that the Warren Court's use of criminal procedure to serve other goals was doomed to failure: "[I]t is simply not possible to maintain a system of limited resources that effectively separates the guilty from the innocent, deters government misconduct, and daily proves our commitment to fair procedures for their own sake."[76]

Seidman's conceptual criterion for a Burger Court counter-revolution is the adoption of a pure guilt or innocence model of criminal procedure. Although conceding that the Court rhetorically embraced such a model, Seidman correctly pointed out that the Burger Court's treatment of habeas corpus[77] and guilty pleas[78] demonstrates that it "has continued to sacrifice the truth in individual cases on the altar of broader social goals. While these goals differ in some measure from those pursued by the Warren Court, the underlying process remains the same."[79] The validity of Seidman's conclusion that "the overall thrust of the Burger Court's criminal procedure decisions are best

72. *Id.* at 441.
73. *Id.* at 436-37, 445.
74. *Id.* at 442.
75. *Id.* at 445 (emphasis added).
76. *Id.* at 443.
77. *See id.* at 449-470.
78. *See id.* at 470-483.
79. *Id.* at 446.

understood in terms of continuity rather than change"[80] depends on the existence of a pure guilt or innocence model of American criminal procedure. If our procedural system must inevitably serve functions that prevent "establishing a process focusing on individualized guilt and innocence,"[81] then the continuity between the two Courts that Seidman emphasized reflects an inherent feature of our criminal justice system. If no Court could adopt such a model, it certainly should not be used as a criterion to evaluate the differences between the two Courts. Instead, one would examine the relative weight the two Courts attached to criminal procedure's guilt determination function when it conflicts with other goals served by our system. We cannot begin to make such a comparison without a clear conception of the functions served by American criminal procedure.

II. THE FUNCTIONS OF AMERICAN CRIMINAL PROCEDURE

A. DETERMINING SUBSTANTIVE GUILT—HISTORICAL FACT RECONSTRUCTION AND MORAL EVALUATION

Criminal procedure must provide a process that promotes the goals of the substantive criminal law. Accordingly, an analysis of criminal procedure's functions is inextricably interwoven with one's vision of these substantive goals. Most commentators assume that the primary goal of any criminal process is to discover the "truth." But what "truth" are we trying to discover? To many, the concept of truth-discovery implies that guilt is an empirical fact ready to be discovered and verified. Debate then focuses on what processes best promote the detection and reliable determination of historical facts.

Equating the substantive criminal law's concept of guilt with historical fact would be defensible if crimes were defined solely in terms of the defendant's acts. But the criminal law usually refuses to predicate criminal liabilty on acts alone.[82] Such a restrictive definition of substantive guilt would erode one of the major distinctions between criminal and civil liability: Only the former imposes a special moral stigma of community condemnation. Criminalizing acts alone would also greatly enhance the state's power to intervene in the lives of its citizens. Accordingly, the substantive criminal law's definition of guilt protects individual autonomy and preserves the moral force of the criminal sanction by requiring some showing of the defendant's moral culpability.

Our substantive criminal law requires a moral evaluation of the actor's conduct by including some mental element (e.g., purpose, knowledge, recklessness, or negligence[83]) in its definition of most offenses and by its recognition of

---

80. *Id.* at 445.
81. *Id.*
82. *See generally* G. WILLIAMS, CRIMINAL LAW: THE GENERAL PART (2d ed. 1961).
83. The Model Penal Code definition of recklessness is as follows:

A person acts recklessly with respect to a material element of an offense when he consciously disregards a substantial and *unjustifiable* risk that the material element exists or will result from his conduct. The risk must be of such a nature and degree that, *considering the nature and purpose of the actor's conduct and the circumstances known to him*, its disregard involves a *gross deviation from the standard of conduct* that a law-abiding person would observe in the actor's situation.

198   THE GEORGETOWN LAW JOURNAL   [Vol. 72:185

affirmative defenses that either justify the defendant's conduct or excuse it.[84] Since substantive guilt includes both facts and value judgments about the actor's moral culpability, criminal procedure must provide a procedural mechanism that reliably reconstructs historical facts and morally evaluates their significance. The combination of these two procedural functions—reliable historical fact reconstruction and moral evaluation—cannot be equated with "truth-discovery."

Admittedly, in many criminal prosecutions, guilt or innocence will depend solely on a contested issue of historical fact. When a defendant presents an alibi defense or claims a mistaken eyewitness identification, she is disputing the "truth" of the state's factual claim that she committed the proscribed conduct. But, even in these cases, criminal procedure reconstructs facts in a manner that expresses an error-deflection preference.[85] At least in theory, our system prefers erroneous acquittals over erroneous convictions. Consequently, it requires compelling proof that the defendant engaged in the proscribed conduct to provide maximum protection of the substantively innocent. Recognizing the fallibility of any human process used to reconstruct facts, criminal procedure deliberately places the risk of factual error on the state to protect the integrity and moral force of a guilty verdict.[86]

Thus, when commentators describe the primary function of criminal procedure as "truth-discovery," they provide an oversimplified and misleading account of how our system is designed to determine guilt. The "truth-discovery" label ignores the moral content and force of substantive guilt and the resulting need for a process that evaluates the moral quality of the defendant's actions.

B.   PROMOTING THE AIMS OF PUNISHMENT

Once guilt is reliably established, criminal procedure must provide a process that determines the appropriate disposition for the guilty offender. In theory, the substantive criminal law has already decided the most important aspects of this question. The legislature determines the kind and potential degree of punishment involved for each offense and the identity of the sentencing authority. The legislature's sentencing system should reflect its underlying view of the purposes served by the criminal sanction—retribution, specific and general deterrence, incapacitation, or rehabilitation. For example, if the legislature views

---

MODEL PENAL CODE § 2.02(2)(c) (Official Draft 1962) (emphasis added).
   The Model Penal Code definition of negligence is as follows:

> A person acts negligently with respect to a material element of an offense when he *should be aware* of a substantial and *unjustifiable* risk that the material element exists or will result from his conduct. The risk must be of such a nature and degree that the actor's failure to perceive it, considering the nature and purpose of his conduct and the circumstances known to him, *involves a gross deviation from the standard of care that a reasonable person would observe in the actor's situation*.

Id. § 2.02(2)(d) (emphasis added). As the italicized language demonstrates, the adjudicator must make moral and social value judgments when it applies these two "mental elements" to the facts it reconstructs.

   84. *See generally* Robinson, *Criminal Law Defenses: A Systematic Analysis*, 82 COLUM. L. REV. 199 (1982).

   85. Professor Lawrence Sager coined the phrase "error-deflection" to describe this procedural bias in a conversation with the author.

   86. *See In re* Winship, 397 U.S. 358, 364 (1970).

rehabilitation and/or incapacitation of the dangerous offender as the most important aims of the criminal sanction, it will probably choose a relatively indeterminate sentencing structure that gives a parole board most of the real sentencing power. If the legislature views retribution and general deterrence as the paramount goals, it is likely to adopt a more determinate sentencing scheme that limits the judge's sentencing discretion.

The criminal process should be structured to promote the legislature's sentencing system and goals. First, the procedural mechanism used to determine substantive guilt should provide the sentencing authority with some of the information it needs to make an appropriate sentencing decision. Second, the guilt-determining process should minimize the effect of the parties' tactical choices upon appropriate sentencing decisions.[87] Finally, criminal procedure should protect the substantive criminal law's proportionality principle—that the defendant's degree of punishment not exceed his "just deserts"[88] —by providing some check against legislative abuse of its sentencing powers.

Up to this point, we have examined the substantive criminal law objectives that criminal procedure should promote.[89] However, the functions of American criminal procedure extend beyond vindication of substantive criminal law goals.

C. AMERICAN CRIMINAL PROCEDURE'S INDEPENDENT FUNCTIONS

1. Allocation of Power to Resolve Dispute

Our accusatorial system structures criminal proceedings as an adversarial contest between the state and the accused in which the parties themselves control, for the most part, the course of the dispute. To provide a workable dispute-resolution mechanism, American criminal procedure must allocate power in a manner that implements the system's judgments about which state officials, institutions, and community representatives are best suited to investigate, apprehend, charge, adjudicate, and sentence. These institutional competency judgments will reflect in part political norms (e.g., separation of powers, federalism) about the appropriate structure and distribution of government authority. These judgments will also be influenced by the need to allocate scarce resources efficiently. Some officials must distribute the scarce resources society gives to the criminal justice system in a manner that promotes procedure's goals with minimal allocative inefficiency. All of these factors will affect how

---

87. *See* Alschuler, *The Changing Plea Bargaining Debate*, 69 CALIF. L. REV. 652, 652-89 (1981).

88. *See* Solem v. Helm, 103 S. Ct. 3001, 3010-11, 3016 & n.32 (1983). *Solem* resurrected eighth amendment proportionality analysis that the Burger Court had seemingly abandoned for non-capital offenses in Rummel v. Estelle, 445 U.S. 263 (1980).

89. As Griffiths points out, our accusatorial system appears to assume an irreconcilable conflict between the state and the individual. He suggests that the substantive criminal law could punish offenders without status degradation if its goal were to reconcile the two parties. *See* Griffiths, *supra* note 3, at 371-91. If the criminal law's primary goal were to reintegrate offenders into society, the criminal process might use procedures that would implement a resolution by consensus about the individual's future conduct. Resolution by consensus would encourage an examination of the offender's total situation rather than focusing solely on her past acts and blameworthiness. Such a process might also use mediation techniques that encouraged all interested members of the community to participate. Negotiation and compromise might constitute an integral part of such a dispute-resolution mechanism.

American criminal procedure allocates power and protects its distribution by preventing one actor from encroaching on the powers of another.

2. Legitimation

Regardless of how a criminal justice system characterizes the nature of the dispute between the state and the individual, it cannot resolve the controversy without exercising coercive power over individuals. Since the state monopolizes the use of physical violence, it must validate its monopoly by providing impersonal criteria for resolving conflicts with its citizens. Some of these impersonal criteria flow from the substantive criminal law's definition of guilt. Criminal procedure can also attempt to justify the state's use of coercion[90] by articulating fair process norms that place some substantive and procedural limits on the state's exericse of power.

Some of these fair process norms (e.g., compelling proof of guilt, timely and final resolution of the dispute, independent adjudication, assistance of counsel) are valued in part because of their instrumental effect on the system's outcome. These process norms contribute to good results—the reliable conviction of the guilty and the exoneration of the innocent—by providing a means for realizing the commands of the substantive criminal law. But, "in legal ordering man does not live by results alone."[91] Criminal procedure also articulates fair process norms that have value independent of their "result-efficacy."[92] Most of these fair process norms operate as substantive and procedural restraints on state power to ensure[93] that the individual suspect is treated with dignity and respect. The content of these dignitary norms should reflect society's normative aspirations, embodied in its positive laws, customs, religions, and ideologies about the proper relationship between the individual and the state.[94] Some of these fair process norms (e.g., grand jury review of the prosecutor's charging decision) also promote political values like community participation[95] that affect criminal procedure's institutional competency judgments. Finally, some of these norms also reflect procedural values (e.g., procedural regularity, ra-

---

90. I am not suggesting that the only way or even the most effective way the state can ethically validate its use of coercion in the criminal process is by articulating fair process norms. The dominant political ideology of the state may itself serve this legitimation function. American criminal procedure's preoccupation with abuse of power issues reflects a basic theme in liberal political theory that views government authority with suspicion. In contrast, socialist political theory assumes that the interests of the state and the individual are in harmony and that state officials will exercise their power to promote society's general welfare. Consequently, one would expect that socialist criminal procedure would not need to rely primarily on fair process norms to ethically validate the state's use of coercion.

91. Summers, *Evaluating and Improving Legal Processes—A Plea for Process Values*, 60 CORNELL L. REV. 1, 51 (1974).

92. *Id.* at 2.

93. *See infra* text accompanying note 108.

94. For a discussion of the values courts could use to give meaningful content to the dignitary theory of due process in admistrative law, see Mashaw, *Administrative Due Process: The Quest for a Dignitary Theory*, 61 B.U.L. REV. 885, 898-906 (1981).

95. For arguments as to why the grand jury screening function and its defects should be taken seriously, see Arenella, *Reforming the Federal Grand Jury and the State Preliminary Hearing to Prevent Conviction Without Adjudication*, 78 MICH. L. REV. 463 (1980) [hereinafter cited as Arenella, *Reforming the Federal Grand Jury*] and Arenella, *Reforming the State Grand Jury System: A Model Grand Jury Act*, 13 RUTGERS L.J. 1 (1981) [hereinafter cited as Arenella, *Reforming the State Grand Jury System*].

tionality, and intelligibility) that underlie society's conception of the rule of law.

Our Bill of Rights offers several examples of constitutional fair process norms that have value independent of their "result-efficacy." For example, the fourth amendment protects the individual's liberty and property from unreasonable government seizures. It also protects several distinct substantive privacy "interests," such as informational privacy,[96] privacy of place,[97] and physical privacy.[98] Finally, the fourth amendment promotes notions of procedural fairness and regularity by identifying and regulating those circumstances in which the state may justifiably intrude upon these substantive interests.

Similarly, the privilege against self-incrimination promotes both substantive values (e.g., individual dignity, mental privacy, and some notions of consensualism[99]) and procedural norms (e.g., adversarial guilt determination[100]) whose protection may impair the system's guilt-determination function. The privilege partially[101] shields the individual from the state to ensure that the dispute will be resolved in an impersonal manner that prevents the outcome from simply reflecting the state's superior power and resources.[102]

The sixth amendment's right to counsel promotes procedural fairness, regularity, and rationality by ensuring formal equality of access to the system. Although the right to counsel may contribute to more reliable outcomes, it has value independent of its result-efficacy because it promotes the individual's meaningful participation in the process. This independent process value explains why the Supreme Court has recognized the individual's constitutional right to represent herself.[103] While the right to counsel usually enhances the individual's capacity to participate in the process, this value is lost when the state forces the individual to accept "assistance" she does not want.[104] The Court constitutionalized the right of self-representation even though this fair process norm could impair other process values (such as procedural rationality) and the reliability of the process' outcome.[105] The state may deny this right to a competent[106] defendant only in those cases when the defendant's conduct

---

96. *See* Katz v. United States, 389 U.S. 347, 350-53 (1967) (fourth amendment protects intangible oral communications).

97. *See* Payton v. New York, 445 U.S. 573, 583-90 (1980) (fourth amendment protects sanctity of home).

98. *See* Schmerber v. California, 384 U.S. 757, 766-72 (1966) (fourth amendment protects physical privacy and dignity).

99. *See* Arenella, *Reappraisal, supra* note 58, at 40-42, 49.

100. *See, e.g.,* Fisher v. United States, 425 U.S. 391, 405-09 (1976).

101. The privilege protects only against testimonial compulsion, not against compulsion designed to elicit physical evidence. *See* Schmerber v. California, 384 U.S. 757, 760-65 (1961) (withdrawal of blood and use of blood analysis not testimonial or communicative).

102. It is tempting to explain the privilege as an inevitable feature of an adversarial system preoccupied with rules that ensure a fair battle between the contesting parties. Such an explanation, however, ignores the fact that most inquisitorial systems recognize some form of the privilege because it protects substantive values as well as procedural norms tied to adversarial guilt adjudication. Of course, if the dominant political ideology views confession to state authorities as a positive value that promotes social cohesion, the legal system might define these substantive values quite narrowly to bar only physical coercion of incriminating responses.

103. Faretta v. California, 442 U.S. 806 (1975).

104. *Id.* at 820-21.

105. *Id.* at 839-40 (Burger, C.J., dissenting).

106. The Court articulated minimal criteria for competency. A defendant need not have the skill

seriously jeopardizes other fair process norms such as procedural regularity (e.g., "the dignity of the courtroom"[107]).

One can take American criminal procedure's protection of fair process norms at face value as an ethical prerequisite of a just legal system that places some substantive and procedural restraints on the state's exercise of power. Or, one can explain this legitimation function from an instrumentalist perspective. To perform its dispute-resolution function effectively, American criminal procedure must provide a mechanism that settles the conflict in a manner that induces community respect for the fairness of its processes as well as the reliability of its outcomes. From this instrumentalist perspective, the most important consideration is how the process appears to the community. Given this definition of legitimation, criminal procedure need not in fact consistently respect these fair process norms, but it must create the appearance of doing so.[108] Regardless of one's explanation for why American criminal procedure performs this legitimation function, its presence suggests that the fairness of the state-individual interaction in the criminal process cannot be defined solely in terms of procedures that contribute to good substantive criminal law results. Simply put, American constitutional criminal procedure values and protects fair process norms even when they impair procedure's guilt-determination function.

a.   Legitimation and the Exclusionary Rule Debate

If the legal order takes these fair process values seriously, it must provide some sanction for their violation. But why should the sanction be located within the criminal process when the violation produces reliable evidence of substantive guilt? Why should criminal procedure frustrate substantive criminal law goals if remedies outside the criminal process could compensate individuals whose "rights" have been violated and deter state officials from abusing fair process norms in the future?

Defenders of the fourth amendment exclusionary rule often answer this question by challenging the effectiveness and utility of civil remedies.[109] Although I share their doubts, I do not share their unstated premise that the exclusionary rule debate only raises empirical considerations about the tangible costs and benefits of criminal versus civil remedies.[110] What is at stake in this debate is whether American criminal procedure should serve an independent function that impairs its capacity to vindicate substantive criminal law

---

and experience of a lawyer to be deemed "competent." He should, however, "be made aware of the dangers and disadvantages of self-representation, so that the record will establish that 'he knows what he is doing and his choice is made with eyes open.'" *Id.* at 835 (citing Adams v. United States *ex rel.* McCann, 317 U.S. 269, 279 (1942)). In other words, the defendant must "knowingly and intelligently" forego the relinquished benefits of counsel's assistance. *Id.* (citing Johnson v. Zerbst, 304 U.S. 458, 464-65 (1938)).

107. *Faretta*, 422 U.S. at 834-35 n.46.

108. Those who believe the legitimation function simply creates the *appearance* of fairness concede that criminal procedure must occasionally promote fair treatment in fact to support the image.

109. *See* Mertens & Wasserstrom, *Foreword: The Good Faith Exception to the Exclusionary Rule: Deregulating the Police and Derailing the Law,* 70 GEO. L.J. 365, 406-10 (1981).

110. *See* Kamisar, *Does (Did) (Should) The Exclusionary Rule Rest on a "Principled Basis" Rather than an "Empirical Proposition"?,* 16 CREIGHTON L. REV. 565, 618-20 (1983).

goals.[111]

American courts touch upon this normative question when they refer to "judicial integrity" rationales for the fourth amendment's exclusionary remedy. Unfortunately, the courts have rarely described the normative content of this concept or explained its functional significance. As a result, some American commentators[112] and Supreme Court Justices[113] have recently dismissed the "judicial integrity" rationale as a question-begging cliche.

Indeed, the "judicial integrity" label is misleading because the issue is not whether the courts are "condoning" improper executive action or whether they are "vicariously responsible" for the executive's misconduct. The issue is not the court's integrity but the criminal process' integrity as a self-regulating legal order.[114] Justice Brandeis eloquently described this rationale in his famous *Olmstead* dissent:

> If the government becomes a lawbreaker, it breeds contempt for the law; it invites every man to become a law unto himself; it invites anarchy. To declare that in the administration of the criminal law the end justifies the means—to declare that the Government may commit crimes in order to secure the conviction of the private criminal— would bring terrible retribution.[115]

In essence, Justice Brandeis was reminding us that the rule of law must reject the view that the end justifies the means. Our criminal justice system's moral legitimacy rests to some degree on its willingness to replace brute force with legal rules that limit the means government may use to pursue laudable ends.

At stake in the fourth amendment exclusionary rule debate is our view of the fourth amendment itself. What type of fair process norm is it? One way of answering this question is to suggest that the fourth amendment rests on a process-integrity rationale. According to this rationale, the fourth amendment regulates the balance of power between the state and the individual to protect substantive and procedural values that are as important to society as the effi-

---

111. It is hard imagine a criminal procedure system that does not attempt to allocate scarce resources efficiently, distribute power, and determine substantive guilt. It is possible, however, to construct a procedural model that articulates fair process norms but refuses to remedy their violation by excluding reliable evidence of substantive guilt. Consequently, the fact that our system and some inquisitorial systems occasionally exclude evidence obtained in violation of a fair process norm does not prove that the vindication of fair process norms within the criminal justice system is an *inherent function* of *any* procedural system. *See supra* note 90.

112. *See, e.g.,* Loewy, *The Fourth Amendment as a Device for Protecting The Innocent,* 81 MICH. L. REV. 1229, 1268 n.177 (1983) ("Preservation of judicial integrity, if not entirely out of judicial favor, is little more than a makeweight argument.").

113. *See, e.g.,* United States v. Peltier, 422 U.S. 531, 537-38 (1975) (judicial integrity not offended if law enforcement officials reasonably believed conduct in accordance with law).

114. Accord State v. Davis, 666 P.2d 802 (Or. 1982), where the Oregon Supreme Court noted that the process-integrity rationale for excluding evidence is

> not identical with a concern with "judicial integrity" that also is expressed in some Supreme Court opinions. The object of denying the government the fruits of its transgression against the person whose rights it has invaded is not to preserve the self-regard of judges but to preserve that person's rights to the same extent as if the government's officers had stayed within the law.

Id. at 806-07. *See also* State v. Sheridan, 121 Iowa 164, 166-67, 96 N.W. 730, 731 (1903).

115. Olmstead v. United States, 277 U.S. 438, 485 (1928) (Brandeis, J., dissenting).

cient repression of criminal conduct. Instead of justifying the exclusionary rule as a "remedy" designed to deter future constitutional violations, this process-integrity rationale validates the rule because it places the state and the individual, as far as possible, in the position they would have been in had the state not exceeded its constitutional authority.[116] Exclusion of evidence that the state[117] has obtained by violating the defendant's fourth amendment rights is the only response that serves this regulatory purpose. Viewed from this perspective, it is the fourth amendment itself, and not the exclusionary rule, that deliberately hinders more "efficient" crime control practices to protect citizens' privacy, property, and liberty interests.[118]

---

116. The Oregon Supreme Court recently adopted this rationale. *See* State v. Davis, 666 P.2d 802, 806-07 (Or. 1982); *supra* note 114. *See also The Exclusionary Rule Bills: Hearings on S.101, S.751 and S.1995 Before the Subcomm. on Criminal Law of the Senate Comm. on the Judiciary*, 97th Cong., 1st & 2d Sess. 372-77 (1982) (testimony of Prof. Yale Kamisar).

Judge Wilkey points out quite correctly that the courts have never interpreted the fourth amendment to achieve this objective. *See* Wilkey, *The Exclusionary Rule: Costs and Viable Alternatives*, 1 CRIM. JUST. ETHICS 16, 22-23 (1982) The state is not required to return illegally seized contraband, and the Supreme Court has consistently permitted courts to try defendants who were brought within the court's jurisdiction by "forcible abduction." *See* Frisbie v. Collins, 342 U.S. 519, 522 (1952); Wilkey, *supra*, at 22-23. I suspect the real reason that courts have shied away from a process-integrity rationale of the fourth amendment is the extent to which it would impair crime control interests. For example, the process-integrity view of the fourth amendment would mandate exclusion of unconstitutionally seized evidence from both pretrial and post-trial proceedings.

The difficulties of confining the scope of the process-integrity rationale, coupled with its deliberate impairment of crime control values, have prompted the courts to adopt an instrumentalist view that values the fourth amendment for its capacity to promote general protections of citizens' rights *in the future*. Once the government violates the fourth amendment in a criminal prosecution, the instrumentalist rationale asks what remedy will promote the deterrence of future police misconduct. Under this rationale, excluding reliable evidence of substantive guilt is a very costly remedy that only makes sense in those circumstances where the rule's future speculative benefits of deterrence clearly outweigh its present tangible costs.

Justice Stewart uses this instrumentalist perspective to defend the exclusionary rule. Stewart, *The Road to* Mapp v. Ohio *and Beyond: The Origins, Development, and Future of the Exclusionary Rule in Search and Seizure Cases*, 83 COLUM. L. REV. 1365, 1393 (1983). He argues that there must be some effective remedy for the violation of constitutional rights and that at present the exclusionary rule is the only remedy that provides sufficient incentives to prevent *future violations* of the fourth amendment. *Id.* at 1383-92. While I agree wholeheartedly with his conclusion, this instrumentalist perspective permits the Court to recognize impairment of crime control interests as a cost of the exclusionary rule *instead* of an inevitable cost of the fourth amendment itself. Indeed, this instrumentalist perspective permits the Supreme Court to speak of "judicial integrity" being impaired by the vindication of fourth amendment principles in cases when the police have acted in good faith. *See* Illinois v. Gates, 103 S. Ct. 2317, 2342 (1983) (White, J., concurring) (absent "bad faith" government misconduct, excluding reliable evidence of guilt impairs court's integrity by "undermining public confidence in the reasonableness of the standards that govern the criminal justice system"). For an excellent critique of this instrumentalist perspective, see Schrock & Welsh, *Up from* Calandra: *The Exclusionary Rule as a Constitutional Requirement*, 59 MINN. L. REV. 251 (1974).

117. Judge Wilkey argues that adoption of the "judicial integrity" rationale would force courts to exclude evidence obtained unlawfully by *private* parties. *See* Wilkey, *supra* note 116, at 23. His argument rests on the mistaken assumption that the system excludes evidence to protect the *Court's* integrity. However, the process-integrity rationale supports the "private" party exception to fourth amendment regulation. Because the state has not violated substantive and procedural constraints on its exercise of power, admission of evidence seized by a private party does not implicate the balance of power between the state and the individual with which the fourth amendment is concerned.

118. Justice Stewart defends *Mapp* on deterrence grounds but insists that it is the fourth amendment itself that deliberately impairs police power to pursue crime control objectives. *See* Stewart, *supra* note 116, at 1384-85. Justice Stewart notes:

Similarly, the [exclusionary] rule has been criticized for hindering the police in the performance of their duties. Once again, this criticism is properly reserved for the fourth amendment. The exclusionary rule places no limitations on the actions of the police. The fourth amend-

Allowing the government to pay tort damages for its failure to comply with the fourth amendment hardly seems consistent with this process-integrity view of the fourth amendment. Compensating victims of government misconduct would constitute an appropriate supplemental remedy. But exclusive reliance on civil remedies would permit criminal justice officials to "profit" from their deliberate violations of the rules that regulate the balance of power within the criminal process. Permitting the state to use the fruits of such misconduct to prove substantive guilt undermines the very notion of our criminal process as a self-regulating legal order.

b. Legitimation: A Comparative Perspective

No one would deny that American criminal procedure's protection of fair process norms sometimes has the *effect* of frustrating substantive criminal law goals. However, many observers would challenge my view that this result is the justifiable consequence of an independent function of criminal procedure. Pointing to inquisitorial systems, they might suggest that my analysis suffers from cultural myopia. Consider Chief Justice Burger's claim that inquisitorial systems do not exclude reliable evidence of substantive guilt to protect other societal interests.[119] Indeed, some commentators have used the inquisitorial system's commitment to "truth-discovery" to criticize American criminal procedure's apparent willingness to frustrate substantive criminal law objectives.[120] Their critique implies that criminal procedure should focus exclusively on the reliable adjudication of substantive guilt. In other words, fair process norms merit protection *within the criminal process* only if they contribute instrumentally to the promotion of good substantive criminal law "results."

Let me anticipate their arguments. First, they would contend that viewing the criminal process as a dispute-resolution mechanism is an idiosyncratic aspect of American criminal procedure. Our accusatorial system structures criminal proceedings as an adversarial contest between the state and the accused.

---

ment does. The inevitable result of the Constitution's prohibition against unreasonable searches and seizures and its requirement that no warrant shall issue but upon probable caue is that police officers who obey its strictures will catch fewer criminals. That is not a political outcome impressed upon an unwilling citizenry by unbeknighted judges. It is the price the framers anticipated and were willing to pay to ensure the sanctity of the person, the home, and property against unrestrained governmental power.

Id. at 1393.
Justice Stewart rejects the process-integrity rationale for the fourth amendment because it rests on a value judgment that freeing the criminal is a lesser evil than permitting the government to profit from its illegal activity. *Id.* at 1383. Stewart suggests that neither the text of the fourth amendment nor historical practices provide any evidence that the Framers "constitutionalized" this value judgment. *Id.* Yet, if Justice Stewart is right, how can he assert that the fourth amendment, and not the exclusionary rule, deliberately impairs efficient crime control in order to protect citizens' rights? This view of the fourth amendment itself reflects the same value judgment. Moreover, to view the choice as freeing a criminal or ratifying government misconduct ignores the fact that the government would not have faced this "choice" if it had complied with the fourth amendment's strictures in the first place. For an alternative explanation of why courts have rejected this process-integrity rationale, see *supra* note 116.
119. *See* Bivens v. Six Unknown Named Agents, 403 U.S. 388, 415 (1971) (Burger, C.J., dissenting) (noting that neither England nor Canada use exclusionary rules).
120. *See, e.g.,* Wilkey, *The Exclusionary Rule: Why Suppress Valid Evidence?*, 62 JUDICATURE 214, 216-18 (1978).

Since accusatorial ideology assumes the two parties have inherently conflicting interests and unequal resources, it is preoccupied with regulating the balance of advantage between the state and the accused to ensure a fair battle.[121] Since the parties control the course of both the investigation and the trial, "truth-discovery" is only the incidental by-product of a system that views dispute-resolution as its primary objective.[122]

Pointing to inquisitorial systems, these critics might then argue that criminal procedure need not frustrate substantive criminal law goals. In contrast to our dispute-resolution model, inquisitorial systems view the criminal process as an official inquiry in which state officials take primary responsibility for determining whether the defendant has committed a crime. Instead of two partisan investigations designed to produce evidence favorable to a particular party, state officials conduct an objective investigation to determine the truth. They are responsible for finding exculpatory as well as inculpatory information and must disclose all information uncovered to the defendant before trial. Since the paramount objective of inquisitorial procedure is "truth-discovery," most relevant sources of information, including questioning of the accused, are explored at the investigatory stage. Unlike her accusatorial counterpart who acts as an umpire at trial to ensure that the parties abide by the rules of the contest, the inquisitorial judge conducts the course of the nonadversarial trial. The judge's objective is to discover the truth by examining all sources of relevant information, including the defendant.[123]

This somewhat idealized description of inquisitorial criminal procedure creates the impression that continental procedure focuses exclusively on vindicating substantive criminal law goals. Recent research has convincingly demonstrated, however, that some European jurisidictions are willing to exclude reliable evidence of substantive guilt to protect fair process norms articulated in constitutional and statutory safeguards.[124]

For example, West German courts will exclude reliable evidence of guilt if the state obtained it by means of brutality or deceit.[125] Their authority to exclude such evidence derives from the *Rechtsstaatsprinzip*—the constitutional principle of a state governed by the rule of law.[126] This principle

> affords a fair trial before a legally appointed and independent judge in which constitutional guarantees are observed; specifically the dignity of the person, the right to free development of the personality, the freedom of the person, the equality before the law . . . as well as the prohibition against inhumane treatment. The right to a fair procedure also guarantees the accused the right to free counsel in serious

---

121. *See generally* Griffiths, *supra* note 3.
122. *See* Nesson, *Reasonable Doubt and Permissive Inferences: The Value of Complexity*, 92 HARV. L. REV. 1187, 1194 (1979).
123. *See generally* L. WEINREB, DENIAL OF JUSTICE: CRIMINAL PROCESS IN THE UNITED STATES (1977); Langbein & Weinreb, *Continental Criminal Procedure: "Myth" and Reality*, 87 YALE L.J. 1549 (1978).
124. *See* Bradley, *The Exclusionary Rule in Germany*, 96 HARV. L. REV. 1032, 1033 n.5 (1983) (list of sources).
125. *Id.* at 1033-34. It is unclear how frequently West German courts actually exclude evidence under this principle. *Id.* at 1039-41.
126. *Id.* at 1034.

cases if he can't afford to pay . . . .[127]

Evidence seized in violation of this principle must be excluded automatically, "regardless of its probative value or the seriousness of the crime under investigation."[128] The analogy between West Germany's *Rechtsstaatsprinzip* and our concept of due process, which excludes probative evidence obtained by police "conduct that shocks the conscience,"[129] is striking.[130] Moreover, West German courts have justified their exclusion of this evidence on grounds of judicial integrity. Automatic exclusion is necessary "to preserve the purity of the judicial process."[131]

If the *Rechtsstaatsprinzip* principle is not violated, West German courts still possess constitutional authority to exclude reliable evidence of guilt if its admission would violate the defendant's constitutionally protected privacy interests. Unlike the *Rechtsstaatsprinzip* principle, exclusion under *Verhältnismässigkeit* (principle of proportionality) is not automatic.[132] Instead, West German courts must balance the defendant's privacy interests against the need for the evidence and the seriousness of the crime. Balancing these factors may lead to the exclusion of reliable evidence that the police *lawfully* seized because West German courts use the proportionality principle to protect the substantive value of privacy, not to deter police misconduct.[133] The violation of statutory safeguards concerning witness privileges, wiretapping, and the defendant's privilege against self-incrimination also may lead to the exclusion of reliable evidence of substantive guilt.[134] Professor Bradley's examination of West Germany's exclusionary rules[135] leads him to draw the following conclusions:

> [C]ontrary to the traditional view, Germany in fact has a well-developed system of exclusionary rules founded on constitutional principles and statutory provisions. The German and the American exclusionary rules both reflect the fundamental principle that relevant evidence must occasionally be excluded to safeguard constitutional rights, but the rules sometimes differ significantly in the scope of protection that they afford. The German rule, for example, is less stringent than the American rule in excluding evidence derived from

---

127. *Id.* at 1039 (quoting T. KLEINKNECHT, STRAFPROZESSORDNUNG Einleitung ¶ 19 (33d ed. 1977)).

128. *Id.* at 1040.

129. *See* Rochin v. California, 342 U.S. 165, 172 (1952).

130. If this analogy extends to the rules' applications as well as their rationale, one would expect very few West German judicial decisions excluding evidence on this ground.

131. Bradley, *supra* note 124, at 1034, 1047.

132. *Id.* at 1041-43.

133. *Id.* at 1042. In a conversation with the author, Professor Langbein insisted that West Germany's constitutional exclusionary rules bear no resemblance to American exclusionary rules because only the latter exclude reliable evidence of guilt to deter future police misconduct. The primary reason we wish to deter such conduct, however, is because it impinges on privacy interests protected by the fourth amendment. Finally, regardless of the primary motivation for invoking such a rule, both accusatorial and inquisitorial systems recognize that criminal procedure must occasionally serve goals that impair its capacity to determine guilt reliably.

134. *Id.* at 1049-63.

135. Unfortunately, Bradley lumps together both constitutional exclusionary rules and testimonial privilege rules under his definition of "exclusionary rules."

improper searches of the home, and the failure to give *Miranda*-type warnings to suspects generally will not result in exclusion in Germany. On the other hand, in comparison to their American counterparts, the German courts afford significantly greater protection to witnesses with personal or professional ties to the defendant and are stricter in suppressing evidence obtained in violation of wiretapping statutes. The German courts have also defined a doctrine of personal privacy that will cause certain private material, such as diaries, to be excluded even when such material has been obtained legally. The two systems converge, however, in their treatment of coerced confessions and evidence obtained through brutality or deceit.[136]

Whether one examines the constitutions, statutes, or judicial decisions of West Germany or the United States, one finds a criminal process that does far more than simply determine instances of the substantive criminal law's breach. Regardless of how the state characterizes its criminal justice system, it uses the criminal process in part as an instrument of coercion and social control. Inquisitorial and accusatorial systems attempt to validate the state's use of coercion by using criminal procedure to protect social values that have little to do with procedure's guilt-determination goal. To perform this legitimation function, inquisitorial systems must make moral and political judgments about how much power state officials should be given over citizens of the state and how to respond when state officials intrude upon important societal values. To articulate these fair process norms, inquisitorial systems, like their accusatorial counterparts, must consider society's normative aspirations about human relations embodied in its constitution, statutes, customs, religions, and ideologies. While inquisitorial systems are less willing than our system to vindicate fair process norms at the expense of good substantive criminal law "results,"[137] some of them clearly recognize the need to do so.

Whether this legitimation function requires the realization or just the appearance of a process that treats human beings, including the guilty, with dignity and respect, the "bottom line" remains the same: There is, at present, no pure "guilt or innocence" model of American criminal procedure. Constitutional criminal procedure serves other goals—efficient allocation of scarce resources, power allocation, and the protection of fair process norms—that may impair its function of reliably determining substantive guilt. Having identified these independent functions, we are ready to evaluate the procedural significance of the Burger Court's shift towards a "crime control" perspective.

---

136. *Id.* at 1064.

137. Some empirical studies of the American exclusionary rule suggest that our criminal justice system rarely excludes reliable evidence of substantive guilt. *See* COMPTROLLER GENERAL OF THE UNITED STATES, REP. NO. GGD 79-45, IMPACT OF THE EXCLUSIONARY RULE ON FEDERAL CRIMINAL PROSECUTIONS (1979). The exclusionary rule's real impact is felt in the plea bargaining process where the potential success of a suppression motion becomes a negotiating chip that defense counsel may use to secure greater sentencing or charging concessions from the state. In such cases, the exclusionary rule's impact on the ultimate sentencing disposition may still impair the substantive criminal law's punishment goals.

III. RECONSTRUCTING PACKER'S DUE PROCESS AND CRIME CONTROL "MODELS"—IDENTIFYING THEIR CONFLICTING IDEOLOGICAL IMAGES OF OUR CRIMINAL JUSTICE SYSTEM'S FUNCTIONS

A. PACKER'S CRIME-CONTROL AND DUE PROCESS MODELS

The Burger Court is undoubtedly more interested than its predecessor in using the criminal process to effect broadscale crime prevention and control, although the extent of even this change is easy to overstate.[138]

Most commentators would readily agree with Professor Seidman's observation about the Burger Court's preoccupation with crime control. To understand why Seidman minimized the importance of this change, it is necessary to explore the conventional "models" some criminal justice scholars have used to explain overarching judicial trends in American criminal procedure.

Many American scholars have relied on Professor Herbert Packer's crime control and due process models to identify the competing values served by American criminal procedure.[139] Writing near the end of the Warren Court era, Packer's professed objective was to articulate two distinct and competing "normative models" "that permit us to recognize explicitly the value choices that underlie the details of the criminal process."[140] Packer identified two value systems, the crime control and due process models, which reflect

the normative antinomy at the heart of the criminal law. These models are not labeled Is and Ought, nor are they to be taken in that sense. Rather, they represent an attempt to abstract two separate value systems that compete for priority in the operation of the criminal process. Neither is presented as either corresponding to reality or representing the ideal to the exclusion of the other. The two models merely afford a convenient way to talk about the operation of a process whose day-to-day functioning involves a constant series of minute adjustments between the competing demands of two value systems and whose normative future likewise involves a series of resolutions of the tensions between competing claims.[141]

After describing some general concerns about legality and the adversarial system that underlie both value systems, Packer summarized the central values and presuppositions underlying each model.

1. Crime Control Model

The crime control model sees the criminal process' most important function to be the repression of criminal conduct. The model puts a premium on the speed and efficiency with which the process operates to punish those defend-

---

138. Seidman, *supra* note 8, at 437.
139. *See, e.g.,* C. WHITEBREAD, CRIMINAL PROCEDURE 6-8 (1980).
140. H. PACKER, *supra* note 19, at 153.
141. *Id.*

ants who have committed the proscribed act, the "factually guilty"[142] in Packer's terminology. To be efficient and speedy in a system that lacks sufficient resources to deal with the vast number of cases that must pass through it, the crime control model prefers the informal, ex parte, administrative factfinding of the police and prosecutor to the more cumbersome adversarial determination of guilt at trial.[143] The model trusts state officials to screen out the "factually innocent." Those not screened out are presumptively guilty.

> The supposition is that the screening processes operated by police and prosecutors are reliable indicators of probable guilt. Once a man has been arrested and investigated without being found to be probably innocent, or, to put it differently, once a determination has been made that there is enough evidence of guilt to permit holding him for further action, then all subsequent activity directed toward him is based on the view that he is probably guilty.[144]

The indictment imprints the presumption of guilt and the guilty plea prevents it from being upset by the application of factual guilt-defeating doctrines at trial.[145] Moreover, the guilty plea enhances the finality of this administrative determination of guilt by reducing the defendant's opportunity to challenge his conviction.[146]

2. Due Process Model

Unlike the crime control model's exclusive preoccupation with the suppression of criminal conduct, Packer's due process model concentrates on the problem of how best to limit official power over the individual. This preoccupation with limiting state power reflects the due process model's concern with "the primacy of the individual,"[147] the stigma of the criminal sanction, and the possibilities of abuse inherent in official power.[148] This concern over state power and its abuses explains why the due process model uses the criminal process to police itself by its formal commitment to the concept of "legal guilt."[149]

> According to this doctrine, a person is not to be held guilty of crime merely on a showing that in all probability, based upon reliable evidence, *he did factually what he is said to have done*. Instead, he is to be held guilty if and only if these factual determinations are made in procedurally regular fashion and by authorities acting within competencies duly allocated to them. Furthermore, he is not to be held guilty, even though the factual determination is or might be adverse to him, if various rules designed to protect him and to safeguard the integrity of the process are not given effect.[150]

---

142. *Id.* at 165.
143. *Id.* at 160, 162.
144. *Id.* at 160.
145. *Id.* at 162.
146. *Id.*
147. *Id.* at 165.
148. *Id.* at 165-66.
149. *Id.* at 166.
150. *Id.* (emphasis added).

The due process model prefers adversarial adjudication over an administrative determination of guilt for two reasons. First, trial adjudication is seen as a more reliable factfinding mechanism.[151] Second, the police and prosecutor lack the competence and willingness to apply factual guilt-disabling doctrines when they make their administrative determination of guilt.[152] In contrast to the empirical presumption of factual guilt underlying the operation of the crime control model, the due process model relies on a normative presumption of legal innocence.[153] The due process model limits state power over all suspects, including the factually guilty, by forcing the state to prove its case in an adjudicative forum that will provide maximum protection to the factually innocent and maximum assurance that the state has respected the defendant's rights in securing its evidence and proving its case.[154]

Taken at face value, Packer's two "models" appear to describe in an overly simplified and dichotomized form how our system determines guilt by adversarial trial adjudication or by plea bargaining.[155] The due process model describes how a small percentage of criminal prosecutions receive the system's full process. Regardless of whether the defendant is "factually guilty," her "legal innocence" is presumed until the state proves her "legal guilt" at trial. The crime control model describes how our system has relied on plea bargaining to process the vast majority of criminal prosecutions.

While Packer's models identify some of the values furthered by trial adjudication and plea bargaining, they are not procedural models because they do not offer a coherent vision of how to structure the American criminal process.[156] Neither "model" identifies the specific functions of American criminal procedure nor fully explains how these functions would be served or thwarted by a "due process" or "crime control" value perspective.

More significantly, Packer's models create the erroneous impression that American criminal procedure is concerned solely with the question of which party, the state or the individual, should get the advantage in their adversarial contest. As John Griffiths observed, Packer's models suggest that "the crucial question for criminal procedure so conceived is what bias to build into the rules. This is where Packer's models differ . . . . What he gives us is a single Battle model with two possibilities of bias."[157]

The crime control model appears to be a simple restatement of the tendency of *any* criminal justice system to resist legal restraints in the pursuit of procedure's primary objective of punishing the guilty offender.[158] Thus, some commentators view the crime control model as a shorthand description of the law

---

151. *Id.* at 163-65.
152. *Id.* at 167.
153. *Id.* at 167-68.
154. *Id.* at 166-67.
155. It would be a mistake to view the two processes as completely independent of each other. The plea bargaining process reflects in part the parties' prediction of the trial's likely outcome. *See also supra* note 137.
156. *See* Damaska, *supra* note 3; Goldstein, *Reflections on Two Models: Inquisitorial Themes in American Criminal Procedure,* 26 STAN. L. REV. 1009 (1974); Griffiths, *supra* note 3.
157. Griffiths, *supra* note 3, at 367-68.
158. Goldstein, *supra* note 156, at 1015.

enforcement community's value perspective.[159] The due process model appears to lack any positive procedural content apart from its general concern about limiting state power over the individual.[160] As Professor Damaska correctly pointed out, Packer's due process perspective is not a procedural model because it is "conceptually impossible to imagine a criminal process whose dominant concern is a desire to protect the individual from public officials."[161] In other words, Packer's models appear to restate in abstract form the tension in our system between efficient guilt-determination and the protection of the defendant from overreaching state power.[162]

Packer's models encourage us to compare Warren and Burger Court decisions by evaluating the degree of bias the Courts interject in the defendant's or government's favor. By implicitly relying on this simplistic perspective, commentators end up trivializing the differences between the two Courts. For example, Kamisar, Israel, and Saltzburg appear to be defining a judicial counter-revolution as one where the Court promotes law enforcement interests (e.g., crime control values) without regard to the accused's procedural rights (e.g., due process values).[163] Similarly, Seidman suggests a judicial counter-revolution would have occurred if the Burger Court had refused to enforce due process norms by excluding reliable evidence of guilt.[164] Since the Burger Court has continued to protect due process norms that impair procedure's guilt-determination function, it can be viewed, like its predecessor, as engaging in a process of accomodation between the defendant's rights and the state's interests in effective law enforcement.[165] At this level of abstraction, the fact that the Burger Court gives more weight than its predecessor to crime control values suggests only that the Burger Court is more likely than the Warren Court to rule in the government's favor.

To understand why the Burger Court's shift toward a crime control perspective implicates procedural goals apart from the allocation of bias preferences, we need to develop more fully these competing value systems and identify their procedural implications. The next section reconstructs Packer's two "models" by examining how each value system makes distinct and conflicting normative claims about the validity of specific procedural functions and the relative weight that should be attached to valid procedural objectives that con-

---

159. Griffiths, *supra* note 3, at 362 n.14. Equating the crime control model with the police's perspective creates the erroneous impression that only the due process model has ideological content. This view raises a troubling question about how one can explain the discrepancy between our normative ideals (e.g., due process norms) and how our system actually functions in most cases. One commentator has answered this question by suggesting that due process ideology is a form of "false consciousness." According to Rudovsky, our due process norms legitimate an unjust system by providing an idealized and distorted image of its functions and values. Rudovsky, *The Criminal Justice System and the Role of the Police*, in THE POLITICS OF LAW 242, 242-43 (D. Kairys ed. 1982). For a critique of this view, see *infra* note 231.

160. Damaska, *supra* note 3, at 575.

161. *Id.*

162. Since Packer's due process model emphasizes equality and fair adversarial process norms, some American scholars have used it to describe the ideals espoused by the Warren Court. *See, e.g.,* C. WHITEBREAD, *supra* note 139, at 5-7.

163. *See* Kamisar, *supra* note 1, at 68-91; Israel, *supra* note 6, at 1416-25; Saltzburg, *supra* note 2, at 154-58.

164. Seidman, *supra* note 8, at 437.

165. *Id.* at 437, 497-503.

flict with each other. We shall see that these two reconstructed "models" actually describe competing ideological visions of how our system should serve criminal procedure's functions.

B. RECONSTRUCTING PACKER'S MODELS[166]

1. Vindicating Substantive Criminal Law Goals—Promoting Reliable Guilt-Determination and Punishment Goals

If one accepts the validity of Packer's distinction between "factual" and "legal" guilt,[167] one can understand the commonly-held perception that the crime control model better serves the substantive criminal law's goals. Packer created the erroneous impression that substantive guilt simply requires a procedural mechanism that reliably reconstructs historical facts.[168] Given this limited conception of substantive guilt, it is hard to see why an adversarial adjudication of historical facts is necessarily more accurate than an administrative determination of facts by law enforcement officials followed by a negotiated guilty plea. After all, in an adversarial proceeding, the independent adjudicator hears only what the parties decide to present as evidence. Trial tactics, constitutional restraints, and concerns about prejudicial impact may exclude a great deal of relevant evidence from the trial that was considered by the police and the prosecutor in making their own determination of "factual guilt." Moreover, the trial's stringent proof beyond a reasonable doubt standard deliberately increases the risk that a "factually guilty" defendant will be acquitted to provide maximum assurance that the factually innocent will not be convicted.

Accordingly, one must agree with Damaska that the due process model's preference for adversarial adjudication simply reflects that model's "negative" objective of limiting state power over individuals, including the "factually guilty."[169] Packer's definition of "legal guilt" also supports this view. A person is not legally guilty until his factual guilt has been demonstrated in a forum, the criminal trial, that has the competence and inclination to apply factual guilt defeating doctrines that protect the accused and the integrity of the process. In contrast, the crime control model secures the conviction of the "factually guilty" by encouraging defendants to forfeit their factual guilt defeating[170] claims in exchange for some sentencing concession.

---

166. In reconstructing these two models, I am not attempting to create two ideal procedural models. One can easily imagine an ideal due process model that prefers inquisitorial to adversarial adjudication. Similarly, it may be possible to construct an ideal market-negotiation model whose concern for efficiency, speed, and finality does not frustrate substantive criminal law goals. My reconstructed models describe two competing ideological visions operating within our present criminal justice system.

167. Many legal actors make this distinction and rely upon it to justify their practices. *See* Arenella, *Reforming the Federal Grand Jury, supra* note 95, at 503-07.

168. Ironically, in an early section of his book, Packer recognized the substantive criminal law's moral content and force. *See* H. PACKER, *supra* note 19, at 73-75. Yet, in his discussion of the due process and crime control models, he never refers to how the procedural process promotes these concerns.

169. *See* Damaska, *supra* note 3, at 575-76.

170. The guilty plea does not forfeit all claims that prevent the state from establishing factual guilt. *See, e.g.,* Menna v. New York, 423 U.S. 61, 62-63 n.2 (1975); Blackledge v. Perry, 417 U.S. 21, 28-29 (1974).

To see how a reconstructed due process model promotes the substantive criminal law's objectives, we must correct Packer's definition of guilt. By implicitly equating "substantive guilt" (e.g., engaging in the proscribed conduct with the requisite intent under circumstances that do not justify or excuse the conduct) with "factual guilt" (e.g., engaging in the proscribed conduct), Packer ignored the moral quality of substantive guilt. For example, Packer characterized the insanity defense as a legal guilt requirement. According to Packer's definitions, the legally insane actor is "factually guilty" but "legally innocent." The insane actor is not "substantively guilty," however, because he lacks the requisite moral culpability to be blamed for his conduct.[171] Indeed, that is why the verdict in insanity cases is "not guilty by reason of insanity." No purpose is served by labeling the insane actor or the individual who justifiably kills in self-defense as "factually guilty" apart from conveying the mistaken notion that substantive guilt rests solely on the factual question of whether the defendant engaged in the proscribed conduct.

Packer's concept of "factual guilt" is a misleading and dangerous fiction. By erroneously reducing guilt to an empirical question, Packer encouraged an overly simplistic view of the criminal process as a "truth-discovery" mechanism. But the "truth" cannot be discovered until some determination has been made about the actor's moral culpability.[172] Moreover, Packer's use of this fiction obscured the positive procedural content of the due process model. Once we use a proper definition of substantive guilt (e.g., engaging in the proscribed conduct with the requisite intent under circumstances that do not justify or excuse the conduct), we can readily see how a reconstructed due process model promotes the substantive criminal law's objective of deliberately inflicting suffering on individuals who deserve to be punished. The due process model's legal guilt doctrine restates our system's theoretical commitment to the principle of adversarial[173] guilt adjudication. Legal guilt is simply susbstantive guilt as well as it can be determined by a fallible procedural process that strives to protect the substantively innocent while simultaneously serving other independent procedural functions.[174]

Damaska's well-founded criticism[175] of Packer's due process construct as a "negative" model does not apply to our reconstructed due process model. The model's commitment to an independent adjudication of substantive guilt reinforces the moral content and force of the criminal sanction in several different respects. For example, the due process model requires the state to prove the

---

171. *See generally* Arenella, *Reflections on Current Proposals to Abolish or Reform the Insanity Defense*, 8 AM. J.L. MED. 271 (1982) [hereinafter cited as Arenella, *Reflections*]; Arenella, Book Review, 80 COLUM. L. REV. 420 (1980) (reviewing H. FINGARETTE & A.F. HASSE, MENTAL DISABILITIES AND CRIMINAL RESPONSIBILITY (1979)) [hereinafter cited as Arenella, Book Review].

172. *See* Arenella, *Reforming the Federal Grand Jury, supra* note 95, at 465-66 n.6.

173. I am not suggesting that an "ideal" due process model must endorse adversarial guilt adjudication. I do believe that such a model of criminal procedure should provide for some form of independent adjudication to promote subtantive criminal law goals. *See infra* text accompanying notes 197-202. The reconstructed due process model described in the text simply reflects our system's ideological preconceptions about the most appropriate form of guilt adjudication. *See* Griffiths, *supra* note 3.

174. Arenella, *Reforming the Federal Grand Jury, supra* note 95, at 465-66 n.6. For a slightly different definition that relies on factual guilt terminology but comes close to my definition of legal guilt, see Alschuler, *supra* note 87, at 707, 709 n.152.

175. *See* Damaska, *supra* note 3.

defendant's guilt beyond a reasonable doubt. This stringent standard of proof reflects the moral significance that our society attaches to the criminal sanction. We are willing to make factual errors in the defendant's favor to ensure that the state's most coercive and stigmatizing sanction is applied only to those individuals who are certainly blameworthy.[176]

The model's commitment to lay adjudication also promotes substantive criminal law goals. The jury's prerogative to acquit against the weight of the evidence is not simply an inevitable by-product of lay adjudication. After all, the criminal process could limit jury nullification power by adopting civil jury-control devices, such as directed verdicts, special verdicts, and judgments notwithstanding the verdict. One could argue that the absence of these devices in criminal procedure reflects the system's unwillingness to limit the criminal trial jury to the role of factfinding.[177] Indeed, juries may nullify the law because their function extends beyond simply applying legal norms to the facts. They may negate the substantive criminal law's clear application to a particular defendant in cases in which they believe applying the legislative standard would be unjust.[178]

Lay adjudication provides a safety-valve review of the legislature's original criminalization decision. In theory, the legislature's definition of the crime reflects a community judgment that violation of the rule justifies state interference because an individual has culpably chosen to disregard important societal interests. The legislature's rule, however, may be overinclusive—some examples of its breach may not demonstrate the defendant's culpability and/or the harm normally associated with violation of the rule.[179] In the alternative, the legislature's original criminalization decision may no longer comport with the community's sense of justice. In theory, the legislature should respond to changing community standards by repealing outdated offenses that no longer appear sufficiently blameworthy or dangerous in the public's eye. In practice, however, legislators are often reluctant to repeal archaic crimes out of fear that their constituents may construe repeal as a symbolic expression of legislative

---

176. *See In re* Winship, 397 U.S. 358, 372 (1970) (Harlan, J., concurring).

177. *See* Westen, *The Three Faces of Double Jeopardy: Reflections on Government Appeals of Criminal Sentences*, 78 MICH. L. REV. 1001, 1012-18 (1980). Although directed verdicts are used against both plaintiffs and defendants in civil cases, and against the prosecutor in criminal cases, their use against defendants in criminal cases is universally assumed to be unconstitutional. *Id.* This refusal to apply civil jury-control devices to the criminal jury suggests that jury nullification is not only a power but also a right. *Id.*

178. In Gregg v. Georgia, 428 U.S. 153 (1976), the Court noted:

In order to repair the alleged defects . . . it would have to be required that . . . [i]f a jury refused to convict even though the evidence supported the charge, its verdict would have to be reversed and a verdict of guilty entered or a new trial ordered since the discretionary act of jury nullification would not be permitted . . . . Such a system, of course, would be totally alien to our notions of criminal justice.

Id. at 199-200 n.50. *See also* Standefer v. United States, 447 U.S. 10, 22 (1980) ("The absence of these remedial [jury-control] procedures in criminal cases permits juries to acquit out of compassion."). *See generally* Scheflin & Van Dyke, *Jury Nullification: The Contours of a Controversy*, 43 LAW & CONTEMP. PROBS. 51 (1980).

179. *Cf.* MODEL PENAL CODE § 2.12(2) (Official Draft 1962) (De Minimus Infractions) (empowering court to dismiss prosecution when it finds that defendant's conduct "did not actually cause or threaten the harm or evil sought to be prevented by the law defining the offense or did so only to an extent too trivial to warrant the condemnation of conviction").

approval of such conduct. Consequently, legislatures are more likely to expand the scope of the substantive criminal law in response to community pressure than to repeal outdated offenses.

American criminal procedure responds to this legislative defect by giving both the prosecutor[180] and the jury the power to decriminalize a particular defendant's conduct that is not sufficiently "blameworthy" or "dangerous" to justify state interference with the individual's freedom of action. Admittedly, juries may occasionally exercise this right in a manner that promotes community prejudice more than the defendant's just deserts. But, the jury's power to apply a more lenient standard than the positive law demands reflects the substantive criminal law's objective of only punishing those defendants who are morally culpable in the community's eyes.

We have seen how a reconstructed due process model serves substantive criminal law policies. But, does its preference for an independent adjudication of guilt serve these policies as well as the crime control model's reliance on negotiated settlements? Defenders of plea bargaining explicitly or implicitly rely on crime control values to support their contention that negotiated settlements achieve substantive criminal law goals more efficiently than independent adjudications.

First, some advocates of plea bargaining rely on the fictitious concept of "factual guilt" to argue that negotiated settlements produce more accurate determinations of "guilt" than those produced by the vagaries of trial adjudication. For example, Professor Easterbrook argues that requiring adjudication in all cases would not provide us with clearer information about guilt to justify the resulting loss in efficiency. Easterbrook explains:

> There are too many variables at work, from the stacked burden of proof to the vagaries of testimonial evidence, for trials to convey the "truth" with regularity. Most trials end in a verdict of guilt or innocence, but this is simply a way of suppressing uncertainty. Trials produce a verdict by rounding up to one (guilt) or down to zero (innocence) a probability that hovers in jurors' minds somewhere between 0.999 and 0.51. . . . Plea bargains reflect the probabilities case by case; trials disguise probabilities in individual cases . . . .[181]

By erroneously equating substantive guilt with a factual probability judgment, Easterbrook, like Packer, strips the substantive criminal law of its moral content and reduces the function of trials to "a process of mandatory rounding"[182] of factual probability judgments. Establishing that negotiated settlements produce more efficient determinations of "factual guilt" than trial

---

180. *See, e.g.,* UNITED STATES DEP'T OF JUSTICE, PRINCIPLES OF FEDERAL PROSECUTION 9 (1980).

181. Easterbrook, *Criminal Procedure as a Market System,* 12 J. LEGAL STUD. 289, 316-17 (1983).

182. *Id.* at 317. Easterbrook's conclusion that trial outcomes tell us nothing more than what we learn from negotiated settlements in a more efficient manner reflects his assumption that we value a particular process solely for its instrumental tendency to achieve accurate results with minimal allocative inefficiencies. His defense of plea bargaining on efficiency grounds does not address the critique of plea bargaining made in this article that the process of negotiation undermines the moral content and force of the substantive criminal law. *See* Langbein, *Torture and Plea Bargaining,* 58 PUB. INTEREST 43, 55-56 (1980).

adjudication does not demonstrate that plea bargaining promotes substantive criminal law objectives better than trial adjudication.

One can, however, defend the crime control model's preference for negotiated settlements of guilt without relying on its fictitious concept of "factual guilt." A crime control advocate can concede that substantive guilt requires a procedural process that morally evaluates the defendant's conduct but insist that negotiated compromises of the dispute perform this function. Both the prosecutor and the defense counsel must assess the moral significance of the facts in order to predict the jury's likely evaluation of the defendant's moral culpability. Evaluations of the defendant's degree of culpability will influence the prosecutor's selection of the charge and the sentencing disposition to which the parties agree.

One obvious response to this claim is to dispute its assumption that the parties' evaluation of the defendant's degree of culpability plays a significant role in shaping the ultimate bargain. Negotiated compromises concerning the charging decision[183] or sentencing "recommendation"[184] often reflect and promote institutional, financial, and tactical considerations[185] that have little bearing on what the defendant did, or his culpability in doing it. Consequently, negotiated settlements may frustrate the substantive criminal law's punishment goals by exaggerating the effect of the parties' tactical choices upon appropriate sentencing decisions.[186]

But, let us dismiss these practical objections for a moment and imagine a procedural system without these institutional defects. In our ideal system, defense counsel has the resources, financial incentive, and inclination to make an adequate investigation of potential defenses. Moreover, the discovery rules of our ideal system provide counsel with sufficient information about the strength of the prosecution's case to make an informed judgment about the likely outcome at trial. Since we are engaging in fantasy,[187] let us also assume that guilty pleas in our ideal system approximate trial outcomes in terms of their results except that the defendant who pleads guilty gets a minor sentencing

---

183. The absence of any effective limits on prosecutorial discretion in filing charges permits the prosecutor to enhance the government's plea bargaining position by charging the defendant with more serious crimes than the facts in a particular case warrant. Prosecutorial overcharging is also encouraged by the rule that the defendant cannot be convicted at trial for more serious charges than those contained in the formal accusation. See generally L. WEINREB, DENIAL OF JUSTICE: CRIMINAL PROCESS IN THE UNITED STATES 57-58 (1977); Alschuler, The Prosecutor's Role in Plea Bargaining, 36 U. CHI. L. REV. 50 (1968).

184. See generally M. MILLER, W. MCDONALD & J. CRAMER, PLEA-BARGAINING IN THE UNITED STATES (1978). For a vivid example of how negotiating tactics may distort the ultimate sentencing outcome, see Bordenkircher v. Hayes, 434 U.S. 357 (1978), and infra note 186.

185. See Arenella, Reforming the Federal Grand Jury, supra note 95, at 508-12.

186. See, e.g., Bordenkircher v. Hayes, 434 U.S. 357 (1978). After charging the defendant with uttering a forged check for $88 and offering a five-year sentencing recommendation to induce a plea, the prosecutor made good on his threat to charge the defendant under a habitual offender's statute authorizing life imprisonment when the defendant rejected the prosecutor's initial offer. Id. at 358-59. Although the prosecutor thought five years was an appropriate sentence for the original charge, the Burger Court found that the defendant's life imprisonment sentence for insisting on his right to trial did not violate the due process clause. Id. at 363-64. As Justice Stewart observed, "While confronting a defendant with the risk of more severe punishment clearly may have a 'discouraging effect' on the defendant's assertion of his trial rights, the imposition of these difficult choices [is] an inevitable—and permissible—attribute of any legitimate system which tolerates and encourages guilty pleas." Id.

187. See Arenella, Reforming the Federal Grand Jury, supra note 95, at 508-12.

concession for saving some of the state's scarce resources. Does the *process* of negotiation where the parties settle the dispute themselves promote the substantive criminal law's goals as well as the *process* of adjudication where a disinterested third party has the authority to make a binding decision? Which type of dispute-resolution process best reflects the values and goals of the substantive criminal law?

If criminal law's objective were simply to maximize deterrence of criminal conduct with minimal allocative inefficiency, one could defend negotiation as an appropriate dispute-resolution mechanism. Indeed, Professor Easterbrook offers just such a defense.[188] He views plea bargaining as a necessary element of a well-functioning market system that is constantly striving to set the optimal price of crime.[189] This price will depend upon such variables as the frequency of the offense, the rate of apprehension, and the cost and probability of conviction. Since these factors are constantly changing, Easterbrook argues that we need a system that is sufficiently flexible to adjust the price of crime over time in reponse to changing conditions.[190] Having assumed that prosecutors usually try to maximize the deterrence available from their resources, Easterbrook concludes that relatively unregulated prosecutorial discretion and plea bargaining practices are necessary if the market system is to set the optimal price of crime.[191]

Viewing criminal procedure as a market system may[192] justify plea bargaining if one accepts Easterbrook's and the crime control model's assumption that the substantive criminal law's primary objective is to promote deterrence with minimal allocative inefficiency. But, this market-system justification for plea bargaining ignores the criminal law's moral content and oversimplifies its punishment goals. American criminal law imposes suffering and stigma on the defendant, at least in part, because of a societal judgment that the defendant deserves such treatment.[193] Moreover, the criminal law's moral content deliberately limits the state's capacity to deter future criminal acts. We do not

---

188. Easterbrook, *supra* note 181.

189. *Id.* at 308-09.

190. *Id.* at 296.

191. *Id.*

192. Of course, one may challenge Easterbrook's description of our criminal process as a market system by pointing out instances in which the system does not produce deterrence with minimal allocative inefficiencies. Easterbrook himself concedes the possibility of "market-failures." *Id.* at 300. For example, prosecutors may not always try to "maximize the deterrence available from" their budgets. *Id.* But, he insists that any systematic attempt to regulate the parties' conduct will impair the market's capacity to set the optimal price of crime efficiently on a case-by-case basis. Finally, he argues that the worst market-failures can be remedied by judicial invalidation of unconscionable contracts. *See, e.g.,* Santobello v. New York, 404 U.S. 257, 262 (1971) (if prosecutor fails to live up to his side of bargain, court may invalidate the agreement for failure of consideration).

I believe that "market-failures" occur far more frequently than Easterbrook recognizes. As Professor Schulhofer observed in a conversation with the author, Easterbrook fails to consider how the legislature's refusal to fund sufficient prison space may impair the prosecutor's ability to set the optimal price of crime on a case-by-case basis. Nor does he consider how the legislature's refusal to provide sufficient financial remuneration for appointed defense counsel may impair the system's efficiency. Indeed, looking at criminal procedure as a market system is useful to the extent that it highlights major structural defects in the market that may prevent it from functioning in a manner that maximizes deterrence with minimum allocative inefficiencies.

193. *See supra* text accompanying notes 82-86.

criminalize the blameless offender who commits dangerous acts,[194] and the blameworthy offender's degree of punishment does not rest solely on how much punishment will efficiently serve incapacitation or general deterrence objectives.[195] The offender's moral culpability not only justifies the state's use of him as a means to promote these objectives, it provides a ceiling on the severity of punishment that can be imposed to maximize society's future welfare.[196]

Plea bargaining undercuts these distinctive moral aspects of the criminal law. First, negotiated dispute resolution "privatizes"[197] the dispute by empowering the parties themselves to resolve it without any significant involvement by either the public or the courts. Second, negotiated settlements permit the parties to resolve questions concerning the appropriate degree of liability that should attach to the defendant's acts. Such party compromises destroy any notion that an objective societal determination of moral guilt has been made.[198] Worse, negotiation dilutes the moral force of the criminal sanction by treating questions concerning the offender's just deserts as a negotiating chip whose value lies primarily in how it affects the parties' rational adjustment of litigation risks.[199] Consequently, plea bargaining may distort the legislature's labeling of offenses and frustrate its sentencing objectives. Finally, the negotiation process undermines the moral legitimacy of the system in both the defendant's and public's eyes.[200]

In contrast, an adjudicatory process reflects the values that the substantive criminal law is trying to promote. It reinforces the moral content of substantive guilt by forcing the state to offer compelling proof of the defendant's guilt to a disinterested third party in a public forum. Regardless of whether the adjudicatory mechanism uses inquisitorial or adversarial procedures, it provides a process that has its own moral-educative effect on both defendants and the public. A public trial, if fairly conducted, sends its own message about dignity, fairness, and justice that contributes to the moral force of the criminal sanction.[201] Finally, independent adjudication promotes the criminal law's punishment goals by assuring that an objective social determination of the actor's just deserts will be made by either a community body or by a judicial official before the state is given the right to use the defendant as a means to promote society's future welfare. Thus, the substantive criminal law's moral content and punishment goals require a procedural process that provides some form of independent adjudication for those defendants who wish to contest their culpability.[202]

---

194. *See generally* Arenella, *Reflections*, *supra* note 171; Arenella, Book Review, *supra* note 171.

195. *See* Solem v. Helm, 103 S. Ct. 3001, 3010-11 (1983).

196. *Id.*

197. Admittedly the prosecutor represents the state, but I do not share Easterbrook's assumption of complete identification between the prosecutors' interests and those of the public.

198. *See* Alschuler, *supra* note 87, at 703-07.

199. *Id.* at 704-06.

200. *See* Alschuler, *supra* note 32, at 38 n.209 (discussing public perception of the moral legitimacy of the system).

201. *See* Richmond Newspapers, Inc. v. Virginia, 448 U.S. 555, 584 (1980) (absent some compelling necessity justifying closure, public must have access to criminal trials, even when both prosecution and defense have requested that trial be closed).

202. Alschuler, *supra* note 87, at 705. Indeed, a powerful argument can be made for the proposition

Of course, establishing that the process of adjudication reflects and promotes substantive criminal law goals better than negotiated settlements does not demonstrate that *adversarial* guilt adjudication serves these goals better than negotiated settlements in a world of scarce resources. Many actors in the legal system who espouse due process values have begrudgingly accepted plea bargaining as a "necessary evil." They argue that our system must rely on plea bargaining to resolve most disputes because we cannot afford to provide criminal trials to all defendants who wish to contest their culpability. The conventional wisdom is that our system "can offer a trial to all only if few accept the offer."[203]

The "necessary evil" defense of plea bargaining reveals some fundamental flaws in our reconstructed due process model. The model's Achilles' heel is its failure to offer a practical vision of how to implement procedure's independent functions. For example, we have seen that criminal procedure must efficiently distribute the criminal justice system's scarce resources so that the system can process a high volume of cases from arrest to conviction. However, due process ideology equates "maximal efficiency" with "maximal tyranny."[204] Such rhetoric may have an appealing ring, but it completely ignores the system's resource constraints.

Moreover, due process ideology's preoccupation with potential abuses of executive power produces a truncated vision of the system's fair process norms. Since due process ideology relies on the availability of judicial review before and after conviction to protect those fair process norms that check executive power, the model's demand for a "timely" and "final" resolution of the dispute "is . . . very low."[205] "Timeliness" and "finality," however, are themselves fair process norms that criminal procedure must protect. Protracted litigation may impair both the reliability of the process' outcome and the substantive criminal law's sentencing objectives.[206] Delay may also produce unwarranted pretrial deprivations of liberty. Apart from their impact on the system's re-

---

that some abbreviated form of independent adjudication should occur in those cases in which the defendant freely confesses his guilt. *See* Langbein, *Land Without Plea-Bargaining—How the Germans Do It*, 78 MICH. L. REV. 204, 218-22 (1979).

Of course, one might argue that defendants who choose to plead guilty in order to secure some sentencing concession do not "wish" to contest their culpability. This argument might have some force in a system that does not deliberately impose substantially increased sentences on those defendants who exercise their constitutional right to trial. Ours is not such a system. Even if one agrees with Easterbrook that such sentencing differentials between plea and trial convictions are rationally efficient, their efficiency does not resolve the normative question of whether it is appropriate to view constitutional rights in economic terms as something that the individual can sell for some benefit. Efficiency analysis cannot answer the normative question involved in assessing what is "coercion" or what burdens the state may impose on an individual for exercising a "right."

The more troubling question is whether one can defend plea bargaining as an appropriate mechanism for vindicating substantive criminal law goals in a system that does not significantly penalize individuals for exercising their constitutional rights. In other words, if the state did not coerce individuals into pleading guilty, and if competent defense counsel had the resources, information, and inclination to investigate each case and make an intelligent evaluation of the trial's likely outcome, would it serve any useful purpose to require an independent, albeit abbreviated, adjudication of guilt? My own tentative answer is that the process of negotiation still conveys the wrong symbolic message about the distinctive nature of the criminal sanction.

203. L. WEINREB, *supra* note 123, at 82.
204. H. PACKER, *supra* note 19, at 166.
205. *Id.* at 164.
206. *See* Barker v. Wingo, 407 U.S. 514, 519-23 (1972).

sults, "timeliness" and "finality" are fair process values that contribute to the system's capacity to resolve disputes in an authoritative manner. As Professor Summers pointed out, "a dispute-settling process that is always subject to 'reruns' of the same issues is deficient as a process."[207]

These defects may not have destroyed the due process model's utility at an earlier period of our history when criminal trials were fairly simple and expeditious affairs that gave most defendants their "day" in court.[208] But the modern adversarial jury trial is far too complex and time-consuming to be used as the system's routine method for dispute resolution. Unless we allocate more resources to the judicial system and reform trial procedures to make them more efficient and speedy, the due process model's full promise will rarely be realized. Obviously, our criminal justice system has taken a different route. Instead of allocating more resources and streamlining modern trial procedures, it has encouraged the development of an alternative dispute-resolution method, plea bargaining, which takes speed, efficiency, and finality concerns very seriously.

The interesting question is why our criminal justice system has made this particular choice. If many of the legal actors in our system actually share the due process model's preference for an independent adjudication of guilt, why have they accepted, albeit reluctantly, plea bargaining as our system's primary dispute-resolution mechanism? Their answer, of course, is that they have no real choice: plea bargaining is "evil" but "necessary" because our society cannot afford to provide adversarial guilt adjudication in all cases in which the defendant wishes to challenge his culpability. Although they do not explicitly endorse crime control values, they are "realists" who recognize the "facts of life."

Where do these "facts" come from? Most prosecutors insist they could not do their jobs without plea bargaining. Understaffed Public Defender organizations agree. Chief Justice Burger claims that even a ten percent decline in convictions produced by plea bargaining would double the number of trials held in this country.[209] Scholars repeat such misleading statistics[210] to support their conclusion that society cannot afford to abolish plea bargaining.[211] Slowly but surely, the crime control advocate's original claim that our system's survival depends upon plea bargaining becomes conventional wisdom.

It is beyond the scope of this article to challenge these "facts of life." Professor Alschuler has already done so.[212] In his most recent article on plea bargaining, he suggests that our system "could provide three-day jury trials to all

---

207. Summers, *supra* note 91, at 27.
208. *See* Langbein, *Shaping the Eighteenth-Century Criminal Trial: A View from the Ryder Sources*, 50 U. CHI. L. REV. 1, 115 (1983).
209. Burger, *The State of the Judiciary*, 56 A.B.A. J. 929, 931 (1970).
210. As Professor Alschuler points out, Chief Justice Burger's statistics are misleading in several respects. For example, they ignore the transaction costs of plea bargaining that would be eliminated by its abolition. *See* Alschuler, *Implementing the Criminal Defendant's Right to Trial: Alternatives to the Plea-Bargaining System*, 50 U. CHI. L. REV. 931, 938 (1983) [hereinafter cited as Alschuler, *Right to Trial*].
211. I confess to being one of those commentators who have glibly repeated such "facts." *See* Arenella, *Reforming the Federal Grand Jury*, *supra* note 95, at 524.
212. Alschuler, *Right to Trial, supra* note 210.

felony defendants who reach the trial stage by adding no more than $850 million to annual criminal justice expenditures";[213] an amount that is "less than what the Law Enforcement Assistance Administration recently spent annually on improving state criminal justice."[214] Eleven years earlier, a national study group concluded that "[t]he basic problem is not financial; the cost of a model system of criminal justice is easily within the means of the American people."[215] Of course, we may choose not to spend the necessary resources to implement the due process model's vision. The decision to allocate more of our scarce resources to the criminal justice system rests ultimately on a normative value judgment about whether the benefits of protecting due process values in all cases outweigh the costs to society.

The "necessary evil" defense of plea bargaining skirts this normative decision by falsely assuming that our society could not possibly pay for streamlined trials in most cases. This defense of plea bargaining is particularly powerful because it denies the existence of any real choice to due process advocates who might push for reform if they thought it were feasible. Instead of seeing plea bargaining as a legally contingent phenomenon that could be changed, they view it as an inevitable feature of the criminal justice system that they must begrudgingly accept.

Crime control ideology contributes to this defense of plea bargaining by affecting our vision of the "evil" that is "necessary" when we accept plea bargaining as our primary dispute-resolution mechanism. By encouraging the notion that guilt is essentially a factual probability judgment, crime control ideology obscures the nature and significance of the substantive criminal law values that are jeopardized by our plea bargaining system. There is considerable irony here. For many, plea bargaining's major appeal is its hostility to those fair process norms, like the fourth amendment exclusionary rule, that impair the system's capacity to reliably determine substantive guilt. By encouraging negotiated settlements, the crime control model dilutes[216] the impact of these substantive guilt-defeating norms. Concededly, in such cases, it is accurate to say that the crime control model partially serves substantive criminal law goals because it applies criminal sanctions to morally culpable offenders. But those who defend plea bargaining as a necessary "evil" fail to appreciate that this "benefit" of negotiated settlements is outweighed by the many ways in which our present plea bargaining system frustrates substantive criminal law policies.

The hidden costs of crime control ideology extend beyond its impairment of substantive criminal law goals. Crime control ideology also offers a radically different vision of how American criminal procedure should perform its independent functions.

---

213. *Id.* at 936. I suspect that Alschuler's $850 million figure underestimates the necessary increased expenditure, but I agree with his conclusion that our society could afford to implement the due process model if trial procedures were streamlined.

214. *Id.* at 948.

215. RESEARCH AND POLICY COMMITTEE OF THE COMMITTEE FOR ECONOMIC DEVELOPMENT, REDUCING CRIME AND ASSURING JUSTICE 16 (1972).

216. *See supra* notes 137 & 155.

2.   Institutional Competency and Power-Allocation Judgments

Criminal procedure must allocate power in a manner that implements the system's judgments about which state officials are best suited to investigate, charge, adjudicate, and sentence. Since the due process and crime control models make different judgments about institutional competency, they allocate power quite differently.

Due process ideology views executive power with suspicion. Reflecting a basic theme in liberal political theory, it regulates governmental power in part by diffusing it. Investigatory, adjudicatory, and sentencing powers are given to different legal actors in order to provide a system of checks and balances. The model's requirement of an independent adjudication of guilt preserves its distribution of power by confining law enforcement officials to the role of investigation, apprehension, and accusation. It also reinforces the legislature's selection of the appropriate sentencing authority by preventing the prosecution from controlling the sentencing disposition through a negotiated bargain.

Since due process ideology mistrusts executive power, it allocates considerable power to the judiciary and the community to review the executive's decisions. Judicial power is necessary to vindicate the system's fair process norms. Lay adjudication gives the community's surrogate an opportunity to review the legislature's criminalization decisions and the prosecutor's charging decision when it makes its own independent moral culpability judgment. By granting the community considerable adjudicatory power, the due process model reinforces the political value judgment that the disposition of society's most serious sanction should not be left exclusively in the hands of legal professionals.

Crime control ideology expresses a basic faith in the decentralized exercise of power by criminal justice officials. Consequently, the crime control model dramatically shifts the allocation of power in our criminal justice system. First, it severely limits the community's power by confining lay participation in most cases to the grand jury: an ex parte proceeding dominated by the prosecutor.[217] Second, it enhances prosecutorial power by deregulating it. The crime control model must create and validate considerable incentives to induce negotiated settlements in most cases. The model's major incentive is the sentencing differential between conviction after trial and conviction following a guilty plea. Efficient implementation of this incentive system rests on the prosecutor's untrammeled use of his charging and plea bargaining discretion. To get "the maximum deterrent punch out of whatever resources are committed to crime control,"[218] the prosecutor must be free to set the "optimal price"[219] of crime on a case-by-case basis without interference from the courts.[220]

---

217. *See* Arenella, *Reforming the Federal Grand Jury, supra* note 95, at 496-98.

218. Easterbrook, *supra* note 181, at 290.

219. Professor Easterbrook defines "optimal price" as the price which is "just high enough to require offenders to pay for all the harm their crimes inflict on the rest of us." *Id.* at 292.

220. In theory, the court is free to reject the prosecutor's sentencing recommendation. In practice, courts realize that frequent exercise of their prerogative would undermine the system's capacity to induce a high percentage of guilty pleas.

3. Legitimation: Articulating and Protecting Fair Process Norms

The due process and crime control models offer very different and truncated conceptions of the system's fair process norms. Since due process ideology mistrusts executive power, it emphasizes those fair process norms that limit state power over the individual and sleights those fair process norms such as "timeliness" and "finality" that may limit the court's ability to regulate executive conduct. Procedural safeguards like the privilege against self-incrimination and the proscription against unreasonable searches and seizures take center stage in the due process model because they protect the integrity of the process. Vindication of these process norms at the expense of reliable guilt-determination reflects the model's normative claim that criminal procedure should promote independent goals that may impair its guilt-determination function.

In contrast, crime control ideology suggests that criminal procedure should function exclusively to punish the guilty. It values fair process norms primarily for their instrumental tendency to promote good "results"—the conviction of the guilty in a manner that promotes deterrence with minimal allocative inefficiency. This result-oriented instrumental view of procedure's fair process norms helps promote the model's deregulation of prosecutorial power before conviction. Since crime control ideology trusts the prosecutor to use her charging discretion wisely and efficiently, it rejects procedures that would regulate her discretion because they would impair the system's efficiency.

For example, crime control ideology *justifies* the rubberstamp quality of most grand jury screening. A truly independent grand jury would serve no procedural function under the crime control model because it would impair the prosecutor's capacity to allocate scarce resources efficiently. To "market" ideologues like Professor Easterbrook, the grand jury

> is a procedure-free body because procedural strings on prosecutorial discretion are costly but serve no function. The incentives of the prosecutor may be imperfect, but grand jurors are responsible to no one at all and lack the information needed to make intelligent comparative decisions about who should be prosecuted.[221]

Of course, if fair process norms also functioned to protect other values such as meaningful community participation in the process and community review of executive power, one might take the grand jury's role and defects a little more seriously than does Easterbrook.[222]

Crime control ideology's limited vision of procedure's fair process norms also enhances executive power by weakening the justification for factual guilt-defeating process norms like the fourth amendment's exclusionary rule and the privilege against self-incrimination. Crime control ideology views these individual rights from a utilitarian perspective that defines their content in light of their functional impact on society's capacity to promote social control. This consequentialist perspective encourages the courts to balance the individual's interests against competing public policy considerations before recognizing a

---

221. Easterbrook, *supra* note 181, at 308.
222. *See* Arenella, *Reforming the State Grand Jury System, supra* note 95, at 7-9.

right or fashioning a remedy for its violation.[223] Crime control ideology views these individual rights not as "defensive shields," but as "ingredients of public policy"[224] that are recognized and protected only if they contribute, on balance, to society's general welfare.

Crime control ideology's consequentialist perspective also explains its *positive* vision of what constitutes a fair process before conviction. The crime control model must articulate fair process norms that provide some assurance to the community that defendants who plead guilty have in fact engaged in criminal conduct. Thus, the model provides for a symbolic public ritual, a plea hearing, at which the defendant usually confesses his guilt. Moreover, the court must satisfy itself that a "factual basis" for the plea exists and that no "improper" inducements or "threats" have "coerced" the defendant into confessing his guilt.[225]

Crime control ideology justifies the fairness of the negotiation process preceding the plea hearing by relying on contractual and adversarial fair process norms. Evidence of these ideological justifications can be found in Supreme Court references to the parties' "equal bargaining power"[226] and "mutuality of advantage."[227] These contractual metaphors reflect the model's ideological image of criminal procedure as a market system in which the parties themselves settle the dispute efficiently by drawing up a contract.

The fairness of this contractual process rests on two related assumptions. First, crime control ideology relies heavily on the adversarial role of defense counsel as the vigorous advocate of her client's interests. The defendant is "free" to reject the prosecution's offer. Crime control ideology presumes that the defendant's acceptance of the offer upon the advice of competent counsel reflects the client's intelligent and voluntary choice.[228] Second, crime control ideology justifies the process by pointing out how its *outcome* benefits both parties. The state saves considerable expense and secures the conviction of a "factually guilty" defendant that it might not have obtained at trial. Defense counsel's participation in the process ensures that the bargain better serves the defendant's interests than going to trial.[229] In most cases, this "benefit" is the

223. I am not suggesting that a due process court would not engage in a balancing analysis of competing interests before interpreting the substantive scope of constitutional rights. It is impossible to avoid definitional balancing when a court interprets the substantive scope of vague language like "probable cause" and "compelled . . . to be a witness against himself." I am suggesting that the types of factors recognized as relevant to the inquiry, and the weight accorded them, will be influenced by the court's ideological preconceptions. For specific illustrations of this thesis, see *infra* text accompanying notes 297-309. *See also infra* notes 259, 287-88, & 311.
224. *See* Klare, *Labor Law as Ideology: Toward a New Historiography of Collective Bargaining Law*, 4 INDUS. REL. L.J. 450, 469 (1981) (describing two opposing strands of liberal theory of rights—defensive shields or ingredients of public policy).
225. *See* Arenella, *Reforming the Federal Grand Jury, supra* note 95, at 512-19.
226. *See* Bordenkircher v. Hayes, 434 U.S. 357, 362 (1978).
227. *See id.* at 363.
228. In *Bordenkircher* the Supreme Court stated: "Defendants advised by competent counsel and protected by other procedural safeguards are presumptively capable of intelligent choice in response to prosecutorial persuasion, and unlikely to be driven to false self-condemnation." *Id.* at 363 (citing Brady v. United States, 397 U.S. 742, 758 (1970)). *See also* McMann v. Richardson, 397 U.S. 759, 770-71 (1970).
229. *See* McMann v. Richardson, 397 U.S. at 769-71.

sentencing differential between conviction after a guilty plea and conviction after trial.

To summarize: Our reconstructed crime control model does more than simply describe how the system determines guilt in most cases. Nor can it be reduced to a restatement of *any* system's proclivity to avoid the rigorous demands of its formal process by fashioning more speedy, efficient, and informal methods of resolving state-citizen disputes. A comparison of how the models implement criminal procedure's functions reveals two competing descriptions of the criminal justice system's legal ideology. Our reconstructed models describe a set of values, beliefs, and ideas about the functions of American criminal procedure that is held by legal actors and that is reflected in the system's institutions and practices. Moreover, both ideologies serve a prescriptive function. Legal actors use the models' values to make conflicting normative claims about the validity and content of specific procedural functions and the relative weight that should be attached to such functions when they conflict with each other. Each model offers an ideological image of how our criminal justice system should function.

These competing visions of criminal procedure's functions are useful to the extent that they succeed in explaining how a particular legal ideology may validate the system's goals, influence its legal rules, affect its actual practices,[230] or color the community's perception of those practices.[231] Of course,

---

230. The dynamic between legal ideology and legal practices cannot be reduced to a linear model that focuses solely on the question of how ideology influences Supreme Court doctrine that in turn may alter existing practices. Ideology is a form of consciousness that may affect the practices of *legal actors* regardless of doctrinal developments. For example, ideological preconceptions influence legal actors' "empirical" perceptions of the system's practices as well as the actors' evaluation of their desirability. *See supra* text accompanying note 203 (discussing defense of plea bargaining as a necessary evil).

Consequently, one cannot measure the impact of the Warren Court's due process revolution on the system's daily performance by simply examining how much the Court's doctrines altered existing legal practices. One must also consider the extent to which due process norms may have stimulated legislative reforms and influenced the professional training and norm structure of police, prosecutors, defense attorneys, lower court judges, and law students. For example, Professor Israel suggests that the Warren Court's

> general emphasis on protecting the rights of the individual contributed substantially to various reforms in the criminal justice process that have benefited the accused. For example, the decisions of the Warren Court, combined with the pressures resulting from racial confrontations, called our attention to the need for a higher degree of police professionalism. . . . Decisions of the Warren Court also contributed, I believe, to a higher degree of professionalism among lawyers in the criminal justice field. Those decisions presented criminal law as an area of intellectual and social challenge, and this, in turn, induced more able lawyers to enter that field, particularly in the offices of public defenders and prosecuting attorneys.

Israel, *supra* note 6, at 1424 n.438. All of these professional, institutional, and attitudinal changes had an impact on the system's legal actors and practices.

Similarly, one would have to examine how the Burger Court's crime control ideology has affected legal actors' norms and practices to measure that Court's impact on the criminal justice system's performance. My own impression is that the Burger Court's ideology reflects and confirms a belief system that many legal actors already possess. I agree with Professor Amsterdam's observation that:

> To a mind-staggering extent—to an extent that conservatives and liberals alike who are not criminal trial lawyers simply cannot conceive—the entire system of criminal justice below the level of the Supreme Court of the United States is solidly massed against the criminal suspect. Only a few appellate judges can throw off the fetters of their middle-class backgrounds—the dimly remembered, friendly face of the school crossing guard, their fear of a crowd of "toughs," their attitudes engendered as lawyers before their elevation to the bench, by years of service as prosecutors or as private lawyers for honest, respectable business clients—and iden-

neither model can be used to predict how the Supreme Court will fashion legal

tify with the criminal suspect instead of with the policeman or with the putative victim of the suspect's theft, mugging, rape, or murder. Trial judges still more, and magistrates beyond belief, are functionally and psychologically allied with the police, their co-workers in the unending and scarifying work of bringing criminals to book.

Amsterdam, *supra* note 33, at 792. If this observation is correct, it provides a partial explanation for why the Warren Court's successes were so modest. It also suggests that the Burger Court's ideology will not change existing legal practices as much as provide a justification for them.

231. One critical legal studies commentator has explained the discrepancy between our system's due process ideals and its day-to-day functioning by arguing that due process ideology is a form of false consciousness that legitimates an oppressive criminal justice system. David Rudovsky argues that

[t]he most significant social impact of the constitutional principles of due process and equal protection is not their effect on crime, which is minimal or non-existent, or even the basic fairness they can and do provide in some circumstances. Rather, it is the appearance of fairness they lend the criminal justice system, as well as their legitimation of a class- and race-biased judicial process. Indeed, a critical view of each aspect of the criminal justice system, including the criminalization of conduct, police investigation, arrest, prosecution, and incarceration, reveals the very significant degree to which these protections are unrealized promises.

Rudovsky, *supra* note 159, at 242-43.

According to critical legal theorists, legal ideology may promote false consciousness by incorporating false beliefs about the system's values, processes, and purposes. The beliefs may be false because the ideology relies on inaccurate or insufficient information (e.g., our criminal justice system is fair because most defendants get their day in court). More importantly, ideology may encourage "epistemic" mistakes by falsely characterizing a normative value judgment as a factual one (e.g., value preference for adversarial guilt adjudication transformed into empirical statement that such a procedure determines guilt more accurately than inquisitorial trials). Such epistemic mistakes contribute to false consciousness by encouraging individuals to see a legally contingent phenomenon that could be changed—our present unduly complex and time-consuming trial procedure—as a necessary and inevitable fact that the individual must accept. Like individual pathology, legal ideology may also induce false preferences or false values, (e.g., state and individual interests are irreconcilable, criminals are enemies of the state who must be stigmatized and exiled from the community; *see generally* Griffiths, *supra* note 3), that prevent individuals from either seeing or acting in their "true interests."

To demonstrate due process ideology's false consciousness, a critical legal theorist must establish that the ideology either incorporates false beliefs, has a "tainted origin," or functions in a reprehensible manner by inducing the community's acceptance of and obedience to an unjust system. It is at this juncture that critical legal theory's critique becomes opaque. The few critical legal scholars who have examined our criminal justice system have failed to recognize the possibility that two distinct legal ideologies may be used to "legitimate" our criminal justice system.

For example, in his brilliant essay on ideology in criminal procedure, John Griffiths does not recognize that the crime control model conveys a distinct ideological vision of the functions served by criminal procedure that differs substantially from the due process model. Griffiths, *supra* note 3, at 362 n.14. Instead, he views the two models as simple restatements of the competing values underlying our adversarial "Battle Model" of criminal procedure. *Id.* at 367-68. Consequently, some of his criticisms of the "Battle Model's" false consciousness (e.g., failure to consider how procedure must be designed to promote substantive criminal law goals, failure to value process norms for their symbolic and educational effect, failure to treat the guilty as well as the innocent with dignity and respect), *id.* at 376-91, are actually examples of crime control ideology's preconceptions concerning criminal procedure's functions.

Rudovsky, on the other hand, appears to assume that the realization of many due process norms would produce a criminal justice system worthy of community respect. Rudovsky's thesis is that due process ideology *functions* in a reprehensible manner by legitimating a class- and race-biased criminal justice system. Rudovsky, *supra* note 159, at 242-43. His critique of due process ideology begs several important questions. First, he does not explain why any *legal* ideology would have a more powerful effect on citizens' perceptions of the system's fairness than their own political and moral belief systems. Second, he ignores the fact that the Warren Court's due process ideology reached the public through media and political filters that emphasized those fair process norms restricting police powers. This point raises another problem with Rudovsky's thesis—the public was hostile to those due process norms that impaired effective crime control. At a time of escalating crime rates and public anxiety about a breakdown in law and order, the Warren Court's due process ideology may not have constituted a very effective legitimation device in the public's eyes. Once we distinguish between due process and crime

doctrine in a particular case. Many of the Warren and Burger Court Justices cannot be fairly characterized as "due process" or "crime control" ideologues. Moreover, the political and historical context in which the cases arise may force even a "due process" or "crime control" Justice to join a decision that does not reflect his or her own ideological preconceptions about how our system should function. Finally, stare decisis, statutory and constitutional language, and the need to reach a consensus to decide a particular case (even if no coherent rationale has been developed) also influence doctrinal development.[232] All of these factors temper the value of ideological explanations for Supreme Court decisionmaking.

Nevertheless, these two reconstructed models are useful because they provide a more coherent analytical framework to evaluate judicial trends in criminal procedure. Instead of asking whether the Burger Court has protected individual rights or whether the Warren Court enhanced police powers, these models invite us to focus on how the two Courts' decisions have defined and accomodated criminal procedure's competing functions. Presumably, a Court sympathetic to crime control values would identify and weigh these conflicting functions quite differently than would a "due process" Court. Part IV tests that thesis.

IV. EVALUATING JUDICIAL TRENDS IN CRIMINAL PROCEDURE

One can readily see why the Burger Court has not adopted a pure "guilt or innocence" model. American criminal procedure serves independent functions—distribution of power, allocation of scarce resources, and protection of fair process norms—that would prevent any Court from "establishing a process focusing on individualized guilt and innocence."[233] Consequently, demonstrating that the Burger Court has occasionally vindicated values that impaired the system's capacity to reach accurate results in individual cases is not very illuminating.

To compare the two Courts' approaches, one must examine whether the Warren and Burger Courts recognized these other procedural functions, how they implemented them, and what relative weight the two Courts gave them when they conflicted with each other or with the system's capacity to determine guilt. Such a comparison would require a detailed and comprehensive review of both Courts' criminal procedure decisions. This section does not attempt such a Herculean task. Instead, it identifies several distinctive programmatic and doctrinal themes[234] that a Court sympathetic to due process or crime control values might pursue. Both the text and the footnotes to this

control value systems as distinct ideologies, one could argue that Rudovsky has attacked the wrong target. In some respects, the Burger Court's crime control ideology offers a far more convincing example of legal ideology that attempts to legitimate existing legal practices by appealing to values that the public shares and understands.

232. *See* Easterbrook, *Ways of Criticizing the Court*, 95 HARV. L. REV. 802, 821-22 (1982).

233. Seidman, *supra* note 8, at 445.

234. Many of the specific programmatic and doctrinal themes discussed in this section are not inherent fixtures of either model. They are strategies that a Court might adopt in a particular historical/political context to promote its vision of how the criminal process should function.

section evaluate the extent to which Warren and Burger Court decisions actually reflect and promote these themes.

A. PROMOTING OR DISCOURAGING AN INDEPENDENT ADJUDICATION OF GUILT

The due process model relies heavily on the trial's adversarial adjudication of guilt to promote its vision of criminal procedure's functions.[235] Consequently, one would expect a due process court to reduce those systematic pressures that discourage defendants from exercising their right to trial adjudication.

Although Warren Court decisions reflected this due process theme, the Court's commitment to trial adjudication was tempered by its concern about an overburdened criminal justice system. The Court did attempt to reduce law enforcement pressures that discourage defendants from exercising their right to trial adjudication. Both *Miranda*[236] and *Massiah*[237] viewed the suspect's privilege against self-incrimination and the defendant's right to counsel as defensive shields that protect the accused from pressures to confess that might thwart the need for an independent adjudication of guilt.[238] Moreover, the Warren Court cast considerable doubt on the constitutionality of plea bargaining by repeatedly finding that the state could not penalize defendants for asserting their privilege against self-incrimination[239] or their right to trial.[240]

However, the Warren Court never used its penalty model to declare plea bargaining unconstitutional. Instead, it left this escape hatch open by ducking the question of plea bargaining's constitutionality.[241] Ironically, the Warren Court's due process revolution may have indirectly contributed to the systemic pressures favoring negotiated settlements because it occurred during a period when "the volume of criminal cases commonly doubled from one decade to the next, while judicial resources increased only slightly."[242] Granting defendants more rights and enhancing the procedural opportunities for their vindication increased defendants' bargaining power and the state's incentive to avoid

---

235. This undue reliance on the trial stage to ensure a fair process before conviction is a major defect of our accusatorial criminal justice system. *See* Arenella, *Reforming the Federal Grand Jury, supra* note 95, at 521-23.

236. Miranda v. Arizona, 384 U.S. 436 (1966).

237. Massiah v. United States, 377 U.S. 201 (1964).

238. *See infra* note 254.

239. In Griffin v. California, 380 U.S. 609 (1965), the Warren Court ruled that the privilege against self-incrimination protected a criminal defendant from being put to the choice of testifying at trial or having his silence used against him as evidence of guilt. *Id.* at 614. The Court found that the state's imposition of such a choice violated Griffin's privilege against self-incrimination by penalizing its exercise. *Id.* The Warren Court used this penalty rationale to invalidate state investigatory practices that automatically imposed serious or even moderate economic sanctions on individuals who refused to waive their privilege. *See, e.g.*, Gardener v. Broderick, 392 U.S. 273, 278-79 (1968); Garrity v. New Jersey, 385 U.S. 493, 497-98 (1967). If it had wished to do so, the Warren Court could have used this penalty model of fifth amendment compulsion to invalidate state practices that "penalized" the defendant's exercise of his privilege when he refused to plead guilty.

240. The Warren Court applied its view that state-imposed burdens on the exercise of constitutional rights are unconstitutional in United States v. Jackson, 390 U.S. 570, 583 (1968). In *Jackson* the Court invalidated a statutory scheme that potentially imposed a greater penalty (capital punishment) on defendants who exercised their right to jury trial than on defendants who pleaded guilty. *Id.* at 591.

241. *See infra* note 324 and accompanying text.

242. Alshuler, *supra* note 32, at 5.

trials and appeals that might decrease the rate of conviction.[243] Although the guilty plea rate did not dramatically increase during the Warren Court era, the Court's due process revolution may have forced prosecutors to give greater concessions simply to keep guilty plea rates constant.[244]

The Warren Court's ambiguous support of this due process theme is not suprising given the major defects of our reconstructed due process model. First, the model fails to give sufficient weight to speed, efficiency, and finality values. Second, the model's heavy dependence on adversarial guilt adjudication to allocate power, vindicate fair process norms, and determine guilt assures its ultimate failure unless significant additional resources are allocated to the judicial system and trial procedures are streamlined.[245] The Warren Court could neither allocate the resources nor make all of the structural changes needed to provide a more speedy and efficient form of independent adjudication. Thus, the Court could not, by itself, fully implement the model's vision of a fair criminal process.[246]

The crime control model actively discourages trial adjudication because it does not promote deterrence with minimal allocative inefficiency. Adjudicating guilt in most cases would impair its goals of speed, efficiency, and finality. It also would prevent prosecutors from setting the optimal price for crime on a case-by-case basis. Worse, trial adjudication would increase the number of factually guilty defendants who escaped criminal liability. Consequently, one would expect a Court sympathetic to crime control values to accept plea bargaining, not as a "necessary evil," but as a positive feature[247] of our criminal justice system.

Burger Court plea bargaining decisions reflect these crime control themes. The Court's ideological justifications for plea bargaining, the parties' "equal bargaining power" and "mutuality of advantage," embody the crime control model's view of criminal procedure as a market system in which the parties themselves efficiently settle the dispute.[248] At the doctrinal level, the Court has adopted a utilitarian view of the defendant's right to trial that balances the defendant's "interests" in asserting her right against crime control values that favor a more efficient, speedy, and final resolution of the dispute.[249] The Burger Court has used this balancing analysis to validate the state's deliberate imposition of significant burdens on the defendant's right to trial in order to induce negotiated settlements in most cases.[250]

---

243. *Id.* at 38.

244. *Id.* at 39-40.

245. Absent such reforms, the courts should provide greater protections of these due process norms in the pretrial screening process. *See generally* Arenella, *Reforming the Federal Grand Jury, supra* note 95, at 521-23, 529-34, 558-79.

246. The Warren Court can be faulted, however, for its failure to address effective assistance of counsel issues. The due process model's promise cannot be realized if defense counsel do not adequately represent their clients' interests.

247. *See* Santobello v. New York, 404 U.S. 257, 261 (1971) ("Disposition of charges after plea discussions is not only an essential part of the [criminal] process but a highly desirable part for many reasons.").

248. *See supra* note 226.

249. The Burger Court has frequently noted that the Constitution does not bar "every government-imposed choice in the criminal process that has the effect of discouraging the exercise of constitutional rights." Chaffin v. Stynchcombe, 412 U.S. 17, 30 (1973).

250. *See supra* note 186.

B. PROMOTING OR DISCOURAGING JUDICIAL REGULATION OF CRIMINAL JUSTICE OFFICIALS

1. Interpreting the substantive scope of regulatory fair process norms

Apart from the trial, the due process model relies on the judiciary to implement its vision of a fair criminal process. Judicial review provides the opportunity for interpretation and protection of those fair process norms that regulate the conduct of criminal justice officials. Thus, one would expect a due process court to increase the opportunities for effective review of official conduct.

Unlike its equivocal support of trial adjudication, the Warren Court's work strongly reflected this due process theme. The Court constitutionalized many aspects of criminal procedure.[251] It paid special attention to those constitutional process norms, like the fourth, fifth, and sixth amendments, that regulate the balance of power between the state and the accused before conviction. The Warren Court broadly interpreted the substantive scope of these process norms to enhance the opportunity for judicial regulation of law enforcement conduct.[252]

---

251. Using the selective incorporation doctrine, the Warren Court applied the following Bill of Rights safeguards contained in the fourth, fifth, sixth, and eighth amendments to the states: Mapp v. Ohio, 367 U.S. 643, 655-56 (1961) (fourth amendment exclusionary rule); Malloy v. Hogan, 378 U.S. 1, 6 (1964) (privilege against self-incrimination); Benton v. Maryland, 395 U.S. 784, 794 (1969) (ban against double jeopardy); Klopfer v. North Carolina, 386 U.S. 213, 222-23 (1967) (right to speedy trial); Duncan v. Louisiana, 391 U.S. 145, 149-50 (1968) (right to jury trial); Gideon v. Wainwright, 372 U.S. 335, 344-45 (1963) (right to appointed counsel for indigent defendants in felony prosecutions); Pointer v. Texas, 380 U.S. 400, 406 (1965) (right to confront witnesses); Washington v. Texas, 388 U.S. 14, 19 (1967) (right to compulsory process); Robinson v. California, 370 U.S. 660, 667 (1962) (ban against cruel and unusual punishment).

252. Professor Alschuler has suggested that the Warren Court's attempt to regulate police conduct through decisions like *Mapp* and *Miranda* "involved the Court in intense political controversy, but their immediate impact on the everyday administration of criminal justice was probably small." Alschuler, *supra* note 32, at 37 n.209. To support his claim, Alschuler cited a section of a book by Professor Jerome Skolnick that evaluates the exclusionary rule's impact on police behavior, J. SKOLNICK, JUSTICE WITHOUT TRIAL 223-43 (1966), and a Yale student note that evaluated *Miranda*'s impact on New Haven police interrogations conducted immediately after *Miranda* was decided, Note, *Interrogations In New Haven: The Impact of Miranda*, 76 YALE L.J. 1519 (1967).

Neither source fully supports Alschuler's speculation that the Court's decisions had little impact on police behavior. Skolnick pointed out several reasons why the exclusionary rule often fails to deter illegal police conduct that the police see as reasonable given their own norm structure. J. SKOLNICK, *supra*, at 224. Skolnick also insisted, however, that the exclusionary rule will affect police conduct "where prosecution is contemplated," especially in serious criminal cases. *Id.* at 224-25.

The Yale study found that *Miranda* warnings did not appear to impair the New Haven police's ability to elicit incriminating admissions from criminal suspects. Note, *supra*, at 1613. The authors offered several explanations for why the warnings had such little impact, including the manner in which they were given, the suspects' nervousness in a crisis situation, and their lack of knowledge about the effect of their cooperation. *Id.* at 1613-14. The note correctly concluded that the warnings by themselves cannot possibly eliminate the "inherently coercive atmosphere" of police custodial interrogation. *Id.* at 1613. The authors suggested that *Miranda*'s promise of putting the suspect on equal footing with the police can only be realized if suspects consult with counsel "before the police begin questioning." *Id.* at 1614-15.

Of course, such a requirement would be effective because it would drastically reduce the number of criminal suspects who would waive their *Miranda* rights. But, the Warren Court was not attempting to eliminate confessions in *Miranda*. As Yale Kamisar has pointed out, *Miranda* permits

the police to conduct "general on-the-scene questioning" even though the person questioned is both uninformed and unaware of his rights. It allows the police to question a person in his home or office, provided they do not restrict the person's freedom to terminate the meeting. . . . The Court might have held that the inherent pressures and anxieties produced by arrest and detention *and nothing more* are substantial enough to require neutralizing warn-

For example, the Court took a generous view of what constitutes a search or seizure regulated by the fourth amendment.[253] It provided an expansive definition of fifth amendment compulsion[254] to protect the accused from pressures to

---

ings. But it did not. Thus, . . . *Miranda* leaves them free to hear and act upon "volunteered" statements, even though the "volunteer" neither knows nor is advised of his rights.

Kamisar, *supra* note 1, at 66-67 (emphasis added).

   While the Court claimed that the warnings were necessary to eliminate the inherent coerciveness of police custodial interrogation, its objectives were far more modest and pragmatic. The warnings inform suspects of the scope of police authority over them. They give notice of "rights" that the suspect may assert. The warnings do not eliminate, but do reduce the police's decided advantage over criminal suspects. *See* Note, *supra*, at 1615. Finally, the *Miranda* decision reminded the police that there would be some judicial review of their interrogation techniques. *Id.*

   Viewed from this more modest perspective, the question of *Miranda*'s impact on police practices cannot be answered by looking at the results of police custodial interrogation. Instead, one must ask whether *Miranda* made the actual process fairer than it was before suspects were notified of their rights and given the option to terminate police custodial interrogation. The authors of the Yale note conceded that, if one measured *Miranda*'s impact by the degree to which it reduces the police's advantage over criminal suspects, *Miranda* "may succeed in that limited purpose." *Id.* at 1615.

   Skolnick's study of how legal norms influence police behavior and the Yale study of *Miranda*'s impact on police custodial interrogations actually reach similar conclusions about the effect of Warren Court decisions on police conduct. Both studies suggest that Warren Court decisions like *Mapp* and *Miranda* changed police behavior but not as dramatically as the Warren Court might have hoped. The Warren Court did not transform the day-to-day functioning of police investigations and interrogations, but its decisions did improve the fairness of the process.

   253. *See* Katz v. United States, 389 U.S. 347, 353 (1967). Several commentators have used *Katz* as an example of the Warren Court's willingness to protect law enforcement interests by constitutionalizing electronic surveillance. *See* Kamisar, *supra* note 1, at 64. But, a "victory" for the government cannot be equated with a crime control decision. *Katz* extended the scope of fourth amendment regulation by adding reasonable expectations of privacy to the list of interests protected by the amendment. 389 U.S. at 353. Indeed, *Katz* is an excellent example of the Warren Court's pragmatic approach to criminal procedure. It could have found that electronic surveillance was a type of search and seizure activity that was always unreasonable because of its indiscriminate and intrusive nature. Kamisar, *supra* note 1, at 64. The Court also might have adopted Justice Black's literalist approach that conversations were not "effects" that could be seized. *Katz*, 389 U.S. at 365-66 (Black, J., dissenting). Instead, the Court chose a middle ground by subjecting electronic eavesdropping to fourth amendment regulation.

   254. Several commentators have suggested that the Warren Court simply applied preexisting federal constitutional norms to new procedural contexts. *See* Seidman, *supra* note 8, at 440. This view understates the degree to which the Warren Court expanded the concept of fifth amendment compulsion. It may have been logical for the Court to apply the privilege against self-incrimination to the police station. However, the Court's generous interpretation of what constitutes fifth amendment compulsion in *Miranda* indicates that less pressure is needed to render a statement *compelled* under the privilege than is necessary to make a statement *involuntary* under the due process clause. *See* Arenella, *Reappraisal*, *supra* note 58, at 50-53.

   Moreover, the Warren Court extended fifth amendment protections to an individual's decision to remain silent. *See supra* note 239. The Court was quite willing to assume that a criminal suspect's silence constituted a proper invocation of the privilege. Having made this assumption, the Court invalidated state attempts to make evidentiary use of the individual's pretrial or trial silence. According to the Court, such evidentiary inferences penalized the individual for exercising his privilege. *See* Miranda v. Arizona, 384 U.S. 436, 468 n.37 (1966) ("It is impermissible to penalize an individual for exercising his fifth amendment privilege when he is under police custodial interrogation. The prosecution may not, therefore, use at trial the fact that he stood mute or claimed his privilege in the face of accusation."); Grunewald v. United States, 353 U.S. 391, 423-24 (1957) (unanimous Court used supervisory power to reverse federal conviction when defendant questioned at trial about his invocation of privilege before grand jury).

   The Warren Court's "penalty model" cases reflect three basic assumptions about the relationship between silence and the privilege against self-incrimination. First, they appear to assume that the privilege grants the individual a positive right of silence. Second, these cases suggest that this right to silence applies with equal strength in all procedural contexts in which the individual risks self-incrimination by responding to state inquiries. Finally, the penalty model condemns any state-imposed burden on the right's exercise, even if the burden imposed is not sufficiently severe to compel the individual immediately to give incriminating testimony against herself. Without explicitly saying so, the Warren Court's penalty model embraced a very broad view of fifth amendment compulsion by encompassing any state

confess that may thwart the need for an independent adjudication of guilt at trial. It applied the sixth amendment's right to counsel to early stages of the criminal prosecution where counsel could function, not only as an advocate, but as a defensive shield to prevent or witness improper police conduct.[255]

In contrast, crime control ideology trusts executive power and seeks to deregulate it. It values process norms primarily for their capacity to promote good results—the conviction of the factually guilty in a manner that maximizes deterrence and allocative efficiency. Thus, one would expect a crime control court to narrow the substantive scope of those process norms that impair the state's capacity to detect and punish criminal activity quickly and efficiently.

The Burger Court's treatment of fourth[256] and fifth amendment issues left unresolved by the Warren Court reflects this deregulatory theme. The Court has enhanced law enforcement's investigatory powers by narrowing the range of police actions that would qualify as a search[257] or seizure[258] regulated by

---

action that impairs the individual's "free choice to admit, to deny, or to refuse to answer," Lisenba v. California, 314 U.S. 219, 241 (1941), potentially incriminating state inquiries.

None of the penalty model's basic premises withstand close scrutiny. First, the privilege does not convey some indivisible right that merits equal protection from state impairment in all contexts. The privilege protects both substantive values (e.g., mental privacy, human dignity, and moral autonomy) and accusatorial process norms (e.g., fair state-individual balance of advantage, adversarial determination of guilt). *See* Arenella, *Reappraisal, supra* note 58, at 36-38. The degree to which these fifth amendment values are implicated by state-compelled choices depends upon two factors: Whether the state-imposed burden affects criminal or civil adjudication and the nature of the state's interest furthered by the burden. *See* Heldt, *The Conjurer's Circle: The Fifth Amendment Privilege In Civil Cases*, 91 YALE L.J. 1062, 1082-87 (1982). Second, neither the privilege's history nor language ("compelled to be a witness against himself") supports the penalty model's assumption that the privilege conveys a right to silence as an unqualified entitlement that the government must affirmatively protect. *See* California v. Byers, 402 U.S. 424, 427-31 (1971). Instead, the privilege prohibits the state from confronting individuals with choices that place undue pressure on their right to avoid compelled self-incrimination. What constitutes undue pressure must rest upon one's view of the underlying policies served by the privilege and the weight to be attached to the state's interests in gathering reliable information from its citizens. The Warren Court's absolutist approach begged all the critical questions involved in determining what constitutes fifth amendment compulsion by ignoring the need to consider these competing interests. *See infra* note 260 (evaluating Burger Court's treatment of fifth amendment compulsion).

255. *See* United States v. Wade, 388 U.S. 218, 236-37 (1967). Although Wade's lineup occurred after his indictment, the Court's rationale clearly applied to line-ups conducted prior to the filing of formal charges. *See* Kamisar, *supra* note 1, at 69. The Court concluded that counsel's presence was necessary because "it appears that there is grave potential for prejudice, intentional or not, in the pre-trial line-up, which [absent counsel's presence] may not be capable of reconstruction at trial." *Wade*, 388 U.S. at 236. Consequently, counsel's presence was needed to "*avert prejudice* and assure a meaningful confrontation at trial." *Id.* at 236 (emphasis added).

256. The Supreme Court decided nine search and seizure cases last term. Seven of those nine decisions reversed lower court decisions in the defendant's favor. Judge Charles Moylan characterized the government's record as seven victories and two ties because the Court upheld some of the government's contentions in Florida v. Royer, 103 S. Ct. 1319 (1983), and United States v. Place, 103 S. Ct. 2637 (1983). *See* 33 CRIM. L. REP. (BNA) 2408, 2409 (Aug. 17, 1983) (ABA panel discussion on search and seizure law; *see also infra* notes 258-59 (evaluating *Royer* and *Place*).

257. Although assumption of risk analysis begs the normative question involved in determining an individual's justifiable expectation of privacy, the Burger Court has used this rationale to support its conclusion that an individual has no "legitimate expectation of privacy" in information that he "voluntarily" exposes to private third parties. *See* United States v. Knotts, 103 S. Ct. 1081, 1085-87 (1983) (tracking public movement of chemical drum in car by monitoring signals from electronic beeper attached to drum not fourth amendment search); Smith v. Maryland, 442 U.S. 735, 742-45 (1979) (police use of a pen register to record numbers dialed from individual's home phone not fourth amendment search); United States v. Miller, 425 U.S. 435, 442-443 (1976) (no reasonable expectation of privacy in checks and deposit slips customer conveys to bank).

The *Knotts* case graphically illustrates how the Burger Court has narrowed *Katz*'s reasonable expectation of privacy test by using assumption of risk analysis. The Court simply assumed that the elec-

234   THE GEORGETOWN LAW JOURNAL   [Vol. 72:185

the fourth amendment. It also has expanded the range of police searches and
seizures that could be justified on the basis of reasonable suspicion instead of
probable cause.[259] Finally, the Court has narrowly defined the types of state-
imposed choices that constitute fifth amendment compulsion, thereby enhanc-

---

tronic beeper conveyed information that was voluntarily exposed to anyone wishing to engage in visual
surveillance of the car's public movements. *See Knotts,* 103 S. Ct. at 1085-86. Of course, if this were
true, the government would not need to rely on such tracking devices. Beepers are valuable investigatory tools because they convey information that the government could not otherwise obtain unless a
legion of agents lined all possible roads that the car might take. As Professor LaFave points out,

> The use of an electronic tracking device permits a much more extended and thorough surveil-
> lance of an individual than would otherwise be possible. Moreover, especially as this equip-
> ment becomes more sophisticated, less expensive, and more readily available, there is the risk
> that it will be utilized to carry out a volume of surveillance activity far beyond that which
> would otherwise be feasible with available manpower and resources. It is precisely this poten-
> tial for surveillance of such amplitude which merits the conclusion that the use of beepers
> must be subjected to some Fourth Amendment constraints.

LaFave, *Fourth Amendment Vagaries (of Improbable Cause, Imperceptible Plain View, Notorious Privacy, and Balancing Askew),* 74 J. CRIM. L. & CRIMINOLOGY — , — (Winter 1983) (forthcoming).
    Admittedly, the Warren Court also relied on assumption of risk analysis when it found no fourth
amendment violation in Hoffa v. United States, 385 U.S. 293 (1966). But, Hoffa did, in fact, choose to
trust his associate, a government informant. *Id.* at 302-03. It strains credulity to talk of the bank customer in *Miller* having any choice about exposing his checks to bank officials "unless he wants to avoid
taking part in the economic life of contemporary society." Kamisar, *supra* note 1, at 278 n.73. If the
Burger Court had consistently applied this mode of analysis to all information that citizens "voluntarily" exposed to other private parties, the fourth amendment would only protect the informational
privacy interests of hermits. *See generally* Grano, *Foreword—Perplexing Questions about Three Basic
Fourth Amendment Issues: Fourth Amendment Activity, Probable Cause, and the Warrant Requirement,*
69 J. CRIM. L. & CRIMINOLOGY 425, 428-44 (1978).
    The Burger Court also has used the standing doctrine to narrow the scope of police investigatory
actions that defendants can challenge as illegal searches. *See* Rakas v. Illinois, 439 U.S. 128, 148-49
(1978) (legitimate presence in car does not, by itself, give passenger justifiable expectation of privacy in
car's passenger compartment). Finally, the Court's treatment of "consent searches" expands the range
of police investigatory practices that will escape fourth amendment regulation. *See* Schneckloth v.
Bustamonte, 412 U.S. 218, 243 (1973) (Court suggests that when police lack probable cause to arrest or
search, "the community has a real interest in encouraging consent").
    258. One way of reducing the fourth amendment's regulation of police investigatory actions is to
broaden the category of police-citizen encounters that do not qualify as fourth amendment seizures. In
Florida v. Royer, 103 S. Ct. 1319 (1983), the Court accomplished that goal. A majority of the Justices
agreed that no seizure occurs when law enforcement officers approach a person at an airport, identify
themselves, and request and obtain the individual's airline ticket and driver's license. *Id.* at 1326, 1337
n.3. According to a majority of the Justices, this consensual encounter became a fourth amendment
seizure only after the agents told Royer of their suspicions that he was transporting narcotics and asked
him to accompany them to a police room. *Id.* at 1326.
    Royer apparently adopts Justice Stewart's test in United States v. Mendenhall, 446 U.S. 544 (1980),
that a person is seized "only if, in view of all the circumstances surrounding the incident, a reasonable
person would have believed that he was not free to leave." *Id.* at 554. Of course, many "reasonable"
citizens will feel obliged to respond to police questions because of the officer's inherent authority. If the
Court took this approach, however, most police-citizen encounters would qualify as fourth amendment
seizures. To avoid this result, the Court's seizure test requires something more than the ordinary pressures generated by any police-citizen encounter. *See id.* at 555. However, the agents' request for
Royer's driver's license and airline ticket added pressure extending beyond the average citizen's inclination to comply with police authority. It strains reality to suggest that the average airplane traveller
would feel free to walk away when a federal agent has obtained his plane ticket.
    259. *See* Michigan v. Long, 103 S. Ct. 3469, 3480-82 (1983) (*Terry*'s authorization of protective
search for weapons gives police right to frisk passenger compartment of car even though driver in
police control outside car). As Yale Kamisar has suggested, "lower courts will have little difficulty in
viewing . . . [the *Long* case] as one that enables police to make vehicle searches without probable cause
incident to virtually any lawful stopping of a vehicle." J. CHOPER, Y. KAMISAR, & L. TRIBE, *supra* note
69, at — (forthcoming). *See also* United States v. Place, 103 S. Ct. 2637, 2644 (1983) (majority of
Justices conclude that *Terry* stop rationale permits "warrantless seizures of personal luggage from the
custody of the owner on the basis of less than probable cause, for the purpose of pursuing a limited

ing the state's authority to place considerable pressures on criminal suspects to disclose evidence of their guilt before trial.[260]

The Burger Court's sixth amendment jurisprudence defies characterization because the Court has promoted both due process and crime control themes in different procedural contexts.[261] On the one hand, the Burger Court has expanded *Massiah*,[262] a Warren Court decision reflecting the due process view of counsel as a defensive shield warding off state actions that might thwart the need for an independent adjudication of guilt.[263] On the other hand, the Court's decision in *Kirby v. Illinois*[264] that criminal suspects have a right to

---

course of investigation, short of opening the luggage, that would quickly confirm or dispel the authorities' suspicion").

Both *Long* and *Place* reflect "an emerging tendency on the part of the Court to convert the *Terry* decision into a general statement that the fourth amendment requires only that any seizure be reasonable." *Id.* at 2652 (Blackmun, J., concurring in judgment). Instead of viewing *Terry* as an isolated exception to the probable cause requirement, the Burger Court appears willing to promote an ad hoc judicial balancing test to judge the reasonableness of police investigatory practices.

Moreover, in judging the reasonableness of the officer's action, the Court has failed to require consistently that the officer's action "be strictly circumscribed by the exigencies" and "limited to that which is necessary." *Terry*, 392 U.S. at 26. Indeed, in *Long*, the Court suggests that the police need not "adopt alternate means to ensure their safety in order to avoid the intrusion involved" in a *Terry* frisk. 103 S. Ct. at 3482. *Long* actually encourages police to avoid less intrusive procedures to minimize danger so that they can search the passenger compartment without probable cause. Similarly, in Illinois v. La-Fayette, 103 S. Ct. 2605 (1983), the Court concluded that it was not unreasonable for police to search containers in the arrestee's possession as part of a routine inventory procedure incident to the individual's incarceration. *Id.* at 2611. The Court rejected the lower court's assumption that an inventory search of containers was unreasonable when less intrusive alternatives were readily available (e.g., sealing the defendant's shoulder bag in a box and placing it in a secure locker) that would preserve police security, deter theft, and protect against false claims of lost or stolen property. *Id.* at 2610. *But cf.* Florida v. Royer, 103 S. Ct. 1319, 1325 (1983) (investigatory methods used in *Terry* stop "should be the least intrusive means readily available to verify or dispel the officer's suspicion in a short period of time").

260. For example, Justice White's opinion in Fisher v. United States, 425 U.S. 391 (1976), suggests that the privilege against self-incrimination may not bar the state from compelling *the production* of incriminating testimony from the accused as long as the state compulsion does not force the accused *to create* an incriminating testimonial response. *Id.* at 409-11. In *Fisher* the IRS issued a summons for individual tax records that were possessed by the taxpayer's accountant. *Id.* at 393-95. These records contained no testimonial declarations of the defendant. *Id.* at 409. However, Justice White suggested that the taxpayer's privilege against self-incrimination would not have been violated even in a case where the taxpayer himself was ordered to produce papers containing his testimonial declarations as long as his compliance with the summons did not implicitly authenticate the accuracy of the records' contents. *Id.* at 410 n.11, 412-13.

In his concurring opinion, Justice Marshall apparently assumed that Justice White's implicit authentication rationale would prevent the government from subpoenaing the individual's incriminating testimonial records. *Id.* at 432 (Marshall, J., concurring in the judgment). In subsequent cases, however, the government has attempted to eliminate this potential problem by offering to immunize any implicit testimonial authentication of the subpoenaed records. *See, e.g., In re* Grand Jury Empanelled March 19, 1980, 680 F.2d 327, 337 (3d Cir. 1982), *cert. granted sub nom.* United States v. Doe, 103 S. Ct. 1890 (1983). If the Supreme Court upholds this practice, *Fisher* will have destroyed the landmark holding of Boyd v. United States, 116 U.S. 616 (1886), that the privilege bars the government from forcing an individual to produce his private incriminating testimonial papers. *Id.* at 634-35.

261. For an example of the Burger Court's promotion of due process ideals, see Argersinger v. Hamlin, 407 U.S. 25, 36-37 (1972) (sixth amendment right to counsel applies to all misdemeanor trials when actual imprisonment is imposed upon conviction).

262. 377 U.S. 201 (1964).

263. *See* United States v. Henry, 447 U.S. 264, 274 (1980); Brewer v. Williams, 430 U.S. 387, 400-01 (1977). Although these decisions directly contradict basic crime control themes, their pragmatic effect on law enforcement's investigatory powers is not significant. Since the sixth amendment right to counsel does not attach until formal adversarial proceedings have begun, *Brewer*, 430 U.S. at 398, the government may circumvent the *Massiah* rule by delaying commencement of these proceedings.

264. 406 U.S. 682 (1972).

counsel only at line-ups conducted after the formal commencement of adversarial proceedings promoted several crime control themes such as speed, finality, and deregulation of police conduct.[265] Admittedly, *Kirby* undercuts a procedural right designed to protect the factually innocent. But this perspective overlooks the fact that trial courts retain the power under the due process clause to exclude out-of-court and in-court identifications when the trial court believes that a factually innocent defendant has been mistakenly identified.[266] Thus, *Kirby* is not inconsistent with a crime control court's preoccupation with factual guilt. Instead, the decision reflects the Burger Court's hostility to prophylactic rules that may exclude reliable evidence of factual guilt in a particular case in order to protect factually innocent defendants in future cases. In essence, the Burger Court trusts the police to use fair identification procedures. It trusts trial courts to exclude unreliable identifications in those cases in which police procedures produce an inaccurate identification.

2. Promoting or Discouraging the Use of "Exclusionary Rule" Remedies

Due process ideology values fair process norms like the fourth and fifth amendments in part because they impose some limits on the means the government may use to pursue its crime control objectives. Exclusionary "remedies" reflect its commitment to a model of criminal procedure that serves functions apart from vindicating substantive criminal law goals. Consequently, a "due process" Court would view exclusionary remedies as an ethical prerequisite of a fair criminal process that treats all criminal suspects with a modicum of dignity and respect. In contrast, a "crime control" Court would be more willing to remedy violations of process norms in those few cases where their breach raised the spectre that a factually innocent defendant might have been convicted.[267] If the state violated regulatory fair process norms, a crime control Court would prefer to use civil remedies that do not frustrate the system's capacity to determine guilt reliably.

The Warren Court's treatment of the fourth amendment's exclusionary rule provides only partial support of this due process theme. The Court never justified the rule solely on process-integrity (e.g., "judicial integrity") grounds,[268]

---

265. *Id.* at 690-91; *see also* United States v. Ash, 413 U.S. 300, 316-21 (1973) (no right to counsel at *post-indictment* photo display because display can easily be reconstructed at trial and display not a trial-like confrontation).

266. *See* Manson v. Braithwaite, 432 U.S. 98, 112-14 (1977) (trial court should apply totality of circumstances test to determine reliability of identification). The due process totality of the circumstances test permits trial courts to exclude unreliable eyewitness identifications in a particular case while preventing the exclusion of eyewitness testimony that may be accurate but was clearly the product of an unnecessarily suggestive procedure.

267. *See, e.g.,* Chambers v. Mississippi, 410 U.S. 284, 295, 302 (1973) (denial of right to cross-examine witnesses calls into question the "integrity" of factfinding); Ashe v. Swenson, 397 U.S. 436, 445-46 (1970) (state collaterally estopped from retrying defendant for robbery of multiple victims when defendant acquitted of robbing one victim).

268. In Mapp v. Ohio, 367 U.S. 643 (1961), the Court stated:

> But, as was said in *Elkins*, "there is another consideration –the imperative of judicial integrity." [citing Elkins v. United States, 364 U.S. 206, 222 (1960)]. The criminal goes free, if he must, but it is the law that sets him free. Nothing can destroy a government more quickly than its failure to observe its own laws, or worse, its disregard of the character of its own existence.

Mapp, 367 U.S. at 659.

and some of its decisions were inconsistent with this due process theme.[269] Instead, the Court adopted an instrumentalist view that values the fourth amendment primarily for its capacity to protect citizens' rights in the future. Once the government violates the fourth amendment, this perspective focuses on whether the "remedy" of excluding evidence from the criminal process will promote specific future results, such as the deterence of police conduct that violates citizens' privacy, liberty, and possessory interests. The Warren Court used this consequentialist perspective in *Mapp* to defend its application of the federal exclusionary rule to the states. According to the Court, the exclusionary rule is the only remedy that provides sufficent incentives to prevent future violations of the amendment.[270]

The Burger Court has also adopted an instrumentalist view of the fourth amendment. The Court has focused primarily on whether the future deterrent benefits secured by applying the exclusionary rule outweigh its present tangible costs to reliable guilt-determination. Although the Burger Court has not reversed *Mapp*, its apparent decision to retain the exclusionary rule while limiting its practical effect on reliable guilt-determinations is not inconsistent with crime control ideology.

Total abolition of the rule might[271] impair criminal procedure's legitimation function. As Chief Justice Warren observed in *Terry*, a judicial ruling "admitting evidence in a criminal trial . . . has the necessary effect of legitimizing the conduct which produces the evidence, while an application of the exclusionary rule withholds the constitutional imprimateur."[272] While the Burger Court has eschewed any independent judicial integrity rationale for the rule, some Justices have recognized the symbolic purpose served by a rule that expresses disapproval of some means the government may use to promote crime control interests. The Court's apparent willingness to exclude evidence seized by officers acting in "bad faith" serves this symbolic function as well as reflecting the Court's view that the rule only acts as an effective deterrent in such cases.[273]

Although both Courts have recognized that exclusionary rules serve a legitimation function, they have defined that function quite differently. A Court's view of the type of government misconduct that ethically mandates the exclusion of reliable evidence will be shaped by the historical and political context in which challenges to governmental authority arise. In the 1960's, racial, so-

---

269. In Linkletter v. Walker, 381 U.S. 618 (1965), the Supreme Court refused to apply *Mapp* retroactively: "*Mapp* had as its prime purpose the enforcement of the Fourth Amendment through the inclusion of the exclusionary rule within its rights. This, it was found, was the only effective deterrent to lawless police action. . . . We cannot say that this purpose would be advanced by making the rule retrospective." *Id.* at 636-37.

270. *See supra* note 269; *see also* Stewart, *supra* note 116.

271. Even if the Burger Court reversed *Mapp*, other constitutional fair process norms remain that serve this function. For example, the Court could invalidate some offensive police practices because the means employed "shocked the conscience." *See* Rochin v. California, 342 U.S. 165, 172 (1952).

272. 392 U.S. at 13. Once again, there is ambiguity in the term "legitimizing." I suspect that Chief Justice Warren was referring to police perceptions that their conduct must be lawful if the Court admits the evidence they had obtained. Some impressionistic research supports Warren's conclusion that the use of civil remedies coupled with judicial admission of unconstitutionally seized evidence will encourage the police to believe falsely in the legality of their investigatory actions. *See* Loewenthal, *Evaluating the Exclusionary Rule in Search and Seizure*, 49 U. Mo. K.C. L. REV. 24, 39 (1980).

273. *See* Illinois v. Gates, 103 S. Ct. 2317, 2343 n.7, 2344 (1983) (White, J., concurring).

cial, and political unrest challenged the state's moral authority to punish criminal defendants who were perceived by many to be victims of racial and class injustice. The Warren Court responded to this "legitimation crisis" by creating the image, if not the reality, of a self-regulating legal order that could not use the fruits of government misconduct to prove guilt.

The Burger Court has responded to a different crisis. It is no longer fashionable to speak of indigent criminal defendants as victims of racial and economic inequalities. Today, the public sees itself as the victim of a system that does not appear to provide a tolerable degree of protection from street crime. Excluding reliable evidence of guilt in cases where the police acted in "good faith" now may have a "delegitimizing" effect[274] because it confirms the public's impression of a system that is all too willing to protect the victimizer instead of the victim.

In its fourth amendment jurisprudence, the Burger Court has responded to these political forces by recognizing the symbolic need for a rule that places some limits on government power while simultaneously contracting the substantive scope of those limits. The Burger Court has moved toward this goal in several different ways. First, it has narrowed the substantive scope of the amendment itself to deregulate police investigatory practices that do not substantially intrude upon the individual's fourth amendment interests.[275] Second, it has discouraged any effective appellate review of a magistrate's or trial court's probable cause finding by articulating a relatively standardless definition of probable cause.[276] Given such an elastic definition, the magistrate or reviewing court can covertly adopt their own good faith exception to the fourth amendment by finding probable cause whenever the police acted in good faith on information arising above mere suspicion.[277] Finally, the Burger Court has limited the scope[278] and effect[279] of *Mapp*'s exclusionary rule by adopting a

---

274. *Id.* at 2342 (absent bad faith government misconduct, excluding reliable evidence of guilt impairs Court's integrity by "undermining public confidence in the reasonableness of the standards that govern the criminal justice system").

275. *See supra* notes 257-59.

276. *See* Illinois v. Gates, 103 S. Ct. 2317 (1983). In *Gates* the Court overruled the *Aguilar-Spinelli* test for evaluating probable cause based in part on hearsay information and adopted a totality of circumstances test. *Id.* at 2332. An informer's "veracity" and "basis of knowledge" remain relevant factors but neither's absence precludes a finding of probable cause. *Id.* Justice Rehnquist characterized probable cause as a "fluid concept—turning on the assessment of probabilities in particular factual contexts—not readily, or even usefully, reduced to a neat set of legal rules." *Id.* at 2328. As Wayne LaFave observed: "The salient characteristic of *Gates* is that it contemplates greater deference at the suppression hearing and appellate review stages to the judgment of the officer or magistrate who made the initial probable cause determination." LaFave, *supra* note 257, at — (forthcoming).

277. *Gates* requires a magistrate "to make a practical, common-sense decision whether . . . there is a fair probability that contraband or evidence of a crime will be found in a particular place." 103 S. Ct. at 2332. Judicial review of the magistrate's determination is limited to determining that the magistrate had a "substantial basis for conclud[ing] that probable cause existed." *Id.* (quoting Jones v. United States, 362 U.S. 257, 271 (1960)). Given the majority's conclusion that "[t]here are so many variables in the probable cause equation that one determination will seldom be a useful 'precedent' for another," *id.* at 2332 n.11, *Gates* essentially insulates the magistrate's determination of probable cause from effective judicial review as long as the police have presented something more than bare bone conclusions of criminal activity to the magistrate. In effect, *Gates* has recognized a good faith exception to the exclusionary rule by relying so heavily on the magistrate's good faith in assessing probable cause.

278. *See supra* note 52 and accompanying text.

279. *See* United States v. Havens, 446 U.S. 620, 627-28 (1980) (unconstitutionally seized evidence may be used to impeach testifying defendant's credibility).

balancing analysis to determine when the rule should be applied. The Court has balanced the rule's speculative deterrent benefit against its tangible impairment of crime control values to justify its refusal to apply the rule in most cases.[280]

The Burger Court's treatment of the fifth amendment's exclusionary rule reflects the same themes. While the constitutional status of the fourth amendment's exclusionary rule remains in doubt, the privilege against self-incrimination[281] contains its own constitutionally-mandated exclusionary "remedy." To prevent a defendant from being a "witness against himself" at her criminal trial, the privilege prohibits the state from making any evidentiary use[282] of the defendant's incriminating testimony that was the product of fifth amendment compulsion.[283] The Burger Court has limited the impact of the privilege's exclusionary rule by narrowing the range of state-compelled choices that constitute fifth amendment "compulsion."[284]

---

280. For a powerful critique of this interest-balancing analysis, see Kamisar, *supra* note 110, at 645-67.

Explicit adoption of a good faith exception to the fourth amendment's exclusionary rule would promote the same objectives. By retaining the rule, the Burger Court could sustain the image of a self-regulating legal order. By refusing to exclude reliable evidence of guilt because of a "technical" "good faith" police error, the Court could avoid undermining public confidence in the criminal justice system.

281. "No person . . . shall be compelled in any criminal case to be a witness against himself." U.S. CONST. amend. V.

282. *See* New Jersey v. Portash, 440 U.S. 450 (1979); Kastigar v. United States, 406 U.S. 441, 453 (1972).

283. Not all state-compelled choices that induce individuals to give incriminating testimony against themselves constitute fifth amendment compulsion. The privilege only proscribes those state-compelled choices that significantly impair the values protected by the privilege. In order to constitute fifth amendment compulsion, the state-compelled choice must be designed to elicit incriminating testimony from the individual by imposing significant burdens on those individuals who fail to give such testimony. Thus, when the state compels an individual to choose between giving physical incriminating evidence against himself or suffering some penalty for not doing so, no fifth amendment compulsion is involved because this particular state-compelled choice is designed to elicit physical evidence that is not protected by the privilege. *See* Arenella, *Reappraisal*, *supra* note 58, at 48-52, 56-58 (explaining why state-compelled choice of taking a blood alcohol test or having refusal to do so used as evidence of guilt does not violate privilege). The Supreme Court adopted this view of fifth amendment compulsion in South Dakota v. Neville, 103 S. Ct. 916, 923 (1983).

284. The Warren Court embraced a very broad view of fifth amendment compulsion in cases like Griffin v. California, 380 U.S. 609 (1965). The Court concluded that state-compelled choices that penalized individuals for asserting their privilege constituted fifth amendment compulsion even though the penalty was not sufficiently severe to compel the individual to make an immediate incriminating testimonial response. *Id.* at 614. *See generally* Arenella, *Reappraisal*, *supra* note 58, at 30-53.

In contrast, the Burger Court does not assume that every state-imposed burden on the privilege's exercise constitutes a violation of the privilege. For the Burger Court, fifth amendment compulsion only occurs when the state-imposed burdens are sufficiently severe to compel the accused to incriminate himself to avoid imposition of the burdens. The Court has referred to such instances as "core" violations of the privilege. When they occur, the Burger Court will not allow the state to make any evidentiary use of the incriminating testimony that resulted from such choices. *See* New Jersey v. Portash, 440 U.S. 450, 459 (1979). Since *Miranda* violations do not constitute core violations of the privilege, the Burger Court has permitted the state to make evidentiary use (e.g., impeachment) of statements obtained in violation of *Miranda* safeguards. *See* Oregon v. Hass, 420 U.S. 714, 722-24 (1975) (statement taken following proper *Miranda* warnings may be used to impeach defendant's testimony at trial even though interrogation continued after request for lawyer); Michigan v. Tucker, 417 U.S. 433, 447-50 (1973) (witness' testimony admissible at trial even though his identity was derived from statements obtained in violation of *Miranda*); Harris v. New York, 401 U.S. 222, 225-26 (1971) (statement taken following defective *Miranda* warnings may be used to impeach defendant's testimony at trial).

3. Promoting or Discouraging Effective Judicial Implementation of Regulatory Process Norms

To affect the system's day-to-day functioning as well as the parties before it, a due process Court must be something more than the system's superego. Effective judicial implementation of due process values will depend, in part, on the Court's ability to create prophylactic and remedial safeguards that alleviate some of its own institutional limitations as a regulator of law enforcement conduct. Thus, a due process Court might adopt a remedial strategy that would affect both the doctrinal form of regulatory process norms and the procedural contexts in which these norms can be raised to challenge convictions.

At the doctrinal level, the Warren Court implemented this remedial strategy by using, when possible, rules rather than standards to define the content of fair process norms and the circumstances under which they can be waived.[285] Articulating fair process norms in rule form strengthened the Court's regulatory function in three respects. First, rules provide clearer guidance to law enforcement officials. Second, the Court often defined the rule's content to promote prophylactic concerns about deterring future abuses of state power.[286] Third, since rules are somewhat more determinate[287] in their operation than standards requiring case-by-case balancing, they are less easily circumvented by lower courts that wish to dilute their effect on the government's capacity to detect and punish criminal activity efficiently.[288]

A due process Court might also increase the procedural opportunities for judicial articulation and application of regulatory process norms. The Warren Court took an expansive view, for example, of its supervisory authority over the administration of criminal justice in the federal courts. The Court used this power to promote process-integrity concerns beyond those required by the Constitution.[289] The lower federal courts occasionally used their supervisory authority to regulate federal law enforcement efforts by reversing convictions or excluding evidence obtained in violation of statutory or judicial safeguards.[290]

Finally, the Warren Court's remedial strategy prompted it to take an expansive view of the federal courts' authority under the writ of habeas corpus to resolve constitutional claims denied by state courts.[291] Although repetitive

---

285. *See generally* Chase, *The Burger Court, the Individual, and the Criminal Process: Directions and Misdirections*, 52 N.Y.U. L. REV. 518, 561-88 (1977).

286. *Wade*, 388 U.S. at 237-39; *Miranda*, 384 U.S. at 476-79.

287. Defining a fair process norm in rule form still requires courts to engage in definitional balancing of the rule's operative terms. Consequently, Warren Court decisions using the rule form did not escape Burger Court contraction of the rule's scope. The Burger Court simply defined the rule's operative conditions (e.g., "criminal prosecution," "jury trial") more narrowly than did the Warren Court. *See* Chase, *supra* note 285, at 569-72, 574-83.

288. For example, the Warren Court adopted a rule approach in *Miranda* because the due process "totality of the circumstances" test had permitted lower courts to find confessions "voluntary" in cases of dubious constitutionality. *See* Kamisar, *supra* note 1, at 65.

289. *See, e.g.*, Mallory v. United States, 354 U.S. 449, 455 (1957) (Court reverses conviction because of violation of FED. R. CRIM. P. 5(a) requirement of arraignment "without unnecessary delay").

290. *See, e.g.*, Birdsell v. United States, 346 F.2d 775, 782 n.10 (5th Cir.) (court might exclude evidence obtained when federal officials induced foreign police to engage in conduct that "shocked the conscience"), *cert. denied*, 382 U.S. 963 (1965).

291. *See, e.g.*, Fay v. Noia, 372 U.S. 391, 406 (1963) (Constitution invites "generous construction" of

habeas litigation impairs comity, speed, efficiency, and finality norms, the Warren Court concluded that these costs to the system were outweighed by the need to protect fair process norms in a more "neutral" federal forum. This expansive view of the writ alleviated the Court's limited capacity to review criminal cases by promoting a dialogue between the lower federal courts and state courts concerning the elaboration of constitutional norms.[292] For similar reasons, the Warren Court also articulated stringent waiver standards in habeas cases to ensure that deficiencies in the defense counsel's performance at the state level did not bar the defendant's access to a federal forum.[293] The Warren Court's remedial strategy to protect fair process norms partially explains the Court's conclusion that the regulatory purposes served by "dialectical federalism" outweighed finality, speed, efficiency, and comity concerns.

In contrast, a crime control Court might pursue its deregulatory objective by limiting opportunities for judicial implementation of norms that impair the state's capacity to detect and punish factually guilty offenders. At the doctrinal level, Burger Court decisions that have relaxed the "waiver" standard for fourth[294] and fifth amendment rights[295] reflect this crime control theme. The Court has sleighted concerns about whether the individual intelligently relinquished these rights by refusing to give them any dispositive weight. For example, in fourth amendment consent searches, the Court focused on the question of voluntariness. It adopted a standard that permits lower courts to find valid consent searches in all cases when law enforcement officials did not coerce the individual into giving up his rights.[296]

A crime control Court's deregulatory objective might also influence the Court's choice of constitutional authority for analyzing challenges to specific practices. If not bound by precedent, the Court might prefer to apply the due

---

power of federal courts to dispense writ); Jones v. Cummingham, 371 U.S. 236, 243 (1963) (parole conditions sufficient restraint of freedom to allow for invocation of writ).

292. *See generally* Cover & Aleinikoff, *supra* note 31.

293. *See* Fay v. Noia, 372 U.S. 391, 438 (1963) (federal court can adjudicate constitutional claim despite state procedural forfeiture unless defendant "deliberately bypassed" valid state opportunity to raise claim).

294. *See, e.g.,* Schneckloth v. Bustamonte, 412 U.S. 218, 246-48 (1973) (Court refuses to apply "knowing and intelligent" waiver standard from Johnson v. Zerbst, 304 U.S. 458, 468-69 (1938), to consent search case; adopts voluntariness test instead).

295. *See, e.g.,* Jenkins v. Anderson, 447 U.S. 231, 238 (1980) (fifth amendment not violated when defendant's prearrest silence used to impeach credibility of defendant's trial testimony). To justify its decision, the Burger Court resurrected Raffel v. United States, 271 U.S. 494 (1926). *Jenkins*, 447 U.S. at 235-36. In *Raffel* the defendant was tried twice. 271 U.S. at 495. At his first trial, a government witness testified that Raffel made an inculpatory statement. Raffel did not testify. *Id.* After the government witness repeated his testimony at Raffel's second trial, Raffel took the stand and denied making the inculpatory statement. *Id.* The Supreme Court held that the use of Raffel's silence at the first trial to impeach his credibility did not violate the fifth amendment because Raffel had "waived his prior assertion of the privilege by testifying at the second trial." *Id.* at 497-99.

If taken seriously, *Raffel's* retroactive waiver rationale would permit prosecutors to impeach a defendant's trial testimony by referring to his prior invocation of the privilege before the grand jury. *But cf.* Grunewald v. United States, 353 U.S. 391, 424 (1957) (Court relies on its supervisory authority to bar cross-examination of testifying defendant's prior assertion of privilege before grand jury because prejudicial impact of such comment outweighs its minimal probative value); Simpson v. Florida, 418 So. 2d 984, 986 (Fla. 1982) (reversible error for prosecutor to cross-examine defendant concerning defendant's failure to testify before grand jury).

296. *See* Schneckloth v. Bustamonte, 412 U.S. 218, 248-49 (1973). The Burger Court refused to acknowledge that consent searches involved a "waiver" at all. *Id.* at 245-46. A "consent" search was "unreasonable" only if the state coerced the individual into consenting to the search. *Id.* at 248.

process clause rather than some more specific Bill of Rights provision.[297] Since due process clause analysis requires judicial balancing of competing interests, it gives the Court greater leeway to find that crime control values outweigh the defendant's interests.

Warren and Burger Court cases considering whether the state may make evidentiary use of a suspect's or defendant's silence illustrate this point. The Warren Court viewed the issue as raising a fifth amendment problem. In *Griffin v. California*[298] and *Miranda v. Arizona*[299] the Court adopted an absolutist approach that barred the state from penalizing the defendant's assertion of the privilege.[300] Although the Warren Court's penalty model begged important questions,[301] it at least recognized that evidentiary use of a suspect's or defendant's silence raised a fifth amendment issue.

The Burger Court has chosen to analyze this issue primarily under the due process clause. In *Doyle v. Ohio*[302] the Court ruled that the due process clause barred the state from using a defendant's postarrest silence following the receipt of *Miranda* warnings to impeach his trial testimony.[303] The Court concluded that it would be fundamentally unfair to allow this practice given the *Miranda* warnings' implicit assurance that a suspect would suffer no burden for exercising his *Miranda* rights.[304] In *Fletcher v. Weir*[305] the Court used this estoppel rationale to support its ruling that "[i]n the absence of the sort of affirmative assurances embodied in the *Miranda* warnings," no fundamental unfairness occurs when the state uses the defendant's postarrest silence to impeach his trial testimony.[306]

By applying due process clause analysis, the Burger Court could focus on whether specific government acts (e.g., the giving of *Miranda* warnings) had induced the suspect's silence "by implicitly assuring the defendant that his silence would not be used against him."[307] According to the Court, *Miranda* warnings "induce" silence and offer this implicit assurance.[308] This analysis, however, never addresses the fifth amendment question raised in any case in which the state makes evidentiary use of a suspect's silence. Does the privilege itself offer suspects the assurance that their silence will not be used against them? If the *Miranda* warnings simply notify the suspect that he may properly invoke his privilege by remaining silent, why shouldn't the suspect's postarrest silence preceding *Miranda* warnings also be construed as a proper exercise of the privilege?[309]

---

297. *See* Chase, *supra* note 285, at 561-62.
298. 380 U.S. 609 (1965).
299. 384 U.S. 436 (1966).
300. *Miranda*, 384 U.S. at 468 n.37; *Griffin*, 380 U.S. at 615.
301. *See supra* note 254.
302. 426 U.S. 610 (1976).
303. *Id.* at 618.
304. *Id.*
305. 455 U.S. 603 (1982) (per curiam).
306. *Id.* at 607.
307. *Id.* at 606.
308. *Id.*
309. Even when the Burger Court has recognized that state evidentiary use of a suspect's silence raises a fifth amendment issue, it has failed to identify the specific fifth amendment values impaired by the state's practice. In Jenkins v. Anderson, 447 U.S. 231 (1980), Justice Powell summarily rejected Jenkins' claim that the privilege prohibited the state from using his prearrest silence to impeach his trial

By grounding its balancing analysis in due process terms, the Burger Court has skirted a difficult fifth amendment question. Resolution of that question might require the Court to balance *fifth amendment values* against competing state interests. But, no valid doctrinal purpose is served by resorting to the due process clause as the legal foundation for the Court's balancing analysis. Whether a state-imposed burden on the individual's exercise of his fifth amendment privilege is "fundamentally fair" rests ultimately on the Court's view of the purposes and values served by the privilege, the extent to which these values are being impaired by burdening its exercise, and the state's justification for imposing this burden. Relying on due process concerns about fundamental fairness simply permits the Court to engage in an ad hoc balancing of the interests at stake in a particular case without attempting to articulate a coherent normative theory concerning the proper application and scope of the privilege against self-incrimination.

A crime control Court might also interpret a specific Bill of Rights provision in the form that best suits its deregulatory objective. For example, the Burger Court has tended to interpret the fourth amendment as articulating general standards of reasonable police conduct.[310] Implementation of this approach allows the Court to engage in a case-by-case balancing analysis of competing governmental and individual interests. The indeterminacy of such ad hoc balancing permits the Court to give considerable weight to crime control values in deciding whether a particular police investigatory action was reasonable under the circumstances.[311] The fact-specific nature of such balancing tests insulates

---

testimony. Justice Powell never conceded that Jenkins' prearrest silence was protected by the privilege. *Id.* at 236 n.2. Instead, Justice Powell used a balancing analysis to demonstrate why the state's justification for burdening any applicable fifth amendment right outweighed the burden's impairment of fifth amendment values. *Id.* at 238. Justice Powell found that the state's interest in promoting reliable truth-discovery justified imposing this burden. *Id.* But, Powell never identified the specific fifth amendment value impaired by the imposition of this burden. Instead, he resuscitated Raffel v. United States, 271 U.S. 494 (1926) (*see* note 295), to justify the Court's holding that this was a permissible burden because Jenkins had "waived" any prior assertion of the privilege by taking the stand. *Jenkins*, 447 U.S. at 238.

It is hard to overestimate the significance of *Jenkins* and *Fletcher* for fifth amendment jurisprudence. Read together, they reflect the Burger Court's refusal to recognize a criminal suspect's silence as a valid assertion of the privilege that cannot be used against him. Apparently, in the absence of *Miranda* warnings, a suspect must explicitly invoke the privilege in response to police inquiries. Sophisticated criminal suspects might evade *Fletcher* by immediately announcing at the time of arrest that they have a defense but wish to invoke their privilege and talk to a lawyer first. However, many criminal suspects will fail to invoke their privilege *explicitly* until they have received notice of their "rights." Yet, *Fletcher* encourages police to delay giving such notice. If police immediately warn the suspect after his arrest of his *Miranda* rights, *Doyle* prevents the state from using his postarrest silence at trial to impeach his credibility. If, however, the police fail to give *Miranda* warnings until they are ready to start interrogation at the station house, the suspect's postarrest silence that preceded the receipt of warnings becomes a valuable impeachment tool for the prosecution.

310. The Warren Court, on the other hand, emphasized the warrant clause to justify its view that the major criterion of a reasonable search and seizure would be the presence of probable cause and a search warrant unless exigent circumstances made it impractical to secure one. While the lower courts must still engage in a balancing analysis to determine whether probable cause and exigent circumstances are present, such an approach created a presumption that warrantless searches or seizures without probable cause were per se unreasonable. *See* Saltzburg, *supra* note 2, at 160-62.

311. *See supra* note 259. United States v. Villamonte-Marquez, 103 S. Ct. 2572 (1983), provides a striking illustration of this approach. The Court applied *Terry*'s balancing test to justify its conclusion that custom officials' statutory authority to randomly stop and board any vessel on United States navigable waters was a "reasonable" seizure under the fourth amendment despite the absence of any reasonable suspicion or administratively established neutral selection procedure. *Id.* at 2582. The Court found that the government's interest in assuring compliance with documentation requirements out-

lower court decisions from effective appellate review,[312] thereby giving lower courts considerable discretion in determining how to implement fourth amendment norms.

Of course, the Burger Court has not always chosen to articulate fourth amendment norms as principles rather than rules. On several occasions, the Court has adopted a "bright-line" rule and justified its decision by pointing out how rules provide clearer guidance to police than standards. In many of these cases, however, the Court's bright-line rule has promoted a deregulatory objective because the rule has enhanced police investigatory powers.[313]

The Burger Court has also pursued its deregulatory objective by reducing the procedural opportunities for judicial review of process norms that regulate prosecutorial and police conduct. For example, the Court usually has not exercised its supervisory authority to place judicial restraints on executive investigatory power beyond those imposed by the Constitution.[314] Nor has the Court used its supervisory power to supplement constitutional or statutory exclusionary rules.[315] Moreover, the Court has discouraged federal courts from using their supervisory power to reverse convictions in order to remedy violations of judicially mandated safeguards unless their violation impaired the reliability of the trial's outcome.[316]

---

weighed the individuals' fourth amendment interests. The Court justified this conclusion by pointing out that federal law had not provided for external registration markings like that used by states for auto registration. *Id.* at 2580-82. In other words, the government's failure to provide a more visible registration system for vessels justified a significant intrusion of fourth amendment interests. As the dissenters remarked, "It is unseeemly at best for the Government to refrain from implementing a simple, effective, and unintrusive law enforcement device, and then to argue to this Court that the absence of such a device justifies an unprecedented invasion of constitutionally guaranteed liberties." *Id.* at 2590 (Brennan, J., with Marshall & Stevens, JJ., dissenting).

312. Such ad hoc balancing tests permit magistrates and trial courts to adopt their own version of a good faith exception to the fourth amendment's exclusionary rule by allowing them to consider the officer's good faith as a covert criterion of reasonableness. *Cf. supra* note 277.

313. *See, e.g.,* Belton v. New York, 453 U.S. 454, 460 (1981) (search incident to arrest of car passengers includes entire passenger compartment (including containers) within their immediate control at time of arrest even though passengers outside vehicle at time of search and have no real access to car's interior).

314. *See* United States v. Payner, 447 U.S. 727 (1980). Even though the government deliberately manipulated the fourth amendment standing doctrine by intentionally violating the rights of a third party to obtain evidence against the defendant, the Court held that the lower courts could not use their supervisory power to exclude such evidence. *Id.* at 733. Despite Warren Court precedent suggesting that the courts should use their supervisory power to promote "judicial integrity" concerns, the Burger Court found that the major rationale for invoking supervisory authority in *Payner* was deterrence and that the fourth amendment's standing doctrine had already taken that interest into account. *Id.* at 736 n.8.

315. *See, e.g., Payner,* 447 U.S. 727 (1980).

316. *See* United States v. Hasting, 103 S. Ct. 1974 (1983). The Seventh Circuit had reversed Hasting's conviction because the prosecutor had violated *Griffin* by indirectly referring to the defendant's failure to take the stand. United States v. Hasting, 660 F.2d 301, 303 (7th Cir. 1981). In a strained reading of the lower court's grounds for reversal, the Supreme Court concluded that the Seventh Circuit "without so stating . . . was exercising its supervisory powers to discipline the prosecutors of its jurisdiction." 103 S. Ct. at 1978. The Court then concluded that lower courts cannot use their supervisory powers to reverse trial convictions when the prosecutor's error was harmless beyond a reasonable doubt. *Id.*

Hasting provides an excellent example of how the Burger Court values fair process norms primarily for their tendency to contribute to reliable convictions. Under the Court's analysis, deliberate prosecutorial misconduct that flaunted judicial guidelines for fair procedures only justifies reversal when the trial's outcome is affected. As Chief Justice Burger observed,

Supervisory power to reverse a conviction is not needed as a remedy when the error to which

Finally, the Burger Court has limited the federal courts' habeas corpus power to reverse criminal convictions.[317] Citing comity concerns,[318] the Court has restricted the federal courts' capacity to reevaluate the facts relied upon by the state courts to justify their rulings.[319] In the fourth amendment context, dialectical federalism holds no special appeal to the Burger Court.[320] Repetitive litigation of these norms does not improve the accuracy of the system's results, but it does impair the Court's speed, efficiency, and finality objectives. For similar reasons, the Burger Court has given far greater weight than the Warren Court to state procedural forfeiture rules.[321] Relaxing the waiver standard in habeas cases has reduced the federal courts' authority to apply factual guilt-defeating process norms in cases where the defense counsel failed to comply with state procedures. The Court's ambiguous formulation of "cause" and "prejudice" standards for evaluating when a state procedural forfeiture precludes federal habeas relief reflects the Court's special concern about factual guilt and its reliance on counsel to protect the defendant's interests. The Court appears willing to restrict habeas relief to those exceptional cases where the state forfeiture was a product of defense counsel incompetence[322] and the constitutional claim raised the possibility that a factually innocent defendant had been convicted.[323]

---

it is addressed is harmless since by definition, the conviction would have been obtained notwithstanding the asserted error. *Further, in this context, the integrity of the process* carries less weight, for it is the essence of the harmless error doctrine that a judgment may stand only when there is no "reasonable possibility that the [practice] complained of might have contributed to the conviction."

Id. at 1979 (emphasis added) (citing Fahy v. Connecticut, 375 U.S. 85, 86-87 (1963)).

If the Supreme Court were to apply this limited view of judicial supervisory authority to pretrial prosecutorial misconduct, the federal courts would not be able to dismiss indictments based on flagrant prosecutorial misconduct violating judicially-imposed safeguards if such misconduct did not affect the trial's outcome.

317. *See, e.g.*, United States v. Frady, 456 U.S. 152, 166-67 (1982); Engle v. Issac, 456 U.S. 107, 135 (1982); Rose v. Lundy, 455 U.S. 509, 522 (1982); Wainwright v. Sykes, 433 U.S. 72, 87 (1977); Stone v. Powell, 428 U.S. 465, 494 (1976).

318. Although the Burger Court has consistently relied on comity values to justify some of its habeas decisions, it has not been reluctant to reverse state court decisions favoring the defendant that arguably rested on independent and adequate state constitutional grounds. *See* Michigan v. Long, 103 S. Ct. 3469, 3480 (1983) ("[W]hen the adequacy and independence of any possible state law ground is not clear from the face of the opinion, [the Court] will accept as the most reasonable explanation that the state court decided the case the way it did because it believed that federal law required it to do so.").

319. *See, e.g.*, Marshall v. Lonberger, 103 S. Ct. 843, 850 (1983) (federal habeas court must afford high measure of deference to state court's factual findings and must find that court's findings lacked even "fair support" in record in order to reject them); Sumner v. Mata, 449 U.S. 539, 550 (1981) (habeas petitioner must establish by convincing evidence that state court's factual determination erroneous, unless state court determination not fairly supported by record or one of seven conditions listed in 28 U.S.C. § 2254(d) exists).

320. *See* Stone v. Powell, 428 U.S. 465, 494 (1976).

321. *See, e.g.*, Engle v. Isaac, 456 U.S. 107, 135 (1982); Wainwright v. Sykes, 433 U.S. 72, 97 (1977). The Court has precluded federal habeas relief unless the defendant can establish both "cause" for his failure to raise the claim at the state level and "prejudice" to the trial's outcome. *Engle*, 456 U.S. at 129. Although the Court has been less than clear about what constitutes "cause," it has abandoned the deliberate bypass test of *Fay v. Noia* in most procedural contexts. *See supra* note 293 (discussing *Fay*'s application of deliberate bypass test).

322. The Burger Court has found that "cause" for failure to object at trial is not established by the defense counsel's lack of awareness that such a constitutional claim could be made or the futility of presenting such an objection. *See* Engle v. Isaac, 456 U.S. 107, 130, 134 (1982).

323. The Burger Court has applied its "cause" and "prejudice" analysis to constitutional claims that raise the possibility that a *substantively innocent* defendant may have been convicted. *See Engle*, 456

To summarize: The Warren Court's criminal procedure case law reflects some, but not all, of the major doctrinal and programmatic themes of our reconstructed due process model. The match is far from perfect. After all, the Warren Court avoided deciding the constitutionality of plea bargaining[324] and it did not always pursue its regulatory objective with equal fervor, as fourth amendment cases like *Hoffa*,[325] *McCray*,[326] and *Alderman*[327] amply demonstrate.

Similarly, it would be foolish to suggest that all Burger Court decisions reflect and promote crime control themes. The Burger Court has not always attempted to deregulate law enforcement conduct.[328] Indeed, in its sixth amendment jurisprudence, the Burger Court has strengthened the Warren Court's effort to regulate investigatory activities designed to elicit incriminating testimony from defendants after adversarial proceedings have begun.[329] Dialectical federalism is still alive in habeas cases not dealing with fourth amendment claims where no state procedural forfeiture rule applies. Not all fair process norms are forfeited by a defendant's guilty plea.[330] Nor does the Court always ignore the moral content of substantive guilt.[331] Finally, the Burger Court has recognized that process norms may merit constitutional protection even though they protect values such as equality,[332] racial justice,[333] the

---

U.S. at 124-25 (defendant may forfeit right to challenge erroneous allocation of burden of proof on self-defense claim). However, Justice O'Connor conceded in *Engle* that "the nature of a constitutional claim may affect the calculation of cause and actual prejudice." *Id.* at 129. In other words, federal courts retain the power to vindicate a federal constitutional claim that raises the distinct possibility that an innocent defendant has been erroneously convicted. *See, e.g.,* United States v. Frady, 456 U.S. 152, 172 (1982) (Court finds no prejudice based on overwhelming evidence of Frady's guilt).

324. *See, e.g.,* United States v. Carlino, 400 F.2d 56, 58 (2d Cir. 1968), *cert. denied,* 394 U.S. 1013 (1969); Cooper v. Holman, 356 F.2d 82, 85 (5th Cir.), *cert. denied,* 385 U.S. 855 (1966); Pinedo v. United States, 347 F.2d 142, 147 (9th Cir. 1965), *cert. denied,* 382 U.S. 976 (1966); People v. Darrah, 33 Ill. 2d 175, 181-82, 210 N.E.2d 478, 482 (1965), *cert. denied,* 383 U.S. 919 (1966); Green v. State, 327 P.2d 704, 706 (Okla. Crim. App.), *cert. denied,* 358 U.S. 905 (1958); Bailey v. MacDougall, 247 S.C. 1, 14, 145 S.E.2d 425, 432 (1965), *cert. denied,* 384 U.S. 962 (1966).

325. Hoffa v. United States, 385 U.S. 293, 302-03 (1966) (government use of informer to discover incriminating evidence not a fourth amendment "search" when informer invited by defendant into hotel suite and defendant relied not on security of hotel room but on misplaced confidence that informer would not reveal wrongdoing).

326. McCray v. Illinois, 386 U.S. 300, 304-05 (1967) (informer's privilege justifies government's failure to disclose informer's identity at pretrial hearing challenging existence of probable cause; neither sixth nor fourteenth amendments require disclosure of informer's identity at such a hearing).

327. Alderman v. United States, 394 U.S. 165, 171-72 (1969) (fact that evidence seized in violation of fourth amendment used against defendant not sufficient grounds to give defendant standing to complain about violation; only those defendants whose personal fourth amendment interests were affected by government conduct may challenge constitutionality of such conduct).

328. *See, e.g.,* United States v. United States Dist. Court, 407 U.S. 297, 321, 324 (1972) (neither "domestic security" exception of federal wiretap statute nor inherent powers of President to combat domestic organizations attempting to overthrow government justify absence of prior judicial approval of search or electronic surveillance of such domestic groups).

329. *See, e.g.,* United States v. Henry, 447 U.S. 264, 274 (1980); Brewer v. Williams, 430 U.S. 387, 400-01 (1977).

330. *See* Menna v. New York, 423 U.S. 61, 62-63 (1975) (per curiam) (double jeopardy claim not forfeited by guilty plea).

331. *See* United States v. Scott, 437 U.S. 82, 97 (1978) (insanity defense negating defendant's culpability considered a factual guilt or innocence related claim).

332. *See* Bearden v. Georgia, 103 S. Ct. 2064, 2073 (1983) (court may imprison probationer who failed to pay fine despite bona fide efforts only if alternative measures inadequate to meet state interests in punishment and deterrence; contrary action would violate fundamental fairness of fourteenth amendment by depriving probationer of constitutional freedom through no fault of his own).

defendant's meaningful participation in the criminal process,[334] and community participation[335] that do not necessarily enhance the reliability of the system's outcomes.

All of these decisions demonstrate that neither reconstructed model offers a complete description of the similarities and differences between the two Court's criminal procedure decisions. The two models simply provide a more useful analytical framework for evaluating judicial trends in criminal procedure. Using these models to compare the Warren and Burger Court decisions highlights some significant differences between the two Courts' views of the functions served by American criminal procedure. The Warren Court's generous interpretation of regulatory fair process norms, like the fourth and fifth amendment, and its willingness to remedy their violation by excluding reliable evidence reflected the Court's view that the process was as important as the outcome. The Burger Court's treatment of these regulatory norms reflects several distinctive themes of crime control ideology: judicial deregulation of state and federal criminal justice officials, hostility to fair process norms that impair the state's capacity to detect and punish the factually guilty, and a pronounced tendency to view individual rights from a utilitarian perspective that defines their content in light of their functional impact on the system's capacity to promote social control.

Perhaps the Warren Court's most significant message about criminal procedure's functions lay in its attempts to reinforce the notion that the criminal process should treat individuals with dignity and respect even if such treatment occasionally impairs the accuracy of the system's outcomes. Unfortunately, this is not a message that our community readily accepts when its beneficiary is a "criminal" with whom we cannot identify and its consequence is a loss in efficient crime control. The Supreme Court will always engender considerable hostility from both the public and the law enforcement community when it uses the criminal process to vindicate these norms.[336] What is most frightening about the Burger Court's approach to criminal procedure is its apparent unwillingness to reinforce consistently this basic premise that the end of efficient crime control does not justify the means used.

CONCLUSION

The debate about whether a Burger Court counter-revolution has occurred highlights a glaring deficiency in criminal justice scholarship: the failure to identify the functions served by American criminal procedure. By relying on misleading cliches to describe those functions, many commentators have

---

333. *See* Rose v. Mitchell, 443 U.S. 545, 558-59 (1979) (claims of discrimination in selection of grand jury members cognizable in federal habeas corpus action as valid ground for setting aside criminal conviction).

334. *See* Faretta v. California, 422 U.S. 806, 836 (1975); *supra* text accompanying notes 103-07.

335. Globe Newspaper Co. v. Superior Court, 457 U.S. 596, 606-07 (1982) (to deny first and fourteenth amendment right of public access to criminal trials, state must show denial necessitated by compelling government interest and that denial is narrowly tailored to serve government interest); Richmond Newspapers, Inc. v. Virginia, 448 U.S. 555, 580-81 (1980) (plurality opinion) (absent overriding interest articulated in findings, first and fourteenth amendments guarantee public right to attend criminal trials).

336. J. SKOLNICK, *supra* note 252, at 229.

couched the debate in terms that lead to obvious and thoroughly unilluminating conclusions.

This article has addressed that deficiency by attempting to identify several distinct functions served by criminal procedure. The reader may disagree with my definition of these functions or with my conclusion that the Burger Court's perception and implementation of them differs substantially from the Warren Court's approach. But one thing is certain. Without a clearer understanding of criminal procedure's functions, we cannot begin to make any useful comparison of the two Courts' approaches to criminal procedure.

[15]

The Role of Ideology in Prisoners' Rights Adjudication: Habilitative Prison Conditions and the Eighth Amendment

JAMES E. ROBERTSON*

*Society has a right to punish, but not to brutalize, to deprive of liberty, but not to expose to filth and corruption; and if it is obstinately insisted upon that government, as such, has no obligation to correct the morals of convicts, it is, at all events, its sacred duty not to lead them to certain ruin, and society takes upon itself an awful responsibility, by exposing the criminal to such moral contagion that, according to the necessary course of things he cannot escape.***

I. INTRODUCTION

Many areas once thought to be inappropriate subjects for adjudication have recently come within the purview of the judiciary. Judicial involvement in policy-making has expanded dramatically, especially during the past three decades. One area in which judicially supported policy reform has occurred is in the conditions of prison confinement. Prior to the 1970's, courts regularly invoked the "hands-off" doctrine, a doctrine of non-intervention in the administration of prisons.[1] However, by 1970, judges could no longer reconcile the hands-off doctrine with the shocking conditions revealed in prisoner

* Associate Professor of Sociology & Director, Corrections Program, Mankato State University; B.A., University of Washington, 1972: J.D., Washington University, 1975; M.A., California State University, 1979; Diploma in Law Oxford University, 1988. Presently, Professor of Corrections, Mankato State University, Minnesota State University System.

** Lieber, *Preface* to G. DE BEAUMONT & A. DE TOCQUEVILLE, ON THE PENITENTIARY SYSTEM IN THE UNITED STATES AND ITS APPLICATION IN FRANCE 15 (R. Lantz ed. 1964).

    1. The hands-off doctrine states that "[t]he courts have no function to superintend the treatment of prisoners in the penitentiary, but only to deliver from prison those who are illegally detained there." Sarshik v. Sanford, 142 F.2d 676, 676 (5th Cir. 1944). Three rationales supported the hands-off doctrine: 1) judges lack expertise in correctional matters; 2) judges did not possess adequate remedies for correctional deficiencies; and 3) conditions of confinement were privileges, not rights, and thus beyond the scope of judicial review. Berger, *Withdrawal of Rights and Due Deference: The New Hands Off Policy in Correctional Litigation*, 47 UMKC L. REV.

law suits.[2] A decade of lower federal courts activism followed, in which the federal judiciary brought about dramatic changes in the constitutional status of inmates.[3] While the United States Supreme Court initially accepted this expansion of inmates' rights,[4] by the close of the 1970's the Court returned to a position of advocating judicial restraint in correctional adjudication.[5] In the current decade, the

---

1, 2-5 (1978). For a critique of the hands-off doctrine, see Comment, *Beyond the Ken of the Courts: A Critique of Judicial Refusal to Review the Complaints of Convicts,* 72 YALE L.J. 506 (1963).

    2. Idleness, violence, disease, overcrowding, arbitrary decision-making by correctional staff, and a plethora of lesser shortcomings have historically plagued the nation's jails and prisons. As Justice Powell observed, "[t]he history of our prisons is in large measure a chronicle of public indifference and neglect." Saxbe v. Washington Post, 417 U.S. 843, 861 n.7 (1974) (Powell, J., dissenting). *See* Greenberg & Stender, *The Prison as a Lawless Agency,* 21 BUFFALO L. REV. 799 (1972); Hirschkop & Millemann, *The Unconstitutionality of Prison Life,* 55 VA. L. REV. 795 (1969).

    3. *See, e.g.,* Newman v. Alabama, 559 F.2d 283 (5th Cir. 1977) (reasonably adequate food, shelter, clothing and sanitation), *rev'd in part on other grounds sub nom.* Alabama v. Pugh, 438 U.S. 781 (1978); Bowring v. Godwin, 551 F.2d 44 (4th Cir. 1977) (psychiatric care); United States v. Wyandotte County, Kansas, 480 F.2d 969 (10th Cir. 1973) (racial segregation); Sostre v. McGinnis, 442 F.2d 178 (2d Cir. 1971) (freedom of speech); Hodges v. Klein, 421 F. Supp. 1224 (D.N.J. 1976) (procedural due process required in administrative segregation decisions), *aff'd,* 562 F.2d 276 (3d Cir. 1977); Teterud v. Gillman, 385 F. Supp. 153 (S.D. Iowa 1974) (freedom of religion), *aff'd sub nom.* Teterud v. Burns, 522 F.2d 357 (8th Cir. 1975); Goldsby v. Carnes, 365 F. Supp. 395 (W.D. Mo. 1973) (due process required in disciplinary proceedings); Palmigiano v. Travisono, 317 F. Supp. 776 (D.R.I. 1970) (searches of inmate mail); Holt v. Sarver, 309 F. Supp. 362 (E.D. Ark. 1970) (totality of deplorable conditions imposes cruel and unusual punishment), *aff'd,* 442 F.2d 304 (8th Cir. 1971). Several commentators have chronicled lower federal court intervention in state correctional matters. *See, e.g.,* Fair, *The Lower Federal Courts as Constitution-Makers: The Case of Prison Conditions,* 7 AM. J. CRIM. L. 119 (1979); Note, *A Review of Prisoners' Rights Litigation Under 42 U.S.C. § 1983,* 11 U. RICH. L. REV. 803 (1977); Comment, *Confronting the Conditions of Confinement: An Expanded Role for Courts in Prison Reform,* 12 HARV. C.R.-C.L. L. REV. 367 (1977).

    4. Between 1970 and 1977 the Supreme Court held that inmates had limited rights in a number of realms. *See* Morrissey v. Brewer, 408 U.S. 471 (1972) (due process in parole revocation hearings); Procunier v. Martinez, 416 U.S. 396 (1974) (free communication); Wolff v. McDonnell, 418 U.S. 539 (1974) (due process in prison disciplinary hearings); Estelle v. Gamble, 429 U.S. 97 (1976) (medical care); Bounds v. Smith, 430 U.S. 817 (1977) (access to the courts); Jones v. North Carolina Prisoners' Labor Union, Inc., 433 U.S. 119 (1977) (implicitly suggesting that inmates have associational rights); *see also* Lee v. Washington, 390 U.S. 333 (1968) (constitutional prohibition of racial segregation applies to prisons).

    5. *See* Bell v. Wolfish, 441 U.S. 520, 547 (1979) ("Prison administrators

Court's prisoners' rights decisions have contracted the constitutional protections accorded inmates in lower federal court decisions.[6]

This article seeks to broaden our understanding of prisoners' rights adjudication by exploring the role of correctional ideology in the evolution of inmates' constitutional status. The following hypothesis is proffered: that the expansion and recent contraction of prisoners' rights represents in part the changing ideological structure of penology. This hypothesis will be inductively tested by examining the evolving constitutional status of habilitative prison conditions, that is, conditions that do not result in the physical, emotional, or social degeneration of inmates.[7] Advocates of habilitation contend that while the state is not constitutionally obligated to rehabilitate prisoners, the eighth amendment prohibition of cruel and unusual punishment requires that jails and prisons prevent the *degeneration* of their wards. Formulated in activist lower federal court decisions,[8] the concept of constitutionally mandated habilitative prison conditions became a potent vehicle for prison reform prior to 1981. That year, in *Rhodes v. Chapman*,[9] the Supreme Court expressed a correctional ideology incompatible with habilitation as a constitutional right of inmates.

. . . should be accorded wide-ranging deference . . . ''); Jones v. North Carolina Prisoners' Labor Union, Inc., 433 U.S. 119, 136 (1977) (''[C]ourts should allow the prison administrators the full latitude of discretion. . .''). Writing in 1980, one commentator concluded that the Court had erected a "new hands-off doctrine: the Court will not deny jurisdiction, but the negative results based on the principle of wide-ranging deference to administrative discretion will now achieve the same result as the previously discredited jurisdictional bar." Robbins, *The Cry of Wolfish in the Federal Courts: The Future of Federal Judicial Intervention in Prison Administration*, 71 J. CRIM. L. & CRIMINOLOGY 211, 219 (1980) (footnote omitted).

6. *See, e.g.*, Hewitt v. Helms, 103 S. Ct. 864 (1983) (administrative segregation requires minimal due process procedures, even if a protectable interest is found to exist); Jago v. Van Guren, 454 U.S. 14 (1981) (no protectable interest in early parole release, hence no hearing required prior to denial of parole); Connecticut Bd. of Pardons v. Dumschat, 452 U.S. 458 (1981) (prisoner with mere hope for, but no right in commutation of his life sentence); Rhodes v. Chapman, 452 U.S. 337 (1981) (prison overcrowding does not constitute cruel and unusual punishment).

7. *See generally* Note, *Laaman v. Helgemoe: Degeneration, Recidivism, and the Eight Amendment*, 3 VERMONT L. REV. 243 (1978) (The right against degeneration is a bold expansion of the eighth amendment and may encourage judicial intrusion into the prerogatives of the executive and judicial branches of government.).

8. *See, e.g.*, Battle v. Anderson, 564 F.2d 388, 395 (10th Cir. 1977); Laaman v. Helgemoe, 437 F. Supp. 269 (D.N.H. 1977); Barnes v. Virgin Islands, 415 F. Supp. 1218 (D.V.I. 1976). Each of these decisions held that the totality of prison conditions resulted in the probable degeneration of inmates and thus imposed cruel and unusual punishment.

9. 452 U.S. 337 (1981).

II. The Original Eighth Amendment And The "Monomanie" Over The Penitentiary

The eighth amendment prohibition of cruel and unusual punishment was drafted in response to the brutal corporal punishments of Stuart England.[10] When the abortive rebellion of the Duke of Monmouth against King James II failed, the "Bloody Assize" of 1685 followed: to be hanged, then while still alive, to be disembowelled, beheaded, and quartered was the fate of those guilty of treason.[11] In seeking to prohibit such practices, the drafters of the eighth amendment acted to limit the exercise of macro-power, a form of power that works immediate, manifest and foreseeable harm upon the body of criminal offenders.[12]

By the middle of the nineteenth century, imprisonment had replaced corporal punishment as the principal criminal sanction.[13] As Beaumont and Tocqueville observed, a certain class of reformer had "caught the *monomanie* of the penitentiary system."[14] The penitentiary was intended to rehabilitate the offender through the enclosure, segmentation, and inspection of space.[15] In the prison a new form of power was born—micro-power, a power exercised within the bodies of offenders rather than from above them.[16] In contrast to macro-power, micro-power works latent and often unintended punishments

---

10. *See* Note, *The Cruel and Unusual Punishment Clause and the Substantive Criminal Law*, 79 Harv. L. Rev. 635, 636-37 (1966); Note, *The Effectiveness of the Eighth Amendment: An Appraisal of Cruel and Unusual Punishment*, 36 N.Y.U. L. Rev. 846, 846 (1961). The eighth amendment states: "Excessive bail shall not be required nor excessive fines imposed, nor cruel and unusual punishments inflicted." U.S. Const. amend. VIII.

11. *See* Granucci, *Nor Cruel and Unusual Punishments Inflicted: The Original Meaning*, 57 Calif. L. Rev. 839, 854 (1969). *See generally* W. Emerson, Monmouth's Rebellion (1951).

12. The concept of macro-power, as used in this article, is derived from the writings of French social scientist Michel Foucault. He contends that power can take many generic forms. One may view macro-power as a generic form of power whose most dramatic expression is capital punishment. *See* M. Foucault, Discipline and Punish 32-103 (1975). *See generally* A. Sheridan, Michel Foucault (1981). The concept of macro-power is further discussed *infra* in the text accompanying notes 15-17.

13. "The substitution of imprisonment for torture and death was the most revolutionary step in the entire history of punishment for crime." G. Killinger & P. Cromwell, Penology v (1973).

14. G. de Beaumont & A. de Tocqueville, On the Penitentiary System in the United States and Its Application in France 80 (R. Lantz ed. 1964).

15. *See generally* M. Foucault, *supra* note 12, at 135-230; M. Foucault, Power/Knowledge 37-62 (1980).

16. The concept of micro-power, which is juxtaposed to macro-power, is based

upon the psychology of the offender. This power has found institutional expression in the attributes of confinement; Gresham Sykes' concept of "the pains of imprisonment"[17] arising from deprivations of liberty, autonomy, goods and services, heterosexual contact, and security can be viewed as manifestations of micro-powers.

Whereas corporal punishment gave way to the "monomanie" of the penitentiary, the judiciary restricted the scope of the eighth amendment to punishments involving "torture or a lingering death"[18] through a formalistic mode of legal reasoning.[19] Fidelity to precedent dictated that only the brutal corporal punishments of Stuart England should be prohibited as cruel and unusual punishment.[20] Even excessive prison terms were not considered unconstitutional under the eighth amendment; as the Kansas Supreme Court observed, the amendment prohibited "the kind of punishment, and not . . . its duration."[21] In a century that saw the substitution of incarceration for corporal punishment, the eighth amendment became impotent in the face of

upon Michel Foucault's concept of "the micro-physics of power." Foucault asserts that a complex web of power relations exist in the prison that invest, train, and mark the body. These powers operate on the "modern soul:"

This real, non-corporal soul is not a substance; it is the element in which are articulated the effects of a certain type of power. . . .On this reality reference, various concepts have been constructed and domains of analysis carved out: psyche, subjectivity, personality, consciousness, etc.; on it have been built scientific techniques and discourses, and the moral claims of humanism.

M. FOUCAULT, *supra* note 12, at 29-30. For an analysis of DISCIPLINE AND PUNISH see A. SHERIDAN, *supra* note 12, at 113-63.

17. G. SYKES, THE SOCIETY OF CAPTIVES 63-83 (1958).

18. Wilkerson v. Utah, 99 U.S. 130, 136 (1878).

19. "Legal reasoning is formalistic when the mere invocation of rules and the deduction of conclusions from them is believed sufficient for every authoritative legal choice." R. UNGAR, LAW IN MODERN SOCIETY 194 (1976). Legal formalism is thus rule-centered, asking judges to "find" rather than "discover" the law. The mode of reasoning assumes that legal rules are of determinate scope and application. *See generally* Horowitz, *The Rise of Legal Formalism*, 19 AM. J. LEGAL HIST. 251 (1975); Kennedy, *Legal Formality*, 2 J. LEGAL STUDIES 351 (1973).

20. *See, e.g.*, Wilkerson v. Utah, 99 U.S. 130 (1878) (Shooting as a means of execution did not impose the terror or pain of disembowelling, burning alive, or other practices prohibited by the eighth amendment.); *In re* Kemmler, 136 U.S. 436 (1890) (Electrocution did not violate the eight amendment because it is not "manifestly cruel" punishment, unlike crucifixion.); *see also* Weems v. United States, 217 U.S. 349, 389-400 (1910) (White, J., dissenting).

21. State v. White, 44 Kan. 514, 519, 25 P. 33, 35 (1890), *quoted in* Weems v. United States, 217 U.S. 349, 405 (1910)(White, J., dissenting). As Justice White's dissent makes clear, the Court in *Weems* had clearly departed from precedent in reading a proportionality requirement into the eighth amendment prohibition of cruel and unusual punishment. *See Weems*, 217 U.S. at 398-413 (White, J., dissenting).

micro-power:[22] legal formalism dictated that the amendment check only abuses of macro-power.

In *Weems v. United States*[23] the Supreme Court freed the eighth amendment from the constraints of legal formalism. Weems, a minor customs official in the Philippines, had been convicted by a Philippine court of falsifying a government document. He was sentenced to a prison term of fifteen years at hard labor, to be followed by lifetime surveillance and perpetual loss of civil rights. The Supreme Court held that Weems' sentence amounted to cruel and unusual punishment. Writing for the majority, Justice McKenna implicitly overruled precedent to find punishments grossly disproportionate to the crime violative of the eighth amendment. In place of a static meaning, he gave the amendment a dynamic, variable content:

> Time works changes, brings into existence new conditions and purposes. Therefore a principle to be vital must be capable of wider application than the mischief which gave it birth. This is peculiarly true of constitutions. They are not ephemeral enactments, designed to meet passing occasions. . . .The future is their care and provisions for events of good and bad tendencies of which no prophecy can be made. In the application of a constitution, therefore, our contemplation cannot be only of what has been but of what may be.[24]

The *Weems* decision inaugurated a purposive, result-oriented interpretation of the eighth amendment. Whereas formalistic legal reasoning is rule centered, concerned with the institutional autonomy of law, and more committed to procedural regularity than substantive justice, purposive legal reasoning subordinates precedent to desired results and is more responsive to social attitudes and pressures as sources of legal theories.[25] While legal formalism aspires to value neutrality, its purposive counterpart overtly engages in the selection of competing values.[26] Future Supreme Court decisions would read

---

22. *See* T. COOLEY, A TREATISE ON THE CONSTITUTIONAL LIMITATIONS WHICH REST UPON THE LEGISLATIVE POWER OF THE STATES OF THE AMERICAN UNION 694 (8th ed. 1927).

23. 217 U.S. 349 (1910).

24. *Id.* at 373. *See generally* Mulligan, *Cruel and Unusual Punishments: The Proportionality Rule*, 47 FORDHAM L. REV. 639 (1979); Comment, *The Eighth Amendment, Beccaria, and the Enlightenment: An Historical Justification for the Weems v. United States Excessive Punishment Doctrine*, 24 BUFFALO L. REV. 783 (1975).

25. *See* P. NONET & P. SELZNICK, LAW AND SOCIETY IN TRANSITION 53-113 (1978).

26. Procedural or substantive notions of justice become important as purposive forms of legal reasoning are adopted, and they in turn give impetus to those varieties of argument. For policy-oriented legal discourse forces one to make explicit choices among values, and the pursuit of procedural

purposiveness into the substantive protections of the eighth amendment by requiring punishment to further a "valid penal function."[27] The federal courts would thus secure a constitutional basis for determining which penal goals are legitimate and for scrutinizing the conditions under which punishment is administered.

III. FROM REHABILITATION TO HABILITATION

The Supreme Court in *Weems* expressed concern that unless the legislative power to fix prison terms was restrained by the eighth amendment, "zeal for a purpose, either honest or sinister" might lead to cruelty.[28] Ironically, enlightened penology of the period decreed the indeterminate sentence to be "the first condition of civilized criminal jurisprudence;"[29] rehabilitation had gained ideological hegemony.[30] The rehabilitative ideology called for individualized treatment of offenders and thus advocated the use of broad discretionary powers by sentencing courts and correctional personnel. Unlike the power of the minimal state, power exercised in the name of rehabilitation could be trusted to do good; benevolence had no limits.[31] For the judiciary, long accustomed to benign neglect of prisons, the rehabilitative ideal affirmed its hands-off attitude toward prison practices.

The ideological hegemony of the rehabilitative ideal collapsed during the 1970's. A "massive desertion from the rehabilitative ideal and its assumptions" occurred in public, political, and academic

---

or substantive justice requires that rules be interpreted in terms of ideals that define the conception of justice.
R. UNGAR, *supra* note 19, at 195.

27. Coker v. Georgia, 433 U.S. 584, 593 (1977); Estelle v. Gamble, 429 U.S. 97, 103 (1976); Gregg v. Georgia, 428 U.S. 153, 183 (1976).

28. 217 U.S. 349, 373 (1910).

29. Lewis, *The Indeterminate Sentence*, 9 YALE L.J. 17, 19 (1899).

30. *See* F. ALLEN, THE DECLINE OF THE REHABILITATIVE IDEAL 6 (1981) ("[I]t is remarkable how widely the rehabilitative ideal was accepted in this century as a statement of the aspirations for the penal system, a statement largely endorsed by the media, politicians, and ordinary citizens.") A detailed examination of the rise of the rehabilitative ideology is presented in F. CULLEN & G. GILBERT, REAFFIRMING REHABILITATION 45-83 (1982).

31. Historian David Rothman attributes this trust in the state to the Progressives' belief that the state, not individual self-interest, could define the common good and make the individual free from domination by the private sector. This trust in the state finds expression in the extensive discretion given the juvenile court, one of the many contributions of the Progressives to the modern criminal justice system. Rothman, *The State as Parent: Social Policy in the Progressive Era*, in DOING GOOD 69-95 (1978).

circles.[32] Two competing ideologies emerged from its rubble, each attacking the rehabilitative ideal.

The first ideology, labeled as liberal, focuses on protection of prisoners' rights.[33] The liberal ideology rejected the rehabilitative ideal when it redefined rehabilitation as treatment having the appearance of benevolence but the substance of oppression. Proponents adopted the belief that enforced therapy works an improper intrusion on the prisoners' autonomy and provides a rationale for the exercise of unchecked governmental power. As it addresses the administration of the nation's prisons, contemporary liberal penal ideology relies on three basic precepts: first, that prisons are at best necessary evils which should incarcerate only those offenders too dangerous to remain in the body politic; second, that the rights of inmates can be protected only if the conduct of prison officials is carefully scrutinized by the judiciary; and third, that inmates are entitled to the maximum degree of liberty compatible with the security of the prison.

The second major assault on the rehabilitative ideal has been labeled as conservative and emphasizes protecting society rather than either rehabilitating the offender or safeguarding the criminal's civil rights.[34] The conservative ideology perceives rehabilitation as

---

32. Allen, *The Decline of the Rehabilitative Ideal in American Criminal Justice*, 27 Clev. St. L. Rev. 147, 149-50 (1978). Allen traces the decline of the rehabilitative ideal to "cultural events" which undermined its legitimacy among the public and its constituents. Among these events were: the perception of increasing crime; hostility to authority arising from the civil rights movement, Vietnam war, and Watergate affair; the increased social distance between the public and the prison population brought about by the rising percentages of non-white inmates; and the equation of criminal penalties with the oppression of Blacks. F. Allen, *supra* note 30, at 29-31; *see also* Halleck & Witte, *Is Rehabilitation Dead?*, 23 Crime & Delinq. 372 (1977); Serrill, *Is Rehabilitation Dead?*, 1 Corrections Magazine 21 (1975).

33. *See* F. Cullen & G. Gilbert, *supra* note 30, at 104-25. The liberal penal ideology finds its foremost expression in American Friends Service Committee, Struggle for Justice (1971). Other influential expressions of the liberal penal ideology include D. Fogel, ". . . We Are The Living Proof . . ." (2d ed. 1979); J. Mitford, Kind and Usual Punishment (1973); McAnany, *Justice in Search of Fairness* in Justice As Fairness 22-51 (1981); Rothman, *Of Prisons, Asylums, and Other Decaying Institutions*, 26 Pub. Interest 3 (1972). *See generally* Bayer, *Crime, Punishment, and the Decline of Liberal Optimism*, 27 Crime & Delinq. 169 (1981).

34. *See* F. Cullen & G. Gilbert, *supra* note 30, at 91-104. Unlike the liberal penal ideology, the conservative perspective did not benefit from any publication as articulate and comprehensive as American Friends Service Committee, *supra* note 33. The tenor of the conservative penal ideology finds expression in E. van den Haag, Punishing Criminals (1975); J. Wilson, Thinking About Crime (rev. ed. 1983); *see also* Miller, *Ideology and Criminal Justice Policy: Some Current Issues* in Classes, Conflict and Control 3-38 (J. Munro ed. 1976). The conservative penal

accomplishing little more than the coddling of criminals. For conservatives, offenders are not sick and thus do not require rehabilitation; rather, they are rational actors who engage in crime because lenient punishments fail to deter them. Regarding the administration of prisons, contemporary conservative penal ideology advances two propositions. First, prisons properly impose harsh, punitive conditions of confinement because inmates should experience incarceration as severe retribution. Accordingly, the body politic should not grant inmates constitutional rights which ameliorate retribution. Second, prison administrators, being best qualified to control the dangerous felons who inhabit prisons, should be accorded extensive discretionary powers.

Along with the decline of the rehabilitative ideology prisons experienced a minor revolution as federal courts dramatically expanded the number and scope of prisoners' rights.[35] The lower federal courts stood at the forefront of the judiciary's reform of the nation's jails

---

ideology draws heavily from the "Crime Control Model" of criminal justice in that both are based on the belief that "the repression of criminal conduct is by far the most important function to be performed by the criminal process." H. PACKER, THE LIMITS OF THE CRIMINAL SANCTION 158 (1968). What this article describes as the conservative penal ideology can be seen as the application of Packer's Crime Control Model to the administration of prisons. In turn, those critics of the rehabilitative model, whom Gordon Hawkins calls "rigorists," embody the values of conservative penal ideology:

> The term "rigor" denotes severity and strictness, and in speaking of rigorism I refer to the belief that severe treatment and strict discipline should be the basic elements of strict prison programs. Critics who adopt this viewpoint are not usually overly concerned about human rights or humanitarian values. Their dissatisfaction with the correctional treatment model stems from a different ideological basis. For them, that model is misconceived not because it involves some lack of respect for individual rights but because it is seen as representing a misguided and sentimental departure from older and sounder punitive principles.

G. HAWKINS, THE PRISON 12 (1976).

35. Battle v. Anderson, 564 F.2d 388 (10th Cir. 1977) (habilitative environment); Bonner v. Coughlin, 517 F.2d 1311 (7th Cir. 1975), *cert. denied*, 435 U.S. 932 (1978) (search and seizure); Adams v. Carlson, 488 F.2d 619 (7th Cir. 1973) (access to the courts); Woodhous v. Virginia, 487 F.2d 889 (4th Cir. 1973) (protection from inmate violence); Walker v. Blackwell, 411 F.2d 23 (5th Cir. 1969) (freedom of religion); Jackson v. Godwin, 400 F.2d 529 (5th Cir. 1968) (racial discrimination); Jackson v. Bishop, 404 F.2d 571 (8th Cir. 1968) (corporal punishment); Hamilton v. Covington, 445 F. Supp. 195 (W.D. Ark. 1978) (protection from fire hazards); Pugh v. Locke, 406 F. Supp. 318 (M.D. Ala. 1976) (habilitative environment), *aff'd as modified sub nom.* Newman v. Alabama, 559 F.2d 283 (5th Cir. 1977), *rev'd on other grounds sub nom.* Alabama v. Pugh, 438 U.S. 781 (1978); Wright v. Enomoto, 462 F. Supp. 397 (N.D. Cal. 1976) (procedural due process in administrative segregation decisions), *aff'd mem.*, 434 U.S. 1052 (1978); Carter

Criminal Policy Making

and prisons.[36] Hardly any aspect of prisoner life was considered to be beyond the ken of these courts during the 1970's. For a time, the Supreme Court accepted the views of the lower federal courts: during the 1970's the Court upheld lower federal court rulings giving inmates limited rights of expression,[37] association,[38] and access to the courts,[39] and to medical care[40] and procedural due process in parole revocation[41] and prison disciplinary actions.[42] However, in recent years, this trend has been reversed as the Court has attempted to erect a new hands-off doctrine through a policy of broad deference to the conduct of correctional officials.[43]

One result of this lower federal court activism was the development of a legal theory by which the right to habilitative prison conditions was anchored in the Constitution. Since *Pugh v. Locke*,[44]

---

v. McGinnis, 351 F. Supp. 787 (W.D.N.Y. 1972) (procedural due process in disciplinary decisions); Sawyer v. Sigler, 320 F. Supp. 690 (D. Neb. 1970) (medical care), *aff'd*, 445 F.2d 818 (8th Cir. 1971).

36. The efforts of the lower federal courts to reform prison conditions have been described and analyzed by numerous commentators. *See, e.g.*, Fair, *supra* note 3; Robbins & Buser, *Punitive Conditions of Prison Confinement: An Analysis of Pugh v. Locke and Federal Court Supervision of State Penal Administration Under the Eighth Amendment*, 29 STAN. L. REV. 893 (1977); Note, *Eighth Amendment Challenges to Conditions of Confinement: State Prison Reform by Judicial Decree*, 18 WASHBURN L.J. 288 (1979); Comment, *supra* note 3.

37. Procunier v. Martinez, 416 U.S. 396 (1974).

38. Jones v. North Carolina Prisoners' Labor Union, Inc., 433 U.S. 119 (1977).

39. Bounds v. Smith, 430 U.S. 817 (1977).

40. Estelle v. Gamble, 429 U.S. 97 (1976).

41. Morrissey v. Brewer, 408 U.S. 471 (1972).

42. Wolff v. McDonnell, 418 U.S. 539 (1974); Baxter v. Palmigian, 425 U.S. 308 (1976).

43. *See* Hewitt v. Helms, 103 S. Ct. 864 (1983); Jago v. Van Curen, 454 U.S. 14 (1981); Connecticut Bd. of Pardons v. Dumschat, 452 U.S. 458 (1981); Rhodes v. Chapman, 452 U.S. 337 (1981); Bell v. Wolfish, 441 U.S. 520 (1979); Jones v. North Carolina Prisoners' Labor Union, Inc., 433 U.S. 119, 137 (1977); Montanye v. Haymes, 427 U.S. 236 (1976); Meachum v. Fano, 427 U.S. 215 (1976); *see also* Berger, *supra* note 1; Calhoun, *The Supreme Court and the Constitutional Rights of Prisoners: A Reappraisal*, 4 HASTINGS CONT. L.Q. 219 (1977); Robbins, *supra* note 5; Robertson, *The Constitutional Rights of an Inmate at an Administrative Segregation Proceedings: Hewitt v. Helms and the Withdrawal of Prisoners' Rights*, 11 OHIO N.U.L. REV. 57 (1984). The extent that recent Court decisions have actually restrained the lower federal courts remains largely unexplored. *See* Robertson, *When the Supreme Court Commands, Do the Lower Federal Courts Obey? The Impact of Rhodes v. Chapman on Correctional Litigation*, 7 HAMLINE L. REV. 79 (1984) (The impact of Supreme Court decisions on the lower federal courts is lessened by divisions within the Court, a vague majority opinion, and policy preferences of lower federal court judges that are at odds with those of the Court.).

44. 406 F. Supp. 318 (M.D. Ala. 1976), *aff'd as modified sub nom.* Newman

several federal courts have accepted the theory that inmates are entitled to habilitative conditions under the eighth amendment.[45] The basis for this theory can best be expressed as a syllogism. The major premise asserts the Supreme Court's identification of cruel and unusual punishment as the "unnecessary and wanton infliction of pain"[46] and its demand that punishment serve a legitimate penal goal.[47] The minor premise posits that confinement under conditions "where degeneration is probable and self-improvement unlikely"[48] increases the probability of an inmate's recidivating and eventually suffering additional punishment in the form of future incarceration. From the major and minor premises, one may conclude that inmates are protected under the cruel and unusual punishment clause from prison conditions making degeneration probable and self-improvement unlikely because allowing such debilitative conditions amounts to an unnecessary infliction of suffering which serves no legitimate penal goal. As one court put it, "[p]unishment for one crime, under conditions which spawn future crimes and more punishment, serves no valid legislative purpose and is so totally without penological justification that it results in the gratuitous infliction of suffering in violation of the Eighth Amendment."[49]

---

v. Alabama, 559 F.2d 283 (5th Cir. 1977), *rev'd in part on other grounds sub nom.* Alabama v. Pugh, 438 U.S. 781 (1978):

> While courts have thus far declined to elevate a positive rehabilitation program to the level of a constitutional right, it is clear that a penal system cannot be operated in such a manner that it impedes an inmate's ability to attempt rehabilitation, or simply avoid physical, mental or social deterioration.

406 F. Supp. at 330.

45. *See, e.g.,* Madyun v. Thompson, 657 F.2d 868, 874 (7th Cir. 1981); Battle v. Anderson, 564 F.2d 388, 403 (10th Cir. 1977); Williams v. Lane, 548 F. Supp. 927, 931 (N.D. Ill. 1982); Hendrix v. Faulkner, 525 F. Supp. 435, 525 (N.D. Ind. 1981); Heitman v. Gabriel, 524 F. Supp. 622, 627 n.4 (W.D. Mo. 1981); Ramos v. Lamm, 485 F. Supp. 122, 131-32 (D. Colo. 1979), *aff'd in part, vacated in part, and remanded,* 639 F.2d 559 (10th Cir.), *cert. denied,* 450 U.S. 1041 (1980); Laaman v. Helgemoe, 437 F. Supp. 269, 324-25 (D.N.H. 1977); Barnes v. Virgin Islands, 415 F. Supp. 1218 (D.V.I. 1976).

46. Gregg v. Georgia, 428 U.S. 153, 173 (1976).

47. *See, e.g.,* Coker v. Georgia, 433 U.S. 584, 592 (1977) (A punishment is cruel and unusual if it "makes no measurable contribution to acceptable goals of punishment."); Gregg v. Georgia, 428 U.S. 153, 183 (1976) ("[T]he sanction imposed cannot be so totally without penological justification that it results in the gratuitous infliction of suffering.").

48. Laaman v. Helgemoe, 437 F. Supp. at 316.

49. *Id.* (quoting Gregg v. Georgia, 428 U.S. 153, 183 (1976)).

Habilitation is an expansive right, covering all aspects of confinement. The totality of prison conditions acquire constitutional significance: unconstitutionality is measured by aggregating the effects of confinement.[50] The prison is perceived as an microcosm, in which the diverse realms of an inmate's life are joined together under the concept of his or her habilitative welfare.

The right to habilitative prison conditions requires that prisons do more than merely abstain from certain actions. Affirmative obligations are acquired and the extent of these obligations has been variously articulated. For example, *Pugh v. Locke*[51] mandated minimum constitutional standards in the following areas: (1) living space; (2) segregation and isolation areas; (3) classification; (4) mental health care; (5) protection from violence; (6) living conditions; (7) food service; (8) correspondence and visitation; (9) educational, vocational, and employment opportunities; (10) physical plant facilities; and (11) staff ratios and training.[52] In contrast, *Laaman v. Helgemoe*[53] employed two interacting variables: (1) the probability of degeneration; and (2) an accommodation among the rehabilitative, deterrent, and security functions of the institution in question.[54] With regard to the latter variable, no single goal, such as security alone, would justify degenerative prison conditions. Instead, the institution must strike a balance among the three functions. Once the probability of degeneration is determined by examining the totality of prison conditions, remedial action is to be considered against the backdrop of the rehabilitative, deterrent, *and* security functions of the penitentiary.[55]

---

50. The totality approach permits a finding of cruel and unusual punishment through an assessment of the aggregate impact of various prison conditions even though no one condition itself violates the eighth amendment. All conditions that contribute to the finding become subject to judicial remedy. Consequently, the totality approach allows courts to impose comprehensive reforms upon federal and state prisons. *See, e.g.*, Madyun v. Thompson, 657 F.2d 868, 874 (7th Cir. 1981); Laaman v. Helgemoe, 437 F. Supp. 269, 322-23 (D.N.H. 1977); *see also* Robbins & Buser, *supra* note 36, at 920.

51. 406 F. Supp. 318 (M.D. Ala. 1976), *aff'd as modified sub nom.* Newman v. Alabama, 559 F.2d 283 (5th Cir. 1977), *rev'd in part on other grounds sub nom.* Alabama v. Pugh, 438 U.S. 781 (1978).

52. *Id.* at 332-35. Illustrative of the detailed requirements of these constitutional minimums are: 1) that single occupancy isolation cells have at least 60 square feet of living space; 2) that all inmates be provided a storage locker and lock; and 3) that there must be either one urinal or one foot or urinal trough for every 15 prisoners.

53. Laaman v. Helgemoe, 437 F. Supp. 269 (D.N.H. 1977).

54. *Id.* at 316-17.

55. *Id.*

The affirmative obligations imposed upon the prison in order to foster habilitation dramatically redefine the boundaries of cruel and unusual punishment. Manifest and intentional inflictions of harm are no longer requisite features of unconstitutional punishment. Protection against degeneration requires the definition of punishment to include the unintended and latent harms inflicted by the prison as a "total institution."[56] In the prison power works not only upon the "body" but also at the "capillary" level, identified as "the point where power reaches into the very grain of individuals, attitudes, their discourses, learning processes and everyday lives."[57] Consequently, penal deprivations that once passed constitutional muster become suspect. For example, in *Laaman v. Helgemoe*,[58] the court concluded that the New Hampshire State Prison violated the habilitation standard even though it found inmates to be "adequately warehoused."[59] The court reasoned that the aggregate impact of "inadequate" or "insufficient" food service, isolation cells, fire protection, medical services, educational and vocational programs, and classification system "costs a man more than part of his life; it robs him of his skills, his ability to cope with society in a civilized manner, and, most importantly, his essential human dignity."[60] One commentator placed this decision at the "forefront of constitutional reform" because of its extension of the eighth amendment to non-shocking prison conditions.[61]

The Supreme Court did not address the constitutional status of habilitative prison conditions until its decision in *Rhodes v. Chapman*.[62] *Rhodes* demonstrated that a majority of the Court did not accept the ideological position which the lower federal courts embraced when formulating their concept of an eighth amendment right to habilitation. It is to this subject that this article next turns.

IV. *RHODES v. CHAPMAN*: A REFLECTION OF IDEOLOGICAL CONFLICT

The introduction of purposive legal reasoning into adjudication of eighth amendment issues has permitted the judicial selection of

---

56. A total institution is "a place of residence and work where a large number of like-situated individuals, cut off from the wider society for an appreciable period of time, together lead an enclosed, formally administered round of life." E. GOFFMAN, ASYLUMS xiii (1961).

57. M. FOUCAULT, *supra* note 15, at 39.

58. 437 F. Supp. 269 (D.N.H. 1977).

59. *Id.* at 306.

60. *Id.* at 325.

61. Note, *supra* note 7, at 256-57.

62. 452 U.S. 337 (1981).

ideological values under the aegis of defining cruel and unusual punishment. However, according to Professor Roberto Ungar, "[as] purposive legal reasoning and concerns with substantive justice begin to prevail, the style of legal discourse approaches that of commonplace political or economic argument."[63] Upon collapse of the rehabilitative consensus, a scramble to fill the void left in the ideological environment surrounding prisoner law suits between the conservative and liberal penal ideologies ensued. The resulting clash found expression in the contrasting views about the nature and function of imprisonment expressed by members of the Supreme Court in *Rhodes v. Chapman.*[64]

At issue before the Court in *Rhodes* was the constitutionality of double-celling inmates at the Southern Ohio Correctional Facility. The trial court[65] and the United States Court of Appeals for the Sixth Circuit[66] both held that double-celling at the facility inflicted cruel and unusal punishment. The Supreme Court reversed. Justice Powell, writing for the majority, concluded that double-celling at the prison did not impose "conditions intolerable for prison confinement."[67] Justice Brennan, joined by Justices Blackmun and Stevens, concurred.[68] Only Justice Marshall dissented.[69]

Despite their nearly unanimous agreement that conditions at the Ohio prison did not impose cruel and unusual punishment, the five Justices supporting the majority opinion and three in concurrence differed over the proper function of the penitentiary. Justices Brennan, Blackmun, and Stevens accepted habilation as a constitutional right; and while Justice Powell's majority opinion did not explicitly reject this position, it did embrace ideological tenets incompatible with grounding habilation in the Constitution.

---

63. R. UNGAR, *supra* note 19, at 199.

64. 452 U.S. 337 (1981). For other analyses of *Rhodes*, see Note, *Prison Overcrowding and Rhodes v. Chapman; Double-celling by What Standard?*, 23 B.C.L. REV. 713 (1982); Note, *Constitutional Law—"Double Celling," Under All Circumstances, Held Not Violative of Eighth Amendment's Cruel and Unusual Punishment Clause*, 12 CUM. L. REV. 728 (1982); Comment, *Prison Overcrowding as Cruel and Unusual Punishment: Rhodes v. Chapman*, 66 MINN. L. REV. 1215 (1982).

65. Chapman v. Rhodes, 434 F. Supp. 1007 (S.D. Ohio 1977), *aff'd*, 624 F.2d 1099 (6th Cir. 1980), *rev'd*, 452 U.S. 337 (1981).

66. Chapman v. Rhodes, 624 F.2d 1099 (6th Cir. 1980), *rev'd*, 452 U.S. 337 (1981).

67. Rhodes v. Chapman, 452 U.S. 337, 348 (1981).

68. *Id.* at 352-58 (Brennan, J., concurring). In addition to joining Justice Brennan's concurrence, Justice Blackmun wrote a separate concurrence. *Id.* at 368-69 (Blackmun, J., concurring).

69. *Id.* at 369-77 (Marshall, J., dissenting).

A. THE CONCURRING OPINION

Justice Brennan viewed habilitative prison conditions as a right guaranteed by the eighth amendment: "When 'the cumulative impact of the conditions of incarceration threatens the physical, mental, and emotional health and well-being of the inmates and/or creates a probability of recidivism and future incarceration,' the court must conclude that the conditions violate the Constitution."[70] His attitude toward the habilitative function of incarceration outlined a constitutional theory in accord with the basic tenets of the liberal penal ideology, as can be seen through an analysis of those tenets.

1. The Degenerative Nature of Imprisonment

The first precept of the liberal penal ideology is that imprisonment results in the degeneration of inmates. As one leading liberal critic of rehabilitation writes, "[p]risons brutalize inmates, humiliate them, and educate them in the ways of crime."[71] While the liberal penology does not advocate abolition of prisons, it does condemn the evils wrought upon the offender by imprisonment and would counter them by making prisons no more punitive than demanded by the need for security and internal order. Rather than emphasizing direct government intervention to achieve this goal, supporters of the liberal ideology would empower inmates with the constitutional rights necessary to redress the degenerative nature of imprisonment.

Justice Brennan's acceptance of habilitation as a right granted inmates via the eighth amendment represents the translation of this first precept into constitutional expression. Mirroring liberal penal ideology's condemnation of the degenerative aspects of imprisonment, Brennan concludes that cruel and unusual punishment is imposed when conditions of confinement endanger "the physical, mental, and emotional health and well-being of the inmates."[72] For Justice Brennan, degeneration is not merely to be condemned; he supports the view

---

70. *Id.* at 364 (quoting Laaman v. Helgemoe, 437 F. Supp. 269, 323 (D.N.H. 1977)).

71. *See* Rothman, *supra* note 33, at 13; *see also* AMERICAN FRIENDS SERVICE COMMITTEE, *supra* note 33, at 33:

We submit that the basic evils of imprisonment are that it denies autonomy, degrades dignity, impairs or destroys self-reliance, inculcates authoritarian values, minimizes the likelihood of beneficial interaction with one's peers, fractures family ties, destroys the family's economic stability, and prejudices the prisoner's future prospects for any improvement in his economic and social status.

72. *Rhodes*, 452 U.S. at 364 (Brennan, J., concurring) (quoting Laaman v Helgemoe, 437 F. Supp. 269, 323 (D.N.H. 1977)).

that inmates should be given a positive constitutional basis upon which to protect themselves rather than relying on the benevolence of prison administrators.

2. Distrust of Discretionary Power

The liberal penal ideology perceives the discretionary power of prison officials as being readily abused.[73] To support this second precept, advocates of the liberal penal ideology look to the destructive effects of the hands-off doctrine upon prison conditions: the unchecked powers of prison officials have resulted in administrative lawlessness, with officials exercising their powers in arbitrary ways.[74] Consequently, judicial oversight of prison officials is vital if their conduct is to be expected to comport with fundamental fairness. A return to the hands-off doctrine would subject inmates to the abuses spawned by absolute power.

Similarly, Justice Brennan's concurrence reflects a distrust of discretionary powers long used and abused by prison officials. He noted that by 1981 conditions in individual prisons or entire penal systems in nearly half the states had been found unconstitutional,[75] and that legislators and prison administrators, who were "entrusted in the first instance" with the operation of prisons, were to blame.[76] Like the liberal critics, Justice Brennan viewed judicial intervention as both necessary and beneficial: "[T]he courts have emerged as a critical force behind efforts to ameliorate inhumane conditions [in prisons]. Insulated as they are from political pressures, and charged with the duty of enforcing the Constitution, courts are in the strongest

---

73. The perception that prison officials had been corrupted by their vast powers is vividly presented in Greenberg & Stender, *supra* note 2.

74. *See, e.g.*, Jackson v. Bishop, 404 F.2d 571 (8th Cir. 1968) (whipping of prisoners); Wright v. McMann, 387 F.2d 519 (2d Cir. 1967) (solitary confinement of a naked prisoner in unsanitary conditions); Holt v. Sarver, 309 F. Supp. 362 (E.D. Ark. 1970) (gross overcrowding, pervasive filth, and rampant violence), *aff'd*, 442 F.2d 304 (8th Cir. 1971). Egregious prison conditions have not disappeared from the nation's prisons. *See, e.g.*, Hendrix v. Faulkner, 525 F. Supp. 435 (N.D. Ind. 1981) (inmates suffered "genuine privations and hardships," *id.* at 524); Ruiz v. Estelle, 503 F. Supp. 1265 (S.D. Tex. 1980) (staff brutality, failure to protect inmates from assaultive prisoners, overcrowding, and numerous other conditions resulting in cruel and unusual punishment), *modified*, 650 F.2d 555 (5th Cir. 1981), *aff'd in part and rev'd in part*, 666 F.2d 854 (5th Cir.), *modified*, 679 F.2d 1115 (5th Cir. 1982); Gilmore v. Lynch, 319 F. Supp. 105 (N.D. Cal. 1979) (failure to provide adequate access to the courts).

75. *Rhodes*, 452 U.S. at 353 (Brennan, J., concurring).

76. *Id.* at 354.

position to insist that unconstitutional conditions be remedied, even at significant financial cost."[77]

3. Maximizing the Liberty of Inmates

The third of the interrelated precepts of the liberal penal ideology provides that inmates should have the maximum amount of liberty compatible with the security of the prison. As liberal penologist David Fogel states, "[a]ll the rights accorded free citizens consistent with mass living and the execution of a sentence restricting the freedom of movement should follow a prisoner into prison."[78] Legal scholars refer to this precept as the "least restrictive means doctrine."[79] Since liberal penologists distrust governmental paternalism, they believe that inmates are best protected when they retain their fundamental civil rights. Imprisonment is in and of itself sufficient punishment.

Justice Brennan's acceptance of habilitative prison conditions as a requirement of the eighth amendment indirectly embraces this final precept of contemporary liberal penology.[80] The concept of habilitation is premised on the belief that people are sent to prison *as* punishment, not *for* punishment. Separation from society is punishment enough; in order to preserve the surviving liberty interest inmates must be protected from further harm in the form of degenerative prison conditions. By espousing habilitation as a prisoner's right, Justice Brennan envisions an eighth amendment which prevents unnecessary acts of intrusion into an inmate's liberty interest.

B. THE MAJORITY OPINION

While Justice Brennan's acceptance of the right to habilitative prison conditions reflects the influence of the liberal penal ideology

---

77. *Id.* at 359. Elsewhere in *Rhodes* Justice Brennan observes that "the lower courts have learned from repeated investigation and bitter experience that judicial intervention is *indispensable* if constitutional dictates—not to mention considerations of basic humanity—are to be observed in the prisons." *Id.* at 354.

78. D. FOGEL, *supra* note 33, at 202 (emphasis deleted).

79. The doctrine of least restrictive alternative requires government to achieve a desired end in a manner that does not unnecessarily intrude on constitutionally protected rights. *See* Singer, *Sending Men to Prison: Constitutional Aspects of the Burden of Proof and the Doctrine of the Least Drastic Alternative as Applied to Sentencing Determinations*, 58 CORNELL L. REV. 51, 55-59 (1972). For a history of the doctrine, see Zlotnick, *First Do No Harm: Least Restrictive Alternative Analysis and the Right of Mental Patients to Refuse Treatment*, 83 W. VA. L. REV. 375, 385-91 (1981). *See also* Note, *The Least Restrictive Alternative in Constitutional Adjudication: An Analysis, a Justification, and Some Criteria*, 27 VAND. L. REV 971 (1974).

80. *See Rhodes*, 452 U.S. at 364 (Brennan, J., concurring).

on the Supreme Court, the values embodied in this ideology are not subscribed to by a majority of the Court. Justice Powell's majority opinion in *Rhodes v. Chapman* rejects the constitutional basis for habilitation, favoring instead the conservative ideological tenets. A review of these tenets illustrates his acceptance of the more conservative point of view.

1.   Prisons Should Be Experienced as Harsh, Foreboding Institutions

The conservative penal ideology seeks to legitimate the prison as a punitive institution.[81] From this perspective, the rehabilitative ideal is flawed because it denies society an opportunity to impose retribution upon offenders. Furthermore, supporters of the conservative ideology believe that harsh prison conditions will serve to deter offenders, who are rational actors weighing the pains and pleasures to be gained from criminal enterprise. According to the late J. Edgar Hoover, the criminal fears " 'certain, unrelenting punishment.' " He continued:

> "That is what he understands, and nothing else, and that fear is the only thing which will force him into the ranks of the law-abiding. There is no royal road to law enforcement. If we wait upon the medical quacks, the parole panderers, and the misguided sympathizers with habitual criminals to protect our lives and property from the criminal horde, then we must also resign ourselves to increasing violence, robbery, and sudden death."[82]

Justice Powell's majority opinion in *Rhodes* incorporates this perspective. He interpreted the eighth amendment's prohibition of cruel and unusual punishment as requiring only "the minimal civilized measure of life's necessities"[83] within the prison, a standard that falls considerably short of mandating habilitative prison conditions. Furthermore, Justice Powell defined "life's necessities" with reference only to the physical welfare of inmates, excluding consideration of their mental, emotional, and social well-being.[84] Conditions that are "restric-

---

81. *See* G. HAWKINS, *supra* note 34, at 12-16 ("The rigorists advocate a sternly repressive, vigorously disciplined, punitive regimen for the prisons." *Id.* at 12.).

82. Address by J. Edgar Hoover, Daughters of the American Revolution Annual Convention (April 23, 1936), *quoted in* E. SUTHLERLAND & D. CRESSEY, PRINCIPLES OF CRIMINOLOGY 361 (10th ed. 1978).

83. *Rhodes*, 452 U.S. at 347.

84. In assessing the impact of overcrowding on inmates, Justice Powell appears to have been exclusively concerned with finding concrete evidence of immediate, physical harm. Unlike Justice Brennan's concurrence, the majority opinion fails to consider the long-term, latent impacts of overcrowding on the mental and emotional health of inmates. *Compare id.* at 347-48 *with id.* at 361-64 (Brennan, J., concurring).

tive" and "harsh" become simply part of the penalty to be paid by offenders.[85] Finally, Justice Powell's opinion expanded the range of legitimate incarceral goals to include "punish[ing] justly," an apparent euphemism for retribution.[86]

2. *Prison Officials Should Have Extensive Discretionary Powers*

The conservative penal ideology is little concerned with the rights of inmates.[87] Instead, it focuses on the "right" of society to punish offenders. Consequently, prisons should be houses of discipline and prison authorities should be severe disciplinarians: only then will retribution and deterrence be realized. To accomplish this task, prison administrators require extensive discretionary powers. Judicial "interference" unwittingly serves to counteract retribution and deterrence because it permits prisoners to use litigation to sap the disciplinary powers of the prison staff.

Justice Powell's opinion in *Rhodes* articulates the conservative tenet that prison officials should be allowed to operate their prisons largely unhindered by the courts. He wrote that "[t]his Court must proceed cautiously,"[88] that the Court's ruling must not be based on " 'a court's idea of how best to operate a detention facility,' "[89] and that "courts cannot assume that state legislatures and prison officials are insensitive to the requirements of the Constitution or to the perplexing sociological problems of how best to achieve the goals of the penal function in the criminal justice system."[90] While Justice Powell did not preclude judicial intervention under any specific circumstance,[91] the tenor of his opinion suggests that the judiciary's intervention in prison matters has been too extensive. In his view, the time for judicial retreat from expanding prisoners' rights has arrived, and he would be its harbinger.[92]

---

85. *Id.* at 347.
86. *Id.* at 352.
87. *See* G. HAWKINS, *supra* note 34, at 12.
88. *Rhodes*, 452 U.S. at 351.
89. *Id.* (quoting Bell v. Wolfish, 441 U.S. 520, 539 (1979)).
90. *Id.* at 352.
91. *Id.* "Courts certainly have a responsibility to scrutinize claims of the cruel and unusual confinement. . . .When conditions of confinement amount to cruel and unusual punishment, 'federal courts will discharge their duty to protect constitutional rights.' " (quoting Procunier v. Martinez, 416 U.S. 396, 405-06 (1974)).
92. *See* Aronson, *Prisoners' Rights*, 1982 ANN. SURV. AM. L. 79, 83 (1982) ("The majority's call [in *Rhodes*] for greater deference may be seen as removing the threat that certain prison conditions will be declared unconstitutional. . . .");

V. DISCUSSION

This analysis of prisoners' rights adjudication reveals the close relationship between judicial decision-making and the ideological structure of contemporary penology. One does not see the operation of autonomous legal norms; the substantive content of the eighth amendment arises from the interrelationship between the legal and social systems. The courts, located at the nexus between law and the broader society, acquire important policy-making powers.

The conflict between the liberal and conservative ideologies has found expression in judicial interpretations of the eighth amendment. Constitutional theories in support of each of these ideologies have developed and have been integrated into a hierarchical judicial system that vests in the Supreme Court ultimate jurisdiction to constitutionally resolve the underlying normative conflict. Whereas the majority opinion in *Rhodes v. Chapman* did not explicitly repudiate the habilitative standard, it did embrace incongruent values. *Rhodes* also indicates that a new consensus is in the making, one which emphasizes the retributive function of incarceration and re-establishes the limited role of the courts in overseeing prison administration.

As an arena for normative conflict over the function of the penitentiary, and as an instrument for integrating this conflict into existing legal framework, judicial interpretation of the eighth amendment appears to operate within what has been termed a "paradigm of conflict functionalism" by sociologist Lewis Coser.[93] This paradigm views society as having a consensual basis that is periodically weakened by conflict over the distribution of scarce resources. Coser asserts that the less rigid the social system, the more capable it is of revitalizing

---

Eighth Amendment—A Significant Limit on Federal Court Activism in Ameliorating State Prison Conditions, 72 J. CRIM. L. & CRIMINOLOGY 1345, 1346 (1981) ("'[W]ith *Rhodes*, the Court effectively undermined federal court leadership in pressing for improvements in state prisons across the country.'").

93. L. COSER, THE FUNCTIONS OF SOCIAL CONFLICT (1956). Coser believes that conflict plays a critical role in maintaining group cohesion. Consequently, he stands apart from most conflict theorists, who define conflict as a source of social change. Coser identifies two forms of conflict, external conflict and internal conflict. External conflict, such as a war between nation-states, makes individuals acutely aware of their national identity by introducing a negative reference group, the enemy nation-state. *Id.* at 33-38. Internal conflict, which is addressed in this article, occurs within a society or an institution. Coser asserts that the cohesion of a society or an institution can be revitalized by internal conflict. *See id.* at 39. For a detailed critique of Coser's paradigm, see J. TURNER, THE STRUCTURE OF SOCIOLOGICAL THEORY 159-78 (1978).

existing norms or creating new ones to accommodate conflict and to promote a new consensus. Consistent with Coser's model, the normative basis of American penology has been dominated by the rehabilitative ideal. The consensus over rehabilitation, however, did not obscure its two functions, one manifest, the other latent: the manifest function embraced the rhetoric of the rehabilitative ideal whereas the latent function promoted an orderly prison and retributive prison conditions.[94] When liberals and conservatives were no longer able to reconcile the manifest and latent functions of rehabilitation, they redefined the rehabilitative ideal as the noble lie. Consequently, the consensus, made possible by agreement over and acceptance of both the manifest and latent functions of rehabilitation, collapsed. Conflict over the function of the penitentiary, once resolved through these dual functions of the rehabilitative ideal, has entered the legal arena for resolution because the open-ended, flexible nature of modern eighth amendment interpretation readily allows for the translation of ideological conflict into varying views as to the function of the cruel and unusual punishment clause.

Controversy surrounds Coser's paradigm of conflict functionalism due largely to the fact that he fails to identify for whom the "conflict" is "functional." While Coser portrays a system that seeks harmony, radical criminologists describe a criminal justice system dominated by a ruling elite.[95] From their perspective, the expansion of prisoners' rights is functional to the degree it promotes the perception that the judiciary and the other instruments of class domination, one of which is the prison, are legitimate institutions of social control. However, this article does not seek to resolve the controversy regarding conflict functionalism, but rather intends only to suggest that the emergence and retrenchment of, if not retreat from, the expansion of prisoners' rights involves an ideological conflict which was introduced to the legal system through the interface of law and society.

---

94. *See* D. ROTHMAN, CONSCIENCE AND CONVENIENCE 10 (1980) ("In the end, when conscience and convenience met, convenience won. When treatment and coercion met, coercion won."); D. ROTHMAN, THE DISCOVERY OF THE ASYLUM 240 (1971) ("The promise of reform had built up the asylums; the functionalism of custody perpetrated them.").

95. *See, e.g.*, B. KRISBERG, CRIME AND PRIVILEGE: TOWARD A NEW CRIMINOLOGY (1975); CRITICAL CRIMINOLOGY (I. Taylor, P. Walton & J. Young eds. 1975); Platt, *Prospects for a Radical Criminology in the United States*, 1 CRIME & SOC. JUST. 2 (1974); Quinney, *The Production of a Marxist Criminology* 2 CONTEMPT. CRISES 277 (1978).

VI.   CONCLUSION

Courts do not function in an ideological vacuum; they connect law and society by interweaving normative discourse with legal rules and principles. Ultimately, judicial interpretations of the Constitution involve factual assessments filtered through political, social, and moral precepts of society.[96] Just as the ideology of laissez-faire influenced the Supreme Court between 1890 and 1923,[97] so have penal ideologies shaped the adjudication of prisoners' rights. The constitutional right to habilitative prison conditions identified in the lower federal courts mirrors the principles of liberal penal ideology and demonstrates the influence of this ideology on the prisoners' rights revolution of the 1970's. However, during the 1980's, the influence of conservative penal ideology has been strongly felt in correction litigation as judges are asked to select among controverted conceptions of incarceral punishment. *Rhodes v. Chapman* evidences the clash of these two ideologies in the judicial forum and the dominant influence of the conservative penal ideology within the Supreme Court.[98]

---

96. *See* B. CARDOZO, THE NATURE OF THE JUDICIAL PROCESS 168 (1921) ("The great tides and currents which engulf the rest of men do not turn aside in their course, and pass the judges by."); Powell, *The Logic and Rhetoric of Constitutional Law*, in ESSAYS IN CONSTITUTIONAL LAW 89 (R. McCloskey ed. 1957) ("Judges have preferences for social policies, as you and I. . . .They are warmed by the same winter and summer and by the same ideas as a layman is.").

97. *See,. e.g.*, Adkins v. Children's Hospital, 261 U.S. 525 (1923); Lochner v. New York, ·198 U.S. 45 (1905); Allgeyer v. Louisiana, 165 U.S. 578 (1897); *see also* G. WHITE, THE AMERICAN JUDICIAL TRADITION 165-66 (1976).

98. The Court's decision in Hewitt v. Helms, 103 S. Ct. 864 (1983), demonstrates that the ideological division over prisoners' rights in *Rhodes* is not an anomaly. *Hewitt* addressed two questions: first, when, if at all, does the due process clause of the fourteenth amendment apply to the removal of inmates from the general prison population to administrative segregation?; and second, if due process is applicable, how much process is due segregated inmates? Justice Rehnquist's majority opinion applied a narrow definition of the reach of due process within the prison, holding that administratively segregated inmates must look to a state-created liberty interest to trigger due process safeguards. *Id.* at 870-71. As to the process due segregated inmates, Justice Rehnquist outlined procedures providing few meaningful safeguards against arbitrary decisions to remove inmates to segregated quarters for administrative reasons. *Id.* at 874. The probable effect of *Hewitt* is to give prison officials extensive discretionary powers in determining when the security of the prison or the safety of inmates requires the segregation of prisoners. Four Justices dissented: Justice Marshall, who also dissented in *Rhodes*; Justices Stevens and Blackmun, who joined Justice Brennan's concurrence in *Rhodes*; and Justice Brennan.

Generally, the *Hewitt* majority and dissenting opinions reflected the tenor of the conservative and liberal penal ideologies respectively. Justice Rehnquist, speaking for the majority, emphasized that conviction essentially extinguished the liberty interest of inmates. In contrast, Justice Stevens, author of the dissenting opinion, spoke of a broad liberty interest that survived conviction. *Id.* at 877-80 (Stevens, J., dissenting). While Justice Rehnquist expressed deference to the conduct of prison officials, Justice Stevens sought to safeguard inmates against abusive uses of state power. In weighing the competing merits of institutional authority and prisoners' rights, the majority and dissenting opinions employed contrasting ideological standards.

Part IV
Case Studies

[16]

THE BRITISH JOURNAL

OF

CRIMINOLOGY

| Vol. 35 | Winter 1995 | No. 1 |

THE OPENING STAGES OF CRIMINAL JUSTICE POLICY MAKING

PAUL ROCK*

This article describes how commonplace policy making is organized by a series of dialectical processes that transform the first, tentative ideas of officials and researchers into objective, anonymous policies dispersed throughout the criminal justice system.

A number of small structures and processes animate the very core of the routine politics of criminal justice. They have such a marked effect on the formulation of policy in its opening stages, the stages before legislation and implementation, that they explain much of its character. They deserve attention.

Those structures almost certainly permeate other areas of policy development as well, but I propose to confine myself to the workings of the world with which I am most familiar, the criminal justice system. More particularly, I shall base my description on a succession of linked empirical studies of 'bottom-up' policy making in government departments in Canada and England and Wales between the late 1960s and the early 1990s, drawing on published research on policies for victims (Rock 1986, 1990) and prosecution witnesses (Rock 1993) initiated in the 1980s, on the origins and development of the Home Office Programme Development Unit's first initiative in the early 1990s (Rock 1994), and on the decision taken by the Prison Department in the late 1960s to transform Holloway Prison for women into a secure hospital.

It would be best to define the precise focus and limits of this article. My objectives are circumscribed. I shall not deal much with the *content* of policy making: the history and empirical detail of four of the five initiatives are described at length in books and an article elsewhere. In the comparatively abstract argument of a short paper, I propose merely to stand back to examine a few of their more formal properties. And, in doing so, I shall concentrate on the everyday policy making that is stirred less by big events in the outside world than by the commonplace internal processes of bureaucracy itself.

* Department of Sociology and Mannheim Centre, London School of Economics.

PAUL ROCK

This will be an analysis of routine policies that rise slowly, inconspicuously and methodically through 'the system' (although all prolonged episodes of policy making have their dramas and the history of the rebuilding of Holloway Prison was undoubtedly punctuated by grave crises). This is not an article about the social organization of Royal Commissions and the grander public committees, and it does not discuss the responses of politicians to sudden public disasters such as riots, murders and prison escapes. Neither, should it be stressed, can it be an article about some of the very newest and as yet largely unanalysed modes of policy making.

The organization and politics of criminal justice policy making are currently in flux. One source of change has been a partial turning away from the once standard processes of internal consultation, from committee meetings, briefings and circulating files, towards procedures that are more fragmentary, centrifugal and loosely bounded. Portions of criminal justice policy making have become somewhat less cohesive, coherent, controlled, and centralized as they come under the sway of devolution, 'contracting out', Next Steps Agencies and external consultants. Although the consequences and dimensions of that shift are uncertain and deserve close scrutiny, the new procedures were not at present in any of the initiatives I studied and they cannot be the subject of informed discussion here. At most, it may be said that they co-exist with the older methods in ambiguous relation, those older methods still remaining, if only for a while, as the officials' core recipe knowledge of how to do things.

The newest modes of policy making are themselves the fruits of a new politics of populism, moralism, and the market. Attempting to reform such matters as the organization of the police and prisons, the incarceration of young offenders, and the 'right to silence', a number of Home Office ministers appear recently to have been impelled by a strong sense of the political, by personal volition, a doughty common sense, and appeals to what are thought to be popular sentiment. They have consulted and conferred less often with the experts, distrusting the professionals, the criminologists, officials, and practitioners, who used to define much of the character of crime and criminal justice policy. One cabinet minister, John Redwood, was reported to have remarked in April 1994 that 'there were few in the universities ready to ask the new questions. Where was the criminologist who could explain the crime rate and tell us what to do about it?' (*The Times*, 25 April 1994). Ministers seem now to act more quickly and impulsively. Theirs has become the politics of the general will idiosyncratically conceived and it, too, co-exists uneasily with the standard forms of policy making that are the focus of this article.

Such departures from conventional conduct have occasioned dismay amongst many of the senior officials and baronial powers of the criminal justice system. They are a clear flouting of stock bureaucratic judgements about how things should be done, of what Bittner once called 'the [official] sensibility of esthetic appreciation [which] is summoned for direction, information and control in various concrete situations' (Bittner 1965: 252–3). And it has been an outcome that things *have* begun to go quite manifestly wrong in criminal justice policy making. There has been audible and often effective opposition to the new style inside and outside Parliament (even from the Lord Chief Justice and from former Conservative Home Secretaries such as Lord Whitelaw), visible retreats in policy (particularly in the case of the 1991 Criminal Justice Act) and a frequent loss of face. The reverses of Home Office policy have been politically embarrassing, representing just that public discomfiture of ministers and senior officials

CRIMINAL JUSTICE POLICY MAKING

that civil servants sought traditionally to avoid,[1] a proof perhaps of the wisdom of the older methods. It is possible to suppose that they will eventually be superseded by a greater reliance on the cautious, safe, and orthodox pattern that I analyse in this article.

The Beginnings of Routine Policy Making

Let me describe the ingredients of that pattern. Even within a substantial government department such as the Home Office or the Ministry of the Solicitor General of Canada, proliferating tasks and the division of labour bring it about that only a small number of officials can devote themselves to a specific area of policy, especially at first when the area may not have received much in the way of departmental recognition and resources. The very newest areas are unlikely to be treated as a part of the established division of labour at all, but as an additional task to be allotted to officials already occupied with other matters. To be sure, the numbers of officials in attendance will swell as a piece of policy making becomes more urgent, complex, and immediate in its demands, as political alliances are sought and new boundaries are explored, but the formative early life of a policy can rarely be nurtured by more than a few people. Many policies, and certainly those policies whose trajectory is described as 'bottom-up', advancing from officials to ministers, begin by acquiring their identity in the aspirations, imaginations, relations, and activities of perhaps three or four individuals.

Those small policy-making worlds tend to lack permanence and stability. Quite by design, 'high-flying' Home Office officials are moved from post to post about every three or four years to prevent them 'going native' and to afford them a panoptic vision of ever-wider reaches of government. The officials of other governments (of Canada, for example) may not be shuffled about so methodically, but it is inevitable that they will also change position as they fall ill, become pregnant, pursue their careers, receive promotion and secondment, and retire.

A stable group may well be intellectually fertile, and it can certainly foster commitments and loyalties, but it is the instability of the small group that seems to provide the stronger immediate catalyst for the innovation and diffusion of ideas. People on the move take their histories, expertise, and experience with them, carrying knowledge from site to site. They are prone to transfer, contrast, mix, and refashion the larger common sense and practices of the organizations in which they have worked. It is often the newly-arrived official, seeing parts of the world with a questioning eye, who proposes change. So it was that Irvin Waller, Director of Research in the Ministry of the Solicitor General of Canada, imported the evangelism of the National Organization for Victims Assistance, the American victims movement, in the 1970s; Christopher Nuttall, the new Director of Research and Statistics at the Home Office, and his colleague, Christine Lehman, carried the idea of programme development from Canada and the United States into the Home Office in the late 1980s; and Joanna Kelley, a former governor seconded to the Prison Department as Assistant Commissioner at the end of the 1960s, took her ambition to remodel Holloway Prison into the

---

[1] One senior official involved in the Holloway Redevelopment Project informed a meeting in June 1975 that he was 'responsible to the public to ensure that public money was well spent. Put more defensively, [I have] a duty to protect the Prisons Board and the Permanent Under-Secretary from the possibility of public and Parliamentary criticism'.

PAUL ROCK

heart of penal policy making. They injected old ideas and procedures into new settings where they no longer seemed to be quite so old.

In the small world of the policy maker, personal character, influence, and reputation count. Policies will not and cannot be anonymous there. Rather, they will be the acknowledged offspring of particular people. Thus, the rebuilding of Holloway Prison was linked inextricably with the person of Kelley, Programme Development with Nuttall, and the Justice for Victims of Crime Initiative with Waller, the man once called Mr Victims by his colleagues in the Ministry of the Solicitor General of Canada (see Rock 1986: ch. 4).

A new venture is then liable to become regarded as the symbolic property or adjunct of a named individual or small group of individuals, part of their material self, and *its* worth and prospects will rest in part on *their* social and professional standing, the one colouring the other. What is done for and to a proposal at first may also stand as a response to its proponent, the seemingly impersonal work of policy making actually being transacted quite personally, a set of transfigured social relationships being affected, as are all relationships, by feelings of admiration, friendship, animosity, jealousy, and obligation. The progress of policies themselves will be blocked, diverted, or accelerated in the play of social interaction, the one being a mirror of the other.

Of obvious importance in those early phases is the structural position of the innovating individual or individuals. The more powerful and senior they are, the more unambiguously their formal responsibilities seem to bear on a new proposal, the smoother will be the path of the initiatives they promote. But such a marriage between projector, role, and project is rarely complete. Whilst officials are liable to be most knowledgeable and enthusiastic about matters directly salient to their work, bringing about a convenient coupling of inspiration and duty, bright ideas also have a way of arising unplanned in chance meetings, casual conversations and unexpected juxtapositions that confound the neat boundaries of the division of labour. Indeed, many proposals will be so new that they fail to find a ready home at all (in the mid-1980s, for instance, no government department in England and Wales had formal responsibility for assisting prosecution witnesses who appeared in court). It is inevitable that new ideas will often have to enter an environment which is not formally prepared for them, an environment that consists of activities approved, funded, and targeted at other things altogether. It is also inevitable that the officials who would promote those ideas, just as commonly seem to be stuck in the wrong place or in the not-quite-right place for the task at hand.

Something can always be achieved by rhetoric. Policy making occupies a world of paper and words, of argument and efforts to persuade. The highest praise one Home Office official can give another is to say that he or she is 'good on paper'. Confronted by a misalignment between formal responsibility and aspiration, between the new idea and its environment, officials can improvise, stretching arguments about the limits and terms of mandates and precedents to accommodate the new, discovering and enhancing useful consistencies, differences, and continuities. At the very germination of the Canadian Justice for Victims Initiative, for instance, before the Solicitor General had given any formal commitment to help victims, it was politically inconceivable for policies for victims to advance under their own name. They had instead to be smuggled in under the cloak of the older, established policies of crime prevention and the promotion and dissemination of good police practice.

4

CRIMINAL JUSTICE POLICY MAKING

The first appearance of any new policy may then be more than a little odd, forced, as it were, to parade in disguise. And that disguise will be real enough in its consequences, being quite capable of constraining and moulding what can be done politically and practically. In Canada, it was to be a while before measures could be proposed for victims that were not seen manifestly to address the ends of crime prevention and the enhancement of police practice.

There are other deformations. Appearing to serve older ends, new policy issues will have in effect to fill the crevices offered by approved mandates, tasks, and duties. They may be diffracted and scattered as they enter an existing pattern of work and thought. In the Home Office, for example, policies for victims surfaced simultaneously in crime surveys as a means of 'improving the criminal justice database'; as an instrument of a reparative justice that was supposed to replace the fine as a sanction against the poor and unemployed defendant; and as the recipients of criminal injuries compensation that had been intended to buy off the angry victim of violence. That was how expertise about victims was officially organized and approved: it was piecemeal and incoherent, and it proved difficult indeed to reformulate and synthesize so that radically newer and larger images of victims and their needs could be considered.

I have argued that new ideas must often remain somewhat cloaked, incoherent, unfocused, and undeveloped until they have been allowed to become an explicit object of attention. Matters cannot be taken far without formal sanction. They cannot come properly into their own, and little money will be spent in their name, until they have been confirmed in the proper manner by a high official or, more effectively still, by a minister. Indeed, it is part of the bureaucratic art of persuasion that new ideas appear unfocused and unformed at first: they are *supposed* to be so until they receive political authority (it is, after all, the politician who must present the decision, become publicly identified with it and then answer for it to the wider world). Were it to seem otherwise, it might be thought that there had been an act of *lèse majesté*, a pre-empting of the senior's right to judge, govern, and make changes. Decisions must always seem to flow down from those who are accountable, not rise fully formed from obscure officials below.

Mandates

Political approval translates an idea into a political mandate, an internal notion into an external action, and 'going to ministers' is a transition for which there has to be considerable preparation.

In instances of bottom-up policy making, the setting where new ideas were engendered may well be structurally distant from the settings in which they will be inspected and approved by senior officials or politicians. They may stem at first or second hand from research or from what Canadians call 'program delivery', from the activities of those whose chief duty is not to write policy papers at all. Theirs will be the language of research and practice, a language ill suited to the drafting of policy papers, and it is a characteristic complaint of policy officials and politicians that researchers do not know how to speak or write for purposes of political action.

Policy proposals have their own idiom. They must be transformed into a semblance of the reasonable, consistent, solid, and coherent, transformed, indeed, into something rather more coherent and solid than those who draft them might privately concede

5

them to be. Drafting is a delicate skill. On the one hand, proposals must be given a history, a teleology, and secure links with established policies. They must seem reasonable, safe, and sensible, something worth pursuing, a plausible 'next step' that follows from mandates and manifestos, a step, moreover, that is unlikely to embarrass ministers or expose them to untoward criticism. Yet, on the other hand, they must also seem new and important enough to warrant exciting ministerial interest and perhaps even ministerial patronage, sufficiently distinctive to permit politicians to win 'some ink' as Canadian officials would put it. And all the while, as I have observed, proposals cannot be allowed to seem *too* solid, closed, or well argued because ministers would then think that they have been denied their right to decide and influence policy. Proposals must thus be at once convincing and open, new and not-so-new, clear and ambiguous, coherent and loose.

Above all, policy proposals must be phrased politically. That is, they must be designed to win approval from the powerful individuals and organizations that can impede or accelerate their progress, from other politicians and from 'practitioners' in the criminal justice system in particular. Those 'practitioners'—'private sector' organizations and police forces, probation services, prisons, judges and magistrates, prosecutors and lawyers, and all their representative organizations—compose a wary array of loose-coupled bodies that continually eye and treat with one another and with government at their centre. They are, in effect, a loose mass of significant others that retain what one former Home Secretary, Douglas Hurd, described as an 'independent interdependence'. They are neither autonomous nor subservient. They cannot be controlled by government, they do not control government themselves, but they do mediate the decisions of government, sometimes translating them beyond recognition; they are usually taken to be authorities about matters of government policy; they can reverse and transform what government does (the fate of the 1991 Criminal Justice Act being a prime instance), and ministers neglect them at their peril. Placating them is the first political imperative.

The second imperative is to allow ministers to appear consistent, reasonable, and plausible in the presentation and defence of their policies. The work of Canadian Solicitors General and British Home Secretaries is fraught. It is the dirty work of society (see Hughes 1971), the work from which others choose usually to draw back. It centres on the exercise of violence and coercion, the restraining of those who do not wish to be restrained, the investigation of guilty knowledge, and the routine management of pain, anger, distress, and injury. Allegations of brutality towards demonstrators, immigrants, prisoners and offenders, of negligence in the handling of cases, and of indifference to the victim and public abound. Dirty work is marked by a potential for criticism and scandal (another Home Secretary, James Callaghan, recalled how he used to 'switch on the radio news at seven o'clock in the morning mainly to find out what examples of alleged unfair treatment had cropped up during the night as a result of a Home Office decision' (Callaghan 1983: 15)).

Further, the dirty work of criminal justice is not only flawed by its inability to do much that is demonstrably effective, but it also gives rise to a proliferation of unintended consequences when things *are* attempted: recall that the suspended sentences designed to reduce the prison population merely enlarged it; that the unit fines supposed to restore fairness in sentencing were represented publicly and forcefully as most unfair; and that the short, sharp shock of penal reform was reported actually to

6

CRIMINAL JUSTICE POLICY MAKING

be liked by its recipients. New proposals must be offered gingerly because it is often safer to do very little or nothing at all for fear of things appearing to go wrong.

The third imperative is to hasten other objects sought by government. The politics of criminal justice are but part of a wider pattern of commitments and objectives. In Canada, for instance, federal criminal justice policies were pursued as much for their capacity to strengthen the integrity of the federal system as for any impact they might have on lesser problems of crime and justice. Indeed, federal–provincial relations (for which there was a separate Cabinet office) superseded much else. So it was that a policy emanating from the Ministry of the Solicitor General or the Ministry of Justice in Ottawa could not be allowed to estrange politicians from the provinces, and from Quebec or the western provinces above all, by seeming to encroach on their rights and sensibilities. In England and Wales, there has been for a long while an overriding political imperative to curtail public expenditure and enhance 'efficiency', and criminal justice policy cannot be seen to run markedly counter to it. At the very least, public rhetoric must contain some ostentatious reference to parsimony.

In all this, it may be seen that the argument of policy making does not necessarily model itself on the reasoning of criminology and the social sciences. That reasoning is of lesser importance. It is politically immaterial. Of course, politicians and senior officials do generally tend to want the tacit reassurance that what they are asked to endorse will not run foul of the good sense of criminologists and junior criminal justice practitioners. They would like to assume that they are supported at critical points by a largely invisible body of experts and expertise. They do not wish to appear foolish. But political argument has its own style which does not defer to social science (political speeches and briefing papers are not punctuated by scholarly citations but by references to political endorsements and the possible reactions of powerful institutions and constituencies). It may even be a little casuistical on occasion. In the Prison Department of the 1960s, for example, policies for women were frequently represented as *sui generis*, having no bearing on policies for men and establishing no precedents, because women offenders were themselves *sui generis*. In April 1969, Lord Stonham argued in a speech 'women are a special case requiring forms of treatment which are not necessarily suitable for men. They are special not because they are women but because the woman who risks a custodial penalty is a comparative rarity and thus justifies consideration as a special case'. It probably mattered little whether such an argument was always put with full conviction, whether officials did really imagine that women offenders were significantly different. What mattered was that an argument based on a difference between the sexes could sometimes help to take policies forward within the Home Office of the time.

If criminological reasoning is not always paramount, neither is criminological reasonableness. The discourse of politicians about criminal justice is sometimes less rational and utilitarian ('causative' is Christie Davies's word (Davies 1990)) than moralising, and the two forms of argument do not necessarily converge. Ministers act from moral conviction, political need, and personal opportunism. Their response to much scholarly research, and especially to contradictory research undertaken by their own staff, will be to ignore it, or to wish that it had never been conducted, and, if it *had* been conducted, never published. At a press conference held on 6 January 1994, for instance, the Prime Minister championed the superiority of common sense to 'fashionable theories' about moral conduct. The following day, again exhorting common sense, he was reported by the BBC to have talked about 'airy-fairy theories for dealing with criminals'. Criminology may be as much a political hazard or nuisance as a guide in the politician's world.

Committees as Modes and Models of Action

Seminars, surveys, literature reviews, and fieldwork supply the criminologist's knowledge, but it is the committee that chiefly supplies the knowledge and methodology of policy makers and politicians. Committees are the stock instrument of government: they put flesh on the first, deliberately vague arguments of submissions to senior officials or ministers; they develop, protect, and shepherd ideas through successive stages of the political process; they enlarge the number of organizations seen to have a manifest interest in an issue; they may ultimately be responsible for the implementation of policy; and, in all this, they have their own detailed phenomenology.

The very composition of a new committee is usually intended to convey political meaning to a knowing audience. In the distrustful world of criminal justice, a world built on conflict and competition, the members of a committee tend to be appointed expressly to reassure powerful onlookers that they and their stance have been recognized and incorporated, that a balance has been struck between jarring interests, that the committee will not be the creature of any faction. There are stock configurations: in England and Wales, the probation service is used conventionally to play the part of the offender's champion, the symbolic counterweight to the police, and probation officers will often be found facing police officers in committee meetings; in Canada, a geographically gargantuan federal state riddled with complicated political jealousies, federal officials will be matched by provincial officials, state representatives by representatives of the 'private sector', the eastern provinces by western provinces, and men by women (and Canadian committees are much more substantial, abundant, and prolix than those to be found in England and Wales. Indeed, the Canadian delegations to United Nations congresses on matters of crime and control are amongst the very largest of all.)

Thus recruited and so aligned, the members of a committee act in part to embody the policy maker's expectation of how a new issue might make its political mark on the world. They are an anticipation of who will receive and define the issue; of who will implement it or impede its implementation; of who, in short, must be won before it can succeed. They display a careful political iconography, an encoded statement of the kind of thing the policy must become. It matters less that they do not always contain those who consider themselves the wisest and most experienced men and women in criminal justice, the criminologists and professors of criminal law perhaps, than that they represent a conspicuous obeisance to the institutions that could do their fledgling issue harm.

Forming a committee confirms an important transfer of ownership and it is not without its existential costs for the original small group of officials who engendered a policy. In Canada especially, where it is not considered unseemly to display personal commitment to the ends of policy making, officials sometimes found it difficult to relinquish 'their' issue to others (and especially to others who appeared to have no great regard for the task); to share information, materials, and sources; in short, to lose control over their creation. At various critical opening phases of the history of the

CRIMINAL JUSTICE POLICY MAKING

Canadian Justice for Victims of Crime Initiative, for example, some officials chose to cling to what they had themselves set in motion, impeding its movement to the next stages of what, in Ottawa, is always an elaborately figured sequence of policy development. It was as if they claimed to know and care much more about victims than could any of their successors, the officials and politicians who had shared none of the early investments, experiences, and relations that had infused the beginnings of a new and enthralling area of policy development. Of course, in doing so, they were behaving a little perversely, but they did find it hard to forego what had become symbolically a piece of themselves. Transitions are always difficult.

I have argued that by convention government committees contain the formal representatives of institutionally-embedded interests and practices thought likely to bear significantly on a new policy. They are devised to draw outsiders in, to anticipate and accommodate their views, to implicate them practically and symbolically, perhaps even to transform them into agents who will turn to work on their own parent institutions, and to present them as reassuring tokens of the kind of policy that is considered to be in the making.

Outsiders may do much to promote an issue, they may enlarge the number of its supporters, they will bring fresh knowledge, methods, and ideas to bear, but they will always be included at a price. Those who invite them in will be obliged to surrender some of their ability to define an issue and control how it is treated (and they will be obliged to do so gracefully). The very logic and content of policy making can begin to acquire what seem to be alien forms as the new members work on the original, core idea and transform it into their own property.

Who is invited to draft shapes what will be said. In this sense, policy proposals may be read as transcriptions of the social structure of the committee that considered them. For instance, Status of Women Canada was a federal government organization entrusted with vetting relevant policy papers submitted to Cabinet in the late 1970s and early 1980s, and its representatives were invited as a matter of course to become members of policy-making committees within the Ministry of the Solicitor General. As routinely, almost all criminal justice policy proposals emanating from that Ministry would make conspicuous reference to the interests of women. The Home Office has no commerce with an English counterpart of Status of Women Canada and it does not make such visible genuflections to women. The papers of the Canadian Justice for Victims of Crime Initiative, an initiative addressed to all Canadian victims, were heavily laden with images of crimes against women and with allusions to the special needs of women. Home Office proposals on victims at large were not thus 'gendered' (although, to be sure, there have been other, discrete Home Office initiatives on rape and domestic violence). It was just so with federal–provincial relations, relations between the state and private sector, links between the eastern and western reaches of the nation, and the like. Canadian policy proposals tend to be vastly more ornate and lengthy than their British counterparts, and they make many more detailed references to political mandates and obligations. In so doing, they are a mirror of the greater complexity of relations within that divided, cumbersome federal state. Canadian officials themselves seem to be significantly more conscious of the art and artfulness of policy making. They treat their work as a mystery which demands the greatest attention. They talk incessantly about themselves and their activities as 'process persons'. The British official is, by contrast, less visibly prone to self-examination.

9

PAUL ROCK

Over time, a committee can become rather more than a simple aggregation of diverse interests. It can become a social group with a sense of joint purpose, a history and a distinctiveness that sets it apart from the larger world (including the institutions from which its members were themselves recruited). The experience of working together for a period of time on a single project under a common name recognized by others can lead members to share an identity and the beginnings of a subculture. So it was that the chairman of the Holloway Redevelopment Project Group recorded in his first, unpublished progress report in March 1969 that 'I regard continuity of membership . . . as important in contributing to the development of a loyalty to the group and the project as such. In such a major enterprise it is necessary that the key contributors should feel personally identified with its success'.

What is one chairman's process of personal identification is another's 'going native', and it is just that risk of their representatives 'going native' which can occasion anxiety amongst staff working in other institutions, leading to the periodic replacement of personnel and the deliberate disruption of continuity.

A committee is a way of seeing, and it is a way of seeing, moreover, that is quite purposefully cultivated as members set to work constructing narratives to strengthen and elucidate themselves and their project (a task especially valuable for those who are newcomers to the policy area and who require rapid briefing). One such narrative will centre on an issue's place in the larger history of criminal justice policies. I have argued that issues are often forced to begin their life in strange clothing, being represented as attempts to promote other goals already approved. I have also argued that they will have been deliberately phrased in an underdeveloped and ambiguous form. At the outset, they can seem more than a little confused and ill defined to the naive eye.

It is the job of early committee papers to undo some of that vagueness, to give workable concreteness and definition to an issue and its resolution. In giving them greater solidity, a committee will begin to acquire what is, in effect, the political equivalent of its navigational bearings. Like most elaborate projects in everyday life, policy making is experienced *in situ* as an emergent, indeterminate, anxious, and uncertain process, buttressed by no guarantees of success. At the very beginning, not much will be known about an issue and the problems that will be encountered, it is difficult to predict outcomes, and the manufacture of a semblance of structure and direction is an indispensable first step. From time to time thereafter, there are likely to be further reinterpretations of structure and direction as key officials leave and their successors take stock of their new position. In early 1974, for example, the security advisor to the Holloway Redevelopment Project changed and, with his leaving, there came a significant revision of the new prison's security provisions.

If briefings confer structure and direction, it can never be forgotten that the committee's political mandate was underdeveloped, and that the committee has no licence to change its fundamental import. Re-drafting cannot be free. It must, instead, build carefully on what was originally approved, retaining the statement's sense and, indeed, much of its phrasing, returning pointedly to its principal themes, piling detail on a narrow base. It will begin by locating itself in time, giving itself what McHugh called a retrospective-prospective reading (McHugh 1968).

Retrospectively, it will search for a past, for the precedents and early stirrings that explain how it was that a policy issue arose and the committee came to be formed at all. I remarked how, before they are approved, issues tend to be cultivated as instances of

10

CRIMINAL JUSTICE POLICY MAKING

other policies altogether, and I gave the instance of Canadian victims who were first helped in the name of improving police efficiency. There will be no need to resort to such flags of convenience once a firm political mandate has been secured. To the contrary, such a mandate will enable policy makers to look back and claim other policies and near-policies as part of their own legitimating history. What had been disguised will then be revealed as the clear forebear of policies now in the making. It is as if policies must begin their lives with a false identity imposed by others, but that they will come in time to force others to become part of *their* solipsism, histories switching back and forth in sympathy with changes of political fortune.

The reconstruction of the past can become quite bold on occasion, particularly when it is conducted by a bureaucrat fired with zeal for a cause. Things that might have been thought quite peripheral will then be retrieved and claimed historically, being awarded a teleology in which they become the ancestors and antecedents of a present politics. For instance, papers advancing the growth of policies for victims and reparative justice refer quite routinely to Moses and Hamurabi, to Solon and the Anglo-Saxon moot.

Prospectively, a committee must plot a course based on bureaucratic and political schedules so that patterns of work can be planned and difficulties forestalled. Any piece of policy making requires that its papers will be presented to a succession of meetings and its decisions co-ordinated with those of parallel bodies. Politicians and civil servants work to lesser and greater timetables. There is the round of the parliamentary year and the Public Expenditure Survey and, within it, the smaller rounds of departmental and interdepartmental meetings. Such schedules present a strong teleology for any policy making, laying out an exact sequence of actions that must be undertaken if a committee is to succeed in its task. They reduce uncertainty by preparing a future. They impart a clear, formal logic to policy making: *this* paper must be ready for *that* meeting with *this* argument. They specify much of the content of policy making: a paper must contain recommendations consonant with other recommendations, declarations, and manifestos already agreed by ministers and government. They give a pulse and a rhythm to policy making; *this* meeting on a particular date will be succeeded by *that* meeting of another date and then by yet another meeting thereafter. They give an unambiguous goal for the opening stages of most policy making; most probably a successful submission to Cabinet and Treasury. They give a political audience for policy making; laying out what is, in effect, a chain of significant others who must be addressed effectively if matters are to go forward and prosper. They give duration to policy making. In short, they furnish a strong grammar and choreography which will impress themselves on what must be done.

It is a consequence that policies are fairly homologous within states. They follow set forms of argument that carefully refract the contours and history of the political world through which they are steered. The more complex that world, the more complex must policies and policy documents themselves be. I have already observed that Canadian federal policies deferred to the rights of women and natives; to the private sector; and to the provinces. They were taken before Status of Women Canada, interdepartmental and federal–provincial meetings, and conferences with voluntary organizations. The working year of Canadian officials could be described as a great, orderly spate of meetings, and the wordy policy documents that emerged at its end were replete with bows and curtsies to all the bodies that had been so fulsomely consulted. The Home Office official, by contrast, tends traditionally to reckon with fewer outside powers,

11

PAUL ROCK

attend fewer meetings, communicate chiefly through internal files, and produce fewer, shorter, and more simply-structured briefing papers.

An accompanying step is neither prospective nor retrospective but synchronic. Policy officials may search about them publicly for information about the character of the issue that has newly to come into view, to establish what others are doing in its name. Such a quest also leads to the creation of a narrative about what the issue now amounts to as a practical problem. It would have been compromising to have conducted it before, in advance of formal permission to proceed, because a premature public display of interest might have been misinterpreted by outsiders as a political willingness to act. Besides, policy officials, busy as they often are, have little enough time to interest themselves in affairs to no profit. They tend to present themselves as officially deaf to problems not officially recognized (although unofficially, of course, things may be otherwise, and research staff, entrusted with a different role, are expected to have a reasonably broad knowledge of what is afoot in criminology and criminal justice).

When a policy matter lies wholly within the government's domain, when those liable to be affected are all state employees and state dependants, it may well be the case that officials take it that they know enough to proceed without much visible enquiry. Deafness will prevail. In the instance of the rebuilding of Holloway, for example, consultations were made rather late in the life of the initiative. Plans were quite far advanced when the shape of the new prison was finally disclosed to the public in 1971, three years after the decision was announced in Parliament. And consultations about the new prison were described by those involved as perfunctory indeed. (Even in the instance of rebuilding Holloway, an institution in an urban area, government officials were not quite sovereign: local authorities, Members of Parliament, and residents' groups protested vehemently about the use of scarce land for a prison, and they had to be appeased a little).

In other cases, the political endorsement of a new issue ends indifference. Officials who had formerly been inattentive can become very attentive indeed as they move rapidly to accumulate stocks of knowledge about an area. Government departments have routine techniques for the purpose: research officers or consultants will be set to work compiling 'literature reviews'; money will be allocated to found 'resource centres'; old files and speeches will be trawled; and conferences will be organized. In all this, it is apparent that officials seek to amass, list, and categorize information to furnish a pragmatically useful description of what is being done in and around an issue. But, in such a public amassing of data, they will always accomplish more than mere description. Theirs is a world pregnant with meaning. It will be scanned by politicians, practitioners, and critics and, with a peculiar intensity, by research, voluntary, and statutory organizations continually hungry for money. Officials have to proceed in the full understanding that their every act will be read as a possible sign of shifting government intentions. Indeed, they will knowingly act to signify.

Formal public enquiry stirs up multiple meanings. It is a practical method of advertising that a government or department is considering whether to move in on a social problem (and it may be initiated precisely to invite pressure to move). It will be interpreted as a running indication of the kinds of plan that government has in mind for that problem. It brings into official view those who are the target of enquiry, laying them out within a framework supplied by the state, emphasizing certain facets and

CRIMINAL JUSTICE POLICY MAKING

suppressing others. It encourages those target organizations to examine themselves, to ask whether they are, in fact, inhabitants of the world supposed to centre on that problem and in that manner, whether, indeed, they recognize the problem as an entity that should be so defined at all.

Take one instance: the manner in which the composition of a conference will define a problem. Inclusions, exclusions, timings, and orders of appearance count. When, for example, the mounting of a crime survey was first mooted at a conference organized by the Home Office in early 1981, no invitation to attend was issued to members of the fledgling National Association of Victim Support Schemes, the body responsible for aiding victims of crime. It was thereby made abundantly clear that crime surveys were not supposed to illuminate the character of victims or the experience of crime. They were instead taken to be a method of improving what was called the 'criminal justice data base'.

Conferences have their own manifest phenomenology. They signify that a problem has been acknowledged by government; they define its ingredients and its social constituents; they bring those constituents together and present them to one another, perhaps for the first time, and under a common name, in the hope, perhaps, that they will come to recognize a common identity and purpose; and they act as an audience, response, and catalyst for the decisions that officials will prepare (the teleology of an approaching speech is a powerful means of eliciting public commitments from ministers and senior civil servants, and conferences are frequently organized precisely for that end).

In this search for information and convening of meetings, officials can stretch out quite far to encompass organizations and people who may not have considered themselves parts of the emerging policy issue, and who may indeed resent the belated attempt of central government to determine who and what they really are. After all, such official definitions tend to arise late in the careers of those organizations, usually after they have become established under their own chosen names. One example is given by the Home Office Programme Development Unit that set about funding community-based projects in 1991 by inviting the submission of original proposals to reduce criminality and domestic violence. Its chief object was to discover and foster something of the vernacular criminology currently being practised by local groups. It was fired by a broad Conservative ministerial interest in revitalizing the moral fabric of the family and by the civil servant's interest in the social engineering of 'headstart' and other programmes devised to compensate for social disadvantage. What it *did* meet was a wholesale lay interest in the 'empowerment' of the young, an interest that echoed the Big Bang of the radical liberation movements of the 1960s.

Similarly, when the governments of Canada and of England and Wales set about formulating policies for victims, they encountered groups and individuals who had made little use of the word 'victim', who did not at first conceive themselves to be part of the politics of crime and criminal justice, and who resisted efforts to become incorporated into what appeared powerfully to be another's reality. Those who worked with abused children, assaulted women, and incest and rape survivors, did not enter willingly into the politics of *victims*. Victims, crime, and criminal justice were not central to their vocabulary. They had their own rival political history which was not to be shed lightly.

Such encounters take place on uneven ground because the state has the greater

13

PAUL ROCK

ability to define and reward, especially when those on the boundaries of its newly-proclaimed policies are ill organized, poor, and lacking in substantial authority within the criminal justice system. Yet organizations can and do answer back. It would be most undiplomatic of officials and politicians to rebuff their conceptual challenges too roundly, particularly when they hope to enlist members of the organizations to support them, to give them legitimacy and to do some of the work that the implementation of a policy will require.

Policy Making as a Dialectical Process

At every successive stage of the policy-making process, then, issues will be dressed and proffered to a larger group for inspection, collaboration, and the possibility of symbolic co-ownership, and, at every stage, officials cannot be certain about what that larger group might do. The process is emergent; not quite within the official grasp. If the group's response is not a simple repulse, policy proposals must receive at least some token imprint to register that officials have deferred to the group and heeded what it has said. The whole amounts to a dialectic in which policies enter the public domain step by step, being sent out to ever-wider social circles and presented for possible acquisition, and returning each time transformed. In Canada, a country so vast it must depend on a major decentralization of the criminal justice system, those social circles extend out into the provinces, municipalities, and the private domain, and they are wooed quite assiduously. In England and Wales, the array of circles is smaller, tighter, and more nearly confined to the state, but there must conventionally be consultation with ACPO and ACOP, the Lord Chancellor's Department and the Lord Chief Justice, the Magistrates' Association and perhaps, very tentatively, with friendly bodies in the private sector defined by the Home Office as 'house-trained'. There is a British dialectic too and, if it is ignored, ACPO, ACOP, the Magistrates Association and the others can round on government. They did so quite fiercely in the aftermath of the 1991 Criminal Justice Act.

Policy Making as Reflective Action

The dialectic and its forms are familiar to officials, being the very stuff of statecraft. They deploy presentation and signification to propel subjects through the sequence of phases that will transform them into entities fit for political action. Policies are the effect of an accumulation of stimuli.

Officials cannot always wait patiently for the right stimulus to arise and do its work precisely at the appropriate time. They intervene continually, nursing the dialectic, and they do so by standing back to reflect on the pace, direction, appearance, and impact of their own actions. In what the Canadians call a 'paper world', they use the medium proper to policy making: the manipulation of argument and rhetoric. They objectify themselves, their work, their artefacts and their environment, transforming them all into materials for symbolic management. The world of policy making is then itself reflexive, becoming a thing to be embellished and arranged, goaded into action by stimuli which it has itself created and planted. In Weick's phrase (Weick 1982), officials work to enact their own environment: they engender the apparently objective conditions to which they themselves must respond, and, in responding, carry matters

14

CRIMINAL JUSTICE POLICY MAKING

forward. I described how ministers would be asked to speak on particular themes, committing them to make the public utterances and perhaps even the commitments that officials would draft for them. Entire conferences will be organized to elicit just such a speech. More obvious still is the 'planted' parliamentary question to which there will be a prepared answer, and officials speak with occasional pride and amusement about the replies they drafted for their own questions. Policy making thus turns round on itself, and officials in those states where such a process is especially elaborate may be heard talking about themselves talking, referring to themselves quite impersonally as a third party.

It must be noted that timetables do not always unfold smoothly and officials cannot always be in command of events which they have themselves engineered. Criminal justice policy making is so extensive, unpredictable, and fragmented that they cannot foresee just what may happen about them. In this sense, policies are set in an intricate and volatile environment of other initiatives and events that are also on the move, and their fate will be shaped by the manner in which officials can use that environment to political effect. Theirs must be an opportunistic world that rewards the alert and the persuasive. They are strategists preoccupied always with what they call the 'windows of opportunity' that come and go before them, strategists who try to employ ingenious arguments to manoeuvre their candidate policies into place when the time is right.

So it is that fledgling policies are often obliged to ride to success in the wake of other, more mature political movements and rhetoric will be devoted to the effort of harnessing them together. In *A View from the Shadows* (1986), for instance, I showed how the Canadian Justice for Victims of Crime Initiative, designed for all victims, men and women, acquired its political momentum from the women's movement and its campaigns against rape and battering. A bundle of policies for Canadian victims was advanced within the Trojan horse of a proposed federal initiative to help assaulted women, and, being thus transported, it had to take its timing from another initiative altogether.

So it is, too, that policies must often be hurried for promotion when the propitious occasion presents itself, however unexpected that occasion may be. The National Association of Victim Support Schemes received major government support in 1986 in response to a sudden funding crisis induced by that same government's imminent abolition of a number of the Association's prime patrons, the metropolitan authorities. And the Canadian Justice for Victims of Crime Initiative was assembled rapidly in 1981 because it could be represented as a new, inexpensive venture that could be funded at the very moment when a sum of Treasury money needed to be spent on a cheap policy innovation. Ottawa officials held that the timing was actually not quite 'right', that they were not really prepared at that stage to emerge into the public domain, but financial austerity was looming and money was unlikely to be available when the policies themselves were in a state of greater readiness.

In this and other instances, the intention might well have been to engage in the careful designing, orchestration, and execution of plans, but the practice is as likely to be expedient and improvisatory, and policy itself can become transformed into something makeshift. Many policies have to enter the world premature and incomplete, lacking fine detail and content. It is only after they have been announced that officials can set themselves the task of discovering or inventing quite what has been approved.

15

PAUL ROCK

Conclusion

Policy making is the instrument through which the original, subjective inspiration of a few individuals closeted within a bureaucracy can move out to become a public, anonymous, and objective component of the criminal justice system at large. It proceeds typically by preparing and submitting ideas to an ever greater mass of significant others for judgement and investment, and it turns, first, on the physical and symbolic incorporation of outsiders and secondly, on spinning webs of causality about itself and its projects. It is, in this sense, both its own object, a creature of parthenogenesis, and an object proffered to others for fostering. It would be an otherwise smooth metamorphosis were it not for the sudden lurches and opportunities imposed by uncontrolled problems of timing and context.

REFERENCES

BITTNER, E. (1965), 'The Concept of Organization', *Social Research*, 32.

CALLAGHAN, J. (1983), 'Cumber and Variableness', in *The Home Office: Perspectives on Policy and Administration*. London: Royal Institute of Public Administration.

DAVIES, C. (1990), *From the Sacred Hierarchies to Flatland*. Reading: University of Reading.

HUGHES, E. (1971), 'Good People and Dirty Work', in *The Sociological Eye*, Chicago: Aldine-Atherton.

McHUGH, P. (1968), *Defining the Situation*. Indianapolis: Bobbs-Merrill.

ROCK, P. (1986), *A View from the Shadows*. Oxford: Clarendon Press.

—— (1990), *Helping Victims of Crime*. Oxford: Clarendon Press.

—— (1993), *The Social World of the English Crown Court*. Oxford: Clarendon Press.

—— (1994), 'The Social Organization of a Home Office Initiative', *European Journal of Crime, Criminal Law and Criminal Justice*, 2.

WEICK, K. (1982), 'Enactment Processes in Organizations', in B. Staw and G. Salancik (eds.), *New Directions in Organizational Behavior*. Malabar: Robert E. Krieger.

[17]

Community and the Criminal Justice System

Mary Tuck

The phrase 'the criminal justice system' is so common within the Home Office that it has an internal office abbreviation – 'the CJS'. Everyone knows what these initials mean when used in minutes and memoranda. But the phrase is not in common use elsewhere. Judges, lawyers, prison officials, probation officers or policemen do not habitually perceive themselves as working for 'the criminal justice system'. They see themselves as working within their particular specialist structures.

People at the Home Office have to consider the system as a whole because they know that changes in any one part of it entail changes in another. For instance increased use of cautioning by the police entails a different balance of cases at the magistrates' courts, a different pattern of referral to the higher courts and has effects on the probation service and even the prison population, since the size of that population is so dependent on the processing time of the courts (roughly one fifth of the prison population is on remand). Any desirable reform in any one part of the system almost certainly requires changes in other parts, and these in their turn lead to changes elsewhere.

Such knowledge is inevitably not fully available to those working within particular parts of the system such as the courts, the police service or the prisons.

In a Home Office publication *Tackling Crime*, published in 1989, the then home secretary, Douglas Hurd accepted responsibility for coordinating the criminal justice system. 'The Home Office has many reponsibilities but I am clear that our main job is to lead and coordinate the effort against crime', he wrote. The same words were repeated by his successor in 1990 when the same publication was issued in a revised edition. *Tackling Crime* recognises explicitly that 'coordination' of 'the agencies which make up the criminal justice system' is the responsibility of the Home Office.[1]

But though responsibility is recognised, *Tackling Crime* shows that the machinery is weak. Little can be cited except for 'regular meetings at ministerial and official level' between the Home Office, the Lord Chancellor's Department and the Attorney General's Office, some court user groups in the regions and a programme of ad hoc conferences and seminars set up by the Home Office to encourage cooperation across agencies.

Here is a strange situation: an agreed articulation in a public document signed by successive home secretaries that the criminal justice system *is* a system which needs to be coordinated in some fashion; but a marked inadequacy in the specification of how the agencies which make up this system should relate to each other or how the Home Office can ensure that they do.

Justice versus management

Part of the problem is the very vagueness of the system's goal defined (ingeniously) by the document as 'tackling crime'. There are two very different conceptual models underlying the ways in which 'crime' and 'dealing with crime' are thought about in modern society. These can be described as 'the justice model' and 'the management model'. They operate in different ways within different parts of the system and I shall argue that much of the incoherence of the system is due to unacknowledged conflicts between the two.

By the justice model I do not intend to indicate anything very complex. I am not referring to the concept of 'just deserts' held to underly a specific type of sentencing. I refer simply to the the old fashioned, taken-for-granted common wisdom that the way to deal with crime is to catch criminals, take them to court, judge them and then, if they are found guilty, punish them. If one asked the ordinary man in the street (or the average politician or journalist) how society deals with crime, this would probably be the response: society deals with crime through the police, the courts, and the prisons, catching the guilty and punishing them when caught. Committing a crime is seen as the responsibility of an individual for which he can be punished as an individual. The way to 'deal with' or 'tackle' crime is to deal with the individuals who commit it.

The management model, by contrast, is based on the insight that some crime is inevitable in any society and conceives the task as being to manage, reduce or prevent the amount of crime so as to make its occurrence as little damaging to society as possible. On this model the responsibility for devising ways of 'dealing' with crime falls largely to central administration, which has to measure the efficacy of any particular means of 'dealing' carried out by any of the agencies involved, and to extend or replace it according to its utilitarian value in reducing or preventing the kind of crime which damages society.

The justice model characterises the crown prosecution service, the higher and lower courts and those who serve and work in them such as lawyers and solicitors. They see themselve as 'doing justice'; considerations of managerial efficiency must, if present at all, be thoroughly subordinated to this goal. The Home Office on the other hand is much influenced by the management model. From the Home Office point of view crime is mainly something to be 'managed'; it has to be prevented where possible, but the impossibility of its complete elimination has to be acknowledged. Utilitarian criteria such as the costs of crime and the costs of its prevention and processing must enter into decisions and arrangements. Other criminal justice agencies such as the police, the probation service and the prison service are caught somewhere between the two models.

Of course this account is an over-simplification. The home secretary and the Home Office have this year put before Parliament a Criminal Justice Bill which uses the language of the justice model. The Home Office's necessary role in unifying the system means it has to keep present in its collective mind and its public rhetoric the different models and goals used by all those engaged in criminal justice matters. So the Home Office can never be a creature of the management model alone.

Nonetheless the management model comes more readily and naturally to minds in the Home Office than to minds working in the courts or the crown prosecution service. This can be shown from the Home Office's own research publications.

Justice and management in Home Office research publications
The Home Office is unusual within Whitehall in having had a group of scientific analysts of policy integrated closely into the department over many decades and publishing its work for public scrutiny. This is the Home Office research and planning unit where I myself worked from 1976 to 1989, for the last five years as its head. Those of us who worked in the unit to some extent resented the description of us by outside academics such as Jock Young as 'the new administrative criminologists'.[2] But it is undeniable that much of the unit's effort since its inception in the 1950s has been devoted to developing and improving the managerial model for dealing with crime. This can be shown from the list of Home Office Research Studies. (There are now 120 of them, spanning the decades from 1955 to the present day).

Early work in the 1950s and 1960s concentrated on testing the effects of what I have called the justice model, looking at the effects, if any, on individual offenders of the various disposals of the criminal justice system.

The largely negative results of this phase of work culminated in the mid 1970s with the publication of a Home Office Research Study (HORS No. 35) on the effectiveness of sentencing and HORS No. 36, on the effectiveness of various forms of probation and aftercare treatment. Neither found much impact on subsequent behaviour of the various disposals of the formal criminal justice system.[3]

In the same year, 1976, a new wave of Home Office studies was signalled by the publication of HORS No. 34, *Crime as Opportunity*, which presented for the first time in Britain the theory and practice of 'situational crime prevention'; that is the reduction of crime through the reduction of physical opportunities for its occurrence. From the mid 1970s to mid 1980s *Crime as Opportunity* was followed by further detailed studies in crime prevention techniques by managerial means, many of them reprinted later in two books published by the Home Office, *Designing Out Crime* and *Situational Crime Prevention: From Theory Into Practice*. It is this body of work which lies behind the great popularity of modern crime prevention techniques.[4]

But this was not the only strand of Home Office research in the late 1970s and on through the 1980s. During the same years, a distinguished body of work on the detailed workings and management of the formal criminal justice system was being developed, largely under the influence of Roger Tarling, now the unit's head. HORS No. 46 in 1978 looked at fines in magistrates courts, HORS No. 56 in 1979 at sentencing practice in magistrates courts, HORS No. 71 in 1982 reported on contested trials in magistrates courts.[5] Many of the new series of Research and Planning Unit Papers were devoted to studies of this type. The addition to the unit's strength in 1984 of a group of well-qualified scientific officers with special expertise in systems analysis and computing led to work on modelling the criminal justice system.[6] In 1985 a collected group of studies of management in the criminal justice system was published under the title *Managing Criminal Justice*.[7] This book of readings (published a few years before *Tackling Crime*) opened with a discussion of the reality or otherwise of the concept of 'the criminal justice system'. Under the influence of this theoretical work, the concept of the criminal justice system had become a serious part of Home Office thinking.

So, throughout the 1960s, 1970s and 1980s, the research and planning unit gradually pushed the Home Office in a managerial direction. The effect of Home Office research was to test and discredit the effectiveness of the formal criminal justice system in 'dealing with' crime, and hence by implication to reduce confidence in what I have called the justice model. In its place were developed two frankly managerial techniques. Situational crime prevention offered the hope of reducing crime itself by good management of the opportunity structures. And the new wave of work on

Community and the Criminal Justice System

the criminal justice system and its interactions suggested that the justice
system itself needed to be conceived of in managerial ways.

Another model

In the late 1980s and early 1990s a new strand developed in Home Office
thinking in both research and policy terms. Work in ethnic minority
studies led to a renewed stress on the role of community in creating or
containing crime.[8] Other studies showed that the implementation of
crime prevention measures was itself dependent on social attitudes and
community organisation.[9] Although the British Crime Survey, first
reported on in 1983, had initially been conceived as a means of exposing
the triviality of most crime and the unreliability of police statistics as a sole
guide to the size of the crime problem, by the time the results of the second
wave were published in 1985 it had become a tool for exposing important
area variations in the incidence of crime, of dramatising how much it was
a phenomenon of poor urban areas and hence how closely its existence
was related to social and community factors.[10]

Certainly by the time I became head of the unit in 1986 I was convinced
that under the surface of the 'new administrative criminology' a new way
of thinking, a new community emphasis, was breaking through, an
emphasis to be strengthened in subsequent years by such detailed studies
as HORS No. 96 on schooling and disruptive behaviour, HORS Nos. 106
and 107 on rape and domestic violence and HORS No. 108 on drinking
and disorder in country towns.[11] A conference on communities and crime
was convened by the Home Office Research and Planning Unit in
Cambridge in 1986 and in 1988 the book of readings *Communities and Crime
Reduction* once again confirmed a change in thinking at the centre.[12]
Detailed empirical studies of crime, housing and community were begun
in the late 1980s and some will report later this year.

I believe this new emphasis on community offers a means of
reconciling conflicts beween the justice and management models, and
hence has importance in a discussion of the way forward for the criminal
justice system. But first I need to place the movements of opinion within
the Home Office in the context of a wider debate.

The wider debate

The growing stress on management, both in the research publications and
in the Home Office more generally, is part of a growth of bureaucratic
rationalisation long foreseen and feared by the German sociologist, Max
Weber. In the early 20th century Weber had argued that the rational
exercise of power through bureaucracy was necessary, even inevitable, if
the arbitrary nature of earlier patterns of rule were to be overcome. Weber
did not see this development of bureaucracy as wholly bad. He merely

diagnosed it as inevitable if existing problems were to be solved. But he also expressed fears that the inevitable growth of bureaucracy might create a 'cage of bondage' in which all individuality would be stifled; at worst a total or totalitarian rule, in which people would become mere cogs in a machine, individual problems generalised and formalised into impersonal cases in a bureacratic filing system.

Weber's analyses, Weber's fears have been broadened and developed by later social theorists such as Anthony Giddens and, more particularly, Robert Holton and Bryan Turner, who have applied the Weberian model specifically to the criminal justice system.[13] Are these fears being realised under the influence of 'the new administrative criminologists' in the growth of the managerial model of crime? Many in the legal profession fear that distant management, far from the courts, in pursuit of the elusive goals of economy, effectiveness and efficiency, is losing sight of the need for individual justice. They are afraid for the independence of the law.

There is a tendency among administrators, criminologists and researchers to see all good as on the side of management with its inevitable accompanying bureaucracy, and all drags on progress as caused by an unthinking clinging to older individualist ways of thought by many within the older justice model. There is an opposing tendency among lawyers, judges and the functionaries of the legal apparatus to see all good as on the side of their versions of individual responsibility and of justice thinking, all problems as caused by heartless management. Of course this division is not absolute. There are management minded lawyers; there are administrators driven by a sense of personal justice. Some legal sociologists have shown how the law itself operates increasingly on bureaucratic models; some have suggested it retains its older personalist ideology merely as facilitating myth.[14] The broad divide is, however, there.

It is a deep intellectual and social divide which runs like a fissure through the world of criminal justice. Neither side alone has a monopoly of wisdom. Weber's fears are enough to show us the inadequacy of a purely managerial view of reality. None of us want to live in Weber's 'cage of bondage' – a world where all is settled by specialist expertise. But we cannot throw away the gains of modern knowledge and understanding, of the explosion of expertise about systems. It is no longer possible to take single decisions in isolation without consideration of their effects elsewhere.

Towards a reconciliation
To begin to reconcile these two views we need to develop a better theory of how community affects behaviour.

Purely managerial models rely at bottom on models of economic man and of what has become known as rational choice theory. Man is conceived as economic man, all his actions responsive to the sticks and carrots of perceived rewards or dis-benefits. But of late even rational choice theorists such as Jon Elster have begun to argue that man's actions cannot be explained by sticks and carrots alone. Man is also affected by what Elster describes as 'social norms', that is the ideas and views of his peer group as to how he should behave. This stress on the importance of social norms as a separate variable in predicting behaviour, quite distinct from calculations of expected utilities, has of course been present in social psychological models for many years.[15]

Once social norms are allowed in we are back in a world where behaviour is affected by the social community in which men live.

Such a model is in accord with the empirical facts. We know that the incidence of crime varies markedly by small areas and that the areas which experience most crime are poor council estates and deprived inner-city areas. Within deprived areas we know that the incidence of crime varies by even smaller neighbourhood groupings such as particular housing estates. Throughout the late 1980s it has become clearer and clearer that crime is largely a 'pocketed' phenomenon – rife in some (often very small) local communities, much less of a problem in others. Of course some of the explanation may be 'situational'; opportunities for crime are often greater in poor areas (for instance cash meters for electricity, which encourage theft, are more common there). Some of the explanation may be due to the lower value of 'respectability' as a possible expected utility to those living in such areas; their life chances are perhaps already too poor to be affected greatly by whether or not they fall foul of the criminal justice system. But it has been traditional also to see some of the answer in the sub-culture in such areas. High turnover of tenancies is a known characteristic of 'problem estates', as also is the absence of social interaction and weak family structures. The geographic distribution of crime in the United Kingdom lends credence to the interpretation that its presence or absence is connected with the presence or absence of local social norms against crime or of sufficiently settled communities to either produce or support such social norms. In the United States, Elliott Currie has argued a similar case. He has laid out the need to develop 'a supportive and nurturing human ecology' if crime is to be prevented, and he has suggested that such a programme requires a conscious attention to creating and supporting local institutions of family, work and community.[16]

The most difficult fact to explain about criminal behaviour is why most people most of the time do not engage in it. The 'situational' opportunities are omni-present. The open shelves of supermarkets and department stores groan with easily pocketable goods; citizens walk the streets, casually clutching handbags and briefcases full of money; cars are left parked and untended in car parks all over England; in every suburb whole streets of

houses, stuffed with re-saleable electric goods of some value, are left empty
from morning to night. The strange thing to explain is not that some of
these things are sometimes stolen, but that so many are not. The reason
is unlikely to be simply the deterrent of punishment. The chances of being
caught for casual opportunistic theft are notoriously low. The reasons
must be to do with what Elster calls 'social norms'. Most of us, most of the
time do not engage in criminal behaviour either because it does not occur
to us or we think we should not. These are normative motivations. They
are to do with membership of a community.

As with the criminal, so with the actors in the criminal justice system.
It is true that the manager or the administrator can change the rules of
the professional game so that lawyers or justices' clerks or policemen or
prison officers will behave differently, in ways the manager hopes will be
more adaptive for the smooth running of the system as a whole. But it is
also true that often lawyers or justices clerks' or policemen or prison
officers refuse to respond to the managers' sticks or carrots and go on
behaving in some non-adaptive, non-rewarding, non-maximising fashion,
simply because it is their habit or culture to do so. Sometimes managers
cannot even impose what clearly would be helpful rules, because the
traditions or norms of the institutions or professional groups concerned
make this impossible. It would be a brave bureaucrat, for instance, who
tried to persuade the judiciary that they did not deserve eight weeks'
summer holiday. The customs and norms of professions and institutions
within the criminal justice system are immensely powerful.

A theory of community
To move forward we need to develop a community theory of crime, to put
flesh on the bones of the crucial insight that it is the communities in which
men live that affect their social norms and their behaviours. Neither the
justice schema nor the managerial schema are in themselves sufficient.

Unfortunately community theories have a bad name. As Peter
Willmott has recently documented, the word 'community' has been widely
used in the last decades to describe a multitude of social initiatives, often
loosely conceived. Few of these projects – from community architecture
to community care – have been based on any developed theory of how
communities actually work.[17] If we are to develope a community theory
of crime it needs to be more firmly based. The best source is probably
recent philosophic work on community ethics. The recent revival of
Aristotelian theory in the influential work of Alasdair McIntyre offers a
new framework for thinking about these issues, far richer than the narrow
model of economic man.[18]

In his recent book *After Virtue* McIntyre argues that concepts of 'virtue'
or right action arise, if at all, through common and coherent human social

activities. It is in and through social contexts that we acquire a shared understanding of the meaning of virtue. McIntyre invites us to consider human beings growing up in an ancient heroic society such as that described by Homer. It is necessary for the joint life of that society that men should learn to 'act well' in certain specific ways. Some would need to learn to excel in war as did Achilles, others in keeping the house as did Penelope, others in counsel as did Nestor. But in order to learn to practise these successfully, it is necessary to learn within a tradition, to study earlier best practices in swordsmanship, housekeeping or counselling. It is necessary to learn from and build on the skills of others. But, in turn, to do this needs humility, perseverance, honesty, courage. Without such qualities the individual would be unable to learn from the tradition or to contribute to it. This lived experience, both McIntyre and Aristotle believe, is the source of those habits known as the virtues.

The argument is meant to apply not only to Homeric societies but to all human societies. We can acquire those practices of excellence which living well requires only by acquiring certain habits or qualities collectively known as the virtues. This is as true if the excellence in practice we have to learn is excellence in programming computers or in nursing hospital patients as it is with excellence in swordsmanship or housekeeping. Different practices flourish in societies with different codes or histories; no practices can flourish in societies where the virtues are not valued. So the virtues are both learned from and necessary to all cooperative practices in human society.

McIntyre deals with the relevance of these concepts to the idea of justice. He invites us to consider the project, in any society, of founding a community to achieve a common project. In ancient society such a project might be the founding of a city; in modern society it might be the founding or carrying forward of a school, a hospital or an art gallery. As McIntyre puts it, 'Those who participated in such a society would need to develop two different kinds of evaluative practice. On the one hand they would need to value – to praise as excellences – those qualities of mind or character which would contribute to the realisation of their common good or goods.' In this way the concepts of the virtues arise. But as McIntyre goes on to point out there is a need for a further structure: 'They would also need to identify certain types of action as the doing or production of harm of such an order that they destroy the bonds of community in such a way as to render the doing or achieving of good impossible in some respect at least for some time. Examples of such offences would characteristically be the taking of innocent life, theft or perjury or betrayal.' It is this kind of behaviour which human societies have felt necessary to proscribe as 'crime'. On this view, the central purpose of the criminal law is to proscribe those behaviours that make communal endeavour, not just difficult, but impossible. Criminal law (as against civil law) exists in order to state and enforce those minimal requirements a community has perceived as necessary to its continued existence. Note that the purpose of the criminal law on this view is not to encourage the virtues (to make good men or, to put it another way, to form citizens unlikely to engage in crime); that task lies elsewhere. The purpose of criminal law is to outlaw, proscribe and punish that limited set of actions which are inimical to the very existence of joint practices between fellow members of a community.

Lessons for the criminal justice system

Now apply McIntyre's Aristotelian theory of justice and the virtues to the modern problems of the criminal justice system. The theory implies that neither the justice model nor the management model is in itself sufficient to 'tackle crime' though both (with modifications) are necessary. There is need for a model of community to supply a new more inclusive pattern which, if accepted, could reduce the suspicions those within the justice and managerial models have of each other.

Within such a community model, the ordinary man's justice model would be endorsed, but its limitations made plain. It is, on the community analysis, necessary for some actions such as murder, theft or interpersonal violence to be proscribed by society as a whole on behalf of society as a whole. Such proscription entails the activities of the police and the courts in catching offenders, testing their guilt or innocence and assigning due punishment to the guilty. Such actions are necessary both in justice and for training purposes. The training is of a limited sort and based on fear. 'Training that operates through fear of punishment is the kind of training the law imposes', as Thomas Aquinas, himself a good Aristotelian, put it.[19]

But such training through fear does not go to the root of the matter. Remember that McIntyre distinguishes sharply the proscription of acts that made communal endeavour impossible from the 'encouragement of the virtues'. For men to attain excellence in any endeavour, it is not enough for them to refrain from those disruptive acts properly described as criminal; they must learn to act within a tradition, be it of housekeeping, swordsmanship or computing; and to learn to act communally in this way requires of them the experience of participation in community. 'We learn how to do things by doing the things we are learning how to do'. For a society to be healthy, for the city to succeed, men need the experience of working together; they need to learn through experience to value those habits of trust, co-operation, humility, honesty and fairness ('the virtues') which make learning within a tradition possible.

So the perception of the manager that the activities of the police, the courts and the prisons in catching and punishing offenders do not really 'prevent' crime has some truth in it. The fear of punishment is not in itself enough to deter criminal acts if the chances of getting caught are slight, as they inevitably are in modern society. Crime is only really 'prevented' when men learn to be good. And if McIntyre and Aristotle are right they learn to be good (to practise the virtues) only through joint experience. Unfortunately, too many punishments imposed by the courts make such learning through communal activity more difficult. There is a role for fear. There is a role for punishment. But any society that thinks that only fear and punishment can encourage the making of good men is mistaken.

Community theory carries implications for the nature of punishments imposed by the courts. These, though set on a scale of just deserts, should wherever possible offer the offender the chance of learning the virtues through engaging in joint practices with others. This leads to punishment in the community wherever possible (as advocated in the recent Criminal Justice Act) and where a sentence of custody is unavoidable, to community prisons on the lines advocated by Lord Justice Woolf.[20]

The community analysis also has implications for the management model. The review of Home Office research isolated two strands within the management approach: 'situational crime prevention', the manipulation of the environment so that the rewards of crime are less easy to gain; and management across criminal justice agencies, adjusting rewards and disincentives so as to encourage more efficient processing.

Situational crime prevention has proven gains to offer. There will be a continuing need to improve, update and extend its techniques in a constantly changing world. But too much should not be hoped of these techniques. From the point of view of community theory, they do not go to the heart of the matter. The discouraged offenders have not learned virtue. They have simply had the terms of a non-virtuous calculation altered. The problem of 'displacement' remains; when one easy opportunity is blocked off, the calculating offender, blind to norms against criminal behaviour, may simply seek another. Such a process, if it occurs, will take time; the gains made by situational crime prevention are meanwhile real. But 'removing the occasions of sin' (to use an old phrase), though a sensible strategy, will never in itself be a sufficent one for containing crime.

As for the efficient management of the criminal justice system, a body of useful empirical knowledge has been built up (largely through the work of the Home Office Research Unit) which shows how the alteration of rules at one point in the system can have far-reaching effects at other parts of the system. Such results have been a proven aid to economy and efficiency. Without them and the various initiatives to which they have given rise (such as the introduction of time limits, the growth in police cautioning or the encouragement of community disposals) it is arguable that the criminal justice system of Britain would long ago have collapsed in disarray. There is a need for more work on the often obscure interactions of the ramifying apparatus of the system, and more understanding of how the results of such work can be fed into practice.

But community theory suggests that such manipulations will never be entirely successful unless, in addition, the problems of the social norms of the various agencies within the criminal justice system are addressed. The great block to either studying the interactions of the justice system or implementing the results of such study has been the attitudes of agencies within the system, especially the police and the judiciary who hold most firmly to what I have called the justice model. Early work by the Home Office and the Oxford Institute of Criminology on understanding judicial sentencing patterns was aborted in the 1970s because it was felt by the judiciary to be threatening. Despite the welcome development of the Judicial Studies Board, the culture of the higher judiciary and of the courts of appeal is still inimical to neutral research on the workings of the courts. Although the police have a much better record in collaborating with empirical studies, the Association of Chief Police Officers has over the last decade shown a more suspicious attitude to research and now refuses to allow access to students without carefully sifting their research applications.

The reasons for such suspicions are not entirely ignoble. They do not stem merely from defensive self-interested obfuscation. There is a real fear, certainly among lawyers and to an extent among policemen, that the managers, the bureaucrats, want research only because they do not understand the justice aims of the system – a belief that the managers (often named just as 'the Home Office') think of everything simply in terms of cost cutting and are intent only on cheese-paring exercises which would inevitably ruin the capacity to 'do justice'.

Some of the rhetoric of those engaged in management studies of the criminal justice system strengthens this view. It is sometimes said that the formal criminal justice system is irrelevant to controlling or preventing crime, that it is just an expensive formal charade, which should be run as cheaply as possible. To men whose lives have been spent upholding and practising the formal system, this is a threatening heresy. The judiciary believe deeply that the administration of criminal justice is a necessary part of a civilised society; when they resist management-oriented research they see themselves as defending the historic need to 'do justice'. Similarly, many among the police believe deeply that 'the war against crime' or 'catching criminals' is an essential job. They see themselves as a thin blue line against chaos. Suspecting (with reason) that the bureaucrats do not quite accept this picture, they suspect 'research' as a strategy to shred away their reason for being.

Community and the Criminal Justice System

To resolve these anxieties entails moving beyond the instinctive opposition between those thinking in either the justice or the managerial mode. The community model suggests that both ways of thinking are valuable, indeed essential, but that neither alone holds the full truth about how to 'tackle crime'. We need both a confident criminal justice system (to catch, try and punish those offenders whose acts endanger the community) and maximal efficiency in the techniques of preventing crime and managing inter-actions across agencies. But bureaucratic ingenuity in managing the interaction of rewards and penalties will never in itself be enough to effect change. Real change demands an understanding of the role of social norms, an understanding of the role of community.

Community theory leads to a whole new agenda. Neither the justice model nor the management model has much to offer when it comes to addressing the question sometimes described as 'the criminality of the offender' or 'social crime prevention'. Essentially the question is how best to arrange society to discourage crime. Here community theory implies a definite strategy: that of encouraging, especially among potential offenders, the joint practices of living community. Only in this way will men learn the necessary norms (to use Elster's language) or learn the habits of virtue (to use McIntyre's language). Habitual offenders characteristically suffer from poor parenting, weak families, lack of engagement with school or work group. Characteristically they come from urban areas marked by anonymity, geographic mobility and weak community ties. Far too many of them are graduates of our child care system. We need to find ways to give such young men the experience of working together with others on joint projects in an environment where law-breaking is not habitual. Such a task should not be beyond us.

Practical implications
Can the theoretical arguments I have been advancing be of any practical use in reducing the present antagonisms in the system of criminal justice?

I believe they can. The prime need is for a common articulation of goals across the system. The time has passed when the courts, the police, the probation service, the prison service and the other agencies of the system can perceive themselves alone as ships that sail in the night, only occasionally hailing each other across the dividing seas. We need to build a confident common culture between all those who work in criminal justice.

This is very near to the diagnosis of the Home Office in the booklet *Tackling Crime*. But we need to build further and more energetically on the arrangements there described. Some suggest that the answer is a Ministry of Justice, responsible for co-ordination across the justice system. But such a ministry would almost inevitably become a creature of the lawyers, influenced solely by the justice model. It would risk losing those managerial insights which have largely been developed outside the legal field by theorists and practitioners within the Home Office. A Ministry of Justice headed by a senior lawyer would be rather like a Department of Health headed by a senior doctor – a disastrous recipe for inefficiency. But a Ministry of Justice headed from outside the legal establishment would not command the confidence of the legal profession and would be seen as a creature of the management model.

No departmental reorganisation will be sufficient to heal the deep conceptual divides in our arrangements for tackling crime. The necessary coordination cannot be imposed or directed. It must grow (as all virtues must grow) through the interaction and joint practices of the various agencies themselves.

In accomplishing this task, the programme of conferences between representatives of different agencies already started by the Home Office (and described in *Tackling Crime*) is a good beginning; but the programme needs to be expanded and developed. The best way to do this would be to set up an institution formally independent of any department of state with the remit of facilitating contacts, conferences and consultations betweeen the various parts of the system. It could be called the National Institute of Justice. It would need only a small permanent secretariat, but this would have to be at a sufficiently senior level to engage with senior officials elsewhere in the system. Ideally the institute should also have the power to commission research or special analyses of statistics in its own right. Although independent of any of the main departments of state it would need close ties with the Lord Chancellor's Office, the Home Office and the Attorney General's Office and the senior judiciary. Such an institute could probably most suitably answer directly to the home secretary and be funded on the Home Office vote.

Such a National Institute of Justice would act as a supplement and support to the national and local forums for joint consultation across the criminal justice system recommended by Lord Justice Woolf. The creation of such forums for consultation was a central recommendation of the recent Woolf Inquiry into Prison Disturbances, to which I was an assessor. Those who participated in the Inquiry were convinced of the need to improve machinery for co-operation and interaction across the system.

But no amount of interaction will finally solve current divisions, until some common model of what we are all up to gains general acceptance. More conversation does not always mean more consensus; sometimes it means more conflict. Thinking about crime and criminal justice is currently bedevilled by a conflict between those on the one hand who stress the justice model and suspect anyone interested in managerial efficiency of insensitivity to the claims of justice; and those on the other hand who regard crime as something to be 'managed' and sometimes give the impression of perceiving the work of the courts and the traditional justice system as an expensive charade. They need a common language.

This article is a first step towards providing such a language. To complete the task will require much further work. But I am confident that when a solution is found it will be built around what I have described as the community model for thinking about crime.

References
1. Home Office, *Tackling Crime*, first published September 1989, second edition August 1990.
2. The phrase 'administrative criminology' has been used by Jock Young. See for instance *Realist Criminology*, Gower, 1987.
3. On the effectiveness of the justice model see S.R. Brody, *The Effectiveness of Sentencing: a Review of the Literature*, HORS No. 35, 1976; and M.S. Folkard and D.E. Smith, *IMPACT: Intensive Matched Probation and After-care Treatment, the Results*, HORS No. 36, 1976.
4. On situational crime prevention see P. Mayhew, R.V.G. Clarke, A. Sturman and J.M. Hough, *Crime as Opportunity*, HORS No. 34; R.V.G. Clarke and P. Mayhew (editors), *Designing Out Crime*, 1980; K. Heal and G. Laycock (editors), *Situational Crime Prevention: From Theory Into Practice*, 1986.
5. On the workings of the criminal justice system see P. Softley, *Fines in Magistrates' Courts*, HORS No. 46, 1978; R. Tarling, *Sentencing Practice in Magistrates' Courts*, HORS No. 56, 1979; J. Vennard, *Contested Trials in Magistrates' Courts*, HORS No. 71, 1982.
6. On modelling the criminal justice system see the following Research and Planning Unit Papers: S. Rice, *Criminal Justice System Model: Magistrates' Courts Sub-Model*, RPU Paper No. 24, 1984; P. Morgan, *Modelling the Criminal Justice System*, RPU Paper No. 35, 1985.
7. D. Moxon (editor), *Managing Criminal Justice: a Collection of Papers*, HMSO, 1985 brings together a number of studies on the management of the criminal justice system.
8. For work in the ethnic minority area see P. Stevens and C.F. Willis, *Race, Crime and Arrests*, HORS No. 58, 1979; S. Field et al, *Ethnic Minorities in Britain*, HORS No. 68; M. Tuck and P. Southgate, *Ethnic Minorities, Crime and Policing*, HORS No. 70, 1981.
9. See in particular T. Hope, *Implementing Crime Prevention Measures*, HORS No 86, 1985.
10. On the British Crime Survey see M. Hough and P. Mayhew, *The British Crime Survey: first report*, HORS No. 76, 1983, and M. Hough and P. Mayhew, *Taking Account of Crime*, HORS No. 85, 1985.

11. Among studies of society and crime see J. Graham, *Schools, Disruptive Behaviour and Delinquency*, HORS No. 96, 1988; L. Smith, *Domestic Violence*, HORS No. 107, 1989; and M. Tuck, *Drinking and Disorder*, HORS No. 108, 1989.

12. T. Hope and M. Shaw (editors), *Communities and Crime Reduction: a Book of Readings*, HMSO, 1988.

13. A. Giddens, *The Consequences of Modernity*, Oxford University Press, 1991. For an application of Weberian theory to the criminal justice system see J. Holton and B.S. Turner, *Max Weber on Economy and Society*, 1989.

14. See for instance N. Lacey et al, *Reconstructing Criminal Law*, Weidenfeld and Nicolson, 1991.

15. For an account of the importance of norms in rational choice theory see J. Elster, *The Cement of Society: a Study of Social Order*, Cambridge University Press, 1989. For earlier social psychological models see, M. Fishbein and I. Ajzen, *Belief, Attitudes, Intentions and Behaviour*, Addison Wesley, 1975 also M. Tuck, *How Do We Choose?*, Methuen, 1976.

16. E. Currie, *Confronting Crime: an American Challenge*, Pantheon Books, New York, 1985.

17. P. Willmott, *Community Initiatives: Patterns and Prospects*, Policy Studies Institute, 1989.

18. A. McIntyre, *After Virtue: a Study in Moral Theory*, Duckworth, 1981.

19. *Summa Theologiae: a Concise Translation*, St Thomas Aquinas, edited T. McDermott, Eyre and Spottiswoode, 1989.

20. *Prison Disturbances, April 1990*, report of an Inquiry by Lord Justice Woolf and Judge Stephen Tumim, HMSO, 1991.

[18]

International Journal of the Sociology of Law 1994, **22**, 181–202

Government Strategies for Community Crime Prevention Programmes in England and Wales: A Study in Failure?

BARRY LOVEDAY

Institute of Police and Criminological Studies, University of Portsmouth, U.K.

As recorded crime statistics demonstrate, the rise in crime has occurred against consistently higher spending on law and order services. The majority of offences are property (and opportunistic) crime and it is clear that increased resources for police services or prison places are not likely to substantially impinge on the crime rate. The growth in crime which, in 1990 alone, saw the steepest rise in crime since records began in 1851 does not appear amenable to traditional crime control strategies (Criminal Statistics 1993 HMSO).

The failure of earlier crime control strategies has increasingly directed government attention towards crime prevention. This became apparent when in the 1980s the traditional authoritarian certainties of social control and incarceration failed to achieve any significant reduction in crime rates and were reluctantly superseded by the Thatcher government by crime prevention initiatives.

The emergence of crime prevention as a significant strategy for crime reduction has proved however to be problematic for the Conservative government. It has had to confront the fact that local government is more able to develop an effective co-ordinating role in crime prevention than central government departments. The evidence of the 1980s nevertheless indicates that central government has sought to by-pass local government with its crime prevention strategies. This has reflected a more general policy involving the contraction of local authority responsibility for most services.

The determination to avoid local authority involvement is demonstrated by a cursory examination of government initiatives in crime prevention

0194–6595/94/030181 + 22 $08.00/0

182   B. Loveday

through the 1980s. With major programmes such as Safer Cities and Crime Concern have gone numerous initiatives involving *inter alia* inner city task forces, city action teams (CATS), the Urban Programme, Enterprise Zones, Estate Action Teams, which have been developed by the Department of Trade and Industry and the Department of Environment. The Home Office in the 1980s was heavily committed to developing Neighbourhood Watch and the extension of police force responsibility for crime prevention. This has come via the Home Office Crime Prevention Unit and the Police Crime Prevention Centre at Stafford. But in each case, the responsibility of the individual was stressed by government, as was the need for private sector intervention. It was apparent early on that ideology informed the government strategy with its clearly defined objective of encouraging private sector involvement while marginalising local government.

The most significant Home Office initiatives so far have been Neighbourhood Watch (and other watch schemes): Safer Cities and Crime Concern. Local authority involvement was to prove incidental in each case, playing a secondary role to that of the central department. The police service, for example, was given primary responsibility for establishing and sustaining Neighbourhood Watch. Safer Cities is heavily dependent on a professional team headed by a local co-ordinator employed by the Home Office and under the line management of that Department's Head of Crime Prevention Unit (King 1989).

Crime Concern with the Chief Executive and staff based in Swindon, makes no claims to be community based at all. Its director is appointed by the Home Secretary and its primary purpose appears to be to attract private funding to sustain whatever programmes are thought to be appropriate by its own board.

The Safer Cities initiative has shown the strengths and weaknesses of central department initiatives. Started in 1988, the Safer Cities programme has benefited from the commitment exhibited by local co-ordinators and steering committees. Yet, as 1994 approached, and with it the end of Home Office funding for a number of Safer Cities projects, there was no evidence to indicate that the local business community was prepared to assume responsibility for them. In Birmingham, for example, "the largest Safer Cities project to date in the country", the primary purpose of its final year was to try to encourage businesses to "take a lead role in devising the successor body to Safer Cities" (Birmingham Safer Cities Project Report 1989/1993).

To date there is little evidence to suggest that local business has been forthcoming in this vital area (Interview, Chairperson of Birmingham Safer Cities Project, March 1993).

Unless therefore the local authority can be persuaded to take on these programmes, they effectively end as central funding is withdrawn.

The failure to sustain the Safer Cities programme highlights the variety of short term initiatives started by government departments during the 1980s. In the late 1980s there were so many initiatives that they came to resemble little more than public relations exercises for the department concerned. The result was to create confusion at local level as to which body was responsible for what programme. Alongside Safer Cities and Crime Concern for example, exists the DTI's Inner Cities Task Force and the DoE's Urban Programme, City Action Teams, and Estate Action Teams. All of these, as a subsequent and highly critical report was to identify, are free standing schemes which suggested a propensity for government departments to promote *ad hoc* initiatives (Morgan Report 1991).

The Morgan Report concluded that these initiatives had furthermore, usually been implemented without any consultation with other government departments or with local authorities. Indeed the degree of overlap and duplication, when added to the absence of consultation, presents a picture in which a plethora of bodies set up their own objectives irrespective of those pursued by other departmental agencies. Where, as in the larger cities, all the agencies are engaged in crime prevention activity, the problem of the absence of local co-ordination becomes immediately apparent. At the present time at least three central departments and a large number of local services (police, probation, social services, magistrates courts etc.) are involved in situational crime prevention programmes. At this time it is still unclear just how many agencies are operating in the field and how co-ordination of these activities is achieved, if indeed it is achieved at all.

The Morgan Report on Safer Communities

In response to the growing difficulty of co-ordinating crime prevention activity the Home Office established a working group on safer communities chaired by James Morgan in 1991. Its aim was to evaluate current crime prevention initiatives and to make recommendations concerning methods of co-ordinating those activities. It reported in August 1991. In an open indictment of existing arrangements its report highlighted the confusion and duplication surrounding central government initiatives along with the absence of any permanency of those initiatives. The Morgan Report argued the need for clear local authority involvement if only because it "controlled important services and resources which need to be committed in accordance with a multi-agency strategy for community safety" (Morgan Report 1991).

The Morgan Report also recommended that local authorities should be given statutory responsibility for development and stimulation of community safety and crime prevention programmes. It argued that the local authority should work alongside the police service. But this was not the

184   *B. Loveday*

message that the government wanted to hear. Nor at this time was a report from the National Audit Office helpful. This report was highly critical of police failure to develop an effective crime prevention strategy. It concluded that the evidently low status which crime prevention enjoyed in the police service meant that the police would be unlikely to develop an effective crime prevention programme. Less than half of 1% of police establishment was directed to crime prevention duties which did not exactly demonstrate a strong police commitment to a crime prevention strategy (Loveday 1991).

The low status accorded by the police to crime prevention is of interest if only because of the government's strong desire to push responsibility for crime prevention towards the police throughout the 1980s. If this was a government goal in the late 1980s then it has not been achieved. Interestingly, in this context, some chief officers were to refer to the 'third world status' accorded to the Crime Prevention Centre based in Stafford. This may only reflect the low status accorded overall to crime prevention in Britain which is reinforced by a spending profile which allocates around 2% of total spending on Criminal Justice to crime prevention.

The Morgan Report (1991) identified the limitations in current crime prevention initiatives and recommended local authority primacy. To achieve this it intended that local authorities should be given responsibility for inter-agency co-ordination of crime prevention programmes. There was a need for extra funding, the report concluded, and a code of practice to encourage good practice in a multi-agency approach. The Morgan Report also argued that there was a need for consistency in the development of crime prevention programmes. The consistency which the local authority could provide, would be in marked contrast to central government initiatives which were characterised by "the opportunistic and haphazard identification of problems often undertaken without analysis in an effort to be seen to be doing something" (Morgan Report 1991: p. 21).

The carefully considered conclusions of the Morgan Report were always likely to conflict with the long term centralising strategy of the government. It would appear that crime prevention policy will continue to be determined in Whitehall rather than the town hall. The commitment to centralisation of policy making has been most recently demonstrated by the Home Office's creation of a national board for crime prevention. Elected local authority members have been excluded from board membership.

This suggests that the plethora of initiatives which characterised the 1980s and early 1990s may well continue despite the questionable value of these initiatives and doubt as to their long (or short) term impact. The low status accorded to local government in crime prevention was also exhibited in the 1993 White Paper on police reform.

Within a set of proposals to remove the police service from local government, bringing to an end the last vestige of local accountability, the

White Paper made it clear that crime prevention would continue to emphasise police initiatives and those of central government departments. Thus the public were encouraged to join and support Neighbourhood Watch schemes which the police service would support by providing advice and assistance. In addition, new Watch schemes in high crime residential areas would follow the completion of a pilot project organised by and answerable to Crime Concern, "the independent crime prevention organisation" (White Paper on Police Reform 1993).

Local crime prevention panels were to be expanded but membership was to include "police officers, business people, Neighbourhood Watch scheme members and representatives of the probation and education services". To encourage the active participation of citizens the White Paper suggested there should be a new kind of partnership between the public and the police. The White Paper proposed an extension of police service charters which would explain the level of service which the force areas would provide and also provide "telephone numbers and contact points for members of the public". The educative role of the charter was not overlooked as, in addition to seeking the public's views on the levels of service, police force charters would explain how people could help the police to fight crime (White Paper on Police Reform 1993).

Communities should be encouraged to give police their full support in tackling crime through involvement in local consultative groups, Neighbourhood Watch schemes, victim support or other groups. It was noticeable that local elected members did not loom large in the government's prescription for crime prevention within the White Paper. Each of the groups identified consisted of nominees or self-selected members. Both had only tenuous links with the local authority.

Local police authorities have in the past exercised control over consultative committees outside London by selection of police authority members as chairpersons. Their ability to do so will be curtailed as the number of elected members is substantially reduced as a result of the Police and Magistrates Court Act 1994. This decision was particularly difficult to comprehend given the considerable emphasis placed elsewhere on the need for community consultation. The government believes such consultation can be achieved in a variety of ways which exclude locally elected representatives. These include public opinion and consumer surveys along with reference to the views voiced by local police consultative committee members. How representative of local opinion consultative groups are is a matter of speculation. But as with so much else, the views of local businessmen will be assiduously cultivated by a government which accords them an almost oracle status. Whether this status is warranted is a matter of debate. For a government which is unable to conceive of functions and services outside of a market context, the business element can be expected to assume greater future salience. One consequence of

186   B. Loveday

this could be that private sector provision begins to assume a greater significance in the crime prevention field. It is perhaps of interest here that the Adam Smith Institute which initiated the pressure on government to establish private prisons has already pressed for the provision of private security patrols in high crime residential areas. If, in future, local police commanders are able as a consequence of devolved budgets to buy in services at a local level, then private security patrols could become more common. This is anyway a likely development along with the expansion of the special constabulary to 30 000 members which the government has set as a new target for police forces (White Paper on Police Reform 1993).

Crime Prevention in France

The rejection of local authority primacy which characterises the present government's approach to crime prevention, contrasts strongly with the strategies developed elsewhere in Europe. In France, for example, a highly centralised and traditionally *dirigiste* system has allowed for development of a far more sophisticated strategy exhibiting greater policy coherence than anything developed to date in Britain. Following the reports of the Bonnemaison Committee on crime prevention, successive French governments (from the left and right) have pursued a consistent policy in relation to crime prevention. These have involved central and local government bodies and also voluntary organisations (King 1991).

As Michael King has recently emphasised the Bonnemaison report was based on both rational analysis and a greater recognition of contemporary problems, both social and economic which substantially influence patterns of delinquency and criminal behaviour (King 1991). The Bonnemaison report identified problems of social integration, living conditions, and employment as being particularly important in explaining social dislocation and delinquency in France.

The French experience in the implementation of crime prevention policy also provides a sharp contrast to the 'programme' pursued by the British government. In France, the primary motor of crime prevention has come through Local Community Crime Prevention Councils, chaired by locally elected mayors. The immediate location of crime prevention within a local government structure has influenced the implementation of policy. Local agencies are better able to co-ordinate the activities of a variety of services. A policy of decentralisation to local communities has encouraged further policy integration within local government. This has created a more efficient programme to deal with juvenile delinquency and the problem of social breakdown in the suburbs of France's largest cities. Recognition of social problems as a cause of social dislocation provides a marked contrast to the British government's position. In France the nature of the problem precluded the use of the criminal justice system. The police, the courts, probation and prison services were not thought able to influence, in any significant way, the underlying forces of social breakdown manifested in French society.

Activation of social services along with education and amenities, was identified as a strategy more likely to influence the environment and confront the problem of social breakdown. The Bonnemaison report identified problems of social isolation and alienation as causes of criminal behaviour. It argued that both occurred most often among immigrants and the young unemployed (King 1991).

This sustained the salience accorded to the crime prevention programme nationally by successive governments in France. It also sustained a policy of co-operation and partnership between central and local government in the development of community councils. Interestingly, little emphasis in France has been placed on the private sector or privately-financed organisations. The collaborative approach to crime prevention has been reflected in a mix of funding sources. This provides a stark contrast to Britain where the emphasis has been placed on private sector involvement in crime prevention programmes. This optimism has, to date, proved somewhat misplaced. The private sector has failed to respond to crime prevention initiatives. The approach to funding in France has had one important consequence identified by Michael King. As he argues

> "the partnership ideal means in practice that no one government ministry or local government department is exclusively responsible for funding any particular project. Accountability, therefore, is not directed to the funding body but to the crime prevention council or councils (national, departmental, or local) which organise the funding and approve the project." (King 1991)

The accountability of crime prevention projects come through a crime prevention council at local level rather than a distant central department. Additionally there has been a policy of decentralisation of policing responsibilities. In France the 1980s saw the development of municipal police which have responsibility for a wide range of service functions, including that of general surveillance patrols in the towns. A municipal police training school at Orange (Vacluse) now provides training for officers from a variety of backgrounds (*Le Monde* 13/12/93). In France administrative decentralisation has therefore taken a variety of notable and innovatory forms. This again presents a marked contrast to Britain where government policy has centralised decision making within central departments. In France the underlying strategy has been based upon the recognition of the value, within a previously highly centralised state, of locally accountable services and bodies. These are closer to the problems which confront contemporary urban society than departments based in Paris.

188   *B. Loveday*

Chasing the Dragon

The French experience of crime prevention policy provides a remarkable antidote to the often belligerent prognostigations on crime control exhibited by the current British government. This aggressiveness (now apparently institutionalised within the Conservative Party) was to reach new heights at the 1993 party conference. In a speech designed to raise the Government's flagging popularity among its most loyal supporters, the Home Secretary provided what he described as a "comprehensive programme" to "quell a tidal wave" of concern over rising crime. He was to identify 27 measures aimed at shifting the balance "from the offender back to their victims". These were to form the basis of the 1994 Criminal Justice Act. They included ending the right of silence; DNA testing; new powers to evict squatters; tightening of bail laws; tougher sentences for juvenile offenders and also building six new private prisons. Within the 1994 Criminal Justice and Public Order Act provision is made for new 'floating structures' to cater for the expanding prison population which will be a consequence of the implementation of these new measures. What passed for a crime prevention programme was of particular interest however. Proposals included the return of voluntary village constables and the creation of 20 pilot schemes to monitor their effectiveness in 'combating burglary'. These, along with the decision to reduce bail to offenders, appeared to encapsulate the government's crime prevention strategy. Describing the policy as

> "the most comprehensive programme of action against crime that has ever been announced by any Home Secretary."

Michael Howard went on to state that it represented

> "Action to prevent crime; action to help the police catch criminals; action to make it easier to convict the guilty; action to punish them once they are found guilty... and this is just the first instalment." (*Daily Telegraph* 7/10/93)

A programme which encompassed a war on crime against hunt saboteurs, terrorists, bail bandits, squatters, and 'new age' travellers have all the ingredients of an '*opera bouffe*' rather than a deliberate and considered statement of policy. Unfortunately the Home Secretary's performance at the 1993 party conference worked all too well. His proposals were received with 'rapturous' applause by conference members, it was reported in the popular press. The popular press identified the proposals as an election winning programme and a declaration of war on "the muggers, the robbers and the rapists" who made Britain unsafe. Popular press reports openly referred to the Home Secretary as someone who "understands that the object of the criminal justice system is not to ensure that no innocent person is wrongly punished, but that the guilty never go unpunished." (*Daily Express* 7/10/93)

If Howard's programme was designed to mobilise the extreme political Right then it appeared to have succeeded. The unasked question at the 1993 party conference was what impact would this have on the problem of crime in contemporary Britain? In his conference speech the Home Secretary was to commit himself publicly to a policy of prison expansion. Privatisation and prison expansion are now, once again, central to the government's Law and Order programme. It must be seen therefore as an element of its 'crime prevention' strategy.

This strategy was itself reinforced by the Prime Minister's speech at the 1993 conference. In it he sought to return, he claimed, "to core values of self discipline, respect for the law, traditional education and personal responsibility". In words which were to return to haunt both Mr Major and his party, he demanded that the nation "go back to basics" and return to "those old commonsense British values that should never have been pushed aside". The central key of this programme was to be "tough on crime". As the Prime Minister stated

"policy must be dictated by the needs of justice not the number of prison spaces we happen to have available on any given day. Better the guilty behind bars than the innocent penned in at home." (*The Independent* 9/10/93)

Whether the government's law and order prescriptions will reduce crime remains a matter of contention. Perhaps uniquely in the history of contemporary criminal justice, government proposals have united almost all the practitioners against it. But some response from a 'Law and Order' government was clearly necessary. Evidence demonstrating the crisis of crime confronting contemporary Britain came in a variety of ways. A Home Office survey published in 1994 was to discover, for instance, that in many deprived areas in Britain the fear of crime was so great that half the population would not go out alone after dark. The survey showed that between a quarter and a third of people aged between 16 and 25, of low socio-economic status and living in deprived areas, never went out alone at night. Three quarters of young people, it discovered, said they felt unsafe in doing so. These responses among so young an age group where fear of crime is usually low, were surprising and an indication of the magnitude of the crime problem confronting many residents in Britain's deprived urban areas (Leiter, Shapland & Wiles 1994).

Crime statistics also demonstrated the widening incidence of burglary offences in the early 1990s. Shire counties in the 1990s overtook urban

190   *B. Loveday*

areas in the league tables of recorded offences. It has been in middle class suburbs and rural areas that crime rose at the fastest rate in the early 1990s (*The Observer* 5/12/93).

Burglary and auto crime were offences which constituted a high proportion of the crime epidemic which embraced Britain in the 1980s and into the 1990s. It also became clear that traditional crime control methods had not succeeded in reducing even the rate of increase in recorded crime. This was best demonstrated by Home Office figures of recidivist rates provided in 1993. Reconviction rates for offenders convicted of domestic burglary sent to prison demonstrated that within one year of release 43% could be expected to re-offend. Within two years 65% of offenders released from prison could be expected to be reconvicted for a further offence (*The Independent on Sunday* 17/10/93).

These figures questioned the Home Secretary's claim that it was time for the criminals to live in fear by greater use of prison and that 'prison works'. But Home Office advice on the doubtful value of much of the government's programme has either been rejected or ignored by ministers (*Independent* 24/4/94).

This reflected the programme's value as a populist call to the Tory faithful rather than an informed policy objective. The government's policies, particularly over designating the police in the White Paper on Police Reform and the Police and Magistrates Court Act 1994 as, primarily, 'crimefighters' was to be challenged by a head of the Home Office's criminal justice division. The Home Secretary, in response, distorted the argument of his critic rather than offering a rational defence of his own policy (*The Guardian* 11/1/93).

Government policy on the problem of crime has been explained elsewhere by the Home Secretary in some detail. A speech to a 1993 party conference fringe meeting made by the Home Secretary, provided a platform. The Home Secretary continued to blame the crimewave on the collapse of individual responsibility, the decline of the two parent family, and a growing dependency on the welfare state.

As a consequence of this, the police, the probation service, and prisons were "simply picking up the pieces for the failure of others". Parental failure, he went onto argue, was particularly significant as some parents failed to teach their children "the difference between right and wrong." Additionally schools did not appear to insist on effective discipline while the church had failed to foster 'moral values'. Presumably to encourage the latter, the Home Secretary went on to suggest reform to cap income support for unmarried mothers who had a second or third child. Studies showed, he claimed, that it was the absence of a father that did most damage and fostered criminality (*The Guardian* 6/10/93).

Back to the Real Basics

The litany of personal failure which characterises government's explanations for crime are, however, increasingly difficult to sustain. This is because Britain's 'dangerous places' are closely linked to severe economic decline and social dislocation engendered by it. In many former industrial areas the phenomenon of second or third generation unemployment has become a reality. This could be highly significant, not just in terms of crime, but also in terms defining the role and status of the male as breadwinner and symbol of authority (Campbell 1993).

Some indication of the 'basics' experienced by communities caught up in the spiral of urban decline have been recently identified by commentators. In the North East, social dislocation has been as severe as anywhere. The Benwell estate in Newcastle has, for example, experienced social dislocation as a result of economic decline. As has been argued

> "Here there are three generations of unemployment. Officials put the number of men out of work at 31.1 percent in the Benwell estate and 58.6 percent in the West City estate. The real figure is even higher. On the nearby Scotswood estate, research by community workers found that only 20 percent had full-time work, leaving 8 out of 10 families on benefit or low pay and living on or below the poverty line." (*The Independent* 24/2/93)

One consequence of this has been the social disintegration of the area as the more economically mobile have left it. This has stimulated further criminal behaviour as social controls have progressively broken down. Indeed in Britain, high burglary rates appear to be good indicators of economic decline and social breakdown. This decline in Newcastle has been recorded by commentators

> "On the Benwell estate the rows of Victorian back-to-backs are nightly disintegrating into a ghetto. Down darkened streets are the hulks of burnt out homes and shops. Others stand boarded up and vandalised in what has become a crime ridden slum. A glimpse of light behind a boarded up window suggests someone in refuge." (*The Independent* 24/2/93)

In these (and other) areas of England's former industrial base, the problems are much the same. Young people now gain through crime and street culture everything that they would previously have gained in work. This includes money, excitement, and peer group respect. It remains a matter of speculation as to whether any of the 27 proposals on crime paraded by the Home Secretary at his party conference and encapsulated in the 1994 Criminal Justice and Public Order Act, could expect to make even the most marginal impact on the problems confronting residents on these estates and the dozens like it which have proliferated across Britain

192   *B. Loveday*

over the last decade. These areas would appear to require high levels of both public and private inward investment rather than the crime control programme espoused by the present government.

The contrast with European experience and crime prevention policy is also noticeable. Positive programmes in Europe include crime reduction strategies, public employment, and the improvement of local amenities. In Britain none of these programmes have materialised to date and the government continues to rely on single departmental initiatives which appear to achieve little. Strategies which are most likely to succeed would be those involving the local authority in the co-ordination of better and more comprehensive local services. These would include improved housing, amenities and facilities for the young. It would encompass better health care and opportunities for work. The government appears only able to emphasise the need for law and order along with individual responsibility. In doing so it has relinquished any responsibility for the social crisis which afflicts many of our urban communities. Nor has the government any intention of involving the state to help ameliorate the harsh conditions which are now an everyday basic reality for a growing number of the urban poor. Unlike France, it has no intention of establishing partnerships with local government to tackle the underlying malaise occasioned by economic decline and social dislocation. This might be thought unfortunate as much of the problem may be associated with government policy over two decades of market orientated strategies. These strategies have recently been explained more fully by the Home Secretary to party loyalists.

Mr Howard's Civil Society

In his recent Disraeli lecture Michael Howard has outlined his government's approach to what he describes as the provision of public goods and collective wants (*The Times* 28/2/94). These can best be achieved, he claimed, by the recreation of a sense of obligation and duty among individuals as 'good neighbours'. Individual obligation must replace collectivist action which, he believes, has created communities characterised by alienation, lack of confidence, and crime. In state collectivist communities (i.e. urban housing estates), he argued, crime rates are high. In communities where "voluntary collective action is most apparent", the community, he concluded, is stronger and the crime rate is lower. To encourage voluntary collective action the aim should be, he argued, to roll back the state to provide greater scope for individuals to get involved. Involvement in schools, playgroups, and environmental societies would be one expression of that. School governorships and the membership of housing associations would be another means of involving the community. In each case, voluntary community activity should replace collective provision. Howard also emphasised that 'the community' did not mean local government. He stressed that "the government's opponents mistakenly equate local communities with local authorities". A policy of voluntary activity should permeate the strategy of the government "where the voluntary sector could expect to provide nursery education along with help for the elderly". Voluntary collective action should extend to crime prevention activity. But the latter may be based on an overly optimistic assessment of the effectiveness of Neighbourhood Watch. As Howard argued

> "The growth and success of Neighbourhood Watch is an excellent example of government's encouragement of new ideas. There are now 115 000 schemes covering five million households. In some areas where police are stretched, volunteers have banded together to patrol. I have just visited such a scheme in Sandwich only recently. By quietly patrolling the streets, local residents have cut the burglary rate significantly." (*The Times* 28/2/94)

The Home Secretary believes this kind of initiative should be extended. It might include the creation of Farm Watch or Business Watch to "share information and keep an eye out for suspicious activities". But it will join Pub Watch, Bicycle Watch and Car Watch as the government's primary crime prevention strategy in what appears to be a voluntary surveillance society. Not to be outdone in the surveillance league, the Education Secretary has identified 'Truancy Watch' as a further responsibility of an ever watchful public. These initiatives allow for the withdrawal of the state and its 'coercive' apparatus. They emphasise the importance of family and neighbourhood which, with local voluntary collective activities, will allow England to finally become "one nation".

Yet the examples provided by the Home Secretary appear to confine voluntary collectivism to communities whose residents might be expected to be relatively wealthy, well integrated, and employed. It is his view that because these communities exhibit such voluntary collective action they are areas of high confidence and low crime. This has apparently nothing to do with the relative economic security enjoyed in largely middle class high income suburban areas. It is, however, the proclivity of residents within these areas to volunteer their time for a variety of social duties. According to Howard poor urban areas should not blame economic decline but the coercive intervention of the state for high crime and the social disintegration they now experience. While this argument is difficult to sustain, it does provide a useful 'exit point' for a government which refuses to accept any relationship between crime, unemployment and an economic policy pursued at a huge social cost for more than a decade.

The argument presented by the Home Secretary also reaffirmed his identification of individual responsibility as the basic explanation for criminal activity. This now extends, however, to the need for the individual to volunteer time to protect both his own interests (and that of the commu-

194   *B. Loveday*

nity) by direct involvement in street patrols. Middle class vigilantism, which
he encourages, may question the role of the police as law enforcers who act
as paid professional intermediaries and who respond to calls for service
from members of the public. For the Home Secretary much of this could
apparently be left to voluntaristic groups which would assume greater
responsibility for law enforcement. But the Home Secretary's experience of
voluntary collective action has been confined to overtly middle class, high
income areas. It remains a matter of speculation if he would offer similar
support to aggressive vigilantism which has characterised the activities of
resident groups in declining areas. Here, vigilante activity has resulted in
physical attacks and serious injury to suspected offenders.

Back to Berberis

The government's evident difficulty in responding to the crime problem
was highlighted subsequently by the Prime Minister. Addressing a Conservative Party local government conference in 1994 he was to reflect on
the law and order programme initiated by his government. The problem of
crime continued to be a central issue to many people. He added

> "As I go round the country one subject resonates more clearly than any
> other—a concern up and down the country that people have about
> crime. This year we have the most comprehensive legislation for years
> to crack down on crime to give the courts and police the power they
> need." (*The Observer* 27/2/94)

But more could be done locally. Referring to a number of initiatives taken
by local authorities, Mr Major went on to contradict the Home Secretary in
highlighting the importance of local government in the fight against
crime. He told Tory activists that councils could play a big part in the war
against crime. He emphasised that the government would be issuing
guidelines on "planning that would help councils cut crime". One matter
addressed was how the Prime Minister expected local authorities to reduce
crime. He identified street lighting, closed circuit television, and tower
block entry phones as examples. He also argued that putting, as in the
London Borough of Ealing, 'gates in estate alleyways', would cut domestic
burglaries substantially. This was

> "Not expensive. Not difficult. Just plain common and garden sense.
> Back to basics you might say. And that is just one of the things councils
> should do." (*The Observer* 27/2/94)

The remarkable insight into local government strategy for crime prevention offered by the Prime Minister was not however confined to 'alleyway
gates'. In what must be viewed as a bizarre proposal for a national leader,

Mr Major was to encourage the planting of berberis, buckthorn, and pyrocamphor, "prickly barbs", to deter burglars. He went on to suggest that closed circuit television could extend surveillance and deter the criminal. He added

> "We are out to stop the criminal and the best way to do that is to spot him before he strikes. Closed circuit television cameras have proved they can work. We need them wherever crime is high."

Despite the claim to originality, the Prime Minister's proposals (other than that of berberis) were not new. Most of the initiatives had been implemented some time before by local authorities. But with crime as a sensitive issue in successive local elections, it was incumbent for the Conservative Leader to identify a crime policy of some kind at the local authority level. The gimmickry of Mr Major's speech was however no substitute for a strategic and comprehensive crime prevention programme for local government. That issue had been highlighted in the 1991 Morgan Report which the government has continued to ignore. The arguments presented within the Morgan Report have yet to be seriously challenged by government ministers. However any new programme involving local government would seriously undermine the long term policy of the Thatcher and Major governments. This policy, to reduce the status and functions of local authorities in England and Wales, has been pursued over 15 years. Any alteration in course now would question the emphasis placed on voluntary collective activity (as a substitute for public service provision) identified by the Home Secretary in his Disraeli lecture. The Prime Minister's 1994 Local Government speech, described at the time as being "as devoid of content as the delivery was of passion", was really designed to motivate local activists at a difficult time for the Conservative Party, and was not a new departure for the government in its relationship with local authorities. As has been argued in a recent Home Office publication, crime prevention need not include local government at all and can be made specifically a community responsibility. As the Home Office Crime Prevention Minister has argued elsewhere

> "The government's crime prevention statement announced our intention to enhance our support for local communities who wish to develop their own crime prevention strategies." (George 1994)

Causes of Crime: The Official View

More recently another government minister has reiterated the view that crime was linked neither to poverty nor to unemployment. If an explanation for crime was sought, he has argued, it would be found in 'wickedness and greed'. As he stated

196   *B. Loveday*

> "Some of the so-called cultures which have sprung up in our country
> reject all decency and civilised values. The cultures of the house-
> breaker, the hippy, the hoodlum. The bulk of thieving today, of course,
> has nothing to do with poverty. It is a result of wickedness and greed."
> (*The Times* 21/3/94)

The minister's statement provides a further example of condemning
patterns of behaviour which are held to be beyond the influence of the
state. It also continues to explain criminality in terms of individual
pathology or collective moral decline. Of particular interest, however, is
the same minister's view on the motivation of offenders. He argued that

> "Almost nobody today robs to buy food and they do not mug to buy
> school clothes for their children. No degree of poverty in Britain today
> forces people into crime to subsist. We should not confuse rising
> expectations and demands with poverty." (*The Times* 21/3/94)

Recent research evidence continues to challenge these conclusions. Home
Office research in 1990 was to identify a close and sustained link between
types of offence and the economic cycle (Field 1990). Research in 1994 was
to demonstrate a close correlation between burglary offences and levels of
unemployment among males of between 16 and 25 years of age (Dickinson
1994). More recently a leading insurance company has, in its annual
report, linked levels of theft with unemployment rates (*The Guardian*
24/2/94). These research findings suggest the crime prevention activity
whether provided by voluntary collective action or the state will not of itself
provide a long term solution to what appears to be a growing problem.
Interestingly, within the Home Office, officials have identified an issue of
relative deprivation and have concluded that the most effective policy in
reducing crime among young offenders would appear to be to give them
employment (*The Independent* 8/4/94).

Underlying factors which are linked to relative deprivation, generational
and structural unemployment will require a more comprehensive strategy
than the present government is ever likely to provide. In addition the
absence of future employment opportunities for the young in the declining industrial areas make it less appropriate to explain criminal activity by
way of "wickedness and greed". David Hunt's prognostications on the
issue of wickedness seemed only a banal repetition of those of John Patten
when Home Office minister under Mrs Thatcher.

Despite a barrage of official argument to the contrary and consistent
ministerial attempts to play down the link between unemployment and
crime, the public still believes that a link does exist between unemployment and crime (*The Times* 21/3/94).

A recent MORI poll has demonstrated the impact of crime and the
public perceptions of it, along with the growing chasm in Britain between

government rhetoric and the realities of crime. The poll demonstrates that despite the government's efforts, fear of crime has continued to rise and that respondents named unemployment as a primary cause of crime. The poll showed that 77% of respondents were afraid of having their homes burgled. Fifty-six percent feared having their home or possessions vandalised. The assessment of likely victimisation identified by the 1994 poll provided graphic evidence of government failure.

The public's perception differs substantially from that of government on many law and order issues despite its explanations for crime. The same MORI poll found that unemployment and drugs were together blamed by most people as the key causes of crime. Unemployment was most frequently quoted as a cause of crime and showed that respondents thought unemployment a 'major cause' of crime. Parental discipline, lenient sentencing, and alcohol as explanations of crime were not as salient. Also, only 16% of respondents believed that absent fathers or single motherhood were a cause of crime. More significantly, in light of the Criminal Justice and Public Order Act (1994), only 14% of respondents believed that jailing more offenders would cut crime. The poll did show, however, that the public continued to believe the single most important measure to reduce crime would be to increase the number of police on the beat. One editorial concluded '87% of those questioned would like more police on the beat, a view more prevalent among the lower social classes, [sic.]' (*The Times* 21/3/94).

This response accords with victimisation rates identified in the 1992 British Crime Survey. The 1992 BCS demonstrated that the highest victimisation rates occurred in the most deprived areas, usually large urban public housing estates. In these, the fear of crime may not exaggerate the likelihood of victimisation. It is in these areas that voluntaristic collective action, identified by the Home Secretary, will apparently provide an effective alternative to the repressive "state apparatus of the police". But these areas are likely, in the foreseeable future, to remain either dependent on public police services or to develop a culture of aggressive vigilantism which may go some way beyond the polite street patrols identified by Mr Howard in Sandwich, Kent.

Without the encouragement of Mr Howard's Disraeli lecture, vigilante groups have already appeared in these high crime areas. The absence of police in these areas, which may explain the rise of vigilantism, raises a further question. If the police are seen to be primarily crime fighters, what programme of action could be most successfully applied in such areas by the police service? Could a 'strategy for poverty' be developed by the police to respond to the high victimisation rates in Britain's most deprived and 'dangerous' places?, Beatrix Campbell's recent evidence from Britain's dangerous places suggests that police services are rarely in evidence in areas where the need is greatest (Campbell 1993).

It is clear that these issues go well beyond the government's simplistic notions of crime fighting and its public relations exercises dressed up as crime prevention policy. They require the government to face up to the consequences of major economic decline and growing dislocation which its own policies may have encouraged. They require the state to engage in public provision of services and strategies to begin to reverse the decline in Britain's poorest areas. This requires more than the artifice of youth training schemes which, while massaging the unemployment figures, offer nothing to those required to join them. There is a need for strategic vision on behalf of government to improve the life chances of the poor. This will be more constructive than nostalgic imagery encompassed within the back to basics campaign of John Major, to which he thinks society should return. The back to basics campaign suggests a government which has already abrogated any responsibility for the current crisis which its market approach has helped to generate.

Conclusion

The government's crime prevention programme remains unambiguous. It will not support policies which would enhance the status of the local authority. Thus in what a Home Office minister recently described as "Phase 2 of the Safer Cities programme", 10 towns and cities have been identified for fresh funding. These programmes will, however, be co-ordinated and run directly by either Crime Concern or NACRO. It also remains the view of the Home Secretary that Safer Cities has proved to be a great success. Yet the optimism exhibited by ministers over Safer Cities, may be misplaced. Private funding has been difficult to generate in those cities involved in the first stage of the programme. Similarly, government optimism concerning Neighbourhood Watch remains high. A Home Office minister has recently referred to the five million households now involved in the schemes and their success "in areas as socially disparate as Wythenshawe in Manchester and Hampstead in London" (George 1994). It is however the next stage of the Neighbourhood Watch programme which is likely to prove of greater interest. This involves street patrols by Neighbourhood Watch members. The Home Office is actively involved in developing a code of conduct with ACPO to assist Citizen Patrols where Watch members initiate patrol activities. This programme only reflects the Home Secretary's encouragement of voluntary action in crime prevention. The extent to which these voluntaristic activities begin to confront the crisis experienced by residents of urban high crime areas remains problematical. As the 1992 British Crime Survey demonstrated, the risk of crime differs substantially in terms of area (British Crime Survey 1992).

The BCS data demonstrate that those areas where the Home Secretary's 'voluntaristic community groups' are most likely to be found remain low

Community Crime Prevention Programmes   199

Table 1. Relative Rates of Crime and Attempted Crime

	Burglary	Auto crime around home	Theft from person
Low Risk			
Agricultural areas	20	20	50
Modern family housing	60	70	70
Other middle-status housing	70	100	60
Affluent suburban housing	70	70	70
Better-off retirement areas	70	80	70
Medium Risk			
Older terraced housing	120	160	100
Better-off council estates	90	110	120
Less well-off council estates	150	160	100
High Risk			
Poorest council estates	280	240	200
Mixed inner metropolitan areas	180	190	340
High-status non-family areas	220	150	250
Indexed national average	100	100	100

Source: British Crime Survey 1992

risk areas. These are classified by the BCS as Low Risk areas with crime rate
levels well below the national average (see Table 1). Those at greatest risk
of victimisation, according to the BCS, are residents in Britain's poorest
council estates where burglary rates are three times the national average
and where auto crime and theft from the person are twice as likely to occur
(High Risk, see Table 1). The BCS data identify issues which confront the
government's market approach and also raise questions about the future
strategy of local authorities and the police. The data suggest, for example,
that if the police are to be seen as 'crime fighters', they will need to develop
a 'strategy for poverty' which offers some security for residents in high
victimisation areas. This might be thought a more productive strategy than
the withdrawal of police service identified by Beatrix Campbell. One
approach might include adoption of a 'problem solving approach' where
the police use local information to identify underlying problems generating criminal activity. This would be a more productive policy than
encouraging vigilantism which the government appears to want to legitimise. But if the police are to develop a strategic response to poverty they
need to do so in terms of an inter-agency approach linked to the local
authority. As the Morgan report suggested

> "The evidence provided by the report indicates that progress towards
> community safety has been most impressive where the local police
> commander has encouraged and supported local authority police

executives in taking an active and leading part in co-ordinating a multi-agency approach." (Morgan Report 1991: para 6.1)

Because it has control of important services and resources, which need to be committed for a multi-agency strategy, the report concluded that the local authority should assume responsibility in conjunction with the police, for future community safety development. As the local authority is concerned about its total environment it should also devise stategies to protect that environment. As was argued

> "For these reasons, the working group recommends that in the longer term, local authorities working in conjunction with the police should have clear strategic responsibility for the development and stimulation of community safety and crime prevention programmes." (Morgan Report 1991: para 6.9)

The Morgan Report recommendations also appear to offer a sensible and workable alternative to the market and increasingly, maverick approaches pursued by the Home Secretary.

At the 1993 Conservative Party conference, the Prime Minister appealed to a nostalgic ideal of England. This image is now rather alien to contemporary urban experience. A recent report on the growing need to protect public service staff from the threat of indiscriminate violence in Britain's inner areas provides graphic evidence of how government policies consistently underestimate the problems of social and economic decline. The British Medical Association has, for example, discovered that one in 12 family doctors had suffered an assault while on duty during the previous two years. Its 1994 report concluded

> "Last December, bullet-proof glass windows were installed in a practice's new premises in Stockwell, South London, where ten GPs are based. During the previous 18 months a local GP had been robbed at gunpoint in his surgery, a second threatened with a shotgun by a patient who wanted to register with the practice." (*The Observer* 27/3/94)

The same report noted that

> "This year ambulance crews in Manchester were issued with bullet-proof vests because of growing violence that they face." (*Observer* 27/3/94)

These snapshots of the reality of everyday urban life show it is far removed from the sentimentalism exhibited by John Major. It suggests that intervention, rather than withdrawal of the state, is emphatically needed.

Community Crime Prevention Programmes 201

Civil society does not rest on strident individualism or, as Mr Howard would believe, on voluntary collective activity. Civil society does not rest either on notional values of the market. It is based on the ability of the state to regulate the market and protect the weakest from its worst excesses. As has been argued by Perkin, the free market could not exist but for the state. Without regulation to set the terms of the market, it would collapse into chaos, allowing the strong to take what they like from the weak. As Perkin has argued

> "Thus the state itself, far from being the enemy of freedom is its source and origin. Freedom can be positive as well as negative, freedom to do and be without molestation or exploitation by other citizens as well as freedom from state intervention. Freedom from all state interference is freedom for criminals, thieves and frauds. Civil society itself exists by reason of the state, without which it would descend into a Hobbesian state of nature, the war of all against all." (Perkin 1989)

In the context of urban decline, ever higher rates of deprivation and victimisation, then state intervention becomes more necessary not less. This may be needed as the 'trickle down' effects of tax cuts for the wealthy and the market mechanism together fail to provide economic opportunities for those who experience the worst effects of a market system. Poor housing, the impact of broken homes, unemployment, along with domestic violence, alcohol and drug abuse are now recognised as major factors explaining crime. While state intervention at local and central level might be opposed by supporters of the market, public intervention is needed and is best achieved at local authority level. A wider public interest now requires the state at both central and local level to intervene to deal with the growing inequalities and deprivation that characterise contemporary English society. A market system which has generated a crisis of both social relations and crime, now needs the intervention of the state to deal with those problems generated by it and for which it has no satisfactory solutions.

References

Birmingham Safer Cities Project Report (1989–1993) Home Office: London, p. 5.
British Crime Survey (1992) HMSO: London.
Campbell, B. (1993) *Goliath: Britains Dangerous Places.* Methuen: London.
Criminal Statistics (1993) HMSO: London.
Dickinson, D. (1993) *Occasional Paper. University of Cambridge.* Cambridge.
Field, S. (1990) *Trends in Crime and their Interpretation,* HMSO: London.
George, B. (1994) *Policing and Security 2000 and Beyond.* Conference held at the House of Commons: Westminster, 28 March 1994.
Morgan Report (1991) Standing Conference on Crime Prevention: *Safer Commu-*

202   *B. Loveday*

nities: The local delivery of crime prevention through the partnership approach. Home Office: London.

King, M. (1989) *Social Crime Prevention à la Thatcher.* The Howard Journal of Criminal Justice **24**(4) Blackwell: Oxford.

King, M. (1991) *The Political Construction of Crime Prevention: a contrast between the French and British Experience.* In *The Politics of Crime Control* (Stevenson, K. and Cowell, D.) Sage: London.

Loveday, B. (1991) *Police and Government in the 1990s. Social Policy and Administration,* **25**, No. 4.

Leiter, M., Shapland, J. & Wiles, P. (1994) *Drug Usage and Drugs Preventions: The Views and Habits of the General Public.* HMSO: London.

Perkin, H. (1989) *The Rise of Professional Society in England Since 1880.* Routledge: London, pp. 12–13.

White Paper on Police Reform (1993) *The Government Proposals for the Police Service in England & Wales.* Cmd 2281, HMSO: London.

[19]

International Journal of the Sociology of Law 1980, **8**, 149–164

The Future of Control Systems-the Case of Norway*

THOMAS MATHIESEN

Institutt for Rettssosiologi,
Universitetet i Oslo, 3, Norway

On 26 May 1978, White Paper No. 104 On Criminal Policy – the "Criminal Policy Paper" – was issued by the Norwegian Cabinet. A paper which had been commenced several years earlier had thereby finally been made public. In advance, the public debate concerning the long awaited "Criminal Policy Paper" had been comprehensive: in the course of a year and a half – from November 1976 to the publication of the Paper – 1300 smaller or larger articles on the "Criminal Policy Paper" or closely related topics had been published in the Norwegian press. And from 18 February to 18 April 1978 – two months of continuous debate just before the publication – the four large Oslo newspapers alone produced 150 metres of newspaper columns on the topic. Rarely has a White Paper been so thoroughly debated *before* its publication [1].

One hundred and thirty-seven years earlier – in 1841 – another recommendation was published concerning the criminal policy of Norway. This was the "Account of the State of Norway's Punitive Institutions and Care

---

*Paper presented to the Conference of the European Group for the Study of Deviance and Social Control, Copenhagen 1979.

The present paper is a translation of the final chapter – Chapter 10 – of the author's book *Den skjulte disiplinering* ("The Hidden Disciplining"), which appeared in Norwegian with Pax Publishers in 1978.

The paper deals with a recent Norwegian White Paper on Criminal Policy, and the control policies which that White Paper may suggest for the future. It should be mentioned, as a context to readers from other European countries, that during the late nineteen-seventies comprehensive white papers on criminal policy have appeared in all of the four Nordic countries – Finland, Sweden, Denmark and Norway. The Finnish and Swedish white papers are to a considerable extent "neo-classical" in orientation, emphasizing a return to the classical principles of imprisonment. The Danish and Norwegian white papers contain more of a "control orientation" which is described and analysed for Norway in the present paper. The difference between the two sets of white papers is not dealt with in the present paper, but constitutes an obvious further subject of analysis. The two main lines of development which the four white papers suggest, may in fact occur together and complement each other. This possibility is dealt with on a general level in the final section of this paper.

0194–6595/80/020149+16 $01.00/0

150   *T. Mathiesen*

of Prisoners as well as Opinion and Recommendation Concerning a Reform in Both, According to the Pattern of Foreign States", which was published that year in Christiania (the former name of Oslo). A long debate also took place before the publication of that report.

For a long time, widespread discontent had existed in political and professional circles concerning the state of affairs in the prisons and correctional houses of the time. The number of prisoners had been rising – in absolute numbers and per capita – during all of the first part of the 19th century, and even if the rise had been related to the great shift in legislation – from corporal punishment to incarceration – which Michel Foucault describes in *Discipline and Punish*, it must have appeared ominous to the people of the time. The fact that the figures peaked around the middle of the century (in 1843, to be exact), and that they slowly but steadily declined again in absolute figures as well as per capita as the year 1900 approached (after which they stabilized and remained more or less stable up to our own time), could not be known at that time [2]. Something had to be done, and something was in fact in the making. As early as around 1820, a medical doctor – and later professor – by the name of Fredrik Holst went abroad to study what was being done there with criminals. In 1823 he published a book, bearing the title "Reflections on the Newer British Prisons, Especially With Regard to the Necessity of an Improvement in Prison Care in Norway". Holst was concerned with the unsavoury circumstances of the prisoners. He presented the prisons and the correctional houses as inhuman institutions. And he was deeply concerned with the fact that the institutions did not contribute to the general improvement of the prisoners. He advocated the notion of the penitentiary: the inmates were to serve their sentences in complete isolation – in silence and religious contemplation – whereby they would turn to better thoughts. Holst was made a member of the Commission on Punitive Institutions, which was established in 1837.

The Commission worked for about four years – about as long as the Ministry of Justice took to prepare the "Criminal Policy Paper" of our own time. In July 1841 the "Opinion and Recommendation", totalling 707 pages, appeared, printed in black letter types. The "Opinion and Recommendation" contained a devastating critique of the punitive institutions of the time. The institutions were found to be completely unsuited to their task: the administration was poor, the officers were too few and too poorly paid, the buildings were miserable, there was unrestricted intercourse between the prisoners day and night, and – not least – discipline was virtually non-existent. The closing down of all of the old punitive institutions, both in the fortresses and in the correctional houses, was most urgently recommended, and the construction of seven new prisons built according to the principles adopted in Philadelphia, with a total capacity of 2100 prisoners, was requested. These prisons, it was maintained, should be built in the course of a 20-year period. A prison for men in Christiania should be the first institution. It was estimated that the building

The future of control systems 151

programme would altogether cost over 1.5 million Rix-Dollars (coin used up to 1873 and worth about one American dollar), but according to the Commission it would be a good investment.

The Ministry of Justice declared its agreement in all essentials with the Commission, and agreed that a start should be made with a prison for males in Christiania, able to house 500 prisoners. The Committee on Criminal Matters in Parliament also agreed, but maintained that the construction period should be stretched to 25 years, and that a smaller prison should be the first institution. The Committee recommended an appropriation for a prison for women, housing 240 inmates, in Christiania. In 1842 the appropriation was made by Parliament, construction started in 1844, and on 5 May 1851 *Botsfengslet* received its first prisoner.

As we know today, Botsfengslet became a prison for men, and remained the only new Philadelphia prison in Norway – the rest of the construction programme was not carried out. There were probably several reasons for this – including the above-mentioned peaking of the prison figures, and the fact that the economic burden of the construction programme was great. But throughout the eighteen-fifties and sixties, as many as 56 smaller "cell prisons" (district prisons) were established throughout the country, giving room for a total of about 800 prisoners.

The basic principles of prison reform during the first part of the 19th century have been described and debated elsewhere [3]. So have the economic and societal background explaining why reform came when it did [4]. Here I only repeat that it was reform with European dimensions. In Norway we borrowed the ideas from, among other places, England, and we were a little behind in time, but not much. I also briefly repeat that the most basic principle of the new programme emphasized religious discipline: the prisoners were to repent – in isolation and silence – and thereby turn to better thoughts – improve. The whole architecture of the new prisons revolved around this principle [5]. The principle received overwhelming support at the time, for example in the above-mentioned "Opinion and Recommendation" of the Norwegian Commission on Punitive Institutions. A single political figure in Norway – MP, Ludvig Kr. Daa – criticized this Norwegian penitentiary reform, with its emphasis on isolation, for what it was: a brutal and gruesome method of punishment, also "for its time". He maintained that the Commission on Punitive Institutions had refrained from reporting results which did not speak in favour of the principle of isolation. However, Daa did not win support for his view, and remained alone [6].

Let me now point out one aspect of the basic principle of this 19th century reform which is often overlooked, but which I believe is crucial: the basic principle of the reform was distinctively *individualistic*. By this I mean that the disciplining, through the criminal justice system, of that part of the working class which was registered as criminal, took place *as a disciplining of individuals*; a disciplining of the law-breakers "one by one". The individualistic nature of the

152   *T. Mathiesen*

disciplining was so pronounced that total isolation of the individual prisoner was, to repeat, regarded as being the very foundation of the system.

I emphasize that the individualistic principle, also known earlier but systematized through the great mid-nineteenth century reform, constituted the main basis for penal practice throughout that century and into our own. The external form certainly changed: while *the notion of religious repentance* prevailed during the breakthrough of the prison reform, *the notion of treatment* prevailed during the first part of our own century, *the notion of work* (with modern industrial prisons like the Norwegian Ullersmo and the Swedish Kumla) prevailed from 1960 on, and *the notion of schooling* prevailed (at least in Norway) during the nineteen-seventies. An analysis of the shifts between these ideological justifications would be interesting, but must wait till some other time [7]. Here the point is that the individualistic principle has been central regardless of concrete ideological form [8]; the disciplining of those of the working class who have been registered as law-breakers has all the time primarily taken place as a disciplining of them individually.

What can be said about the background of the individualistic criminal policy? The question is obviously complex. Let me point to one set of circumstances which I believe has had significance.

The individualism contained in penal policy has been a part of a basic individual-liberal mode of thought which has prevailed in a general sense far into our own century. Generally speaking, an individual-liberal interpretation of human behaviour may be maintained as long as the behaviour of the individual appears rational in relation to the external conditions which constitute the framework of the behaviour. This also holds for an individualistic interpretation of crime: individualism in penal policy is a principle which may be maintained as long as people's criminal acts may be explained as *in themselves understandable – however unacceptable – individual reactions to the environment.*

For a long time it has been possible to interpret crime this way. The question of whether the various individualistically oriented theories of crime have been wrong or not, is not the issue here. The point is that the basic individualistic precondition contained in all of the theories has appeared reasonable against the general background that the object of the crime – usually private material property in one form or another – *has appeared as an object which the offender would understandably want.*

More explicitly, it is obvious that the thefts of the last century – at that time, as now, constituting the main bulk of registered crime – were to a significant degree crimes of need. And if they were not understood as such, they were at least seen as understandable, materially oriented acts. The same conception has been able to prevail far into our own century. Against this background it has been the "obvious" thing to maintain an individually oriented criminal policy: it has been the obvious thing to react primarily to – and to try to discipline – the individual who has stolen.

Another possibility was theoretically present: the authorities of the time might have instituted policies to ameliorate the material situation of potentially criminal groups. Such a "societal" policy would, however, have run counter to basic political principles of early (and, as we shall see, also late) capitalism. The disciplining of individuals remained the main way out.

This brings us to our own situation, and to our own "Criminal Policy Paper". After the last World War, Norway and a good many other capitialist countries have seen a more or less unequalled economic growth, which also has entailed an increase in the standard of living for large groups of people. Such an increase in the standard of living is no "kind gift" from capitalism, but basically the result of capitalism's own need to be able continually to sell more. But disregarding this, and regardless of the fact that the growth is now beginning to show its limits and limitations, the development has created a new situation in criminal policy: the large mass of traditional crime – the thefts – may no longer as easily be explained as understandable materially oriented acts, committed by individuals against the background of their total material situation. To be sure, the sociologist may still argue that theft, especially in the recidivist form, is associated with a lack of material resources and with material need [9]. But in the light of the general material growth, it is politically very difficult to uphold such a lack and such a need as a basic causal principle.

If the crimes of theft had largely remained on the same level (or, even more, if their number had gone down) it would still probably have been possible to continue rather undisturbedly the reliance on the old, individually oriented types of sanctions. The problem, however, is that coinciding with the most successful period of growth in the history of capitalism, *the registered theft-rate has increased by leaps and bounds.* The result is, that the State stands without a reasonable explanation of – and without measures which may be expected to be effective towards – a pattern of behaviour which – through its dramatic increase – *in fact is beginning to threaten the legitimacy of the regime.* A shift in understanding and in measures seems near at hand [10].

And it is precisely such a *shift of understanding and of measures* which the "Criminal Policy Paper" of 1978 foreshadows. Let me emphasize right away: far from a complete shift is announced. Imprisonment is to a very large extent maintained as a measure despite its lack of efficiency – and despite the fact that this lack of efficiency is pointed out in the Paper [11]. But the new departure which is intimated is probably important in terms of principle and long-term policy.

First, a few words about the new understanding of crime in the "Criminal Policy Paper". The old individually oriented understanding is abandoned, a "societal" understanding has taken its place. It is emphasized that crime may "be traced back to structural and organizational features of society" (p. 77 in the Paper).

In more detail, a societal understanding of crime is emphasized which maintains that crime manifests itself as a consequence of weakened "social control". The industrialization and urbanization which our society has

154   *T. Mathiesen*

witnessed, especially after World War II, has presumably brought with it such a weakened "social control". This point of view runs through the Paper as a whole, and a separate chapter is devoted to it under the title "Societal conditions and the causes of crime" (Chapter 7).

What is the effect of the emphasis on weakened "social control" as the cause of crime? There are two effects. In the first place, it brings crime back to the sphere of rationality. In the last century and far into our own century, crime – especially theft – could be explained as an understandable materially oriented act. By emphasizing weakened "social control", crime may again be given a rational explanation. Secondly, and simultaneously, this emphasis provides an opening for new measures which may be instituted. Because if society's "social control" is so weakened that crime flourishes, it is *natural to try precisely to strengthen society's "social control"*.

A weakening of society's "social control" is not the only possible "societal understanding" which would have brought crime back to the sphere of rationality. Another basic hypothesis, namely that social problems – including crime – are external symptoms of being expelled – especially of being expelled from work life – in our society, would also have had this function. However, such a basic hypothesis would not – if it was taken seriously – have opened the way for new measures which might appropriately have been instituted: if mechanisms of expulsion of this kind were behind the problems, it would in fact be necessary to change fundamentally the very system of production in society. This is a type of measure which would be inconceivable as a state measure in a capitalist society. But *increased "social control", on the background of a presumed preceding weakening of this "control", is conceivable as a state measure in such a society* [12].

Thereby the new societal understanding of the "Criminal Policy Paper", and the measures foreshadowed in it, are *integrated into a social democratic understanding of society and politics*. This is actually not so strange – after all, a social democratic Government has drafted the Paper. The interesting fact is that with the "Criminal Policy Paper", criminal policy is being integrated into the series of fields in which a social democratic policy has superseded an individualistic mode of thought. The similarity with the development of the social democratic economic policy, which took place before and after World War II, is striking: an economic policy based on an individualistic, liberal understanding of society broke down. A new interventionist state policy developed on the basis of a new, and less individualistic understanding. But all the time a policy was maintained which did not break basically with the framework conditions.

Criminal policy is – with the "Criminal Policy Paper" – perhaps the last field of society to be "social – democratized".

Now, it must be added that the concrete instructions of the "Criminal Policy Paper" as to measures, on the basis of the new understanding of crime, are actually sparse. The new viewpoint is expressed many times, but largely in general terms. But on three points the Paper is concrete.

The first point concerns the proposal to appoint a "Council of Crime Prevention". Following a pattern from Sweden and Denmark, "the establishment of a Norwegian crime preventive council" (p. 91) is advocated. "The Council", it is emphasized, "must itself be able to initiate the bringing forth, and the communication, of knowledge and viewpoints concerning the relationship between society and crime . . . The Council is in general supposed to function as a meeting place where representatives of important institutions [områder] in society come together and draw attention to how developments in their own field influence the development of crime" (p. 91). In the light of the societal understanding which the Paper relies on, it is in other words fairly clear – if not directly stated – that a Norwegian "Council of Crime Prevention" certainly is to have "social control" as its topic of concern. In this respect, the Swedish and Danish models are clear. Furthermore, the Council is to have a corporative structure: "If the Council is to function according to its goal, it is important that the members have a broad basis of experience. They should, among other things, have ties to industrial life, the labour market, and district development, schools and social policy institutions, in addition to the traditional criminal justice system. The Council should also comprise representatives of those research branches which are particularly important in relation to criminal policy issues" (p. 91). The corporative structure of the Council is linked directly to its mandate: "If the Council is to operate according to its broad societal goal, it is important that the traditional criminal justice system does not dominate the composition of the Council" (p. 91).

The second point concerns the proposal for a development of "crime care in the community". A further integration of the aspects of "control" and "help" of probation is advocated: "The Ministry of Justice assumes that a division of labour in probation and parole work, for example between social agencies and the police (the help and the control functions respectively) should not be carried out despite the conflict situations which an integration apparently implies" (p. 145). An integration of the two aspects is underlined through the proposal "that crime care in the community should *be integrated in the Ministry of Justice,* more precisely as a section which also comprises the present tasks of the Prison Department" (p. 147, the Ministry's italics). At the same time, there may "according to the opinion of the Ministry . . . also be reason to consider whether one should introduce a *special* measure which consists of *sentencing directly to supervision,* but without an alternative imprisonment" (p. 146, the Ministry's italics).

The third point concerns the proposal to develop the structure and efficiency of the police. The development of the structure and efficiency of the police, which has included a centralization and militarization of the force, has been taking place – under the social democratic regime – all through the seventies [13]. The White Paper devotes considerable space to increased police efficiency, though words like centralization and militarization are not used. "The police,"

156   *T. Mathiesen*

according to the White Paper, "play a central role in society's protection against crime. This role has several important aspects. First of all the police are to prevent crime. If this succeeds, the punitive system does not need to come into effect. Thereby, a great deal is gained. Through their preventive activities, the police are to attempt to make the criminal law more efficient as a means of influencing people's behaviour" (p. 56).

All of these statements – and several more of them – emphasize the significance of establishing a "balance" between the weakened societal "social control" which presumably is the cause of crime, and the State's own control measures. There is, in other words, an emphasis on establishing a balance between a *weakened informal social control* and *the State's formal control*. Let me give a few quotations which strongly underline the creation of such a balance. In the lengthy chapter on "Societal Conditions and the Causes of Crime" (in a section called "Barriers to Crime") it is stated, for example:

> The organized formal control which probably most directly influences people's behaviour, is the responsibility of the police. Society's need for this type of control increases as informal social control is being weakened (p. 77).

The same point is also emphasized this way:

> Generally we have grounds for saying that people are becoming continually more alien to each other in modern industrial society, whereby social control in the smaller groups is also weakened. The result is a greater need for public control agencies, though they cannot fully compensate for informal social control (p. 77).

And this way:

> If one wishes to reduce the extent of crime in society, it is therefore important both to improve the possibilities of control in the immediate environment [naermiljøet], and to invest in the development of various public control agencies (p. 77).

And finally, this way, in connection with society's technological development – e.g. automobilization:

> The development of new technical measures and forms of production has, to repeat, contributed to a weakening of informal social control in society. There is reason to believe that a further development in the same direction will place still greater demands on the public, formal control system. The question, then, is how great a control task society after a while may manage to take on, and also how much public control is desirable. If society is going to manage to limit the development of crime, we must – in the time to come – be more disposed towards reducing *the possibilities* which

people have of committing unwanted acts in a series of crime areas. This must be done through political decisions in areas which traditionally have not been viewed in relation to the development of crime. Also the general development in the direction of increased public participation and review within a continually larger number of areas of social life contributes indirectly to a new form of "social control" (pp. 78–79).

In short: in three concrete respects, and also in general terms, the "Criminal Policy Paper" suggests new measures on the basis of the new political understanding of crime. They are all *geared towards increased formal control, out there in society, as a balancing of weakened informal control.*

Some threads may be tied together. The great reform in the first part of the century which preceded ours built on an individualistic understanding of crime and foreshadowed an individualistic system of measures, with radical punitive isolation as a central method. The consideration of reform towards the end of the present century [14] builds on a societal understanding of crime, and foreshadows intensification of the general and official societal control system, out there in society. Another societal understanding – with an emphasis on the mechanisms of expulsion which in the last instance may be traced back to the dynamics of work life and mode of production – could have led to measures in the direction of fundamental change in this very mode of production. When confronted by this possibility, a social democratic State naturally halts – now as at earlier turning points in history. With "weakened social control" as a theoretical point of departure, measures which in no way imply such a fundamental change, but which in fact probably support prevailing relations of production, may be defended and introduced.

Some of the measures may certainly still show signs of being individualistic – like a conceivable future network of measures and types of compulsion in the mental health system, in the system for care of alcoholics and drug addicts, and in the proposed "crime care in the community" which was mentioned above. Concerning these measures, Foucault's perspective on the prison-like features "diffusing" into outside society will truly be an apt perspective [15]. But other conceivable measures may move fully away from individualism, and focus on *control of whole groups and categories* – through planned manipulation (with good intentions of establishing "brakes on crime") of the everyday life conditions of these groups and categories. TV cameras on subway stations and in supermarkets, the development of advanced computer techniques in intelligence and surveillance, a general strengthening of the police, a general strengthening of the large privately run security companies, as well as a whole range of other types of surveillance of whole categories of people – all of this is something we have begun to get, and have begun to get used to. These forms do not represent a further development of the individualizing prison form, but rather a certain break with it – just as the prison in its time broke with physical punishment [16]. The new, genuinely societal forms of control – where whole

158   *T. Mathiesen*

groups and categories are controlled – may be woven together with the prison-like offshoots into a total control system.

   The change of thinking from the great reform during the first part of the last century to the principles of reform towards the end of our own century, at the same time mirrors a change *from open to hidden discipline*. It was one of the marks of individual liberalism that its disciplining not only was individualistic, but at the same time still relatively *open*. The disciplining was focused, as a direct measure, on the individual, and could thereby be clearly recognized by him or her, and by others in the environment. It is one of the marks of social democracy that its disciplining not only is societal, but – precisely on the basis of the specific type of societal understanding which underlies it – that it is also *hidden*. The new control out there in society is either completely outside the individual's range of vision, or at least quite a bit less visible than the control forms of pure individual liberalism.

   To this I must, before I conclude, add a couple of points. In the first place it must be emphasized clearly, once again, that the "Criminal Policy Paper" neither goes very far in actually suggesting a reduction of imprisonment nor very far in suggesting concrete non-individual and more hidden societal controls as alternatives to imprisonment. It is my personal political opinion that the former is bad and the latter is good. Secondly, it must also be emphasized that it will not be easy for the interventionist social democratic state (which has developed over time, and which functions in a social democratic way regardless of whether the concrete government comes from this or that bourgeois party) in the immediate future to find control forms out there in society which in fact will function effectively against crime. My view, at any rate, is that a "combatting of crime" must, as a necessary if not sufficient condition, involve deep alterations of the central mechanism of expulsion in our mode of production – bankruptcies, mergings, rationalizations and reductions of output – which in turn follow from the basic competitive and profit-oriented premise of the mode of production [17]. To repeat, the social democratic State halts in front of such alterations; the mechanisms are ameliorated, not abolished.

   But the inefficiency of the control forms may in fact stimulate their growth: their inefficieny my long be utilized as a background for developing new and "better" social controls. The inefficiency of imprisonment was for a long time used in this way: simply as a justification for building more and larger prisons.

   In the late capitalist, social democratic states, with state interventionism as a main characteristic, we may in other words – and this is of course a speculation – see the development of a new societal control policy as our own century draws to its close – just as we some decades ago saw the development of a new – social democratic – economic policy. The great change in criminal policy during the century preceding ours, was a rapid change – it was completed in 50–75 years. It is difficult to say whether the change which we are suggesting towards the year 2000 and thereafter will take place as rapidly. But with the technological level of our time the possibility is present. If I were to venture a prediction, it would firstly be that the real prisons will live on for a rather long time. The prisons have important functions in society, and evidence from Sweden, Denmark, Norway, England, and United States indicates that prison figures are again on the rise – after temporary downward trends [18]. But in terms of support and legitimacy, the prisons will be backed by less and less enthusiasm. At the same time – this is my secound and main prediction – the external or societal control system will gradually expand and become continually more extensive and inportant [19]. The expanding external control system will, this is an additional prediction, paradoxically provide the old prisons with some new legitimacy: in the shadow of the new control system with its increased emphasis on the efficent control of whole categories of people, the prisons will regain a sense of rationality as a kind of last resort, used unwillingly against the utterly uncontrollable. In this way the control system as a totality may *expand rather than shrink* as a consequence of "progressive" political initiatives such as the Norwegian "Criminal Policy Paper".

Interspersed with the new external or societal control system, other elements may develop. It is something of a criterion of social democracy that it searches for, and finds, arrangements which to some degree ameliorate the most acute problems which people have, while the given basic structure – which creates the problems – is cemented. The ameliorating aspects at the same time have a legitimating function for the regime. Such a "double character" developed in connection with the new economic policy of the Thirties and Forties, and it may be developed again in the social control field. The conceivable future control arrangements may, for example, be combined with certain types of collective state intervention in the form of insurance or compensation to the victims of crime. We already see the beginning of such arrangements todays, and they may have a corresponding function of softening criticism against the regime in the field of crime.

The future control system, which we only see in outline in the "Criminal Policy Paper", may – if it develops – have great political consequences. A developed state interventionist criminal policy may fuse with the general hidden political control – and thereby disciplining – which is developing in society [20].

All the more important, from a general political point of view, becomes the opposition to the development of the criminal policy control system. By way of conclusion, a few words should be said about this opposition. Ten years ago [21] the State had no integrated policy in the penal field. The field was regarded as a technical, narrowly defined professional area. At that time it was possible for a conscious political opposition to "break through", and to win the struggle for abolition of forced labour for alcoholics (abolished in Norway in 1970), abolition of the youth prison system (abolished in Norway in 1975), etc. – all of this *without* the State in advance having secured prison-like "alternatives" to these systems. Today the State *has* begun to formulate an integrated policy – symbolized by the "Criminal Policy Paper" – and if the

160   *T. Mathiesen*

analysis which is presented above is anywhere near correct, it will be significantly more difficult to "break through" in this way in the decades to come. Put differently, the future opposition in penal and control policy must be highly alert to the development of "alternative" arrangements of control. So we were earlier as well: we continually emphasized the importance of not giving control "alternatives" of an even more dangerous kind a chance to appear elsewhere [22]. But now a double-tracked race must be run *in practice as well:* now we must, also in practice, not only conduct our struggle against the prison mode of control, but in direct opposition to the development of the "alternative" arrangements as well.

Thereby the field of labour will be expanded. And – to repeat – be of much greater general political significance than just a few years ago.

Postscript

After the completion of this article (early 1979), a change took place on the criminal justice scene in Norway: during a general cabinet "overhaul" in the social democratic party in the Fall of 1979, the minister of justice who stimulated and presented the "Criminal Policy Paper" was given another ministerial post, while a new minister of justice was installed. In political circles and in the press the change was widely viewed as a shift from a "radical" to a "conservative" minister of justice, caused by the mounting public criticism of the former minister, and her "Criminal Policy Paper", for its radical stance in criminal policy matters.

Indeed, the press– primarily emphasizing the aspects of the Paper stressing de-penalization (see footnote 11) - had managed to define the Paper as very radical. And the new minister of justice quickly took a different view of the content of parts of it. In a Parliamentary debate early in the Fall of 1979, and in various newspaper interviews, he came out forcefully *against* an adoption of any of the (mild) suggestions for de-penalization contained in the Paper. In particular, he went against the suggestion of revising the use of imprisonment for theft – see details in footnote 11 above.

At the same time, the new minister *advocated* – in rather vague terms – "reviewing the Criminal Policy Paper, focusing on what is best in it for future use in practical criminal policy" (*Aftenposten*, 3 November 1979). In this and similar statements the new minister in other words took a *selective* stand to the Paper.

On this basis there is, indeed, *an even greater chance that the "control aspects" of the Criminal Policy Paper will be focused on and made into practical policy, while the "de-penalization aspects" will be further reduced in importance.* If this occurs, the tendencies indicated in the present article will be given further impetus.

The shift on the ministerial level, and its above-mentioned possible consequence, shows the danger involved in relying on the hope that a government policy paper eventually is adopted *as a whole.* Rather, the process of political debate and legislation is *selective,* in the sense that proposals running counter to prevailing political tendencies are easily weeded out while proposals supporting such tendencies are focused on and enhanced.

For that reason, a well-intentioned policy paper may, in the end, be used for aims which were originally unintended.

Notes

1 A content analysis of the press material has been undertaken: Randi Hirsch (1979), *Kriminaljournalistikk – salg, politikk eller saklig informasjon?,* Inst. for Sociology of Law: Oslo.

2 Denmark and Sweden witnessed rather similar trends. The data on the rise and fall of the prison figures are presented by Nils Christie (1966) in De fratagbare goder, *Tidsskrift for samfunnsforskning,* pp. 119–130. Christie explains the shifts in prison figures as reflecting changes over time in "penal values".

3 See George Rusche and Otto Kirchheimer (1939), *Punishment and Social Structure,* Russell & Russell: New York. Michel Foucault (1977), *Discipline and Punish,* Penguin Books Ltd.: London. Thomas Mathiesen (1972), Fengselsvesenets ideologi 1600–1970, in Aslak B. Syse (ed.): *Kan fengsel forsvares?,* Pax: Oslo, pp. 10–34.

4 See George Rusche and Otto Kirchheimer, *op. cit.,* and in contrast to them, Leif Petter Olaussen (1976), Avspeiler straffen arbeidsmarkedet?, *Sosiologi Idag;* see also Thomas Mathiesen (1977), *Rett og samfunn,* Pax: Oslo, pp. 72–95.

5 See Foucault *op. cit.*

6 See Ludvig Kr. Daa (1843), *Har Amerikas Erfaring bevist de Pensylvanske Faengslers Fortrinlighed?,* Krohn & Schibsted: Kristiania.

7 Some viewpoints on the question may be found in Thomas Mathiesen: "Fengselsvesenets ideologi 1600–1970", *op. cit.*

8 There have been certain ameliorations of the individualistic principle – for example the attempts of the nineteen-sixties at creating "therapeutic communities". But the attempts have been ameliorations, not breaks with the basic principle.

9 See for example Flemming Balvig (1977), Alternativer til frihedsstraf, *Information,* 10 October.

10 The fact that registered theft has increased during recent years, appears with great clarity in one of the appendices to the "Criminal Policy Paper" – see Leif Petter Olaussen: "Vedlegg I" in the Paper.

Olaussen shows that between 1835 and 1955 the number of people punished for crimes (after 1923 including those with charges withdrawn) increased and decreased in cycles between 150 and 275 per 100,000 inhabitants in the country. Also in absolute figures, the number only showed a weak and uneven increase. From 1955 on, however, the curve per 100,000 inhabitants only shoots up, in 1968 the normal "upper limit" of 275 registered criminals per 100,000 inhabitants is bypassed, "and the increase has continued, even if somewhat more hesitantly during the last 3–4 years". (Olaussen, p. 183.) The absolute figures also show an unmatched increase after 1955. Through the whole period it is theft which has dominated the picture. "And the dominance of the thefts has become continually greater, the proportion of the thefts increasing from 65.9% of all crimes in 1957 to 74.7% in 1976. Accordingly theft must occupy a central position in an analysis of Norwegian crime". (Olaussen, p. 198.)

162   *T. Mathiesen*

Olaussen points to a relationship between the above-mentioned increase in thefts on the one hand and a marked increase, from the end of the nineteen-sixties, in paid theft insurance premiums on the other (p. 201). An increase in the number of those having an insurance may have contributed to the increase in the number of registered thefts, because more people may gain something be reporting thefts to the police. To the State, however, it is all the time the quantity of registered – known – crimes which is threatening to legitimacy. In addition, the insurance companies may very well be among the institutions which concretely press for a change in the direction of new measures in criminal policy.

11 Elsewhere I have given an account of how insignificant the "Criminal Policy Paper's" suggestions concerning reduced imprisonment are: see Thomas Mathiesen (1978), Berget som fødte en mus, *Dagbladet*,31 May. I emphasize that I do not provide a full review of the content of the "Criminal Policy Paper" in the present paper. For the benefit of non-Scandinavian readers I here add a listing of the main suggestions and recommendations for reduced use of imprisonment contained in the White Paper:

It is suggested that *the age of criminal reponsibility* should be raised from 14 to 15 years, after a 3–5 years transition period (to give the authorities "a reasonable adjustment period") and on the condition that a strengthening of the social apparatus "takes place before new legislation concerning the minimum age is put into effect". *The use of remand* is recommended reduced to "a smaller extent than presently", but the recommendation is not made concrete because a committee report on remand is awaited. *The minimum period of punishment* – today 21 days – it is recommended, should be reduced, for example to seven days, but it is admitted that such a reduction "will only constitute a small contribution to the reduced use of imprisonment". *Imprisonment for theft* is recommended to be revised, but the recommendation is not made concrete. *Imprisonment for life*, it is suggested, should be abolished, but this reform is suggested in order to create the possibility of renewed prison sentencing of life-termers who have committed new offences behind the walls. At present such offenders can only be sentenced to isolation, which, it is suggested should be abolished as a penal sanction (but retained as an administrative measure). *The use of security* for so-called "abnormal" offenders – an indeterminate measure used against a relatively small group – should be virtually abolished. The proposal concerning "security" is the most clear-cut "anti-prison proposal" of the whole White Paper. In addition, some alternatives to imprisonment are suggested – especially "community service". British experience with "community service", however, indicates that the sanction for a majority becomes an alternative to conditional sentences, whereby it constitutes an increase rather than a decrease of the total criminal justice control system – see Home Office Research Study No. 39, 1977. None of the suggestions or recommendations is binding on the Government. They are presented as a basis for debate in Parliament. At the time of writing – early 1979 – that debate has not yet taken place, despite the fact that the White Paper appeared in May 1978. The debate is expected to take place in 1980.

12 The "Criminal Policy Paper" could have found considerable theoretical and empirical support for an "expulsion view" of crime in Knut Halvorsen (1977), *Arbeid eller trygd?*, Pax: Oslo. The work is not even mentioned in the bibliography of the "Criminal Policy Paper".

I mention that also an "expulsion view" may be "incapsulated" or "co-opted" and used as a basis for measures which hardly change the dynamics of production. We have seen this happen in various fields of social policy. It is this understanding taken in full seriousness, and followed up in full consequence (as in Halvorsen's book), which creates the opportunity for measures of a kind which transcend the existing order.

13 An account and analysis of the development of the Norwegian police may be found in Thomas Mathiesen (1978), *Politikrigen*, Pax: Oslo. See also Hakon Lorentzen (1977), Politioppusting - aktører, interesser og strategier, *Retfaerd*, pp. 7–26.

14 And almost to the year "1984".

15 See Foucault, *op. cit.,* final chapter; see also Thomas Mathiesen (1978), *Den skjulte disiplinering,* Pax: Oslo, Chapter 9.

16 Foucault (in *Discipline and Punish, op. cit.*) emphasizes that imprisonment also entails the surveillance of large numbers by the few, and that modern techniques of surveillance in outside society thereby are a "continuation" of the prison form. I think this emphasis overlooks the even more basic – historical – difference between control of single individuals and generalized control of groups or categories.

17 Evidence favouring this view seems to be increasing. For Norway I refer to Thomas Mathiesen (1975), *Løsgjengerkrigen*, Sosionomen: Oslo, pp. 122–136, which shows in detail the great increase in bankruptcies, mergings and rationalizations during the "growth years" of the nineteen-sixties, and to Leif Petter Olaussen: "Vedlegg I" to the "Criminal Policy Paper", pp. 194–195, which shows a rather clear relationship between the number of bankruptcies and registered crime between 1865 and 1940. See also Knut Halvorsen (1977), *Arbeid eller trygd?*, Pax: Oslo. But of course, the concrete links between the mechanisms of the production system and traditional criminal behaviour and/or criminal careers remain unravelled, and much research remains to be done.

18 One reference may be given by way of example: *Prison Statistics – England and Wales* (1978), Her Majesty's Stationery Office: London, p. 14. Excepting Norway, all of the countries mentioned saw a decline in their prison figures in the beginning of the nineteen-seventies, followed by new upward trends in the late seventies. The upward trend is particularly conspicuous in England and the United States.

19 A similar prediction concerning the external or societal control system has been presented in Stanley Cohen (1977), Prisons and the Future of Control Systems: From Concentration to Dispersal, paper presented to the European Group for the Study of Deviance and Social Control: Barcelona. See also Stanley Cohen (1979), The Punitive City: Notes on the Dispersal of Social Control. Paper presented to the European Group for the Study of Deviance and Social Control: Copenhagen.

20 The latter measures of control – of which political surveillance and tendencies towards "Berufsverbot" are only two – are discussed at length in the book from which the present paper is taken. See Thomas Mathiesen, *Den skjulte disiplinering, op. cit.* See also Thomas Mathiesen (1980), *Law, Society and Political Action*, Academic Press: London, final chapter.

21 The Norwegian organization KROM – organizing prisoners and others in opposition to the official criminal policy – was founded exactly ten years before the "Criminal Policy Paper" was published.

22 See Thomas Mathiesen (1974), *The Politics of Abolition – Essays in Political Action Theory*, Martin Robertson: London, pp. 83–100.

164   *T. Mathiesen*

References

Balvig, F. (1977) Alternativer til frihedsstraf. *Information,* 10 October.

Christie, N. (1966) De fratagbare goder. *Tidsskrift for samfunnsforskning,* pp. 119–130.

Cohen, S. (1977) Prisons and the Future of Control Systems: From Concentration to Dispersal. Paper presented to the European Group for the Study of Deviance and Social Control: Barcelona.

Cohen, S. (1979) The Punitive City: Notes on the Dispersal of Social Control. Paper presented to the European Group for the Study of Deviance and Social Control: Copenhagen.

Daa, L. K. (1843) *Har Amerikas Erfaring bevist de Pensylvanske Faengslers Fortrinlighed?* Krohn & Schibsted: Kristiania.

Foucault, M. (1977) *Discipline and Punish.* Penguin Books Ltd.: London.

Halvorsen, K. (1977) *Arbeid eller trygd?* Pax, Oslo.

Hirsch, R. (1979) *Kriminaljournalistikk Ø salg, politikk eller saklig informasjon?* Institute for Sociology of Law, mimeo: Oslo.

Lorentzen, H. (1977) Politiopprusting – aktører, interesser og strategier. *Retfaerd,* pp. 7–26.

Mathiesen, T. (1972) Fengselsvesenets ideologi 1600–1970. In *Kan fengsel forsvares?* (Syse, A. B., Ed.). Pax: Oslo, pp. 11–34.

Mathiesen, T. (1974) *The Politics of Abolition.* Martin Robertson: London.

Mathiesen, T. (1975) *Løsgjengerkrigen.* Sosionomen: Oslo.

Mathiesen, T. (1977) *Rett og samfunn.* Pax: Oslo.

Mathiesen, T. (1978) Berget som fødte en mus. *Dagbladet,* 31 May.

Mathiesen, T. (1978) *Den skjulte disiplinering.* Pax: Oslo.

Mathiesen, T. (1979) *Politikrigen.* Pax: Oslo.

Mathiesen, T. (1980) *Law, Society and Political Action.* Academic Press: London, (forthcoming).

Olaussen, L. P. (1976) Avspeiler straffen arbeidsmarkedet? *Sosiologi Idag,* pp. 33–40.

Rusche, G. & Kirchheimer, O. (1939) *Punishment and Social Structure.* Russell & Russell: New York.

Date received: September 1979

[20]

SOCIAL CONTROL AS A POLICY: PRAGMATIC MORALISM WITH A STRUCTURAL DEFICIT

JOLANDE UIT BEIJERSE AND RENÉ VAN SWAANINGEN

Erasmus University, Rotterdam

INTRODUCTION

I T CANNOT be said that British commentators of Dutch penal policy are biased in any way or present an incorrect picture. Indeed, not infrequently, such external observations make Dutch scholars aware of national peculari- ties that they might otherwise tend to take for granted (Rutherford, 1986; Downes, 1988). Although being overall very well informed, the limitation of such an outsider's approach lies in the fact that authors mostly have to rely on those materials which are available in the English language (and these are not fully representative), and in the fact that it is also tempting to 'use' examples from another country as proof of a possible utopia of reason and tolerance – which, moreover, refers to the relatively mild penal climate in the Netherlands which existed prior to the 1980s and during which time was dramatically rejected. The enthusiastic reception of the 1985 Dutch White Paper 'Society and Crime' ('Samenleving en Criminaliteit') in Britain, does indeed give the impression that the post-war era of reductionism and decarceration still exists in the Netherlands. Keith Bottomley has argued that this 'fascinating document . . . calls for radical redirection, instead of simply more of the same'. The Dutch White Paper 'enunciated a set of clear principles' and would 'stand in sharp contrast to the pragmatic and management oriented statements of criminal policy by British governments in recent years' (Bottomley, 1986: 200, 213, 199).

SOCIAL & LEGAL STUDIES (SAGE, London, Newbury Park and New Delhi), Vol. 2 (1993), 281–302

'Society and Crime' was, however, not only greeted with enthusiasm in Britain, nearly every Dutch political party, as well as many academics, were equally positive. The plan might indeed contain 'a carefully constructed strategy' (Bottomley, 1986: 209), but since its *concrete* merits remained rather vague, we should have immediately become suspicious about the interests which lay behind such a strategy. Among other things, the White Paper stresses civic responsibility with regard to crime prevention. In this respect, a distinction is made between petty crime – for which the criminal justice system should be treated as a last resort – and more serious forms of crime – for which the classical repressive approach should be intensified. With this bifurcation, a range of totally different measures – ranging from social policy to a triplification [*sic*] of prison capacity – was presented to parliament as one overall policy. Political parties with, until then, rather different views on criminal justice could on the one hand all remain focused on their particular hobby horses, while, on the other hand, were able to accept the White Paper as a whole. The initial enthusiasm from the academic side should be primarily understood in the context of policy changes in research funding – Dutch universities have become rather dependent on external financing, and 'Society and Crime' promised an important 'well' of funding (van Swaaningen et al., 1992).

In this article we evaluate the *actual* effects of five years' experience of crime prevention as proposed by 'Society and Crime'. We first outline the content of the so-called 'radical redirection' and 'clear principles' of the White Paper with regard to petty crime – leaving aside the plan's paragraphs on 'serious crime', for which a tougher approach was advocated. Subsequently, we examine how several crime prevention projects actually function in practice with reference largely to our own research in a working-class neighbourhood in Rotterdam, and briefly making some comparisons with an English and a German study, we put the problem of petty crime in its socioeconomic context.

A Short History of Dutch Policy on Petty Crime

In 1983, an advisory committee on petty crime was set up – the Roethof Committee. The prevalence of petty crime was considered to be an important element of the deterioration of, mainly urban, life. The Roethof Committee Green Paper offers some interesting perspectives in this respect. It begins by problematizing the concept of petty crime as such. Instead of presenting it as an abstract notion, the Committee differentiates between the various types – petty violence and threats, shoplifting, burglary without serious damage, bicycle theft, vandalism, soccer-related vandalism, illicit use of public transport and minor traffic violations. For clarity's sake, we refer to these problems here as 'everyday crime'. While noting a steep increase of these problems since the 1960s, the Roethof Committee proposes an intensification of various forms of social control. An important premise of the Committee's report was that the declining importance in people's lives of institutions like the school, church or family had not been replaced by an increase in any other form of social control.

Furthermore, the opportunity to commit petty crimes was seen to have increased because of a growing anonymity in terms of social relations and, because in a situation of increasing affluence, there are simply more goods to steal. In its report the Committee accepts that everyday crime could well be caused by problems such as unemployment, but declares this aspect beyond its terms of reference (Commissie Kleine Criminaliteit, 1984).

The basis of the Roethof Green Paper lies in notions of social control as developed by Travis Hirschi (1969). It has been argued that Hirschi's control theory has been so broadly applied in the Netherlands because it is simple enough for even politicians to understand, because it can be easily translated into policy terms and because of the flexibility of the concept of social control as such: if you fire enough rounds you're bound to hit something (Bruinsma, 1990). All the political parties have given their own particular interpretation of social control. The Christian Democrats refer to the human inclination to evil and the need to curb it. They point to the so-called 'social centrefield' (*maatschappelijk middenveld*), that is, that part of society we have virtually daily direct contact with, as the level of society at which direct forms of informal social control are situated. The Social Democrats stress unemployment as an important cause of petty crime. In the tradition of Willem Bonger, they view the communal responsibility for a just social order as the main form of social control. By cutting social welfare budgets the government has indeed achieved the crime statistics it deserves, they argue. This stance was strongly opposed by the Liberal Conservatives, who maintain that it is the welfare institutions which have failed in their alleged preventive duties. For them, the principal form of social control remaining as a serious option is techno-prevention (K. Brants, 1986; C. Brants, 1993).

The focus of the Roethof Committee was to stimulate *social* prevention[1] by revitalizing social control at the level of neighbourhoods, schools, soccer clubs, and so on. Social control should consequently be implemented by persons whose normal occupational duties encompass a wider field than that of the police – such as social workers, teachers, sports coaches, among others – because control should not be a task in itself, but an implicit part of other important activities. Furthermore, the Green Paper advocated a reorganization of the urban environment so that people could feel safer in public places. All political parties agreed with these recommendations. Such widespread agreement, it has been argued, is also rooted in the Dutch tradition of paternalism, in which great value is attributed to 'caring' forms of supervision. The notion behind this national appeal to self-constraint is that people will 'voluntarily' subject themselves to the 'norms' if they can be convinced that it is in their own (communal) interest to do so (C. Brants, 1993). This also seems to be an important reason why in Dutch social control agencies, behavioural and welfare specialists have traditionally played a far more important role than lawyers (Blankenburg and van de Bunt, 1986).

The section of 'Society and Crime' which referred to petty crime was indeed based on the Roethof Report, but the authors of the White Paper gave a more instrumentalist and judicial orientation to the Committee's recommendations. In Hirschi's theory, social control ranges from direct institutional control to indirect forms of control which are related to personal bonds and various other attachments to society. Hirschi stresses the role direct *personal* relations play with regard to crime and crime prevention. In the Roethof Report, the emphasis on informal social control is well recognized, but the replacement of 'implicit agents of social control' by various administrative officials in 'Society and Crime' seems to misrepresent basic Hirschian assumptions. Whereas the Green Paper focused on the meso-level of society (the neighbourhood, schools, clubs, etc.), the White Paper stresses the responsibility of the mayor, the chief of police and the public prosecutor. Essentially, crime prevention is thereby made the responsibility of these partners in the so-called 'trilateral consultation' at the local level, and now consists of both preventive and repressive measures. The genius behind this White Paper, Jan van Dijk, characterizes this approach as an example of a new pragmatic moralism about crime (van Dijk, 1987). With this creative transformation, a nostalgia for the preventive role of social control mechanisms inherent in the traditional pillarized Dutch society of the 1950s became again an implicit part of judicial policy (C. Brants, 1993; Boutellier, 1991).

The policy on everyday crime was now presented as administrative prevention – which could be seen as the Dutch equivalent of the British multi-agency approach. In nominal accordance with the recommendations of the Roethof Committee, three guiding principles of administrative prevention were adopted: (1) occupational control by bus-drivers, janitors, shop staff, sports coaches, youth workers, etc. with regard to potential offenders; (2) urban planning and development which takes limiting the opportunity to commit crime into account; and (3) reinforcing social integration, particularly with regard to the younger generation (Ministerie van Justitie, 1985).

Here we can indeed still distinguish three elements of control theory: social control, opportunity and attachment – notions of commitment, involvement and beliefs were interpreted as inherent in the last 'crime stopper' – attachment.

ORGANIZING PREVENTION PROJECTS: CONFLICTING INTERESTS AND ACADEMIC PROSTITUTION

Before any concrete decision was made with regard to implementation, politicians debated for some time on the cost-effectiveness of the various measures. If one were to adopt the proposed wide view of crime prevention, which ministry would carry the financial burden, the Ministry of Justice or the Ministry of the Interior? The government decided to set up an *inter*departmental fund of 45 million guilders (approximately £17,500,000) to subsidize 'promising local initiatives of administrative crime prevention' for the period 1986–90.[2] In November 1985, all provincial and local authorities were invited to apply for such a subsidy. Criteria for the funding of any project were that it should (1) be of a so-called 'integrative', i.e. multi-agency, nature; (2) have the approval of the trilateral consultation (between the police, the Department of Public Prosecution and the mayor); (3) introduce a 'new' approach; and (4) be evaluated scientifically. The ministries expected that after a positive evaluation, local authorities would be prepared to continue a project on a permanent basis at their own expense (Storm van's Gravesande and de Vries, 1986).

The various applications for funding showed how broad, but also how *restrictive*, the interpretation of 'administrative prevention' could be. Formally, all projects had to fit into one of the three guiding principles of social control, but since these were not explained in any great detail, local officials tended to interpret them in their own way, i.e. distorting the rhetoric of 'Society and Crime' so that it would tie in with local projects. A wide variety of already existing projects vaguely to do with crime were suddenly referred to as 'administrative prevention', and the government accepted most projects at face value – under the sole condition that they should be subject to academic research.

It was the first time that scientific evaluation was made a condition for receiving a subsidy for the implementation of a national policy. Unfortunately, the process by which this evaluation was to take place was possibly even more obscure than the guiding principles of administrative prevention. Two types of evaluation were distinguished: (1) organizational evaluation – what, where, how, for whom, etc.; and (2) effect evaluation – with regard to reoffending, etc., but there was no indication as to what standards any such evaluation should be judged against. This implied that even the criteria for the success or failure of a project were left to the interpretation of the individual researcher. From the viewpoint of academic freedom this might still seem a logical approach, but when the actual outcome of research has direct financial and political implications, academic credibility and personal interests can easily come into conflict.

Many of the crime prevention projects were merely a continuation of plans which practitioners and local politicians had already agreed upon. In most cases, *they* were *already* convinced of the effectiveness of their particular ideas, and in such cases it is hard to convince people of a need for any critical examination. When a scientific evaluation is a condition for receiving money in the first place, and only a *positive* evaluation is needed to get any money for a follow-up, it's not hard to see that those who are politically and practically responsible do not want to risk 'their' project failing its evaluation and are therefore not really interested in any serious academic analysis. The academic is therefore perceived as the outsider, and an evaluation only takes place because it is a formal obligation.

The experience of our own department in its research for 'Society and Crime' illustrates perfectly that the project initiators' co-operation with academics was indeed to a large extent motivated by the possibility of acquiring funding for projects which had virtually been implemented already. One of these projects was the installation of electronic warning systems for shopkeepers. The inventor and distributor of these systems was actively involved in the acquisition of funding for the project. Yet another representative of private enterprise who entered the crime business was hired to take practical measures, ranging from provision of bicycle parking places to drawing up a 'criminal map' of the area. This person started immediately, which meant that not a single research result could even be taken into account, since the research had yet to get under way (Fijnaut et al., 1991)!

The preoccupation with previously planned projects and the possibility of acquiring funding for them illustrates the lack of any interest whatsoever in the nature of existing problems or their causes. In a preliminary examination of six 'Society and Crime' projects oriented towards crime in shops and shopping centres, we found that in most cases virtually no preparatory study had been made regarding the frequency or the nature of the problems the project aimed to tackle. Most 'analyses' were based on the results of a rather simplistic and methodologically incoherent questionnaire which the police had distributed among shopkeepers. These questionnaires mainly contained questions about the incidence of shoplifting, the frequency of reporting such occurrences to the police and, almost incidentally, about threats and violence accompanying shoplifting. In most of these cases no further research was initiated (Moerland and uit Beijerse, 1988).

Paradoxically, research activities by commercial advice bureaux really started to flourish. Universities, being increasingly dependent on externally financed research, have also shown willing to sell their academic soul for a nickle and a dime to such political interests, but when private enterprise enters 'the business', the academic prostitution is complete. A large proportion of the 45 million guilder subsidy was spent on such 'scientific' evaluation. Private advice bureaux generally charged large sums for their quasi-scientific blessings but at the same time, their customers were quite satisfied (uit Beijerse et al., 1990a). There was rarely any supervision over the *quality* of the research. Practical implications played such a dominant role, that no one paid much attention to any qualitative considerations, or in fact to the research findings themselves. In reality, the result was that anyone who wanted to initiate any project vaguely related to the problem of crime in general and who had been able to get local authority support, could virtually do what he or she wanted with the money.

Concrete Results of 'Society and Crime' Projects

Now the experimental period of five years has come to a close, and with over 100 crime prevention projects in more than 90 local communities having received subsidy, it is interesting to look at their practical results. Also, the Ministry of Justice's 'meta-evaluation report' itself cannot really be called positive. Many of the projects have not even succeeded in developing any qualitative standards by which to judge their effects. The quality of internal evaluation (by police, local government or project managers themselves) was generally lower and less critical about how such projects functioned than was the external evaluation. In fewer than one-third of the reports did the evaluation contain *any* useful information about the effect on the incidence of crime, and only half of *these* results were considered to be reliable. The ministerial researchers have concluded bitterly that the years of work, effort and enthusiasm put into the development of a differentiated administrative-judicial programme of crime prevention, has resulted in an attempt at 'the prevention of vandalism and thefts in car parks, shopping centres and schools, committed by juveniles' (Polder and van Vlaardingen, 1992).

As we have shown, measures were sometimes undertaken before any research had been carried out. Usually, initiators of such projects based their plans solely on complaints about one particular type of offence, for example shoplifting or vandalism. The project managers did not take into account that when people complain about certain events which they call 'crime', this does not necessarily mean that such events can be understood as such in legal terms, or that such highlighted legal variables are indeed the real or even the key elements of the problems they were dealing with. People can feel uncomfortable or insecure for many different reasons, but the most easy and generally accepted complaints are those which are expressed in *terms* of crime. The somewhat unspecific questions on 'experience of crime' which were generally posed, were consequently followed by rather limited control measures, which tended to leave the real problems untouched.

As researchers of a 'Society and Crime' project in Rotterdam, we were also confronted with this preoccupation with certain 'crimes' and presupposed repressive responses. Where we concluded that shoplifting as such was only a problem for a few large chain-stores (mostly supermarkets) who had chosen an intrusive sales strategy, most of the practical measures were still strictly confined to shoplifting, for example a course was set up in which all shopkeepers, small retailers included, could learn how to prevent shoplifting. Few people showed any interest in the course: in spite of active recruitment fewer than 10 percent of all shopkeepers chose to participate. Simplifying the method of reporting shoplifting to the police was another measure which was implemented. The police set up a system by which such offences could be reported by telephone, and a quicker judicial procedure for shoplifters was made possible. Nonetheless, these 'preventive'(?) measures were seldom used. They were initially set up because shopkeepers had complained that reporting these offences cost a lot of time, and that in the final event shoplifters were rarely prosecuted. By discussing this issue with the shopkeepers, we found out that they believed that the police released shoplifters in a shorter space of time than the time it had cost them to hand them over to the police in the first place. Our conclusion was, however, different; the shopkeepers' annoyance was merely due to their being unacquainted with the criminal procedure. Shopkeepers interpreted a physical 'release' by the police as an acquittal, whereas in reality in the Netherlands it is the *general* rule that the suspect is released until their trial unless certain legal and social circumstances require that he or she is remanded in custody. If there had been a genuine desire to do something about this problem, it would have been simpler and more appropriate to inform the shopkeepers about (the rationale behind) this procedure first (uit Beijerse et al., 1987; Moerland and uit Beijerse, 1988; Fijnaut et al., 1991).

The fact that project managers hardly ever change their minds after any research results, but stick steadfastly to their original plans, might also have something to do with their connections or obligations to other parties or people involved in the project; or perhaps there are political motivations behind it, in the sense of being seen to be already 'doing something about the problem'. National political considerations could also well have hindered any real integrative approach. Within governmental bureaucracy, 'justice' is the only 'growth industry', while in all other departments, budgets, such as social welfare, are being cut; so the chances of a project's financial success increase if measures are of a more judicial nature (Fijnaut, 1991).

When we look at the more than 100 projects, an integrative, or multi-agency, approach of crime prevention, as originally proposed, can barely be distinguished. Looking at the three guiding principles of administrative prevention, we must conclude that most of the measures are oriented towards restricting the opportunity to commit a crime. A number of other measures are confined to supervision, mostly applied as a rather repressive form of prevention. And the third principle, reinforcing the younger generation's integration into society, has hardly been implemented at all. One-third of the measures are called 'person-oriented' – mostly towards juveniles – but they mostly had very little to do with the recommendations of the Roethof Committee in this respect. Measures like providing information about the criminal justice system, controlling truancy, settling criminal cases more quickly and developing non-custodial sanctions for juveniles can hardly be regarded as means to strengthen their attachment to society. Only some of the measures undertaken, for instance the provision of aid to so-called risk groups of juveniles and the establishment of leisure-time projects for young people, could be interpreted (with some stretch of the imagination) as such, but then the desirability of such initiatives still completely depends on the specific way in which they are executed (Bruinsma, 1992). The risk of the punitive city comes particularly close here.

CRIME PREVENTION IN A WORKING-CLASS AREA IN ROTTERDAM

The involvement of local government in the so-called 'social centre-field' did not lead to any common multi-agency initiative to resolve the more inherent social problems in the weaker parts of society, but merely to a dispersal of repressive social control to areas beyond the police and judiciary. It became clear that people were only willing to take action as long as it concerned their own personal interests or those of the organization they represented. When the perceived problems turned out not to be those expected, there was neither the willingness nor the flexibility to change what had already been planned. Neither, apparently, did the people behind these plans possess the creativity to search for a new approach. The final result was that all efforts largely failed to produce any concrete results – or only resulted in a positive outcome for a limited period of time. Possible inherent causes of the problems were not taken into consideration. Where a neighbourhood was policed the crime problem moved on to other areas and found new victims – crime always tends to hit the weak spot in society.

The following is based on our own research in a working-class neighbourhood in the south of Rotterdam.[3] In the first phase of our research, we made use of open interviews in which we tried to encourage different interest groups to tell us about their problems. In this way, we were able to find out which problems *they* considered to be important, in which cases they expected the authorities to act and which problems they could handle by themselves. With this starting point, our approach has similarities with ethnographic studies which have been carried out in Frankfurt (Hanak et al., 1989) or in the London borough of Islington (Jones et al., 1986).

In this first part of our research we focused on a particular shopping street in this neighbourhood, the Boulevard Zuid (uit Beijerse et al., 1987). Complaints about shoplifting, sometimes aggravated, had decided Rotterdam City Council to apply for funding to start a 'Society and Crime' project aimed at reducing crime in this particular street. Preparatory research, consisting of open interviews with sixty shopkeepers, showed, in contrast to the general picture outlined above, that crime *as such* was not considered to be the most crucial part of the problem. The main problem the shopkeepers iterated was a general feeling of insecurity. This actually had to do with the street being polluted by traffic and dirt and made untidy by goods on display in front of the shops. What was striking was that many of these problems were the prime responsibility of the shopkeepers themselves. Small retailers especially complained about the fact that new shops came and went, and that the owners only felt responsible for their own particular premises and not for the street as a whole. An investigation of daily police reports with respect to Boulevard Zuid and a comparable shopping street in a working-class area in the northern part of Rotterdam, shows some striking differences. First, Boulevard Zuid has a higher number of traffic accidents and, secondly, a relatively large proportion of the offenders which are 'caught' here, also live in the immediate area around the street. Other problems were connected to the impoverishment and deterioration of the neighbourhood and the changing character of people who frequented the street. A common complaint was the disturbing presence of hard-drug users, and this was the main cause of the general feeling of vulnerability. The high percentage of so-called foreigners in the population was also perceived as a threat to public safety. These subjective complaints did not reflect any specific racial tension, but were an expression of very general fears of the unknown, and indicated how the older generation especially found it difficult to have a feeling of 'home' when the majority of the population spoke another language, had another religion and other customs. The interviewees often accompanied these remarks with excuses and assurances that they were not racists in any way whatsoever.

The ideas the shopkeepers put forward for reducing the problems were mainly oriented at intensifying co-operation among the shopkeepers themselves. A good example of where such co-operation has failed is the installation of roller-shutters in several of the (larger) shops. After installing the shutters, these shops were indeed secure from burglary and having their windows smashed, but since then these problems have been concentrated on the shops which do not have roller-shutters, i.e. mostly those stores who cannot afford to purchase such means of prevention. Moreover, having shops with roller-shutters along the street only tended to intensify people's feelings of insecurity. Previously, people had been able to walk along the street after closing-time window shopping; now, the roller-shutters are down, people can no longer stroll along glancing at goods on view and, what's more, are reluctant to walk along the street anymore because of the threatening appearance of all those vast areas of iron shutters. Such problems could have been prevented if the shopkeepers had arrived at a collective solution to the problem instead of leaving the problem at their neighbour's door by only taking measures to protect their own premises.

Another suggestion the shopkeepers put forward was to develop some kind of co-operative warning system against 'trouble-makers'. Further proposals to reduce feelings of insecurity included cleaning the street more regularly, creating a more friendly ambience by painting the walls in lighter colours and keeping it neat by not allowing goods to be put on show on the pavement in front of shops. Following that, the shopkeepers suggested some architectural changes to make it more difficult for thieves to commit a crime. Though we accept that these proposals do not, by and large, go beyond the restriction of opportunity or the increase of social control, the shopkeepers did also point to the poor socioeconomic standards of the people who live in the neighbourhood.

This was the main impetus to the second phase of the research into the particular problems of this area (uit Beijerse et al., 1990b). Here we touched upon the more inherent causes of crime. In this phase, people from more than thirty institutions that work for and with the inhabitants of the neighbourhood were interviewed – such as schools, doctors, nurses, police, community centres, residents' platforms, centres for the elderly, youth organizations, Turkish organizations, the municipal welfare bureau and the city housing department. Besides these, about sixty inhabitants of the neighbourhood were also interviewed. The interviews showed that there were two main points on which everyone was in agreement. First, they all show that it is hard to distinguish between crimes as defined under the criminal code and other problems which are experienced as being as annoying as crime. Second, in all interviews, almost naturally, a connection was made between perceived crime and the prevailing socioeconomic conditions in the district, not only in the sense that these facilitate the incidence of crime, but also that they create an atmosphere in which crime is just one of the elements of daily life. For these reasons, we describe below some of the developments that have taken place in the neighbourhood over the years.

The district was built in the 1920s to house people who had come from the countryside to work in Rotterdam harbour. The oldest parts were hastily built, and the results of this quick and cheap building are still visible: narrow and dark streets with small flats having one common entrance. Other parts of the district, which were built when the Social Democrats were in office, provide more space and have more green areas around the houses. In the 1960s, a new group of migrant workers came to the district, this time not from the Dutch but from the Turkish countryside, who were housed in boarding-houses in the oldest parts. The fact that these 'guest-workers' were squashed together in all-male groups – their families weren't with them – in small, badly constructed and maintained houses had several negative side-effects. In the early 1970s the older inhabitants of the neighbourhood complained to the local authorities about the high concentration of boarding-houses for immigrant workers in this particular district, as well as about the overcrowding and the unhygienic conditions. No action was taken. Later, several large fires broke out, in which numbers of Turkish men died. Stirred up by disputes about noise and dirt, in 1974 these social conditions culminated in a riot between the Turkish workers and the white Dutch population, which lasted for a whole three days and during which some Turkish boarding-houses were destroyed. It is hard to comment in any meaningful way here as to what extent latent racist tendencies might have also played a role in the riots, but neither Turkish nor Dutch inhabitants have mentioned racial tensions as a crucial element of the problem. The problem was clearly perceived as being due to the high concentration of immigrant boarding-houses and overcrowding of the apartments, even to the extent of establishing a mosque in a normal flat (van Reenen, 1979: 235–42).

After these events, Rotterdam City Council announced plans for a large-scale urban renewal, which entailed a vast renovation programme of all the houses in the older districts; for reasons the Chicago School could not have foreseen, Rotterdam has not had an old city centre since May 1940. This operation was to have two phases, starting with the oldest districts. The neighbourhood in which we carried out our study was to wait till the second phase of renovation. This waiting period was one of the main causes of the impoverishment and deterioration of the district in the 1980s. In the following we detail the (criminal) problems experienced there and try to indicate the social conditions lying behind them.

First, the neighbourhood suffers from a disproportionately high incidence of theft from houses, cars, public buildings and building-sites. The residents confronted with these problems point to the deplorable housing conditions as the main cause of their troubles; because of the proposed renovation programme, owners stopped maintaining their houses. And because of the bad condition of the houses and because many of them are unoccupied while awaiting renovation, it is particularly easy to break into such places. The streets are, furthermore, so dark, that anyone can break into cars and public buildings relatively unnoticed. Because old age pensions have been cut, many of the elderly residents live a rather lonely and isolated life. This makes them particularly vulnerable to theft or burglary.

We cannot seriously comment here on the cause or nature of, or solution to, the drug problem. To be simplistic for this reason, suffice it to say that it is likely that most of these thefts and burglaries are committed by drug addicts. The stolen goods are often of so little material value that a non-addicted person would not take the trouble to steal them – and run the risk of being caught. Many residents even know who broke into their house or car. It is important to stress that for most of the residents drug addicts do not represent a sort of creature from another planet, but are indeed people whom they have known since they were children! For this reason, some victims of theft, especially the younger residents, prefer to handle the cases on their own, without police intervention. Drug addicts can be held responsible for many of the known cases of theft and burglary in public buildings, as well – especially those in medical centres, where it is often medicines and prescriptions which are stolen.

A second social condition specific to the neighbourhood is the situation of young people. With little hope for a better future, owing to poor education and massive unemployment (especially for immigrants: one-fifth of the white Dutch residents are unemployed and nearly half of the immigrants), many of them have found an alternative challenge in the drug scene. And the illegality of hard drugs causes such high prices, that addiction cannot be supported by legal means alone. Furthermore, the fact that renovation has yet to begin has attracted a group of addicts from other parts of the city, where renovation had been completed and where they consequently find it impossible to get somewhere to live.

Another form of theft which can be distinguished is that from building-sites. Here we can distinguish three forms. The most innocent form is by people living around the building-sites who filch sand, tiles or tools for personal use. A second form can be seen as an exponent of juvenile vandalism. As soon as the old houses to be renovated become vacant, they enter these houses and pinch any valuable materials in order to sell them. A third category are thefts from the newly built but as yet unoccupied houses. Here complete central heating systems, doors, windows and walls all 'disappear'. The relation between these three forms of theft and burglary and the housing conditions is obvious. They will probably cease when the renovation is completed.

Other everyday crimes in the district take the form of aggression and threats. This in part has to do with a general lack of accepted social skills. The city housing department is confronted with people who become aggressive when their particular requests for other (that is, better) houses are refused. The municipal welfare bureau is also victim to aggression and threats when it has to turn down requests for unemployment benefit or refuse to advance money for such benefits. According to the people interviewed, some forms of aggression in the neighbourhood also have to do with the specific subculture of a working-class district: fights between families or neighbours are not uncommon. And it is a kind of tradition that groups of youths quarrel and fight around the community centre as a form of 'gang subculture'. A relatively recent phenomenon is fights between immigrant and Dutch youngsters.

Here a relation with the third condition, demographic developments, is evident. Because of the renovation programme many families moved to the newly built parts of the city. Between 1971 and 1987 the total number of residents decreased by one-third, while the remaining population consists mainly of new residents, many of whom are immigrants who moved into the district in the same period. In 1987 these people (mainly of Turkish origin) made up one-quarter of the population, and in the oldest parts of the district they form the majority of the population. Annoyance caused by dirt, noise and smells, seems to be of even greater importance than the petty crime described above – theft, burglary, aggression and threats. These annoyances are also related to the housing conditions. Because of their proximity, almost every noise can be heard and cooking smells permeate the houses. Such problems from neighbours must have also occurred in former times, but, because the neighbours are 'foreign', because the irritation is caused by people who speak another language and eat different food, is probably why it is now perceived as a problem – for the smell of traditional Brussels sprouts can certainly not be called pleasant either! Further-more, the small houses do not have gardens or balconies in which to put rubbish. Dutch people complain that the immigrants 'dump' their garbage on the streets. The immigrants, for their part, see the Dutch habit of keeping the rubbish inside the house as unhygienic. That is also the way they feel about keeping large dogs in small houses. Together with those Dutch people who do not own dogs, they complain about dog faeces in the streets. Here cultural differences, as well as housing conditions, do play an apparent role. The fact that the Dutch specifically complain about the immigrants could, however, also be related to the fact that most of the elderly are Dutch and most of the youth are immigrants. Elderly people do tend to complain about young people: about their noise their soccer games against their windows, the 'music' blaring from their ghetto-blasters, their tinkering with their mopeds and their throwing empty cans, plastic bags or fast-food plastic trays on the streets.

Another source of annoyance has to do with the presence of the drug scene in the neighbourhood. Trade in illegal hard drugs takes place in several unoccupied buildings and in coffee-shops, but also in drug addicts' houses. The annoyance can become particularly acute when the house of a drug addict is being used for trade, because then the premises are also visited by lots of other people and a rather aggressive atmosphere can be created, especially because there is just the one common entrance. Another side-effect of having drug addicts as neighbours is that this often goes hand-in-hand with neglect of the houses. Because of a continuous need for money, virtually everything from the house which has any value tends to get sold off. Sometimes houses are shared by many people, and because all the money is spent on drugs, bills don't get paid and the electricity is cut off. In that case candles are used to light the place, and this leads to the fear of fire among the neighbours – still remembering the incidents of the early 1970s. In addition to all this, many residents are concerned about the influence the drug scene has on their children. Children quite often come home with used needles, and even one of the very few children's playgrounds in the neighbourhood had to be closed because it had been virtually taken over by drug dealers and users.

These feelings of insecurity and inconvenience may be the most serious consequence of the deprivation mentioned above. Many people, especially pensioners and women, are so afraid that they dare not go out at night and have partially barricaded their houses. Also, because the district has become spatially and socially segregated, people do not feel it is home anymore. Neighbours do not know each other, the limits of their tolerance were passed a long time ago and cultural differences reinforce a mutual incomprehension. People are unhappy about their living conditions which they feel have deteriorated. At the same time, the inhabitants feel neglected and forgotten by the local authorities. The extremely negative way in which people speak about government officials is a striking example of their growing distrust of and disinterest in politics. Many of the white Dutch inhabitants, who traditionally voted for the Labour Party, no longer vote or have switched – sometimes as an act of revolt – to obscure parties on the extreme right. The situation is smouldering.

THE STRUCTURAL DEFICIT OF SOCIAL CONTROL

Of course, the problems we have described are not unique to Rotterdam. They are the general problems of any European urban area. What may be a little more unusual is the fact that a specific national policy is used as a model to tackle these problems at a local level. As we have seen, this policy is strongly oriented towards Hirschian control theory. As would probably have been the case in any other city and country, a restricted approach to control has not proved a suitable means to understand or tackle the real nature of such social problems.

The idea that such a limited perspective is too vague and only globalizes very different lived realities has also been illustrated by the *Islington Crime Survey* (Jones et al., 1986). The left realist researchers analysed the problems in this London borough: they differentiated beliefs about and risks of victimization according to the structure of the neighbourhood and the social class, gender and race of the people interviewed. Left realists can also take the credit for giving back an important place in criminological research to social aetiology. And they have been strong supporters of a socially oriented multi-agency approach which addresses the inherent causes of the problems and the actual victims, the public, the offenders and the relationships between the various agencies. They showed quite convincingly, furthermore, that petty crime is not interclass, but intraclass: it is poor against poor and black against black. For us, it has been important to bear these observations in mind when analysing the shortcomings of the Dutch projects. Our concern with the realists' approach lies, however, in their strong emphasis on policing as a contributor to the solution, which Heinz Steinert has expressed in the following words:

> The only problem we had when reading that book [*What Is to be Done about Law and Order?*] was why all this should be treated as a problem of 'crime' and not as one of racism, the breakdown of community and the general brutality of conduct under deteriorating conditions of living, as was shown in the book itself. And this, as we know, is not just a matter of words, but one of programmes of action; if the problem is one of crime, then the course of action is to get hold of the individual perpetrators and punish them, and the relevant institutions are the police, the judge and the prison. If the problem is the breakdown of the community, then the police will not be the first institution that comes to mind when thinking about how to restore social relations. (Steinert, 1989: 173)

By looking at various social problems in terms of crime, the main focus of the Dutch 'Society and Crime' projects remained a penal approach. This has also made the policy principle of reinforcing social integration, particularly of the (unemployed, immigrant) youth, a dead letter and, instead, has caused the selling of repression as prevention. Without explicitly answering these critics, Jock Young (1992) slightly refined his 'police-centred' approach in his recent 'Ten points of Realism' by prioritizing more structural ways of intervention and, for the time being, leaving 'consensual policing' as a facilitating service. The top–down nature of concepts like crime and social control as such is, however, still not problematized: realism does not deal with such abstractions, Young says.

Yet this analytical problem has also been the starting point for Hanak et al.'s (1989) ethnographic study of petty crime in Frankfurt. These more abolitionist-oriented researchers start by differentiating between crime as conflict and crime as social problem. Their approach of starting with people's lived realities comes closer to the approach *we* have adopted. We also concluded that the people directly concerned are often more than capable of analysing the underlying causes of their problems and even have clear ideas of how these problems could be tackled and prevented. We also drew several similar conclusions to those of Hanak et al. Their contentions that stories of 'winners' and 'losers' in society are at odds with the judicial distinction between victims and offenders, that general annoyances are often perceived as more problematical than 'crime' in the strictest sense, and that sanctioning and policing will first be an unrealistic reaction and second a countereffective one, are supported by our own findings. With them, we would also like to share the idea that many forms of *social conflict* can be settled by mediation – if power differences are equalized and cultural differences explained – but many of the *social problems* were indeed of a more inherent nature and require a more intrinsic approach. Some form of personal participation in crime prevention could, however, still be a means to allay the more exaggerated fears about crime.

When summarizing the range of possible measures the people interviewed in the southern area of Rotterdam have put forward, it is remarkable to see how many of them indeed point to the failures of local authorities and municipal services in dealing with the problems. One proposal is that the department responsible for the renovation plans should redesign the neighbourhood in a more general sense – create more open and green spaces, children's playgrounds and parking areas. Another idea is that the city sanitation department should clean the streets and collect the rubbish more often. The role of the city housing department is often criticized. Many Dutch as well as Turkish people feel that they should have taken care to avoid a concentration of immigrants in one particular part of the district. Others feel that this department is also responsible for the problems of drug addicts selling drugs in their houses. The parents of young children especially often become quite emotional in their anger about the fact that the department could have foreseen that 'junkies' cause problems and could have housed them in buildings without common entrances.

The notion put forward by the Amsterdam sociologist Kees Schuyt, that people tend to act in a similar way as they are treated by the authorities, seems quite appropriate in this respect. As the institutions are increasingly seen as indifferent, disrespectful, abusive and cynically calculating towards the citizens, people tend to 'respond' in similar ways (Schuyt, 1993). The inhabitants of the neighbourhood we researched do indeed feel ignored by the local authorities, and as a reaction they can no longer feel any responsibility for 'their' surroundings. An often heard suggestion from government officials is that people should recover their pride in their district. But how can they be proud when municipal services show nothing but contempt? This is a clear example of what is generally referred to as the 'drifting apart' of citizens and politics.

Hereby we touch upon the least satisfactory part of 'Society and Crime': the (lack of an) explanation as to how the proposed reintegration of citizens into society can be achieved. In the White Paper, this integration is quite restrictively interpreted – within the framework of the already slightly distorted interpretation of Hirschian control theory. A stronger emphasis on the now rather implicit Hirschian notions of commitment to and involvement in social activities would have done no harm. Within Jan van Dijk's pragmatic moralism, the Hirschian notion of beliefs in the conventional order is even less problematized than by Hirschi himself. And it is precisely in this way of making the problem of crime politically harmless, that the major shortcoming of the current discussion of crime prevention lies. Empirical analyses show that it is exactly this belief which cannot be taken for granted. In declaring the problem of unemployment beyond its terms of reference, the Roethof Committee actually blocks a way of resolving the problem: namely a better social integration of young people and the socially deprived (Boutellier, 1991: 227).

Control theory is simply inadequate to explain this (lack of) social integration. We need to resort to other theoretical models. To start with, this lack of social integration could be seen as a consequence of strain; a tension in the psyche of the individual between his or her perceived aspirations and the possibility of achieving them. No matter how many 'American Dreams' one might have, the chances of realizing them are not equally distributed. The implicitly presumed commitment to society and weighing up the risks of whether or not to engage in criminal activities, are not equal factors in the lives of the 'haves' and 'have-nots'. Although strain theory goes some way to explain the lack of social integration, at the same time it remains too oriented towards specific segments of society to be satisfactory in a situation which seems to be largely due to social conditions. At the Groningen Institute of Criminology of Riekent Jongman c.s., a form of strain theory has been developed which is oriented precisely towards those factors which still deter people who live in socioeconomically deprived circumstances from committing crimes, that is, a perception of still having something (a relationship, a job, etc.) to lose in society. From this perspective, the combination of integration and strain is at odds within the rather limited rationale of 'Society and Crime' (Jongman, 1990). Jongman interprets the underpriviledged's lack of integration into society as a consequence of social inequality (Jongman, 1988) and delinquency, subsequently, as an exponent of a latent resistance to stress (Jongman and Timmerman, 1985).

Though Jongman does not extend his critique of social control beyond the penal area, his integration of attachment and strain theories comes close to deviancy theory's critique of control theory, namely that it leaves, next to the aetiological question, the power question untouched (Cohen, 1989). Jongman, however, hardly touches upon more general critical criminological questions regarding the interest various groups have in maintaining the status quo. If this is a group's hidden agenda, they are certainly not going to question the conventional order, but will in fact try to draw attention away from any inherent causes of problems, and focus on micro-level analyses and solutions. And this is exactly what has happened in the 'Society and Crime' projects.

Young people from impoverished neighbourhoods have virtually no positive experiences from which they could derive some basic sense of self-esteem, social status or indeed belief in the justness of the social order. The only place where they feel respected is in their role in a street- or community-group. On the other hand, many of the neighbourhood's women and elderly live a rather isolated life because they feel particularly unsafe on the streets. It is tempting to opt for one particular theory as a frame of reference for one's empirical findings and as a point of orientation for concrete policy recommendations. The complexity of the research material, however, hardly allows for any monocausal explanations, and indeed points to the, albeit limited, relevance of both control and strain theory, as well as the critical social theory of deviance. And even such a materially grounded eclectic combination cannot offer adequate answers to certain questions – like whether a low participation rate in society might be an explanation for a comparatively high fear of crime or whether other factors are of greater importance in this respect. A more differentiated critical analysis of *why* different groups of people have different subjective perceptions of security, would seem particularly appropriate for a further analysis of the social problems in districts like the one we describe.

In a time in which an increasing number of people fail to receive a share in the benefits of society, the current governmental nostalgia about restoring beliefs and commitments by the reinforcement of the norms and values of an idyllic 'caring community' seem quite out of place – it would be more appropriate for these cynical bureaucrats to admit that to believe in a just world is a fundamental delusion (van Swaaningen, 1993). Macro-sociological analyses of the perceived effects of the proposed pragmatic moralism oriented towards such traditional values, indicate that they are quite irrelevant. The belief in the grand narratives of civilization, of the chances the market economy offers to everybody, of the welfare state and indeed of emancipation and the 'success society' has perished. Now so many social ideals have failed – 'great boredom', accompanied by an individualistic consumerism, seems for many the only functional replacement for beliefs and commitments (Kunneman, 1991).

In view of this fundamental legitimation crisis in our present society at the macro-level, it is simply not realistic to expect that social bonds will be strengthened by a moral appeal to the citizens alone (Boutellier, 1991:235). We have already seen that the 'mentality' of the government itself should be held responsible for the much criticized 'normless' mentality of its citizens (Schuyt, 1993). Instead of acknowledging this, the Ministry of Justice is directing its policy towards 'severe government', thereby abandoning the traditional Dutch – and rather adequate we may add! – forms of social control, i.e. pragmatic and normative tolerance (van Swaaningen, 1993). A lot more could be done to strengthen social integration by looking more realistically at and orientating policy more specifically towards social roles and expectations; and recognizing that these vary substantially between the young and old, men and women and the employed and unemployed. Each group has its specific problems and its different material needs which require addressing, if crime, or indeed the fear of crime, is to be prevented. The dominant global orientation towards law and order, crime and punishment and prevention based on a nostalgic and outdated moralism, have been nothing but counterproductive with respect to this third guiding principle of 'Society and Crime'.

Conclusions

Seemingly concrete problems, easily labelled as 'crime', turn out not to be so concrete as they appear at first sight. Crime often turns out to be a projection of quite general feelings of unsafety and dissatisfaction. These feelings are most common in areas where social deprivation is high. As Hanak et al., (1989) concluded in Frankfurt, we have also observed in Rotterdam that it is often relatively small annoyances – *Ärgernisse* – which are the greatest source of people's dissatisfaction with their living conditions and environment. Acts labelled 'crime' are undeniably *one* of these real problems, but because tackling the 'crime problem' has such a high place on the political agenda, *all* socioeconomic misery is translated into a crime discourse – which is the most certain way of receiving political attention. In this way, politicians, instead of acknowledging that the crime problem is an integral part of socioeconomic problems, lead people to interpret crime as something completely distinct from any other social problem and to have unwarranted expectations of the criminal justice system. In addition, the proposed differential, multiagency approach of 'Society and Crime' comes down, in the final event, to law and order. We are generally inclined to call this the depoliticization of the crime problem, but, in fact, it is actually a *very* political technique to combat the symptoms instead of the problems.

One other reason why control theory is so popular in policy debates on crime prevention, which has not been mentioned yet, could be the fact that it does not challenge the penal rationale. In fact, it can be seen as the criminological brother of punishment: both share the assumptions of specific and general preventive effects of control, and both leave the more intrinsic causes of crime untouched; therefore, it is particularly suited to accompany an approach in which judicial and administrative measures should be integrated. In *Causes of Delinquency*, Hirschi (1969) ignores any possible causes of crime which point at economic or social deprivation. This element of control theory is also adopted in the Dutch policy considerations. In addition to a non-aetiological vision, Hirschi also adopts a non-moralistic approach towards crime. And yet this is the point at which 'Society and Crime' takes a different route from Hirschi – and the Roethof Committee.

Control theory also has, however, an *implicit* normative orientation, as social control is seen as a means to make people conform to the conventional values of society. This implicit message was well understood by Jan van Dijk, when he referred to the policy of crime prevention as one of pragmatic moralism (van Dijk, 1987). Gerben Bruinsma has called this move the translation of social control into terms of social adaptation and repressive prevention, by which evil is being projected onto specific groups in society (Bruinsma, 1990). Especially in the multicultural context we have described, such an approach is of no help at all.

Opportunity, the second premise of 'Society and Crime', is treated solely as the pendant of social control in the Hirschian sense. Opportunity makes the thief. Control limits the opportunity. So control limits theft. A policy in which petty crime is perceived purely as a matter of opportunity and control, ignores the fact that power relations form the basis of the problem. Restricting opportunity seems to be an effective solution at first sight, but in practice it generally means that problems are only transplanted to other areas, and perhaps to where society is even more vulnerable.

In the case of the Rotterdam project, it is obvious that all sorts of acts which can be labelled 'crime' are inextricably interwoven into acts which cannot be defined under any specific paragraph in the criminal code. These acts are, however, experienced as extremely annoying, irritating or frightening, but in a judicial framework nothing can be done about them. These problems are closely connected with cultural, socioeconomic, demographic and spatial developments, and therein lies the key to their solution. Many of the opportunities to commit crimes are the byproduct of the renovation programme. Also, for this reason, one cannot individualize these problems to certain (potential) offenders – as is generally the case in the crime prevention projects – but one could certainly limit these events by giving more priority to completing the renovation programme.

In most of the 'Society and Crime' projects, the reality of the problems is simplified to an unacceptable degree, and by doing so it has become rather illusory to expect any structural effects. However, we are afraid that we have to accept that this social control approach fits very well into the general Dutch culture of combining paternalism and pragmatism. And, secondly, we have seen that, especially when finances are involved, the true character of this country of wheelers and dealers and their gratuitous morality comes to the surface: it gives Dutch politics, whose theoretical premises are currently based on not much more than half-baked commonsense notions packaged in crypto-scientific discourse (van Swaaningen et al., 1992), an internal dynamics, which has indeed little to do with the problems it aims to tackle.

In this respect there seem to be indeed very few positive points of distinction with Bottomley's description of the management orientation in Britain (Bottomley, 1986: 199). We hope to have shown that in the implementation of the 'Society and Crime' projects there remains very little 'radical redirection' or any 'clear set of principles'; rather, what we have witnessed is a rather classical case of bifurcation, and an expansion of social control in a punitive city. As the Maastricht criminologist Grat van den Heuvel (1990) comments, the Dutch crime prevention projects and their British counterparts of multi-agency and neighbourhood watch initiatives, are really based on similar considerations, they function in a similar way and they are equally unclear in their content and effect. The only difference is that the Dutch policy papers are more rhetorical and explicit about their *intentions*. And it is this mock clarity which has inspired some English scholars to fantasize about the existence of some promised land (van den Heuvel, 1990).

NOTES

1.   In criminology, we generally distinguish between (1) socio-, (2) techno- and (3) penal prevention. Techno- and penal prevention are both based on the assumption of deterrence, be it with other means (reducing opportunities by technical means,

the threat of punishment). These approaches leave aetiological questions largely untouched. This can also be the case with socio-prevention, but in this form of crime prevention one can also do something about the social causes of the problem. It is this latter area on which we aim to focus. In what way does this phenomenon of socio-prevention distinguish itself from, for example, non-custodial sanctions? We agree that the following stipulative definition is debatable, but when we speak of *sanctions* we refer to an individualized repressive reaction to an act listed in the criminal code, whereas we speak of *prevention* if measures are taken to prevent (potentially criminalizable) social problems in the future without necessarily individualizing such problems by prosecuting individual offenders.

2.   This seems a lot of money, but the extent to which petty crime is 'taken seriously' should be viewed in the correct financial perspective. In 'Society and Crime', these 45 million guilders are put at the disposal of local authorities for initiating prevention projects in the field of petty crime, but for the implementation of the sheer repressive policy on 'serious crime' the government has reserved more than 1 thousand million guilders (approximately £375,000,000) – largely to be spent on prison building – plus still some hundreds of millions guilders on technical police facilities for the same period of time.

3.   The findings mentioned in this paragraph will not specifically be accounted for, since they are all derived from the same research. The interviews mentioned took place in slightly different periods: with the shopkeepers regarding conditions on the street from April to June 1987; with the various organizations on social conditions in the neighbourhood from March to June 1988; and with the inhabitants themselves in May and June 1990. A full record of these interviews, and of the followed methodology, is given in uit Beijerse et al., (1987) regarding the shopping street, and in uit Beijerse et al., (1990b) regarding the neighbourhood.

REFERENCES

Beijerse, Jolande uit, Hans Moerland and Cyrille Fijnaut (1987) *Boulevard Zuid: een winkelstraat met problemen?*, EUR werkdocument No. 1. Rotterdam: Centrum voor Geïntegreerde Strafrechtwetenschap.

Beijerse, Jolande uit, Cyrille Fijnaut and Hans Moerland (1990a) 'De Delicate Positie van de Universitaire Onderzoeker in Bestuurlijke Preventieprojecten', pp. 144–57 in Michel Zwanenburg and Anne Marie Smit (eds), *Kleine Criminaliteit en Over-heidsbeleid*. Arnhem: Gouda Quint.

Beijerse, Jolande uit, Hans Moerland and Cyrille Fijnaut (1990b) *Problemen in een stadsvernieuwingswijk in Rotterdam Zuid*, EUR werkdocument No. 3. Rotterdam: Centrum voor Geïntegreerde Strafrechtwetenschap.

Blankenburg Erhard and Henk van de Bunt (1986) 'Over de maakbaarheid van "criminaliteit" tot beleidsprobleem', *Tijdschrift voor Criminologie* 28: 215–19.

Bottomley, Keith (1986) 'Blueprints for Criminal Justice; Reflections on a Policy Plan for the Netherlands', *The Howard Journal of Criminal Justice* 25: 199–215.

Boutellier, Hans C. J. (1991) 'Criminaliteit als moreel vraagstuk', pp. 223–41 in Paul B. Cliteur et al., (eds), *Burgerschap, levensbeschouwing en criminaliteit*. Amersfoort/ Leuven: De Horstink.

Brants, Chrisje (1993) 'Mickey Mouse in de lage landen: sociale contrôle en verzuilingsideologie', pp. 325–39 in Jan Nijboer et al. (eds), *Criminaliteit als politiek probleem*. Arnhem: Gouda Quint.

Brants, Kees (1986) 'Criminaliteit, politiek en criminele politiek: de Haagse receptie van een nieuwe heilsleer', *Tijdschrift voor Criminologie* 28: 219–35.

Bruinsma, Gerben, J. N. (1990) 'De schaduwzijden van de sociale controletheorie', pp. 17–28 in Michel Zwanenburg and Anne Marie Smit (eds), *Kleine Criminaliteit en Overheidsbeleid*. Arnhem: Gouda Quint.

Bruinsma, Gerben J. N. (1992) 'Macht en onmacht van bestuurlijke preventie; enkele kanttekeningen en suggesties', *Justitiële Verkenningen* 18(2): 21–35.

Cohen, Stanley (1989) 'The Critical Discourse on "Social Control"; Notes on a Concept as a Hammer', *International Journal of the Sociology of Law* 17: 347–59.

Commissie Kleine Criminaliteit (1984) *Interim-rapport*. Den Haag: Staatsuitgeverij.

Dijk, Jan J. M. van (1987) 'Het actieplan als proeve van pragmatisch moralisme', *Justitiële Verkenningen* 13(6): 13–20.

Downes, David (1988) *Contrasts in Tolerance; Post-War Penal Policy in the Netherlands and England and Wales*. Oxford: Clarendon.

Fijnaut, Cyrille (1991) 'The Disconnection of Social Policy and Crime in the Netherlands', paper presented at the NACRO Conference 'Social Problems and Urban Communities', Edinburgh.

Fijnaut, Cyrille, Hans Moerland and Jolande uit Beijerse (1991) *Een winkelboulevard in problemen; samenleving en criminaliteit in twee Rotterdamse buurten*. Arnhem: Gouda Quint.

Hanak, Gerhard, Johannes Stehr and Heinz Steinert (1989) *Ärgernisse und Lebenskatastrophen; über den alltäglichen Umgang mit Kriminalität*. Bielefeld: AJZ.

Heuvel, Grat van den (1990) 'Samenleving en criminaliteit in Nederland en Engeland', pp. 83–9 in Michel Zwanenburg and Anne Marie Smit (eds), *Kleine Criminaliteit en Overheidsbeleid*. Arnhem: Gouda Quint.

Hirschi, Travis (1969) *Causes of Delinquency*. Berkeley, CA: University of California Press.

Jones, Trevor, Brian MacLean and Jock Young (1986) *The Islington Crime Survey; Crime, Victimisation and Policing in Inner-City London*. Aldershot: Gower.

Jongman, Riekent (1988) 'Over de Macht en Onmacht van de Sociale Contrôle', *Tijdschrift vor Criminologie* 30: 4–31.

Jongman, Riekent (1990) 'Over de geringe omvang van criminaliteit', pp. 31–47 in Cyrille Fijnaut and Pieter Spierenburg (eds), *Scherp toezicht, van 'Boeventucht' tot 'Samenleving en Criminaliteit'*. Arnhem: Gouda Quint.

Jongman, Riekent and Harrie Timmerman (1985) 'Criminaliteit als Verzet; motivatie en remmingen', *Tijdschrift voor Criminologie* 27: 303–19.

Kunneman, Harry (1991) 'Wissels in het moderniseringsproces', pp. 77–89 in Paul B. Cliteur et al. (eds), *Burgerschap, levensbeschouwing en criminaliteit*. Amersfoort/Leuven: De Horstink.

Ministerie van Justitie (1985) 'Samenleving en Criminaliteit; een beleidsplan voor de komende jaren'. Den Haag: Staatsuitgeverij.' (In English summary as 'Society and Crime: A Policy Plan for the Netherlands'. The Hague: Ministry of Justice 1985.)

Moerland, Hans and Jolande uit Beijerse (1988) 'Projecten rond overlast en criminaliteit in winkels en winkelcentra: een aanzet tot inventarisatie', pp. 19–51 in Hans Moerland et al. (eds), *Projecten rond overlast en criminaliteit in winkels en winkelcentra*, EUR werkdocument No. 2. Rotterdam: Centrum voor Geïntegreerde strafrechtswetenschap.

Polder, W. and F. J. C. van Vlaardingen (1992) *Preventiestrategieën in de praktijk; een meta-evaluatie van criminaliteitspreventieprojecten*. Arnhem: Gouda Quint.

Reenen, Piet van (1979) *Overheidsgeweld; een sociologische studie van de dynamiek van het geweldsmonopolie*. Alphen a/d Rijn: Samsom.

Rutherford, Andrew (1986) *Prisons and the Process of Justice*. Oxford: Oxford University Press.

Schuyt, Kees (1993) 'De omweg van de onverschilligheid', pp. 29–35 in Jan Nijboer et al. (eds), *Criminaliteit als politiek probleem*. Arnhem: Gouda Quint.

Steinert, Heinz (1989) 'Marxian Theory and Abolitionism; Introduction to a
    Discussion', pp. 172–91 in Bill Rolston and Mike Tomlinson (eds) *Justice and
    Ideology; Strategies for the 1990s*, working paper No. 9. Belfast: EGSDSC.
Storm van 's Gravesande, A. and R. de Vries (1986) 'Bestuurlijke preventie', *Tijdschrift
    voor Criminologie* 28: 323–38.
Swaaningen, René van (1993) 'Levensbeschouwing, burgerschap en criminaliteit; een
    ethisch reveil?', *Recht & Kritiek* 19(1): 86–93.
Swaaningen, René van, John Blad and Reinier van Loon (1992) *A Decade of
    Criminological Research and Penal Policy in the Netherlands; The 1980s: The Era
    of Business-Management Ideology*, EUR working document No. 4. Rotterdam:
    Centre for Integrated Penal Sciences.
Young, Jock (1992) 'Ten Points of Realism', pp. 24–69 in Jock Young and Roger
    Matthews (eds), *Rethinking Criminology; The Realist Debate*. London: Sage.

[21]

Journal of Criminal Justice, Vol. 13, pp. 307–319 (1985)
Pergamon Press, Printed in U.S.A.

CONGRESS AND CRIMINAL JUSTICE POLICY MAKING: THE IMPACT OF INTEREST GROUPS AND SYMBOLIC POLITICS

BARBARA ANN STOLZ

School of Justice
The American University
Washington, D.C. 20016

ABSTRACT

This article explores the congressional criminal justice policy-making process in the United States, using efforts toward federal criminal-code revision and capital punishment as case examples. It examines how interest groups and symbolic politics affect criminal justice policy and thereby attempts to enhance understanding of the political realities of criminal justice policy making. Based on the findings reported here, an approach to criminal justice policy making is recommended. This approach builds on the disjointed incremental model found in the political science literature and should facilitate criminal justice policy makers in becoming more effective participants in the legislative process.

Although criminal justice administration in the United States is primarily a state and local, rather than a federal, function, Congress does make criminal justice policy. Little attention, however, has been paid to how it does so. This article examines congressional criminal justice policy making in the context of efforts toward federal criminal-code revision and capital punishment. Repeatedly, Congress has tried and failed to pass legislation in these two areas. Specifically, the article focuses on how interest groups and symbolic politics have affected these policy efforts. Such an analysis contributes to our understanding of the political realities of criminal justice policy making. Based on the findings reported here, an approach to criminal justice policy making is recommended. It builds on the disjointed incremental model found in the political science literature and may help criminal-justice-policy advocates become more effective participants in the legislative process.

POLITICAL ANALYSIS, CONGRESS, AND CRIMINAL LAW

Political science has emphasized the necessity for political analysis on two levels—the tangible and the symbolic. The former level focuses on how political acts provide people with tangible rewards and the latter on what political acts mean to the public (Edelman, 1964:2; Arnold, 1935; Lasswell and Kaplan, 1952, Edelman, 1971; Anton,

1967). One of the foremost writers on
symbolic politics (Edelman, 1964:42) has
postulated that every instance of policy
formulation involves a "mix" of both symbolic effect and the rational reflection of
interests in resources, although one may be
dominant in a particular case. Since understanding any political act requires analysis
on both levels, it follows that criminal
justice policy making must be so examined.

Tangible benefits tend to be distributed
to well-organized groups, called interest
groups. Political interest groups are defined as groups whose shared activities
include attempts to influence decisions
made within the public policy-making system (Greenwald, 1977:15). The role of
these groups in policy formation at the
state and national level has been well
documented in the political science literature (Bentley, 1908; Trumen, 1951; Gross,
1953; Huitt and Peabody, 1969; Greenwald, 1977). How to measure their effect,
or their influence, however, has been debated without resolution (Dahl, 1961; Milbrath, 1963; Greenwald, 1977).

For this study, the congressional staff
interviewed were asked to define influence.
They emphasized a group's ability to have
its concerns given serious consideration by
congressional members. This could mean
ensuring that specific legislative provisions
reflected the group's interest, but it could
also mean stopping legislation. Congressional staff were primarily concerned with
the former type of influence.

Symbolic rewards tend to be distributed
to the less-organized public. They are the
means by which those unable to analyze a
complex situation rationally may adjust to
it through stereotyping, oversimplification,
and reassurance (Edelman, 1964:40). Symbols, thus, derive their meaning from an
audience's response rather than from the
act itself. The case study of federal capital-
punishment legislation indicates that a symbolic component of congressional death
penalty legislation exists and emcompasses
three functions: a "model" for the states,
reassurance, and moral education. (Stolz,
1983).

METHODS

The case method[1] was used to investigate
the legislative process surrounding efforts
toward federal capital-punishment legislation between 1972 and 1982[2] and toward
criminal-code revision between 1971 and
1982.[3] In each case, hearing records and
other congressional records were employed
in the analysis. Between 1976 and 1982, the
author also observed numerous hearings
and mark-up sessions on each piece of
legislation. Interviews with members of
Congress and congressional staff clarified
and expanded the information gathered
from written sources.

The capital-punishment hearings provided the basis for determining which members of Congress had been most actively
involved in the issue. Sixteen members were
identified as activists between 1972 and
1982, having introduced capital-punishment
legislation, been involved intensively in
hearings, or been recognized by other members as active on the issue. These activists
were asked to respond to a questionnaire;
nine (six House members and three Senate
members) did. Five were pro-capital punishment, four were against.

A semi-structured questionnaire, a technique used effectively by political scientists
(Huitt and Peabody, 1969:28), was used.
Questions were designed to evoke information regarding the rationale for the member's
interest in the issue, explanations for general
congressional interest, interest-group participation and influence, and perceptions of
the effect of the legislation. Several staff
members who had worked extensively on the
issue were also interviewed.

In the case of criminal-code revision,
written records underscored the prevalence
of interest-group participation but not the
significance of that involvement. To determine interest-group influence, a reputa-
tional technique was used. Staff members
were asked, first, to define influence. They
were then asked to identify the groups they
felt had influenced the reform process and
to describe how the groups had accomplished this. The same groups were named

repeatedly. Representatives of most of these groups were subsequently interviewed. All interviewees concurred on how the groups influenced the substance of the criminal-code legislation and, for the most part, on who was influential. To further investigate symbolic concerns, interviews were conducted with key House, Senate, and Justice Department staff.

THE ROLE OF INTEREST GROUPS IN THE CRIMINAL JUSTICE POLICY-MAKING PROCESS

The hearing records on criminal-code revision and capital-punishment legislation in the House and Senate indicate that diverse groups testify on criminal justice legislation (Hearing on H.R. 6869 Part III, 1977; Hearings on S. 1382, 1978; Hearing on H.R. 13360, 1978, among others). These include legal and criminal justice professional associations (e.g., the American Bar Association, the National Black Police Association, the International Association of Chiefs of Police, the National Legal Aid and Defender Association); reform groups (e.g., the National Council on Crime and Delinquency); representatives from state agencies (e.g., state attorney-generals); civil liberties organizations (e.g., the American Civil Liberties Union and the National Committee Against Repressive Legislation); and issue-related organizations (e.g., the National Coalition to Ban Handguns and the National Coalition against the Death Penalty). Organizations whose primary interest is not criminal justice, such as church, media, labor, and business groups also testified and lobbied on criminal-code revision and capital punishment. Although government agencies are not usually classified as interest groups, they do articulate their interest in criminal justice legislation. In this article, therefore, governmental agencies, whether executive or judicial, are categorized as interest groups. The Justice Department and the Judicial Conference testified on the criminal code repeatedly.

Criminal-code revision addressed the con-

cerns of numerous groups. Both House and Senate staff felt that many of these groups had had their interests met, but only a few were designated as influential. These included: the U.S. Justice Department, the American Bar Association, the American Civil Liberties Union, the Business Round Table, the National Association of Manufacturers, the Association of General Contractors, the National Committee Against Repressive Legislation, and the AFL-CIO. Representatives of interest groups, when interviewed, concurred with the assessment of congressional staff.

In contrast, although various groups testified in the death penalty deliberation, they were not perceived as influencing the process. Thus the following two sections focus on the groups involved in criminal-code-revision efforts; specifically, on their goals and techniques.

Goals

The groups participating in the process of criminal-code revision exhibited different types of goals. Interests were broad, narrow, concrete, solidary, or purposive. The nature of their goals affected each group's ability to influence the process.

The three groups with the broadest criminal justice interests were the Justice Department, the American Civil Liberties Union (ACLU), and the American Bar Association (ABA). Since the Justice Department is generally responsible for implementing federal criminal justice legislation and is thus the primary constituency concerned about criminal-code revision, the breadth of its interest is not surprising. The Department also purports to speak for the public interest. Both publicly and privately, the Department was the most active participant in the revision process and, according to many, the most influential, particularly in the Senate. The description of the ACLU by some interviewees as a "shadow Justice Department" with a liberal persuasion indicates the breadth of the ACLU's involvement. The basis for their involvement in the code and other criminal justice legislation is, according to organizational sources, the ACLU's view that criminal law is the most fundamental type of legislation because it sets limits on people's behavior. The American Bar Association was primarily concerned with encouraging, for the "public good," modernization and rationality in the criminal justice system. These three groups—the Justice Department, the ACLU, and the ABA—supported the concepts of modernization and comprehensive reform but opposed and sought changes in a broad range of specific provisions. The ACLU, in particular, was a vocal critic of many sections of the criminal-code revision.

A fourth group exhibiting a broad interest in the bill was the National Committee against Repressive Legislation (NCARL). Unlike the ABA, the ACLU, and the Justice Department, the NCARL opposed the omnibus approach of the bill as well as specific provisions. They argued that an omnibus bill forced members of Congress to vote for provisions they did not like.

Most groups, however, expressed only narrow interests, seeking action on a few specific provisions that affected them directly. The AFL-CIO was concerned with issues such as labor extortion. The Judicial Conference, the body governing the administration of the federal judiciary, testified on provisions establishing sentencing guidelines and a sentencing commission (Congressional Quarterly Service, 1979:603). Prison-reform groups and church groups sought alternatives to incarceration. The press was concerned about first-amendment rights. Business groups lobbied for or against provisions affecting corporate interests. During the decade of legislative debate, more groups became aware that the legislation could potentially affect them and entered the process in support of specific interests. Interviewees did not perceive the specific and limited nature of those concerned or the diversity of groups interested to be unusual in this policy area. Moreover, they did not feel that the narrowness of a group's interest made it less influential.

Among the groups designated by staff and other groups as influential were not only the Justice Department and legal organizations, but groups whose primary concern is not criminal justice. Criminal justice reform groups or representatives of specific minority interests were not considered influential (although one might argue that the ACLU represents such concerns). Business groups, however, were viewed as highly successful in having their demands met. Yet their interests were not only narrow, but parochial. While the pursuit of their interests affected the criminal justice system, these groups were not primarily concerned with good criminal justice policy, but with protecting business interests—a parochial concern.

Goals may also be concrete (e.g., monetary), solidary (e.g., psychological, ideological rewards), or purposive or altruistic (e.g., civil liberties) (Greenwald, 1977:52). The groups participating in criminal-code revision varied along this dimension as well. Church groups, the Moral Majority, and criminal justice reform groups articulated purposive concerns, such as the abolition or retention of capital punishment or the abolition of prisons. The goals of the Moral Majority were also solidary; they hoped to move others in society toward their ideological position. Another example: the Business Round Table, an association of business executives from 180 companies, opposed sentencing reforms that would permit novel sanctions, particularly restitution, arguing that the ineffectiveness of traditional punishment (e.g., fines and prison) had not been proven. The concern of this organization appeared to reflect a fear of the potential effects of novel sanctions on its members, since providing restitution for the victim of a crime means that the complaining witness has a direct economic stake in the outcome of a criminal trial. This could prove expensive in cases of corporate crimes (*Hearings before Subcommittee on Criminal Justice on H.R. 6869*, 1978: Vol. 3, 2602–03).

Staff indicated that the practicality of a group's goals was most important to them. If a group presented its position as nonnegotiable, that group was considered impractical and would be written off. Similarly, if congressional members perceived a group's goals as unattainable, then the group was viewed as impractical and received less attention. Clearly, concrete goals are more likely to be practical than are solidary or purposive goals. Those groups identified as having practical goals that could be negotiated were perceived by staff to be influential. The Justice Department, the ACLU, the ABA, the Business Round Table, the Chamber of Commerce, the Association of General Contractors, the National Association of Manufacturers, and the AFL-CIO had such goals.

The list of influential groups did not include the Judicial Conference, although this organization spoke for the federal judges and testified more than most other groups. They would not, however, compromise; therefore, their demands were not viewed as practical. The Moral Majority's interests, similarly, could not be negotiated. The National Council on Crime and Delinquency, perhaps the most notable national criminal-justice-reform group, was also perceived as having impractical interests.

Groups having impractical goals did appear to be influential in stopping legislation. Most interviewees attributed the failure of S. 1630 of 1983 to the Moral Majority. Many of the positions of this group—for example, the inclusion of the death penalty—were viewed as impractical. Other complaints of the group were vague—for example, they claimed the bill was "soft on crime"—and in their vagueness, non-negotiable and impractical. The blocking of S. 1 of 1973 and 1975 was attributed by several interviewees to the National Committee Against Repressive Legislation. Their goals, too, were perceived as impractical.

Techniques

Staff also indicated that the techniques used by a group affected its ability to influence criminal justice policy. Many groups testify at hearings. While hearings provide a forum for airing issues publicly and sometimes attract the press, both congressional staff and the representatives of interest groups agreed that testifying, no matter how often, does not signify that a group is influential. Rather, a group's ability to influence policy was believed to be affected by the use of other techniques and informal mechanisms. These were categorized as: internal access, expertise, group membership, and external influences. The criminal-code case indicates that the utility of a specific technique depends on whether a group wants to amend or block passage of a bill.

Internal access means that some groups seek access to congressional members who serve as spokespersons for their interests. The Moral Majority had the support of Senators Helms, McClure, and Denton during the 97th Congress. The ACLU had advocates in both the House and Senate.

Expertise is a resource that groups can use to aid congressional members and staff. Influential groups, including the ABA, the ACLU, and the Justice Department, as well as business groups, indicated that they prepared written recommendations and documentation to support their position. Such efforts were viewed as assisting staff.

Interviewees also indicated that follow-up discussions with congressional staff and members were essential. The failure of groups such as the Judicial Conference to achieve their goals was attributed, in part, to their not having followed up testimony with informal meetings.

Organizations with a membership barraged members of Congress with letters, an approach political scientists have labeled the shotgun method (Key, 1964: 135). They also asked some of their more influential members to contact specific congressional members; this is known as the rifle approach (Key, 1964:134). The National Committee Against Repressive Legislation used the shotgun approach, mustering strong grass-roots opposition to S. 1 of 1973 and 1975. The Business Round Table provided written statements from members' companies for specific congresspeople, a rifle approach, to support their concerns.

Groups also use external influences, including other organizations and the press.

Coalitions have existed on both sides of the criminal-code issue at various times. On the left, the National Committee Against Repressive Legislation informed other groups how their interests were affected by the bill, often garnering the support of those organizations. During the 96th and 97th Congress, a coalition emerged on the right. The "Library Court" held meetings at which representatives of various conservative groups were told how the bill affected their interests. It is unclear how influential these coalitions were. Such efforts may create the impression of possible grass-roots opposition, convincing some congressional members that voting on such controversial legislation may not be wise; consequently, coalition activities may explain inaction on legislation.

Groups use the media to draw attention to their concerns. Jack Landau of the Reporters Committee publicized First Amendment concerns in S. 1. The Moral Majority used the press to focus attention on S. 1630. Supporters of criminal-code-revision bills also used the press. Editorials chastizing the House for its slow deliberations appeared after the Senate passed S. 1437 in 1978.

In summary, on the level of interest-group politics, the case material on the criminal code indicates that a variety of groups with different types of goals participate in criminal justice policy making. Not all participants are influential. Influence depends on the practicality of goals and the ability to use certain informal techniques successfully. However, simply examining criminal justice policy from the perspective of interest groups does not fully explain the criminal justice policy making process.

SYMBOLIC POLITICS[4]

The second level of political analysis is the symbolic. In the criminal-code-revision efforts, certain issues appeared to be of concern primarily because of their symbolic significance to the public. Federal death penalty provisions, both within the code and in separate legislation, were perceived as symbolic efforts rather than as being di-

rected toward meeting interest-group needs. Interviews indicated further that legislation could perform one or more symbolic functions: as a model for the states, as reassurance, or as moral education.

Model for the States

Both supporters and opponents of capital punishment, when interviewed, asserted that federal capital-punishment legislation was important because it provided a model for the states. With respect to federal criminal justice agencies, this role of the federal government has been acknowledged by policy makers. For example, the development of the Federal Bureau of Prisons as a model for the states was supported by the National Advisory Commission on Criminal Justice Standards and Goals (1973: 606–03), and the Law Enforcement Assistance Administration and the Office of Juvenile Justice and Delinquency Prevention were created to promote change by providing monies for programs in states and communities, based on federal notions of good policy (*Conference Report on Juvenile Justice and Delinquency Prevention Act of 1974:2*, 40–44; Juvenile Justice and Delinquency Prevention Act of 1974: PL 93–415: Juvenile Justice Amendments of 1977: PL 95–115; Omnibus Crime Control and Safe Streets Act of 1968: PL 90–351; Shanahand and Whisenand, 1980:55; Gibbons et al., 1977:3). What the interviews indicated was that this perception of the federal government as a model did not refer simply to federal agencies, but also extended to federal criminal law in general. Such legislation was intended to demonstrate, by example, what a criminal law and penal system should include. Since capital punishment is the most extreme form of punishment, it was perceived to be a significant component of the model.

While agreeing on the importance of federal capital-punishment legislation as a model, opponents and proponents disagreed on the substantive content of that model. Supporters believed that the ultimate crime deserves the ultimate punishment. The death penalty should be part of the federal system because it is an essential component of any good penal system. In contrast, opponents felt the federal government would be setting an enlightened example by not imposing this sanction. Both sides perceived the content and function of the model as important because the legislation was thought to exemplify good criminal justice policy.

Moreover, by creating the impression that Congress is attempting to deal with the problem and can demonstrate how to do so, Congress may, at least symbolically, enhance its power position vis-a-vis the states. The need for the federal government to generate such an impression of power may explain why some proponents interviewed expressed concern over the failure of Congress to act on the death penalty. They suggested that inaction created an image of the federal government as "behind" the states. Similarly, the failure of Congress to pass criminal-code-revision legislation, when many of the states have revised their codes, diminishes Congress's symbolic position as a leader.[6]

The Reassurance Function

A second symbolic function is public reassurance. Edelman (1964:38) explores the general concept of the *reassurance function* and postulates that symbolization induces a feeling of well being and reduces tension. Using the example of regulatory statutes (and their administration), he explains that political activities can convey a sense of well being to the onlooker because they suggest vigorous activity, although there may be, in fact, inactivity (Edelman, 1964:38). In the criminal justice area, "getting tough" efforts—i.e., increasing penalties—are purportedly the last hope of crime control because of their perceived deterrent effect (Zimring and Hawkins, 1973:18–19), but they may also perform a *reassurance function*. That is, they suggest that "something" is being done about crime, whether or not that "something" is an effective deterrent. The audience to be reassured is

that segment of the public who see and think in terms of stereotypes, personalization, and oversimplification and who cannot tolerate ambiguous, complex situations (Edelman, 1964:31).

A statement by the current chairman of the Senate Judiciary Committee provides an excellent example of belief in the dual function of the "getting tough" position as it relates to capital punishment:

> The death penalty must be restored if our criminal justice system is to effectively control the increasing number of violent crimes of terror. The confidence of the American people in our criminal justice system must also be reclaimed and the imposition of the death penalty can restore such confidence. (*Congressional Record*, January 23, 1979, daily edition)

Supporting capital punishment is an example of the "getting tough" posture. The first sentence quoted above implies that the intended audience is those who would commit violent acts but who would be deterred by the death penalty. The second sentence indicates a belief that reinstituting capital punishment would restore public confidence in the criminal justice system because it would reassure people that something is being done about crime.

Congressional opponents of capital punishment also recognize the significance of the reassurance function. This point was illustrated by the interviewees' descriptions of what they felt would happen if death penalty legislation were to come to the Senate floor during the 97th Congress. Opponents were expected to introduce an amendment to substitute "life imprisonment without parole" for the death sentence in the proposed bill, rather than to try to kill the bill outright, because of a perceived need to reassure the public that Congress was dealing with crime.

The interviews also indicated a public misconception about federal law that might enhance the reassurance effect of a federal death penalty as well as a misconception about federal criminal law in general. A segment of the public perceives federal law as nationalizing policy. According to this misconception, a federal death penalty statute would result in the nationalizing of the death penalty for any murder, when in fact, such a statute would apply only to certain federal cases. As a consequence of this misconception, the passage of federal death penalty legislation could ensure a greater sense of well being.

In the context of criminal-code revision, opposition to the repeal of the Logan Act[5] reflected symbolic concerns directed toward public reassurance. Proponents of the repeal argued that the act reflected symbolic concerns directed toward public reassurance and that the act was a useless appendage, since it had never been enforced. Opponents of the repeal emphasized that, although the law was unenforceable, it was perceived as a public policy statement. Maintaining the law reassured the public (particularly in the midst of international crises such as the Iranian hostage situation) that the conduct of international affairs was vested in the executive branch of government rather than in the private citizen (U.S. Congress, *Criminal Code Pending Matters*, July 2, 1982).

Both the death penalty and the Logan Act underscore the significance that the need to reassure the public may have in maintaining or repealing a statute.

The Moral Educative Function

While criminal justice scholars debate whether or not the criminal law performs a moral educative function (Andanaes, 1974; Zimring and Hawkins, 1973; Arnold, 1935), the case studies of both the death penalty and criminal-code revision indicate that members of Congress act as if it does. Perceiving criminal law as performing a moral educative function reflects a belief that criminal law communicates a message to the public, socializes, and, in the case of federal law, indicates a national moral consensus.

Interviewees, both proponents and opponents, concurred that a federal death penalty law performed this function, but did not agree on the message communicated. Proponents of capital punishment believed the death penalty communicates society's ultimate disapproval. By associating "the ultimate punishment" with a crime, the death penalty emphasizes the distinctiveness of the acts for which it is imposed. Moreover, a federal death penalty statute carries particular weight because of the perception that it reflects a national consensus.

A message is not only communicated to offenders, but also to "law-abiding" citizens. The death penalty is believed to reassure "those who do right," by distinguishing them from "the criminals." In the words of one congressional proponent, it is a "catharsis for the law abiding." This view has been articulated by Berns (1979:507), who argues that criminal law works by praising as well as by blaming.

The opponents of the death penalty who were interviewed, while agreeing that federal capital-punishment legislation communicates a message, reached different conclusions. Capital punishment was felt to "legitimize the taking of life under certain circumstances." In so doing, capital punishment contributes to the level of violence in society. Some opponents were also concerned about the message communicated when the wrong person is executed. The tangible consequence of such an act to the individual executed is evident, but the miscarriage of justice also communicates a message to the "law-abiding citizen" that obeying the law does not necessarily protect the individual from unjust punishment.

Opponents believed abolition of federal capital punishment would communicate a complex message, but they preferred this message. First, abolition was perceived as a statement against violence. Second, abolition would transmit the notion that economic and social injustice are partially responsible for crime and that, therefore, society must bear a share of the responsibility.

A related question is whether or not the law has to be enforced in order to communicate a message. In the case of capital punishment, the proponents interviewed indicated it did, but they did not suggest how frequently. If, however, one considers the debates that can ensue over laws that have never been enforced, implementation of the law appears to be a lesser concern. Some legislators interviewed believed that tinkering with existing laws indicates that policy has changed, thereby communicating approval where there has once been disapproval. These legislators, therefore, opposed changing even those laws that have never been and may never be enforced. The aforementioned debates over the repeal of the Logan Act illustrate this point clearly.

SUMMARY AND IMPLICATIONS

Examining congressional criminal-code-revision and capital-punishment efforts from the perspectives of interest-group involvement and symbolic politics suggests a complex policy-making process. It indicates that criminal justice policy may be influenced by pressure from groups or by the need to respond to public concerns rather than by rational, comprehensive policy making.

With respect to interest-group politics, it was found that the groups most influential in having their interests incorporated in legislation included not only the Justice Department and the American Civil Liberties Union, but organizations with parochial concerns who had no interest in general criminal justice policy. These influential groups had practical, negotiable goals.

Moreover, a group's use of various techniques affects its ability to influence policy. Giving formal testimony rarely influences legislative outcomes; using informal techniques effectively, can. Those seeking specific changes, such as the ACLU and the Justice Department, relied on internal access and expertise. These techniques meshed well with "practical" goals. Those wishing to stop bills—groups such as the National Committee Against Repressive Legislation and the Moral Majority—relied heavily on grass-roots-oriented techniques. These techniques, used in conjunction with "impractical" goals, were effective. Groups

identified by interviewees as noninfluential even though they testified often (e.g., the Judicial Conference and the National Conference on Crime and Delinquency) had impractical goals and did not use informal techniques to follow up their testimony.

Ultimately, the breadth of criminal-code legislation and the diversity of narrow interests concerned has ensured a steady flow of groups whose interests have had to be considered by congressional staff and members. This suggests that criminal justice policy may be the result of brokering interests rather than of conscious planning.

On the symbolic level, three functions of legislation were described: a model for the states, reassurance, and moral education. These functions are primarily directed toward the public. In trying to reassure the public, to provide a model, or to educate, Congress may focus on policy issues that have little importance in the actual functioning of the criminal justice system, and even less in crime reduction, but that communicate to the public or to the states (1) what good policy is and (2) that the federal government is in control and is working on the problem. With respect to policy outcomes, analysis on the symbolic level helps explain why ineffective policies, e.g., the Logan Act, are maintained; why no decision is made on certain issues, e.g., capital punishment; and why policy makers may advocate seemingly unacceptable policies, e.g., why capital punishment opponents accept life imprisonment.

Together, the findings on both levels of analysis further suggest that it is easier to block policy than to effect policy changes. Neither the death penalty bills nor the federal-code bills have passed both houses of Congress. Criminal justice legislation may be blocked because of demands from an overwhelming variety of narrow interests. Or, interest groups with "impractical" concerns not included in the legislation may thwart the legislative process using grass-roots techniques. The symbolic component may make a particular criminal justice policy the subject of intense public concern. Since congressional members dislike controversy, the legislation of such a policy may be avoided or limited in scope. A possible exception to this scenario might occur in a case where the public reaction to an issue is strong and where most legislators agree with that reaction. Congressional efforts to reform the federal insanity defense in response to the Hinckley verdict may prove to be a case in point.

The potential for blocking comprehensive criminal justice policy (omnibus legislation) is even greater. The scope of such legislation—i.e., the number of issues included—means that such legislation affects more interested parties. Symbolic issues (even those having little significant impact on the criminal justice system) incorporated in such legislation may be sufficiently volatile to preclude passage of the total package. Over the last decade, numerous symbolic issues have been removed from the proposed criminal-code legislation, with the agreement of both liberals and conservatives, on the grounds that leaving these issues in would jeopardize the entire package.

At first glance, the primary conclusion to be drawn here is that comprehensive criminal justice policy making is impossible. A less drastic conclusion may be warranted, however, if these findings are used to construct a policy-making strategy.

COMPREHENSIVE CRIMINAL JUSTICE POLICY MAKING: A FEASIBLE APPROACH

A policy-making strategy should include five components: breaking down major changes into smaller components; introducing those changes as solutions to clear, but limited, problems; if necessary, creating crises and the need for solutions; when possible, making changes simultaneously; and reintegrating the smaller components. This strategy constitutes a planned incremental approach to comprehensive change. That is, a major policy change need not be presented as major, particularly if doing so generates opposition, but may be proposed piecemeal.

Introducing major changes in small increments may still evoke opposition. Change rouses less controversy, however, if it is presented as a solution to a clearly perceived problem. For example, community corrections reforms, presented as a means to reduce costs or to relieve conditions for special cases, should be accepted more readily than those same reforms introduced as a master plan to change correctional policy.

The reform should be clearly related to the problem, and the problem should be clearly perceived. This may mean creating the impression that there is a crisis, in order to accelerate response time and give the opposition less time to mobilize.

Traditional planning approaches focus on sequencing the steps toward change. Often, however, incremental changes can be undertaken simultaneously. This is particularly true if the responsibility for particular changes can be divided, e.g., among different subcommittees. Simultaneous action increases the speed at which change can occur, thus reducing the opportunity for the opposition to organize.

The final step—reintegration—is vital when a major change is broken down into smaller components. Broad policy goals should mesh. The specification of mechanisms for implementation may be deferred to the implementation stage, leaving this aspect of the decision-making process to the administrators of the change. The advisability of delegating reintegration to the administrators varies from decision to decision, depending on the anticipated responsiveness of the implementing agencies.

What is being advocated here is a strategy that expands an approach some political scientists have recommended for years— i.e., disjointed incrementalism (Lindblom, 1959, 1979; Braybrooke and Lindblom, 1970). The model involves adjusting means to ends, a never-ending series of attacks on problems, and successive efforts at policy analysis. This approach reflects the realities of pluralist politics, which is the type of politics found in criminal justice.

Lindblom's model presents new considerations for criminal justice policy planners

(Smith and Klosterman, 1980), some of which run counter to principles that policy planners have perceived as essential. Critics have argued that Lindblom's approach is limited because it describes the process rather than providing a planning tool. As presented in this paper, the model is more than description; it is a planning tool that calls for the intentional breaking down of larger decisions, for molding policies into solutions, for creating crises, and for reintegrating components deliberately. Such an approach may enable criminal justice planners to plan in the context of legislative-process realities.

CONCLUSION

This article is a beginning in the study of the process of federal criminal justice policy making. It examines this process from two perspectives, that of interest-group influence and that of symbolic politics. Certain groups do influence the making of federal criminal justice policy, but the most effective groups may be less concerned with criminal justice policy than with parochial concerns. Symbolic concerns may focus more attention on issues of interest to the public but may have less bearing on the substance and operation of the criminal justice system. The process seems more likely to produce either no legislation or limited compromises than to produce well-planned policies. An understanding of the process, however, suggests an alternative approach to comprehensive (omnibus) criminal justice planning, based on the disjointed incremental model.

Further research on Congress and criminal justice policy is needed. There is a broad range of federal criminal justice concerns that may reflect different types of politics. With respect to the process of policy making, the role of congressional staff and the relationship of congressional members' goals to public policy should be examined, as they have been in other policy areas. As a beginning, however, applying the findings and recommendations presented in this article should enhance the quality of criminal-justice-policy advocates' participation in the highly political, criminal justice policy-making process by increasing awareness of what that process is rather than of what it should be.

ACKNOWLEDGMENTS

I thank Peter Hoffman for reading and commenting on earlier drafts. An earlier version of this paper, "Congress & Criminal Law: Symbolism, Interest Groups, Motivation and Change," was delivered at the annual meeting of the Academy of Criminal Justice Sciences, March 1982.

NOTES

[1] A detailed presentation of the capital-punishment study is found in Stolz (1983) and of the criminal-code revision in Stolz (1984).

[2] The time period 1972–1982 was chosen because both legislation to abolish and to reinstitute capital punishment were considered; thus both pro and con forces introduced legislation and dominated the process.

[3] The time period includes the entire recent congressional criminal-code revision effort.

[4] Because of space limitations, this section is organized according to the categories of analysis. A more formal case-study presentation and a detailed discussion of the symbolic functions are found in Stolz (1983).

[5] The Logan Act of 1979 (18 U.S. Code 953) forbids private citizens undertaking diplomatic correspondence or intercourse with a foreign power with intent to influence conduct in relation to controversies with the United States.

[6] A limited crime bill did pass Congress in 1984. While its passage supports the arguments presented in this article, the bill passed too late to be included in the analysis.

APPENDIX

Congressional Documents and Related Sources

U.S. Congress. Debate on Capital Punishment. *Congressional Record.* January 23, 1979 (daily ed.), p.S. 419.

U.S. Congress. House. Committee on Judiciary. *Capital Punishment Hearings before Subcommittee 3 of the House Subcommittee on Judiciary on H.R. 8414,*

8483, 9486, 3243, 193, 11797. 92nd Cong. 2d sess., 1972.

U.S. Congress. House. Committee on Judiciary. *Sentencing in capital cases. Hearings before Subcommittee on Criminal Justice of the House Committee on Judiciary on H.R. 13360,* 95th Congress, 2d sess., 1978.

U.S. Congress. House. Committee on Judiciary. *Legislation to revise and recodify federal criminal laws. Hearings before Subcommittee on Criminal Justice of the House Committee on Judiciary on H.R. 6869,* 95th Congress, 1st and 2d sess., 1977–1978. Parts 1–3.

U.S. Congress. House. Committee on Judiciary. *Reorganization and reauthorizing the Law Enforcement Assistance Administration. Hearings before Subcommittee on Crime of the House Committee on Judiciary.* 95th Congress, 2d sess., 1978.

U.S. Congress. House. Committee on Judiciary. *Criminal code pending matters.* Mark-up before House Committee on Judiciary. 96th Congress, 2d sess., July 2, 1982. (Observed)

U.S. Congress. House. Committee on Judiciary. *Report of the Subcommittee on Criminal Justice on recodification of federal criminal law.* Subcommittee on Criminal Justice of the House Committee on Judiciary, 95th Congress, 2nd sess., 1978.

U.S. Congress. House. Committee on Judiciary. *Report on the Criminal Code Revision Act of 1980 on H.R. 6915.* 96th Congress, 2d sess., September 25, 1980.

U.S. Congress. House. *Conference report on Juvenile Justice and Delinquency Prevention Act of 1974 to accompany S.821.* 93rd Congress, 2d sess., 1974: No. 93-1298.

U.S. Congress. Senate. Committee on Judiciary. *Hearings on reform of the federal criminal law before the Subcommittee on Criminal Law and Procedures.* 92nd Congress, 2d sess., 1972.

U.S. Congress. Senate. Committee on Judiciary. *To establish constitutional procedures for the imposition of capital punishment. Hearings before Subcommittee on Criminal Laws and Procedures of the Senate Committee on the Judiciary on S.1382.* 95th Congress, 1st sess., 1977.

U.S. Congress. Senate. Committee on Judiciary. *To establish rational criteria for imposition of capital punishment. Hearings before Senate Committee on Judiciary on S.1382.* 95th Congress, 2nd sess., 1978.

U.S. Congress. Senate. Committee on Judiciary. *Capital punishment. Hearings before Senate Committee on Judiciary on S.114.* 97th Congress, 1st sess., 1981.

U.S. Congress. Senate. Committee on Judiciary. *Report of Senate Committee on Judiciary to accompany S.114.* 97th Congress, 1st sess., 1981.

Hearings before House Subcommittee on Criminal Justice and Senate Subcommittee on Criminal Law and Procedures on the Federal Criminal Code. Observed personally between 1974 and 1982.

Congressional Quarterly Service (1971). Criminal laws reform. *Congressional Quarterly Almanac:* 793. Washington, D.C.: Congressional Quarterly.

Congressional Quarterly Service (1975). Subcommittee approves criminal law reform. *Congressional Quarterly Almanac:* 541. Washington, D.C.: Congressional Quarterly.

Congressional Quarterly Service (1977). Criminal code revision. *Congressional Quarterly Almanac:* 602–04. Washington, D.C.: Congressional Quarterly.

Congressional Quarterly Service (1978). Senate passed code bill dies in House. *Congressional Quarterly Almanac:* 165–73. Washington, D.C.: Congressional Quarterly.

Congressional Quarterly Service (1980). Criminal code bills die in both chambers. *Congressional Quarterly Almanac:* 393–

Congress and Criminal Justice Policy Making: The Impact of Interest Groups and Symbolic Politics 319

95. Washington, D.C.: Congressional Quarterly.

REFERENCES

Andanaes, J. (1974) *Punishment and deterrence.* Ann Arbor, MI: University of Michigan Press.

Anton, T. (1967). Roles and symbols in the determination of state expenditures. *Midw Jour Pol Sci* 11:27–43.

Arnold, T. (1935). *The symbols of government.* New Haven, CT: Yale University Press.

Braybrooke, D., and Lindblom, C.E. (1970). *A strategy of decision: Policy evaluation as a social process.* New York: Free Press.

Bentley, A. (1908). *The process of government.* Reprint. Cambridge, MA: Belknap Press, 1967.

Berns, W. (1979). *For capital punishment.* New York: Basic Books.

Clausen, A. (1973). *How congressmen decide: A policy focus.* New York: St. Martin's Press.

Congressional Quarterly Service (1979). Senate judiciary reports criminal code bill. *Congressional Quarterly Almanac,* 363–69. Washington, D.C.: Congressional Quarterly.

Dahl, R. (1961). *Who governs?* New Haven, CT: Yale University Press.

Edelman, M. (1964). *The symbolic uses of politics.* Chicago: University of Illinois Press.

———. (1971). *Politics as symbolic action: Mass arousal and quiescence.* New York: Academic Press.

Gibbons, D.C.; Thimm, J.L.; Yoste, F.; and Blake, G.F., Jr. (1977). *Criminal justice planning.* Englewood Cliffs, NJ: Prentice-Hall.

Greenwald, C. (1977). *Group power: Lobbying and public policy.* New York: Praeger.

Gross, B. (1953). *The legislative struggle: A study in social combat.* New York: McGraw-Hill.

Hawkins, G. (1972). Punishment as moral educator. In *Contemporary punishment,* ed. R. Gerber and P. McAnany. Notre Dame, IN: University of Notre Dame Press.

Huitt, R., and Peabody, R. (1969). *Congress: Two decades of analysis.* New York: Harper and Row.

Key, V.O. (1964). *Politics, parties, and pressure groups.* 5th ed. New York: Thomas Y. Crowell.

Lasswell, H. and Kaplan, A. (1952). *Power and society: A framework for political inquiry.* London: Routledge and Kegan Paul.

Lindblom, C.E. (1959). The science of muddling through. *Pub Adm R* 19:79–99.

———. (1979). Still muddling, not yet through. *Pub Adm R* 39:517–24.

Milbrath, L. (1963). *The Washington lobbyist.* Chicago: Rand McNally.

National Advisory Commission on Criminal Justice Standards and Goals (1973). *Corrections.* Washington, D.C.: U.S. Government Printing Office.

Sapir, E. (1934). Symbolism. In *Encyclopedia of the Social Sciences,* ed. Edwin R.A. Seligman, vol. 14, 492–95. New York: Macmillan.

Shanahan, D. T. and Whisenand, P. (1980). *The dimensions of criminal justice planning.* Boston, MA: Allyn and Bacon.

Smith, R.A., and Klosterman, R.E. (1980). Criminal justice planning: An alternative model. *Criminol* 17:403–18.

Stolz, B. (1983). Congress and capital punishment: An exercise in symbolic politics. *Law and Policy Quarterly* 5:157–79.

———. (1984). Interest groups and criminal law: The case of federal criminal code revision. *Crime Delinq* 30:91–106.

Truman, D. (1951). *The governmental process.* New York: Knopf.

Zimring, F., and Hawkins, G. (1973). *Deterrence: The legal threat in crime control.* Chicago: University of Chicago Press.

Part V
Emerging Issues

[22]

The Howard Journal Vol 26 No 1. Feb 87
ISSN 0265–5527

Abolitionism and the Politics of 'Bad Conscience'

WILLEM DE HAAN
Professor, Criminologisch Instituut der Vrije Universiteit, Amsterdam

Abstract: Image and reality of criminal justice in The Netherlands differ to a considerable degree. The causes for the relatively mild penal climate in Holland have to be taken into account, if a potential successful strategy to preserve that climate is to be developed. The discussion about the merits of abolitionism, currently held within the Dutch League for Penal Reform, is dealt with in detail.

It will hardly have come as a surprise that the Second International Conference on Prison Abolition[1] was to be held in The Netherlands, considering the remarkable reputation this country seems to have as 'a classic case of decarceration' (Downes 1982). Penal reformers from all over the world continue to visit our country, take a look at our prisons, talk with prison directors, chiefs of police, scholars, social workers, activists, and sometimes even prisoners. Subsequently, they present their impressions to their constituencies of policy-makers, politicians and activists at home. From their reports, The Netherlands emerges as a model of humane criminal justice administration. Apart from its surprisingly low incarceration rate, the friendly, relaxed atmosphere inside the small-scale penitentiaries is highly praised (Smith 1984). Numerous comparative studies have also been dedicated to The Netherlands in which conclusions were reached like: 'The Netherlands is achieving a *de facto* abolition of prisons' (Doleschall 1977, p. 52) or 'The courts continue this evolutionary system of prison abolition simply by sentencing less people to shorter terms' (Dodge 1979, p. 151). Nice as this would be, reality is unfortunately different and – as is so often the case – also more complicated. Furthermore, these authors refer to circumstances as they were during the 1970s, ignoring the major changes which have taken place since then. These reasons should warrant an updated discussion of the image and reality of criminal justice in The Netherlands. I would suggest that such a discussion is also indispensable for the current discussions around penal reform strategies which are waged within the Dutch League for Penal Reform. It is only when we take the reasons for the relatively mild penal climate in The Netherlands into account, that efforts to preserve that climate can hope to be successful. Nevertheless, in this paper my primary intention is a slightly different one.

In the first part of the paper, I shall demonstrate why the incarceration rate has never been a good barometer for the penal climate in The Netherlands. Before taking a look at the recent shift in penal policy, I shall touch briefly on the reasons for the fact that the penal climate in The Netherlands still deserves to be called 'relatively mild'. Then I shall deal with the policy changes presently facing Dutch penal reformers. In view of the fact that these policy changes are strongly reminiscent of neo-conservative criminal justice policy found both in the U.S. and U.K. in recent years, it can be interesting for Dutch penal reformers to see how progressives, radicals and liberals in these countries have tended to react to the policies in question. A brief characterisation of these reactions will be presented in the second part of the paper. Finally, I shall provide a summary of the discussion presently waged in the Dutch League for Penal Reform in which the potential merits of abolitionism for the League's position towards the current penal policy in The Netherlands is being debated.

The Dutch Penal Climate: Image and Reality

The reputation enjoyed by The Netherlands for its mild penal climate is based primarily on the remarkable low incarceration rate, that is, the number of prisoners per 100,000 inhabitants.[2] To conclude that our country has a mild penal climate on the basis of the small average size of our prison population is rather premature, however. Obviously, the number of prisoners at any moment serves as a very rough indication of how often people are sentenced to prison and for how long. Insight is still required concerning the extent and nature of the criminal behaviour, the selection processes within the penal system itself, and the frequency and duration of the prison sentences being administered (Steenhuis, *et al.* 1983). Whenever possible, other penal sanctions should also be included in the evaluation of the penal climate. The regime within the penitentiaries might even be a better indicator. Perhaps, the general level of repression can also be used as a good indicator for the penal climate.[3] The scarcity of detailed data often results in extremely global comparisons between countries. The risk is considerable that reality becomes seriously distorted. In other words, theories which try to explain such problematic differences are lacking a solid empirical foundation. Consequently, they rarely prove to be more than wild guesses. In order to achieve some insight into what the penal climate in The Netherlands is really like, some data on the frequency and duration of prison sentences will now be provided.

It is a fact that between 1965 and 1975 the prison population decreased by about 30%. However, the number of prison sentences administered in the course of one year, as well as the number of prisoners who have been in custody during that year, continuously increased for several more years.[4] Thus, the relatively small prison population can not be viewed as resulting from a relatively low number of prison sentences. The real cause resides in the fact that from the 1950s on, the average duration of prison sentences continuously decreased (Heijder 1974). The number of brief sentences (less than one month) increased between 1950 and 1970 by 50%.[5] In the same period, the percentage of prison sentences of one year or more decreased from 12% of all unsuspended prison sentences to hardly more than 4% (Tulkens 1979). Thus, the overall picture of the prison sentences given was that they were relatively more frequent, but less severe. Whether this means that our penal climate is mild, however, remains questionable. Strictly speaking, a comparison should be based on both the percentage of offenders receiving prison sentences and the average duration of these sentences, whereby the average severity of the offence should also be taken into account. However, even when we proceed in such a systematic way, an unequivocal conclusion would not be possible. This is due to the fact that so much depends on one's view concerning the value of short- and long-term prison sentences, the aims and effects being intended, and how the ultimate results should be interpreted. I shall return to this point later. Let it suffice at this point to say that any comparison of the penal climate in different countries based on incarceration rates alone is bound to be biased. Despite the fact that the Dutch penal climate is, relatively speaking, an undeniably mild one, the incarceration rate still gives an overly flattering picture. Moreover, the question arises inevitably as to how long it will stay that way. I shall return to this issue later.

Explaining Leniency

Criminologists and scholars of jurisprudence have continuously raised the issue of how it is possible that a highly industrialised and over-populated urban society like The Netherlands can manage to confine such small groups in prisons. There has been considerable speculation concerning the underlying reasons for this disproportionately small prison population. One theory, for instance, explains the relatively lenient penal and sentencing policy in The Netherlands as a manifestation of the cultural tradition of Dutch 'tolerance' and our acceptance of deviant minorities. This culture of tolerance is viewed as a structural feature of Dutch society; a society which has been traditionally structured along religious, political and ideological rather than class lines. The important denominational groupings created their own social institutions in all major public spheres. This process, which has been called 'pillarisation' is responsible for transforming a pragmatic, tolerant attitude into a requirement (Lijphart 1975; Moerings 1983). Thus, there has always been a structural basis for a certain amount of tolerance toward deviancy.

Another closely related explanation can be found in the exceptionally low level of class struggle in The Netherlands. There has never been a strong workers' movement because trade unionism was also organised and, consequently, divided in terms of the religious, political or ideological background of their members. Due to the absence of any overt class struggle that could have posed a serious threat to the social order, the ruling class was able to permit itself the luxury of being 'tolerant'. By offering social services, a responsive state was able to integrate flexibly problem populations and oppositional forces into the system. In this way, the social and political basis for a reticent criminal justice policy was

17

established (Hess 1983, p. 93). Since the integrative functions of the social system had obviously been met, there was no necessity for establishing social cohesion by stigmatising and incriminating deviants. Thus, Dutch society never had to engage in a 'war on crime' so that its members could become united. It was not necessary to invoke such grounds for a solidarity which had already been accomplished by other means (Downes 1982, p. 341).

These socio-cultural and socio-political theories enhance one another as a historical explanation for the relative leniency of the Dutch penal climate. They can also explain why the capacity of penal facilities has not been structurally enlarged in the last one and a half centuries (van Ruller 1981). What they fail to explain, however, is why this tolerance, as expressed in sentencing practices, has apparently increased during the post-war period, that is, increasing proportions of cases have been waived, decreasing proportions are being sent to prison at all, shorter sentences are being imposed. More specific explanations seem warranted.

One basis for all this is that the ever present necessity for political parties to form coalitions prevents them from using penal policy issues for their specific party interests. The interlocking character of party coalitions results in an effective political neutralisation and, thus, in a reticent penal policy (Johnson and Heijder 1982). This theory is flawed, however, by the fact that the 'pillarised' structure and the accompanying 'politics of accommodation', regarded as the essential context in which Dutch leniency must be seen, have gradually been disintegrating since the mid 1960s. Moreover, it is not clear just which connections in the political domain have led to the changes in sentencing policy ultimately resulting in the remarkably low incarceration rate (Downes 1982, p. 343). It seems likely that the relative mildness of Dutch penal policy and sentencing practices during the post-war era is a much more complicated pheno-menon than has been assumed so far. Any explanation would, then, have to take into account a multitude of factors. Another possibility would be to interpret the relative mildness, particularly of sentencing, not so much as an intended consequence of deliberate policy, but rather as a contingent result of the interplay of myriad factors, that is, the development of a welfare state, the impact of mass media, and penal reforms (Hulsman 1978). On the other hand, the problem with such a large-scale account is that it explains everything and nothing at the same time. It is hardly possible to decipher in any detail to what extent single factors do, in fact, contribute to accomplishing mild sentencing. These factors themselves could stem from the same causes as does the phenomenon they are supposed to explain (Downes 1982, p. 344). In order to account for the developments in the 1950s, 1960s, and 1970s, the explanatory power of those factors directly relating to prosecution and sentencing practices, seems superior. Particularly the mentality and philosophy of the Public Prosecutor and the judiciary could be important, considering the extensive discretionary powers of these bodies.[6] A shared community of values does seem to underpin prosecution and sentencing. Central to this 'occupational culture' is the distinctly negative value placed upon

18

imprisonment, which is viewed as, at best, a necessary evil, and, at worse, as a process likely to inflict progressive damage on a person's capacity to re-enter the community.[7] As one Dutch scholar of the philosophy of law suggests, this negative attitude toward imprisonment pervades the whole penal culture in such a decisive way that Dutch penal law could be characterised as 'classicist with a bad conscience' (Langemeijer 1973, p. 66). It is conceivable that it is precisely this 'bad conscience' which explains why prison sentences and particularly long-term prison sentences have been demanded, imposed, and administered with reluctance. The roots of this notably negative attitude towards imprisonment can generally be localised in the work of one particular group of penal law scholars.

The Utrecht-School

In the 1950s, the Utrecht-School set the standards for the penal climate in the decades to follow. Their opposition to long-term imprisonment and advocacy of rehabilitative measures have had a tremendous impact. Existing ideas concerning the goals, possibilities and limits of criminal justice began to change (Bianchi 1975, p. 53; Kelk 1983, p. 158). The critical attitude promoted by the School pervaded the Public Prosecutor and the judiciary to such a degree, that it remained even in the 1960s and 1970s when high hopes concerning the positive effects of rehabilitation on offenders had to be abandoned. Whereas the School is not the only source of anti-penal thinking in The Netherlands,[8] it has undoubtedly reinforced this critical attitude (Downes 1982, p. 348). It is worth noting that the negative attitude toward imprisonment held by the School was not based on any critical social theory of criminal law and society. Instead, the School's anti-penal outlook stemmed from their existential philosophical background assumptions (Bianchi 1974). Their reformist endeavours were primarily motivated by a strong empathy with the delinquent as fellow human being. Central to their thinking was the notion that the convict is, on the one hand, a person needing help and, on the other hand, entitled to certain basic rights. In other words, compassion and a sense of humanity supplied the main motive for the School's critique of institutions and conditions which did not do justice to the delinquent. The same factors also underpinned the struggle to humanise the administration of criminal justice. This was, of course, all well within the framework of the legal order (Moedikdo 1976, p. 114). That this purely humanitarian critique has nevertheless, and maybe even necessarily been extraordinarily effective, can be illustrated by the following example.

At the end of the 1950s a study of the harmful effects of long-term imprisonment was published in which the author, a member of the Utrecht School, allowed prisoners to speak for themselves (Rijksen 1961). In this way, he presented a picture of the administration of criminal justice in The Netherlands as seen through the eyes of suspects and convicts. The author took the position that the time had finally come to take a critical but serious look at how criminal justice is viewed by the

19

prisoners themselves (Rijksen 1961, p. xiii). The book's presentation of statements by convicts caused a shock. The government was so horrified that it bought up the entire first edition of the book and placed its distribution safely in the hands of the Justice Department. Remarkably enough there were no protests against this confiscation and censorship. The book was reissued a few years later, when it once more had an immediate and tremendous impact.[9] If it were true that the direct influence of the Utrecht-School on contemporary criminology, criminal law, and jurisprudence is negligible (Moedikdo 1976, p. 144), then we may have to conclude that it must have been the convicts themselves who saddled prosecutors and judges with a 'bad conscience'. It cannot be denied that the School has been oriented outspokenly toward penal reform and has neglected more or less any systematic theorising. On the other hand, it may also be true that direct confrontations are the only way to appeal to the conscience of the criminal justice authorities. I shall deal with this later on. Whatever the case may be, we may rest assured that the relatively mild penal climate in The Netherlands has not been the result of persistent abolitionist struggle. In fact, we would have to say that the opposite has been true. It is only recently that there has been a growing interest in The Netherlands for radical abolitionist ideas. Moreover, this interest seems to go hand in hand with a marked shift in penal policy.

A Classic Case of Recarceration?

In the last few years, changes can be observed in penal policy which raise the question of how long the relatively mild penal climate in The Netherlands can continue to exist. A considerable cooling of this climate has already been noted. Criminal justice policy has taken an expansionist rather than a reductionist line (Rutherford 1984). Punishment is no longer seen as a 'necessary evil', but as a 'normal' response to criminal behaviour. In the field of crime control, 'minor' and 'serious' crimes are differentiated. Rights of suspects in criminal procedures are sacrificed increasingly in the interest of effective crime control. The capacity of penitentiary facilities is being adapted currently to the growing 'demand' (Hulsman 1984). The number of prison cells has been enlarged from 3,000 in 1975 to 3,900 in 1981, when a special task force concluded that a shortage of prison cells still existed requiring an additional 100 every year. In 1983 this figure was updated to 189 additional cells per year. In 1985, the total capacity had already reached 4,800 cells, although a shortage of hundreds of cells was still claimed. For the years to come, it has been decided to make approximately 300 additional cells available every year. It is argued that the 'demand' resulting from prosecution and sentencing practices has to be met in order to safeguard the credibility of the rule of law. In particular, the independence of the judiciary in a constitutional state is supposed to be at stake here. Judicial orders have to be obeyed strictly and consistently. In a governmental policy plan, 'Society and Criminality', recently submitted to parliament, these tendencies can be identified immediately.[10] The policy which is presented in the plan is a

20

differentiated one. Prevention and control of criminality are different according to the seriousness of the offences. Petty crime is preferably to be controlled in a preventive way, whereas serious crime is to be combatted solely by repressive means. Whereas prevention and control of petty crime are considered a matter concerning both citizens and the state, the fight against serious organised crime is the exclusive domain of the state. It is assumed that The Netherlands faces grave danger because of internationally organised, professional crime. This contention is based on 'a definite impression' presently existing within the police and the justice departments. Even though facts and figures are not available, the government feels that serious organised crime, particularly the drug trade, has to be combatted more vigorously. No less than an 'utmost effort' will be necessary to curtail the currently increasing danger of a widespread and deep-seated underworld in Dutch society. The Netherlands must be prevented from becoming an attractive resort for internationally organised, professional crime due to its reluctant crime control and relatively mild penal climate. Furthermore, it should be noted that these criminals frequently display an open disrespect for the law. To endure this would contribute to further erosion of norm awareness among the citizenry. In order to avoid additional disruption to the image of criminal law, a series of special measures needs to be taken. Installation of special District Bureaux of Criminal Investigation and a further expansion of the prisons' estate capacity are the most important ones. In order to reach the stated goal of at least 7,100 cells by 1990, four to five new prisons have to be built within the next few years. Once this project has been completed, the prison system will have enlarged its total capacity by 135% since 1975. Foreign observers will probably not be terribly impressed by these changes presently taking place within Dutch penal policy. After all, what are five prisons with 250 cells each compared to the hundreds of prisons and thousands of cells being built in the U.S. and U.K.? However, when viewed from a historical perspective, this current expansion of cell capacity in The Netherlands is extremely unusual. For about a century and a half, the total capacity has always remained at the level of 4,000–5,000 prison cells (van Ruller 1981). Penal reformers in The Netherlands regard these plans, therefore, as a historical break with a long tradition of tolerance and lenient criminal justice. Moreover, they are racking their brains to see if they can find something which might at least slow down these processes. It is in this light that the increased interest in what has been taking place in other countries in past years must be seen. Until not so long ago, this was not particularly relevant for the Dutch situation. Now it is urgently so. This is why there is now increased interest in how penal reformers in other countries have reacted to similar shifts in their respective penal policies.

Neo-Conservatism and the Progressive Response

It has been noted by various authors that criminal justice policy in The Netherlands today is showing certain similarities with the neo-conserva-

21

tive penal policy as manifested in various Western countries, especially in the U.S. in the last decade.[11] In the second part of this paper, I shall provide a brief characterisation of neo-conservatism in penal policy. Special attention will be given to changes in the ideas about crime and punishment upon which new policy is based. Finally, I shall describe how progressives, Marxists, liberals and abolitionists have reacted to the policy shift. Obviously, these are little more than some general impressions based on relevant literature. They will, however, hopefully suffice to show the tension which also marks the present discussion about the possibilities and limitations of penal reform in The Netherlands.

Neo-Conservative Penal Policy

Since the emergence of neo-conservatism, law-and-order campaigns are well on their way towards eliminating even minimal reforms in criminal justice and corrections previously gained. It was, in fact, partly due to the law-and-order issue that the right came into power in the first place. The groundwork for its success in the ideological battlefield around issues of crime and crime control had already been laid in the mid 1970s by conservative and liberal scholars. They maintained that since rehabilitation obviously didn't work, retribution and deterrence had to be reaccepted as indispensable elements of criminal justice. Moreover, they claimed that punishment (including the death penalty) did have a deterrent effect on crime and that incapacitation of offenders on a large scale would greatly reduce crime as a major problem in society. The necessity of deterrence and retribution for the credibility of criminal law enforcement and the maintenance of the social order was particularly stressed (van den Haag 1975). The theory that crime could be reduced to a considerable extent by (selectively) incapacitating lawbreakers, however, marked the breakthrough in penal policy (Wilson 1975). These successful attacks on liberal penal philosophy have put the politicians in a position to launch that very policy that we have observed since the second half of the last decade. Deviant behaviour was recategorised and certain forms of conduct were again made punishable by law. A distinction was made between the truly bad who deserve prison and the not-so-bad who are to be kept out of the criminal justice system and subjected to other programmes. The attempt was made to minimise public fear of burglary and 'street crime' by punishing substantially these offences. In this way, the public fear of crime was used to pursue a penal policy based on the concepts of deterrence and retribution (Michalowski 1983). As we know now this policy has led to a dramatic increase in the prison population, rapidly deteriorating prison conditions, subsequent outbreaks of violence and a growing number of (attempted) suicides. Taken together, these developments constitute what might be called a prison crisis.

Neo-Realism in Progressive Criminology

Confronted with the electoral success of neo-conservative criminal justice

22

policy, 'radical' or 'critical' criminology was treated in no uncertain terms to a hard lesson in the facts of life. Critical criminologists had not been able to come up with convincing solutions for the problems experienced by large segments of the population. Their alternatives to criminal justice remained abstract and impractical. By skipping too lightly over street crime, critical criminology gambled on its credibility and lost. The entire field of crime as a political issue changed hands and became the concern of neo-conservative criminology. In addition, this gave neo-conservative politicians the chance to put some new lyrics to the old, familiar tune of how valuable punishment is for the prevention of crime. Of course, they could present this with success to their constituencies who had been feeling pretty much left out in the cold when it came to their day-to-day problems with crime.

At present, critical criminologists seem to be involved in a process of political reorientation. They are engaged in the reconstruction of socialist criminology as well as a socialist position on crime control. The formulation of a programme of both short- and long-term penal reforms is high on their list of priorities at the moment. In an attempt to recover lost ground, proposals have been made like: no more expansion of prison facilities; reduction of long-term prison sentences; strengthening the legal position of both suspects and prisoners; the large-scale application of programmes for preparing prisoners for their return to society; re-evaluating priorities concerned with criminal investigation and prosecution and replacing them with a greater concern for injustices like violence against women and minorities, racism and discrimination, corporate violations of safety and environmental precautions, corruption, fraud, etc. Community programmes are advocated as a way to combat and prevent crime. 'Authentic' forms of justice in communities and neighbourhoods are also being propagated. And, last but not least, they are arguing for changes at a structural, socio-economic level, that is, full-scale employment. In recent years, such 'realistic' reform programmes are there for the taking (Taylor 1981; Gross 1982; Currie 1982; Bute 1982; Platt 1982; Michalowski 1983; Lea and Young 1984). Their realism entails, among other things, the recognition that 'crime really is a problem', that 'we must take crime control seriously' and that 'punishment can sometimes be justified for a violation of the law' (Greenberg 1983; Lea and Young 1984). Oddly enough, the concrete proposals mentioned before are strongly reminiscent of those made earlier in the sixties and seventies by moderate penal reformers. However, those reformers have not been standing still either. They have also adjusted their positions to changing realities and have come up with their own brand of 'realism'. Their 'realism' expresses itself in the neo-classical approach which they have begun to endorse (von Hirsch 1983). Impressed by both the harshness of neo-conservative penal policy and the disappointing results of rehabilitation programmes, liberal criminologists have come to the conclusion that their current priority is to defend what has already been achieved against attacks from right-wing politicians.[12] Particularly the legal position of suspects and convicts is in jeopardy. In accordance with their classic-

23

liberal philosophy of criminal justice, prison sentences as such are not
seen as problematic, but rather the question of due process in sentencing
and correction is seen as the main issue. Justice is interpreted in such a
way that only those who really 'deserve' it have to be punished and even
then only according to the seriousness and the circumstances of the
offences. As soon as sentencing begins to take place along the lines of this
'justice model,' current proponents of the proportionality principle hope
to see punishments reduced.

Abolitionism

My contention has been that left-wing criminologists – whether Marxist,
socialist, or liberal – and sociologists of criminal law have been moving
steadily towards the right and now seem to be advocating even neo-
positivist or neo-classical views. The more pragmatically oriented,
however, appear to be moving in just the opposite direction. I am
referring to the family members of (ex-) convicts, church groups engaged
in support work, and individuals actively struggling for prison reform.
They call themselves 'abolitionists'. Abolitionism in the U.S. belongs to a
tradition which is almost completely non-existent in Europe.[13] Abolitionists regard the struggle for abolition of prisons as their historical mission,
as a continuation and fulfilment of the struggle against slavery which was
waged by their forbears. Imprisonment is seen as a form of blasphemy.[14]
They regard crime primarily as the result of the social order and advocate
drastically reducing the role of the criminal justice system as well as
finding 'public solutions for public problems'. Their belief is that
reconciliation, not punishment, is the appropriate reaction to crime. A
minimum of coercion and interference with the personal lives of those
involved and a maximum amount of care and service for all members of
society is advocated. Moreover, they believe that individual and collective
forgiveness is only possible within a caring community. At the same time,
a long-term strategy in the form of a three-step 'attrition model' should be
followed. To begin with, as far as prisons are concerned they strive for a
total freeze on the planning and building of prisons. Furthermore, as
many categories of convicts as possible should be decarcerated, that is,
released from prison. Finally, as many categories of lawbreakers as
possible should be excarcerated, that is, kept outside prison.[15]

The political significance of American abolitionism is hard to gauge.
Considering the developments in the U.S. in the recent past, however, it
seems that its impact has not been particularly significant. Some of the
radical criminologists and sociologists who previously defended abolitionist positions in the early seventies, are presently engaged in discussions
about the pros and cons of the 'justice model' (Greenberg 1983;
Humphries 1984). They remain radical, but this time in their rejection of
abolitionism as an example of 'bizarre politics', 'disastrous strategy' or a
'dangerous ultra-leftist adventure (Platt 1982; Greenberg 1983). In order
for any serious reform movement to get off the ground, reality has to be
faced. According to the progressive criminologist, abolitionists are simply

24

blind dreamers with their ideas about easy alliances between peace groups, anti-nuclear groups, anti-fascist and anti-racist groups, women's groups and gays, etc., all united under the banner of prison abolition. It is argued, moreover, that abolitionist ideas lack serious class analysis and attention hasn't been paid to appropriate organisational forms. Such wishful thinking unfortunately does not create the solutions needed for real and serious problems. In conclusion, progressive America seems to be standing somewhat desperately and with deplorably empty hands by the wayside as the reactionary roll-back passes them by. Having been forced into a defensive position, the left is scarcely able to stop the right from revising those criminal justice reforms which had previously been won. In this situation, they have even given up former doubts about the legitimacy of prison sentences and begun to accept them as, more or less, 'realistic'. Now the prison system is criticised in terms of the inhuman conditions in overcrowded institutions, and the ineffectiveness and high costs of mass imprisonment as a strategy for crime control. On the other hand, the abolitionists, acting out of the courage of their convictions and a strong sense of moral righteousness, continue to take a firm stand against imprisonment and deny it any legitimacy whatsoever.

Abolitionism and the Dutch League for Penal Reform

Following this brief overview of the different reactions to neo-conservative law-and-order politics, particularly in the U.S., we can now address the question of which of these reactions would be most appropriate for the current Dutch situation. In the final section of this paper I shall report on a discussion presently being waged within the Coornhert-Liga – the Dutch League for Penal Reform – concerning the merits of an abolitionist approach to criminal justice and penal reform. The second conference on prison abolition served as an occasion for the League to discuss abolitionism.[16] More specifically, the question was raised as to whether future interventions might gain in strength and coherence if they were based on an abolitionist approach. Before we turn to this issue, however, a brief overview of the League's history is in order.

Without a doubt the Coornhert-Liga has contributed considerably to the creation and maintenance of a penal climate in The Netherlands in which critical thought on criminal justice and penal reforms was accepted (Kelk 1983, p. 161). Since its inception in 1971, however, two questions led to a certain amount of division among the members of the League. The first was a theoretical one concerning the direction penal reform should take. The second one was a political strategy issue. The theoretical issue brought forth a difference in opinion as to whether a legal 'human rights' approach toward continued formalisation should be followed or whether it was better to take a behavioural science and 'human relations' approach and deformalise criminal justice (Buiting and Jörg 1983, p. 136). From a legal point of view, crime control was seen as relatively unproblematic. The specific juridical issue concerns the accomplishment of crime control in accordance with those autonomous principles or rights which constitute

25

the legal character of criminal justice in the first place (Peters 1972). From a behavioural science point of view, however, it is the purposive administration of criminal justice, that is, crime control which is considered as problematic. Criminal justice is seen as a system which created social problems rather than resolving them (Hulsman 1976). The juridical approach aims at strengthening the legal position of suspects and convicts, whereas the behavioural science approach gives priority to the reduction of prison sentences through depenalisation and decriminalisation. The second controversy in the League concerned the question of whether a strategy should be followed toward long-term, fundamental changes or immediate changes (Kelk 1983, p. 160). In the present situation, we can expect with reasonable certainty, to see abolitionist ideas, which have always appealed to the 'human relations' faction, coming to the fore with increased vigour. On the other hand, it is conceivable – if not probable – that the neo-realistic 'justice model' will appeal to the more legally-oriented 'human rights' faction. I shall be dealing mainly with abolitionism and with the 'justice model' since the reform proposals by neo-marxist criminologists and sociologists in the U.S. have not evoked controversy among Dutch penal reformers.

Abolitionism as a Theoretical Perspective

Even if we stretch our imagination, there is nothing remotely like a European equivalent of the abolitionist movement at present. At best, a free-floating theoretical perspective can be observed, looking for a social movement to take it under its wing. As theoretical perspective, abolitionism pinpoints the failures within the current criminal justice system; that is, by demonstrating the negative effects of a penal law frame of reference and by showing the impossibility of ever achieving goals like deterrence and crime prevention. At the same time, however, abolitionism is a 'sensitising theory', presenting both a fundamentally new view on the criminal justice system as well as a corresponding discourse (Scheerer 1984; Hulsman 1985). It shifts the focus from the criminal justice system to the surrounding social networks and institutions as well as to the various forms of conflict management and dispute resolution used in these contexts. In this way, abolitionism can reveal social possibilities for dealing in a rational way with unjust behaviours which have been overlooked so far or under-rated from a legal point of view (Bianchi, forthcoming).

Abolitionism as a Political Strategy

From a political point of view abolitionism can be seen as a strategy of negation. This approach is based on the claim that the successful struggle for the abolition of the prison system requires a strategy of strictly negative reforms, these being the only ones which do not contribute to the maintenance or the legitimation of criminal justice (Mathiesen 1974). This strategy has been elaborated into a general political 'strategy under late capitalism'. The original uncompromising position has thereby given way to a pragmatic attitude. A strategy aiming at purely negative reforms has been refuted as ultimately leading to resignation. On the contrary, a strategy has to be followed which alternates between offensive and defensive activities (Mathiesen 1980). Offensive abolitionist action uses radical, transformative demands as its starting point. Defensive abolitionist work departs from concrete issues within delimited fields or areas and is followed by the pursuit of new structures. Especially in periods of increasing political repression, this course seems necessary to protect what has been gained in the reform struggle against attacks. However, in order to prevent the movement and its ideas from being absorbed by the system, it must strive for both short-term realistic and long-term Utopian goals. Social movements will have to alternate reformist and revolutionary strategies. The two aspects must be emphasised 'all along' (Mathiesen 1980, p. 265).

For a Pragmatic Abolitionism

Concerning the relevance of abolitionism – as a possible theoretical perspective, political strategy or moral appeal – for future activities on the part of the Dutch League for Penal Reform, I would like to offer the following suggestions. Critics have repeatedly pointed to the embarassing lack of adequate theory behind numerous proposals for applying other than the conventional penal forms of conflict management. It is my contention that abolitionism has an interesting contribution to make for enlarging such proposals' theoretical scope, even though it is at present hardly more than a 'sensitising theory' requiring elaboration itself. One particularly promising feature of abolitionism is that it directs our attention to other, more rational reactions to socially problematic behaviour.[17]

As a political strategy, abolitionism has the merit of warning us against overly optimistic expectations concerning short-term, positive reforms. Unfortunately, it also tends to deny positive reforms any significance, except in the maintenance and legitimation of present criminal justice. Because of this rigidity, abolitionism as a political strategy has to be refuted. The League for Penal Reform may better stick to the pragmatic attitude which has enabled it to achieve such remarkable results in the past. It would be preferable, however, if this pragmatic strategy could be combined with a radical theoretical perspective. Whereas the theoretical perspective of abolitionism aims at the abolition of the penal system as a whole, experiments and positive reforms are nevertheless valuable, if only for their moral and political significance (Cohen 1985, pp. 236–72). Strictly speaking abolitionism as a moral appeal is incompatible with the goals of the League. According to the statutes, criminal justice and penal policy are to be evaluated on the basis of 'rational' criteria alone. I would suggest that moral points of view must not be excluded completely. It seems conceivable that this level may provide even more opportunities for working against the threatening return of authoritarian penal policy and repressive criminal justice.

27

The Politics of 'Bad Conscience'

Any strategy aimed at preserving a mild penal climate in The Netherlands will have to start with an analysis of the origins of our particular circumstances. As we have seen, the relatively mild penal climate has been the result – at least, in part – of the judiciary's deeply rooted conviction that long-term imprisonment has serious and damaging effects. In this final section, I shall toy with the idea that the negative attitude in The Netherlands towards long-term imprisonment – what I have been calling our 'bad conscience' – makes it relatively hard to justify punishment at all. Up until now the concepts of treatment and rehabilitation have provided a justification for punishment by masking the very character of it, that is, the deliberate infliction of pain. These options, however, are rapidly deteriorating in terms of their credibility as deterrence and retribution come to the fore. However, even with a sophisticated justification of punishment the deliberate infliction of pain in the form of long-term imprisonment remains a bitter pill to swallow for the Dutch. This is especially true for those who bear the actual responsibility of sentencing: the judiciary. Considering the 'bad conscience' which has influenced classical penal law decisively in the past decades, a simple return to neo-classical concepts like deterrence and retribution does not seem possible. Consequently, a deficit remains in the legitimation of prison sentences. It is not unimaginable however, that under the influence of current shifts in thinking about crime and punishment, the judiciary may be tempted into lulling their 'bad conscience'. By grabbing onto legal principles and values like 'proportionality' and 'just deserts', they may be prepared to cross the line and begin accepting the sentencing of offenders to serve time in prison as their moral duty. There is reason to fear that the specifically juridical approach endorsed by the second generation of the same Utrecht-School which originally created that 'bad conscience', could become counterproductive under the present circumstances. Any one-sided accentuation of the formal legal position of suspects in criminal procedure could lead easily to the legitimation of that very administration of criminal justice which it intended to criticise. Considering the present tendency to accept imprisonment as an inevitable, necessary, 'normal', legitimate and even moral reaction to crime it is particularly important to keep this danger in mind. I do not wish to create the impression that the present approach by the Utrecht-School is identical with the neo-classical 'justice model'. Clearly, those who now endorse the 'due process' approach of the School do not in any way intend to legitimate the criminal justice system. However, it cannot be denied that there are similarities between the 'due process' and the 'back to justice' approach. Moreover, if we recall earlier enthusiastic exclamations issuing from the ranks of the general deterrence proponents when the School's 'due-process' programme was first pre-sented, we should not be surprised by such unintended consequences.[18] In order to curtail the danger just described, it seems necessary to me that the specifically juridical approach be placed in a more encompassing social theory. Moreover, the abolitionist perspective can be particularly useful in this respect. As theoretical perspective, abolitionism could serve to counter-balance the growing inclination to accept once again the intentional infliction of suffering as 'realistic'. Abolitionism has this potential due to its inherent 'moral rigourism' (Christie 1982). In conclusion, I would like to plead for a politics of 'bad conscience', that is, let's make it as difficult as possible to justify punishment and let's do that in every way conceivable. In every discussion about the justification of punishment, the last line of defence is that there is no alternative. It is my contention that by showing that there are several alternative ways to deal rationally with socially problematic conduct, we can make it difficult to present punishment as an indispensable reaction to crime. In this way an environment in which a 'bad conscience' can continue to thrive is maintained.

The specific merits of the 'due process' approach are invaluable here, for example, in adding a legal quality to informal procedures. In this way, the Utrecht-School with its particular expertise, could make a major contribution towards the maintenance of the relatively mild penal climate which may still be found in The Netherlands. Reviving the humanitarian spirit of the original Utrecht-School and replicating their traditional stance are not enough, however, if we intend to make if difficult to justify imprisonment. It is imperative to incorporate their 'ethical humanism' in a more encompassing critical theory of criminal law and society.

Notes

[1] An earlier version of this paper was presented to the Second International Conference on Prison Abolition held in Amsterdam, 24–27 June 1985 (see Bianchi and Van Swaaningen, forthcoming). I wish to thank Richard/Abel, Constantÿn Kelk, and Karl Schumann for their helpful comments. Special thanks to Kathy Davis who did the translation.

[2] In 1974, the rate of incarceration of 21 prisoners per 100.000 inhabitants was one of the lowest in the world (see Dodge 1979, p. 258). According to the data issued by the Council of Europe on 2 February 1985, the incarceration rate had increased to 34.0. Compared with U.K. 90.0, F.R.G. 99.7, France 79.7, Italy 77.5, Denmark 68.0, Sweden 58.0, and Norway 50.7, this was still relatively low (Council of Europe 1985, p. 22).

[3] It was noted, for example, that the Dutch resolve their social crises with remarkably less repression (Hess 1983).

[4] The number of prisoners at the end of the year were subsequently: 1965: 3,358; 1970: 2,419; 1975: 2,359. The number of unsuspended prison sentences: 1965: 19,983; 1970: 21,775; 1971: 23,069; 1972: 23,100; 1973: 21,657; 1974 no data available; 1975: 19,649. In that last year, the waiting list for people convicted to short sentences had grown to 14,400.

[5] In 1970, about 57% of all prison sentences were for one month or less. In 1975, this percentage had increased to 75%. In the same year, about 96% of all prison sentences were for half a year or less.

[6] Public prosecutors are not elected, but appointed by the Crown. Consequently, they are subordinate to the political authority of the Minister of Justice. Nevertheless, the Public Prosecutor has acquired a central position in the administration of justice and operates more or less independently.

[7]   Downes and Mitchell found this on the basis of interviews with some 25 judges
      and public prosecutors (Downes 1982).
[8]   Moedikdo also maintains that the influence of the Utrecht-School on post-war
      developments has primarily been indirect and that various attempts to soften
      the administration of criminal justice would have occurred even without the
      Utrecht-School (Moedikdo 1976). Moedikdo and Downes both come to the
      conclusion that further research is called for in order to reconstruct the
      intellectual history of the School (Downes 1982; Moedikdo 1976).
[9]   Downes and Mitchell report that several of the judges and prosecutors
      mentioned the book (Downes 1982).
[10] This policy plan has been analysed in another paper (De Haan, 1986).
[11] According to Hulsman it's 'quite clearly the same tendency' (Hulsman 1984, p.
      216). The political commentator Kuitenbrouwer remarked nastily, but to the
      point, that the above-mentioned policy paper was a rerun of the law-and-order
      campaign 'which had already left a path of destruction in its wake in other
      countries' (Kuitenbrouwer 1985).
[12] Originally the attack on the idea of rehabilitation had a different goal.
      Certainly Martinson had shown that rehabilitation programmes did not
      provide any serious evidence of reduced recidivism of offenders. He also
      concluded from this that rehabilitation of offenders was just a myth serving to
      mask the appalling conditions in American penitentiaries. However, Martin-
      son advocated that prisons continue to serve the protection of the public
      against really dangerous offenders. Except for these cases prisons could best be
      torn down, since they are simply impossible to ameliorate. Neo-conservatives
      have merely taken Martinson's arguments and applied them to their theories of
      deterrence and retribution (Martinson 1972, 1974).
[13] Abolitionism as a social movement must be differentiated from the theoretical
      perspective as found in current discussions in Western Europe (Scheerer 1984).
[14] The first article of the abolitionist catechism states: 'Imprisonment is morally
      objectionable and indefensible and must therefore be abolished' (Morris 1976,
      p. 11).
[15] A moratorium on the building of prisons is presented as the single most
      important step towards a fundamental reform of the prison system.
[16] The last part of the present paper has its origins in a position paper which was
      written for the League on invitation. I am grateful to Job Knap – president of
      the Coornhert-Liga – who invited me to co-operate and to the other members of
      the Board of the Dutch League for Penal Reform who stimulated the project
      while it was in progress.
[17] Parenthetically, it might be wise to discard the predicate 'abolitionist' for
      starters and substitute another one like, for instance, a 'reflexive' approach to
      crime and punishment. In this way, misunderstandings could be avoided. It
      would be clear that we are not referring here to a political strategy or to
      negative reforms only (Gouldner 1970; Bianchi 1980).
[18] As Peters, leading spokesman of the School, has noted: 'Ideas which are right
      in principle are especially suited to justifying wrongs, to presenting them in a
      much nicer way, and ultimately to getting them accepted, even by those who
      are the victims of those very same ideas' (Peters 1976, p. 190).

References

Bianchi, H. (1974) 'Naar een nieuwe fenomenologische kriminologie', *Nederlands
   Tijdschrift voor Criminologie, 16*, 97–112.

30

Bianchi, H. (1975) 'Fenomenologie in flashback', *Nederlands Tijdschrift voor Criminologie, 17*, 131–6.

Bianchi, H. (1980 *Basismodellen in de Kriminologie*, Deventer: Van Loghum Slaterus.

Bianchi, H. (forthcoming) *Justice as Sanctuary*, Amsterdam: Kugler.

Bianchi, H. and Van Swaaningen, R. (Eds.) (forthcoming) *Abolitionism. Towards a Non-Repressive Approach to Crime* (Proceedings of the Second International Conference on Prison Abolition), Amsterdam, Free University Press.

Buiting, B. and Jörg, N. (1983) 'Criminal justice in the Netherlands 1970–1980', *Contemporary Crises, 7*, 135–54.

Bute, J. (1982) 'Crime and community: strategies for the left', *Crime and Social Justice, 18*, 34–6.

Christie, N. (1982) *Limits to Pain*, Oxford: Martin Robertson.

Cohen, S. (1985) *Visions of Social Control*, London: Polity Press.

Council of Europe (1985) *Prison Information Bulletin No. 5, June*, Strasbourg: Council of Europe.

Currie, E. (1982) 'Crime and ideology', *Working Papers*, 26–35.

Dodge, C. (1979) *A World Without Prisons*, Lexington, Mass.: Heath.

Doleschall, E. (1977) 'Rate and length of imprisonment: how does the United States compare with the Netherlands, Denmark and Sweden?', *Crime and Delinquency, 23*, 51–6.

Downes, D. (1982) 'The origins and consequences of Dutch penal policy since 1945; a preliminary analysis', *British Journal of Criminology, 22*, 325–57.

Gouldner, A. (1970) *The Coming Crisis of Western Sociology*, London: Heinemann.

Greenberg, D. (1983) 'Reflections on the justice model', *Contemporary Crises, 7*, 313–27.

Gross, B. (1982) 'Some anti-crime proposals for progressives', *Crime and Social Justice, 17*.

Haag, E. van den (1975) *Punishing Criminals*, New York: Hill and Wang.

Haan, W. de (1986) 'Explaining expansion: the Dutch case', *Working Papers in European Criminology, 7*, 1–16.

Heijder, A (1974) 'The recent trend toward reducing the prison population in The Netherlands', *International Journal of Offender Therapy and Comparative Criminology, 18*, 233–40.

Hess, H. (1983) 'Editorial', *Contemporary Crises, 7*, 91–3.

Hirsch, A. von (1983) ' "Neoclassicism", proportionately and the rationale for punishment: thoughts on the Scandinavian debate', *Crime and Delinquency, 28*, 52–70.

Hulsman, L. (1976) ' "Civilizing" the criminal justices system: strategies to reduce violence in society' (Address given at the Annual Meeting of the Howard League), London: Howard League.

Hulsman, L. (1978) 'The relative mildness of the Dutch criminal justice system: an attempt at analysis', in D. Fokkema, *et al.* (Eds.) *Dutch Law for Foreign Lawyers*, Deventer: Kluwer.

Hulsman, L. (1984) 'Een brief aan wim. . . een plaatsbepaling', in: |*Recht op scherp. Beschouwingen over Handhaving van Publiekrecht Aangeboden aan Prof. Mr. W. Duk*. Zwolle: Tjeenk Willink.

Hulsman, L. (1985) 'Strafrechtelijk beleid en planning', in: *Liber Amicorum Th. W. van Veen*, Arnhem: Gouda Quint.

Humphries, D. (1984) 'Reconsidering the justice model', *Contemporary Crises, 8*, 167–73.

Johnson, E. and Heijder, A (1982) 'The Dutch deemphasize imprisonment: a sociocultural and structural explanation', in: D. Chang (Ed.), *Criminology: A Cross-Cultural Perspective*, Durham N.C., Carolina: Academic Press.

31

Kelk, C. (1983) 'The humanity of the Dutch prison system and prisoners' consciousness of their legal rights', *Contemporary Crises, 7,* 155–70.

Kuitenbrouwer, F. (1985) 'Te veel nadruk op toezicht, te weinig op dienstverlening', *N.R.C. Handelsblad, 22,5.*

Langemeijer, G. (1973) 'De toekomst van onze rechtspleging', *Nederlands Juristenblad,* 61–7.

Lea, J. and Young, J. (1984) *What is to be done about Law and Order?,* Harmondsworth: Penguin.

Lijphart, A. (1975) *The Politics of Accommodation,* 2nd ed., Berkeley and Los Angeles: University of California Press.

Martinson, R. (1972) 'The paradox of prison reform', *New Republic, 3,* 1–29.

Martinson, R. (1974) 'What works? Questions and answers about prison reform', *The Public Interest, 35,* 22–54.

Mathiesen, T. (1974) *The Politics of Abolition,* London: Martin Robertson.

Mathiesen, T. (1980) *Law, Society and Political Action: Towards a Strategy under Late Capitalism,* London: Academic Press.

Michalowski, R. (1983) 'Crime control in the 1980s: a progressive agenda', *Crime and Social Justice, 20,* 13–23.

Moedikdo, P. (1976) 'De Utrechtse School van Pompe, Baan en Kempe', in: C. Kelk, *et al.* (Eds.), *Recht, Macht en Manipulatie,* Utrecht: Spectrum.

Moerings, M. (1983) 'Protest in the Netherlands: developments in a pillarized society', *Contemporary Crises, 7,* 95–112.

Morris, M. (Ed.) (1976) *Instead of Prisons: A Handbook for Abolitionists,* Syracuse, New York: Prison Research Action Project.

Peters, A. (1972) *Het Rechtskarakter van het Strafrecht,* Deventer: Kluwer.

Peters, A. (1976) 'Recht als vals bewustzijn, in: C. Kelk, *et al.* (Eds.), *Recht Macht en Manipulatie,* Utrecht: Spectrum.

Platt, T. (1982) 'Crime and punishment in the United States: immediate and long-term reforms from a Marxist perspective', *Crime and Social Justice, 18,* 38–45.

Rijksen, R. (1961) *Meningen van Gedetineerden over de Strafechtspleging,* 2nd ed., Assen: Van Gorcum.

Ruller, S. van (1981) 'Het aantal gevangenen in Nederland sinds 1837: een analyse van 140 jaar gevangenisstatistieken', *Tijdschrift voor Criminologie, 23,* 209–23.

Rutherford, A (1984) *Prisons and the Process of Justice: The Reductionist Challenge,* London: Heinemann.

Scheerer, S. (1984) 'Die abolitionistische perspektive', *Kriminologisches Journal, 16,* 90–111.

Smith, P. (1984) 'If it can happen here: reflections on the Dutch system', *Prison Journal, 58,* 847–50.

Steenhuis, D., *et al.* (1983) 'The penal climate in the Netherlands: sunny or cloudy?', *British Journal of Criminology, 23,* 1–16.

Taylor, I. (1981) *Law and Order: Arguments for Socialism,* London: Macmillan.

Taylor, I. (1982) 'Introduction to the | justice model discussion', *Contemporary Crises, 6,* 1–15.

Tulkens, H. (1979) *Some Developments in Penal Policy in Holland,* Chichester: Barry Rose.

Wilson, J. (1975) *Thinking About Crime,* New York: Basic Books.

[23]

IN PURSUIT OF THE VERNACULAR: COMPARING LAW AND ORDER DISCOURSE IN BRITAIN AND GERMANY

LUCIA ZEDNER

Corpus Christi College, Oxford

We need, in the end, something rather more than local knowledge. We need a way of turning its varieties into commentaries one upon another, the one lightening what the other darkens. (Geertz, 1983b: 233)

CRIME HAS BEEN increasingly politicized in Britain, held up as a metaphor for social disorder and a manifestation of political rupture.[1] Law and order has become the currency of heated cross-party debate and, since 1979, a staple of general election manifestos. As a corollary, social problems (from education and employment to housing and the environment) are increasingly described in terms of crime. Recast as truancy, unemployment, homelessness and urban degeneration, these wider social issues attract attention only insofar as they are deemed to threaten social order. As crime figures supplant unemployment statistics or mortality rates as indicators of the health of the nation, the question arises whether debates about growing inner-city violence or spiralling prison populations are really just about crime or rather express some deeper unease.

The anxieties articulated by discourses of law and order extend beyond experiences of victimization or the rational anticipation of harm. This lack of fit between the 'realities' of the crime problem and the space it occupies in the national psyche is not readily explained (Müller-Dietz, 1993: 57–9). In seeking to

SOCIAL & LEGAL STUDIES (SAGE, London, Thousand Oaks, CA and New Delhi), Vol. 4 (1995), 517–534

Criminal Policy Making

Lucia Zedner

understand why so much political capital is invested in British discourses of law and order, comparisons are made with Germany, a country similar in many respects, yet whose legal culture is markedly different. The case for comparison here rests on the observation that the high profile of law and order has become so deeply embedded in British culture as to appear self-evident. Where immersion in one legal culture tends to entrench uncritical assumptions, exposure to other possible ways of seeing and shaping the world not only excites us out of the torpor of parochialism but demands that we regard our domestic topography anew.[2] Awareness of the 'other' (assumptions, values, languages and forms) obliges us to recognize the contingency of our own laws and legal practices, and makes it difficult to maintain uncritical adherence to the dogmas of our own legal culture (Lacey, 1995).

In this article, I seek to illustrate some theoretical and methodological problems entailed in reconciling sensitivity to local difference with the generalizing imperatives of the comparative. I critically examine the appeal to universalism in comparative law and go on to consider the demands made by Clifford Geertz that we should recognize the value of 'local knowledge' (Geertz, 1983b), offering some thoughts both on the methodological difficulties of this approach and its potential gains. I then return to compare law and order discourses in Britain and Germany, looking particularly at the vocabularies of order and disorder and at current political debates surrounding the role of the state in maintaining order in both countries.

Some Issues in Comparative Method

Comparative research often starts from the premise that legal systems are of the same genus differing only in varieties of form (Langbein, 1974, 1977; Langbein and Weinreb, 1978). Comparison here proceeds upon the basis of two distinct assumptions. First, that there are essential principles, structures, procedures and goals which constitute the 'universals' of any legal system (Zweigert and Kötz, 1992: 20). Weigend, for example, asserts that 'some structural components of the criminal process seem to be universal and independent of procedural ideology' (Weigend, 1980: 418). Second, and by implication, it avers that external appearances of difference are no more than surface traits concealing the universal core beneath. According to this view, the task of comparison is to distinguish 'the skeleton common to all modern procedural systems' while revealing 'significant differences in their muscles, viscera, and organs' (Ingraham, 1987: x). This use of zoological analogy should alert us to the dangers of attempting to derive conclusions about human society by adopting the methodological assumptions of natural science.

The universalizing imperative is not confined to comparative studies of procedure or doctrinal law but arises also in respect of parallel approaches to legal culture. The rule of law, the principle of legality, the demands of fairness and the requirement of equality are all adduced as constants of the 'western legal tradition', as if from the fog of local culture one can distil universal legal truths

(Zweigert and Kötz, 1992: 20). Several possible interpretations of this universalizing approach suggest themselves. It may be that it conceals a disguised hegemonic project and that the avowed search for global legal concepts barely cloaks a powerful colonizing impulse. This intellectual imperialism may arise from a covert, perhaps often quite unconscious, assumption of the superiority of our own legal culture as a means of making sense of the world.[3] Or, it may simply be that, as comparative scholars, we derive comfort from seeking out the familiar in alien surroundings and structuring the world in terms derived from our native culture. Unchecked, this impulse leads us to grasp at the apparently like and to leap at similarity in an overeager bid to make sense of the world. It is an impulse which, as others have reminded us (Evans-Pritchard, 1963; Downes, 1988;Nelken, 1992), we would do well to resist. If the comparative project is to produce anything of value we need to develop an acute sensitivity to the peculiarities of the local. There, however, we should not rest like bewildered tourists awed by the unfamiliar and the exotic but go on to discover ways of interpreting and comparing this local knowledge (Nelken, 1994b: 226).

With rare exceptions, we regard one country from the perspective of the other. This partiality places objectivity and neutrality beyond our grasp, for, however dedicated and determined researchers we may be, it is rarely possible to attain equivalent familiarity with two cultures. We are necessarily the child of the one and, at best, the distant cousin of the other. Anthropologists have long attempted to escape this partiality by immersing themselves in the life and culture of the community that they wish to study (Malinowski, 1926), but the 'insider' knowledge promised by such immersion proves elusive. The posthumous publication of the diaries of Bronislaw Malinowski revealed that the master of such techniques was himself often disillusioned and alienated from those he studied (Malinowski, 1967). This raised the disturbing question 'if it isn't, as we had been led to believe, through some sort of extraordinary sensibility, an almost preternatural capacity to think, feel, and perceive like a native ... how is anthropological knowledge possible?' (Geertz, 1983a: 56).

Abandoning the, probably impossible, task of seeking to understand from 'the native's point of view', aspiring comparativists might be better advised to concentrate on the externally observable modes by which the 'natives' construct their social world. Instead of attempting to inhabit the minds of those under scrutiny, this approach would focus on the external form, colour and timbre of legal discourse. If pursued with close attention to the context against which legal debates take place, this approach reveals how legal discourse serves as an interpretive and structuring device – a means by which people seek to make legal 'sense' of conflict, confusion and disorder. Stressing the symbiotic relationship between law and its locality, it develops an avowedly circular account of law as responsive to and constructive of the environment out of which it arises.

Making legal discourse our primary focus raises particular methodological problems of interpretation and transcription. When local articulations of law are rephrased through the vocabularies and grammatical structures of an alien legal language, nuances of meaning and subtleties of intonation may be lost. This raises the puzzle posed by Piers Beirne: 'How then can we render intelligible, in our terms, the values and institutions of another culture, a culture whose language and concepts differ from our own?' (1983:384).[4] Anthropologists have long grappled with the problem of language as one of the unresolved problems of the comparative endeavour (Hooker, 1975:11–12). Bohannan even suggested that they should undertake comparison in the mechanistic neutrality of computer language (quoted in Hooker, 1975:11). This is surely a false solution predicated upon the spurious assumption that there can be a context-free, culturally neutral or universal language. Legal concepts, rules, procedures and institutions, however, are not free-floating entities, unfettered by the vocabulary and grammar which gives expression to them.[5] The languages in which local legal sensibilities are formed and expressed are both products and producers of their environment: language inevitably is culturally specific.

The conclusion that legal discourse is contingent upon local environment and communicable only in its native-tongue, risks slipping into cultural relativism (Beirne, 1983), suggesting that legal norms, rules and practices simply mirror the landscape in which they are situated, reflecting back the political, social or moral pigments of their surroundings. They are perhaps better understood as conscious attempts to impose meaning and order upon chaotic landscapes. Here we might agree with Geertz that 'It is this imaginative, or constructive, or interpretative power, a power rooted in the collective resources of culture rather than in the separate capacities of individuals . . . upon which the comparative study of law, or justice, or forensics, or adjudication should . . . train its attention' (1983b:215). In what follows, this challenge is applied to a comparative analysis of constructions of law and order in Britain and Germany in the hope that juxtaposing the legal discourses of one country against the other may prove illuminative in the ways suggested.

THE POLITICS OF LAW AND ORDER IN BRITAIN AND GERMANY

Law and order debates in Britain and Germany reproduce local assumptions about the role of the state in the maintenance of social order but, as we shall see, they are also determinative of them. In Britain 'law and order' occupies an increasingly important place in political debate. It has a life independent of criminal justice policy and, at times, almost independent of crime itself, embracing a bundle of ideas which have had varying prominence at different moments and from different political perspectives (Downes and Morgan, 1994:183). Conservative Party rhetoric of the past 15 years asserted a determination to induce and enforce in the general population respect for the rule of law (Conservative Party, 1979; Brake and Hale, 1992).

Significantly, in Britain, threats to social stability are largely envisioned as internal to the body politic. Historically crime has been conceived as an issue of social class. Nineteenth-century anxieties about the perishing and dangerous classes[6] may now be expressed in different vocabularies, but the over-riding conviction is that the primary threats to social order come from within and below (Downes and Morgan, 1994:201–2). Youth crime, thanks partly to intense coverage by the British media, is seen as the primary threat to order today.[7] Failure of parental responsibility as a cause of youth crime (Home Office, 1990: 40) is attributed most commonly to those lower down the social scale, to working mothers leaving latchkey kids to fend for themselves or single-parent families abandoned by irresponsible fathers. Discussions about falling moral standards, increasing sexual promiscuity and the breakdown of family life link these micromanifestations of dissolution to wider social transformations and decline (Reiner and Cross, 1991).

The debate in Germany has, until recently, been markedly more muted. The German concept of *Innere Sicherheit* (lit. 'inner security') is suggestively different from its counterpart 'law and order' and warrants further examination (Beste, 1983). Administratively, it connotes that area of public life which is the responsibility of the *Innen Ministerium*.[8] Its role in maintaining internal security parallels that of the German Foreign Office in defending against external threats. Paradoxically, however, the primary threats to internal order are themselves conceptualized as external. This predisposition was fed by the breakup of the Soviet bloc which cast former East European states in the role of exporters of crime to Germany. At the same time, however, within Germany the disruptions accompanying the process of reunification and the *gesellschaftliche Umwälzung* ('social upheaval') in the former East German *Länder* blurred the distinction between internal and external in ways which have important connotations for the concept of *Innere Sicherheit* (Kury, 1992a).

Another significant contrast is that *Innere Sicherheit*, unlike law and order, refers less to public manifestations of moral or political disorder than to perceived threats to individual and collective feelings of security. *Innere Sicherheit* does convey something of 'order' but, unlike its British counterpart, this order lies largely in the subjective perception of the individual (Arnold, 1993). As such it is regularly used by criminologists and opinion pollsters in Germany seeking to establish perceptions of safety levels within the community, of personal safety and, more narrowly, of fear of crime (Kury et al., 1992b). That debates about law and order should be constructed around public feelings of insecurity reflects the normative presumption that the law's purpose is to foster social integration. Public expressions of insecurity are thus considered to be an indicator of disintegration and represent a failure of law (Heiland, 1992: 46). Thus, whereas in Britain discourses of law and order and debates about fear of crime are distinguishable and far from mutually dependent, in Germany the two are encapsulated in a single term. *Innere Sicherheit* seems to embrace the public and the personal, state and private concerns about order and disorder.

CONSTRUCTIONS OF DISORDER

These differences in national discourses of law and order have interesting implications for the ways in which sources of disorder are identified and the 'crime problem' itself is constructed. In Britain, crime is associated with specific social groups, in particular the young, the poor and unemployed, certain ethnic minorities (though significantly not others) and, increasingly, those whose lifestyle or activities are deemed to threaten public order. This last group was made the particular focus of the Criminal Justice and Public Order Act 1994, described as 'a comprehensive toughening up of the law relating to those with marginal or somewhat unorthodox lifestyles – squatters, new age travellers and Gypsies as well as more mainstream dissenters and protestors who engage in aggravated trespass' (Smith, 1995:19). The much vaunted endorsement of 'traditional' values of self-reliance, respect for property and respectability under Conservative ideology fosters an 'increasing intolerance ... towards those minorities who pursue lifestyles that deviate from the supposed "norm" whether through choice or circumstance' (Campbell, 1995:36). These groups are clearly located within British society, though some, whether by virtue of their poverty, ethnic origin or lifestyle are ascribed marginal status. Significantly, for the purposes of comparison, while socially or even morally, these groups may be posited as nominal outsiders, there is little question as to their national identity.

Perceptions of what constitute prevailing crime problems derive in part from the identification of these groups as a source of potential menace. In part too, they are the product of extensive coverage by British media of public-order problems, interpersonal and sexual offences and even routine offences of car theft, household burglary and petty theft. Although general perceptions of threats to social order are fed by a daily diet of crime extensively reported in the British press, what constitutes the subject of prevailing interest or concern at any given time varies. Too often it is determined by media-inspired 'moral panics'[9] or the occurrence of unusual or particularly horrifying crimes which attract enormous media coverage.[10] This intensity of reporting has several consequences: it distorts public perceptions (particularly concerning the prevalence of serious crimes) and raises public anxiety out of line with actual risk (Hough and Mayhew, 1983:23; Maxfield, 1984:3); it fuels a public debate highly populist in tone and has a disproportionate impact on the development of criminal justice policy.

In Germany, by contrast, the mass of traditional crimes which so preoccupy in Britain draw comparatively little media coverage. Crime-related stories occupy much less space in press, radio and television reporting and, as a consequence, attract less political attention and fewer resources. The result, according to one academic commentator, is that 'police investigation of these acts and actual prosecution of offenders is near zero' (Hassemer, 1993). We can only speculate how far this apparent absence of political will and concurrent decline in enforcement depresses the crime statistics, further reinforcing the impression that traditional types of crime no longer threaten social order. An obvious difficulty here is how one might render comparable the quantity, quality and impact of media reporting of crime stories in the two countries.[11] Even if one could satisfactorily count airtime or the column inches of national newspapers, what might it signify? Media coverage might owe as much to the structure of press ownership or the legal constraints upon broadcasting companies as to popular or political interest. More elusive still is the impact of the media on public perceptions of what threatens social order, property or personal integrity.

To say that crime is little reported is not to deny that crime is a matter of political moment in Germany. Germany's supposed vulnerability at the crossroads between former East and West Europe makes it an obvious target for cross-border crimes. The continuing influx of immigrants from developing and East European countries, arising partly from social upheaval there and partly from the relative openness of German immigration policies, is deemed to constitute a major threat to social stability in Germany today. Those who come as *Ausländer* continue to be identified as such, however long they remain in the country. Thus the much-debated problem of *Ausländerkriminalität* has become a conceptual 'hold-all' not only for offences committed by foreigners but for those by immigrants, asylum seekers and even by those born in Germany but, for example, of Turkish descent (Walter and Kubink, 1993). The threat they are deemed to pose to traditional moral and social order is thus constructed as external or, at very least, foreign despite the geographical location of these groups *within* Germany.[12] Curiously, the rising number of violent attacks on foreigners by German nationals contrive to excite grave moral concern (Gehrmann et al., 1994) and yet also to feed the perception that foreigners are themselves concurrently both focus and source of disorder. Despite its lack of conceptual clarity, *Ausländerkriminalität* is widely invoked, particularly by the media, and only rarely subject to critical scrutiny (P-A. Albrecht, 1994).

As one might anticipate, quite a different body of offences captures the political imagination in Germany. International and organized crime most dramatically threatens the German sense of *Innere Sicherheit*, and it is with smuggling, money-laundering, drug-trafficking, complex fraud and offences against immigration laws that parallel political debates are engrossed (Hassemer, 1992, 1994). These crimes, not mugging or joy-riding or trespass, preoccupy, despite the fact that, unlike everyday property or public-order offences, they are far removed from the experience of ordinary Germans.

Constructions of crime and, more particularly, of what threatens order are clearly very different in Britain and Germany and their respective preoccupations inform and shape both political debate and criminal justice policy. There is, here, an acknowledged circularity in that perceptions of what threatens law and order themselves determine the allocation of police resources, the practice of the courts and the direction of legislative programmes. These in turn ensure that it is those types of crime which most preoccupy which are most vigorously policed and most commonly prosecuted. This self-reinforcing logic makes it impossible to test domestic perceptions of disorder against the 'truth' of criminal statistics, for these may be as much an indicator of political will as of any social reality. As David Nelken observes,

> the problem of finding cross cultural criteria for isolating and identifying such variables for the purpose of demonstrating differences in legal culture is not merely technical. Such variables as rates of crime . . . are already the product of (unknown) cultural processes which make it impossible to use them to explain cultural differences. (1994a)

In accepting that apparently objective variables like crime statistics are themselves social constructs, we should not deny their illuminative potential

Criminal Policy Making

LUCIA ZEDNER

altogether. Read less as the facts of crime but rather as indices of public perception, policing practices and judicial response, statistics have quite a different story to tell about the nature of local legal culture.

SOURCES OF SOCIAL ORDER

In both Britain and Germany, the increasing pace of social change is seen to threaten those institutions historically considered essential to the maintenance of social order (Brake and Hale, 1992; Kury, 1992a). Disorder both manifests itself in and is simultaneously intensified by disruptions to family, church, school and community. Dwindling numbers of households organized around traditional family structures, declining church attendance and the dissolution of once stable communities are all adduced as signals and sources of social disruption.[13] There are, however, significant differences in how and where these disruptions are located within the political rhetoric of crime control in the two countries. These differences are best illustrated by examining the location and attribution of responsibility for the maintenance of order in recent British and German debates.

Traditionally, debates about order maintenance in Britain focused primarily on the role of the state. Over the past decade, however, the British government itself increasingly sought to divest itself of this responsibility. Families, schools, churches and the media have all been encouraged to recognize their potential contribution in upholding social stability and repairing the 'moral fabric' (Shapland and Nuttall, 1993: 163). In the 1983 general election, the Conservative Party manifesto declared 'It is teachers and parents – and television producers too – who influence the moral standards of the next generation' (Conservative Party, 1983). The message here was clear: that as a society we could no longer expect the onus for maintaining order to lie solely with central government nor with the formal agencies of criminal justice (Crawford, 1994: 498–9). An interdepartmental circular published in the following year was hailed as a landmark in expressing the government's view that preventing crime was 'not simply a matter for the police' (Home Office, 1984; Bottoms, 1990: 3). This shift was variously interpreted. On one view it rests on a genuine belief in the potential of informal mechanisms of social control to solve problems which lie 'deep in society'. On another, more sceptical, view it represents a covert admission of the failure of governmental strategies to combat rising crime rates, to prevent the decline of the inner city or to avert industrial unrest (Lacey and Zedner, 1995: 305).

This more pessimistic interpretation recognizes the political dangers inherent in the high-profile law and order discourse of the 1980s. Having raised awareness and expectations in this regard, the government found its political credibility imperilled when its own law and order policies failed to work. Diffusing political responsibility out from the formal apparatuses of the legal system to the community, by supporting informal and voluntarist efforts and by encouraging citizens to protect themselves, to engage in crime prevention and to co-operate with community-based penalties, served to deflect attention from government (King, 1989). Since the mid-1980s, the British public have been ever more loudly encouraged to participate in local Neighbourhood Watch schemes, to buy home-security devices and alarms, to secure their personal property and to modify their behaviour in ways which might limit their exposure to risk (Brake and Hale, 1992: 11; Home Office, 1989). Evoking notions of 'active citizenship' this rhetoric has sought to promote a greater sense of responsibility for maintaining order within the community and to foster active co-operation with the formal agencies of policing in responding to crime. Public-information literature carrying slogans such as 'Together we can crack crime' invite public participation in activities once largely reserved to the police (Home Office, 1989). More insidiously, rising-crime rates are repackaged as providing evidence not of the failure of law enforcement but of the negligence of the general public in protecting their property and persons.

In Germany, by contrast, the stark divide between notions of public and private responsibility for order maintenance remains strong. The Welfare State is largely intact and its functions, including the maintenance of social order, are for the state alone. To quote one German observer: 'Germans are *staatsgläubig*, they place their trust in government institutions and kow-tow to authority' (Glatzer et al., 1992: 238; see also Damaska, 1986). In turn the powers of the state are, at least at a rhetorical level, enshrined in and delimited by law. When compared to the British, Germans seem to have higher expectations of government and to evince great faith in the *Rechtstaat* which reserves regulation firmly to the legal sphere (Eser, 1989: 14).[14] As the responsibility of the state, order and the sanctioning of those who threaten its preservation must be pursued consistently (von Hirsch and Jareborg, 1991). The consequence is that the potential for informal crime control has, historically at least, been very little debated (H-J. Albrecht, 1993: 40; Vahlenkamp, 1989).

Confronting the prevailing paradigm of the *Rechttsstaat* are emerging discussions about the possibilities of *lokale Justiz*. Of a very different key to debates about the role of community in Britain, *lokale Justiz* recognizes the declining capacity of the state to ensure *Innere Sicherheit* at the very same time that demands by the public for greater security become more insistent (Heiland, 1992: 46). They recognize also that social problems vary by locality and that the values and interests of society are also locally dependent.[15] In part, this new discourse merely reflects existing practice: police react differently to drug-taking on the streets of large cities than they do in rural areas. In part, it arises also from recognition that crime problems can effectively be studied only at the local level and that solutions to them must necessarily also be sensitive to local conditions and local needs (H-J. Albrecht, 1992: 40 ff; Karger, 1992). This approach is not only methodologically important but, necessarily, has implications for the development of the *Kriminalpolitik*.

Quite how the informality and fragmentation promised by appeals to the local can be squared with continuing adherence to demands of legality is currently the subject of some debate (P-A. Albrecht, 1988). In Germany, however, calls for *lokale Justiz* do not entail direct involvement of the community of the sort implied by British penal discourse. Partly because the charity or voluntary sector is underdeveloped by British standards (Glazter et al., 1992: 90–5), partly because historically, there has been relatively little involvement of lay elements in the criminal justice process[16] and, perhaps, most importantly, because issues of social order are thought to be matters to be resolved at the level of the *Länder* (H-J. Albrecht, 1993: 41), there has been little discussion about the possible role of the community in this respect. Thus much which in Britain would be described as 'community crime prevention' or 'punishment in the community' is in Germany the preserve of criminal justice professionals. Diversion initiatives (*Diversion*), mediation projects (*Täter-Opfer-Ausgleich*) and community service schemes (*Gemeinützige Arbeit*) abound in Germany but with little lay involvement and little explicit discussion of their relationship to the communities they serve (H-J. Albrecht, 1992: 35). Nor would it be thought appropriate for the state to resign its responsibilities to nonprofessionals or volunteers.

Another reason for the continuing reservation of policing activities to the state is that, as we have seen, the primary focus of political concern lies with categories of crime different from those in Britain. Whereas advocating citizen foot-patrols makes some sense as a means of combating street offences, such as car theft and domestic burglary, such measures would be patently inappropriate to meet prevailing concerns in Germany about organized crimes such as fraud, money-laundering and drug-trafficking (Gropp, 1993). Such crimes, often highly sophisticated, complex and largely hidden from public view, suggest quite other tactics. Moreover, their gravity and the threat which they are deemed to pose to the security of the state justify powerful countermeasures. Long-term intelligence-gathering and police surveillance, extensive telephone-tapping, data collection, computerized descriptive profile-searching, undercover operations and the protection of witnesses all form part of the so-called *Grosser Lauschangriff* ('Great Bugging Operation') which is currently said to be central to German criminal justice practice.[17]

Some telling comparisons may be made between the prevailing discourse in the two countries. Many of the most widely publicized and most often-discussed crime-control initiatives in Britain are unashamedly low tech, involving no more than the invitation to citizens to 'walk with a purpose'.[18] By contrast the 'Great Bugging Operation' in Germany promotes high-tech state of the art strategies carried out by professional surveillance and intelligence officers. Whereas the foot-patrols and community-based initiatives forwarded in Britain are visible and largely reserved to the public sphere, the surveillance strategies now being promoted in Germany are avowedly covert. As a corollary, whereas recent crime-control initiatives in Britain reserve their gaze to the public activities of those surveyed, those in Germany have the potential, at least, to intrude into the most private moments of citizens' lives. Whereas crime control in Britain is increasingly said to be the responsibility of private citizens, private organizations and that amorphous entity the 'community', in Germany these activities are reserved not only to the state but increasingly to an alliance between criminal and intelligence services.[19]

At the level of political rhetoric, these contrasts are impressive, but we would do well neither to overdraw them nor to assume that they reflect similarly sharp contrasts in actual practice. British police also employ undercover-surveillance techniques and maintain extensive computerized databases. German police still undertake traditional patrols seeking out traditional crimes. The striking difference, however, is that these practices attract little political interest or media debate in either country.

IMPLICATIONS FOR CRIMINAL JUSTICE

Whereas, in the late 1980s, the prevailing discourse of criminal justice policy in Britain was generally liberal in tone, a dramatic shift in political mood (both within the Cabinet and the Home Office) in the early 1990s ensured a sharp change in direction. The avowed commitment to parsimony in the use of penal sanctions, which culminated in the Criminal Justice Act 1991, was displaced by a bald reassertion of confidence in imprisonment. Since the re-election of the Conservative Party in 1992, the government has pressed for greater certainty of punishment and the imposition of harsher penalties on the grounds that offenders were too often allowed to get away without sanction. This swing was intensified by the arrival in the office of Home Secretary of Michael Howard who, at the 1993 Conservative Party Conference, announced an action plan proposing 27 separate changes to the law. In support of these changes he declared in a fiercely populist speech:

> The silent majority have become the angry majority. . . . You have shown that only the Conservative Party can give that majority a voice. . . . In the last 30 years, the balance in the criminal justice system has been tilted too far in favour of the criminal and against the protection of the public. The time has come to put that right. I want to make sure it is criminals that are frightened, not law-abiding members of the public.[20]

Opposition parties, fearful that they would be seen as 'soft on crime' and in a tactical bid to wrest the mantle of law and order from the Conservatives, also shifted rhetorical key. The Labour Party declared itself 'tough on crime and tough on the causes of crime' (Labour Party, 1993: 13). Although the slogan alludes to the social circumstances which give rise to offending, the declaration would seem an unprecedented endorsement of punitive policies by a party of the Left in Britain.

This shift in discursive approach across the political spectrum manifests itself in various concrete consequences. The courts appear to have responded to perceived public demands by handing down tougher noncustodial and longer custodial sentences. The prison population has risen steadily since the end of 1992 and is likely to rise further.[21] The Criminal Justice and Public Order Act 1994, promoted at the Conservative Party Conference 1993 as a means of giving 'greater protection for communities, property owners and private citizens', introduced an array of new offences and increased sentences for many existing ones.[22] Yet again, the Labour Party not only failed to oppose the passage of the bill but gave their active support.[23]

More generally, community penalties have been condemned on the question-able grounds that they 'have failed to command the confidence of the public' (Home Office, 1995:11) and are to be made 'tough and demanding' leaving offenders 'wet, tired and hungry' (Criminal Justice Minister David Maclean, quoted in *The Guardian* 13 October 1994; Home Office, 1995). Similarly, custodial sentences are no longer reviled as 'an expensive way of making bad people worse' (Home Secretary Douglas Hurd speaking in 1990) but warmly applauded on the highly questionable grounds that 'prison works' (Home Secretary Michael Howard speaking in 1993). This extraordinary shift in rhetorical key is not reflective of some new-found faith in the instrument of the prison but rather reproduces a significant change in the perceived goals of incarceration. The prison 'works', but in one limited sense only: it excludes from society those who threaten its security. In this respect, the prevailing political rhetoric is explicitly and avowedly disintegrative.

In Germany, by contrast, parallel social elites have, at least until very recently, pressed for movement in broadly the opposite direction. Decriminalization, decarceration, waiving of sanctions, mitigation of sentences, diversion, medi-ation and reparation have been the primary currency of penal debate over the past decade. In the early 1980s, German prosecutors and judges resolved to reduce the prison population and secured a steady fall of about 3.5 percent per annum over the next five years (Graham, 1990:150), without any legal change or intervention by politicians, academics or the media.[24] Moreover, whereas in Britain the assertion, made with increasing vigour, that 'society deserves a rest' from the depredations of offenders has been invoked to justify increasing recourse to exclusionary custodial sanctions, in Germany penal policy-making has been oriented instead toward 'shaping a system of sanctions in a manner as minimally destructive as was unavoidably necessary and as favourable to social reintegration as was feasible' (Eser, 1989:14). Thus *General Prävention* as a central aim of German penal law was distinctively cast as embracing reintegrative aims (Kaiser, 1988:10). This approach has been challenged by recent political developments.

A central issue of current debate is how far earlier liberal aspirations can and will be maintained in the aftermath of reunification. Increases in fear of crime and the perception of risk (particularly in the new Federal states) are arguably more telling pressures than actual rises in crime.[25] Discussions about the social causes of crime and the rehabilitative potential of penal orders have receded (P-A. Albrecht, 1994:265). In their place are increasingly strident demands for the toughening of criminal law, procedures and penal sanctions. This swing was promoted primarily by the Catholic Democratic Union (CDU, 1994) but supported for the first time also by the Social Democratic Party (SPD). The SPD voted, for example, in support of powers permitting extensions to the electronic surveillance of suspected criminals under recent legislation.[26] As in Britain, the valuable political capital vested in securing public acceptance as a party capable of combating crime has, it would seem, proved an irresistible lure even for parties of the Left. In their demands for the introduction of tougher measures to fight crime, the politicians found widespread support among the police at every level

(Hassemer, 1994: 333). Support has come also from the Federal Criminal Office (*Bundeskriminalamt*), from the Criminal Offices of the *Länder* and from the police unions. Equally predictable, opposition has come both from civil liberties organizations and from academics critical of the extension of state powers entailed (Lisken, 1994). Their impact, however, has been limited. Unlike in Britain where opposition to the 1994 Criminal Justice and Public Order Act (outside the House of Commons) was vociferous, the *Verbrechensbekämpfungsgesetz* 1994 provoked little public debate and no public demonstrations or protests. The immediate outlook is similarly quiescent, as one German professor observed 'I see no sign of the discussion moving back into a more basic rights-orientated phase'.[27]

CONCLUSION

In this article, I began from the premise that comparative research may enable us better to understand the complex relationship between legal and 'local' culture or what Clifford Geertz somewhat inelegantly, but aptly, terms 'legal imminglement' (1983b: 215). Throughout the article, comparison has been used to illustrate the ways in which legal discourse is both reflective and simultaneously constructive of its local environment. By juxtaposing differing legal sensibilities, namely the discourses of law and order in Britain and Germany, I have tried to show how they may be used as reciprocal commentaries upon each other. Juxtaposition is no substitute for analysis, but it does reveal the illuminative possibilities of comparison. Allowing the one to act as a foil to the other serves to highlight aspects of the two domestic debates which, I suggest, might otherwise have remained in shadow, unremarked.

NOTES

This article was originally presented at the Workshop on 'Comparing Legal Cultures', University of Macerata, Italy, 18–20 May 1994 and owes much to discussions there with David Nelken and the participants of the Workshop. It arises from a project on 'Social Order, Criminal Justice and the Appeal to Community in England and Germany' currently being carried out with Nicola Lacey, Birkbeck College, London, as part of the Economic and Social Science Research Council (ESRC) 'Crime and Social Order' programme. Many of my ideas were stimulated by fruitful discussions with Nicola Lacey. I would also like to thank our research assistant Michael Jasch; Gerhard Dannemann, University of Oxford; Brad Sherman and Michael Power, London School of Economics; and Hans-Jörg Albrecht, University of Dresden. I am grateful to the Max Planck Gesellschaft for awarding me a research stipend and with it the opportunity to spend a sabbatical at the Max Planck Institut, Freiburg, in 1993.

1. Stanley Cohen, with his customary perspicacity, made this the theme of his lecture 'Crime and Politics: Spot the Difference', the London School of Economics Centenary Lectures in Law and Society, 9 May 1995.
2. This realization appears to be a powerful motivation of much legal anthropology and it is to this literature I turn in seeking methodological and conceptual guidance.

3.   As Hill observes: 'the Western legal tradition reveals a strong commitment to certain values, such as individual liberty, freedom of contract, and private property, and while Zweigert and Kötz do not expressly endorse these values, they nonetheless take them for granted' (1989: 106).

4.   Beirne goes on to conclude: 'we can only understand the social life of other cultures through the prism of our own linguistic and conceptual apparatus' (1983: 385).

5.   As Gadamer observes 'We can only think in a language, and just this residing of our thinking in a language is the profound enigma that language presents to thought' (1976: 62).

6.   Terms used first by mid-nineteenth-century social commentators like Mary Carpenter and Henry Mayhew to denote those strata at the very bottom of the social order whose members threatened, or were perilously close to threatening, the security of those above.

7.   As, indeed, it has been historically. See Part 4 'Making Sense of "Law and Order" Myth' in Pearson, 1983.

8.   Which, significantly, publishes a journal entitled *Innere Sicherheit*.

9.   A term coined by Stan Cohen in respect of annual street-fighting between Mods and Rockers in British seaside resorts (Cohen, 1972), but which has been successively applied to the 'mugging crisis' of the 1970s (Hall et al., 1978), to the 'Cleveland affair' concerning the sexual abuse of children in the 1980s, and to outbreaks of car theft and 'joy-riding' by the youth of deprived housing estates in the early 1990s.

10. An obvious example here is the killing of two-year-old James Bulger early in 1993 by two young school boys. Both at the time of its occurrence and during the protracted trial which followed, the case attracted blanket coverage by all news media.

11. Nelken provides some important insights into the difficulties of 'measuring' legal culture (Nelken, 1994a).

12. In a fascinating account of the political discourse of protest-policing in 1980s Berlin, della Porta describes how the violent demonstrators who threatened public order were described 'as young criminals, *Chaoten* that came from *outside* Berlin in search for violence' (emphasis added) (della Porta, 1993: 11).

13. Although these changes may be overplayed by reference to romanticized visions of past social institutions which were never quite so cohesive, supportive or restraining as their protagonists would have us believe (Davidoff, 1976: 144).

14. Coupled to the notion of the *Rechtsstaat* is that of the *Sozialstaat*, which secures to the state full responsibility for social governance and has, according to one view, provided the grounds for increasing intervention by the state into the social body (P-A. Albrecht, 1988).

15. Discussions about significant variance in the characteristics, politics and values of the *Länder* may even raise doubts about using the nation-state as unit of comparison.

16. With the exception of the work of *Laienrichter* and *Schöffen*, the criminal justice system is highly professionalized. The police too see themselves as a highly professionalized force of crime-fighters with a history very different from the ancestry of the British bobby as a 'good citizen in uniform'.

17. All the German contributors to a day conference on 'Punishment and Politics in Britain and Germany', Goethe Institut, London, June 1994, were anxious to stress the centrality of the *Grosser Lauschangriff* to current German *Kriminalpolitik*.

18. In 1993, Home Secretary Michael Howard urged Britain's 115,000 Neighbourhood Watch Schemes to mount civilian street patrols – a proposal which provoked a furious response from senior police who condemned this as an invitation to vigilantism. 'Vigilantes urged as police strength cut' *The Guardian* (6 December).

19. Laws safeguarding the division between criminal and political intelligence gathering have been severely eroded; under the *Verbrechensbekämpfungsgesetz* (1994), German secret-service agents are allowed to pass on information disclosed by telephone monitoring in foreign countries to the police and prosecution service.
20. Howard speaking at the Conservative Party Conference 1993.
21. The prison population rose between November 1992 and November 1994 by 7501 (17 percent) and by March 1995 stood at 51,243, exceeding its previous all time high in 1987. The prison population is currently projected to reach 56,000 by 2002.
22. For example, offences relating to squatting, trespass, mass assembly and many other aspects of public order, to poaching and to fisheries, to the misuse of drugs and firearms.
23. Labour leader Tony Blair declared 'we do not oppose the strengthening of the criminal justice system – on the contrary we actively support measures that actively strengthen the system' (quoted in *The Guardian* 8 October 1994).
24. Though they were certainly applauded in their efforts by many academics (Feest, 1988; Kaiser, 1990).
25. On the lack of fit between actual risks and levels of fear see interview with Helmut Kury 'Die Angst vor Verbrechen übertrifft die Wirklichkeit' *Frankfürter Allgemeine Zeitung* (19 January 1995), p. 10.
26. *Gesetz zur Bekämpfung der organisierten Kriminalität* the 'Act for Combating Organized Crime' (1992) and the *Verbrechensbekämpfungsgesetz* the 'Suppression of Crime Act' (1994).
27. Professor Winfried Hassemer speaking at the day conference on 'Punishment and Politics in Britain and Germany', Goethe Institut, London, June 1994.

References

Albrecht, H-J. (1992) 'Gemeinde und Kriminalität', pp. 33–54 in H. Kury (ed.) *Gesellschaftliche Umwälzung: Kriminalitätserfarhungen, Straffälligkeit und soziale Kontrolle*. Freiburg: Eigenverlag Max Planck.
Albrecht, H-J. (1993) 'The State of Knowledge in the Federal Republic of Germany', pp. 33–47 in P. Robert (ed.) *Crime and Prevention Policy*. Freiburg: Eigenverlag Max Planck.
Albrecht, P-A. (1988) 'Das Strafrecht auf dem Weg vom liberalen Rechtsstaat zum sozialen Interventionsstaat', *Krit V*: 182–209.
Albrecht, P-A. (1994) 'Das Strafrecht im Zugriff populisticher Politik', *Strafverteidiger* 5: 265–9.
Arnold, H. (1993) 'Kriminalität, Viktimisierung, (Un-)Sicherheitsgefühl und Wohnzufriedenheit', pp. 1–33 in G. Kaiser and H. Kury (eds) *Kriminologische Forschung in den 90er Jahren*. Freiburg: Eigenverlag Max Planck.
Association Internationale De Droit Pénale (1981) *The Criminal Justice System of the Federal Republic of Germany*. Toulouse: Érès.
Barak-Glantz, I. L. and E. H. Johnson (1981) *Comparative Criminology*. Beverly Hills, CA: Sage.
Beirne, P. (1983) 'Cultural Relativism and Comparative Criminology', *Contemporary Crises* 7: 371–91.
Beirne, P. and J. Hill (1991) *Comparative Criminology: An Annotated Bibliography*. New York: Greenwood Press.
Beste, H. (1983) *Innere Sicherheit und Sozialforschung*. Münster: Lit Verlag.
Bottoms, A. (1990) 'Crime Prevention Facing the 1990s', *Policing and Society* 1: 3–22.
Brake, M. and C. Hale (1992) *Public Order and Private Lives: The Politics of Law and Order*. London: Routledge.

Burnham, R. W. (1993) 'The Promise and the Perils of Comparative Criminology', *Howard Journal of Criminal Justice* 23: 67–72.
CDU (1994) *'Offensive 2000' Innere Sicherheit und Verbrechensbekämpfung*. Bonn: CDU.
Campbell, S. (1995) 'Gypsies: The Criminalisation of a Way of Life?', *Criminal Law Review* 28–37.
Cohen, S. (1972) *Folk Devils and Moral Panics: The Creation of the Mods and Rockers*. London: MacGibbon & Kee.
Cole, G. F. et al. (eds) (1987) *Major Criminal Justice Systems: A Comparative Survey*. Beverly Hills, CA: Sage.
Conservative Party (1979) *The Conservative Manifesto*. London: Conservative Party.
Conservative Party (1983) *The Challenge of Our Times*. London: Conservative Party.
Crawford, A. (1994) 'The Partnership Approach to Community Crime Prevention: Corporatism at the Local Level?', *Social & Legal Studies* 3(4): 497–519.
Damaska, M. (1986) *The Faces of Justice and State Authority*. New Haven, CT: Yale University Press.
Davidoff, L. et al. (1976) 'Landscape with Figures: Home and Community in English Society', in A. Oakley and J. Mitchell (eds) *The Rights and Wrongs of Women*. Harmondsworth: Penguin.
della Porta, D. (1993) 'The Political Discourse on Protest Policing: Italy and Germany from the 1960s to the 1980s'. Unpublished paper.
Downes, D. (1988) *Contrasts in Tolerance: Post-War Penal Policy in the Netherlands and England and Wales*. Oxford: Oxford University Press.
Downes, D. and R. Morgan (1994) 'Hostages to Fortune? The Politics of Law and Order in Post-War Britain', pp. 183–232 in M. Maguire et al. (eds) *The Oxford Handbook of Criminology*. Oxford: Oxford University Press.
Eser, A. (1989) 'A Century of Penal Legislation in Germany', pp. 1–26 in A. Eser and J. Thormundsson (eds) *Old Ways and New Needs in Criminal Legislation*. Freiburg: Eigenverlag Max Planck.
Eser, A. and B. Huber (1985, 1987, 1990) *Strafrechtsentwicklung in Europa, Volumes 1, 2, 3*. Freiburg: Eigenverlag Max Planck.
Evans-Pritchard, E. E. (1963) *The Comparative Method in Social Anthropology*. London: Althone Press.
Feest, J. (1988) *Reducing the West German Prison Population: Lessons from the West German Experience*. London: NACRO Occasional Paper.
Gadamer, H-G. (1976) 'Man and Language', pp. 59–68 in H-G. Gadamer (ed.) *Philosophical Hermeneutics*. Berkeley, CA: University of California Press.
Geertz, C. (1983a) '"From the Native's Point of View": On the Nature of Anthropological Understanding', in C. Geertz *Local Knowledge: Further Essays in Interpretive Anthropology*. New York: Basic Books.
Geertz, C. (1983b) 'Local Knowledge: Fact and Law in Comparative Perspective', pp. 167–234 in C. Geertz, *Local Knowledge: Further Essays in Interpretive Anthropology*. New York: Basic Books.
Geertz, C. (1988) *Works and Lives: The Anthropologist as Author*. Oxford: Polity Press.
Geertz, C. (1993) 'Thick Description: Toward an Interpretive Theory of Culture', pp. 3–30 in C. Geertz (ed.) *The Interpretation of Cultures*. London: Fontana.
Gehrmann, W. et al. (1994) 'Bürger im Zugzwang', *Die Zeit*: 17–22.
Glatzer, W., K. O. Hondrich, H-H. Noll, K. Stiehr and B. Wörndl (1992) *Recent Social Trends in West Germany 1960–1990*. Frankfurt: Campus Verlag.
Graham, J. (1990) 'Decarceration in the Federal Republic of Germany', *British Journal of Criminology* 30: 150–70.
Hall, S. et al. (1978) *Policing the Crisis: Mugging, the State, and Law and Order*. London: Macmillan.

Gropp, W. (ed.) (1993) *Besondere Ermittlungsmaßnahmen zur Bekämpfung der Organisierten Kriminalität.* Freiburg: Eigenverlag Max Planck.

Hassemer, W. (1992) 'Kennzeichen und Krisen des modernen Strafrechts', *Zeitschrift für Rechtspolitik* 10: 378–83.

Hassemer, W. (1993) 'Danger Cannot Justify All Countermeasures', *Die Zeit*, 3 December.

Hassemer, W. (1994) 'Aktuelle Perspektiven der Kriminalpolitik', *Strafverteidiger* 6: 333.

Heidensohn, F. (1991) 'Introduction: Convergence, Diversity and Change', pp. 3–13 in F. Heidensohn and M. Farrell (eds) *Crime in Europe.* London: Routledge.

Heiland, H-G. (1992) 'Modern Patterns of Crime and Control in the Federal Republic of Germany', pp. 45–67 in H-G. Heiland et al. (eds) *Crime and Control in Comparative Perspective.* Berlin: De Gruyter.

Heiland, H-G., L. I. Shelley and H. Katoh (eds) (1992) *Crime and Control in Comparative Perspective.* Berlin: De Gruyter.

Herrmann, J. (1987) 'The Federal Republic of Germany', in G. F. Cole et al. (eds) *Major Criminal Justice Systems.* Beverley Hills, CA: Sage.

Hill, J. (1989) 'Comparative Law, Law Reform and Legal Theory', *Oxford Journal of Legal Studies* 9: 101–15.

Home Office (1984) *Crime Prevention.* HO Circular 8/1984. London: Home Office.

Home Office (1989) *Practical Ways to Crack Crime: The Handbook.* London: HMSO.

Home Office (1990) *Crime, Justice and Protecting the Public: The Government's Proposals for Legislation.* London: HMSO.

Home Office (1995) *Strengthening Punishment in the Community: A Consultation Document.* London: HMSO.

Hooker, M. B. (1975) *Legal Pluralism: An Introduction to Colonial and Non-Colonial Laws.* Oxford: Clarendon Press.

Hough, M. and P. Mayhew (1983) *The British Crime Survey: First Report.* London: HMSO.

Ingraham, B. L. (1987) *The Structure of Criminal Procedure.* London: Greenwood.

Kaiser, G. (1988) 'Criminology in the Federal Republic of Germany in the 1980s', pp. 3–15 in G. Kaiser, H. Kury and H-J. Albrecht (eds) *Criminological Research in the 80s and beyond.* Freiburg: Eigenverlag Max Planck.

Kaiser, G. (1990) 'Recent Developments in Criminalization and Decriminalization in West German Penal Policy', *EuroCriminology* 3: 27–45.

Karger, T. (1992) 'Vergleichende Kriminalitätsforschung: National repräsentative versus Gemeinde-Stichproben', pp. 99–113 in H. Kury (ed.) *Gesellschaftliche Umwälzung: Kriminalitätserfahrungen, Straffälligkeit und soziale Kontrolle.* Freiburg: Eigenverlag Max Planck.

King, M. (1989) 'Social Crime Prevention à la Thatcher', *The Howard Journal* 28(4): 291–312.

Kury, H. (ed.) (1992a) *Gesellschaftliche Umwälzung: Kriminalitätserfahrungen, Straffälligkeit und soziale Kontrolle.* Freiburg: Eigenverlag Max Planck.

Kury, H. et al. (1992b) *Opferfahrungen und Meinungen zur Inneren Sicherheit in Deutschland.* Wiesbaden: Bundeskriminalamt.

Labour Party (1993) *Partners against Crime: Labour's New Approach to Tackling Crime and Creating Safer Communities.* London: Labour Party.

Lacey, N. (1995) 'Contingency and Criminalisation', pp. 1–27 in I. Loveland (ed.) *The Frontiers of Criminality.* London: Sweet & Maxwell.

Lacey, N. and L. Zedner (1995) 'Discourses of Community in Criminal Justice', *Journal of Law and Society.* 22: 301–25.

Langbein, J. (1974) 'Controlling Prosecutorial Discretion in Germany', *University of Chicago Law Review* 41: 439–67.

Langbein, J. (1978) *Comparative Criminal Procedure: Germany.* Paul, MN: West Publishing Co.

Langbein, J. and L. Weinreb (1978) 'Continental Criminal Procedure: Myth and Reality', *Yale Law Journal* 87: 1549–69.

Leigh, L. H. and L. Zedner (1992) *The Royal Commission on Criminal Justice Research Study No. 1: The Administration of Criminal Justice in the Pre-Trial Phase in France and Germany*. London: HMSO.

Lisken, H. (1994) '"Sicherheit" durch "Kriminalitätsbekämpfung"', *Zeitschrift für Rechtspolitik* 2: 49–52.

Malinowski, B. (1926) *Crime and Custom in Savage Society*. New York: Kegan Paul.

Malinowski, B. (1967) *A Diary in the Strict Sense of the Term*. London: Athlone Press, (reprinted 1989).

Maxfield, M. G. (1984) *Fear of Crime in England and Wales*. Home Office Research Study no. 78. London: HMSO.

Müller-Dietz, H. (1993) 'Die soziale Wahrnehmung von Kriminalität', *Neue Zeitschrift für Strafrecht* 2: 57–65.

Nelken, D. (1987) 'Criminal Law and Criminal Justice: Some Notes on Their Irrelation', pp. 139–75 in I. Dennis (ed.) *Criminal Law and Criminal Justice*. London: Sweet & Maxwell.

Nelken, D. (1992) 'Law and Disorder: A Letter from Italy', *Socio-Legal Newsletter* 8: 6.

Nelken, D. (1994a) 'Can Legal Culture Be Measured? A Theoretical Agenda', paper presented at the Workshop on 'Comparing Legal Cultures', University of Macerata, Italy 18–20 May 1994. Forthcoming in D. Nelken (ed.) *Comparing Legal Cultures*. Aldershot: Dartmouth.

Nelken, D. (1994b) 'Whom Can You Trust? The Futures of Comparative Criminology', pp. 220–43 in D. Nelken (ed.) *The Futures of Criminology*. London: Sage.

Pearson, G. (1983) *Hooligan: A History of Respectable Fears*. London: Macmillan.

Reiner, R. and M. Cross (eds) (1991) *Beyond Law and Order: Criminal Justice Policy in the 1990s*. London: Macmillan.

Shapland, J. (1991) 'Criminology in Europe', pp. 14–23 in F. Heidensohn and M. Farrell (eds) *Crime in Europe*. London: Routledge.

Shapland, J. and C. Nuttall (1993) 'The State of Knowledge in the United Kingdom', pp. 155–70 in P. Robert (ed.) *Crime and Prevention Policy*. Freiburg: Eigenverlag Max Planck.

Smith, A. T. H. (1995) 'The Criminal Justice and Public Order Act 1994: The Public Order Elements', *Criminal Law Review*: 19–27.

Tomasson, R. F. (ed.) (1985) *Comparative Social Research, Volume 8: Deviance*. London: JAI Press.

Vahlenkamp, W. (1989) *Kriminalitätsvorbeugung auf kommunaler Ebene*. Wiesbaden: Bundeskriminalamt.

von Hirsch, A. and N. Jareborg (1991) *Strafmass und Strafgerechtigkeit: Die deutsche Strafzumessungslehre und das Prinzip der Tatproportionalität*. Bonn: Forum Verlag.

Walter, M. and M. Kubink (1993) 'Ausländerkriminalität – Phänomen oder Phantom der (Kriminal-) Politik?', *Monatsschrift für Kriminologie* 5: 306–19.

Weigend, T. (1980) 'Continental Cures for American Ailments: European Criminal Procedure as a Model for Law Reform', pp. 381–428 in N. Morris and M. Tonry (eds) *Crime and Justice, Volume 2*. Chicago, IL: University of Chicago Press.

Weigend, T. (1983) 'Criminal Justice: 2, Comparative Aspects', *Encyclopedia of Crime and Justice* 2: 537–46.

Zedner, L. (1995) 'Comparative Research in Criminal Justice', pp. 8–25 in L. Noaks, M. Levi and M. Maguire (eds) *Contemporary Issues in Criminology*. Cardiff: University of Wales Press.

Zweigert, K. and H. Kötz (1992) *An Introduction to Comparative Law*. Oxford: Clarendon Press.

[24]

Crim.L.R.

Criminal Justice—a European Perspective*

By Heike Jung

University of the Saarland (Saarbrücken)

I. 1993—the beginning of a new era?

The European time-table has focussed everybody's attention on what we have to expect from a more integrated Europe. Europe is no longer restricted to lofty political oratory. It becomes more and more real, has crept not only into our imagination, but also into our professional concerns, planning and deliberations. Of course, historical developments do not occur in the form of sudden changes but rather as a continuous flow which may be speeded up at times by particular events. In this sense, the theme and practice of co-operation and harmonisation has, despite all cross-cultural and systematic differences, reached criminal justice systems long ago. They have been on the agenda at least since the late nineteenth century, when different organisations operated as a platform for the international exchange of ideas in criminal policy,[1] not to speak of the sweeping all-European victory of Beccaria's penal philosophy in the era of the Enlightenment.

Yet, we cannot overlook the fact that the recent movement has brought about a new quality which can be sensed in every sphere of social and professional life, even in the criminal justice system. That the wave of European integration has reached the criminal justice system can pass as an indicator for the advanced stage of this development. Traditionally, criminal law and criminal justice are symbols of state sovereignty, so to speak its very core and centre-piece.[2] Now, not even this last bastion of nationhood seems to hold out any longer.

On the surface, the rise of the European perspective and of European issues has to do with the opening of national borders. This event has been of particular concern for the police and crime control agencies, a preoccupation which has given birth to the so-called Schengen Treaty and constitutes a Leitmotif of Article K. 1 of the Maastricht Treaty. Since the filter function of borders in the field of crime control and detection should not be over-estimated, their opening has more of a symbolic impact which directs our attention to, and sharpens our senses for, European demands and standards in the field of criminal justice. Though the British public may be led to believe the opposite, this development has not been induced by what the tabloid press tends to label "The Brussels bureaucrats." Rather, the reasons are manifold and lie on different levels.[3] To

---

* A revised and slightly extended version of a paper presented at the National Probation Conference at Harrogate on February 26, 1992.
[1] As to the role of the IKV-AIDP (International Association of Criminal Law) *e.g.* Radzinowicz, *The Roots of the International Association of Criminal Law and their Significance* (Freiburg, 1991).
[2] *Cf.* for a more detailed analysis Jung, Sanktionensysteme und Menschenrechte, Bern/Stuttgart/Wien 1992, p.24; Salas, Etat et droit pénal, Droits 1992, No. 15, p.77.
[3] *Cf.* also Tsitsoura, Faut-il un droit pénal européen?, Pouvoirs 1990, p.133.

begin with: criminality has never paid much respect to national boundaries. In the era of international mass communication and travelling, cross-border connections and conflicts have become a routine event. An integrated Europe cannot cope with excessive disparities in the field of criminal law and criminal justice, since they produce unwanted distortions and "oasis"-effects. Also the reservoir of potential criminal law reactions and sanctions is not unlimited. Finally, the international criminal policy system of values and standards, though far from being uniform, has reached a level of compatibility which no longer allows for national escapades. The citizen in Europe whether British, French or German requires in essence—leaving aside technical niceties which flow from the particular national legal set-up—an equal status with regard to basic human rights. The criminal justice system has been the traditional "testing-field" of such concepts of human rights. This holds true in particular for criminal procedure and the system of sanctions, since they are the embodiment of state power, the very target of human rights guarantees. Here, penological concerns come into the picture. For it is self-evident that moving closer together should promote a competition of concepts and a search for common ground in a field which has such a vital impact on individuals and society at large.

The following overview can only allude to some of the issues involved. No pre-fabricated solutions or recipes can be expected in a field which does not lend itself to legal exactitude. I simply want to contribute to the emergence and growth of a European conscience. Of course, such a European conscience should, neither in the field of criminal law nor elsewhere, destroy distinctive characteristics which have grown up over the centuries.[4] Yet, a pluralistic Europe requires a set of meta-standards and the readiness to enter into an international dialogue aimed at gradually enlarging the common ground of criminal policy.

II. Setting the European criminal policy agenda

At present, the perspectives and positions in criminal justice are so manifold and controversial that they should be able to fuel the criminal policy debate for years to come. Whoever believes that today's criminal policy debate can be reduced to a single streamlined formula has not understood what he or she is talking about. The prerequisites and the aims of punishment are as controversial as ever: neo-classical, rehabilitative and abolitionist models rival each other. It is not without significance, in this respect, that at the level of the Council of Europe a more just desert-oriented proposal on sentencing, and a re-appraisal of psycho-social interventions within the criminal justice system are being discussed at the same time. The rediscovery of the victim has added a new quality to the general policy debate.[5] Whereas the Council of Europe's decriminalisation report of the year 1980 highlighted a movement for less criminal law,[6] today moves for criminalisation are perhaps even more popular than moves for

---

[4] Also in favour of a co-ordinated legal pluralism Delmas-Marty, *Le flou du droit* (Paris, 1986), p.333.

[5] *e.g.* Heuni (ed.), *Changing Victim Policy: The United Nations Victim Declaration and Recent Development in Europe* (Helsinki, 1989).

[6] Council of Europe (ed.), "Report on Decriminalisation," Strasbourg 1980.

decriminalisation. Yet again, the rise of "soft" diversion, mediation and reparation strategies flows from the idea that it is not helpful, and even perhaps counterproductive, to let the machinery of criminal justice run at full speed. If you peruse the themes and papers of the last Council of Europe criminological conferences, the discussion tends, irrespective of the particular topic, to centre on the same key words: new social strategies, reparation, mediation, the "healing potential" of the community or, to use the French phrase, "une politique criminelle restauratrice," all together echoing long-forgotten modes of conflict resolution.[7]

Still, progress, or what is considered to be progress, is often sold under the disguise of "law and order" slogans. This may have to do with the fact that our criminal policy debate is haunted by rising crime figures. This seems to correlate with a rising "fear of crime" and an increased demand for personal safety. Politicians as well as the representatives of the criminal justice system operate somewhat as "anxiety barometers"[8] prepared to go for tougher reactions and stiffer sentences. A closer analysis reveals two things, however: the general public's margin of tolerance with regard to more leniency is wider than expected.[9] Also, much is to be said in favour of the thesis that "fear of crime" is only an indicator of people's general set of anxieties ("Lebensangst").[10] Since measures of criminal policy will not really alleviate such underlying anxieties, crime prevention strategies should not be unduly concerned to register every oscillation on the "fear of crime" seismograph.

Whereas some react to contemporary criminal justice problems with a bureaucratic response calling for more efficiency, more coherence and more coordination,[11]) others remind us of the socio-psychological fact that state-based systems of criminal justice are only accepted if they provide for a set of procedural safeguards.[12] Therefore, a human rights approach to the criminal justice system cannot be considered as an antagonist to procedural efficiency, but rather as a complementary element.

All in all, we are confronted with a very colourful mosaic, which is not static but a moving picture. A more realistic approach to rehabilitation clashes with neo-classical models. Diversion, mediation, reparation and community service, which tend to add a new socio-constructive quality to criminal law, clash with a tendency to call for stiffer sentences in particular fields such as drug offences.

The arsenal of criminal sanctions has been continuously refined and enriched. Its application has produced a certain "bifurcation."[13] A variety of "soft"

---

[7] For an assessment from a legal anthropologist's point of view see Rouland, *Aux confins du droit* (Paris, 1991), p.77.

[8] Mathiesen, *Prison on Trial* (London, 1990), p.13.

[9] We owe this knowledge to Walker/Hough (eds.), *Public Attitude to Sentencing*, (Aldershot, 1988).

[10] In this direction see Kunz, *Die Verbrechensfurcht als Gegenstand der Kriminologie und Faktor der Kriminalpolitik* (Monatsschrift für Kriminologie und Strafrechtsreform, 1983), p.162.

[11] Steenhuis, "Coherence and Coordination in the Administration of Criminal Justice," in van Dijk (ed.), *Criminal Law in Action: an Overview of Current Issues in Western Societies* (Arnhem, 1986), p.29.

[12] Hassemer, "Konstanten kriminalpolitischer Theorie," in *Festschrift für Lange* (Berlin/New York, 1976), p.501.

[13] The term was first used by Bottoms, "Reflections on the Renaissance of Dangerousness" (1977) *The Howard Journal of Penology and Crime Prevention* 70 at p.88.

reactions is followed by a sudden escalation to stiff sentences. Likewise, the change in the pattern of reactions leads to a realignment of the clientele. This holds true in particular for probation. Probation officers are increasingly confronted with a group of wrong-doers who tend to have committed serious crimes; they are consequently called upon to monitor reactions, which, though non-custodial by definition, may be of considerable impact on the individual. Indeed, incarceration is, if we look back at the last century, very much on the retreat. Also, informal social control measures, somehow integrated into the formal control pattern, and thus operating in the shadow of the Leviathan, have gained in importance. The emergence of new projects and models in the field of criminal justice at large, to name only reparation and victim-support schemes, emphasise participatory elements or, to use an overworked expression, "community involvement."[14]

III. Harmonisation: desires, devices and obstacles

Harmonisation in the field of criminal justice is a slogan almost everybody subscribes to. This does not mean, however, that everybody is in agreement as to its impact and depth.[15] Certainly, a move towards a European criminal policy can rely on a common European tradition which has been kept alive and carried further by European institutions. The notion of economic union, not to speak of a supranational political union, calls for systems of criminal justice which should not drift too far from each other. A larger market without borders necessitates a new co-ordinated approach to crime control. Citizens have grown sensitive to discrepancies requiring some sort of common ground, even if it may still fall short of a Euro-standard.

Bearing in mind the general political situation, such demands can only be fulfilled by a complex set of devices. A single legislator who could take over this task does not exist. Different European institutions have different fields of manoeuvre which may affect criminal justice to a greater or lesser extent. A full inventory of international treaties will have to be considered. Traditional mechanisms of exchange, such as conferences, working parties and the like, play an important role. Even academic gatherings or organisations may act as a catalyst.

The specificities of harmonisation in the European context are embodied in the particular situation and functioning of Europe's supra-national institutions. There are, however, exceptions to the rule: the Schengen Treaty, presumably the most important single move towards harmonisation, has been negotiated on an inter-state level, outside the framework of the E.C. and the Council of Europe's institutions, though it is meant to provide a basis at least for the E.C. countries.[16] Brussels' influence is more subtle, but still noticeable in the field of

---

[14] As to the theoretical concept of community involvement, *e.g.* Nelken, "Community Involvement in Crime Control" in (1985) 38 *Current Legal Problems* 239.

[15] For a general outlook as to the scope mechanisms and problems of harmonisation *cf.* Jung/H. J. Schroth, "Das Strafrecht als Gegenstand der Rechtsangleichung in Europa," in *Goltdammer's Archiv für Strafrecht* 1983, p.241.

[16] The Schengen Treaty and its repercussions on criminal policy and crime control are dealt with more thoroughly by Kühne, *Kriminalitätsbekämpfung durch innereuropäische Grenzkontrollen?* (Berlin, 1991).

Crim.L.R.   Criminal Justice—A European Perspective   241

criminal justice. The E.C. has no competence in the field of criminal law as such. However, through its guidelines and ordinances it provides for the underpinning of many a criminal statute. Also, the priority of community law may "neutralise" criminal law which is not in conformity with the European regulation. Finally, the Member States are in some instances obliged to protect Community interests by way of criminal legislation.[17] The Maastricht Treaty, though falling short of establishing a supranational competence for criminal law and criminal policy, has defined areas of common concern in the wider field of criminal policy.

Though its legal framework is much looser, the Council of Europe has for some time operated as a powerful agent in the field of criminal justice. It has done so on different levels and in different settings. Above all, tribute has to be paid to the European Convention of Human Rights and Basic Freedoms with the Strasbourg Commission and Court of Human Rights. The Strasbourg judiciary has established a growing set of precedents from which flows a loosely-knit European system of references and guidelines for the domestic jurisdictions.[18] Besides, the Council of Europe has by way of its recommendations spelled out its position on many "hot" and controversial issues, a position which will usually arise from the "filtered" knowledge of its national contributors. Also, the Council of Europe has launched many of the international treaties which have added to the growing net-work of co-ordinated interaction.[19] Lastly, one should not underestimate its importance as a broker of information. Who does not take a look into the Council of Europe's Prison Information Bulletin to see where his or her country stands in the statistical ranking list of detention rates?

When it comes to obstacles of harmonisation we have more or less overcome the short cut defence of "national pride and peculiarities." The next level is marked by the customary claim that the dichotomy between the adversarial and the inquisitorial model accounts for many differences in the actual practice. Such comparisons seem to start from an all too superficial or perhaps purist notion of such models. The common framework of the European Convention of Human Rights and Basic Freedoms, and its interpretation by the Strasbourg Court, has taught us the lesson that the structural problems do not necessarily follow such superficial classifications, but rather run along the line of such meta-principles as fairness, checks and balances, predictability and procedural transparency.

Another familiar dichotomy, that between the principle of compulsory prosecution and the discretion to prosecute, loses its sharpness on further consideration. In Germany, for example, which adheres to the principle of compulsory prosecution, the procedural reality is characterised by a mix of the two approaches, whereas Moody and Tombs have claimed for Scotland where dis-

---

[17] For more details, *e.g.* Langfeldt, *Kriminalpolitik im europäischen Entwicklungsprozeß* (Bewährungshilfe, 1991) p.134 at 136.

[18] As to their impact on criminal law and criminal policy *cf.* Bengoetxea/Jung, *Towards a European Criminal Jurisprudence? The Justification of Criminal Law by the Strasbourg Court* (Legal Studies, 1991), p.239.

[19] Presented by Jescheck, "Möglichkeiten und Probleme eines europäischen Strafrechts," in *Festschrift für Jhong-Won Kim* (Seoul, 1991), p.947 at 955.

cretion prevails that it is rarely exercised in practice.[20] This all goes to show that the law in the books and on the level of lofty principles does not necessarily correspond to the law in practice. Therefore discrepancies at the level of principles should not hinder moves towards harmonisation. Often enough, agreements can be reached more easily if we isolate the concrete problems which may at times be smothered by a set of abstract principles. Most important, harmonisation will get into deep water if it does not have the backing of the legal apparatus, since it is their "esprit de corps" which determines what the law is going to be like.

IV. Who can learn what from whom?

Systems of criminal justice within Europe or even at a world level can no longer remain in splendid isolation, but are tied to each other by reciprocal interests and the pledge to a set of common standards. Openness for comparison and even for takeovers is one thing; to agree on a yardstick for such operations is another thing. Should we focus on the crime rate within a jurisdiction, on its punitiveness or rather on its compliance with human rights standards? I am reluctant to consider the crime rate as a parameter of any particular significance for comparison. This has to do with my scepticism as to the actual influence of the criminal justice system on crime rates best embodied in Nils Christie's formula: "Something ought to follow certain actions—but we do not know what, how much, or in what way."[21] Since criminal justice systems can also be regarded as instruments for the exercise of power over individuals to protect other individuals, the impact on individuals should stand in the forefront. In this sense, criminal policy is by necessity a criminal policy destined for individuals and not for organisations.[22] This implies that it should refrain from any unnecessary harm and rather opt for socio-constructive, instead of merely punitive, solutions. Of course, "punitiveness" as a yard-stick is open for interpretation itself. Should we focus on the number of cases in which the most serious sanction is inflicted, *i.e.* the detention rate? Should we relate this number to the intake into the system, thus considering the proportion of "soft" options within the system? On the basis of any approach which assesses systems according to their quality of human rights protection, detention rates per 100,000 inhabitants—the Council of Europe's parameter—are certainly of significance; they are an indicator of the over-all amount of coercion utilised in the administration of justice.[23]

As far as trend-setting in criminal law reforms is concerned the United Kingdom has a good record. This holds true in particular as regards the development of non-custodial measures starting from the institution of probation around the turn of the century and continuing up to more modern features such as community service orders and compensation and reparation schemes. Though the United Kingdom has thus helped pave the way for reduction of punishment, the

---

[20] Moody/Tombs, *Prosecution in the Public Interest* (Edinburgh, 1982), p.57.
[21] Christie, "Utility and Social Values in Court Decisions on Punishment," in Hood (ed.), *Crime, Criminology and Public Policy. Essays in Honour of Sir Leon Radzinowicz* (London, 1974), p.281 at 290.
[22] The key-message of Schüler-Springorum's *Kriminalpolitik für Menschen*, (Frankfurt a.M., 1991).
[23] *Cf.* Jung, *Sanktionensysteme und Menschenrechte, op cit.*, p.48.

assessment of the British stand in Europe today is somewhat ambivalent. British "export articles" like privatisation in crime control have not been accepted with much enthusiasm lately. New proposals such as electronic monitoring have been rejected more or less out of hand. The new sentencing policy underlying the Criminal Justice Act 1991 has some chance of catching on elsewhere, though the outcome is still uncertain. Also, the United Kingdom does not compare favourably in its over-all use of custody. As of September 1988, the United Kingdom had the highest detention rate among the Council of Europe Member States.[24] English prison conditions have been dealt by a special report of inquiry.[25]

All of a sudden the German experience in criminal justice has become a point of interest.[26] However, a closer scrutiny of the German experience reveals no particular surprise. By and large, the German policy discussion reflects the international trend. If I had to isolate one single characteristic trait, it would be the impressive and consistent record of diverted cases. In 1990, 46 per cent. of all sanctions in adult criminal law were so-called "informal sanctions," in absolute numbers 525,000 out of 1,144,224. In juvenile criminal law, the percentage amounts to 61 per cent., in absolute numbers 123,000 as compared to 201,463.[27] The number of prisoners in custody awaiting trial (or awaiting appeal), another indicator of the general criminal policy climate, has been diminishing over the years. Germany can—despite the fact that the figures seem to be rising again—refer to a considerable over-all decrease (1982[28] : 16,543; 1985: 12,254; 1988: 11,703; 1989: 12,222). All in all, the German criminal justice system has produced a low-key response to rising crime figures. It remains to be seen whether this strategy can be maintained in the face of mounting social pressure in post-unification Germany.

Probably many small changes and modifications have contributed and produced synergic effects. The consistency in development may be owed to the state prosecution service, which controls the intake into and practical working of the German criminal justice system. Though, or perhaps because, German prosecutors are guided by the principle of compulsory prosecution, diversion is being handled as a routine procedure almost like a compulsory decriminalisation. In a way, the prosecution service is about to change its character from a repressive agency to an institution which not only holds the key to decarceration, but also uses it. Up till now the English Crown Prosecution Service has played a rather subordinate role. England seems to vest all her hope in a change of *judicial* sentencing policies. I take it that the Criminal Justice Act 1991 is a move in this direction. I applaud the move in this general direction, notwithstanding my fear that a "just desert" philosophy lends itself too easily to repressive misinterpretation.

---

[24] According to Council of Europe, Prison Information Bulletin June 1990, the U.K. detention rate per 100,000 inhabitants amounted to 97.4. Seemingly, there has been a slight but significant decrease in the mean-time.

[25] Prison Disturbances April 1990, HMSO, London 1990.

[26] e.g. Graham, "Decarceration in the Federal Republic of Germany," in (1990) *British Journal of Criminology* 150.

[27] Cf. Heinz, "Diversion im Jugendstrafverfahren," in *Zeitschrift für die gesamte Strafrechtswissenschaft* (1992), p.591 at 603.

[28] Figures as of March 31.

V. Criminal justice and human rights

A conference staged by the French newspaper *Le Monde* two years ago related criminal justice and human rights to the emergence of a European conscience.[29] Indeed, the human rights concept, though its approach is not limited to criminal law and criminal justice,[30] imposes itself decisively on the understanding and handling of criminal justice. The tendency for human rights issues to play an increasingly important role and to permeate the whole criminal justice system has a number of sources. To begin with, it reflects the general turn towards a rights-oriented approach.

It may be a matter of debate whether this rights-oriented approach is a home-made criminal policy product, or whether it has been imported from jurisprudence, constitutional and public international law. However that may be, traditional compartmentalisation has given way to a more integrated concept of criminal policy to which criminal law, human rights law, comparative law and criminology, jointly contribute. It does not come as a surprise that criminology's orientation towards the human rights model has been acknowledged and advocated in particular by internationally inclined criminologists such as Lopez-Rey, who called for a criminology which should be "subservient to the protection of human rights individually and collectively understood."[31] The same message, though from a different angle, comes from Sir Leon Radzinowicz: "Indeed, one of the most disturbing interconnections brought out in the last 25 years is the one between human rights and penal standards."[32] The human rights-oriented approach is not simply a legal imposition. Rather, there is an increasing body of socio-psychological knowledge explaining why people put such a great emphasis on fairness. Only recently Tyler has produced empirical evidence suggesting that, and explaining why, people insist on fair procedures. In essence, he suggests that respect for status and rights is an essential ingredient to groups which wish to maintain the allegiance of their members.[33] Denials of hearings and being treated without dignity and respect signify a status derogation leading to withdrawal of legitimacy and disrespect for group rules. This may help to calm down the continual calls for greater effectiveness in the criminal justice system.[34] It also strengthens the position of those who believe that alternative social strategies inside or outside the criminal justice system cannot do without a minimum of legal safeguards. This general sensitivity for human rights is reflected in the activity of the Strasbourg Court and Commission. They have

---

[29] Documented in Delmas-Marty (ed.), *Procès pénal et droits de l'homme. Vers une conscience européenne* (Paris, 1992). This theme was also taken up in a more recent conference on "Quelle politique pénale pour l'Europe"; see *Le Monde* of October 28, 1992, p.3.

[30] Delmas-Marty, *Contraintes européennes et politique criminelle. Revue trimestrielle des Droits de l'homme* (1992), p.427 at 433, even speaks of a "recomposition du champ juridique" due to the human rights perspective.

[31] Lopez-Rey, *Crime, Criminal Justice, and Criminology: An Inventory, Federal Probation* (June, 1982), p.12 at 17 (quoted after Hood, "Some Reflections on the Role of Criminology in Public Policy" [1987] Crim.L.R. 527 at 530.

[32] Radzinowicz, "Penal Regressions" (1991) 50 *Cambridge Law Journal* 422 at 428.

[33] Tyler, *Why People Obey the Law* (New Haven/London, 1990), p.174.

[34] *Cf.* the compromise position adopted by the French "Rapport Delmas-Marty" on the reform of the criminal procedure: *Commission Justice pénale et droits de l'homme, La mise en état des affaires pénales* (Paris, 1991), p.122.

turned into guarantors of such human rights standards in the field of criminal justice. The web of decided cases hints at what come close to Euro-standards. Their ever-increasing case-load shows that citizens have become aware of this truly European remedy against the infringement of human rights.

VI. Conclusion

"The moral temper of the public in regard to the treatment of crime and criminals is one of the most unfailing tests of the civilisation of any country." Churchill's famous quotation from his 1910 speech as Home Secretary[35] could still today pass as the Leitmotif for a gradually emerging pattern of European standards of criminal justice. Of course, to some extent such standards will have to remain abstract, allowing for pluralism at the domestic level. Yet it seems to me that the common ground and reciprocal understanding are growing daily.

---

[35] Hansard XIX col. 1354.

[25]

Cambridge Law Journal, 50(3), November 1991, pp. 422–444
Printed in Great Britain

PENAL REGRESSIONS

Sir Leon Radzinowicz*

I. The Projection of a World that Was Never to Be

Baron Raffaele Garofalo's memorable treatise *Criminology* ends (almost as an afterthought) with an Appendix entitled "Outline of Principles Suggested as a Basis for an International Penal Code". In barely twelve pages he formulates: principles of criminal liability; an enumeration of categories of offenders; a system of penalties to be adopted to combat crime; and some basic rules of procedure for bringing offenders to justice.[1] Garofalo was not a cranky, lofty or flamboyant idealist. Together with Cesare Lombroso and Enrico Ferri he was the founder of the famous Positivist School of Criminology launched in Italy towards the end of the nineteenth century. He was a High Court Judge, a tough realist with a sharp and incisive mind. Staunch traditional conservative that he was, he might instead have been expected to advocate that each nation should be free to express its unique individuality through its own distinctive legal and penal edifice.

In the same vein the eminent German scholar and Privy Counsellor Professor Franz von Liszt, the guiding spirit of the prestigious International Association of Criminal Law and an exceptionally acute observer of the European scene, asserted with utmost confidence that it was possible, indeed highly desirable, to promote a unified criminal legislation cutting across national frontiers.[2]

How did they come to believe that all countries (or even a majority of them) would agree to such a radical solution in so complex

---

* LL.D., F.B.A., Fellow of Trinity College, Cambridge; formerly first Wolfson Professor of Criminology and Director of the Institute of Criminology at Cambridge.

This paper is part of a larger work being carried out under the auspices of the Patrick and Anna M. Cudahy Fund, in which I am trying to reassess the development of penal thought and practice during the 63 years I have been involved with it.

[1] Raffaele Garofalo, *Criminology*, pp. 405–416. (First Italian ed. 1885; 2nd ed. 1891; French ed. 1905; translated into English and published in the *Modern American Criminal Science Series* in 1914; reprinted in 1968).

[2] See Franz von Liszt's preface to the first volume of *Die Strafgesetzgebung der Gegenwart,* etc. (1894), pp. xxiv–xxv.

and controversial a sphere as that of criminal jurisprudence and penal legislation? Where should we look for an explanation of such a utopian, and yet by no means isolated, expectation?

The answer lies in the spirit of the time. At the turn of the century it was firmly believed that economic, technical, social and political forces would, in due course, drastically reduce the basic differences which hitherto had existed between countries; bringing them closer to each other and leading them to uninterrupted progress in its widest sense. The study of crime and its control, in unison with all the other key disciplines relating to man in society, would ultimately provide explanations and solutions. These, in their turn, would lead to a set of beliefs and a programme of action which would be accepted and scrupulously followed by the world at large. It was only a question of time before the advance of civilisation would effectively eradicate crime as a mass phenomenon. These beliefs were naturally most strongly held in Europe, then looked upon as the centre of the world. But the persistence of crime, its extent and trends, played havoc with these expansive hopes, revealing them to be no more than unwarranted figments of unreal anticipation. It was not the only factor in their demise, but nevertheless it was one of immense significance, both direct and indirect.

The most recent exemplar of wishful thinking about the contemporary evolution of crime was the contention that demographic shifts, such as fewer births and longer life expectancy, would lead to a lowering of the crime rate in the population as a whole.[3] This proved to be so, but only to a very limited extent and for a very short span of time. The dominant universal trend, with a few exceptions such as Switzerland, or—to provide a perplexing contrast—Japan, is of a steady, substantial increase. It embraces all age-groups, both sexes, fresh recruits to the army of crime as well as its hard core, the recidivists, the non-violent as well as the violent. It has ceased to be an almost exclusive phenomenon of great urban agglomerations and extends all over the country, though naturally with varying intensity, and it embraces virtually all the major categories of infractions. Nor should it be forgotten how woefully incomplete the best of criminal statistics inevitably are. "Statistical crimes" is the term sometimes used to characterise changes in recorded crime that have no basis in

---

[3] "These conclusions of a near-term decline are the direct consequences of the so-called 'baby-bursts', a precipitous decline in fertility from the post-war peak of 3·8 children per woman in the late 1950s to fewer than 1·8 children for women in 1976, the lowest level in American history . . . the relative numbers of teenagers to older people in this country can readily be predicted: they will decline until at least the 1990s. Consequently, any prediction of crime rates that depends primarily on the age distribution of the population shows a levelling or a decline in crime for the near future": see Jan M. Chaiken and Marcia R. Chaiken, "Crime Rates and the Active Criminal" in *Crime and Public Policy*, edited by James Q. Wilson (1983), pp. 11–29 at p. 21.

real changes in the number of crimes actually committed. So much committed crime remains hidden, never coming to the attention of the authorities; or is not reported by the victims; or fails to be properly recorded by the police or other responsible agencies. Even if an offender can be identified there may be no prosecution at all or the offence charged may be transformed by prosecutorial compromises and, of course, may escape conviction altogether in the last phase of judicial proceedings. Thus, in one way or another, the figures made available inevitably grossly underestimate, indeed distort, the reality of crime.[4]

Recent sophisticated research in the United States and England has gone far to reveal its actual amount and kinds through surveys of crime victimisation among the population at large and other devices.[5] But I believe they have not gone far enough in their socio-psychological excavations. In my opinion—and I gladly acknowledge this to be no more than my personal conjecture—when a total view of crime is taken, across the board as it were, the ultimate amount of crime cleared up by a conviction represents no more than fifteen per cent. of the crime actually committed.[6] I also believe that, in many parts of the world, the dark figure, far from diminishing as a proportion of the whole, is increasing faster than that of the crime which finds its way into criminal statistics. This unidentified mass of unpunished criminal behaviour has a negative social impact in as much as it tends to put further strains on public confidence and the feelings of security which are expected to flow from a well regulated system of criminal justice.[7]

Most discouragingly, despite some sharp fluctuations up and down

[4] It was a Japanese student who, at the beginning of the present century, in order to express this hidden reality, coined the word *Dunkelziffer* (see S. Oba, *Unverbesserliche Verbrecher und ihre. Behandlung*, Berlin, 1908, p. 27). Since then, the term made its *tour du monde* and was readily accepted into criminological currency (*le chiffre noir, il ciffro nero*).

[5] Surveys of crime victimisation ". . . ask representative samples of the population about selected offences they have experienced over a given time, whether or not they have reported them to the police . . . They have done much to elucidate the 'truer' level and nature of crime, the extent of unrecorded offences for different crime categories, and in particular the distribution of risks across different groups . . ." See Jan J.H. van Dijk, Pat Mayhew and Martin Killias, *Experiences of Crime across the World* (1990), pp. 2–3.

[6] According to a Committee set up by the American Bar Association under the chairmanship of Professor Samuel Dash, "with the exception of the crime of murder only a small fraction of the serious criminal acts committed in the United States ever enter the criminal justice system, for reasons totally unrelated to constitutional restrictions. The overwhelming majority of these crimes, which keep Americans in fear, are untouched by the work of police, prosecutors, judges and prison officials. Thus out of the approximately 34 million serious crimes committed against persons or property in the United States in 1986, approximately 31 million never were exposed to arrest, because either they were not reported to the police, or if reported they were not solved by arrests . . ." See *Criminal Justice in Crisis* (American Bar Association, Washington, D.C., 1988), p. 4.

[7] For my more detailed views concerning these vitally important subjects, see Leon Radzinowicz, "The Criminal in Society" (The Peter Le Neve Foster Lecture), *Journal of the Royal Society for the Encouragement of Arts* (1964), vol. 112, No. 5100, pp. 916–929, at pp. 916–920; also Leon Radzinowicz and Joan King, *The Growth of Crime* (1977), pp. 31–54.

in recent years, I can see no redeeming feature in the picture I drew some thirteen years ago of the conditions of crime within its international context. If at all, the very grey shadow of the recent past has now conspicuously darkened. To prophesy in social and penal matters is to ignore the wise warning of George Eliot that "among all forms of mistake, prophecy is the most gratuitous". Yet I perceive no indication, however hesitant and timid, that the upward trend, constant and all-pervasive, will alter its course in the foreseeable future. Although the bulk of recorded crime is still relatively trivial and fear of it is often exaggerated, it is nevertheless unreal to deny that crime is a significant social problem.[8]

The vast and painful changes which the Soviet Union and its former satellites will have to undergo will inevitably bring increases in crime of every kind. Forthcoming information, scanty as it is, clearly points in this direction. This world-wide expansion has had a paralysing effect on all layers and levels of the criminal justice system which, as a general rule, even at the most favourable of times, has always been grossly under-developed. The machinery is simply breaking up in its crucial components under the sheer weight of numbers. Nor should one be surprised to note that this chronic "crime-pressure" inevitably also leads to a crystallisation of public opinion against measures of criminal policy inspired by a liberal social outlook and a gravitation towards short-cut solutions usually identified with authoritarian systems of criminal justice.

II. The Spread of Authoritarian Models of Criminal Justice

In the field of criminal justice, in spite of the output of criminological knowledge, the political approach still holds sway. Indeed, in several parts of the world it has become predominant. The authoritarian model of criminal justice is a natural outcome of this tendency and its many visible features are closely interconnected. They are as follows.
   (1) Criminal Codes lack precise definitions of many crimes. The number of acts classified as criminal tends to increase, while, at the same time, the limits of what is permissible are often left deliberately vague. This leaves the door wide open to arbitrary interpretations and retroactive decisions.

---

[8] I was glad to see that the "left realist" criminologists have so firmly endorsed this point of view. See J. Lea and J. Young, *What is to be done about Law and Order* (1984), pp. 11–75 and 262–273 and R. Kinsey, J. Lea and J. Young, *Losing the Fight Against Crime* (1986), pp. 57–63. It seems to me that *The Times* in its spirited leading article "Neither Prevented Nor Cured" (16 April 1991) went much too far in minimising the impact of contemporary crime.

(2) The police act in flagrant conflict with the requirement of legality. There is no emphasis in police recruitment on personal integrity and social responsibility, no independent investigations of complaints, indeed hardly any public accountability. Police forces operate primarily as agents of those who hold the supreme power and not as organs of criminal justice based on the rule of law.

(3) Use and abuse of physical or mental pressures to achieve the objectives of the criminal process is common.

(4) The system of prosecution, trial and sentence lacks a general commitment to openness. The rights of the suspect and the accused to keep silent, not to be forced to confess, and to have independent legal representation, are non-existent or neglected.

(5) Strictly enforced rules of evidence, strictly interpreted and inspired by the principle of the presumption of innocence, are absent or neglected.

(6) There are inadequate guarantees and provisions for appeal against conviction and sentence.

(7) The judiciary is committed to following the wishes of the political rulers and is weak in maintaining its independence and impartiality: public prosecutors and the Bar display a similar attitude.

(8) The criminal is primarily seen as an anti-social individual, in revolt against the laws of the state, a malevolent force to be broken or annihilated. Crime is not perceived as a social phenomenon, society not thought to bear any share of responsibility for producing it. Criminal justice, utterly divorced from social policy, is essentially punitive, even when given the gloss of "re-education".

(9) Retribution, intimidation and elimination are regarded as the dominant functions of penal sanctions. Belief in, and a widespread use of, capital punishment are essential ingredients of criminal policy. The reformative function, although admitted for juveniles is, in practice, grossly restricted.

(10) The entire system of punishment, in sentencing and in enforcement, is consistently harsh and rigid. The general bent of criminal policy is strikingly anti-humanitarian.

(11) Not even lip service is paid to the rights of prisoners and no effort to protect them is deployed. Independent inspection of penal institutions is fiercely discouraged.

(12) Hardly any worthwhile initiative is taken to evolve a humane system of alternative measures, outside the scope of traditional penalties.

(13) The enforcement of criminal justice is not dispensed by the courts only. It can be, and is, also exercised by the executive power, through administrative and police organs, often through the secret police or ruling party, which often have their own coercive confinement centres. This hidden jurisdiction relates to a large area of behaviour vaguely described as anti-social, deviant or parasitic.

(14) Independent public investigations of the working of the system as a whole, or of any part of it, even when abuses and inefficiency are glaring, are hardly ever set on foot. Governmental authorities are extremely reluctant to publish any significant facts or accounts about what is going on in the field of criminal justice.

(15) The entire system is protected not only by secrecy at home but also by isolation from abroad. Developments in other countries are either ignored altogether or presented in a very distorted form.

(16) And finally, independent criminological research is not tolerated. Any research permitted is kept under very strict official supervision. Its mission is to endorse and justify the existing system, its own output hardly ever going beyond shallow and tedious reports.

In sharp and unbridgeable contrast to this authoritarian pattern stands the socio-liberal model of criminal justice. Its ideology can easily be reconstructed by virtually reversing each of these 16 leading characteristics of the authoritarian model. On the other hand, it is much more difficult to identify with precision what constitutes the conservative model. It stands somewhere between the socio-liberal and the authoritarian, containing elements pertaining to both. It can never be assimilated with the former: the areas of contradiction between them are too basic and too striking. It can, however, in certain political and social circumstances, move much closer to the authoritarian formula.

III. THE GRIM REALITY

I cannot claim to have been in all parts and corners of the world, or to have studied them all in depth. But I have travelled enough, observed enough and recorded enough, to be able to characterise their predominant philosophies and practices.

It is Soviet Russia and Nazi Germany which are entitled to claim the credit for evolving and practising the most perfect (and cruel) examples of the authoritarian model of criminal justice. But in at least two-thirds of the member states of the United Nations (and there are 166 of them) criminal justice is administered very much in accordance with this model, though not always in a form so monolithic and so extreme as signalised by my 16 points. Attenuations and adaptations take place to fit particular local traditions and socio-political mutations. A leading student of terrorism commented, a few years ago, that "far from being a fortunately rare exception in an otherwise civilised world, the *coup d'état* is now the normal mode of political change in most member states of the United Nations". "There are now", he continued, "many more military dictatorships in existence than Parliamentary democracies . . . during the last fifteen years there have been some 120 military coups". These military régimes are a mixed bag, but their effects on systems of criminal justice is uniformly devastating, reducing them to the lowest common denominator of arbitrary repression.

In very many parts of the world, including Europe, the system of criminal justice is amorphous, disjointed and stagnant. In many it is torn by chronic turmoil, punctuated by severe convulsions, the inevitable consequence of recurring political and social upheavals. Often there are pious proclamations of goals to be pursued which are flagrantly contradicted by the ugly realities; or else brutality is openly paraded to maximise deterrence and fear. Often the system of criminal justice is perceived and enforced as a self-perpetuating bureaucracy, a self-contained machine deliberately cut off from wider influences and reliable re-assessments. Often, an undoubtedly sincere belief in decent penal standards is overshadowed or, more precisely, overwhelmed by the impact of increasing crime, by financial restrictions, and by the pressure to invest limited resources in attempts to alleviate other, more appealing, social problems.

I am aware that these are harsh statements, but they simply reflect harsh realities. The exceptions to such strictures are very few, accounting for a very small proportion of the countries of the world. There are at least four billion people in the world at present who are as hungry for elementary criminal justice as they are for everyday essential commodities.[9] The annual reports of *Amnesty International* and of *Human Rights Watch*—terrifying but authentic accounts of violations of human rights across the world—are as important, if not more so, as the accounts of the working of criminal justice as a whole. Indeed, one of the most disturbing interconnections brought out in the last 25 years is the one between human rights and penal

---

[9] It is estimated that, each day, the population of the world increases by 225,000 people, and that by about the year 2025 the world population will have doubled, amounting to 9 billion. Will this mass of humanity by then be less deprived of decent criminal justice? I wonder. For an exceptionally lucid overview of the world population, which according to the most recent estimates amounts to about 5 billion, made up of seven units and comprising some 225 countries, see *1988 Demographic Yearbook* (40th ed.), United Nations, New York (1990), pp. 161–169.

standards. They condition and influence each other and neither can achieve satisfactory fulfilment without the other.[10] The famous epigram of Franz von Liszt that "the Criminal Code should be regarded as the Magna Carta of the Criminal" is today too often distorted or ignored altogether.

In these circumstances, meaningful international collaboration in important penal questions frequently comes to a virtual standstill, or is but a skilful camouflage. It was sad to witness the too frequent alliances on this subject between the Soviet bloc and countries of the Third World, aimed at obstructing penal progress. At the international crime conferences sponsored by the United Nations, heads of the official delegations too often read out speeches prepared at home in advance, ignore what transpired during subsequent discussions, have little disposition to give or take, and vote according to easily anticipated alignments. Independent experts have little chance to contribute to the debates, let alone to influence their outcomes. Too many of the resolutions adopted are evasive in language and mean very little. Too often penal questions have become merely political questions and penal expertise is either submerged or subordinated to political expediency. A sincere tribute must be paid to the small but gallant band of officials of the Crime Prevention and Control Branch within the United Nations Secretariat, who show so much resourcefulness and dedication in this kind of atmosphere. In these circumstances the role of non-governmental organisations becomes crucial, and much is expected of them. But here too there is a tendency to keep aloof from the sombre reality which characterises so many contemporary systems of criminal justice.[11]

With the bewildering changes which are taking place in Soviet Russia and its former satellites it is reasonable to expect that a fundamental change in the attitude towards criminal law and its enforcement will follow.[12] But again I am reminded of an unfulfilled

---

[10] For a brief, but illuminating, account of the historical roots of the concept of human rights, see Louis Henkin, *The Rights of Man Today* (1978), pp. 1–30.

[11] The volume of the *Revue Internationale de Droit Pénal* (1982), vol. 53 n.s. nos 3–4, pp. 553–972 entitled "La Philosophie de la Justice Pénale et la Politique Criminelle Contemporaines" may be quoted as an example. It was the product of the work carried out in two international seminars, organised by the International Institute of Criminal Science of Syracuse (January 1981–May 1982) under the auspices of the four major organisations: the International Association of Penal Law; the International Penal and Penitentiary Foundation; the International Society of Criminology; and the International Association for Social Defence. It contains a valuable amount of information, but it is singularly deprived of realism and relevance with respect to the flaws and distortions which affect systems of criminal justice across the world. A similar escapism from reality may be levelled against another volume produced with the purpose of making a comparative review of the preparatory phases of the criminal process. See "La Phase Préparatoire du Procès Penal en Droit Comparé" in *ibid.*, (1985), vol. 56, n.s. nos 1–2, a volume of 380 pages. No more than a few rather timid references to prevailing defects or irregularities can be found in this expansive collection of essays, and yet it deals with a field rampant with flagrant abuses.

[12] In this connection the paper of the distinguished Dutch expert in Soviet criminal matters, Ger.

promise or, perhaps, bland wishful thinking. In 1900, at the close of the International Penitentiary Congress in Brussels, the former chief of the Prison Administration of Imperial Russia presented a statement (obviously officially approved) in which he summarised the report of the Council of the Empire, presided over by Nicholas the Second, concerning the new policy regarding transportation of offenders. It ended as follows:

> The Middle Ages left Russia three legacies—torture, the knout, deportation. The eighteenth century abolished torture, the nineteenth saw the disappearance of the knout, and the first day of the twentieth century will be the last day of a penal system based on deportation.[13]

It is perhaps rather mean to quote this when exhilarating expectations of a brighter future run so high. But the unfulfilled promises of the past, and there were far too many of them everywhere, should not be muted. They too have a message to convey.

IV. THE AMERICAN DECLINE

The report *Criminal Justice in Cleveland* is today virtually forgotten, but many parts of it should be made compulsory reading for all those taking an interest in the penal evolution of America.[14] The document, directed and edited by two eminent members of the Harvard Law School of the period, Felix Frankfurter and Roscoe Pound, presents the first incisive and persuasive account of the gap between the requirement of a rapidly growing urban America and the limited capabilities of its under-developed machinery of justice. And the conclusion reached—to quote Felix Frankfurter—was "the practical breakdown of criminal machinery [which] has its parallel in other cities". The date of the report was 1922. Some thirty years later, more precisely in 1953, the late Mr. Justice Robert K. Jackson threw his influence behind the Ford Foundation's grandiose initiative to launch a nation-wide examination of the entire area of criminal law enforcement by affirming tersely: "Criminal justice [is] the vital problem of the future."[15] A further decade came to a close. Largely in response to Senator Barry Goldwater's passionate rhetoric about

---

P. van den Berg, "Judicial Statistics in a Period of Glasnost" provides an encouraging foretaste of better things to come. See *Review of Socialist Law* (1987), vol. 13, pp. 299–311.

[13] See "Communication de M. Solomon, Chef de la délégation officielle de Russie, sur la suppression de la déportation en Sibérie" in *Actes du Congrés Pénitentiare International de Bruxelles, 1900* (Berne, 1901), vol. 1, pp. 74–82, at p. 82.

[14] *Criminal Justice in Cleveland. A Report* (The Cleveland Foundation, Cleveland, Ohio, 1922). Particularly important is the piece by Roscoe Pound, "Criminal Justice and the American City", pp. 550–654.

[15] See *American Bar Association Journal* (1953), vol. 39, p. 743.

the collapse of "law and order" in America, President Johnson set on foot in 1967 a Commission to provide a sober answer. To my mind the Commission may have inhaled too fervently the intoxicating perfume of the "Free Society" and taken a somewhat too naive and too idealistic a view of the possibility of changing those social conditions which underlie crime as a mass phenomenon within our complex "Not so Free Society". But I have no doubt that, in the scope and quality of the end-product of its labours, the Commission stands out as the most remarkable investigative enterprise of its kind in the twentieth century.[16] At each stage, and at every significant corner of its explorations, it pointed in forcible language to the impending penal crisis. A further 23 years have passed and many more inquiries have come and gone. Yet who can deny that the signals each has projected have proven to be not a clarion call for bold reconstruction, but only another sombre exercise in sterile autopsy? A good system of criminal justice cannot be brought into existence by a statute or a Commission, nor can it be brought into existence by a feverish endeavour extending over a few months or even a few years. It requires a systematic and gradual approach. It is the misfortune of the United States not to have regarded the red signals, just hoping that, by some kind of miracle, crime would fade away and there would be no necessity to modernise the apparatus of criminal justice and to finance it properly.

Nevertheless, to conclude on the basis of this frustrating evidence that the American ways of enforcing the criminal law belong to the authoritarian system would be grossly misguided and unfair. America adheres to the prerequisites of legality—the presumption of innocence, publicity, fair play and public accountability in the processes of prosecution, trial and sentencing—prerequisites which constitute an integral part of the liberal and classical conception of justice. These roots are revered. And little if any obstacle is put in the way of uninhibited and independent enquiries into the working of the system. But the existence of a chronic chasm between what is urgently required and what is scarcely available in the field of criminal policy provides fertile ground for the propagation of all kinds of regressive ideas and short-cut solutions. It accentuates the deeply embedded feeling that criminals deserve nothing but rough treatment. It lowers still further the traditionally low priority assigned to criminal law enforcement as compared with other societal requirements. The

---

[16] The Commission on Law Enforcement and Administration of Justice (established on 23 July, 1965, through Executive Order 11236). Chairman: Nicholas de B. Katzenbach, then the Attorney General. Executive Director: Professor James Vorenberg, subsequently Dean of the Harvard Law School. Main Report: *The Challenge of Crime in a Free Society* (1967). It was supported by an impressive series of *Task Force Reports*—all published.

whole response to crime-control tends to become more crude and more cynical, displaying an increasing disregard for those fundamental considerations of a political, social and moral nature from which the foundations and the operations of the machinery of justice in a democratic society should never be cut off.

What follows is a randomly selected mixed bag of influential judicial decisions and legislative innovations which illustrate this shifting image and direction. A more detailed examination would obviously be out of place here.

Incriminating evidence, assembled illegally, may nevertheless be used in certain cases to facilitate conviction. More precisely, a confession obtained in violation of the *Miranda* rules (but not "coerced" in the traditional phrase) can be used to impeach a defendant's inconsistent testimony on the stand.[17] The Supreme Court has also ruled that the police may act without a warrant to stop and briefly detain a person they think is wanted for the commission of a crime. It was not important to the decision that the person arrested was wanted in another country.[18] In the "school search case" the court held that public school teachers and officials can search a student's purse as long as there are "reasonable grounds" for believing that the search will yield evidence of a violation of the law or of the school's rules. In this case the search turned up evidence of a crime.[19]

Under the new Federal Law, courts are given power to detain in prison before trial defendants charged with all kinds of serious crime, if it is thought necessary to protect "the safety of any other person and the community". Indeed, in certain cases when a Federal judge or magistrate finds enough evidence to justify charging a defendant with a major drug offence, as well as in the case of several other serious offences, under the new law "it shall be presumed" that the accused is dangerous and consequently should be detained, unless he can prove otherwise at a hearing which is not subject to the ordinary rules of evidence. There you have the emergence of a bold and elastic scheme of *preventive detention* before trial.[20]

Under the new rules relating to the insanity defence, the burden of proof has shifted from the prosecutor who, until 1984, had to prove that the defendant was not insane, to the defendant, who now has to prove that he was. This change had much to commend it.[21]

---

[17] See *Harris* v. *New York*, 401 U.S. 222 (1971).
[18] See *United States* v. *Hensley*, 429 U.S. 221 (1985). The "Stop and Detain" case is called by American lawyers the "Stop and Frisk" case.
[19] See *New Jersey* v. *T.L.O.*, 469 U.S. 325 (1985).
[20] On the Federal Preventive Detention Statute see: 18 U.S.C. 3142 (d), (e), (f), (g), enacted in 1984.
[21] See, for the Statute passed in 1984 following John Hinckley's acquittal by reason of insanity for his attempt to assassinate President Reagan, 18 U.S.C. 17. Also, for a very informative

What is highly controversial is the formula which has redefined the meaning of insanity under criminal law. Until the change in the law a defendant could be found not guilty by reason of insanity if a jury determined that, because of a mental disease or defect, he either could not control himself well enough to obey the law, or could not appreciate the wrongfulness of his conduct. Now a successful defence is restricted to the second limb of the formula only. This has virtually amounted to a resurrection of the famous McNaghten rules drawn up in England in 1843 and subjected to intense and fully justified criticism throughout the present century by bodies of the standing of the British *Royal Commission on Capital Punishment* (1949–1953) and the American Law Institute in its *Model Penal Code*.

A radical re-casting of sentencing mechanisms has taken place. The discretion of Federal judges has been sharply curtailed in such a way that they are now expected to apply a narrow range of sentences prescribed for different offences. *Sentencing Guidelines*, as they are designated, have been drawn up by a special *Sentencing Commission*, which will continue to keep an eye on this crucial judicial function. The judges are expected to explain in writing any departures from the guidelines. The prosecution has the right to appeal against any sentences more lenient than those prescribed, though it is only fair to add that defendants will also have the right to appeal against sentences which appear to them to be harsher than those laid down. But, of course, in practice, the prosecutors will have the advantage. In some cases the guidelines have provided for levels of punishment higher than those commonly imposed under the former sentencing system. Parole, as a general mechanism for supervisory discharge, has been abolished, with far-reaching repercussions on many facets of the penal system and penal policy. The courts are still empowered, in individual cases, to order a supervisory period following imprisonment, its maximum length depending on the gravity of the offence. Though this provision salvages something from the parole system, it is very inadequate. The type and length of supervision needs to be decided when the prisoner is about to be released, not at the much earlier time when he is sentenced. The judge is grossly handicapped in making the decision, certainly at that early stage. In a paper by Dr. Roger Hood and myself, published in 1981, we argued against such rigid innovations.[22] Nothing has occurred since which could

---

discussion of the issues involved, Peter W. Low, *Criminal Law* (revised 1st ed., 1990), pp. 209–213. I am indebted to Professor Low for putting me right on a number of points.

[22] See Leon Radzinowicz and Roger Hood, "The American Volte-Face in Sentencing Thought and Practice" in *Crime, Proof and Punishment, Essays in Memory of Sir Rupert Cross*, edited by Colin Tapper (London, 1981), pp. 127–143. For valuable background information on this legislative and administrative movement which has been sweeping across the country, see *Research on Sentencing: The Search for Reform* (edited by Alfred Blumstein, Jacqueline Cohen, Susan E. Martin and Michael H. Tonry), 2 vols. (National Academy, Washington, 1983);

possibly lead me to abandon or modify my views. I agree with the criticisms of the Federal Sentencing Commission re-stated by Jeffrey S. Parker and Michael K. Block and by Andrew von Hirsch, but I would go even further. I regard Sentencing Commissions as having fatal flaws of one kind or another. They should not be regarded as a solution to the problems which face contemporary sentencing policy.[23]

A cluster of proposals to be embodied in criminal legislation was included in the *Model Penal Code* and a number of other devices have been developed in practice to promote the highly laudable objective of doing away with unreasonable disparities in sentencing, yet without altering the role of the judiciary within the constitutional and political framework of the state.[24] But they have never been fully and thoroughly tried out. I must confess that, in spite of admiration for Professor Andrew von Hirsch's intellectual vitality, I continue to be at a loss to understand the ultimate significance of his pet theory of "just deserts", other than that it re-affirms again and again that in any rationally conceived and coherently pursued sentencing activity the principle of proportionality cannot and should not be left out.[25] Nevertheless, I do favour the establishment of a body which would provide regular critical surveys of sentencing practices within the context of the criminal justice system as a whole. Such a body would be able to communicate its findings to all concerned, and particularly to the judiciary. To advise—yes; but not to direct.

The effective moratorium on capital punishment in the United

Sandra Shane-Du Bow, Alice P. Brown, Eric Olsen: *Sentencing Reform in the United States* (National Institute of Justice, Issues and Practices, 1985); and the lively number of *Judicature* devoted to "Criminal Sentencing in Transition" (1984, vol. 68, Nos. 4–5). I am grateful to Professor Walter Gellhorn for having brought this number to my attention. For recent developments, see the well-informed article by Michael Tonry, "Structuring Sentencing" in *Crime and Justice* (edited by M. Tonry and N. Morris, 1988), vol. 10, pp. 267–337.

[23] J.S. Parker and M.K. Block, "The Sentencing Commission, P.M. (Post-Mistretta): Sunshine or Sunset", *American Criminal Law Review* (1989), vol. 27, pp. 289–330, and A. von Hirsch, "Several Sentencing Guidelines: Do they Provide Principled Guidance?", *ibid.*, pp. 367–390.

[24] A fresh convert to the idea comes from England. The Labour Party promises that if it wins the next election, it will establish a "Sentencing Council", either consisting entirely of judges (who would have the power to co-opt others) or, from the start, not limited to the judiciary. Its object would be "to produce a set of sentencing ceilings for different types and grades of offences (*e.g.* different types of burglary, different types of theft) together with principles for use in calculating the precise sentence beneath that ceiling, including principles governing the sentencing of persistent offenders. These recommendations will be issued as practice directions." See *A Safer Britain: Labour's White Paper on Criminal Justice* (January 1990), pp. 13–15. See also the Fabian Tract (No. 522, October 1987) by Stephen Shaw, in which he advocates the creation of a Ministry of Justice, the abolition of the Lord Chancellor's Department and the setting-up of a sentencing council, *Conviction Politics: A Plan for Penal Policy*, pp. 24–25. But for reasons which remain to me unclear he describes these and several other proposals as a programme of "Socialist Penal Policy". Similarly, the several important principles formulated by John Croft (writing from a Conservative Perspective) do not seem to me to be exclusively linked to Conservative ideology. See John Croft, *Croft on Crime* (privately printed, 1990), pp. 6–7 and 28–33.

[25] The most recent article by Professor von Hirsch seems to me to reinforce this contention. See "Proportionality in the Philosophy of Punishment" in *Criminal Law Forum* (Winter 1990), vol. 1, pp. 259–290.

States extended from 1968 until the execution of Gary Gilmore in 1977.[26] Since then its resuscitation has proved to be remarkably viable, to the despair of the abolitionists and the blatant satisfaction of the retentionists. Even its application to young offenders finds many influential allies. The recent initiative of Chief Justice Rhenquist fits the trend. In 1988 he sponsored a Committee under the chairmanship of the former Justice Lewis F. Powell, Jr., to enquire into "the necessity and desirability of legislation directed toward avoiding delay and the lack of finality" in capital cases in which the prisoners had or had been offered counsel. The committee recommended a change in the operation of *habeas corpus* by curtailing the right of convicted defendants to raise constitutional challenges as to the validity of their conviction or sentence. This was aimed, in particular, at multiple appeals at the state level and multiple petitions to the Federal courts.[27] Armed with this recommendation the Chief Justice proposed to change the practice in order to streamline and expedite the execution of capital sentences across the Union. For much too long the existing practice has been a national and indeed an international scandal. The average delay from time of sentencing to time of execution is over seven years and there were occasions when some of those sentenced to death among the more than 2,400 lately on death-row died of causes other than the appointed capital punishment. However, the initiative can in no way be interpreted as a move to reduce the scope of the supreme penalty. Quite the contrary. If accepted it would have the effect of stabilising it by eliminating, or at least considerably reducing, the many shocking aspects of the appallingly long wait on death-row.

The Chief Justice's initiative prompts a rather interesting historical comparison. In England it was the retentionists who, in the middle of the nineteenth century, pressed hard for doing away with public executions and the morbid and sordid "Tyburn spectacle" associated with them. They favoured executions within prison walls, out of public view and in accordance with a business-like, sober and rapid procedure. This, they believed, and with good reason, would make the penalty itself much more acceptable to public opinion. And it was exactly for these reasons that the abolitionists were not keen to support this step.[28]

---

[26] For the "condition" of capital punishment in the United States of America, see the excellent report of Dr. Roger Hood presented to the United Nations Committee on Crime Prevention and Control, *The Death Penalty: A World-Wide Perspective* (Oxford University Press, 1989), pp. 32, 40, 59–61, 63, 69–70, 74–75, 80–82, 85–86, 91–98, 98–116, 121–127, 130–148.

[27] See "Judicial Conference of the United States". *Ad Hoc* Committee on Federal *Habeas Corpus* in Capital Cases. Committee Report and Proposal. (Chairman: Lewis F. Powell, Jr.)

[28] See Leon Radzinowicz, *History of English Criminal Law and its Administration from 1750*, vol. 4 (1968), pp. 343–353.

Pressure and dissent continue. The Chief Justice did not succeed in having his proposals adopted but they have since been incorporated into a Bill sponsored by the Government which also raised nearly a dozen Federal crimes into capital crimes, such as terrorist attacks on aircraft and trains, mail bombings, murders committed in the course of robberies, and genocide. It also proposed to revoke Federal benefits for convicted drug offenders and to impose one-year prison terms for illegal use of steroids. The measure was opposed by a Bill, sponsored by the Democrats, going in the opposite direction. This was a bold attempt to reduce the scope of capital punishment, to free it from the grave suspicion of being influenced by racial discrimination and to ensure that offenders facing the supreme penalty obtain a highly qualified and well-rewarded lawyer. The proposals and counter proposals were considered in a highly charged emotional atmosphere; the very slogan under which they were announced is characteristic: "One Anti-Crime Bill, One Pro-Crime Bill".[29] When the Bills passed the House and the Senate respectively both sides were forced to abandon many of their cherished proposals, so many that ultimately the statute that emerged differed in many essential features from these initial formulations.[30] Thus another political game was played out at the expense of a rationally conceived criminal policy. With hardly any lapse of time the pattern repeated itself.[31]

---

[29] See Dick Thornburgh (Attorney General of the US), "One Anti-Crime Bill, One Pro-Crime Bill" in *Wall Street Journal*, 26 September 1990; William P. Barr (Deputy Attorney General), "Death-Penalty Delay Doesn't Promote Justice", *New York Times*, 5 October 1990, and Editorial, "'Pro-Justice', not 'Pro-criminal'", *ibid.*, 26 September 1990. And last, but not least, Anthony Lewis, "Crime in Politics", *New York Times*, 1 October 1990.

[30] See 47 *Crim. L. Reporter*, 1349–51 (1990); 1060–63 (1990); 1130–31 (1990).

[31] On 26 March 1991 the Supreme Court (by a majority of 5–4) upheld the "good faith exception", allowing evidence seized through a technically faulty search warrant to be used at a trial if the police honestly believed the warrant to be valid. Also, a coerced confession can be admitted as "harmless error" if other evidence is sufficient to prove guilt (see *McCleskey v. Zant*, 111 S. Ct. 1454 (1991)). On 16 April 1991 the court decided (by 6–3) to redefine the doctrine of "abuse of writ", thus severely limiting the right of State prisoners sentenced to death to raise constitutional claims in *habeas corpus* proceedings in the Federal courts (see *Arizona v. Fulminante*, 111 S. Ct. 1246 (1991)). The Bush Administration's Crime Bill will intensify this regressive trend by including a "firearms exception" under which illegally seized weapons could be produced as evidence in Federal trials for violent or serious drug crimes even if the police have no good-faith belief in the legality of the seizure of the guns. It also provides for a considerable extension of capital punishment. Senator J. Biden, the Chairman of the Judiciary Committee and a Democrat, counteracted by announcing his intention to introduce his own Crime Bill. In parallel, hard bargaining has at last led to a modest measure aimed at making it rather more difficult to obtain handguns for illegal purposes. Recently (May 1991), the Supreme Court by a 5–4 majority (*County of Riverside v. McLaughlin*, 111 S. Ct. 1661 (1991)), ruled that people who are arrested without a warrant may be imprisoned for as long as 48 hours (not including holidays and weekends) while awaiting a judicial determination of whether the arrest was proper. A breath of fresh air has been provided by a decision of a Federal Court in San Francisco to dismiss a criminal charge because of the Attorney General Dick Thornburgh's rules issued (June 1989) to Federal Prosecutors allowing talks between Federal Prosecutors and defendants when no defence lawyer is present and his consent had not been obtained. See *United States v. Lopez* 1991 U.S. Dist. LEXIS 7379.

The process of expanding and strengthening the deterrent hand of the machinery of justice is expected to gain further momentum and secure other changes inspired by similar near-authoritarian approaches. The late William French Smith, the Attorney General in President Reagan's administration, made no secret of this: ". . . such landmark federal legislation will serve as a model and a catalyst for powerful anti-crime reform in the fifty states". His successor in President Bush's administration, Mr. Dick Thornburgh, echoed this ethos in more fervent terms: "There is a growing sense among the American people that our criminal justice system is too laden with legal traps and technicalities to deal effectively with the problem . . ." "Unfortunately", he goes on,

> repeated efforts to address fundamental defects in our criminal justice system—to put the rights of victims on a par with those properly accused of criminal behaviour—have historically been tossed aside in exchange for quick political fixes that grab headlines but achieve little. We cannot allow it to happen again.

This is, to put it mildly, an astonishing statement to come from the premier law officer of this great democratic country.[32]

One point, however, needs to be emphasised. The *Comprehensive Crime Control Act* of 1984 which heralded many of the changes just described, was supported by bipartisan votes in both the Senate and the House. Indeed, it is an open secret that the measure could not have been adopted without the consistent, not to say enthusiastic, alliance between the liberal Senator Edward Kennedy, his conservative colleague Senator Strom Thurman, and the coalition drawn up behind the two of them. This reflected a real shift in American public opinion, a shift which cannot be ignored. As long as crime continues to increase, and no lasting upper hand is gained with respect to the criminal aspects of the drug problem, support for authoritarian short-cut remedies and the political demagogy that feeds them are bound to grow and flourish.[33]

---

[32] I would be hard pressed to find a more objective, informative and succinct analysis of the effect (if any) of the exclusionary rule and the *Miranda* decision on the control of crime than the one provided by Samuel Dash's Committee of seasoned experts set up by the American Bar Association. See *Criminal Justice in Crisis* (American Bar Association, Washington, D.C., 1988), pp. 27, *passim*. In December 1990, the Supreme Court in a 6 to 2 decision (Chief Justice Rhenquist and Justice Antonin Scalia dissenting) reaffirmed and in some ways extended the *Miranda* ruling. This rather unexpected decision must have come as a bitter disappointment to the Attorney General and his Deputy: see *Minnick* v. *Mississippi*, No. 89/6332 Supreme Court of the United States, 1990 USU Lexis 6118: 59 U.S. L.W. 4037.

[33] An exceptionally ugly episode of political demagogy, twisting a tragic penal case, occurred during the last Presidential election. I refer to the case of Willie Horton (a black convict with a heavy previous record) who had been "furloughed" in Governor Dukasis's home state of Massachusetts. In the final stage of the campaign he was arrested in Maryland for raping a white woman and stabbing her husband. The electoral campaign committee for Vice-President Bush seized upon the case with unsavoury alacrity and gave it a nation-wide intense publicity to prove the bankruptcy of the social and liberal approaches to criminal justice. Warren E.

The loudly proclaimed objective was to strengthen the deterrent hand of the machinery of justice, to stem the tide of crime and raise the levels of individual and collective security across the land. No hard evidence is forthcoming that this has been achieved to any degree whatsoever.[34] Instead there is no scarcity of solid proof to describe the gravity of the predicament from which the country is suffering. I have been fortunate and privileged to be able to take cognisance of and study the penal evolution of America as part of the international scene in my scholarly and public pursuits over a long period. Most reluctantly I have reached the following five conclusions. First, at no time during these four decades can I point to a stage, however brief, and confidently assert that the machinery of justice was then discharging its major functions in a satisfactory manner. Secondly, taking 1947 as a point of departure, the system has been constantly declining, its basic defects and flaws becoming more and more accentuated, with hardly any redeeming features. Thirdly, this deteriorating trend has not always been moving downwards at a more or less even rate. The performance was already bad during the 1980s but since then the pace of regression has quickened, has turned from bad to worse and now reached its nadir. It has produced a collapse or paralysis of virtually all the vital sectors of criminal justice. In effect, the system would have exploded a long time ago if the sentencing process had not been distorted by the "under the counter" arrangements of plea bargaining, which now operate in nearly ninety per cent. of cases, and the impact of other devices, such as court moratoria on the use of imprisonment because of unconstitutional overcrowding, the erratic use of bail, and the failure to proceed with cases because of the non-appearances in court of the accused, victims or other witnesses. And who can deny that these practices are inimical to the most fundamental objectives of an effective criminal process? Fourthly, even the very considerable juridical advances in refining the criminal law and in defining its constitutional limits could not be expected to have much practical

---

Burger, the former Chief Justice of the United States, was the only man who could authoritatively redress this distortion because of his long-standing support of furlough, but he remained silent for quite a long time. Finally, a written statement from him was released to the Associated Press, but this was just a few hours before the polls closed on the East Coast. It was couched in gentle terms but it stated that "Unfortunately the issue of corrections is never likely to become adequately treated in any political campaign". The tactic of the campaign committee was well calculated: according to the *New York Times* (November 9, 1988), "One voter in five yesterday said that the punishment of criminals was among the issues that mattered most to them, a remarkably high proportion for a Presidential election. And voters who mentioned crime as an important issue went about 2 to 1 for Bush". Governor Dukakis was asked on the screen what he would do if his wife were raped. I am not aware that Vice-President Bush was also subjected to this primitive ordeal.

[34] See, for instance, the solid piece by George C. Thomas III and David Edelman, "An Evaluation of Conservative Crime Control Theology", *Notre Dame Law Review* (1988), vol. 63, pp. 123–159.

impact on the system of criminal justice. Fifthly, I am fully aware that a comparative rating of a particular criminal justice system, especially on an international scale, involves, in the final analysis and determination, a very personal subjective element. Nevertheless, I do not hesitate to affirm that the American system belongs to the lowest category among the democratic countries of the world.

V. The English Crisis

England was almost predestined—to use a much abused word—to provide the English-speaking world with a model of criminal justice, worthy to be admired and if possible to be imitated. "It is a remarkable fact, at least so far as my observation and experience goes", stated Sir Evelyn Ruggles-Brise, well known for his reticence and understatement, "that foreign countries look to England with anxiety and curiosity for the *practical* [his italics] solution of the penal problem. If this is so, our responsibility as a nation is very great."[35] The advantages possessed by England in this respect were many and substantial. The prestige of being the centre of a glittering constellation of many states across the world; the medium size of the country—and experience shows that the quality of a criminal justice system varies inversely to the size of the environment in which it is expected to operate; a lot of national pride and no mean measure of well-being; the stability, coherence and homogeneity of its population; the long tradition of the rule of law, devotion to social service and inclination towards practical philanthropy. Add to this the emerging welfare state and a promise of greater equality and support for the under-privileged; the low incidence of violent crime; hardly any political crime; organised crime virtually unknown and very little drug addiction. Then there was the reluctance to follow rigid doctrinal schools of criminal law and instead a tendency to assess penal matters by empirically minded parliamentary commissions of enquiry. This was a combination of factors which, in their cumulative impact, could not fail to augur well for the emergence of an effective as well as a humane criminal justice system.

Penal evolution between the two wars greatly profited from these conditions. Police forces enjoying a deservedly high standing, a not over-burdened judiciary, a small but exceptionally enlightened group of Home Office officials, a highly motivated probation service, a prison staff neither fragmented nor in conflict with the higher

---

[35] Sir Evelyn Ruggles-Brise, *Prison Reform: At Home and Abroad* (1925), p. 16. Ruggles-Brise was the Chairman of the Prison Commission (the Head of the Penal System) and President of the International Penal and Penitentiary Commission.

authorities, all discharged their responsibilities in harness. There were certainly differences in substance or in emphasis between the major political parties on certain aspects of penal reform, but they hardly ever reached the level of bitter political contest. Agreements were reached because there was a large consensus that this was an area where national interest should prevail over party preoccupation.[36] The system displayed many strikingly progressive factors. There were no long periods of pre-trial detention of persons accused of crime and not put on bail, all cases were swiftly brought to court; young offenders were kept separately from adults at the main stages of criminal law enforcement; very short and very long sentences were drastically restricted; imposition of fines had been re-arranged better to take account of the economic situation of the offender; probation and allied measures were being made use of on a very substantial scale indeed; the borstal system, designed for young recidivists, had a 75 per cent. success rate and was the object of world-wide admiration; attempts were being made to overcome the negative features of prisons by setting up a better system for classifying prisoners into correspondingly different types of institutions; the fact stood out that there was no sharing of single cells by prisoners and the average prison population hardly ever exceeded eleven thousand—the lowest rate among the major countries of the world; flogging and capital punishment were fading away; the sentencing policy, as practised by all kinds of courts, was moving boldly towards depenalisation. It is true that there was an increase in crime, but it was a trend which still caused no public alarm and presented no significant challenge to the machinery of justice.[37]

Today, many of these hopeful factors have been reversed.[38] The deterioration started to be felt after the last war, somewhere in the late 1940s, and has continued at an accelerated pace ever since. Constructive advances have been made, such as sophisticated situa-

---

[36] This is the very vivid impression which I gained when invited to listen to the debate in the House of Commons on the second reading of the Criminal Justice Bill just before the outbreak of the War.

[37] Thus, for instance, in 1900 release with or without conditions was imposed in 17·1 per cent. of cases; in 32·1 per cent. in 1910; in 46·6 per cent. in 1924; and in 55·5 per cent. in 1936. The punishment of whipping which accounted for 7·1 per cent. of all punishments in 1900, dropped to 2·8 per cent. in 1910; to 1·2 per cent. in 1924; and constituted no more than 0·2 per cent. in 1936. The process was no less striking with respect to long-term penal servitude. The percentage of terms of 4 1/2 and 5 years dropped from 30·6 per cent. in 1900 to 14·1 per cent. in 1936; of over 5 years and up to 10 years from 13·7 to 3·9 per cent.; and of over 10 years from 1·4 to 0·2 per cent. For further changes of similar significance in the sentencing structure of the country at that period see Leon Radzinowicz, "Assessment of Punishments by English Courts" in *The Modern Approach to Criminal Law* (vol. IV of *English Studies in Criminal Science*, edited by L. Radzinowicz and J.W.C. Turner, 1945), pp. 100–122. I had discussed these and other changes some years earlier in my report to the Polish Ministry of Justice, part of which was published as "Le Système de Répression Pénale en Angleterre" in *Revue de Droit Pénal et Criminologie* (1939), vol. 19, pp. 1114–1148.

[38] See *e.g.* Lady Blackstone's very effective tract *Prisons and Penal Reform* (1990).

tional schemes for the immediate prevention of crime, in the support given to victims of crime, in the establishment of an independent Crown Prosecution Service, and in the search for viable alternatives to imprisonment—now a central feature of the Government's endeavours to reduce the prison population—much of it emanating from sound criminological research carried out within the Home Office and in the universities and polytechnics, also mainly supported by the Home Office. Nor should one overlook the very substantial recent decline in the number of juveniles and young adults committed to custody. But, at the same time, a growing emphasis is being put on measures inspired by an anti-liberal approach, often similar to those implemented or contemplated in America.[39] Parallel to the idea of "punishment in the community"—itself a vague and elastic concept— there is a trend to undue accentuation of the severity of punishment for violent offences, a trend which is already pushing up the long-term prison population by leaps and bounds. Furthermore the Government has set its face against a proposal, supported by the House of Lords, to abolish the mandatory life sentence for murder. As regards prisons, the proposal of the former Home Secretary, following the violent prison riots, to make prison mutiny a crime is obviously desirable if the existing criminal law armoury is not sufficient to deal with it. The maintenance of law and order within the penal system is as necessary (or perhaps even more necessary) as it is in the outside world. But to paraphrase the well-known dictum of Lacassagne ("Les sociétés n'ont que des criminels qu'elles méritent") it is only realistic and fair to maintain that, as a general rule, "prisons have the mutinies they deserve". And, not unlike the situation in America, the massive upward surge of the totality of crime is the major culprit even if not the only one.[40]

[39] Among the ideas borrowed from America are the privatisation of prisons and the electronic monitoring of offenders. On the former, see my letter to *The Times* of 22 September, 1988, "Principles at Stake in Prison Reform". Perhaps one day K.D. Ewing and C.A. Gearty, the two persuasive authors of *Freedom under Thatcher: Civil Liberties in Modern Britain* (Oxford, 1990) will join hands to ascertain whether a parallel can be discovered in the sphere of the evolution of criminal justice (legislation and practice). For an interesting attempt moving in this direction, see Richard J. Perrill "Margaret Thatcher's Law and Order Agenda", *The American Journal of Comparative Law* (1989), vol. 37, pp. 429–455. The study by Alan Norrie and Sammy Adelman picks up and develops several good points, but their ultimate assessment suffers greatly from a one-sided political approach. See "Conservative Authoritarianism and Criminal Justice in Mrs. Thatcher's Britain" in (1988) 16 *Journal of Law and Society* pp. 112–128.

[40] Total indictable offences recorded by the police were: 438,000 in 1955; 2,106,000 in 1975; 3,706,000 in 1989—a seven-and-a-half-fold increase of 3,268,000. It is true that changes in methods of recording and the incidence of reporting, among other factors, may push "the state of crime" up or down to a very considerable degree (more often up than down). The problem of so-called "statistical crimes" has been known for a long time by numerous students of crime trends and in many countries. One such example, by now ancient, and yet notorious is mentioned in my study "English Criminal Statistics", in *The Modern Approach to Criminal Law* vol. IV of the *English Studies in Criminal Science*, edited by Leon Radzinowicz and J.W.C. Turner, (1945), pp. 174–194, at pp. 179–180, where, as a result of a single change in the method of recording

The Irish Question—that nightmare with a seemingly endless tunnel—is definitely an aggravating factor. Emergency legislation and enforcement—measures closely akin to a state of siege, especially when of long standing—although formally restricted to a particular area of the country, in practice cannot fail to have repercussions on the whole machinery of justice. I found rather astonishing the phlegmatic announcement by Lord Lane, the Lord Chief Justice, of the collapse of the case against the Guildford Four: it will stand as one of the most tragic and unforgivable failures in the history of the English High Court judiciary, a failure which was perpetuated by two momentous unsuccessful appeals. The tragedy of the wrongful imprisonment of the Birmingham Six, at last recognised, fits the same pattern. Lord Lane's response may be indicative of a defensive judicial attitude to failures of justice, but seems also to reflect a hardened public opinion in all matters concerning criminal justice.[41] If the issue of capital punishment were made the object of a referendum now, an enormous majority, perhaps as high as 75 per cent., would be in favour of bringing it back. I am inclined to think that a similar majority could be mobilised in America. It is very much to the credit of Mr. Douglas Hurd, when Home Secretary, to have resisted the pressure from the then Prime Minister—an ardent advocate of capital punishment—and from a powerful section of his own party, including his successor Mr. David Waddington (now Lord Waddington).[42]

There are aspects of the English system such as its prisons which, if viewed within the European context, I would be inclined to rate as coming close to the notoriously inadequate prison organisation of Italy.[43] Without embarking upon a more detailed comparison it is very sad but essential to acknowledge that the English system cannot any longer be displayed to the world at large as a model worthy of inspiration. It would however be incorrect to identify it with its American counterpart. The challenges that it faces, the flaws that it exhibits, bear no comparison with the American predicament.[44] But

---

certain crimes, a real increase of about 5 per cent. in the Metropolitan area had been transformed to a "statistical increase" of 220 per cent.

[41] The articles of Peter Jenkins in the *independent*, 24 October 1989 ("Law as an Enemy of Justice") and of Hugo Young in the *Guardian* of the same date ("Too much Faith in their own convictions"), eloquently expressed, needed to be written and reflected on. And so does the Leading Article in *The Times*, "Blaming Lord Lane", 19 March 1991.

[42] Lord Waddington's successor, Mr. Kenneth Baker, as well as the present Prime Minister, Mr. John Major, both oppose the reintroduction of the death penalty.

[43] I very much hope that prison conditions in England are not as bad as those described by Paolo Graldi in the highly respected newspaper *Corriere della Sera* (1 August 1986, p. 7) "Poggioreale, nostra Caienna metropolitana". To my knowledge, no independent and competent commission has been established in Italy in the past four decades (or even longer) to reveal the real conditions of penal institutions in that country.

[44] The prison population of Great Britain, which was about 11,000 in the period between the two

the fact stands out that English criminal justice is passing through a grave, widely spread, crisis and one which, if decisive action is not taken, threatens to be permanent.[45] The recently published report by Lord Justice Woolf and Judge Tumim is the first positive indicator that this challenge is, at last, being responded to in a bold way.[46]

*   *   *

It may well be that, as regards America, far too many chances of gradually rebuilding the system have been missed, that by now the rot has set in too deeply and that the task of a radical penal renovation, as perceived in sheer financial terms, is not a practical proposition any more. According to Professors Norval Morris and Michael Tonry in 1990 there were more than one million Americans aged 18 and over in prison and jail and more than two and a half million on parole and probation. If one adds those on bail or released awaiting trial or appeal and those serving other punishments such as community service orders, the grand total under the control of the criminal justice system exceeds four million, nearly two per cent. of the nation's adult population.[47] And it is not only the amount as such

---

wars, went up to 20,000 in 1955; 39,800 in 1975 and 48,600 in 1989: a four-and-a-half-fold increase. It went down in 1990 to 45,500. To find reliable comparative prison statistics is even more difficult than crime statistics. Too many states have a vital interest in being discreet or evasive about it. There is such a thing as the "dark figure of prisoners". A census launched by the United Nations some time ago remained largely unanswered (only 48 countries deemed it desirable to respond). It is much easier (though by no means with complete satisfaction) to get information on the prison populations of European countries. *Prison Information Bulletins* regularly published by the Council of Europe (in Strasbourg) go a long way to achieve this objective. I am unable to provide worthwhile data for other parts of the world. In the early 1980s the Russian prison population was estimated at 4 million. And although "no firm data are available on China's prison population, one source estimates that the population there totals at least 3 to 4 million persons", whereas another suggests it may be as high as 20 million. See *International Practices and Agreements concerning Compulsory Labour or Indentured Labour*, United States International Trade Commission, Washington, D.C., 20436, Report December 1984, ch. IX, at pp. 28–32. The Report urges great caution in making, or accepting, prison estimates, especially from the "Non-market economy countries", and it emphasises the necessity of distinguishing between "Convict Labour"; "Forced Labour"; and "Indentured Labour". The penal system of China is nothing less than a form of slavery of the worst kind. The information just discovered by Asia Watch (*Prison Labour in China*, 19 April 1991, New York), proves beyond doubt how the Chinese Gulag labour camps, encompassing millions of convicts, are being used to obtain better entry for their products into the American, Japanese and German markets. The treatment of accused persons and penal conditions in India are as bad as ever. The seeds for advancement were there but they were allowed to die. See the Report by Lieut.-Colonel F.A. Barker, *The Modern Prison System of India*, English Studies in Criminal Science, edited by L. Radzinowicz and J.W.C. Turner, vol. III, (1944), and David J. Rothman and Aryeh Neier, "India's Awful Prisons", in *New York Review of Books*, vol. 38, No. 9, (16 May 1991), p. 53. See also M. Maguire, "The Indian Prison" in D. Whitfield (ed.), *The State of the Prisons—200 Years On* (1991), pp. 30–55.

[45] The definition of "crisis" by the Oxford English Dictionary (the Compact Edition, col. 1, p. 60) provides no great comfort. *Crisis:* "the point in the progress of a disease when an important development or change takes place which is decisive of recovery or death; the turning-point of a disease for better or for worse; . . . a vitally important or decisive stage in the progress".

[46] *Prison Disturbances April 1990*. Report of an Inquiry by the Rt. Hon. Lord Justice Woolf (Parts I and II) and His Honour Judge Stephen Tumim (Part II), Cm. 1456 (1991), "Twelve Central Recommendations", pp. 28–38).

[47] See *Between Prison and Probation* (1990), p. 9.

which is disturbing, but also its steady and appalling rate of increase. Thus in 1976 there were about 200,000 people in federal and state prisons and 140,000 in county jails, a total of about 340,000. In barely 14 years the number exceeded one million, nearly 300 per cent. more. And it would appear that the latest annual increase amounts to 13 per cent. The cost is quite considerable and is increasing. Federal, state and local governments spent $61 billion for civil and criminal justice in 1988—a 34 per cent. increase since 1985. But it is still rather insignificant in comparison with other items of expenditure. Compared with their justice expenditure the authorities spent six times as much on social insurance payments; five times as much on national defence and international relations; four times as much on housing and the environment; and twice as much on public welfare.[48] Although, states the Department of Justice, the cost of justice activities has grown faster than all government spending in recent years ". . . it will amount to only about three cents of every public dollar spent throughout the Nation".[49] The Dash Committee on *Criminal Justice in Crisis* concluded "that the entire criminal justice system is starved for resources".[50] As far as I am aware no sober full-scale projection has ever been made to ascertain what the cost would be of endowing and maintaining a decent system of criminal justice for the America of today. In consequence, it may well be that American society will have to reconcile itself to continuing to be served by a system gripped by a quasi-permanent, deep-seated decline, with sporadic measures taken whenever the need for containment of the onslaught of crime and drugs appears to acquire special urgency. One thing is certain. No fundamental change in the *status quo* will take place unless the approach is freed from short-term considerations and distortions prompted by political expediency. No progress will be forthcoming unless influential and sturdy bipartisan support is secured to make it a matter of "important national concern".[51]

[48] See *Justice Expenditure and Employment, 1988* (NCJ 124132).
[49] Bureau of Justice Statistics Bulletin (1990) NCJ 124132, *passim.*
[50] *Op. cit.* note 32 above, p. 5.
[51] The expression is John Howard's. See his *State of the Prisons in England and Wales* (London, 1777) p. 499.

Name Index

Stonham, Lord 387
Storm van's Gravsande, A. 455
Stuyvesant, Pieter 27, 28
Swaaningen, René van xv, 451–72
Sykes, Gresham 165, 359
Szasz, Thomas 167

Takagi, Paul 31
Tarling, Roger 400
Taylor, I. 41, 497
Thatcher, Margaret 428
Thornburgh, Dick 550
Thurman, Strom 550
Timmerman, Harrie 466
Tocqueville, Alexis de 30, 358
Tonry, Michael xiii, 556
Toombs 529
Tredgold, A.F. 50
Trilling, Lionel 153, 174
Truman, D. 474
Tuck, Mary xv, 397–412
Tulkens, H. 491
Tumim, Judge 556
Turner, Bryan 402
Tyler 532

Ungar, Roberto 368

Vahlenkamp, W. 515
van Vlaardingen, F.J.C. 456
Von Hamel, J.A. 46, 47
von Liszt, F. xii, 46, 535, 542

Vorrink, L. 133

Waddington, David 555
Walker, N. xii, 41
Walter, M. 513
Walton, P. 41
Weber, Max 18, 401–2
Weick, K. 394
Weinreb, L. 508
Weis, K. 133
Weis, S. 133
White, Arnold 51
Whitelaw, William 382
Wiener, Martin J. xii, xiv, 3–16
Wiles, P. 421
Wilkins, Leslie 195
Willmott, Peter 404
Wills, Sir Alfred 52
Wilson, A. 50
Wilson, D. 276
Wilson, James Q. xiii, xiv, 159, 173, 174, 175–81, 496
Windlesham, Lord xii
Woolf, Lord Justice 286–7, 407, 410, 556
Wright, Justice J.S. 161, 167–8

Young, Jock 24, 41, 95, 464, 497
Young, P. 42

Zedner, L. xiv, xv, 507, 514
Zimring, F. xiii, 479, 480
Zweigert, K. 508, 509